African Indigenous Religious Traditions in Local and Global Contexts: Perspectives on Nigeria

A Festschrift in Honour of Jacob K. Olupona

African Indigenous Religious Traditions in Local and Global Contexts: Perspectives on Nigeria

A Festschrift in Honour of Jacob K. Olupona

Edited by

David O. Ògúngbilé

Malthouse Press Limited
Lagos, Benin, Ibadan, Jos, Port-Harcourt, Zaria

© David Olugbenga Ogungbile 2015
First Published 2015
ISBN 978-978-53250-1-0

Published and manufactured in Nigeria by
Malthouse Press Limited
43 Onitana Street, Off Stadium Hotel Road,
Off Western Avenue, Lagos Mainland
E-mail: malthouse_press@yahoo.com
malthouselagos@gmail.com
Tel: +234 802 600 3203

All rights reserved. No part of this publication may be reproduced, transmitted, transcribed, stored in a retrieval system or translated into any language or computer language, in any form or by any means, electronic, mechanical, magnetic, chemical, thermal, manual or otherwise, without the prior consent in writing of the publishers

This book is sold subject to the condition that it shall not by way of trade, or otherwise, be lent, re-sold, hired out, or otherwise circulated without the publisher's prior consent in writing, in any form of binding or cover other than in which it is published and without a similar condition, including this condition, being imposed on the subsequent purchaser.

Acknowledgements

Historical Strands of Religious Interaction in Nigeria [Reprinted from Abubakre, R.D., M.T. Yahya, M.O. Opeloye, R.A. Akanmidu, E.A. Odumuyiwa, P.A. Dopamu and C.A. Dime (eds.), *Studies in Religious Understanding in Nigeria* (Ilorin, Nigeria: A Publication of the Nigerian Association for the Study of Religions, 1993): 129-154]; Politics in an African Royal Harem: Women and Seclusion at the Royal Court of Benin, Nigeria (Reprinted with permission from Berkeley and Los Angeles: University of California Press (In Anne Walthall (ed.) *Servants of the Dynasty: Palace Women in World History, 2008)*; Orisha Traditions in the West [Reprinted with permission from Baylor University Press, Waco, Texas (In Miguel A. De La Torre (ed.), *The Hope of Liberation in World Religions,* 2008)]

Foreword

- Graham Harvey

Religions and the study of religions in Nigeria are vibrant and important matters. The interfaces and interchanges between religions seem to multiply and diversify in relation to other evolving cultural phenomena. Changes in economics, politics, gender relations, ecology, media, international and inter-ethnic relations, and many other facets of Nigeria's complex cultural scene all engage with religions, and vice versa. Meanwhile, Nigeria has continued to produce high calibre scholarship on religions — and to export its scholars and scholarship to other venues of reflection, debate and dissemination. (It is not sufficiently acknowledged that Nigeria led the way in establishing the first department for the study of religions, separate from theology or divinity, before such a seismic disciplinary change occurred elsewhere in the world.) In large part, the Nigerian creation and continuing dynamism of religious studies as a separate field of study relates to a desire to engage with indigenous religious traditions or African Traditional Religions alongside the study of Islam, Christianity and other traditions. It is therefore fitting that this volume honours one of the great scholars of our era: Professor Jacob Olupona. Although he has conducted significant portions of his career outside of Nigeria, he has not separated himself from his colleagues or from interests in religions in Nigeria and elsewhere in Africa. His publications and presentations offer the international scholarly community important critical insights into a range of religious activities, lifeways and ideas originating in Africans and the African Diaspora. For many of us, his work concerned with indigenous religions and their adaptation (forced or willing) to global contexts has been of the highest value. This is not to ignore his contributions to the study of Islam and Christianity, which play immensely important and fascinating roles in Nigeria, West Africa and beyond. Rather, it is to emphasise the fact that what sometimes seems like a marginal topic in the study of religions, namely the study of indigenous religions, can have a considerable impact among our academic colleagues. Professor Olupona leads the way in demonstrating the inestimable value of research and teaching about indigenous religions not only to provide facts about those religions but to advance critical theorising in our discipline.

In this book, David Ògúngbilé has brought together an excellent team of authors who contribute information and debate about cutting-edge matters.

That is, their discussions of material arising among practitioners of indigenous religions generates valuable discussions of issues at the forefront of our discipline. (It is noteworthy that the phrase "practitioners of indigenous religions" might on some counts comprise ninety percent of the population of Nigeria since almost everyone, regardless of their primary religious self-appellation, participates in some "traditional" activities at least some times.) Scholars in neighbouring disciplines will also find inspiration or provocation of thought here. Some of the book's significant issues are: knowledge, representation, materiality, performance, ritual, festival, ethics, politics, gender, ancestry and belonging. But there is much more beside. Everyone will find something close to their chief interests. For me, these are discussions about material and performance cultures in relation to religious lives. But the cross-fertilisation provided by the proximity of such issues to discussions of other matters is what makes this book vital (important and lively). I strongly recommend it to you.

Preface

When David Ògúngbilé sent me his manuscript to examine for writing a preface, it came as a surprise because I was not expecting it, being a scholar on the fringe of religious studies; and as a gift, given the share weight of the deliberations and information in the 25 chapters of the book he courteously extended to me. They were mostly seminar work, enlarging upon the context and importance of African Traditional Religion in literature and social praxis, and offering insights, remarkably new, into the saliency of a specialized body of knowledge in addressing change and developmental concerns, particularly in Nigeria. I quickly realized that it was his way of incorporating me into an intellectual exchange, becoming ingenious, vigorous and intense, distinguished and informed by a multiplicity of approaches and reflective response to historical facts, and ethnographic data, on the destruction and origination of culture, and the adaptive strategies of navigating the experiences of a changing society/world. It was not merely a privilege to have the book, and be drawn, through my comments into the responsibility of sharing the concerns of the authors as to how to predicate an identity in the stream of human and global challenges, but also how to acknowledge and reflect on the arrival of new, stimulating, perspectives that contain their share of illumination, obfuscation, confusion, and discoveries about African belief systems.

May I also say that the fact that this book is a Festschrift in honour of a person I have collaborated with in writing articles (Jacob Kehinde Olupona) makes it also a compelling read for me; and that is not, in any case, because I collaborated with him on intellectual excursions, or that he is a Professor at Harvard University, which is a centre of excellence in knowledge production (although this may invariably matter), rather, it is because Kehinde Olupona has, in various capacities, established in Africa and other continents, several centres of critical reading and reflections on religions, and pioneered a socio-anthropological imagination radically different from the historico-theological bent of the classical scholars on the subject of African religions. He stands apart in a class of his own, in the path-breaking contributions already made, and especially in the spectacular manner of connecting with ongoing reflections, research and debates on how religion shapes the society and how the society itself shapes religion. The arrival of this book is, thus, for me a double gift: that I have the privilege of reading the essays and that I have the opportunity of joining others to celebrate and acknowledge the profundity and impact of one of Africa's best scholars, Jacob Kehinde Olupona.

At the risk of oversimplification, and in spite of the diversity in the thoughts and opinions expressed, and equally of the range of disciplines and topics contained in the book, one can say that the authors have developed a share concern about the role of African Traditional Religion in the processes of development and the context within which it (development) had or is taking place. The book guides us to a deep understanding and appreciation of how Africans in their varied situations grapple with existential problems through philosophical ruminations, complex ritual processes, cultivated memory and organized coping strategies. These concerns are, of course, by no means unique to this manuscript, which builds on the ground-breaking works of other scholars, but it represents an adequate and effective link with ongoing reflections in other disciplines, and offer either divergent, convergent or parallel views. More specifically, the central theme which underlies most of the contributions, explicitly and consciously or implicitly and unconsciously, is the crisis of humans regarding their own creativities, whether this be artistically, administratively, ideologically or organizationally. Their narratives, mythologies and symbolic constructions, as we read in this book, encapsulate an action and reaction that mark and incise the space, physical and virtual, in a way that leaves a deep scar on the mind, about the uneasy movement between the real and the unreal, the truth and the lie, which have bothered men for centuries about the strength and limitations of their capabilities and the strength of their belief.

The authors who have contributed to this book have written the historical, comparative, and ethnographical accounts about various sites marked out by societies for religious reflections and observances; they have made effort as up-to-date as possible so that the reader is exposed to current debates within the societies and in the literary circles; they have written a lucid, readable prose that is engaging, and used data that are richer and more refined to provide more adequate explanatory frames whatever may be the weakness of the general eclectic approach, and we cannot but expect such where forum is available to various levels of competencies, they bring into public attention the emphatic account that is a must read. I grant a humble extension of the freshness, enlightenment and flavour in a book that was a gift to me, to all scholars in Religion, Sociology, Anthropology and History.

Prof. Olatunde Bayo Lawuyi
Department of Archaeology & Anthropology
University of Ibadan

Editor and Contributors

Editor

OGUNGBILE, David Olugbenga, M.A., (Ife), M.T.S. (Harvard), PhD (Ife), is Reader in Comparative Religion and African Religions in the Department of Religious Studies, Obafemi Awolowo University, Ile-Ife, Nigeria. He is Fellow at the Harvard University W.E.B. Du Bois Institute for African and African American. He is a pioneer recipient of American Council of Learned Society/African Humanities Program Fellowship. His teaching interests include Methods and Theories of Religion, Phenomenology, Anthropology, Sociology and Psychology of Religion, and Ethics. He has published extensively in local, national and international outlets. His publications include *Creativity and Change in Nigerian Christianity* (edited with Akin Akinade) (2010). He is contributor to *Encyclopaedia of Religious Rites, Rituals, and Festivals* (2004), *Encyclopaedia of Religion* (2005), *Encyclopaedia of Religion, Communication, and Media* (2006), *Encyclopaedia of Sex and Gender* (2007), *Encyclopaedia of African Religion* (2009). He has also edited (with others) a number of volumes including *Locating the Local in the Global* (2004), *The Humanities, Nationalism and Democracy* (2006), *Rethinking the Humanities in Africa* (2007). His manuscripts, "Divine Manifestation and Human Creativity: Cultural Hermeneutics of Myth, Ritual and Identity among the African People and their Transnational Community and Cultural Memories"; "Performance, and Meanings in Indigenous Festivals and Celebrations among the Yoruba of South-western Nigeria" are being completed.
Web: www.ogungbile.net, Email: dogungbile1@yahoo.com, dogungbile@oauife.edu.ng

Contributors

ADENIYI, Victoria, PhD is Senior Lecturer in the Department of Dramatic Arts, Obafemi Awolowo University, Ile-Ife, Nigeria. Email: vicadeniyi2k4@yahoo.com

ADERIBIGBE Ibigbolade Simon Ph.D. teaches African Religion at the Department of Religion and African Studies Institute, University of Georgia, at Athens. He was, during the spring and summer of 2008, an Adjunct Faculty in Religions of Africa and African Diaspora at Africana Studies Department, University of North Carolina at Charlotte. Aderibigbe was until January 2007, an Associate Professor and Head of Department of Religions, Lagos State University, Ojo, Lagos, Nigeria. He has written and edited many books. He has also contributed articles in reputable Journals and scholarly books. He was editor of Religions' Educator, the Journal of Nigerian Association for the Study of Religions and Education. His current area of research interest is African Religion in Africa and the African Diaspora.

AJIBADE, George Olusola, PhD, is Senior Lecturer, and the current Head of Department of Linguistics and African Languages, Obafemi Awolowo University, Ile-Ife, Nigeria. He is an Alexander Humboldt fellow. He has published extensively in the areas of Yoruba orature and theories of oral performance. Among his major works are *Negotiating Performance: Osun in the Verbal and Visual Metaphors.* (Bayreuth, 2005) and *Finding Female Voices: A Socio-cultural Appraisal of Yoruba Nuptial Poetry* (2009).

AKINTUNDE, Dorcas Olubanke PhD was Reader in New Testament Studies and Women Studies, the immediate past Head of the Department of Religious Studies, University of Ibadan, Nigeria. She was a member of the Concerned African Women Theologians, International Association for Mission Studies, Nigerian Association for Biblical Studies, and African Association for the Study of Religions. She was Assistant Editor of *Orita, Ibadan Journal of Religious Studies*, and the *African Journal of Biblical Studies*. Her research focused on women studies and HIV and AIDS. Among her numerous publications are *The Ministry of Women in Lucan Narratives: A Model for the Christ Apostolic Church, Nigeria* (2001), *Women and the Culture of Violence in Africa* (ed.), "The Attitude of Jesus to the 'Anointing Prostitute': A Model for Contemporary Churches in the Face of HIV and AIDS in Africa," In Isabel A. Phiri, B. Haddad and M. Masenya (eds.) *African Women, HIV/AIDS and Faith Communities* (2003)

AWONIYI, Peter 'Ropo Ph.D. is Senior Lecturer in World Religions in the Nigerian Baptist Theological Seminary, Ogbomoso, Nigeria. His area of research interest is African Culture and Religious Interactions. His current project focuses on Yoruba Christianity in the Context of New Testament Christian Culture. Email: roporomoke@yahoo.com

AYANTAYO, Jacob Kehinde PhD is Senior Lecturer and current Head of the Department of Religious Studies, University of Ibadan, Nigeria. His areas of specialization are religious ethics and interreligious conflict management and peace building. His current research focus is claim and counter-claims to public space and implications for interreligious conflicts in Nigeria. His publications include "Religious Communication in Nigeria and the Challenges to Environmental Management" in the *Journal of Environmental and Culture,* (2006), "The Ethics of Remembering, Memorizing and Documentation of Ifa Divination System among Yoruba

People of Nigeria" in *Journal of Religious Studies* (2006), "Ignorance: the Bane of Interreligious Crisis in Nigeria: An Exposition" in *Journal of Sustainable Development in Africa*, (2008). Email: kehindejacob@yahoo.com

DANFULANI, Umar Habila Dadem, B.A., M.A. Religious Studies (Jos); PhD History of Religions (Uppsala), is Professor, History of Religions and current Dean, Faculty of Arts, at the University of Jos. Among his numerous publications are *Pebbles and Deities: Pa Divination among the Ngas, Mupun and Mwaghavul in Nigeria* (1995), *Understanding Nyam: Studies in the History and Culture of the Ngas, Mupun and Mwaghavul of the Jos Plateau, in Nigeria* (Rüdigger Köpper Verlag, 2003), and *The Sharia Issue and Christian-Muslim Relations in Contemporary Nigeria: Studies on Inter-Religious Relations 15* (2005). He holds a number of fellowships including the prestigious Alexander von Humboldt Stiftung, Germany (from 1997), STINT award, Sweden (from 2000) and IICS Global Scholar, US (from 2010).

DARAMOLA, Yomi PhD is a Reader in the Department of Music, Obafemi Awolowo University, Ile-Ife, Nigeria. His research interests are Ethnomusicology, Traditional (African) Music, and World Music culture. He is a Fulbright Scholar. Among his publications are "Sokoro Sakara: A Contextual and Gender Analysis of Some Offensive Yoruba `Proverbial Songs" in *NEBULA-Online:* (2007), and "Educational and Aesthetic Values in Yoruba Islamic Music" in *Journal of the Association of Nigeria Musicologists* (2008).

DIAKITÉ, Dianne M. Stewart, M.Div. (Harvard), PhD (Union Theological Seminary), is an Associate Professor of Religion and African American Studies at Emory University, where she teaches courses in the graduate and undergraduate curricula. She has taught at The College of the Holy Cross in Massachusetts and at Macalester College in Minnesota. Diakité's research and teaching interests include theologies and religious practices of the African diaspora with particular emphases on African-derived religions in the Americas and the Caribbean; Black, Womanist and Caribbean liberation theologies; theory and method in Black religious studies; and interreligious dialogue among communities in the African diaspora. She is the author of *Three Eyes for the Journey: African Dimensions of the Jamaican Religious Experience* (2005). She has also written a number of articles and essays on various subjects in her field and is currently completing a book manuscript on women in the Orisha Religion of Trinidad. Diakité has studied and lectured in a number of African, Latin American, and Caribbean countries. Most recently, she spent a year and a half conducting research as a Fulbright Scholar (2006-2007) in the Democratic Republic of Congo where she studied the history of religions in Central Africa during the transatlantic slave period and current indigenous religious cultures in the Lower Congo.

EHIANU, Wilson E. PhD in Church History (Ambrose Alli University, Ekpoma). He is lecturer in the Department of Philosophy and Religions in the University of Benin, Benin City, Nigeria. Some of his publications include "Stimuli for Vatican II: Relevance to Christianity in Africa" (2006), "The Church and Agricultural Development in Nigeria" (2006), "Expanding the Frontiers of Ecumenism and Evangelization in Africa: The African Communal Model" (2008) Email: destiny4real2@yahoo.com

IDUMWONYI, Mercy Itohan is a Doctoral Candidate in the Department of Religious Studies, Rice University, Houston, Texas. She specializes in Old Testament. She teaches in the Department of Philosophy and Religions, University of Benin, Benin City, Nigeria. Email: fessyito@yahoo.co.nz

ISIRAMEN, Celestina Omoso PhD is Professor in the Department of Religious Management and Cultural Studies, and presently the Director, University Consultancy Services Unit, Ambrose Alli University, Ekpoma, Nigeria. Her area of specialization is Philosophy of Religion with focus on African Ethics, Feminism, African Humanism, and Inculturation. Her publications include *Abortion and the Nigerian Society: A Legal and Religious Overview* (2004); "Sexuality and Spirituality in the Nigerian Context: A Critical Assessment of Religious Laws, Their Ambiguities and the Way Forward" African Regional Sexuality Resource Centre, (2005), www.arsrc.org. "The African Traditional Religion's Business Ethics: A Paradigm for Spirituality in Global Business Ethical Standard" In N. Capaldi (ed.), *Business and Religion: A Clash of Civilization?* (2005).

JEGEDE, Obafemi Charles PhD is a lecturer in the Department of Religious Studies, University of Ibadan, Ibadan, Nigeria. His areas of interest are African traditional religion and medicine, indigenous religion and development. His most recent book on *Incantations and Herbal Cures in Ifa Divination* (2010). He is currently researching on Oath-taking and Jurisprudence in Yoruba Religion and African Traditional Religion and Democracy. He is a Laureate of Codesria Institute of Health, Politics and Society in Africa and Democratic Governance Institute.

KALU, Ogbu U., PhD was the Henry Winters Luce Professor of World Christianity and Missions, McCormick Theological Seminary, Chicago, Illinois, He was Professor of Church History in the University of Nigeria, Nsukka, Nigeria until 2001. His ground-breaking publications include *Power, Poverty and Prayer* (2000), *African Pentecostalism* (2008).

KAPLAN, Flora Edouwaye S. PhD anthropologist, *emerita* Professor, Faculty of Arts and Science; and founding Director of Graduate Museum Studies at New York University. A Fulbright professor (University of Benin, Nigeria, 1983-1985), her research is ongoing at the royal court. She publishes widely on Benin religion, art and politics, gender, and material culture,. Among sixty-five publications and six books are: *Queen, Queen Mothers, Priestesses, and Power, Museums and the Making of 'Ourselves'*;

(XXX) and "Twice Told Tales: Yoruba Religious and Cultural Hegemony in Benin, Nigeria," in J. K. Olupona & Terry Ray (eds.), *Orisa Devotion as World Religion* (2007). In 1991, Oba *Erediauwa* of Benin, named her *Edouwaye* ("You have come home to Benin"), the first scholar to be so honoured, equivalent to an *Edo* chieftaincy title.

MILLER, Ivor PhD, a cultural historian specializing in the African Diaspora in the Caribbean and the Americas, is currently a Research Fellow at the African Studies Center of Boston University. His most recent book, *Voice of the Leopard: African Secret Societies and Cuba* (UP of Mississippi 2009) is based upon fieldwork in Nigeria, Cameroon, Cuba, and New York City. It documents ritual languages and practices which survived the Middle Passage and evolved into a unifying charter for transplanted slaves and their successors. Current research interests are the pre-colonial formation of the Ekpe (Leopard) Society in West Africa, as well as issues of gender in initiation societies in the African Diaspora. He has also published a book on the early Hip hop movement in New York City. See <afrocubaweb.com/ivormiller/ivormiller.htm> for more.

OGUNNAIKE, Ayodeji is Doctoral Student in African Studies and Religion at Harvard University.

OGUNTOLA-LAGUDA, Danoye, PhD (Lagos State University). Laguda is senior lecturer in the Department of Religions, Lagos State University. His doctoral dissertation is on Determinism and Activities of *Esu* in Yoruba Religious Beliefs. His research interest is on traditional religion and culture, conflicts and peace, oral traditions, religion and media and sociology of religion. He has to his credit articles published in books and journals. His edited book is Religion: Study and Practice in Nigeria (2003). He was the Secretary General of the Nigerian Association for the Study of Religions (NASR), 2002 TO 2006. He is a is a Nigerian Representative of the African Association for the Study of Religions (AASR) and a member of American Academy of Religion (AAR). Email: danoyeoguntola@yahoo.com

OHA, Obododimma, PhD is Professor of English in the Department of English, University of Ibadan, Nigeria. Obododimma Oha teaches Semiotics and Stylistics. He has great interest in indigenous knowledge systems. Detailed information on his scholarship is available on his weblog at http://udude.wordpress.com/

OLADEMO, Oyeronke PhD is Professor in Christian Studies and Women Studies, and current Head of Department of Religions, University of Ilorin, Nigeria. She teaches comparative religion and African Christianity. Her recent book *Women in the Yoruba Religious Sphere* (2003) explores how gender issues play out in indigenous and Christian traditions. She is a Nigerian representative of African Association for the Study of Religions (AASR). Email: wuraolaanike@yahoo.com

ONIBERE, S.G.A. PhD is Professor of African Traditional Religion at the Obafemi Awolowo University, Ile-Ife, Nigeria. He is a leading scholar in African Traditional Religion in Nigeria and he has published numerous articles in local, national and international outlets. His teaching and research interests include anthropology of religion and phenomenology of religion. He has mentored and supervised several doctoral theses, and has served as external examiner to several universities in Nigeria.

PROBST, Peter, PhD is a Professor for African art history and visual culture at the department of art history, Tufts University, USA, where he is also an adjunct professor for anthropology. His interests are memory and monument, modernity and globalization, and cultural heritage politics. He has conducted fieldwork in Cameroon, Malawi, and Nigeria. His latest publication is *Osogbo and the Art of Heritage: Monuments, Deities, and Money* (2011); *African Modernities: Entangled Meanings in Current Debate* (2002); *Between Resistance and Expansion: Explorations of Local Vitality in Africa* (2004); Keeping the Goddess Alive. Marketing Culture and Remembering the Past in Osogbo, *Social Analysis*, Vol. 48/1, (2004); "Picturing the Past: Heritage, Photography and the Politics of Appearance in Osogbo, Nigeria." In Michael Rowlands and Ferdinand de Jong (eds.) *Reclaiming Heritage: Alternative Imaginaries of Memory in West Africa* (2007).

SALAMI, Yunusa Kehinde, PhD is a Professor in the Department of Philosophy at Obafemi Awolowo University, Ile-ife, Nigeria. His area of specialization is Epistemology, while his areas of interest include African philosophy, among others. Some of his publications include "Ethnic Pluralism and National Identity in Nigeria" in Coates Rodney D., (ed.) *Studies in Critical Social Sciences: Race and Ethnicity, Across Time, Space, and Discipline* (2004), "A Politico-Economic Analysis of the Rise in the Phenomenon of Religion in Nigeria" in Feridun Mete *et al* (eds.) *Nigerian Economy: Essays on Economic Development* (2005), and "Yoruba Proverbs and Democratic Ethos" in Mieder Wolfgang *et al* (eds.) *Proverbium: Yearbook of International Proverb Scholarship* (2004).

SANFORD, Mei Mei, PhD (Drew University) lectures in Black Studies Program, College of William and Mary, Williamsburg, VA. She is co-editor (with J.M. Murphy) of *Osun Across the Waters* (2001).

VAN DER MEER, Tony Menelik has been a lecturer in the Africana Studies Department at the University of Massachusetts, Boston for thirteen years. He was an African American Studies major at Northeastern University and studied Community Economic Development at the Graduate School of Business at New Hampshire College (now Southern New Hampshire University) where he received his M.S. Degree. He is currently in the Antioch University PhD Program for Leadership and Change. Tony is a past president for the Boston *Black Political Task Force* and the *Boston Pan African Forum* and is the Co-chair of the *Rosa Parks Human Rights Day*

Committee. He also serves as a founder and the Program Director of the *Cultural Café*, a member of the *African American Master in Artist Residency Program (AAMARP)* – an adjunct program of Northeastern University's African American Studies Department. Tony is also co-editor of the book, *State of the Race, Creating Our 21st Century: Where Do We Go From Here* (2004).

WOTOGBE-WENEKA, Wellington O. is Professor of Religious Studies in the Department of Religious and Cultural Studies, University of Port Harcourt, Nigeria. His works focus on African Traditional Religion with special reference to the Ikwerre people of North Eastern Niger Delta. His writings include comparative analysis of Ikwerre indigenous religion and Christianity. He has edited several articles and edited an important volume *Religion and Spirituality* (2001).

Contents

Preface - Olatunde B. Lawuyi
Foreword - Graham Harvey

I. Issues and Perspectives on African Indigenous Religious Traditions

1. Paradigms and Conceptual Issues in African Indigenous Religious Traditions - *David O. Ògúngbilé* - **1**
2. The Study of Indigenous Religions: Academic Bias and Its Ethical Implications for Interreligious Conflicts - *Jacob K. Ayantayo* - **23**
3. Historical Strands of Religious Interaction in Nigeria - *Ogbu U. Kalu* - **39**
4. Indigenous Tradition in Transition: 'Born Again' Traditional Rulers, Religious Change and Power Contestation - *David O. Ogungbile & 'Ropo Peter Awoniyi* -**69**

II. Knowledge, Power, Vitality and Representations

5. An Epistemic Critique of *Ifa* as a Revelatory Source of Knowledge - *Yunusa K. Salami* - **95**
6. The Drop of Oil that Puts Out the Fire: Orisa Sonponna, Moral Knowledge and Responsibility in the Age of AIDS and Biowarfare - *Mei-Mei Sanford* - **103**
7. Health, Healing and Restoring - *Danoye Oguntola-Laguda* - **111**
8. Shrines and Sovereignty in Religious Life and Experience - *Obafemi Charles Jegede* - **123**
9. Power, Secret Knowledge, and Secret Societies - *Gbola Aderibigbe & Danoye Oguntola-Laguda* - **137**
10. Vestiges of Indigenous Spirituality in the Lives and Experiences of Muslim and Christian Religious Founders and Leaders - *Dorcas A. Akintunde* - **147**
11. Indigenous Voices in the Music Performances of Contemporary Christian and Muslim Missions - *Yomi Daramola* - **163**
12. Portrayal of Indigenous Religion and Ifá Divination in Ola Rotimi's *Gods are not to blame* - *Victoria Adeniyi* - **175**

III. Rites, Rituals and Festivals

13 Comparative Studies of Rites of Passages among the Ngas, Mupun, and Mwaghavul of the Jos Plateau in Central Nigeria - *Umar Habila Danfulani* - **187**
14 Burial Rites and Reincarnation in the Indigenous Tradition of the Ikwerre People of Upper Niger Delta - *Wellington O. Wotogbe-Weneka* - **217**
15 Igue Festival Among the Benin People: Response and Resilience of Indigenous Religion - *Wilson E. Ehianu & Mercy Idumwonyi* - **227**
16 Celebrating Indigeneity in the Shadow of Heritage: Another Version of the Osun Osogbo Festival in Nigeria - *Peter Probst* - **245**
17 Drama, Poetry and Ritual in Zangbeto Festival of the Ògù People of Badagry - *George Olusola Ajibade* - **255**

IV. Ethics, Women and Indigenous Spirituality

18. *Eto*: A Retributive Principle in Owhe Society - *S.G.A. Oseovo Onibere* - **271**
19. *Egbo*: Gating Spiritual Security and Morality in the Igbo Context - *Obododimma Oha* - **279**
20. Indigenous Spirituality, Business Ethics and Contemporary Challenges among the Igbo- *Celestina O. Isiramen* - **291**
21. Women in Yoruba and Igbo Indigenous Spirituality - *Oyeronke Oladeno* - **303**
22. Politics in an African Royal Harem: Women and Seclusion at the Royal Court of Benin, Nigeria - *Flora Edouwaye S. Kaplan* - **313**

V. AIRTs in Diasporic Contexts

23. Orisha Traditions in the West - *Dianne M. Stewart Diakete* - **333**
24. Dilemmas, Controversies and Challenges of African Descendant Ifa Priests and Practitioners in the United States: Some Reflections - *Tony Menelik Van Der Meer (Awo Alakisa)* - **353**
25. Separated by the Slave Trade: Nigerians and Cubans Reunite Through a Shared Cultural Practice - *Ivor L. Miller* - **363**
26. Borderless Homeland: Memory, Identity and the Spiritual Experience of an African Diaspora Community - *David O. Ogungbile* - **389**

Postscript: A Brief Biographical Sketch of Professor Jacob Kehinde Olupona - *Ayodeji Ogunnaike* - **413**

Select Bibliography; **415**
Index - **431**

I

Issues and Perspectives on African Indigenous Religious Traditions

1

Paradigms and conceptual issues in African indigenous religious traditions

- David O. Ògúngbilé

Jacob K. Olupona: a paradigm shift

African Indigenous Religious Traditions (AIRTs): Perspectives on Nigeria has been compiled in honour of the Nigerian scholar of African indigenous religion, Professor Jacob K. Olupona, who has made a huge contribution in the past three decades to the academic study of African indigenous religious traditions. Jacob Olupona is currently Harvard University Professor of African and African American Studies, and Professor of African Religious Traditions in the Divinity School, and the former Chair of Harvard Committee on African Studies.

Olupona has pioneered a unique perspective in the study of indigenous religious traditions which has its basis in his doctoral work published in the Stockholm Studies in Comparative Religion series as *Kingship, Religion and Rituals in a Nigerian Community: A Phenomenological Study of the Ondo Yorùbá Festivals* (1991). This in-depth research, which offers a paradigm for studying the practice of religion as a living experience of the practitioners, has been serving as a canon for research into indigenous religious traditions. Moreover, since his teaching career in the then University of Ife (now Obafemi Awolowo University, Ile-Ife), Olupona has championed a course that transformed and continues to transform religious studies scholarship in African universities through the students that he taught and mentored, the colleagues he interacted with, and the institutions in Africa where he served as adjunct lecturer and external examiner.

He has wielded a strong influence on younger, middle-career, and even older colleagues through his interactions and writings in this field of study. His publications have inspired scholars in the field of Indigenous Religious Traditions and his influence on scholars in African continent, Europe and the Americas is noteworthy. Besides being the pioneer and two-term President of African Association for the Study of Religions (AASR), the position he used to advance the frontier of knowledge in African Indigenous Religions, he has published extensively in this area. Indeed, his publications have been a model to scholarship, not only in religious studies, but also in African studies. His most recent work, *City of 201 Gods: Ile-Ife in Time, Space, and the*

Imagination (2011) which explored the religious traditions in the Yorùbá ancestral city of Ile-Ife, won the Harvard University 2012 Cabot award. It was also in the recognition of his unique and outstanding contributions to scholarship and research in the field of humanities that he was honoured with the Nigerian National Merit Order, one of the most prestigious awards given for intellectual accomplishment by the Federal Government of Nigeria. It was noted that Olupona's research has contributed to national development.

Contemporary issues and current engagements in AIRTs

The present volume which focuses on perspectives on Nigerian indigenous religions covers some ethnic groups across the country where indigenous religious traditions flourish. It also identifies a few communities in the West where African-derived indigenous traditions serve as the marker and definer of the people's cultural identities. Thus, it is noted in the recent times that there is a resurgence and revival of African-derived religions among the people of African descent. Among the most notable are the peoples of Brazil, Cuba, Trinidad and Tobago, Puerto Rico and a good percentage of the Caribbean. Abiodun Adetugbo (2001) points out one important factor, notably the trans-Atlantic slave trade, that was responsible for the production and continuities of African traditions in the Western world.

As the contributions in this volume reveal, African indigenous religious traditions are traditions based on a myriad of experiences and a wide range of practices and performances, and not on set of 'beliefs' as found in Islam and Christianity. Thus, issues engaged here include myth, ritual, festival, ethics and morality, divination, power, secret societies, healing, music, drama and poetry, gender, leadership, etc. from the traditional to the contemporary, from the local to the global, and from the experiential to the expressional. It is important to remark that besides the manifest internal dynamics within African indigenous religious traditions, the traditions are found to have a high degree of resilience and persistence even in the face of Islam and Christianity, altering and redefining the latter, showing certain important fundamental features that make humans what they truly are without them being dismissed as syncretistic. Continuity and change are discovered in indigenous religions in the same way as they are manifest in Islam and Christianity. These are made possible by the flexibility, elasticity and compromise of indigenous religious traditions of the Africans, and of the Yorùbá in particular. In its transnational migratory and diasporic contexts, Africa's indigenous religious traditions have been found to have a strong influence in some parts of the western world.

There is a need for this volume on the African indigenous religious traditions of Nigeria because of the huge diversity of their worldviews. To restate its importance, Nigeria, the acclaimed most populous African nation is central to the definition of indigenous religious traditions within the African and global contexts. The defining factors of its more than 250 ethnic groups are essentially imbued in the nature, contents, components and fundamental features of their indigenous traditions. These have been found to be true with groups such as the Yorùbá, Igbo, Edo, Efik, Nupe, Ibariba, Igbirra, Igala, Itsekiri, Esan, Ibibio, Tiv, Ikwerre, and some places in the Northern and Middle Belt where indigenous religious traditions still flourish. Besides, several aspects of Nigerian indigenous religious traditions have been noted to define and reinforce the nature and practice of African Indigenous Religious Traditions in the New World and particularly among the Diaspora and proselytes of African indigenous religions. That is, Nigerian indigenous traditions underline the spirit and form of indigenous traditions in the Diaspora.

One other fact that reinforces the importance of this volume is the hugeness of indigenous religious traditions of Africa which has not allowed the production of meaningful scholarly works. Most of the existing works that carry the continental or regional nomenclature such as African Traditional Religion or West African Traditional Religion either focus on a group of people or some aspects of indigenous expression leaving out the required depth and intensity that would justify the intended title and expected coverage.

The entire volume offers some theoretical and practical analysis of Africa's immensely rich and deep indigenous religious traditions showing how they manifest and define the identities of different communities within their local and global contexts. The chapters explore the dimensions and diverse expressions of the traditions among some Nigerian ethnic groups and their transnational communities. The volume provides some interpretations of indigenous practices, and examines the resilience, transformations and current resurgence being witnessed within and outside Africa. It also identifies and discusses the challenges posed by Islam and Christianity, the two competing religious forces and the consequences of their complex relationships and interactions. It observes the inspirations derived from the numerous immigrant esoteric religious societies, often termed 'New Religious Movements' (NRMs). Two notable examples are the Olumba Olumba Obu which has its origin and prominence in Calabar, studied by Rosalind Hackett, and One Love Family Movement known as Sat Guru Maharaj Ji Movement located on Ibadan-Lagos Expressway. The volume further highlights and discusses the representations of African indigenous religions in popular culture.

The chapters of *African Indigenous Religious Traditions* cover case studies and aspects of indigenous religious traditions from western, eastern, central, and eastern Nigeria; there are also case studies from the Americas. The significance of this volume lies in its capacity to provide scholars and the readers an understanding of the lived religious experiences of the diverse peoples, and in offering an opportunity for comparative study and analysis in local, national and global perspectives.

The volume is inter- and multi-disciplinary in depth, scope and interpretation. Its contributors are seasoned scholars who are specialists in various disciplines of African studies with focus on indigenous religious traditions of Africa. They are academics who have made significant contributions through their researches and writings to the field of religion as the traditions manifest in cultural, social, political and global contexts. It is important to point out that these scholars engage in what Clifford Geertz (Geertz 1973, Van Herik 1984) describes as "thick description". The contributions reveal a direct contact and experience of the scholars with the religious lives of the people they studied and wrote about. They present real case studies. On the whole, the entire volume provides an overall scheme for the study and analysis in comparative study of religions from the local, national and global perspectives.

Organising principle and coverage of the volume

African Indigenous Religious Traditions: Perspectives on Nigeria provides a paradigm shift from previous scholarship in the discipline. There is no doubt that the works of the early scholars on African Indigenous Religious Traditions have been important reference materials for students and scholars of religion. Within their own world and times, the researchers and scholars who include Parrinder (1968), Mbiti (1969), Idowu (1973), Awolalu and Dopamu (1979), Westerlund (1985), Metuh (1985, 1987), Gehman (1989), etc. have engaged in research activities from such perspectives as theology, anthropology and philosophy, using the nomenclatures that I consider neither appropriate nor representative of their book titles. Each of the scholars had however responded to the academic challenges of their times. Contemporary scholars in the field of philosophy, anthropology, sociology and theology have found their works compelling and useful. It is nevertheless to be mentioned that most of the scholars have been hooked by western paradigms in the classification and structuring of publications on indigenous religious traditions.

Different structures have been suggested in the earlier scholarly writings. Attempts at using those structures or developing another structure for the present volume cannot be done without running a risk of excluding important aspects of the various local, unique and important traditions, thus destroying their essential qualities. The main title 'African Indigenous Religious Traditions' is expressive of the centrality and importance of indigenous traditions in Nigeria. In the recent time and as demonstrated in some of the chapters in this volume, indigenous traditions of some Nigerian communities have been discovered to define and reinforce the Africanness of indigenous religions in the West. Specific references worthy of our mention are Osogbo, Ile-Ife, Oyo and Calabar, Nigerian communities that have continued to inspire and strengthen African indigenous traditions among the Diaspora. The subtitle 'Perspectives on Nigeria' is important in emphasizing the central focus of the volume.

The chapters in this volume represent scholarship in the history of religion, philosophy, linguistics and African languages, ethics, drama, music, women studies, theology, and African American studies. We have therefore adopted, as our organizing principle, the "dimensions of the sacred", provided by the historian of religion, Ninian Smart, as a roadmap for accessing African indigenous religious traditions in designing the present volume. These dimensions are: ritual and practical, narrative and mythological, doctrinal and philosophical, ethical and legal, social and institutional, experiential and emotional, material/artistic, political and economic (Smart 1969, 1996). It is important to mention that each of these dimensions is not treated as a distinct category. Thus, one may discover that the topic addressed by each author identified and discussed aspects of the dimensions as the tradition speaks to him or her. The volume which has twenty-six chapters has five sections. The following paragraphs in this chapter provide an introduction to each of the sections.

Issues and perspectives on African indigenous religious traditions

This first section, which focuses on important issues and perspectives in understanding the contents and contexts of AIRTs, has four chapters. They provide the lens for interpreting the dynamics, change and continuity, the strength and reality, the manifest transformation, and the tenacity of indigenous spirituality on both the individuals and the collectives.

This chapter focuses on conceptual paradigms in indigenous religious traditions of Nigeria. It examines Jacob Olupona as the pioneer of a paradigm shift which began from his doctoral research, an ethnographic work conducted among the Ondo-Yorùbá community. This work resulted in the production of a thesis that paid less attention to earlier works in terms of structure and focus. The uniqueness of Olupona's research activities and writings provide a model for multidisciplinary approach and engaging theoretical framework. This chapter further identifies and provides the new model for doing research and patterns for organizing research outputs in the way that indigenous religious traditions are rescued from meaningless or undue generalisations and reduction of their essences. The chapter pays attention to the importance of both the essence and function of indigenous traditions as lived and practiced by the people.

Jacob Ayantayo examines the problems associated with the academic research and teaching of indigenous religions in tertiary institutions. These problems are primarily associated with the scholars and teachers of these religions who lack the adequate training and necessary methodological skills to conduct the research in this area; added to this is that they are so much attached to their religions of profession which they allow to interfere with their research and teaching. The consequence of this is the gross bias against indigenous religious traditions which they treat with disdain and insult. From an ethical perspective, Ayantayo engages in examining the implications of this bias on the needed interreligious dialogue in a multi-faith nation where religious suspicions become a ready instrument to fight social, ethnic and political differences. Moreover, indigenous religious values which could serve the pragmatic purpose of reinforcing human values are negatively presented by these scholars. Thus, Ayantayo advocates that:

> ...religious scholars should not be biased in their approach to religions different from theirs because such may be contemptuous, blasphemous and disrespectful. In as much as we revere our religion and place it on high esteem, it will be morally wrong to speak evil about other religions. This is important because as our religion is important to us, we should honestly accept that the religions of other people are equally important to them. This is a poser for scholars of religion who at all times should be objective, rational, neutral and courteous in the study of religion qua religion... Therefore, the practice of saying contemptuous things about religions different from ours shall continue to generate conflicts in which there will never be a winner or a loser. This is a poser for all stakeholders in the promotion of interreligious relation and peace building in Nigeria and Africa where interreligious conflicts have been an endemic problem.

In "Historical strands of religious interaction in Nigeria," Ogbu Kalu explores the nexus of multidimensional approaches and their significance to historical researches in understanding religion and nation building. He notes particularly such approaches as phenomenology, sociology and anthropology, identifying their limitations and strengths. Providing the basis for this connection, he illustrates with several scholars and their research works in different communities in Nigeria. One particular interest of this chapter for the volume is the centrality and tenacity of indigenous African worldview on the entire lives of the people of Nigerian communities. He notes the predominance of spiritual forces which leave no profane spaces or times, even in the face of change in state systems and democratic decision-making processes. He writes that "at the core of the changing patterns was a sacralized worldview which drew little difference between the profane and sacred." He further points out the different phases which indigenous religion controls: society or community, economic activities, politics, health, state formation, human values, etc.

Besides indigenous religious traditions, Kalu discusses the history, practice and the different forms of Islam and Christianity in traditional society. Moreover, he examines the interactions of the three religions, particularly in the Independence and post-Independence eras with the aim of suggesting dialogue as an antidote to the obvious social and political tensions and conflicts in Nigeria where the modern and traditional 'publics' operate. In this vein, Kalu provides the nature of the dialogues that could be derived from both the Christian tradition and Islamic roots. While noting the limitations of the dialogues in these two competing traditions, he points out several "elements of traditional religious values in social control models which could still be applicable in modern setting."

Ògúngbilé and Awoniyi's chapter investigates the current trend in traditional political institution. Indigenous communities hold traditional rulers, the *Oba* (king) as the custodians and embodiments of the traditions and customs of the land. By his/her definition, essence and function, the authority of the *Oba* derives from the mythic narrative and ritual activities that establish the community. These are rehearsed and re-enacted in occasional and/or annual festivals. The authors describe the contemporary development where the traditional rulers who have once been installed through the instruments and powers of indigenous tradition now profess and proclaim new-found faith, claiming to have been converted into Christianity or Islam.

Such religious change, it is noted, continues to challenge and transform traditional political institution thus altering and threatening indigenous religious traditions. Ògúngbilé and Awoniyi discuss the patterns of the religious conversion and power contestation, examining the consequences of these on the convert, the community and the indigenous traditions.

Knowledge, power, vitality and representation

Indigenous religious tradition continues to prove its resilience, strength and dynamism through certain modes. From oral to written, from personal to the collective, from experiential to the expressive, from silence to sound, from casual to formal, the extraordinary power of the Nigeria indigenous tradition is expressed in various ways. The eight chapters in this section centre on four important interconnected modes through which NIRTs flourish: knowledge, power, vitality and representation. Yunusa Salami and Mei-Mei Sanford focus on different dimensions and expression of knowledge, one form of the modes. Salami discusses the centrality of *Ifa* in the lives of the individual and the community in the Yorùbá worldview. The 'beingness' and existence of the individual, and the prosperity or otherwise of the individual and the community which are determined, sometimes by the supreme being or the individual, or collectively by both, are known and could only be revealed from the text of *Ifa* called *Ifa* corpus.

The centrality of *Ifa* deity and divinatory techniques in Yorùbá cosmology extend to all areas of existence including health and healing, secret and open societies, politics and power, and the operations within the òrìsà systems. Sanford's chapter, "The drop of oil that puts out the fire: Orisa Sonponna, moral knowledge and responsibility in the age of AIDS and Biowarfare," reflects on the ways "Yorùbá understandings of epidemic disease differ from the Western model." While showing that though Òrìsà Sonponna possesses the potency to heal different kinds of diseases as claimed by the olórìsà and as contained in his *oríkì*, praise poetry, Sanford discovers that òrìsà religion emphasizes human choice as well as human responsibility in soliciting Òrìsà Sonponna's healing. Thus, *Ifa* corpus and oral texts of other òrìsà including Sonponna, Ogun and Osun reveal that moral knowledge and responsibility are crucial to effectuating healing and health.

Oguntola-Laguda discusses holistic nature of the healing and restoration process in traditional medical practice. Illness and sickness in indigenous thought, which may include physiological, moral, spiritual and ontological, is a product of the breakdown in the harmony between human beings and spiritual forces. He further examines Yorùbá traditional health care delivery methods, different types of traditional healing experts among some Nigerian groups, and contemporary trends of neo-traditional healing practices within Pentecostal and Muslim traditions. Laguda submits further that indigenous religious traditions have begun to exert tremendous impact on the practice of western medical practices in Yorùbá and some other African communities even in the rapidly modernizing age.

The chapters by Obafemi Charles Jegede, "Shrines and sovereignty in religious life and experience" and Gbola Aderibigbe and Oguntola-Laguda, "Power, secret knowledge and secret societies," both explicate the dimensions and dynamics of power in and of indigenous religious practices. Jegede's ethnographic study of *Okija* shrine in Anambra State and *Osun* shrine in Osogbo provides helpful case studies to explain the sense, essence and function of shrine as the locus of power. This power extends through metaphysical, judicial, ecological, healing, political, etc. Jegede observes that the shrine, private or corporate, contains elemental forces which are made possible by the instrumentality of the ritual specialists who activate material objects by

> the use of plants, invocation and incantation and songs, thereby making these objects immediately become sacred, transcendental or supernatural. ...[S]ome forms of synergy of herbs with the spiritual objects or symbols and the synchronisation of material objects to bring out the spiritual component to invoke awe and wonder.

The shrine serves several functions. It possesses a uniting energy and offers itself a binding force for the community. It serves as instrument of justice as the shrine is patronized to seek redress, as in the case of *Okija* shrines.

The extraordinary perception and awesome reverence of the shrine is reinforced by the perceived attributes and symbolic importance of the material elements used to build it. Thus, the shrine represents the meeting point of the human, the natural and spiritual entities, and its importance in human affairs takes the aura of sovereignty.

If the shrine presents a dimension of power, secret knowledge and secret societies collectively present another realm of power. Aderibigbe and Oguntola-Laguda discusses the different types and forms of secret societies and how they have been able to wield strong influence and immense power through the esoteric knowledge of the mundane and transcendental world they claim to acquire. The authors suggest that "membership of secret societies in Nigerian religious space has direct relationship to the acquisition and exercise of power." Secret in no small measure opens itself to some pride and respect from those to whom such secrecy is exclusive. Providing a fair classification of three types of secret societies among the Yorùbá, Efik and Igbo, Aderibigbe and Oguntola-Laguda discuss their functions and relevance.

While in most cases secret societies within indigenous religious tradition claim sacredness, their socio-cultural groups are attached to festivals. The authors note that the secret societies function generally to preserve and protect indigenous tradition and institutions. Membership of a secret society, the authors opine, has some psychological effect on the initiate who sees his/her membership in relation to 'class status.' Furthermore, the possibility and advancement in spiritual development and acquisition of magical power(s) serves as a driving force. In the process, the initiate learns new arts. The concluding reflection of the authors is apposite here:

> We observe that apart from social, religious, political and economic motives for wanting to be initiated into secret societies, Nigerians also wish to obtain power with esoteric values…[T]his perhaps makes the secret societies not only a source of power but also an avenue for exercising such power.

How do indigenous religious traditions survive in the face of the competing and rapidly evangelizing efforts of the fundamentalist and Pentecostal, Muslim and Christian missions? We have noted from some of the preceding chapters the biases, by scholars and teachers of indigenous religions, the proselytizing effects on traditional rulers who by design and practice are custodians of indigenous traditions, and the changing face indigenous traditions due to modernization. On the other hand, we have also observed the resilience and vitality of IRTs in healing and health practice and the upsurge and patronage of shrines and continual relevance of secret societies. The following two articles by Dorcas Akintunde and Yomi Daramola discuss the effects of indigenous religion on Islam and Christianity in some Nigerian communities.

Akintunde examines the consequences of colonialism and early Western missionizing efforts that deprived African religion and culture its spiritual space. She highlighted the African indigenous response to this attitude, particularly the production of African indigenous or independent movements. She notes that founders of early indigenous churches "succeeded in creative adaptation of African Traditional Religion" as they "cropped up as a natural development of the meeting of Christian message with the cultures of the African people." These efforts have also been noted with the early and new Pentecostal movements. As it is in Christianity, the establishment of Muslim groups and their adaptation of indigenous practices in their activities express both the compromise and absorbent nature of Nigerian indigenous religion.

Akintunde identifies the baggage of indigenous religious traditions which these church founders and leaders have deployed in developing their doctrines and practices. These indigenous mediums include language and traditional elements and mediums. Not only this, the place accorded the female gender is reflective of the god-goddess complementary operations in African-Yorùbá worldview. The practice of healing is notably a combination of Christian/Muslim and indigenous practices.

The rise in music production in contemporary Nigeria is startling and astonishing. Several issues that emerge from here include the proliferation of self-made and self-proclaimed music evangelists; the mutual borrowing and use of Christian and Muslim religious terminologies in lyrics; and competition and contestation Christian and Muslim singers. However, Yomi Daramola's "Indigenous voices in the music performances of contemporary Christian and Muslim missions" describes the level at which indigenous concepts and ideas are used as materials for musical expressions in Islam and Christianity. Primarily, the chapter shows the resilience and vitality of indigenous rites and festivities in the face of Islam and Christianity which musical cultures have influenced and being influenced by the traditional cultures of the people. The complexity of the mutual influence on the one hand is how Muslim and Christian lyrics denigrate indigenous culture, and on the other hand some indigenous lyrics express the imposing force on indigenous festivals on the people of a community. However the mutual influence goes, it shows the vitality of indigenous religious practices in music.

The question of representation is also an important fact of the nature and essence of indigenous religious tradition. Daramola's chapter could be interpreted as revealing how indigenous tradition has been represented in the lyrical composition of Muslim and Christian musicians. Victoria Adeniyi's own paper "Portrayal of indigenous religion and *Ifa* divination in Ola Rotimi's *Gods Are Not To Blame*" focuses on another critical aspect of representation of indigenous spirituality which reveals the vitality of NIRTs. It is important to point out the centre point of most African and Nigerian literary writings are diverse dimensions of indigenous traditions. A few of the numerous examples of literary writers whose work demonstrated the centrality of indigenous traditions are Daniel Fagunwa and Wole Soyinka.

Using the popular Ola Rotimi's *The Gods Are Not To Blame,* an adaptation of the tragic drama Sophocle's *King Oedipus,* Adeniyi analyses the novel, pointing out the complexity of the human destiny in Yorùbá culture. While providing the operation of *Ifa* divination and its power to alter human destiny, Adeniyi notes that Ola Rotimi uses Greek-oriented model which plays down the significant role of *Ifa* in the resolution of the complexity of freewill and determinism, and alterability or otherwise of human destiny.

It is also important to note that this concept of representation of indigenous religious traditions has become a significant pattern, not only in literary texts, but also in Nigerian secular and Christian home videos.

Rites, rituals and festivals

Rites, rituals and festivals constitute some vital elements in the experience, expression and practice of indigenous religions. Each of these needs to be understood as human, cultural and social phenomena. In all these dimensions, they focus on human transition of life, they are passed on from generation to generation, and they express several levels of human relationships and identity.

Umar Habila Danfulani provides a conceptual framework for defining and understanding ritual and rites of passage, using three communities in Jos Plateau in central Nigeria which indigenous traditions are comparatively less focused in African indigenous religion scholarship as the Yorùbá or Igbo. Danfulani has combined historical, anthropological and phenomenological approach and adopted Cox's taxonomy of rites of passages in presenting calendrical rituals, life cycle rituals and crisis rituals, among the Ngas, Mupun and Mwaghavul. It is important to note that the first category, that is, temporary cycle or calendrical rituals are regarded by the three communities as their ethnic national festivals. Life cycle or life crisis rituals, the second category are the dramatic and ceremonial performance in the life of an individual. It covers important landmarks in the life of a single individual to express the dignity and worth of the person. The third category constitutes the crisis rituals which are community-centred, focusing on the passage of the communities through perilous, difficult and troublesome times in their shared or corporate life. Such events are believed to be beyond the ordinary human control, bordering on the human life in the community.

Danfulani gives vivid illustrations of the different categories of the rituals as lived and practiced by the people of the communities. The author notes that the re-enactment of the rituals informed several festival celebrations which have become a rallying point and have created some sacred spaces in the three communities even till the present time, and in spite of the presence of agencies of change.

Burial rites, to indigenous Africans generally, have a lot of significance for several reasons. Burial rites answer the question regarding the meaning and essence of human life and existence. They provide the reasons for morality and ethical behaviours since it is believed that the dead does not go into extinction but continue to live. The deep and immense rites of transition performed for those who could reincarnate are a proof that the dead is still active in the affairs of human beings. These are regarded to qualify as ancestors and sometimes called 'living dead', for whom family shrines are constructed on their graves. This is the kernel of Wotogbe-Weneka's chapter which engages in the question of burial rites and reincarnation among the Ikwerre people of the present River State. Although he points out that burial rites and reincarnation are "one of the cardinal hallmarks of the indigenous religious belief system of the Ikwerre is the belief in reincarnation," it is important to restate the fact that it is not peculiar to the Ikwerre people. Thus, Bolaji Idowu notes that "...ancestral cults derives from the belief of Africans that death does not write 'finish' to life, that the family or community life of this earth has only become extended into the life beyond..." (1991:186). I should however point out that reincarnation is a complex phenomenon with variations in intensity of practices among the different peoples of Africa. Ikwerre's belief and practices of reincarnation bear some semblance with Buddhist and Hindu belief in *karma*.

Festivals are an important aspect of indigenous religious traditions. As a religious phenomenon, they characterize those dimensions that connect the human, natural and supernatural entities. Their mythic-historical element links the past to the present by providing the raison d'être for the ritual practice(s) and the structure for the re-enactment and reinforcement of present celebrations. The features, including songs, music, chants, drums, prayers, costumes, movements, silence, homage, etc., produce a sort of drama which becomes an occasional or yearly event for the community.

Festivals serve important purposes. Hegemonic festivals celebrate the cultural event or birthday of communities where the community bond is spiritually and socially reinvigorated and the traditional rulership re-enact his/her commitment to the community. Some festivals celebrate the coming of age of boys and girls, while some re-energize the vegetative power of their natural phenomena. In all, the religious ideas of African communities are conveyed through festival celebrations. Wilson Ehianu and Mercy Idumwonyi, Peter Probst, and George Ajibade provide some interpretations of three of such festivals from the Benin, Osogbo and Ogu (Badagry) people respectively.

Ehianu and Idumwonyi examine *Igue* festival which is celebrated among the entire people of Benin kingdom. The authors note that *Igue* festival has existed for well over six hundred years and that it is in it that "the cultural excellence of the Beninese finds crystallization." *Igue*, according to Idumwonyi and Ehianu is the most popular in the kingdom and that it cuts across all the strata of the community including the monarch, members of the palace societies and the entire Benin community.

It is pointed out that Roman Catholic Mission has taken root in Benin for over a hundred and fifty years. However, unlike in many other African communities where Christianity in general has uprooted or destroyed the fabrics of their indigenous celebrations, *Igue* festival has remained resilient in Benin kingdom. One interesting point here is that the two traditions are strong among the people with a common field of playing and the same audience. This is a case of role-playing and role-shifting. What is the crux of the discussion here? The main argument of Ehianu and Idumwonyi is that *Igue* contains important social and cultural ingredients that could be integrated and incorporated into Roman Catholicism to produce a unique tradition and theology that I may describe as *Theologia Beninese* for the people of Benin.

The authors identify and compare some of the socio-cultural elements in *Igue* with those of Jewish indigenous tradition. Ehianu and Idumwonyi argue for assimilation of 'non-idolatrous' aspects of Benin culture into Roman Catholic liturgy and practices, since "there are good principles in African religion and indeed *Igue* festival, which the Beninese cherish irrespective of religious affiliation [which] include religious tolerance, respect for ancestors, priests and constituted authorities." To the authors, this is the basis for 'Inculturation Theology'.

Peter Probst chapter "Celebrating indigeneity in the shadow of heritage: another version of the Osun Osogbo Festival in Nigeria" presents and interprets one of the 'unofficial traditions' that has not been referenced by "the publications of the Heritage Council nor the scholarly literature." Probst describes the ethnography of *Odún Ère* (Image festival), a minor festival, usually celebrated in December, towards the end of the dry season, in Osogbo in honour of *Obaluaye*. *Obaluaye* is the Yorùbá deity of sickness, suffering, anger and heat. The significance of *Osun* and other deities who characterise 'coolness' is for them to plead with and calm *Obaluaye* from his inherent anger to be able spare the people of pain and pestilence of smallpox epidemic.

The activities that make up *Odún Ère* reveal a lot of spiritual (re)energizing of Osogbo landscape towards the preparation of Osun festival which comes up in August. *Odún Ère* expresses the centrality of *Osun* and her diverse spiritual and physical imagery: fertility, femininity, motherhood, sexuality, wealth, wisdom, knowledge, healing, beauty, art, and power. The ritual space, ritual specialists and materials provide an intrinsic link between *Odún Ère* and *Osun Osogbo* that is celebrated in August. The intense ritual activities in *Odún Ère* include washing of the *Ère* (carvings), the decoration of *ère* (sculptures), public presentation and ritual preparation of the *Arugbá* (votary maid) that would carry the sacred calabash in the forthcoming Osun festival. Offering the narrative which is somewhat unpopular in scholarship but which still re-affirms a strong connection with the earlier narrative in a deeper sense, is an important contribution, according to Probst, that "in the framing of identity by notions of heritage and indigeneity, a multiplicity of voices exist." What is of essence in understanding of African indigenous religious tradition is the "sense and meaning that is generated in the process of performance rather than following a 'text'".

As earlier mentioned, religious festivals in Africa contain dramatic and poetic elements that are of social and spiritual significance to the community. George Ajibade discusses the fusion of poetic, religious and dramatic elements in *Zangbeto* cultural festival of the Ògù people of Badagry, Lagos state. This ethnographic work draws data from oral literature and the performance of the festival. The author identifies a shift of traditional theatre from ritual into entertainment among the people. According to Ajibade, *Zangbeto* is a form of theatre employed by the Ògù people as a form of signification and communication through which they reaffirm the beliefs that nourish their community.

Ethics, women and indigenous spirituality

This section which contains five chapters focuses on two main issues: morality and women. Africans are very conscious of the mechanisms that are employed by human beings in living a moral life. Morality, to them, is human as it is divine. It applies to both the human and non-human entities. Morality, from its social dimension, is judged by the principles developed in individual communities to redress antisocial acts and punish offenders including witches, sorcerers, murderers, thieves, adulterer, and so on. Oseovo Onibere, a retired Professor of African Traditional Religion, examines this phenomenon in the chapter titled "*Eto*: a retributive principle in Owhe society." According to him, justice, in Owhe community located among the Isoko of the Niger Delta, is predicated upon the operations of *eto* to ensure "that the evil-doer does not go unpunished." *Eto* which is housed in a shrine involves ritual preparation of material elements by *obueva,* a diviner. *Eto* works on the basis of operator-client agreement, and the consequence is borne by the offender who experiences affliction in his or her body systems. Guilt results! To the Owhe people, this is justice well meted. The offender could only neutralize the effects of *eto* and regain his or her health by consulting the *obueva* who prescribes a number of ritual preparation, and an offended-offender resolution which involves restitution and payment of a huge number of items to the aggrieved party. Onibere concludes that "*eto* is indubitably an instrument of justice, externalizing deities' judgmental attribute among the Owhe people."

Obododimma Oha's chapter, "*Egbo:* gating spiritual security and morality in Igbo context," explores the semiotics of the *egbo*, an ancient mechanism for power balancing and conflict management among the Igbo of eastern Nigeria. The author identifies the relevance of *egbo* to conflict management and ethical re-orientation in contemporary Igbo society. *Egbo* is a ritual gate that is mounted which is however prohibitive of *mmanwu* or *mmonwu,* 'masked spirit' from crossing. *Mmanwu* is regarded as the manifestation of the dead ancestor; it possesses some spiritual power and it is capable of enacting violence which is deployed as an instrument of correction and teaching the disobedience.

Characteristically, masked being or masquerade chases the unmasked human beings in a sort of drama. *Mmanwu* is accorded affection and respect in Igbo culture and indigenous religious tradition. However, *mmanwu* is forbidden from entering through *egbo* and other places of cultural and spiritual significance. Also, *mmanwu* is prohibited from chasing frontally and it halts its aggression wherever it is alarmed of *egbo*. It is also pointed out that *mmanwu* does not enter an *egbo*, and that when sit is necessary, it enters backing in, bowing. This cultural restriction creates some power balancing between spiritual and human beings as possible excesses of *mmanwu*, a spiritual entity, are curbed. For the *mmanwu,* violating a cultural code of conduct as this usually leads to unpleasant consequence. Oha asserts that this phenomenon, "a culturally shared system...provides the possibility of disarming the assailant and also offers solace to the one in danger." This cultural form of control has a Jewish semblance of Cities of Refuge (Num. 35:6-32; Josh. 20:2-3; I Chr. 6:67)

"Indigenous spirituality, business ethics and contemporary challenges among the Igbo" by Celestina Isiramen identifies the indigenous practice of swearing on *Ofo* as the greatest form of oath-taking. This ritual practice, she emphasizes, is a strong means of attesting to the truth, affirming innocence and sincerity and punishing of offender through cursing which could lead to impoverishment, incurable sickness, disinheriting, ostracizing and expulsion. *Ofo* is prepared and empowered through the agency of the *dibia* (diviner). The interest of Isiramen hinges on the centrality of indigenous spirituality manifested in the swearing on *Ofo* and its relevance to Igbo business ethics, drawing a comparative analysis between the traditional and modern business practices.

Isiramen identifies and discusses important and significant deities who are in control of morality among the Igbo. Traditional priests, individual deities and ancestral spirits are actively involved in the execution of the entire aspects of morality. There are numerous shrines which house the symbols of these deities which are ritually empowered for people's patronage and use. Oath-taking is the strongest means of moral control on these shrines. Isiramen notes that several shrines exist among the Igbo for the purpose of justice in business, and that the import of the shrines can be understood as an abode of oath-taking in the honest sealing of business agreement. Besides the Ogwugwu shrines, Okija shrines that have been in existence for over 200 years serve the needed ethical purpose for the people.

The concern of this chapter is the effect of foreign influences, modernity, urbanization and Christianity on indigenous spirituality, particularly the issue of oath-taking that is gradually losing its grip, leading to gross business immoral and unethical behaviour. In recognition of indigenous spirituality and principles in human life and practice, Isiramen suggests an incorporation of indigenous spirituality into business ethics, and a modernization of Igbo indigenous business ethical standards. She believes that the ideals of such values would engender sanity in modern Nigeria.

The second part of this section contains two chapters by Oyeronke Olademo and Oyeronke Olademo which focus on women. Olademo's "Women in Yorùbá and Igbo indigenous spirituality" takes on important definitive issues which are crucial to the understanding of women-gender. Of significance is the theoretical issue on women-gender which includes identity politics that involves a process of manipulation by the state or social forces, culture, symbolism, interpretation of religious texts, and economy. All of these are employed in interpreting women in Yorùbá and Igbo indigenous spirituality.

Olademo examines the Yorùbá worldview and the place of women in indigenous religious practices. She emphasizes that "African gender relationships are usually marked by mutual respect and complementary relations." This is demonstrated in the in women's spirituality as it manifests in their leadership roles, healing practices, spirit possession, fertility rites, goddess worship, and divination practices. She notes the effects of this spirituality on the role and status of women in modern Christianity and Islam in contemporary Africa. Her discussion on Igbo counterpart focuses on the ecological dimension of Igbo women spirituality and their function as mediums and diviners through which they facilitate communication with the divine.

Flora Kaplan's ethnographic essay, "Politics in an African royal harem: women and seclusion at the Royal Court of Benin, Nigeria," describes a complex and enduring system of women's role and status in one of the oldest traditional administrative institutions where the monarch is a semi/demi-god. Central to Kaplan's chapter is the phenomenon of seclusion in the harem, the harem being "a world within the world of the vast palace". One striking note in her discussion is the resemblance with Benin, of many early accounts of palace women in the Middle East, China, India and elsewhere that harems were found up to the twentieth century." The author examines various oral traditions and accounts of the development of royal women and the practice of seclusion. She describes the periods of several monarchs and the role and status of women in each from the oral and photographic materials that were produced at each period. Kaplan notes that the seclusion of the wives of the *Oba* was and is a function of the sacred nature of the *Oba* and their bodily contact with him, thus conferring *Oba*'s sacredness to the women in the harem. Thus, these women are forbidden to be touched by any other man, including their own fathers, brothers, or close relatives, once married to the *Oba*.

The social and political purpose of the harem is that it offers women's groups and visitors, an informal opportunity to hear and respond to petitions and requests confided to them by women and men from different parts of Benin kingdom. She is often knowledgeable of grassroots sentiments and issues that may not yet have reached the *Oba*. The wives of the *Oba*, though in this harem, perform several other important functions that have consequence for the *Oba*, the different segments of the community and the entire community. Their identity is so crucial to the definition of the *Oba* and the community.

AIRTs in Diasporic contexts

That African indigenous religious traditions have been global in scope and influence is obvious. Literatures burgeon on the resilience, persistence, and vitality of indigenous religious traditions. AIRTs continue to make waves across the global. In fact, while it is a truism that certain deep aspects of the tradition continue to lose its flavour and assist the traditions (Islam and Christianity) that came to Africa to become relevant in the continent, AIRTs are being revitalized by and in the Diaspora. It has been remarked that:

> The African spirit proved remarkably resilient in the face of the transatlantic slave trade, inspiring the perseverance of African religion wherever its adherents settled in the New World...Thousands of African Americans have turned to the religion of their ancestors, as have many other spiritual seekers who are not themselves of African descent. (Olupona and Rey 2008: cover page).

Dianne Stewart, in "Orisha traditions in the West," examines the production, influence and strength of African-derived religious traditions, of significance which is *Oriṣa* (correct orthography of *Orisha*), in the Black Atlantic world. She discusses the factors that informed the making of the diverse manifestations of *Oriṣa* traditions in various religious cultures in the Americas, and how this phenomenon continues to reinforce African American identity, a spiritual identity that liberates and binds the dislocated people of color. Devotees of *Oriṣa* have their homes in locations such as Salvador, Matanzas, Caracas, Tegucigalpa, Panama City, Port of Spain, Loiza, New York, South Carolina, Toronto, and Birmingham. Stewart further notes that *Oriṣa* traditions have been empowered by multidirectional movement of African peoples including global expeditions, commercial ventures and evangelical enterprises and spiritual ventures. These have inspired the formation, organization and institutionalization of the International Congress of Orisa Tradition and Culture (Orisa World Congress) where practitioners and scholars of indigenous religions engage in efforts at centralizing and institutionalizing of local *Oriṣa* expressions across the globe in order to protect *Oriṣa* legitimacy. The kernel of Stewart's chapter is that "African religion has all ingredients for liberation thought and praxis" which "is not primarily oriented toward responding to social suffering," but that which "is conceptually framed by theories of African retention and religious syncretism."

The chapter by Tony Menelik Van Der Meer, whose initiate name as *Ifa* priest is Awo Alakisa, is a deep personal reflection of the training, practice and initiation into *Ifa* divination which began in 1976 under several teachers and mentors some of who themselves passed through some trainings and initiations under the specialists who claim legitimacy and authenticity. As a committed practitioner and ardent knowledge-seeker, Van der Meer went into several cities and participated in numerous ceremonies and discussions with priests, priestesses and practitioners of those communities. Not only this, this author mentions that he engaged in the study of Yorùbá *Ifa* literature and *Odu* corpus.

The question of authenticity and legitimacy is perhaps the summary of Van der Meer's essay which bothers on environment. The author identifies the Cuban influence and dominance before the emergence of contemporary Nigerian Yorùbá traditional *Ifa* divinatory practices in the United States. Prior to the emergence of the Nigerian system, the Cuban tradition has common rituals, songs, dances and ceremonies that have been in practice; spiritual items for rituals and propitiation could be purchased convenience stores. While "the rituals and ceremonies are in Spanish, the Cuban system incorporates the Yorùbá language or what can be considered Spanish Yorùbá into their practice." However, the concern of orality which is characteristic of *Ifa*/Orisa tradition, that is, adapting and incorporating the Yorùbá language, of which they are not fluent, into their liturgical practices is problematic.

The above and other issues generate controversies among African descendant *Ifa* practitioners in the United States and more controversy about them from priests and practitioners from other *Ifa*/Orisa practices. Van der Meer points out three of these issues which include the issue of money (fees and service charge), gender (women initiated in *Ifa*, and their roles), and race (the initiation of European Americans and the possibility of their access to the sacred knowledge of *Ifa*.

Van der Meer suggests some measures at overcoming the dilemmas, controversies and challenges for African American descendant *Ifa* practitioners in the United States. Among these is the necessity for building local, state, regional, national and international associations of *Ifa* practitioners. He believes that:

> through local associations African descendant *Ifa* practitioners in United States initiated by different *Ifa/Orisa* families in Yorùbáland will be able to come together to develop, learn and function in a more cohesive and supportive environment. This will allow practitioners to adapt and change epistemologically to the shared experiences.

The author also believes that this initiative would create honesty and engender mutual respect among the African Diaspora and practitioners of indigenous religious traditions in homeland Yorùbá and other communities where African-derived religious traditions exist.

Ivor Miller's "Separated by the Slave Trade: Nigerians and Cubans Reunite through a shared cultural practice" presents and examines an African institution – the Ékpè Leopard Society — from a well-defined source region — the Cross River region of Nigeria and Cameroun, and its historically related Caribbean counterpart — the Abakuá society of Havana and Matanzas Cuba. This essay, an ethnographic-based, centres upon the views of leaders from both societies who have participated in recent meetings to display their traditions to each other in order to find common ground, whether in the confirmation of a shared symbolic vocabulary (called *Nsìbìdì* in West Africa) that includes a system of gestures, body masks, percussion ensembles, chants in a ritual language, geometric signs, and auditory vibrations from within an inner sanctum. It is important to state that these leaders are responsible for the maintenance of these systems, and have privileged access to information about their history and codes.

The author compares Abakuá society which was founded by Africans in colonial Cuba in the 1800s, but today has some 150 lodges and 20,000 members in the port cities of Matanzas and Havana with *Ekpe* (leopard) society of Nigeria and Cameroon. Miller notes that since 2001, Abakuá leaders have participated in a series of meetings with representatives *Ekpe* society who are their major source institution. The focus of this essay is the performance mode of communication which holds that while Abakuá and *Ékpè* do not speak the same colonial languages (Spanish and English respectively), they have been communicating through the performance of *Nsìbìdì*. Miller identifies and describes the processes involved in the performances which include chants, body masks, and percussion which provide the useful data in mapping the cultural history of this trans-Atlantic continuum.

"Borderless Homeland: memory, identity and the spiritual experience of an African Diaspora community" by David Ògúngbilé examines the living experiences of a group people of African descent in the Americas and how they have been negotiating, redefining and reinforcing their identity through an intense spirituality and indigenous religious practices. Drawing from the personal narratives, interviews, focus group discussions and participation in their religious and festival celebrations, Ògúngbilé offers a variety of the bases of interpreting and theorizing the Diaspora discourse. They include issues as memory/imagination, settlers/indigenes (native), centre/border (periphery), insider/outsider, immigrants, and homeland/hostland.

The focus of this essay is that African Americans or people of African descent in the Americas generally, while recognizing the social, political, economic and emotional challenges in their American homeland and the implications of these, engaged in the redefinition of their identity by appealing to a common spiritual root. The current political identity, to them, seems to offer inhuman or subhuman treatment. The spiritual identity which is memorialized in indigenous religious practices, through which certain individuals recognise and realise their essence provides a strong basis for a new 'spiritual' community.

Ògúngbilé summarises brief spiritual autobiographies of a group of individuals who describe themselves in terms of religious community. Notably, the individuals narrate their former and current religious experiences and how they accept indigenous religious traditions and the consequences and challenges of their newfound faith as well as the practices, particularly in their American homeland. These individuals make constant references to their nostalgia of their African homeland and the importance of connecting or reconnecting with some *orisa* (Osun, Sango, *Ifa*, Ogun, etc.) through initiation in Yorùbáland and pilgrimage to some annual Yorùbá festivals in Osogbo, Ile-Ife and Oyo. This spiritual 'root' provides ready transitional networks and global linkages to their 'real' reality through certain markers of spiritual identity including ritual and festivals. It is interesting to note that most of these converts built altars in their homes in America, take on Orisa-related names, and engage in the learning of Yorùbá language and *orisa* songs.

Taken together, the essays in *African Indigenous Religious Traditions in Local and Global Contexts: Perspectives on Nigeria* show the nexus among the different aspects of the human life, viz. the social, cultural, ethical, economic, political, etc. The essays validate the claim of the inseparability of the sacred and the profane, and the spiritual and the material of the African worldview (Idowu 1991). The essays in the volume offer important conceptual and methodological perspectives for scholars of indigenous religions in other African communities to show the manifest uniqueness and diversity, resilience and flexibility, and compromise and resistance in the face of competing forces of Islam, Christianity and globalization.

On a final note, I thank Professor Jacob Kehinde Olupona for deepening me and putting my feet in the field of comparative study of religion. I acknowledge the authors who have contributed to this volume, *African Indigenous Religious Traditions in Local and Global Contexts: Perspectives on Nigeria* which has been produced to honour Jacob Kehinde Olupona, who has devoted his life to teaching, mentoring, researching, and for bequeathing to these and upcoming generations an invaluable asset of knowledge. At the outset of this work, the design of the volume was intended not to be as big as this. A few of the scholars were selected and written. Several who heard about the volume that intended to honour Jacob Olupona felt insulted and cheated, they quickly wrote to show interest in participating in the project by contributing to the volume in appreciation for the commitment of Jacob Olupona to scholarship in African indigenous religious traditions. These include young, middle-career, and older colleagues.

I appreciate Professor Tunde Lawuyi and Professor Graham Harvey who enthusiastically, respectively wrote a prologue and foreword for the volume. I acknowledge the friendship and academic exchanges of my fellows at the W.E.B. Du Bois Institute for African and African American Research at Harvard University, which inspired me to put this volume together; and my Research Assistant at the Du Bois Institute, Lisanne Norman, who read and made comments on the first draft of the papers. I thank my colleagues, too numerous to mention, in the Obafemi Awolowo University, Ile-Ife, Nigeria for playing important and diverse roles in my academics that continue to form me into who and what I am today. To my inestimable jewel, Margaret Olusola Ògúngbilé: thanks immensely for always standing by and following me through all the journeys of my academic and spiritual life.

Selected works of Jacob K. Olupona on indigenous religious traditions

The following are selected major works on African Indigenous Religious Traditions by Professor Jacob Kehinde Olupona:

- *African Religions: A Very Short Introduction* (New York: Oxford University Press, 2014)
- *In My Father's Parsonage: The Story of an Anglican Family in Nigeria.* Ibadan: University Press, 2012
- *City of 201 Gods: Ile-Ife in Time, Space and the Imagination* (Berkeley, Los Angeles & London: University of California Press, 2011)
- *Orisa Devotion as World Religion: The Globalization of Yorùbá Religious Culture* (edited with Terry Rey), (Madison, Wisconsin: The University of Wisconsin Press, 2008)
- *African Immigrant Religions in America* (edited with Regina Gemignani), (New York & London: New York University Press, 2007)
- *Beyond Primitivism: Indigenous Religious Traditions and Modernity*, (edited), (London/New York: Rutledge Press, 2004)
- *African Spirituality: Forms, Meanings and Expressions*, Volume 3 of the World Spirituality: An Encyclopedic History of Religious Quests, New York. (New York: Crossroads Press, 2000)
- *The Study of Religions in Sub-Saharan Africa: Past, Present and Prospects*, (edited), (Cambridge: Roots & Branches and University of Zimbabwe Press, 1996)

- *Religious Plurality in Africa: Essays in Honour of John S. Mbiti*, (edited), (Berlin: Mouton de Gruyter, 1993)
- *Religion and Peace in Multi-faith Nigeria* (African Books Collective Ltd, 1992)
- *African Traditional Religions in Contemporary Society* (edited), (New York: Paragon Press, 1991)
- *Kingship, Religion and Rituals in a Nigerian Community: A Phenomenological Study of the Ondo Yorùbá Festivals* (Stockholm Studies in Comparative Religion, 28), (Almqvist & Wiksell International Stockholm, 1991)
- *Religion and Society in Nigeria: Historical and Sociological Perspectives* (edited with Toyin Falola), (Ibadan, Nigeria: Spectrum Press & Channel Islands, England: Safari Press, 1991)
- There are also numerous entries in encyclopaedias, chapters in books and several articles in journals that are used in institutions all around the world.

References

Adetugbo, Abiodun, *African Continuities in the Diaspora*. Lagos: Centre for Black and African Arts and Civilization, 2001.

Awolalu, J.O. and P.A. Dopamu, *West African Traditional Religion* Ibadan, Nigeria: Onibonoje Press, 1979

Geertz, Clifford, "Thick Description: Toward an Interpretive Theory of Culture," in *The Interpretation of Cultures: Selected Essays by Clifford Geertz* New York: Basic Books, 1973

Gehman, R.J., *African Traditional Religion in Biblical Perspective* Kesho Publications, Kenya, 1989

Idowu E. Bolaji, *African Traditional Religion: A Definition* London: SCM Press, 1973

Mbiti, John S., *African Religions and Philosophy* London: Heinemann, 1969

Metuh, Emefie-Ikenga, *African Religions in Western Conceptual Schemes: The Problem of Interpretation (Studies in Igbo Religion)* Ibadan, Nigeria: Pastoral Institute, 1985

Metuh, Emefie-Ikenga, *Comparative Studies of African Traditional Religion* IMICO Publishers, Onitsha, 1987

Olupona, J. K., *Kingship, Religion and Rituals in a Nigerian Community: A Phenomenological Study of the Ondo Yorùbá Festivals*. Stockholm Studies in Comparative Religion, 28. Almqvist & Wiksell International Stockholm, 1991

Olupona, J.K. and Terry Rey (eds.), *Orisa Devotion as World Religion: The Globalization of Yorùbá Religious Culture* Madison, Wisconsin: The University of Wisconsin Press, 2008

Opoku, Kofi Asare, *West African Traditional Religion*, Accra: FEP International Private Limited, 1978

Parrinder, E. Geoffrey, *African Traditional Religion* Sheldon Press, London, 1968
Smart, Ninian, *Dimensions of the Sacred: An Anatomy of the World's Beliefs.* University of California Press, 1996
Smart, Ninian, *The Religious Experience of Mankind.* New York: Charles Scribner's Sons, 1969
Smart, Ninian, *Worldviews: Cross-cultural Explorations of Human Beliefs* (3rd Edition) Prentice Hall, 1999
Van Herik, Judith, "'Thick Description' and Psychology of Religion" in Robert L. Moore and Frank E. Reynolds (eds.) *Anthropology and the Study of Religion* Chicago, Illinois: Center for the Scientific Study of Religion, 1984
Westerlund, David, *African religion in African Scholarship: A Preliminary Study of the Religious and Political Background,* Studies published by the Institute of Comparative Religion at the University of Stockholm 27. Stockholm: Almquist & Wiksell International, 1985

2

The study of indigenous religions: academic bias and its ethical implications for inter-religious conflicts

- J. Kehinde Ayantayo

Introduction

Beyond the theory of errors in terminology launched by Bolaji Idowu and popularized by other scholars such as Parrinder, Awolalu and Dopamu and other contemporary scholars of African traditional religion, the bias against Nigerian indigenous religious traditions (NIRT) has not been seriously considered with references to its implications for interreligious conflicts in Nigeria. This chapter intends to fill this gap. This becomes pertinent for two reasons: one, the exercise would help provide a subtle way of minimizing possible interreligious conflicts that could arise from bias scholars have raised against Nigerian Indigenous Religious Traditions, which is also an issue in the way scholars pass comment about religions different from the one they practice. This becomes imperative in Nigeria where religion is always volatile. Two, it would provide a good way of approaching or studying the Nigerian Indigenous Religious Traditions (NIRT) in a more pragmatic and objective manner at a time when globalization is playing down values that are not in consonance with Western values.

For the purpose of emphasis, Nigerian Indigenous Religious Tradition (NIRT) is used in this work to refer to the traditional religious practices of the Nigerians, as a branch of African Traditional Religion. It is characterized by beliefs in *God, ancestors, divinities, spirits, magic* and *medicine*. These religious beliefs and practices have been in existence from time immemorial and are still adhered to today by many Africans. It is the religion, which has been handed down from generation to generation by the forbearer of the present generations of Africans. Certain essential facts must be known while speaking of Nigerian Indigenous Religious Tradition. First, it is a religion, because it came into existence like other religions, as a result of human experience and the mystery of the universe. Secondly, Nigerian Indigenous Religious Traditions is traditional because it is an aboriginal and fundamental thing, which is handed, down from generation to generation and is still practiced by living men today. Thirdly, Nigerian Indigenous Religious Tradition is based essentially on oral traditions. It has no written literature, sacred scriptures or creed forms. All we know of the religion comes to us through oral tradition – myths and legends, stories and folktales, songs and dances, liturgies and rituals, proverbs and pithy sayings, adages and riddles. Some of these oral traditions appear in works of art and crafts, symbols and emblems, names of people and places, shrines and sacred places. It is important to note that works of art are not merely for decoration. They usually convey religious feelings, sentiments, ideas and truth. It is important to note that each of the five fundamental beliefs system had and still have great influence in the overall life of an average African society. In all things, they are religious. Religion forms the foundation and the all-governing principle of life for them. It is the Deity who is in control of all the circumstances of life including its changing scenes, its joys, and troubles.

Review of scholars' works

In order to establish fact about academic bias in the study of Indigenous African Religious Traditions, we consider it important to review at least three monumental works of earliest indigenous scholars of African Traditional Religions from which others after them took clue. These are works of Geoffrey Parrinder, Bolaji Idowu and John Mbiti. Parrinder outlines a catalogue of four terminologies that the earlier scholars such as Tylor, E.O. James and Levy-Bruhl used to describe the religion (Parrinder 1977, 7-12). The terms are primitivism, fetishism, animism and polytheism. Primitivism as so used by the scholars presupposes that African religion is the type of religion that has remained primitive even in modern times. Illustrating this argument, Tylor assumes that an animistic philosophy was developed by Africans to explain the causes of sleep, dreams, trances, and death as well as the difference between a living body and a dead one on the one hand and the nature of the images that one sees in dreams and trances on the other hand. In the words of Tylor, the primitive peoples are those without written traditions; who believe that spirits or souls are the cause of life in human beings; and who picture souls as phantoms, resembling vapours or shadows, which can transmigrate from person to person, from the dead to the living, and from plants, into animals, and lifeless object. Fetishism is so used to refer to a form of belief and religious practice in which supernatural attributes are imputed to material, inanimate objects, known as fetishes.

According to Parrinder, none of these terminologies is good to describe because they do not practically represent what the religion stands for in content and context. For this reason he concludes that the use of these terminologies for describing African religion is tantamount to bias, which Western scholars had for the African continent. The bias in Parrinder's judgment is a product of the poor research method the Westerners used to study African Indigenous Religious Traditions. To our mind, the problem inherent in the research method goes beyond bias, because today in Nigeria, it has the potential to provoke interreligious conflicts because the terms are basically derogatory and they also amount to irreverent handling of religions different from the religions practised by Westerners.

Taking his cue from Parrinder, Bolaji Idowu debunks the use of certain vocabulary, such as paganism, savagism, nativism, fetishism, heathenism, idolatry and animism to describe African Traditional Religion. Having explained the philological basis of the terms, he concludes that they are derogatory and abusive nomenclatures and therefore are inappropriate to the content and intent of African Traditional Religion. In replacement of the derogatory names, he suggests some names that the religion could be called such as Olodumareism for the Yoruba, Chukwuism for the Igbo of Nigeria, Onyameism for the Akan, Ngewoism for the Mende of Sierra Leone or Imanaism for the Ruanda-Urundi as the case may be, if we are anglicizing the term (Idowu 1973, 108-136). He however noted that the defect of this style is that we shall be left with names rather than a name. This would further complicate the matter! Naming the religion is one thing, developing positive and objective attitudes to its studies and making objective statement about the intent, content and the context of this religion in scholarship is another thing. Studying religions objectively requires orientation in order to prevent conflicts that are likely to arise from the use of derogatory terms to describe the religion.

Mbiti's monumental work on African religions and philosophy also sheds some light on manifestation of academic bias in the work of earliest scholars who studied African Traditional Religion (Mbiti 1982, 6-14). He notes that African religion and philosophy have been subjected to a great deal of misinterpretation, misrepresentation and misunderstanding. With emphasis, he conjectures that the earlier descriptions and studies of African religions as animism, juju, totemism, fetishism and naturism among others left us with terms, which are inadequate, derogatory and prejudicial. This act he interprets as portrayal of the kind of attitude and interpretation dominant in the mind of those who invented or propagated the different theories about traditional religions. To stem the tide of this academic bias, he recommends an ontological and phenomenological study of African religions believing there is great potential in the use of the method. He adds that African scholars studying African religions should also use scientific tools and methodology, which involve empirical study and fieldwork. It is believed that the method would give them the advantage of being part of the people of Africa and with almost unlimited access to information and language of the people. This approach is considered as the key to serious research and understanding of African religions and philosophy.

The recommendation made by Mbiti has been relatively accepted and practised by some Western and indigenous scholars of African religions. This notwithstanding, some contemporary scholars of religious studies still manifest the bias in their research. This attitude is common among scholars who are at the same time priests and priestess in their various religious denominations. Worse still, some of these scholars say negative things about

African Traditional Religions, which is capable of generating interreligious conflicts among scholars who belong to different faiths.

Bias and its manifestation in the contemporary religious studies scholarship

Bias in scholarship amounts to putting a slant on something so that it reflects one's prejudices and sometimes ignorance and sentimentally oriented views and which do not practically portray a true image of the word or thing being described. As a result, students' knowledge of an academic area becomes corrupted with 'facts' which are not really facts at all, but opinion or at best self-servingly selective facts of the teacher or lecturer as that case may be (Meek 1998). Corroborating Meek on the implications of bias in scholarship, Cathy Young observes that:

> one of the implications of not teaching the student full truth is to alienate them from intellectual life. It is not good for any group of people to spend a lot of time listening only to like-minded others. It is especially bad for a profession whose lifeblood is the exchange of ideas. (Young 2007)

We notice that today some contemporary scholars of religious studies, especially those specialising in comparative religions, Christian, and Islamic studies are still fond of using derogatory terms to describe African Traditional Religion in spite of striking revelation from scholars like Idowu and Mbiti, among others. They do so because according to them, they prefer to identify themselves with the fashionable religions of Islam and Christianity. The resentment against traditional religion and its studies is evident in their writings, teachings and sermons in both secular and non-secular institutions. The same is also visible in indigenous home videos and films where traditional religious beliefs are portrayed as demonic. This development in part, had in one way or the other indoctrinated some scholars so much that they hardly see studying and researching Nigeria Indigenous Religious Tradition as a worthwhile academic enterprise. This perhaps has to a large extent contributed to little research work available on issues relating to Nigeria Indigenous Religious Tradition when it is compared with researches in other fields of religious studies such as New Testament Studies, Old Testament Studies, philosophy of religion, women studies/gender studies comparative religious studies, church history, Christian theology, sociology of religion, social ethics, Islam and dialogue. This is also evident in the infinitesimal number of scholars who specialize in the study of Nigeria Indigenous Religious Tradition in Nigerian universities. This could probably explain the lack of interest that many undergraduate and postgraduate students are showing to studying of the Nigeria Indigenous Religious Tradition. For example, during the compilation of material for this chapter, I interviewed a

number of staff and students in the Department of Religious Studies, and asked the following questions:
Have you ever done research in NIRTs?
If yes, what is the title?
Do you prefer research in NIRTs to ones in other disciplines such as Christian Ethics, Church history, Old or New Testament, Sociology of Religion, Christian theology among others?
Do you see Indigenous Religion as ritualistic, which can discourage you from researching into it?
Do you see research in other field of Religious Studies as more profitable than research in African Traditional Religion?
Do you prefer going to a pastor to a Traditional Religious Priest(s) in search of information in your research work in Religious Studies?
Do you see going to Priests of Traditional Religion as having the capacity to affect your religious faith?
Do you see Nigerian Indigenous Religious Traditions as dead, and as such not worth researching?

Responses to the questions are amazing. They are amazing in the sense that majority of the respondents show negative attitude to the study of NIRT on the grounds that it is ritualistic and that researching it has a tendency to affect their religious faiths. Some of the respondents prefer researching on issues relating to their religious faiths rather than studying NIRT. What we can deduce from this is that such scholars have a problem with separating the wheat from the chaff, that is, they lack the research dexterity and good will that would help them to make a line of demarcation between research in Religious Studies and faith in religions.

Ethical interpretation of bias and its implications for interreligious conflicts

There are three fundamental issues from our exposition of bias some scholars have against Nigerian Indigenous Religious Traditions, which to our mind deserve clarification. First, the bias is tantamount to treating or approaching the religions of others with irreverence. This singular act is capable of generating ripples among religious practitioners because every religious practitioner always places his/her religion in high esteem and would not be happy if anybody of any status treats his religion irreverently. Second, the language, which employs terminologies such as animism, juju, totemism, fetishism and naturism, is negative because it is offensive and in itself has the propensity to generate interreligious conflicts. Appropriating this assertion Iwara remarkably writes that:

> Language is like the atom bomb: depending on the use one makes of it, it can cause widespread devastation, as it can be a source for peace and harmony. So powerful, in fact, is language that it has sometimes been

claimed that the pen is mightier than the sword...This is possible because language impacts heavily on a wide range of domains where human beings have vested interest. For example, language, as public behaviour, influences our assessment of the individuals or group's personality, intelligence, social status, educational attainment, job qualification, identity and social survival. (Iwara 2005:73-74)

Drawing inference from the above, it is arguable that the use of offensive language, be it written and spoken, regarding the description of Nigeria Indigenous Religious Tradition could be interpreted as contemptuous and annoying. This perhaps explains why many religious practitioners oftentimes find themselves engaged in interreligious conflicts in the name of defending one religion over another. Religion is such a sacred thing to religious practitioners that a religious person is always ready to defend his/her religion and possibly die for it if the need arises. Hence, the use of derogatory terms can produce ill feelings and negative attitudes against the religions of other people.

In other words, an expression of religious ignorance is attitudinal and has the capacity to provoke interreligious conflict. The attitude falls within the periscope of the variables of what Galtung labels as ABC Triangle, which is an analytical model that views conflict as a triangle with variables such as attitude, behaviour and contradiction (IDASA 2004, 13). An attitude in this regard manifests in perceptions, misconceptions and emotions/feelings; while behaviour manifests in hostility, fear, threats, coercion and destructive efforts. Contradiction manifests in actual or perceived incompatibility of goals. Each of the variables has their place in academic bias against Nigerian Indigenous Religious Tradition and also has implications for interreligious conflicts because they often raise the question of values.

It is important to note that religious beliefs raise the question of value, which is primary to conflict discourse. Evidence abounds in conflict discourse that differences in value held by people at one time or the other is one of causes of conflicts. These types of conflict are described as value-laden (CRESNET 2001). According to experts they are usually difficult to understand and resolve because they are based on belief systems, which are associated with institutionalized norms and worldview. Most time, people could die for what they believe because such would lead them to self-actualization, which is manifested in a feeling of self-fulfilment, realizing one's full potentials as being productive and creative. On account of this, it is important for scholars of religion to stop writing or saying anything that has capacity to belittle the religions of other people.

The second inference we can draw from academic bias against Nigeria Indigenous Religious Tradition is that it appears that biased scholars could be said to have a possibly narrow view of what religion is and what it is not. Thus on the account of this narrow view, every religious believer thinks that his/her own religion is the only religion worthy to be described as religion while religions of others are not worthy to be described as religions. This calls for a revisit of what religion is, that may move towards giving good orientation to every stakeholder in religious studies so that henceforth they can live in the spirit of mutual respect for one another's religion(s).

On the question of what religion is, it is imperative to note that to provide a universally approved definition of religion is by no means an easy task. This development is not unrelated with the fact that religion involves many beliefs and many ways of holding and expressing these beliefs. The various definitions that have been attempted by various writers are valuable to man's conception of what religion is or should be. Some define religion from sociological, psychological, ethical and phenomenological perspectives. While we cannot discuss all these now, a few of them are worth mentioning. For example, Émile Durkheim in his popular book *The Elementary Forms of the Religious Life* defines religion as a united system of beliefs and practices that are related to sacred things that is, things that are set apart and forbidden. He posits that, the distinguishing mark of religion in its most basic form is not belief in divinity or in the supernatural but the existence of objects considered to be sacred by a group of people (Ritzer 2000: 93). According to him, sacredness is a value that a given society places on objects. Such objects shape and generate the religious feelings of its members, and religiousness is therefore a function of social belonging. Durkheim further notes that another group does not necessarily see the holiest things in the world to one group—its gods, saviours, scriptures, or sacraments—as sacred absolutes. The sociological way by which Durkheim defines religion aptly tells us how different people can interpret what is a religion or not. Still on the subject matter of the sacred, Mircea Eliade argues that believing in the divine foundations of life transforms the significance of natural objects and activities. He conjectures that for a religious man, time, space, the earth, the sky, and the human body can all come to have a symbolic, religious meaning (Ritzer 2000: 93).

From an experiential point of view, Rudolf Otto argues that the experience of the numinous— "spiritual power"—is the distinctive core of religiousness. Such experience is marked by a sense of awe in the face of the mysterious other reality that dramatically intersects our limited, vulnerable existence. According to Otto, it is this reality that religious traditions symbolized by employing concepts such as God. The numinous can be experienced as something fearful and alienating, but also as something comforting with which one feels a certain communion or continuity. He adds that religious ideas such as the wrath of God or the peace of God express these different aspects of numinous experience. In his view, the capacity for such awareness lies within each person, and it is the purpose of religious language and observance to shape and elicit this awareness (Ritzer 2000: 93). Joseph Kenny defines religion as any system that relates man to ultimate values, whether God or something else, and which embodies a creed, a code, a cult and a communion. To him all the four features manifest in all religion (Dzurgba 1987).

What we can generate from the above and which has implications for religious understanding is that each of the definitions is associated with theories or origin of religion. It implies that religion involves belief in a Supreme Being; hence, religion is that which brings or expresses the intimate relationship between the creator and his creatures. There is awareness in man that there is something in him reaching out for close examination with a power, which is the source of real life. Man is so constituted and so conditioned that he must be dependent upon God if his life is to be meaningful and harmonious. It is in religion that man and God communicate. Religion is something resulting in the relationship, which God established, from the beginning of human life between Himself and man. In light of this, Charles K. Kegley remarkably classifies essential features of religion into three: belief, feeling and action. He adds the fact that central to religion is beliefs in God or gods, the nature and destiny of man, the meaning of history and hope for the future (Dzurgba 1987). From this, it becomes clear that no individual or group of individuals has a monopoly of truth regarding what religion is or what it is not.

With this submission, we can argue that every man or every group has the right to define and regard what she or he considers as religion in as much as she or he is convinced about what she/he is doing and in much as she or he does not interfere in the affairs of other people who equally have a right to religious conviction. In conclusion, religion could be likened to a football field where we have many players from both ends of the field. The ultimate desire of every player is to make a score mainly through the goal post. A shot that passes through the goal post and makes a score can come from different directions of the field. By analogy, God could be likened to the goal post, while all the players in the field who attempt the shots, which come from every direction, could be likened to diverse religions of the world. This is an important point for all stakeholders in religion to note.

Solution to the problem of bias

Two issues are to be addressed in proffering solution to academic bias against NIRT. These are research and teaching matters. There is a need to promote sound and objective teaching of NIRT, which implies employment of a good style to pass information across to the students without the teacher imposing his/her religious faith on students. Appropriating the importance of the above assertion Thomas H. Huxley suggests the application of what he terms Methodological Agnosticism in the teaching of Religious Studies. According to him, this theory concerns the limits of what is and what is not knowable. It is a stance that avoids any and all stands on issues of knowledge. It seeks not to establish a position in response to this question but to describe, analyse and compare the positions taken by others (McCutcheon 1999: 215-220). Still on this, Kurt Rudolph adds that:

> To be absolutely clear, one should not add that for the study of religions "God" or "the divine" or "the numinous" does not constitute an object of study. Instead, this study examines the manifold evidence and multiple data for human belief and action which appear in this realm and which one still encounters in living, changing form today, either through personal experience or through reading and study. (Rudolph 2000: 233)

Buttressing this valid point, the Writing Center, University of North Carolina at Chapel Hill writes that: "Religious Studies takes place within a secular, academic environment, rather than a faith-oriented community." Also corroborating this important assertion, which we shall revisit for proper exploration in the latter part of this work, Kurt Rudolph writes:

> ...the study of religion approaches religion and religious data in a way that is completely different from the approach of religion and its faithful advocates. (2000: 232)

For this reason every lecturer of religious studies is not expected to indoctrinate the students who as a matter of fact are mature enough to separate the facts from fictions. Perhaps it is the recognition of this fact that Bruce Lincoln says that reverence is a religious and not a scholarly virtue (Lincoln 2000: 118). Because of the sensitivity of this matter, a scholar of Religious Studies should equip him/herself with at least four factual statements and teaching principles outlined by Michael Pye as criteria to studying religion in a pluralistic religious world. These are:

(1) The study of religions (*religionswissenschaft*- that is scientific study of religion) is not concerned with the search for religious truth, but rather with the description and scientific investigation of religious phenomenon from a "meta-level" that is from the standpoint of independent reflection. This does not imply a claim to be superior to religious truth in any way.

It cannot be the task of the study of religions, therefore to substantiate or disprove truths, which may be contained in religious doctrine.

(3) One's own personal religious experience is not a prerequisite for working in the study of religions and neither is there any obligation to maintain an anti religious attitude (as in the traditions critical of religion deriving from Feuerbach, Durkheim and others).

Since the study of religions does not serve the interests of any religion, it should be distinguished, for example from missiology and apologetics or a theology of religion. (Pye, 2004, 22)

At this juncture, we can then argue that the teaching of Religious Studies should not be persuasive, sympathetic, apologetic or dogmatic, rather it should be critical, analytical, objective, interpretative and explanatory (to borrow the words of J. S. Jensen and L .H. Martin in their description of principles underlying scientific study of religion (Jensen and Martin 1997)). This to our mind can be called ethics of sound teaching and faith detachment.

For instance, a rational attitude is to be adopted during the course of research: being rational we mean being objective and open in research enterprise so that a researcher does not allow his personal religious experience, emotion and sentiment to influence his research observation, report and publication. In this sense, scholars like Helmut Gollwitzer and Rudolf Bultman and later Ninian Smart have proposed such terminologies such as "methodological atheism," "dogmatic atheism" and "methodological neutrality" (Rudolph, 2000). The above suggests that researchers in religious matters should be faith neutral whenever they are carrying out research because according to Pye again, religious scholarship seeks to maintain an unbiased and value–free attitude. The attainment of this calls for openness and objectivity, which in fact intertwine.

There should be emphasis on research methodology, which appropriates sound research ethics. Appropriating research ethics presupposes that a scholarly study of religion involves seriousness, reflection, diligence, painstakingness, hard work, rational thinking, creativity, wit, insightfulness, perceptiveness, awareness, and discernment among others. It is important to note that empirical and rational study of religion requires evaluation of religious truth. This has a good place in the philosophy of religion. For example, this method is capable of mirroring the question of the relations between revelation and reason or faith and reason as reflected upon in all the Western theistic traditions. Reason and rationality has been the subject of debate in endless variations throughout Western intellectual history.

Empirical study also entails historically or socio-scientific studies of documentable phenomena, which go hand in hand with adumbration of the field. That is, the researcher should be able to sieve fact from fictions as regards information collected in the field. This should be done with caution because one of the shortcomings of this method is that it has a tendency to mislead researchers to believe that "religion" is basically a state of mind. To the best of our knowledge, all religious systems exist at least in part, in the mind of its adherents. But these adherents are socially observable. Studying religions empirically therefore, suggests collecting data in the field, which can be documented on the basis of sources open to more than one investigator and consequently studied in a publicly accessible manner. Empirical method as a scientific method suggests:

(i) the systematic search for verifiable data (facts) firmly rooted in prior knowledge and theoretical formulations;
(ii) the production of evidence as opposed to hearsay, opinion, intuition, or common sense;
(iii) following procedures that others can verify and replicate.

This also implies that empirical research findings are testable. In other words, a research is said to be empirical when it studies and draws conclusions about phenomena that are observable. In order to confirm or refute any particular theory, the research must test that theory with relevant empirical observations, or data. For instance a rational attitude is to be adopted during the course of research.

In other words, what scholars of religion must do in order to display or exhibit high level of rationality and objectivity is to adopt what Peter Donovan describes as suspension of belief and disbelief. This implies turning attention away from the contentious or dubious, so as to concentrate on matter open to investigation by agreed procedures; in particular, the careful, sensitive description of the subject matter itself (Donovan 1999:241). Furthermore, research in Religious Studies implies two things namely knowledge of religious language, reverence, sympathy and empathy which have moral flavour. Competence and knowledge of the researcher is another important principle, which should guide every person engaging in meaningful Religious Studies scholarship. It suggests that every scholar must be competent in terms of understanding and having full or deep knowledge about his own religion and the faith of others with whom he interacts. For example, the Muslim who wants to do research in Christianity must have a good understanding of Christian beliefs and practices and even the original language of the Bible, such as Hebrew and Greek, and must be able to do the exegesis of Biblical passages when the need arises. With this, she/he will be in a good position to understand and know the context in which a particular Biblical message is framed. The same goes for a Christian regarding his understanding of Islam. Besides, each of them needs to know fully the occasion that led to a particular statement so that such a statement will not be quoted out of context and thereby lead to misinterpretation. Each researcher should also be conversant with the cultures from which a particular religion evolved.

A researcher or scholar who relies on information gathered from a few books without obtaining additional information from religious leaders of the concerned religion and every other person who has vital information on the subject matter being studied would end up knowing very little of the required information and such a scholar is likely to make erroneous research findings and conclusions.

On the issue of reverence, it is important to note that, religion is a sacred phenomenon and therefore must be accorded reverences due to its sacredness. Therefore the religion of other people with whom we enter into dialogue must be treated with respect, awe, honour, admiration, esteem, and veneration as the adherents of such religion accord it. No religious person will want his religion to be treated with disdain, disrespect, lack of reverence, and impudence. This is so because all religions are very important to their adherents, because it provides them with information about the mystery of the universe and the eternity. Therefore during the process of dialogue, every religious issue should be treated with reverence because each religious person treats his/her religion reverently and would want others dealing with the religion do the same.

Sympathy and empathy in religious studies scholarship goes with tolerance, which entails accommodating the feelings, opinion, assessment, belief, comment, conviction, estimate, idea, impression, notice, point of view, sentiment and way of thinking of a religion being studied and that of their religious practitioners, the researchers of religious practices notwithstanding. For example, when a Christian scholar is studying Islam he/she should go extra mile to find out why and appreciate why Muslims kneel, sit, or bow during prayer without condemning the liturgical practices on the ground that they differ from Christianity. Conversely, Muslim scholar too should appreciate why some Christians jump up, roll on the ground and even weep during prayer without condemning the liturgical practices on the ground that they differ from what occurs in Islam. In the same vein, we need to understand while traditional worshippers bow before objects in their shrines. Rather than condemning these liturgical activities because they are strange to us, we should seek information regarding the feeling of a religious practitioner noting that religion is a personal affair and it usually depends on a person's long-term experience. So, if an adherent of religion jumps up in prayer, it could be that that is the best way for him/her to show appreciation for what God has done for him/her.

Research should be undertaken in accordance with commonly agreed standards of good practice as are laid down in the Declaration of Helsinki, which contains widely accepted principles essential for meaningful and result-oriented research enterprise. It zeroes in three principles, viz: the first is principle of Beneficence ('do positive good') and Non-Malfeasance ('do no harm'), which presupposes that:

(a) It should be scientifically sound and the purpose should be to contribute to knowledge; and (b) that the research should be undertaken and supervised by those who are appropriately qualified and experienced;

The second principle is informed consent which implies that the consent of respondents to research questions especially interview questions should be sought regarding the intent and the context of the questions. This presupposes among other things that:

(a) each potential subject must be adequately informed of the aims, methods, anticipated benefits and potential hazards of the research and any discomfort it may entail; (b) any documentation given to potential participants should be comprehensible and there should be an opportunity for them to raise any issues of concern; (c) consent should be required in writing and records of consent should be maintained; (d) potential participants must be informed that they are free to withdraw consent to participation at any time; (e) there should be a procedure for making complaints and participants should be made aware of this; (f) all participants should be volunteers.

From the above we can deduce that considerable care should be taken where consent is sought from those in a dependent position and it should be made clear that refusal to participate will not lead to any adverse consequences. For example, students must be assured that any decision not to participate will not prejudice in any way their academic progress; (g) any inducement offered to participants should be declared and should be in accordance with appropriate guidelines; (h) consent must be obtained from a legal guardian in the case of minors or any others who do not have the legal competence to give informed consent.

Confidentiality/Anonymity is the third category. It suggests that all research should conform with legislation relating to data protection. In other words, details that would allow individuals to be identified should not be published, or made available, to anybody not involved in the research unless the individuals concerned give explicit consent, or such information is already in the public domain. In addition, all reasonable steps should be taken to ensure that confidential details are secure and great care must be taken where there is an intention to use data collected for one study, for another study. It is important that relevant guidelines are followed.

Bringing ethics to research in NIRT like other aspects of religious studies is rewarding for many reasons. One, it has the capacity to help stem the tide of possible conflicts that may arise from irreverent ways in which a few scholars of religion have treated religions different from their own. Besides, inculcation of the code of ethics would bring about innovation and creativity in religious scholarship enterprise more than before. This would in turn reduce suspicion, bickering and mutual distrust often associated with Religious Studies in the past. Such a good development has tendency to enhance respect and mutual respect within and without religious studies scholarship and among scholars of religious studies, especially in a country like Nigeria that is noted for her religious pluralism. The integration would not only promote inclusive scholarship because more scholars would open up to learn more about religions different from their own since Religious Studies is not about proselytization, but a pure academic work which in the long run would help to widen the horizons of scholars. It is in the light of this provable assertion that Jacob Neusner correctly remarks that the person who knows only one religion understands no religion. Consequently scholars of religious studies would be better equipped with good teaching and research tools that would enable them highlight and discuss the meaningful place religions occupies in solving global problems such as poverty, ethnicity, racism and gender problems.

Concluding remarks

What we are advocating on a final note is that religious scholars should not be biases in their approach to religions different from theirs because such may be contemptuous, blasphemous and disrespectful. In as much as we revere our religion and place it on high esteem, it will be morally wrong to speak evil about other religions. This is important because as our religion is important to us, we should honestly accept that the religions of other people are equally important to them. This is a poser for scholars of religion who at all time should be objective, rational, neutral and courteous in the study of religion qua religion. Granted this, academic scholars should take the lead in educating those who could be described as illiterate on religious matters are religiously ignorant. All should join hands to promote mutual respect as this relates to religion noting that respect begets respect. From ages to the present, religion remains sacrosanct in Nigerian life. Therefore, the practice of saying contemptuous things about religions different from ours shall continue to generate conflicts in which there will never be a winner or a loser. This is a poser for all stakeholders in the promotion of interreligious relation and peace building in Nigeria and Africa where interreligious conflicts have been an endemic problem.

References

A Toolkit: Peace Practice in Nigeria, Abuja; Published by Institute for Democracy in South Africa, (IDASA), 2004

Conflict Management Training Manual, Produced by Conflict Resolution Stakeholders Network (CRESNET), 2001.

Dzurgba, A., *Sociology of Religion*, Ibadan: A Publication of the Department of Adult Education, University of Ibadan, 1987.

Idowu, E. Bolaji, *African Traditional Religion: A Definition*, London: S.M.C. Press, 1973.

Iwara, A.U., "Language and Communication in Conflict Resolution and Peace Building" *Perspectives on Peace and Conflicts in Africa: Essays in Honour of Gen (Dr) Abudusalami Abubakar*, Isaac Olawale Albert (ed.), Ibadan: Peace and Conflicts Studies, University of Ibadan in Collaboration with John Archer Publishers, 2005: 65-79 & 73-74.

Jensen, J. S. and L. H. Martin (eds.) *Rationality and the Study of Religion*, Aarhus, 1997, (Acta Jutlandica LXXII)

Kurt Rudolph "Some Reflections on Approaches and Methodologies in the Study of Religions" In J. S. Jensen and L.H. Martin (eds.) *Secular Theories on Religion: Current Perspectives,* University of Copenhagen: Museum Tusculanum Press, 2000: 231-247.

Lincoln, Bruce, "Reflections on Theses on Method," in J. S. Jensen and L. H. Martin (eds.) *Secular Theories on Religion: Current Perspectives*, University of Copenhagen: Museum Tusculanum Press, 2000: 117-136.

Mbiti, John S., *African Religions and Philosophy*, London: Heinemann, 1982.

McCutcheon, Russell T., "How Do We Know What We Claim to Know?" In Russell T. McCutcheon (ed.) *The Insider /Outsider Problem in the Study of Religion: A Reader,* London: Cassell, 1999: 215-220

Meek, Nigel, *Three Forms of Bias in Academic Instruction* London: An occasional Publication of the Libertarian Alliance, 1998, www.libertarian.co.uk Retrieved from *http://www.libertarian.co.uk/lapubs/educn/educn030.pdf*

Parrinder, Geoffrey, *West African Religion*, London: Epworth, 1977.

Peter Donovan, "Neutrality in Religious Studies" In Russell T. McCutcheon (ed.) *The Insider /Outsider Problem in the Study of Religion: A Reader,* London: Cassell, 1999: 235-247.

Pye, Michael, "The Study of Religions and Its Contribution to Problem-solving in a Plural World", *Marburg Journal of Religion*, Vol. ? No. ?, 2004: ???-???

Ritzer, George, *Sociological Theory*, 4th edition, New York: McGraw-Hill International Editions, 2000.
University of North Carolina at Chapel Hill Writing Center.
(http://www.google.com/search?hl=en&q=Writing+Center%2C+University+of+North+Carolina+at+Chapel).
Young, Cathy, *The Impact of Academic Bias*, | March 8, 2007. This was retrieved from the Internet on Nov 14th 2007. See also
http://www.reason.com/news/show/119026.html

3

Historical strands of religious interaction in Nigeria

- Ogbu Uke Kalu

The task

The burden of this contribution is the role of the religious factor in nation's history. The historian studies religion from the contemporary to the mythical. Interest in phenomenology of religion is limited to the ability of this method in explaining the role of religion amidst competing variables (political and economic) in the understanding of change. The position is more akin to that of a sociologist. The sociologist would ignore issue of validity of religious experience and concentrate on the analysis of the manifestation of the religious factor in social organization. As Evans-Pritchard, an anthropologist put it:

> This then is the task of social anthropologist, to show the relation of religion to social life in general. It is not his task to 'explain' religion.[1]

This goes for the historian too. The task is to delineate the force of the religious factor in pre-colonial, colonial and post-colonial periods of Nigerian history.

Obviously, those time frames are too broad and for the pre-colonial era tends to leave wrong impression that the religious structure was static. Ranger and Kimambo working from the experience of East Africa have drawn attention to a historical study of religion.[2] Religious ideas and rituals evolve through time. for instance, it has been argued that the original Igbo religion consisted of emphasis on *Chi, Ala* (mother earth), *alusi* (spirits) and the ancestors; that the overarching *Chukwu* (supreme god) was in fact propagated by the Nri in their effort to build a sacerdotal hegemony.[3] Scholars may argue the hypothesis but none would deny that some ideas evolve into the

---

[1] E.E. Evans-Pritchard (ed.) *Institutions of Primitive Society* (Oxford: University Press), p. 6
[2] T. O. Ranger & I.N. Kimambo (eds.) *The Historical Study of African Religions* (Berkeley, California: University of California Press, 1972), Intro.
[3] C. Azuonye, "Hgbo Folktales and Evolution of the Idea of Chukwu as the Supreme God of Igbo Religion." *Faculty of Arts, University of Nigeria, Nsukka Lectures*, 1986

prominence either in the course of legitimizing new political structures or as a result of interaction with people with other religious beliefs. Similarly, rituals flourish and wane. The constraints of space and ignorance will not permit an elaborate subdivision of the pre-colonial period.

For the colonial period, a closely delineated periodization would take cognizance of Ayandele's observation that the initial attitude of colonial officers towards traditional rules and cultures bore elements of respect before confidence bred disrespect and iconoclasm.[4] The formulation of cultural policy in the colonial period took some time and, therefore, religion played various roles through to the period of nationalist resistance[5] and decolonization.

The post-colonial period has easily demarcated herself with coups. Each regime created certain identifiable attitudes to religion. The Civil War interlude also raised religion and ethical issues to the fore.

Yet a curious aspect to this enterprise is the neglect of religion in contemporary analyses of Nigerian political history. Perhaps political instability, rapid economic and social changes have produced a Marxist learning in social analysis. It is true that Marxism does not neglect the force of religion but the materialist critique lays more emphasis on the economic structure. Marxist scholars avoid religion in their analysis as Christians avoid opium.

Religion in traditional structure

Our point of departure would be first to clear some historiographical underbrush. History studies man in time perspective. But two dominant trends have been firstly, to study climaxes in the history of communities. The corollary easily focuses on royalty and men of prominence ignoring servants, peasants and the populace who serve as faceless props in the backdrop. A second trend has focused on organization or structures – political and economic. Thus, in Nigeria, for instance, the administrators, their constitutional creations and other change agents as missionaries received enormous attention.

Recent historiography has countered this trend by refocusing on individuals, their thoughts, fears, hopes and survival strategies in the face of a harsh ecosystem. This new trend is important for the understanding of the religious factor. Though a periodization into pre-colonial, colonial and post-colonial has been adopted, the study of the religious factor cannot be stuffed neatly into such time frame nor can it be approached by merely examining the operation of the institutionalized forms within these periods. Religion is permeating in characteristics. We must start from the individual, psychological level – the matrix of persistent attitudes.

---

[4] E.A. Ayandele, "Traditional Rulers and Missionaries in Pre-Colonial West Africa." *Tarikh* 31 (Dec. 1969):23-37
[5] O.U. Kalu, "Formulation of Cultural Policy in Colonial Nigeria" in E. Ihekweazu (ed.) *Traditional and Modern Culture* (Enugu: Fourth Dimension Publications, 1985): Chapter 9.

At the individual level religion serves three basic functions: explanation, prediction and control of space-time events. Man's quest for security induced an urge to understand and explain the undergirding *order* in the world in which he lives. It has been speculated that religion, in fact, arises out of human inadequacy, fear and apprehension with regard to the unknown, the unstructured, the disordered, discordant or inexplicable aspects of nature. Evans-Pritchard in his *Theories of Primitive Religion* quickly dismissed the speculation on origin as unscientific.[6] But there is little doubt that religion has been used to explain order. Such a mental structuring or explanation of how and why things are the way they are, creates security and determines the structure of acceptable values and moral order.

Based on the worldview articulated, it becomes more feasible to predict space-time events. Divination of various, futurological prophecies are all based on religious perception of the moral order. From here it is a short step to the control of space-time events through healing, rain-making and suchlike activities.

Thus, the core of Nigerian traditional societies was not the political, economic or social orders but the worldview which dominated the psyche of individuals. In Marxist jargon, the other aspects were 'superstructures'. We should, therefore, begin a study of the traditional societies by first looking at the Nigerian's perception of his world from which his values are derived and to which his morals are anchored.

The design of a worldview is most feasible with the Kantian model of Time and Space as the basic predicates. Within this perspective, the western scientific perception of Time moves in a linear form from the past through the present to the future: →Past → Present → Future

But the Nigerian's perception of Time is cyclical: life moves from birth through childhood and adulthood to death with a return through reincarnation to birth as the endless cycle repeats (See diagram).

---

[6] E.E. Evans-Pritchard, *Theories of Primitive Religion* (Oxford: Clarendon Press, 1965); cf. O.U. Kalu, "Snake Skins?: Marxist Materialist Critique and African Traditional Religion," (Faculty of Social Sciences Seminar Series, University of Nigeria, Nsukka), 1975.

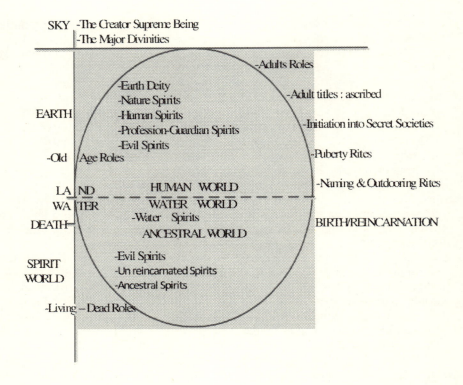

AFRICAN WORLDVIEW (Adapted from Kalu, 1978)

More details of this perception of Time include various rites of passage: from the ululations of parturition follow out-dooring, naming, puberty rituals, initiations into childhood societies, young adult societies and full/male societies – some secret, others open; some ascriptive, others achieved titled societies. Old age brings with it certain responsibilities – political, adjudicatory and so on till death transforms the individual to ancestral roles of protecting the lineage and community from the spirit world. Every dead man does not become an ancestor. Moral prerequisites limit the status to those who have lived clean lives and did not die from inexplicable diseases such as leprosy or smallpox or from brutal death from lightning, falling trees and such-like. Such deaths smack off the anger of the gods and the punishment for concealed crimes. Ancestors reincarnate and start a journey in the human world again. Specific issues about the length of the journey in the spirit world are unclear and unsystematic. But second and third burial ceremonies are used to urge a smooth passage in that world and to ensure an early return.

With a cyclical perception of Time goes a three-dimensional conception of Space. The sky is the abode of the Creator Spirit and the agents who are regarded as major divinities. Some of these are nature spirits such as the sun, moon, etc. The human world is not only inhabited by living human souls but by a number of spirit beings: some major divinities such as the earth goddess, nature deities such as earth, trees, rivers, rocks, human spirits, guardian spirits which look after various professions – farming, hunting, fishing, trading – and ubiquitous evil spirit.

Evil spirits especially the wandering spirits of those who did not receive proper burials also inhabit the spirit world beneath. But this is the abode of the ancestral spirits hence libations are poured on the ground. The ancestors as 'living dead' still protect their human families and are assiduously acknowledged in life events.

A major characteristic of this worldview is the predominance of the spirits, good ones and bad ones. Indeed the perception is a precarious world infested by evil spirits who machinate to thwart the joys of the human world (Kalu 1978). Man, therefore, placates, oblates, pleads, sacrifices, observes taboos and various cleansing rituals in order to harness the resources of the good gods for protection and prosperity.

It is predominantly religious worldview: the world in which we live is not a soulless, physical cosmos inn the Greek sense of *oikos*, rather, it is a spiritualized order. Rattray aptly calls it 'an alive universe'. It is imbued with a moral order which determines and influences man's reaction to the world and to other human beings. Thus, social, political and economic ethics are derived from this worldview.

The history of our pre-colonial world revolves around the various strategies in coping with the varied ecosystems in what later became a nation called Nigeria. Myths of migration trace the paths to various settlements: the imperatives of various ecologies forced changes in economic activities as well as in political arrangements. Some developments elaborated state systems while others utilized segmentary allocation of power or even resorted to democratic decision-making processes. But at the core of the changing patterns was a sacralized worldview which drew little difference between the profane and sacred.

Thus, the society was held together by values which were underpinned by religion. For instance, within the primary level of the family, certain values were inculcated: respect for age was primary; child respected parents and other sibling while the *paterfamilias* played priestly role. Sex and role differentiations while tending towards male dominance was modified by the respect for authority based on age. The movement along the life cycle conferred power and wisdom. Certain personal values form corollaries: hard work, achievement, sense of fulfilment, good neighbourliness, humaneness, honesty, integrity, beauty as character. These were cultivated as antidotes to dysfunctional competitions among sibling and among males and females caused by the enlargement of kinship scale and economic activities and especially inheritance. The dysfunctional elements were quickly explained by the machination of evil forces. Hence, much attention was paid to the possibilities of poisoning, witchcraft, sorcery and such-like.

At the communal level, the clash of interest of various families and men of local prominence was subdued by community-wide age-grades, secret and open societies, sacralization of authority, clear enunciation of wealth and sex differentiations and the cultivation of a priestly case who served as guardians of communal deities. Oracles adjudicated with no possibility of appeal while diviners searched for lost goods, prophesied the future and controlled space-time events for clients.

Religion controlled economic activities. Certain priestly families served the vocational gods, determined the timing for planting and harvesting, protected goods and ensured prosperity. Poor harvests were blamed on angry and offended gods while rituals were used to make amends.

At the political level, there were no secular theories of obligation: gods were the real resources or primary and secondary authority while rulers were spiritualized agents. Certain perceptions of power emerged around the concept of stewardship, especially a humble, moderate and honest use of power. The parts of the ruler's body became linguistic symbols: the head, the eye, the tongue, the arm and the leg. The head was the abode of the spirits; the eye, when opened with certain rituals started to see into the mysteries of life while the tongue delivered justice unless when defiled; the arm achieved either by building or destroying or punishing while the leg aided communication, weaving the dispersed community of families into a whole. Investiture rituals with their elaborate liturgies demonstrate the dominant political values in our pre-colonial world.

Of course, it was not a halcyon world: the explanation of causality by appeal to inscrutable fate, gods and spirits tended to narrow the power base: priests, the wealthy and rulers built an oligarchic concept of power and terrorized and exploited the weak. Witchcraft and sorcery betrayed the level of socio-economic tension in the community while various aspects of social stratification marginalized large section of the community. It could, in fact, be argued that the success of change agents such as the colonial fact was due to the increasing dysfunctional elements or contradictions in the traditional world.

In summary, religion constituted the core ideology in the pre-colonial especially as little notion of secularity existed. Religion served varied functions. Firstly, it served as a force of personality integration so that man found peace with his universe, fellow men and ancestors. This he achieved through thanksgiving and propitiatory sacrifices, libations, observation of taboos, oral and blood oaths and other manipulative ritual acts. Secondly, man cooled his anxieties through prayers and varied types of divination − prophetic and revelatory. Thirdly, religion served as a means of acquiring the good life, material well-being as well as health. Religious rituals secured mental and physical health and warded off evil such as witchcraft and sorcery. Fourthly, religion not only sacralized life and life events but explained the pattern of order. The meaning of life was embedded in religious notions and symbols.

Fifthly, religion underpropped the economic order: the gods protected those who were engaged in economic pursuits, ensured success in economic enterprises, protected materials from roguish eyes and served as source of sanctions in regulating the economic order. Thus rituals determined the pattern of the agricultural cycle. Sixthly, since there was no secular theory of obligation, religion underpropped the political order. Royalty assumed the dual man-spirit personality. Obedience was rooted in religious logic while most instruments of social control were clothed in religious symbolism. Thus, among the Igbo, for an example, the *Ofo* icon assumed immense political and religious significance. It represented truth and justice, it defined status, it evoked loyalty and the certainty that the holder is imbued with moral righteousness and fairness. It left the impression that the supernatural world spoke and governed through the medium of the holder of the *Ofo* stick. Finally religion was sub-served by art - plastic and fine arts − dance, drama, music and entertainment. Once in a while, the god would come as guests to the human world. Masquerades such as the *Egungun, Omabe, Owo* and so on colourfully played out the roles. One area which should deserve attention is the connection between the character and accoutrements of the masquerades and the ecology.

A seventh aspect which would also need closer study is the role of religion in early state formation. Over a decade ago, Abdullahi Smith examined some of the consideration involved in the formation of States in Hausaland. Beyond economic and military considerations he drew attention to the role of religion, especially the significance of the black hills of Hausaland. Following Greenberg, he argued that these were "the dwelling places of the great *iskoki* and may well have been centres of powerful cultural attraction over wide areas", that the Dala hills of Kano, the hills of Kufena and Turunku played similar roles.[7]

To conclude this section with some more general states; the social history of Nigeria moves from a delineation of the core structures in the traditional contexts through the changes wrought by external and internal elements to the modern and complex times. The dominance of religion at the initial point is not peculiar to our society. Indeed, the cyclical perception of time, related to the agricultural season which Mircea Eliade calls "the myth of the eternal return" is evidenced in all preliterate communities.[8] Some values within this context were salient while others were destructive even though they made sense within the total context of the culture. For instance, the incidence of human sacrifice and witchcraft accusation increased with harsh economic fortunes, yet neither of these meant that life was held as cheap. On the contrary, blood was sacred and blood could only be used as a high price to pay for crimes which threatened the existence of the community.

An understanding of development in Nigeria could be achieved by examining whether such salient values survived the forces of modernity in the colonial and post-colonial periods. The perspective here is that enduring culture change must be rooted in the traditional culture of the people by utilizing some values, modifying others while jettisoning those which no longer serve the new times adequately.

Islam in Traditional Society

One school of social anthropology tends to measure the spread of modernity by the demise of religion. It harks back to the Frenchman Auguste Comte whose three stages of civilization was a model which plotted the development path of civilization from a theological phase through a philosophical phase to the dawn of science. This model does not it with the cultural history of Nigeria. Three constraining facts include the incursion of Islam into Northern Nigeria before British presence, the deliberate use of Christianity by the British as an instrument of colonization and the obstinate persistence of traditional religion and the worldview which it underpins. Thus, instead of the demise of religion, a three-way competition between traditional

---

[7] O. U. Kalu, "Precarious Visions: the African's Perception of His World" in O.U. Kalu (ed.) *Readings in African Humanities: African Cultural Development* (Enugu: Fourth Dimension Publishers, 1978): Chapter 3; A. Smith, "Some Considerations relating to the formation of States in Hausaland" *JHSN* 5.3 (Dec. 1970, p. 340

[8] Mircea Eliade, *Patterns of Comparative Religion* (London: 1958 English translations)

religiosity, resurgent Islam and Christianity ensured. Layers of British policies enhanced the prospects of all.

Since the mythical kingdom of Prester John could not be located in West Africa and the French claim for a mission base in West Africa dating to the 11th century is definitely fictitious, Islam arrived before Christianity in Nigeria and should be examined first.

The incursion of Islam has been dated to the 3rd Muslim century or the eighth Christian century. The early development, according to al-Bakri, was in Kanem which is situated to the north-east of Lake Chad. Islam came through trade links with Tripoli in North Africa via Kawar and the Fezzan. However, both al-Bakri and another Arab Commentator al-Muhallabi claimed that as late as the 10th century, the people of Kanem still venerated their king instead of God Most High. It would appear that further widespread of Islam into Hausaland occurred from the late 14th and early 15th century through Muslim traders from the Upper Niger region known by the various names as Wangara, Dhula and Yarse. Gold and kolanut of the forest region were key commodities.

Historians have often pointed to the caution which must be employed in the use of Kano Chronicle; however, this 17th century document contains much detailed information for those interested in the pattern of Islamic expansion in Hausaland. The interest here is rather on the process of Islamization, that is, on the role played by Islam in catalyzing changes in the political, economic and social development of Nigeria. The second area of interest would be on the relative fortunes of Islam during the colonial era.

Robin Horton has pointed out that the process of islamization usually operated in three stages – quarantine, mixing and militant evangelization.[9] The early stages of Islam operated in courts and among trades. Wandering Arab scholars performed many secretarial, administrative and diplomatic roles for rulers while the Arab traders controlled the exchange of foreign goods. The Muslims often lived in exclusive areas and practiced their religious rituals and dietary laws. Indigenous traders who wished to share in the trade were virtually forced to adopt Muslim religion. Cultural adaptation followed trade and gradually Islamic influence spread as initial hostilities cooled.

The famous writing of al-Maghili, "The Crown of Religion Concerning the Obligations of Princes" symbolizes the style of this early period. Al-Maghili arrived in Kano about 1492 on a journey which took him to Mecca, Air, Gao and Katsina. This document which has been compared to Machiavelli, *The Prince,* shows how Islamic influence

---

[9] Robin Horton, "On the Rationality of Conversion." *Africa* 45.3 (1975):219-235; 45.4 (1975): 373-399

started to permeate political ethics. But the comparison ends at the date of writing. Al-Maghili betrays an intriguing aspect of Islamic religion namely, the claim to be a total way of life, subsuming all actions, thought and life style to the mandate of the Qur'an. Instead of the humanist, astute politique of Machiavelli sought to create a theocratic conception of power and governance. His writings later influenced Usman dan Fodio and much of the political and religious history of Northern Nigeria. The Kano chronicle claims that Al-Maghili not only produced a Qur'an but trained over 3,000 teachers who propagated the faith in Hausaland. The exaggeration does not detract from the impact of such wandering scholars on the royal courts.

But Lamin Sanneh has drawn attention to the roots of the mixing st5age: political rulers served two complementary roles. One was to facilitate the introduction of Islam into their states, and the other was to help expose it to local religions. Thus, when Islam finally took root in African societies, particularly in those places where the ruling class were the first to be Islamized, it assumed a flexibility imposed on it by the host environment.[10] In time, many Muslim centres, cut off from outside influences, regressed and became subsumed under the preponderant traditional religious waves. He concluded that Islam relied for its survival on the patronage of the older African traditions hence the diatribes on rulers by the militant orthodoxy of the jihadists. Muslims railed against 'heathenism' while absorbing ingredients of African tradition religiosity for survival. The conflict between Islam and traditional religion remained ambiguous until the jihadists struck.

P.B. Clarke summarizes the matter thus:

> Islam was emerging (in 1600-1800) as a counter-tradition, so to speak, whereas previously it had been accommodationist, assimilationist and prepared to co-exist peacefully with non-Muslim community. Instead of turning completely to mysticism and messianic theories, these Muslim scholars came to insist on the necessity of assuming political authority.[11]

Educated Muslim elite agitated for a more favourable political climate because as a minority they suffered political and economic exploitation. Clarke also argues that the enormous socio-economic changes of the period such as slave trade, importation of firearms and

---

[10] Lamin Sanneh, *Christianity in West Africa: A Religious Perspective* (Maryknoll, New York: Orbis Books, 1985), p. 213
[11] P. B. Clarke, *West Africa and Islam* (London: Edward Arnold, 1982), p. 87

pillaging caused insecurity and created vast opportunities for those with a clear sense of order and ability to offer security.

In summary, the relationship between Islam and traditional societies was an intriguing one. Ibn Bathuta painted a picture of more civilized Arabs rescuing pagan communities of Western Sudan with literacy, diplomatic services, structured government, architecture, elaborate commercial contacts and finance and so on. These are true but it did not take long for traditional values to react and deeply change Islam. For survival, Muslims utilized immense aspects of traditional religion. M.O.A. Abdul has, for instance, shown how Islam borrowed from Ifá divination and Doi has demonstrated a high level of syncretism in Yorúbáland.[12] Islam contributed much in the political and economic lives of communities especially when indigenous rulers saw it as a veritable tool for social change.

Militant Islam and the Colonial Fact

The emergence of the Sokoto Caliphate as a result of the Dan Fodio jihad of 19th century is one of the most significant events in Nigerian history. It set the stage for the application of Islamic principles in state development. Admittedly, throughout the 19th century, the reformers faced problems arising from administration, emigration, succession disputes, internal revolts, external aggression and the formation of rival reformist states such as the Mahdist state in Adamawa. But the jihadists achieved much which has changed the political culture and structure of Nigeria. First, the extension of Islam into the southern forest zone, specifically, north-east Yorúbáland and the establishment of a coherent Islamic state pre-empted the lines of the geographical division of the country in the future. It ensured that the administrative division would have a religious tone (both over and under).

However, the story of Islam in Yorúbáland was not wholly as a result of the jihad. More peaceful patterns of expansion could be detected in Old Oyo, Ilorin, Badagry, Epe, Lagos and so on. The initial agents of propagation were Hausa domestic slaves, Muslim traders and Ijebu merchants. Later, returnee, Muslim, freed slaves from America, Brazil and other places came back with knowledge of English, Portuguese, skills and Brazilian culture. Several reasons could be adduced for the patterns of response: influence of converted rulers and men of prominence, materialist allurements, Islamic tendency to borrow from traditional religiosity, parallels in religious practice such as divinations and use of amulets, enhanced status and authority and the

---

[12] M.O.A. Abdul, "Yoruba Divination and Islam," *Orita* 4.1 (June 1970): 44-56

benefits of Islamic education. Scholars such as G.O. Gbadamosi have delineated the increasing acceptance of Islam in Yorúbáland in the 19th century[13] along these lines.

Secondly, the jihadists reformed Islam in Hausaland and thereby created a powerful centre for political and economic forays. Thirdly, they created in Islamic administrative structure with a central imamate and with an emirate-type of government with a rational, differentiated structure based on emirs, Waziri, amir al-jash and so ensured efficiency. Some traditional officers were, however retained. Fourthly, they created a judiciary which enforced Islamic laws. It is a moot point here whether the enforcement was successful at the initial period. But the shariat was installed with a Qudi. Finally, the jihadists conducted a literacy campaign which ensured that records now exist, women's role through education increased and administrators were nursed.

The jihad and a rationalized Sokoto Caliphate brought religion into the centre of the development of Nigeria. Traditional religiosity persisted. Some rural areas in the emirate remained unislamized but Islamism became a central issue in allocation of power, sharing of resources and constitutional arrangements.

The strength and size of the Caliphate meant an inevitable clash with British colonial expansion. British colonial policy was predicated on certain goals: the establishment of legitimate trade as a remedy to slave trade. The corollary was the old mercantilist policy of acquiring raw materials for industry and opening of markets for industrial goods. The second goal was the establishment of a rational administrative structure and a modern judiciary system. The third was to civilize and build a Pax Britannica. As Fowell Buxton had argued in *African Slave Trade and Its Remedy,* religion was an important vehicle for the civilizing mission. He meant the use of Christianity. Indeed, early British imperialists formed Sudan parties who set out to combat resurgent Islam.

In reality, local and international facts forced a certain pragmatism on the colonialists. The period of formal colonial presence was characterized by rumors of wars, wars and conflicting posturing. The scramble for colonies soon gave to the First World War, uneasy inter-war years, economic depression, another war and a battered Europe reeling under a psychological depression or what T.S. Elliot called a 'wasteland'. The jingoism of G.A. Henry's novels came under a 'shadow'.

In the colonies, manpower and material resources were so scarce that administrators had a paranoid desire to create order and utilize

---

[13] T.G.O. Gbadamosi, *The Growth of Islam among the Yoruba, 1841-1908* (London: Longman, 1978)

indigenous resources in men, materials and structures of governance. The initial hubris backed by racialist notion of the White Man's Burden, Manifest Destiny and other scientific theories of racism had to be abandoned or modified into a more tolerant attitude towards indigenous culture and even religion. For Igboland, this modification in policy could be illustrated with official attitude towards secret societies between 1910 and 1950. For Northern Nigeria, colonial policy moved quickly towards.

Indirect Rule which utilized with few modifications and improvements the structures created by the jihad. Islam was protected in fact grew stronger utilizing the new infrastructure and communication system of the British, Islamic education and legal system became further entrenched.

It could be rightly argued that colonial administrators consolidated the North-South dichotomy in the Nigerian political culture based on a religious touchstone. The situation was not without much irony: the protected Islamic Northerners soon started to protest that the protection from use of English in the educational system, for instance, created a prejudicial gap and was an aspect of how the British underdeveloped the North. The South clobbered the Northern administrators for being more Northern than Northerners. Head or tail, the colonialist lost. In fact two cardinal aspects of the historiography of Islam in Nigeria have been firstly, how Islam spread and assisted communities to develop and secondly, how British administration interrupted, irrepressibly the development path. It is even assumed that the last development path was determined less by inbuilt change of indigenous cultures than by the foreign religion, Islam. Either way, religion became prominent in writing the history of these communities. Perhaps, a more detailed study of Islamic doctrine especially the wide correlation between Islamic practices and traditional religion will explain this abandonment of an Africanist ideology. But the constraints of space forbid adventure into this ambiguity.

Muslim reaction to colonialism at the initial stage was, however, confused. Introverts suffered in silence hoping for a Mahdist saviour. Cultural opposition reared its head in the form of the Bamidele movement in Yorúbáland while a few die-hards resorted to a futile 'planned withdrawal' from British territory, the *hijra*.

Christianity in Colonial Nigeria

The fate of Christianity in the colonial era is a large issue which must perforce be treated cryptically. After the failed missionary enterprise of the Portuguese in the 15th and 16th centuries, Christian presence in

Nigeria received a new vista in the imperial slogan, 'For Gold, Glory and God'. The 'civilizing mission' of 1841 set out to explore the Niger and establish Christian British presence. Two expeditions later, Christian presence on the Niger was firmed up. Meanwhile, the Wesleyans from the Gold Coast and soon the Anglicans moved into Western Nigeria around the 1841/1842.

By 1846 the Presbyterians came from Fernando Po and the Primitive Methodists followed in the 1890s with a host of other smaller bodies at the turn of the century. In the East, the Aro Expedition of 1901/2 forced the British occupation of the hinterland and missionary scramble for the interior. The opening of the roads and building of railroad in 1911/1916 accelerated the pace and determined the direction of missionary expansion.

A number of Nigerian scholars have traced the patterns of expansion: K.O. Dike worked on the Niger Mission, J.F.A. Ajayi and E.A. Ayandele followed on the trail. M. Oduyoye examined the *Planting of Christianity in Yorúbáland*. G.O.M. Tasie did the same for the Niger Delta, Obaro Ikime looked at the Urhobo and Itsekiri with S.U. Erivwo while N.C. Ejituwu worked on the missionary enterprise among the Andoni. A.E. Afigbo pointed to some unacceptable portrayals of the role of the Presbyterians in the Arochukwu expedition. Kalu examined the enterprises of the Presbyterians in the Igbo Cross River Basin and the Primitive Methodists poised on the railroad junctions of Igboland while Felix Ekechi who was a Roman Catholic school teacher, examined the rivalry between the Roman Catholics and the Anglicans in Igboland. The historiography on the Roman Catholic enterprise has been scanty until a crop of books in the 1985 Centenary complemented Ozigbo's doctoral thesis and the over-reliance on Jordan's account of Bishop Shanahan. Before then, only the few pages in Elizabeth Isichei's books with her "Biography of Father Tansi" provided some data. Some materials exist on the seventh Day Adventists by Omolewa and on the Qua Iboe Missions.[14]

---

[14] K. O. Dike, *The Niger Mission* (1962); J.F.A. Ajayi, *Christian Missions in Nigeria, 1841-1892: The Making of An Elite* (London: Longman, 1965); E.A. Ayandele, *The Missionary Impact on Modern Nigeria, 1842-1914* (London: Longman, 1966); Obaro Ikime, "The Coming of the C.M.S. to Itsekiri, Urhobo, and Isoko", *Nigeria Magazine*, 84 (Sept. 1965), 206-215; C.C. Ifemesia, "The Civilizing Mission of 1841", *JHSN*, 2.3 (Dec. 1962): 291-310; S.U. Erivwo, "Christian Churches in Urhoboland", *Orita* 7.1 (June 1973): 206-215; See also Vol. 12.1 (June 1978); *West African Religion* 17.2 (1978): 22-34; G.O.M. Tasie, *Christianity in the Niger Delta* (Leiden: E.J.Brill, 1976; A.E. Afigbo "The Missionaries and the Aro Expedition of 1901/02, *Journal of Religion in Africa* 5.2 (1973): 74-106; O.U. Kalu, "The Battle of the Gods: Christianization of Cross River Igboland", *JHSN* X.1 (1978): 1-18; "Primitive Methodists on the Railroad Junctions of Igboland, 1910-1931" *JRA* 20 (forthcoming); Felix Ekechi, *Missionary Enterprise and Rivalry in Igboland, 1857-1914* (London: Frank Cass. 1972)

The history of Christianity in Northern Nigeria has benefitted from the researches of Crampton, Ayandele, Gbadamosi and Ubah.[15] The Theological College of Northern Nigeria, Bukuru started a number of local church history studies and a few good researches have come from University of Jos. This is neither a comprehensive bibliography nor even a fully descriptive one.

More important is that these materials reveal a generally nationalist tendency, utilizing the resources in the changing historiography of Nigeria. It would appear that much more work has been done on Christian missionary enterprise than on Islam or African Religion. Education in Southern Nigerian ensured this.

The emphasis here is on the process of Christianization and especially the contribution of Christianity to national development. Certain characteristics of Christian presence deserve mention. Missionaries, according to Ayandele, started with an initial deference to traditional African rulers but soon became antagonistic as their confidence grew.[16] This could be explained in part by the relationship with the colonial administrators. Missionaries from British background assumed that they were partners in the civilizing mission. They served variously as path-finders, collaborators and even softened the ground for the colonial process.

Yet their relationship with the government remained ambiguous: both parties differed in their attitude towards traditional cultures. The government in the quest for *order* was willing to allow tradition which was not a competition or a hindrance. For instance, the government was particularly concerned with ritual murder and the machinations of oracles. Oracles could prove to be a source of protest and a challenge to the new judiciary system built on the white man's courts.

The Christians made no such distinctions. They condemned all traditional religiosity with pejorative names such as pagan, heathen, animism and such like fearful European terms. In the end, the missionaries proved to be more destructive of African culture than the imperialist boots which Mabel Segun's poem "The Second Olympus" accused. Indeed, the pursuit of aesthetics and plastic arts soon led the colonial government to build museums, preserve art forms and encourage art craft. The irony was that the Africans themselves were more interested in European goods than in their own products.

---

[15] E.P.T. Crampton, *Christianity in Northern Nigeria* (London: Geoffrey Chapman, 1975); T.G.O. Gbadamosi, "The Establishment of Western education among Muslims in Nigeria", *JHSN* 4.1 (1967): 94ff; E.A. Ayandele, "The Missionary Factor in Northern Nigeria" *JHSN* 3.3 (Dec. 1966); C.N. Ubah, "Problems of Christian Missionaries in the Muslim Emirates of Nigeria, 1900-1928" *Journal of African Studies* 3.3. (1976): 351-372; "Islamic Culture and Nigerian Society" in E. Ihekweazu (ed.) *Traditional and Modern Culture* (Enugu: Fourth Dimensions Publ. 1985): Chapter 16.

[16] E.A. Ayandele, "Traditional Rulers and Missionaries in Pre-Colonial West Africa" *Tarikh* 3 (1969): 23-37.

The irony spilled over into education. The missionaries used educational institutions as a means of evangelization as well as competition among themselves. Education liberated minds had set the tone for modernization, self-awareness and the quest for both cultural and political independence. As Ajayi's subtitle put it, missionaries created the Nigerian elite. Much of these product-content was accidental. It was the colonial government who had in fact used the missionaries to achieve these goals: the government worried about the quality of education and curricula with secular and professional content. She appointed inspectors and gave grants-in-aid to approved schools. Admittedly, the authorities did not hope to breed political agitators but that is exactly what education did. It emancipated. Perhaps it would have achieved more if mission education had not been conservative and inadequate. For instance, missionaries, to a very large extent, ignored technical and vocational training. They ignored the indigenous culture and miseducated the elitist products.

Many charitable institutions were similarly established by missionaries as instruments of evangelization: hospitals, children's homes, agricultural farms for cash crops such as cocoa and so on.[17] These transformed the socio-economic landscape of Nigeria even if the recipients did not remain converted for long.

Indeed, conversion to Christianity was for the most part instrumentalist. People saw Christianity as a means of acquiring wealth, new status, education, contact with Europe and Europeans and government jobs. It rescued some from the harsh elements of the colonial policies. Ayandele illustrates this instrumentalist, materialist approach with the story of the Brass people of the Niger Delta. When trade was good and they served as middlemen, they donated generously to the church and built towering churches. When a crop of whites reacted to a depressed economy, moved into the hinterland and displaced the middlemen, these reacted by appealing to their friend, Queen Victoria. The Queen did not reply and so, Brass people deserted Christianity and returned to the worship of *iguana*.[18]

Admittedly conversion was assisted by the failure of traditional religiosity in certain areas of control successfully space-time events. When the god, Kamalu, could no longer serve Asa people of South-Eastern Igboland, when the priests became rapacious, the worshippers found the miracles of Garrick Braide's agents to be more powerful and

---

[17] Dinker's study, *Profit for the Lord* has shown that certain missions such as Basel Missions utilized commercial enterprises and small-scale industries more extensively in India and Cameroons, as evangelical tools than ethnic missioning in Nigeria.
[18] E.A. Ayandele, "The Missionary Factor in Brass, 1875-1900: A Study in Advance and Recession", *Bull. Soc. For African Church History* 2.3 (1967): 249-257.

changed camps,. Once in a while the traditionalists would lash back at Christianity and the colonial government. The Ekumeku riot, the attacks by secret societies such as *Ekpe*, all these primary forms of resistance proved futile. They may excite nationalist pride but they did not change the course of history.

In any meaningful conceptual scheme in Church History, the Finger of God must be acknowledged. Some converted out of real conviction and grew to be great and daring propagators of the new faith.

The greatest contribution of Christianity was in the field of ethics. Christianity does make the distinction between the things of Caesar and those of Christ. It has a doctrine of Two Kingdoms but it is not so sharply drawn as to reject Christian ethical influence in politics, economic choices/policies and in social organization. Christian influence permeated through adherents who held positions of responsibility. Indeed, the church became a rallying point or a political pressure group. The history of nationalism in the colonial era demonstrates this.

The nationalism of this period was predominantly cultural nationalism. The church was the forum where blacks felt free enough to protest against white dominance. Individuals like James Johnson, Mojola Agbebi, Henry Carr and J. G. Campbell made enormous contributions in raising black consciousness in West Africa. They allied with Gold Coast and Saro comrades such as Casely-Hayford and Mensah Sarbah. They invited Wilmot Blyden to Lagos in 1891 where he delivered his famous lecture, *The Return of the Exile.* Africans, he intoned, must evangelize Africa. The call for the indigenization of the church, the formation of the United African Church and the rapid spread of Aládùrà Churches were evidences of assertive cultural nationalism.

The Christian Churches, therefore, served the roles of providing ethical critique on colonial government policies, producing the educated elite who challenged white dominance and provided the forum for black protest. By the 1920s a purely political organization emerged and the nationalist struggle of the future soon moved from cultural to political goals. The road to independence was built from churchly beginnings.[19]

---

[19] O.U. Kalu, "Waves from the Rivers: the Spread of Garrick Braide Movement in Igboland", *JHSN* 8.4 (1977); "Missionaries, Colonial Government and Secret Societies in S.E. Igboland *JHSN* (1977): 75-90; "Formulation of cultural policy in Colonial Nigeria," in E. Ihekweazu (ed.), *Traditional and Modern Culture* (Enugu: Fourth Dimension, 1985): Chapter 9.

Religion and the Politics of Independence

From the declaration of Independence, two problems confronted Nigeria: one was how to maintain a stable state amidst the competition of the ethnic groups; the second was the harnessing of resources for development. Political scientists of the period such as Apter in *Politics of Modernization* drew a distinction between the politics of mobilization which operated in Ghana and the politics of reconciliation which characterized Nigeria. The former was more authoritarian and unitary. A dominant political ideology subsumed tribes and tongues. In the later, the federal experiment sought to accommodate the periphery with a weak centre. The centre must reflect 'federal character' and must be so weak as to be inoffensive to the myriads of cultures, religions, and adventurers in power.

The force of ethnicity was crystallized in the regional division: a Hausa/Fulani-dominated North, Yoruba-dominated West and Mid-West and Igbo-dominated East. These bore the seeds of instability: the minorities could become restive, and the allocation of power may become contentious. A second problem which emerged directly from this was the problem of a viable Constitution. The nation has, like a boat in a storm, reeled from a British model to American model with army interventions serving as the chorus to each scene. Democracy existed in certain areas of Nigerian culture but not in all. Constitution-making has been a problem because a constitution must reflect, in legal, formal manner, the will of constituents.

Thirdly, the north-south dichotomy bred a cankerworm: who governs or at least holds the reins of power? Pride of heritage buttressed with glorified pre-colonial histories merely confused matters. Fourthly, the 'national cake' mentally left the impression that everyone as well as every ethnic group had a task of collecting her share of the cake.

Thus, the sharing or allocation of resources whether industries, educational facilities or basic infrastructure and amenities turned into dog-fights. Education was particularly important because it was seen as an avenue for the harnessing of the resources of modernity. The 'gap' in acquisition of Western education between various ethnic groups heightened the conflict. Crash programmes, 'quota-system', free education, 'catchment area' are catch phrases reminiscent of attempted solutions.

As has been pointed out in the early part of the paper, the weakness in recent analysis of the socio-political history of Nigeria is the neglect of the religious factor. For one, the emergence of the nation state bred secularism. A concept of religious pluralism had to be embedded in the constitution while the nation was declared a secular state. In spite of the theory, however, power alignment and economic control continued to operate along religious grooves. One would have, if space allowed, illustrated with conversion to Islam from among Igbo of South-Eastern Nigeria as a means of entry into markets and economic enterprises controlled by the northern Muslims just as in the old days of the western Sudanic empires.

Secondly, it became increasingly obvious, especially after much experimentation in constitutional arrangements, punctuated by the dins of military coup d'états, that the building of a nation-state was an ethical matter. Socio-economic policies are matters of choices among competing options. Each option reflects a certain understanding of social justice and the obligation of power. Power itself is neutral and only recognized by the effect. Thus, the only rational question is the responsibility of power: power for whom and wielded by whom and for what purpose?

It was recognized that a viable nation could only be built on a viable national ethic and discipline. The question has been constantly raised whether religion, formal or informal, could contribute in the search for sustaining values. The questions arise from the alternatives of humanistic ethics which leftists or Marxists advocate. Leftist ideologies have urged the viability of humanistic ethics to a society whose roots are embedded in a religious worldview.

The questions also arise from the history of religious groups which as pressure groups also served as dysfunctional factors in the political culture. For instance, in the immediate prelude to independence, the competition between Muslims and Christians, between Roman Catholics and Protestants explained the patterns of voting in election, policies, siting of industries and educational policies and jobs and promotions in the Civil Service. As Elochukwu Amucheazi illustrated with Eastern Nigeria, churches constituted formidable pressure groups.[20]

In more recent times the Sharia Court controversy during the making of the Second Republic is a good example. In April 1979, certain members of the Constituent Assembly, numbering about 82 urged that a Federal Sharia Court of Appeal parallel to the Federal Court of Appeal should be enshrined in the Constitution. The reasoning was as follows: Sharia courts exist in the northern states; religious freedom demands that Muslims should be slowed to use the judiciary system provided in the Qur'an. Opponents saw the matter as religious and political rather than a technical aspect of constitution-making. The 'Middle Belt' members joined with the divided Southerners to oppose

---

[20] E.C. Amucheazi, "A Decade of Church Revolt in Eastern Nigeria, 1956-1966" *Odu* 10 (1974): 45-62.

the new form of jihad. The gulf widened as the Northerners claimed numerical superiority which should be rewarded with control of power. They boycotted the Assembly and almost disrepute the arrangements to return to civil government. The issue was resolved with a compromise; perhaps they realized that the success of the NPN may be endangered by continuing the fight. The ceasefire on the contentious Sharia issue may break down because the constitution provides for the extension of Sharia courts into other regions and wealthy Muslims in the South are capitalizing on the sensitive loophole.

Recently, the covert and overt efforts to register Nigeria as a member of the Organization of Islamic States may re-open old wounds. Abiola has been using his enormous material resources including the Concord Newspaper to keep the members of the Sharia issue alive. In these and more ways, religions have served as dysfunctional factors in the body politic. Regional, economic and political competitions are energized by religious prejudices which even cut across ethnic lines. The colonial fact inadvertently enshrined this while the biographies of the Sardauna of Sokoto, especially the latest by John Paden who had earlier worked o Religion and Politics in Kano, betray the character of religious politics by an arch-protagonist.

The complication over the question arises not just from the reputation of religious practitioners either as priestly underprops of oppressive rulers or as the theologians of theocratic wielders of power. The increasing secularism which harks to opponents of priests in traditional culture through the colonial state builders to new technocrats in modern times, has led to state take-over of certain core-institutions previously controlled by the religious groups. Religion appeared to be under attack mostly from the *nouveaux riches* and the educated elite. Politicians preferred the political kingdom. The only problem was that all these groups soon realized that a nation without strong morality was bankrupt; that moral discipline is a pre-requisite for building a stable nation and for harnessing resources and for curbing greed and corruption. Fela's songs such as "Authority Stealing", "ITT", "Confusion and Perambulation", Okosun's "Which way Nigeria", Wole Soyinka's "I love my country" and a host of others drew sharp attention to the moral collapse caused by petro naira.

Official reactions included cultural revival designed to revamp those common cultural forms which bind. The government instituted programs on Ethical Revolution, War Against Indiscipline and Environmental Sanitation. Each effort sought to harness viable ethics from religious sources for the salvation of the nation.

Moreover, Nigeria has witnessed a revival of religiosity, both Islamic and Christian. Aládurà Churches have proliferated. Para-religious forms such as Grail Message, Godianism and Eckankar, to mention a few have emerged. There is little doubt that all these reflect a deep moral collapse and search for reintegration both personal and communal.

This is to put the matter in a summary fashion by arguing that socio-economic and political stress produce heightened resort to religious solution. For instance, diviners and medicine-men must have had a field day during the elections of the last two republics. In spite of Christianity and Islam the force of traditional religion is still very strong. The other contention is that in the early period of Christian missionary enterprise, conversion of adherence was explained by either novelty or instrumentalist factors. Why is patronage on the increase in the modern period in spite of the loss of novelty and the state take-over of education and charitable institutions and the resurgence of traditional modes of according social status —chieftaincies and title-taking? Besides, church growth (vertical or horizontal) is difficult to measure but there is a general indication that the Aládurà-type are growing faster. Patronage of these groups has broken the bounds of class and income brackets. It is no longer 'the religion of the oppressed' or marginalized or artisans. It is no longer the opium of the masses because the owners of capital are writhing as uncontrollably on the floor as the workers. Traditional explanations no longer hold. This is why two explanations are attempted here, namely, that the breakdown of morality which took place in the last decade, the gyrating economic fortunes of the nation, the large-scale scrambling of social structures, political trauma of the elections have generated an enormous amount of stress and psychological disorientation. This fact has bred a second explanation, namely, the rise of counterfeit religiosity. Many wolves in sheep clothing are exploiting vast numbers of men and women. Religion pays high dividends. Politicians also attempted to exploit religious feelings in their adventures for power.

The irony is that the same religious forms which have caused confusion in the political history of the country also contain viable ethics related to social justice, humility in wielding power, honesty and accountability, freedom and liberty, unity and peace. It should have been necessary to examine the various religious forms either from traditions, the Bible or the Quran to depict the centrality of these values.[21] The failure of these values to permeate the society and inform policy and practice could be explained by the force of secularism, the rapid pace of socio-economic development and the failure by confessors to practice what they preach.

---

[21] See O. U. Kalu, "Religion and Political Values in Nigeria: A Pluralistic Perspective", forthcoming in *Religious Pluralism in Africa* (New York: Pergamon Press, 1986)

The first two factors are rather obvious in the wake of secularism; the Nigerian operates in two 'publics', the modern and traditional. In the effort to weave into international world order, salient values in religion are neglected. Besides, the vagaries of the economy and political experiments intensify communal rivalries. Quite often, these rivalries utilize religious colouring. Recent riots in Northern part of Nigeria could best be explained by narrow ethnic rivalries. However, it must be admitted that there is a certain element in Islam which makes the resort to violence very handy. This is being exploited increasingly at the expense of more conciliatory values. Why?

i. The international character of modern Islamic resurgence;
ii. The explosion of Pentecostal-evangelicalism has provided a forum for erstwhile unconquered peoples and energized Christian proselytization;
iii. The resilience of traditional religion and culture means that there is still a sector of the population to be converted.

The unsettled social, political and economic conditions merely provided catalysts to the rapid competition tin recent years. It must also be added that Islam in Northern Nigeria is more politically alert than Islam in the South of the country. The Yoruba evenly patronize all the three religions and are, therefore more attuned to compromise and dialogue.

Dialogue as an Antidote

The cure to the intensified religious violence is dialogue. The obvious word means more than tolerance or even debate. The original Greek also means reflection and conversation. It is a relationship rather than discourse. As people share in offices and buses, dialogical relationship goes on in everyday interaction. However, it could also be planned through lectures, debates, literature and so on. The goal is to remove the rough edge off religious differences in a secular policy and to tap the salient values which affirm life in all religions. To dialogue we must be rooted in our traditions and yet open to others. We must search for the validation from biblical and qur'anic roots.

It is essential that people should not follow religions blindly especially in the Nigerian context where people imbibed religious traditions through the accident of birth. History teaches that either of the two world religions intruded as an external change-agent at some point in time. Reception was hardly dictated by either reasoned choice or even theological understanding. Each religion accepts change; none is static; so, the opportunity exists to study, to know, to share both affirmed traditions and others. This is the spirit of dialogue.

Dialogue in Christian Tradition

The problem of attitude towards other faiths has been endemic in Christian tradition. In the Old Testament, in spite of efforts to insulate the worship of Jehovah from contemporary Palestinian religions, the traditions which developed into the accepted canons contain massive assimilation of material from the religions of Canaan, Egypt, Babylonia, Persia. The New Testament absorbed Greek traditions and thought-patterns. Paul's attitude to the Epicureans and Stoics of Athens as well as the Greek concept of *logos* which illumined everyone set the tone for the early church.

Constraint of space has forced a cryptic summation of various positions.[22] While the World Council of Churches has made progress in catalyzing dialogue, the conservative tradition espoused by Hendrik Kraemer in 1938 Tambaram Conference persists held sway.[23] The Roman Catholic Vatican II on the other hand took more definite succinct steps towards an affirmation of other religions.[24] Hans Kung may be ahead of his church whose position is better articulated by Karl Rahner but Cardinal Pietro Rossano who headed the Roman Catholic Secretariat for Non-Christian Religions affirmed that the Christians' attitude to world religions should be "one of humility and respect and of frankness in giving witness to Christ, the Word that enlightens every person, *paratus, simper nuntiare, paratus simper doceri* – always ready to announce, always ready to be taught."[25]

To answer the question, why dialogue? The Christian must hope to regain insights through dialogue which had been lost or obscured during the course of a history characterized by triumphalism and suspicion.

This draws attention to the question of how to dialogue because goals determine method. We have stressed rootedness and openness, the need to eschew triumphalism and to banish fear, suspicion and mistrust. Patience is essential since many people cling to their traditions as bedbugs to beddings. Dialogue must start at the grassroots community emphasizing relationship and shared concerns. It is a spiritual odyssey, accepting the otherness of the other and risking conversion. It is a means of indigenizing world religions by

---

[22] See Editorial to *International Review of Missions (IRM)*, 74 No. 296 (Oct. 1985), p. 423
[23] Ibid., 447-479
[24] S.J. Samartha, "Dialogue as a Continuing Christian Concern" in his *Living Faiths and the Ecumenical Movement* (Geneva: WCC Publications, 1971): 153-4
[25] Cit. Cobb, *Beyond Dialogue*, 25. See H. Kraemer, *The Christian Message in Non-Christian World* (Grand Rapids, Kregel Publishers, 1961, 5th Edition) – first edition was in 1938. See Paul Knitter, "Roman Catholic Approaches to other Religions: Developments and Tensions" *Int. Bulletin of Missiological Research*, 8.2 (Ap. 1984).

asking antic questions – what does Christ or Muhammad mean in my culture, in my nation and in the mind of brokenness in our lives and rapid socio-economic and political changes in our society?

Dialogue from Islamic Roots

The Qur'an, the Hadiths and Hadith Qudsi, which is considered less authoritative, all contain clear guidance for a dialogical relationship. Though people tend to see Islam only through the Jihad, the term itself, taken from *salama,* means to submit, to surrender. The Qur'an, therefore, calls all mankind to submit to God. All aspects of life are subsumed into a religious perspective. Another emphasis is on peace and this concept emerges from Islamic anthropology akin to the Christian's. Both refer to the Genesis creation myth:

O men! Behold, We have crated you all out of a male and female, and made you into nations and tribes, so that you might come to know one another (not despite one another) (LX: 8)

Peace is predicated on respect, affirmation of the other person and produces acts of mercy. Indeed, believers are defined as those who do good to or love their neighbours:

On those who believe, and do deeds of righteousness
There is no blame ... For God loveth those who do good (Sura 5:96)

Private and public ethics intertwine. Cardinal principles or pillars in Islam therefore include Zakat and Sadaqah. Charity, sensitivity to the poor, ideal of love and loving-kindness to all people are emphasized. According to the Hadith, Muhammad said, "a man does not believe till he likes for his brother what he likes for himself."
In a very thought-provoking article, Peggy Starkey compared the Christian concept of *agape* in Christian and Islamic traditions and found that:

The belief that people will be judged solely on their deeds towards other people enjoins Muslims to practice self-denial and universal charity. The belief that the God Who will judge them on their works is merciful, loving and omnipotent leads Muslims to humble submission before Allah and to practice of patience, resignation and firmness in the trials of life. Hence from a Christian point of view, the revealed scripture and traditions of Islam meet the criterion of agape insofar as they call for deeds of charity, loving-kindness, forgiveness, selfless giving and mercy toward other human beings.[26]

Moreover, the three cardinal virtues of *al-gist* (equity), *al-adl* (justice) and *al-birr* (kindness) underprop ethics of peaceful neighbourliness and tolerance.[27]

But this is not the whole story: the Muslim is called upon to stand firm for his religion. Zakat is not meant for non-Muslims though other alms are. From Sura 60:1 it appears that one must not be on friendly terms with the enemies of one's faith. Thus, Islam has her own exclusivist clauses. But these are countered by other emphasis. For instance, A. Yusuf Ali who translated the Qur'an with copious footnotes, annotates that "Islam recognizes true faith in other forms, provided that it be sincere, supported by reason and backed up by righteous conduct." Sura 60:7 counters Sura 60:1 by saying that:

> It may be that God will grant love (and friendship) between you and those Whom Ye (now) hold as enemies; For God has power (over all things); And God is oft-forgiving, Most Merciful.

In the footnote Ali observes, "We should hate what is evil but not men as such." The Qur'an draws attention to the common elements in Christianity and Islam (III: 84) and enjoins special consideration for people of the Book:

> And argue not with the People of the Scripture unless it be in a way that is better, save with such of them as do wrong and say, We believe in that which hath been revealed unto us and revealed unto you; our God and your God is one, and unto Him we surrender (XXIX:46).

Finally, just as the Christian combats with the demands of the Great Commission, so does the Muslim with the Da'wah or the Islamic Call. It is a witness that is required of each individual Muslim in the practice of his daily life. One strand is inner-directed to ensure the rooting of the intent of Islam on individuals. The other strand is outward-directed. This strand forbids coercion in matters of faith: "There shall be no coercion in matters of faith." (II: 256). It is emphatic, under all circumstances, in upholding the right of freedom of belief for all

---

[26] Peggy Starkey, "AGAPE: A Christian Criterion for Truth in the Other World Religions", *IRM* 74 (1985): 425-463 (p. 446).

[27] See the elucidation of these ethical strands by Abdulla Omar Nasseef, "Muslim-Christian Relations: Muslim Approach" *Current Dialogue 11* (Dec. 1986): 29-32.

mankind. It also emphasizes the role of human reason in evangelization:

> Call thou (all mankind) unto thy Sustainer's path with wisdom and goodly exhortation, and reason with them in the most kindly manner (XVI: 125).

Thus, the roots of Islamic faith urge a pluralistic religious posture, a rigorous practice of Islamic demands, and yet a dialogical relationship characterized by an inner reflection, spirituality, application of moral ethics to everyday life and intelligent discussions, discourses and debates. Reason is God's most significant gift to man. The use of force to restore orthodoxy or in reaction to enemies is not denied but this is not the only means of evangelization.

Limits to Dialogue

The conclusions so far are that willy-nilly dialogue occurs daily and is not always verbal. However, all dialogical situations are neither perceived, consciously pursued or healthy; some are dialogues of the deaf, blind and jelly fish. This is because there are a number of constraints or limits to healthy dialogue.

At the baseline are traditionalism, suspicion, mistrust and ignorance of other religions bred by years and styles of indoctrination. Thus, doctrines are idealized, traditions are unquestioned, bawderized and stereotypes of other religion are mistaken for the truth and the element of change within each religious tradition is ignored. Since religious feelings run along a deep terrain in the human psyche, encrusted biases produce dismal effects.

Socio-economic stress has often fuelled the quest for orthodoxy and easy resort to violence. Surprisingly, the panels on the Maitatsine revolts merely touched on the socio-economic underpinnings. Student radicalism fuels from the same depot. It is a vicious circle as stress and competition at the socio-economic and political spheres engender religious fanaticism and are, in turn, infected by religion.

Implications for African Religion

The interaction of Islam and Christianity with African Religion has been the staple of scholarly attention; so also has been the analysis or the persistence of resilience of traditional religiosity amidst the onslaught. Scholars have shown that Christian missionaries did not develop a viable cultural policy. Even so, there were differences between catholic and Protestant attitudes and between these and nationalist/Aládurà religious forms. Others have demonstrated a higher level of syncretism in Islam. The implication of a dialogical approach is to draw attention to the salient values in traditional religiosity for national development and for coping with survival problems in our ecosystem. The name-calling and condemnations which E.B. Idowu discussed in his *African Traditional Religion: A Definition* are surely inappropriate. As Hans Kung declared, every human being is under God's grace and can be saved and every world religion is under God's grace and can be a way of salvation: whether it is primitive or highly evolved, mythological or enlightened, mystical or rational, theistic or non-theistic. The burgeoning literature on comparative religions and dialogue has put paid to the old doubts about the authenticity of African Religion. Indeed, modern times have witnessed less conflict with Afrelists because the breakdown of the worldview and structures which Afrel sustained has been weakened by secularity and other competing views and structures. It is the inner ethical and practical core of traditional religiosity which has survived. In "God as Policeman", an effort was made to deal with elements of traditional religious values in social control models which could still be applicable in modern setting.[28] The government has paid attention to the efficacy of traditional medicine. The nation does not need a structured Godianism to harness the resources of traditional religiosity. Rather, dialogue implies a conscious study, debate, understanding, openness and utilization of elements of African Religion which are salient for human development. It is not a static religion and should not be romanticized.

The new dialogical attitude is essential because culture serves as anchor in the midst of rapid change. Viable change occurs when new forms are domesticated. This explains Wilmot Blyden's new perception of Islam in spite of his Christian background. When these religious forms are perceived within their competing resources, one may be sucked into serving as a protagonist but when reviewed within the developmental needs of the African, they become external change-agents with resources which could be harnessed for a different interest – nationalist development and stability. Dialogue, therefore, is a model of indigenization or traditionalization amidst the intensified violence in religious matters.

However, a dialogical relationship does not mean the surrender of cardinal doctrines but the assimilation of elements of truth in other religions. Indeed, the quest for orthodoxy should not produce

---

[28] O. U. Kalu, "Gods as Policemen: Religion and Social Control in Igboland," in J.K. Olupona (ed.) *Religious Plurality in Africa: Essays in Honour of J.S. Mbiti* (Berlin: Mouton, 1992).

controversy precisely because every quest for truth is an enriching, liberating exercise while bawderization produces bias and roots false suspicion. Dialogue is a call to risk the moorings of our religious traditions for our common humanity and national stability. It is an antidote against intolerance and the dysfunctional role of religion in contemporary Nigeria.

References

Abdul, M.O.A., 1970. "Yoruba Divination and Islam," *Orita* 4.1 (June): 44-56
Afigbo, A.E., 1973. "The Missionaries and the Aro Expedition of 1901/02", *Journal of Religion in Africa* 5.2: 74-106
Ajayi, J.F.A., 1965. *Christian Missions in Nigeria, 1841-1892: The Making of An Elite* (London: Longman)
Amucheazi, E.C. 1974. "A Decade of Church Revolt in Eastern Nigeria, 1956-1966" *Odu* 10: 45-62.
Awolalu, J. O., *Yoruba Beliefs and Sacrificial Rites* (London: Longman, 1979)
Ayandele, E.A. 1966. "The Missionary Factor in Northern Nigeria" *JHSN* 3.3 (December)
Ayandele, E.A. 1966. *The Missionary Impact on Modern Nigeria, 1842-1914* (London: Longman)
Ayandele, E.A. 1967. "The Missionary Factor in Brass, 1875-1900: A Study in Advance and Recession", Bull. Soc. for African Church History 2.3: 249-257.
Ayandele, E.A. 1969. "Traditional Rulers and Missionaries in Pre-Colonial West Africa" *Tarikh* 31 (December):23-37
Azuonye, C., 1986. "Ígbo Folktales and Evolution of the Idea of Chukwu as the Supreme God of Igbo Religion" (Faculty of Arts, University of Nigeria, *Nsukka Lectures*)
Clarke, P. B., 1982. *West Africa and Islam* (London: Edward Arnold)
Cobb, *Beyond Dialogue*, 25.
Crampton, E.P.T., 1975. *Christianity in Northern Nigeria* (London: Geoffrey Chapman)
Dike, K. O., 1962. *The Niger Mission*
Dinker, *Profit for the Lord* has shown that certain missions such as Basel Missions
Ekechi, Felix, 1972. *Missionary Enterprise and Rivalry in Igboland, 1857-1914* (London: Frank Cass.)
Eliade, Mircea, 1958. *Patterns of Comparative Religion* (London: 1958 English translations)
Erivwo, S.U., 1973. "Christian Churches in Urhoboland," *Orita* 7.1 (June): 206-215
Evans-Pritchard, E. E. (ed.). ???? *Institutions of Primitive Society* (Oxford: University Press)
Evans-Pritchard, E. E. 1965. *Theories of Primitive Religion* (Oxford: Clarendon Press, 1965)
Gbadamosi, T.G.O. 1967. "The Establishment of Western education among Muslims in Nigeria", *JHSN* 4.1: 94ff
Gbadamosi,, T.G.O., 1978. *The Growth of Islam among the Yoruba, 1841-1908* (London: Longman)

Horton, Robin, 1975. "On the Rationality of Conversion" *Africa* 45.3: 219-235; 45.4: 373-399
Ifemesia, C.C., 1962. "The civilizing mission of 1841", *JHSH*, 2.3 (December): 291-310
Ihekweazu, E. (ed.), 1985. *Traditional and Modern Culture* (Enugu: Fourth Dimensions Publications)
Ikime, Obaro, 1965. "The Coming of the C.M.S. to Itshekiri, Urhobo, and Isoko", *Nigeria Magazine,* 84 (September): 206-215;
Ikime, Obaro, 1972. *The Isoko People: A History Survey* (Ibadan: University Press)
Kalu, O. U. 1986. "Religion and Political Values in Nigeria: A Pluralistic Perspective", forthcoming in Religious Pluralism in Africa (New York: Pergamon Press)
Kalu, O. U. 1992. "Gods as Policemen: Religion and Social Control in Igboland", in J.K. Olupona (ed.) *Religious Plurality in Africa: Essays in Honour of J.S. Mbiti* (Berlin: Mouton)
Kalu, O.U. 1975. "Snake Skins? Marxist Materialist Critique and African Traditional Religion," (Faculty of Social Sciences Seminar, University of Nigeria, Nzukka)
Kalu, O.U. 1977. "Missionaries, Colonial Government and Secret Societies in S.E. Igboland" *JHSN*: 75-90
Kalu, O.U. 1977. "Waves from the Rivers: the Spread of Garrick Braide Movement in Igboland", *JHSN* 8.4
Kalu, O.U. 1978. "Precarious Visions: the African's Perception of His World" in O.U. Kalu (ed.) *Readings in African Humanities: African Cultural Development* (Enugu: Fourth Dimension Publishers): Chapter 3
Kalu, O.U. 1985. "Formulation of Cultural Policy in Colonial Nigeria" in E. Ihekweazu (ed.) *Traditional and Modern Culture* (Enugu: Fourth Dimension Publications): Chapter 9.
Kalu, O.U., ????. "Primitive Methodists on the Railroad Junctions of Igboland, 1910-1931" *JRA* 20
Kalu, O.U., 1978. "The Battle of the Gods: Christianization of Cross River Igboland", *JHSN* X.1: 1-18;
Knitter, Paul, 1984. "Roman Catholic Approaches to other Religions: Developments and Tensions" *International Bulletin of Missiological Research*, 8.2.
Kraemer, H. (1938) 1961 5th Edition. *The Christian Message in Non-Christian World* (Grand Rapids, Kregel Publishers)
Nasseef, Abdulla Omar, 1986. "Muslim-Christian Relations: Muslim Approach" *Current Dialogue 11* (December): 29-32.
Ranger, T. O. & I.N. Kimambo (eds.), 1972. *The Historical Study of African Religions* (Berkeley, California: University of California Press)
Samartha, S.J., 1971. "Dialogue as a Continuing Christian Concern" in S.J. Samartha, *Living Faiths and the Ecumenical Movement* (Geneva: WCC Publications): 153-154
Sanneh, Lamin, 1985. *Christianity in West Africa: A Religious Perspective* (Maryknoll, New York: Orbis Books)
Smith, A., 1970. "Some Considerations relating to the formation of States in Hausaland" *JHSN* 5.3 (December): 340
Starkey, Peggy, 1985. "AGAPE: A Christian Criterion for Truth in the Other World Religions," *IRM* 74: 425-463
Tasie, G.O.M., 1976. *Christianity in the Niger Delta* (Leiden: E.J. Brill)
Ubah, C.N., 1976. "Problems of Christian Missionaries in the Muslim Emirates of Nigeria, 1900-1928" *Journal of African Studies* 3.3: 351-372
Ubah, C.N., 1985. "Islamic Culture and Nigerian Society" in E. Ihekweazu (ed.) *Traditional and Modern Culture* (Enugu: Fourth Dimensions Publ.): Chapter 16.

4

Indigenous tradition in transition: 'Born Again' traditional rulers, religious change and power contestation

- David O. Ogungbile & Peter 'Ropo Awoniyi

> Kingship institution in Africa is not only exalted but is revered because a king is not regarded as an ordinary human being. He is seen as next to God Almighty Himself and is therefore, worshipped and adored...A king is an institution unto himself and has no religion, because he is the custodian of the culture, tradition and beliefs of his people...But civilization has crept into the palace. Some kings now profess one religion or the other...Instead of propagating *Ifa* oracle, they preach the gospel and change the face of the palace. Yet they are convinced that they have not done anything to rubbish the traditional seat they occupy. (Muyiwa Adeyemi, 2010)

Introduction

Nigerian indigenous religious traditions could be understood in whole or in part from the structure, pattern and operation within the traditional political institution embodied in kingship and the palace. Kingship institution and the palace of each community in Nigeria express the depth, diversity and unity of such community. Both also represent the communal identity - cultural, social and religious - of the indigenes, which is reinforced by mythic narrative and ritual activities rehearsed and re-enacted in occasional and/or annual festivals.

However, in recent times, this institution is being challenged and transformed through religious change otherwise termed 'conversion' which some traditional rulers who essentially embody the tradition and customs of the community undergo. The mode and process of conversion of some traditional rulers into Christianity and Islam, sometimes radical, drastic and revolutionary, and sometimes subtle and modest, has been noted to have a wholesome effect on indigenous traditions in contemporary Nigeria. It has continued to alter the religious landscape of the people. The climax of this religious change is visible in the formation of the Associations of Christian traditional rulers in the south-western and south-eastern parts of Nigeria. One of such powerful associations formed in the South-western Nigeria is the Association of the Born Again Christian Obas (AOBACO).

This chapter therefore examines the phenomenon of religious change among some traditional rulers as well as the activities of AOBACO and the impacts of the change on traditional institution and the entire community. It analyzes the subject of power contestation between Indigenous Religious Tradition and Christianity.

Traditional ruler and indigenous traditions

A traditional ruler is a monarch who is regarded as the embodiment and the custodian of the culture, customs and tradition of the people in his domain. Although it has always been assumed and asserted that traditional rulers are male because Nigerian communities are basically patrifocal, current researches have revealed the existence of female traditional rulers among the people of Adamawa, Niger, Ebonyi, Delta, Ondo, Ekiti and Oyo States of Nigeria.[1] Fatai Olasupo, in his current research, noted that "there are three kinds of traditional institutions with females as the heads."[2] First, there is the dual rulership where a female ruler co-exists with her male counterpart. Here the female rules over female-folk while the male rules over the men. This system exists in Ondo and Ekiti States. Second, this system allows only a female person to ascend the throne. This is practised among the Mbada Local Government Area of Niger State and Uwama-Afibu North Local Government Area of Ebonyi State. Third, ascendancy to traditional rulership is open to either of the sexes as we have among the Maya area in Oriire Local Government Area of Oyo State.

Essentially, Nigerian indigenous traditions and cultures carry with them religion; this is why the entire structure of the power of the monarch (king) is ritually and socio-culturally constructed. The monarch is held as sacred, and his/her sacredness is enshrined and reinforced through the process of ritual ordering in the selection, election and initiation (installation and enthronement). In most if not in all cases, kingship institution is hereditary, and the status ascribed on members of the family. Ascendancy to the throne therefore follows what is termed 'royal lineage.' Max Weber has described authority in this system of socio-political arrangement as 'traditional'[3] which relates well with indigenous communities in Nigeria and several places in Africa.

The institution of traditional rulers in indigenous communities is highly respected and greatly revered. Traditional rulers occupy sovereign positions. It needs to be stated however that the different religio-cultural lives and orientations of the three major groups in Nigeria produce different types of traditional institutions. For instance, since Islam is deep-rooted among the dominant Hausa and Fulani groups of northern part of Nigeria due to the

---

[1] See Adekanmbi, Dare, "Showcasing Nigeria's Female Traditional Rulers" 02 June, 2010. *Nigeria Tribune*, October 14, 2010. Fatai Olasupo is on his doctoral programme in the Department of Local Government Studies and Administration, Obafemi Awolowo University, Ile-Ife.
[2] Adekanmbi, Dare, "Showcasing Nigeria's Female Traditional Rulers".
[3] Roth, Guenther & Claus Wittich (eds.), 1978. *Max Weber: Economy and Society*, Vols. 1 & 2, University of California Press, The Regents

activities of Uthman Dan Fodio's Jihad of 1800s, Islam has become the tradition of most communities in the area, having displaced indigenous traditions. Subsequently, in modern Nigeria, Emir is regarded as the traditional ruler of most communities of the Muslim north. For the South-eastern part of Nigeria, indigenous traditions still flourish in a diffused form, a reflection of the nature of the communities. However, most communities in south-eastern part of Nigeria have *Obi* as their traditional rulers.

South-western axis, the third major ethnic group in Nigeria, which is peopled by the Yoruba, has a traditional institution whose monarchical structure appears to be more defined in terms of influence and the power of traditional rulers wielded in their different communities. Understandably, the Yoruba people draw their ancestry from a source; they express certain uniformity in indigenous system of operation. Paradoxically, this is where the notion of the transition of indigenous tradition is strong and where power is intensely contested and competed, between Christian-Muslim traditions and indigenous religious tradition through the activities of the Muslim conservatives and fundamentalists and Christian evangelicals in the recent time. This has resulted in religious change which continues to alter indigenous tradition in an unprecedented way. Thus, our discussion will draw heavily from among the Yoruba group, with illustration from people of other communities.

The sacredness and power of the traditional ruler could be explained from the structure of the traditional political institution and the intense ritual processes and activities through which the king is selected, initiated, and installed. The Yoruba call traditional rulers *Oba* who they regard as semi-divine. An *Oba* is addressed as '*alase ekeji òrìsà*' meaning 'second in command to the *òrìsà* (deities)' who also possesses the like-authority in essence and functions. They are claimed to hold the power of life and death. Their words and utterances are claimed to be invocations sanctioned by the divine. Yoruba traditional rulers hold the Oduduwa primordial myth which claims that Ile-Ife is the source of human origin and creation. They maintain that Yoruba kingship institution derive from, and define Yoruba monarchical ancestry of Oduduwa, the first monarch of Ile-Ife in the present Osun State of Nigeria. Essentially, all other Yoruba communities trace their primordial existence to Ile-Ife.

Secondly, most Yoruba communities have a structure called 'royal lineage' that produces traditional ruler(s). Under a normal situation, no one outside the lineage is considered eligible for the throne of the king. Thirdly, there is a group of kingmakers (seven in most Yoruba communities) who occupy an important position, and play such roles as dictated by the given tradition and historical/mythic origin of their own family origin in the community. Fourthly, there are ritual experts or specialists who are involved in the selection and election of the traditional ruler through the consultation of *Ifa* oracle. They are instrumental to the initiation/installation of the traditional ruler through intense ritual including ritual instructions to the initiate. Fifthly, there are severe taboos that the monarch observes throughout his entire life.

This may include annual and occasional prescriptive seclusion, particularly during the town's hegemonic (traditional) festival(s) such that connects kingship institution to the entire community. A few examples are the *Oṣun* and *Olojo* festivals. Furthermore, as the most sacred semi-divine human being in the community, there is restriction to public appearances and social gathering, including eating in the public.

The paraphernalia and instruments of royal office which include crowns and special caps of different makes and stuff, staff, beads, fans, seats are treated with utmost awe and reverence. The *Oba* in his regalia is usually surrounded by his chiefs as a mark of honour. As soon as an *Oba* is made, his head becomes particularly sacred in a special way; his head is not to be left uncovered. Once crowned, his head becomes raised above other humans. Those who install and crown him must bow or prostrate as a mark of respect to him, as he becomes the 'father' of the entire community. Furthermore, he does not bow his head in respect to any human being even if he is younger than the individual.[4] His occasional outing is usually greeted with great respect and worship. All of these have implications for any claim to religious change or conversion as his new experience and 'newfound faith' affects his entire life and that of this community. It should be mentioned that the phenomenon of conversion has been examined from a number of factors, namely: i) the shattered microcosm, ii) the intellectualist theory, iii) an historical explanation, and iv) a socio-structural explanation.[5] This phenomenon of conversion of traditional ruler will be examined along these and other factors and its implications for indigenous religious traditions.

In indigenous communities, the traditional ruler is at the apex of administration which includes economics, politics, religious, culture and the entire society.[6] The roles of the traditional ruler cover ritual and political aspects of the communities. He leads his community in ritual and cultural practices being part of the oath he swears to during his enthronement. He is obligated to fulfil his allegiance to the deities and his ancestors whom he represents in his universe. His activities are regarded as a re-enactment of those of his predecessors. It is claimed that ruling contrary to the tradition of the land is capable of attracting the punishment of the ancestors and deities of the land which may spell calamities for the entire community. If and when this happens, there would be protest by the community which may lead to

---

[4] Bowing or prostrating by a male, and kneeling down by a female, particularly for an older person are a mark of respect in Yoruba custom. In this case, the *Oba* is considered not only superior to everybody in the land, but also carries the honour and dignity of deities who are usually revered by all.

[5] See Ifeka-Moller, C., 1974. "White Power: Social-Structural Factors in Conversion to Christianity, Eastern Nigeria, 1921-1966", *Canadian Journal of African Studies*, Vol. 8, No. 1: 55-72; Horton, Robin and J.D.Y. Peel, 1976. "Conversion and Confusion: A Rejoinder on Christianity in Eastern Nigeria" *Journal of African Studies*, Vol. 10: 481-497; Ikenga-Metuh, Emefie, 1987 "The Shattered Microcosm: A Critical Survey of Explanations of Conversion in Africa" in Kirsten Holst Peterson (ed.) *Religion, Development and African Identity* (Uppsala: Scandinavian Institute of African Studies): 11-27

[6] Yusuf Turaki, *Foundations of African Traditional Religions and Worldview*. Nairobi, Kenya: International Bible Society Africa, 2001, p. 50.

eventual rejection by the people, and possible banishment.[7] It is important to note that the sacredness of traditional institution is reinforced by the ritual burial of the king in the palace as he essentially becomes an ancestor that is appeased and invoked by his successor.

Indigenous traditions in motion

The advent of Islam c.11-14 centuries and Christianity in 1840s in Nigeria has no doubt altered indigenous traditions and traditional institution in diverse ways. The depths of alteration and influence however differ from community to community depending largely on the attitudes of and level of receptivity by any traditional ruler to the incoming faith at any point in time. The wind of Islam and Christianity has succeeded in blowing through the land, leaving a remnant that could be described as traditional religious people. However, in the recent years, there is a resurgence of indigenous practices although this still remains of little significance compared to the influence of Islam and Christianity.

The most significant area where Islam and Christianity have made deep impression is identity. Notably, a Nigerian is defined along the religious, ethnic and national identity. Beyond the socio-cultural identity, personal identity is perhaps most affected. The most visible sign of religious change which reinforce identity is name-change, and name-bearing. Observations revealed that most Nigerians have Muslim or Christian names as their 'first name'. The implication of this is that traditional rulers like most other indigenes are also not spared of Muslim and Christian influence. That is, most were born into Muslim and Christian families, and have also been tutored in those religious traditions. Thus, the depth of their affiliations to Islam and Christianity readily influences their activities as traditional rulers. But in most cases, coming to the throne, they recognize the challenge they need to face in being re-branded and tutored in kingship and palace tradition through the rites of passage into the new role and position. However and generally, it has always been the case, not until recently, that a traditional ruler sees himself as the custodian of all the religious traditions and practices in his domain. He develops an inclusive and compromising posture and attitude concerning the religious affairs as the ruler of the people.

In recent years, there appears to be a change in the attitude of traditional rulers among the Yoruba. It should be emphasized that for a traditional ruler who is a Muslim, there has been less tension. This could be attributed to several factors including subtle compromise, accommodation, and acceptance of indigenous cultural patterns by Muslim rulers. This probably explains why several notable first-class Yoruba traditional rulers are Muslims and this is visible in their names and title as 'Alhaji'. A few examples are Alhaji Adeyemi II, Alaafin of Oyo and Alhaji Yunusa, *Oba* of Ibadan, Oyo State; Alhaji Rilwan Akinolu, the *Oba* of Lagos, Lagos State; the *Timi* of Ede; *Olobu* of Ilobu,

---

[7] Lois, Fuller, *African Traditional Religion.* Kaduna: Baraka Press, 2001, p. 76.

Ataoja of Osogbo in Osun State, etc.[8] Our research has revealed how the immediate past *Ataoja* of Òṣogbo *Oba* (Alhaji) Iyiola Oyewale Matanmi III through subtle compromise continually presented his royal messages to reinforce a civil religiosity and cultural identity in Ọṣun Òṣogbo annual festival.[9]

From the Christian side, the growth of Pentecostalism has produced a different attitude in some traditional rulers who have already accepted the Pentecostal brand of Christianity, or at some point on the throne, they are introduced to such movements. It may interest one to note that a few communities which desire certain kinds of social developments think less of indigenous religious practices but are ready to accept traditional rulers who could inspire the development of their communities. In such a case, such traditional rulers have their ways in undermining indigenous practices. At the other level, traditional rulers who accept new faith while on the throne usually meet with stiff oppositions of their subjects, particularly the ritual specialists who are custodians of some notable deities since their roles give them identity in the community. This Pentecostal influence on such traditional rulers, through the newfound faith termed 'born-again', is a radical instrument that has altered kingship institution as well as thus indigenous tradition among the Yoruba.

The 'Born Again' phenomenon and the antecedents to 'Born-Again' traditional rulers

Although the term 'born again' has been used in the United States since the 1960s, particularly among the Evangelical Christian Renewal, it was unfashionable in Nigeria until the mid-1970s. It was first noticed among the Scripture Union (S.U.), a group of Christians who established Christian fellowships among the students in secondary grammar schools in the south-western part of Nigeria. The group emphasised the 'born again' experience as necessary condition for salvation. This was drawn from, interpreted and reinterpreted from the encounter of Nicodemus, the Jewish rabbi, with Jesus Christ in the Gospel of John (Chapter 3). The activities of the S.U. were complemented and supplemented by the activities of some American evangelists Billy Graham, T.L. Osborn, J. Otis Yoder and others who sent free of charge large packets of bibles, Christian literatures and manual gramophone containing Christian messages; some also offered free bible certificate courses such as World Bible School. Students of these schools were

---

[8] See for instance H. Shittu and B. Inuwa, "Islam and Traditional Beliefs of the Obas in Yorъbóland" in R.A. Raji, et al. (eds.), *Religion, Governance and Development in the 21st Century* (A Publication of the Nigerian Association for the Study of Religions) Ago-Iwoye, Ogun State, 2006):358-370

[9] Ogungbile, David O., 2003. "Myth, Ritual and Identity in the Religious Traditions of the Osogbo People of Western Nigeria." PhD Dissertation, Obafemi Awolowo University, Ile-Ife, Nigeria. Also, Islam and Cultural Identity in Nigeria: The T ogbo-Yoruba Experience" *Orita: Ibadan Journal of Religious Studies.* Vol. XXX/1-2: 123-137.

encouraged to attend 'bible-believing' churches and get baptised by their priests and pastors.

The zeal and fervency of these youths were seen in the formation of a typical Christian group in the Council Commercial School, Iléṣà, in the present Osun State of Nigeria. Of quick note was the article contributed to the school's magazine by a member of this fellowship. The title which was "Have You Been Born Again?" contained, *inter alia*:

> The meaning of being born again is to accept Jesus Christ as your personal Saviour because you are once under sin and this is the reason why Jesus came into the world because God loves us. He does not want us to perish after accepting Him, we must confess our sins and be baptised both of water and Holy Spirit (Acts 3:37-41; John 3:1-7).[10]

The emphasis is that 'being born again' is the ticket to heaven, the kingdom of God.[11] The drastic experience of 'born again' indicates an attitude of 'this-world rejecting' and 'other-world affirming.' The term is often associated with inward conviction, conversion, new birth, new life, new creation, dying to sin, renewal, spiritual rebirth, regeneration, life-transforming, born of the spirit, birth from above, born of God, etc. One recalls the popular chorus in their worship services:

> There's a great change, since I'm born again/4x
>
> The things I used to do, I do them no more/3x
> There's a great change since I am born again
>
> The food I used to eat, I eat them no more/3x
> There's a great change since I am born again
>
> The dress I used to wear, I wear them no more/3x
> There's a great change since I am born again

In the recent time, the term has become fashionable, adopted not only by different Christian groups who had treated the born again group with disdain, but also by Muslim; it has even assumed a secular usage to denote a change of attitude or reenergizing into a new form of life. It goes with it high emotionalism, activism, militancy, radicalism, revolutionary, and fundamentalism. The born again Christian is uncompromising with regards to his/her new religious experience regardless of the risk to his/her person and social status. The experience of new life thus affects the psyche and the physical appearance of the convert. The new experience, directed by Jesus

---

[10] David Ogungbile, "Have You Been Born Again?" *The Eagle: The Magazine of Council Commercial School*, Vol. VIII, Ilesha, Oyo State, Nigeria, 1977, p. 43

[11] Ibid., p. 44

Christ the new master alone through the scriptural teachings, directs and dictates new actions, aspirations, behaviours, etc.

Perhaps the first noticeable appearance of the claim to a similar experience of 'born again' brand of Christianity by a traditional ruler was *Oba* I.B. Akinyele, the *Olubadan* of Ibadan. Certain important facts are noteworthy about *Oba* Akinyele regarding faith experience and indigenous tradition. Olufunke Adeboye pointedly identified some of these issues.[12] She noted that Akinyele was already influential as Ibadan elite, and also distinguished as an active Pentecostal member who professed his Christian faith openly. He not only practiced and lived his faith among the people, but he was also a peripatetic preacher to some villages in Ibadan to whom he preached the doctrines of holiness, prayers and faith-healing which he received from the Faith Tabernacle, which he also transferred to the Christ Apostolic Church when this movement began in the 1930s. It was recorded that he made convert among the chiefs when he became a chief. His chieftaincy career began in 1936 as a holder of junior title, *Lagunna Balogun*. He later moved through the rank to become the *Balogun,* head chief in 1953, and then to the *Olubadan* in 1955.

It should be noted that ascending to these positions, particularly the *Balogun* and *Olubadan* were not easy for Akinyele. First, by tradition and from pre-colonial experience, the *Balogun* was a warlord whose title, status and symbol of authority had with it strong ritual installation and paraphernalia. Akinyele's faith would not be compromised to accept installation with indigenous ritual neither would he accept to take custody of the *Opa Balogun* which was an instrument or staff of his authority, to be given periodic ritual appeasement. After much trouble from the people and his insistence, Akinyele was allowed to make a silver substitute of the staff which was presented to him on his installation; the people however regarded this as powerless and a mockery to his traditional office. Second, by Ibadan tradition,[13] the upward movement of the *Balogun* to Olubadan was automatic as soon as there was vacancy. His chance was going to be scuttled by the National Council of Nigeria and the Cameroons (NCNC), the party which controlled the Ibadan Council whereas Akinyele was a supporter of the Action Group. He however gained the support of the British Resident who overruled the opposition. One could suggest that Akinyele's exposure to western education was responsible for his final approval as the *Olubadan*. It is noteworthy that even as the *Olubadan, Oba* Akinyele still engaged in preaching and held on to the doctrines of the Christ Apostolic Church which strongly maintained divine healing. Although this earned him disrespect among the traditionalists and political opponents, he was undaunted to his faith. Moreover, his prayers and preaching activities earned the fame as

---

[12] Olufunke Adeboye, "The 'Born-Again' *Oba*: Pentecostalism and Traditional Chieftaincy in Yorʉbóland," *Lagos Historical Review: A Journal of the Department of History & Strategic Studies, University of Lagos,* Vol. 7, 2007:1-20

[13] This is different from most other Yoruba towns where there are specific ruling houses which election and selection of traditional rulers are determined by the ruling houses, kingmakers and *Ifa* oracle.

prayerful king and the king of the people who descended to interact with the common people. On the whole, it was remarkable that *Oba* I.B. Akinyele was the first educated *Olubadan* of Ibadan who also successfully resisted traditional practices attached to indigenous institution.

In the mid-1980s, an interaction with the *Akinla* of Erin reinforced two important facts. When the throne was vacant, the indigenes were interested in having an educated and enlightened king. By this time, *Oba* Akinla was a police officer and a committed member of the Christ Apostolic Church. According to him, though he was a prospective candidate for the throne, he resisted the invitation since he understood the rituals attached to the installation of the king. The people, who expressed the need for social development of the town that could be offered by an enlightened king, waived this for him and got him installed following some Christian prayer rituals.

In the research carried out by Olufunke Adeboye, she interviewed four kings: *Oba* Matthew Oyekale, the *Ola-Aresa* of Masifa Ile; *Oba* Julius Fatanmi, the *Olura* of Ira; *Oba* James Ashaolu Adekeye, the *Onimoji* of Imoji, Kwara State; Olatunde Falabi, the *Akire* of Ikire. Adeboye noted that each of these communities where these *Oba* reigned was desirous of an educated king with the expectation that this would aid physical development. It seemed that there were no educated traditionalists for the throne, hence the ready access for the committed Pentecostal candidates.

A personal reminiscence of the conversion experience of *Oba* Samuel Adelegan Popoola, the *Ogboni* of Ipole in Atakunmosa East Local Government Area of Osun State, presents a different case. *Oba* Popoola, until he joined the Christ Trumpeters' Church, Iléṣà, was an ardent traditionalist who regarded himself as 'an evangelist of indigenous religious traditions', not only in Yorùbáland but also in Nigeria. He went about several communities in Nigeria to inspire people in indigenous traditions. It is also noteworthy that one of his wives who first got converted into this Church in the mid-1990s was a strong traditionalist whose influence in Owari rituals and festival was unsurpassed.

It should be mentioned that by tradition, *Oba* Popoola reigned on a community that was considered the spiritual headquarters of Ijesa kingdom, while Iléṣà was the political or administrative headquarters. History has it that the migratory experiences of the Owa Obokun, the leader of the kingdom, defined those towns in terms of their prominence, status and consequence in Ijesa oral history. An expression "*Ogun Ipole ni an i bo kan to bo t'Iléṣà*" (It is the Ogun festival of Ipole that must be celebrated before that of Iléṣà would be) speaks of the importance of Ipole as the spiritual head of Ijesa kingdom since Ogun festival is the hegemonic festival of the entire kingdom. Thus, together with Owari festival, Ogun Ipole festival was an instrument of identity for the people.

One recollects a question thrown at *Oba* Popoola during a worship service when a prophecy echoed "My child, Popoola, would you help me to destroy Orisa?" The simple response he gave was "Well, this should not be difficult. As long as I do not go about spreading or leading the revival of *Orisa* tradition, it would die." This was perhaps why Akinola laments that "in western Nigeria, many traditional rulers, once famed custodians of indigenous culture, are now acquiring a new identity as 'born-again' *oba*.[14] Though Ipole was relatively small, its position in Ijesa kingdom was strong. The annual festival of Ogun festival of Iléṣà was the first challenge for him, as the *Owa Obokun* of Ijesaland was himself a supporter of indigenous tradition. This started turbulence as Ogun festival of Iléṣà would not be done without the celebration of that of Ipole. *Oba* Popoola took his newfound faith seriously. He attended church and revival services regularly and punctually. Some of his actions demystify traditional institution. Whenever he entered the church or attended any worship services, he removed his cap, shook hands with several members, knelt down in prayers with others and sat with others. His two wives joined the workers' units; one was a strong member of the choir, and the other evangelism unit. Besides her activities in this unit, Mrs. Popoola became a peripatetic evangelist, going about some streets in Ilesa with Bible in her hands at about 5 o'clock in the morning, to preach the gospel. This is termed 'morning cry,'

Another case of public importance readily comes to mind. Sometime in late 1990s, an interdenominational revival service was organized at the Enuwa where traditional rulers in the kingdom were invited. The attendance of the members of his church at the service was intimidating. The number of the church's chorister, which performance was noticeably great, was huge. Some traditional rulers were already seated with their caps on. As the *Ogboni* of Ipole stepped on the revival ground, he removed his cap. The traditional rulers in attendance were dismayed as *Ogboni* was considered superior in status to them. It was noted that some of them also removed their own caps. He was hell-bent as a 'born again' Christian not to compromise his faith until 2004 when he was banished. He was however undaunted and undisturbed. His community however was not pleased with him; first his church activities did not allow him to perform his functions as their ruler, and second, his disregard for the town's festivals complicated the issue. Interestingly, when he was reinstated by the Osun State government in 2007, he re-entered the palace with the opened Bible, Psalm 24 read at all the entrances, with prayer session.[15]

Association of Born-Again Christian Obas (AOBACO) and kingship institution

Although the idea of forming a fellowship of Christian traditional rulers was conceived in 1977 by *Oba* M. O. Oyeyode Oyekale, the traditional ruler of Masifa-Ile, Ejigbo Local Government of Nigeria,[16] the Association of Born

---

[14] G.A. Akinola, "Religion and the Obasanjo Administration"
http://www.utexas.edu/conferences/africa/ads/1543.html Accessed March 1, 2008
[15] Olufunke Adeboye, pp. 1-2
[16] Interview with *Oba* (Dr.) Matthew Olayiwola Oyeyode Oyekale, Adegbookun III, the Ola-Aresa of Masifa-Ile via Ejigbo, Osun State, Nigeria, January 23, 2008.

Again Christian Obas (AOBACO) was inaugurated in May 2000 in Òṣogbo, Osun State.[17] It should be mentioned that *Oba* Oyekale had been born again before his enthronement. According to him, the growth of the fellowship was improved by the activities of the Full Gospel Businessmen's Fellowship (FGBMF), an interdenominational Christian group that organizes its services in forms of talks, social interactions, Bible teachings interspersed with some prayer sessions. Sometime there could be organized deliverance services on request; this however is not common. Its membership is usually drawn from people of high social class including civil servants, bankers, traditional rulers, etc. The FGBMF does not operate on conventional church model. Each chapter has a president. The Fellowship uses hotels and other public places for its programmes which are attended mostly by invitation. *Oba* Oyekale used this medium to bring together other traditional rulers.

Since 2001, AOBACO has become strong such that prospective Christian traditional rulers consult this group for advice.[18] As at 2010, the population of the association has risen to thirty in Osun State alone. It is noteworthy that similar associations of traditional rulers are now found in other parts of Nigeria.[19] For instance, there is the Association of Nigerian Christian Kings in Warri, Delta State and another brand of the association of Christian *Oba* exists in Kwara State.[20]

What are the inspirations for founding such an association? Some of the factors, some remote and some immediate, may be attributed to the new wave and upsurge of revivalism and the activities of the New Religious Movements in Nigeria. Of particular notes are activities of the local, national and freelance evangelists who visit palaces to pray and hold Bible Studies with the royal court, The Redeemed Christian Church of God and its Redemption Camp Holy Ghost activities and Campus Christian fellowships. Some of these traditional rulers have tertiary education in the University during which time they already encountered the 'born again' experience and some of them were already members of Pentecostal groups before they were enthroned. A lot of them see the opportunity to exploit the position to strengthen their personal spiritual experience, and propagate and strengthen Christian faith in their domains sometimes in response to religious competition in other communities or political insecurity.

What is the mission of the Association of Born Again Christian Obas? How does this movement operate? *Oba* (Dr.) Adetoyese Oyeniyi Odugbemi identified the mission of the association thus:

---

[17] Muyiwa Adeyemi, "Why We Formed Association of Born Again Christian Obas" http://www.onlinenigeria.com/chritianlinks/ad2.asp?blurb=54. Accessed 20/11/2010; http://groups.yahoo.com/group/Naija-news/message/2391. Guardian News of Saturday, October 12, 2002. Accessed 17/02/2011
[18] Interview with *Oba* (Dr.) Matthew Olayiwola Oyeyode Oyekale, ibid.
[19] Interview with *Oba* Olatunde Falabi, Akire of Ikire,, Osun State. January 26th 2008.
[20] *Oba* (Dr.) Adetoyese Oyeniyi Odugbemi, the Olufi of Gbongan, Osun State. In Muyiwa Adeyemi "Why We Formed Association of Born Again Christian Obas."

We meet every month for fasting and prayers. We know that we have to pray together since the Bible says we should not neglect the coming together of believers. And, corporate prayers have a lot of effect. So, we believe that we should commit our throne to God regularly. We know that we are operating in a peculiar terrain. In the traditional setting, people believe that an *Oba* should be an *Ifa* priest, must be Chief Imam, also a Christian. But not so with somebody who professes to a particular faith.[21]

In other words, members understand AOBACO as an instrument of change to redirect indigenous tradition and evolve a new tradition that would empower them as an individual and possibly recreate a new religious order that would give new identity. This is more so since most of the members are educated, literate and read the Bible; they have also imbibed the new culture of praying directly to the Supreme Being rather than depend on *Ifa* diviners, the specialists, who serve as intermediaries; they are the only ones who could interpret the message of/from the Divine. It is important to mention that some of these Christian traditional rulers conduct all-night prayer meetings with their family members, and in fact create chapels and prayer cells in their palace. *Oba* (Dr.) Matthew Oyekale added that biblical teachings are the basis upon which these traditional rulers want to rule their subjects and not indigenous ritual prescriptions.[22] To them, it is ungodly and unholy to profess the faith of Jesus Christ and still patronize indigenous religious tradition. There is an emphasis on three important elements: Jesus Christ as the only source of true and real power, the direct access to God the Supreme Being, and the way to eternity which is the ultimate goal of any human being. To them indigenous religion and practice would not guarantee these.

The officers of the fellowship are Chairman, Secretary, and Evangelism Chairman/Treasurer. The programme of activities includes Bible studies, prayer meetings, counselling. Their meeting which is held monthly or as the situation demands is rotated from town to town. During their meetings, they share their problems and pray over them. In most cases some of these problems include persecution due to their non-conformist attitude to lead or participate in indigenous rituals. They occasionally invite renowned evangelists to lead them in Bible teachings and prayer programmes. They collect offerings which they spend for promoting the gospel and for other fellowship expenses. They organize outreach programmes with the purposes of converting souls for Christ.[23]

---

[21] Muyiwa Adeyemi, "Why We Formed Association of Born Again Christian Obas"

[22] Interview with *Oba* (Dr.) Matthew Olayiwola Oyeyode Oyekale, Ola-Aresa of Masifa-Ile via Ejigbo, Osun State, Nigeria January 23rd 2008

[23] Interview with *Oba* (Dr.) Adetoyese Oyeniyi Odugbemi, the Olufi of Gbongan, Ayedaade Local Government, Osun State, January 26 2008.

Responding to demystification, confronting the power shift

In the real sense, the born again phenomenon is a clear case of 'culture clash'. The experience has a great effect and implications for traditional institution in so many ways. As earlier mentioned, the primordiality of any traditional community is instrumental to its organization; this is rehearsed in community ritual. First, kingship institution is reinforced by the voice of *Ifa* that is claimed to have established the community, the primordial mythic narrative and ritual practices, all providing the basis for the collective identity of the community. These are re-enacted and rehearsed during the installation of the *Oba*, the celebration of the community festival, and at any crisis moment. Second, kingship institution has the structure that is bonded by community's commitment, material objectification and symbols. Besides the understanding that royal lines are defined and reinforced by traditional myth and ritual, the players at each level of the structure are ascribed. For instance, kingmakers, traditional chieftaincy title-holders, custodians of different deities define their existence in consequence of their commitment to the tradition; each player holds a title and one or more symbols of authority that are used on different set occasions. Moreover, individual role-players do not act in isolation; he/she acts as a representative of his compound community. It is this understanding that the born again phenomenon that instigates conflict arising from change in kingship institution is challenged, confronted and contested.

The general response from practitioners of indigenous religions who by profession and practice would be regarded as custodians of indigenous traditions is represented in the somewhat sharp reaction of a renowned *Ifa* priest, Chief Ifayemi Elebuibon, the *Araba* of Agbaye to the claims of *Oba* Adedapo Tejuoso, the *Osile* of Oke-Ona, Egba in Ogun State. *Oba* Tejuoso had earlier disclaimed indigenous system of worship emphasizing it as 'idol worship' which he could not be involved in "as doing so would be akin to worshipping children who are quite junior to him."[24] He further said that he had destroyed several objects of worship and that as a born again Christian, a new creature, he "could not have anything to do with the traditional worshippers and their objects of worship any more."[25] Reacting, Elebuibon described this attitude and action:

> As a taboo and the highest height of hypocrisy the monarch's destruction of items of worship by traditional worshippers in his domain...the royal father's action amounted to a sacrilege and an affront on Yoruba tradition and culture...Traditional rulers are regarded as custodians of Yoruba customs and tradition, and therefore must at all times strive to be good ambassadors. In Yoruba tradition, traditional rulers are regarded as

---

[24] Tunde Thomas, "Hypocrite! *Ifa* Priest Blasts *Oba* Tejuoso over Idol Worship Disclaimer," *Weekly Spectator*, April 16, 2006, p. 26
[25] Ibid.

custodians of Yoruba customs, including their sacred objects of worship. *Oba* Tejuoso has provoked our ancestors and deities by his action. In fact, he needs to appease the ancestors over his provocative action...[I]t was not possible for any traditional ruler to be crowned king without undergoing some ritual which of a necessity must include making sacrifice to the deities.[26]

We shall cite a few case studies of responses and reactions against born again traditional rulers to illustrate our point. The reactions range from palace boycott, to open ridicule and disrespect, physical attack on traditional rulers and members of their families, destruction of properties and burning of palace. It is important to stress that even though a few of the born again traditional rulers were reluctant in accepting to be made kings because of their faith commitment, they were persuaded to accept and that they would not be coerced/compelled to take part in any form of indigenous rituals including initiation rites. In fact, *Oba* Matthew Olayiwola of Masifa-Ile, who was born again through The Apostolic Church, claimed to have resisted several attempts to be lured into kingship.[27] He reluctantly "accepted to be king, but on the condition that he would remain a devout Christian."[28] However, three days to his enthronement, one of the elders of the town came to inform him of the "various idols in the community in which they would want (him) to observe and worship ... (and) that by virtue of (his) exalted position as an *Oba*, (he) must be initiated into the Ogboni cult."[29] As soon as he was installed as the king, he was told that it was "an abomination for an *Oba* to shun Ipebi rites of initiation."[30]

Oba Olatunde Falabi, the *Akire* of Ikire in Irewole Local Government Area of Osun State is a member of The Redeemed Christian Church of God. For him, traditionalists made several attempts to harm him because of his refusal to participate in the community's ritual worship. The persecution resulted in the burning down of his palace in 2007.[31] In Ipole, Atakunmosa East Local Government Area of Osun State for instance, the initial reaction to *Oba* Popoola was by his chiefs who boycotted a new modern palace that was built for the town by one of its indigenes. This initial reaction which was less violent took a relatively long time. It appears that the very vibrant evangelical church to which *Oba* Popoola belongs is popular in Ijesaland, and it has energetic members who are always full of activities; the church is considered as protective of the *Oba*. Moreover, *Oba* Popoola has his permanent residence in Ilesa town.

---

[26] Ibid.
[27] One particular incident was in 1974 when he went to his town for his annual leave that some elders of the town called him to a meeting and as soon as he arrived, they saluted him 'Kabiyesi'. See Andy Asemota, "*Oba* Declares War on Ogboni, Witches" *Daily Sun,* November 25, 2006
[28] Ibid.
[29] Ibid.
[30] Ibid.
[31] Interview with the *Olokuku* of Okuku, Olaoluwa Local Government. January 20th 2008.

His Royal Majesty *Oba* Samuel Olufisan Ajayi, the *Odundun Asodedero* I, *Alayetoro* of Ayetoro Ekiti, Ido-Osi Local Government of Ekiti State. *Oba* Ajayi claimed to have 'met Christ', another word for 'born again' in 1997 while he became king in July 2002. He claimed that the people of the town prevailed on him to become the king. According to him,

> When they said I must become the king, I told them that if I am going to become king, it has to be in accordance with the will of God. The race for the obaship tussle started in 1999 but I joined the race in 2001 after seeking the face of God. That year, I had to go to a man of God, Prophet T.O Obadare, in whom I have much faith. He asked me to go and put my name forward.[32]

The only visible signs of his royalty were seat, ìrùkèrè (royal horsetail), devoid of usual items that depict many palaces. In contrary, a copy of the Holy Bible was found on the royal seat, a large portrait of the traditional ruler presented by a Christian prayer warrior group was placed, and over the palace walls were hung Christian almanacs and calendars.

The contestation started shortly after *Oba* Ajayi insisted not to get involved in the nine post-enthronement traditional rites which he considered as the most difficult of the exercise. He was ordered to leave the town after he had declined the performance of the rites. The implication of this was that he would die in about three months. He left the town for a 14-day prayer on a mountain in Kwara State. When he came back to the palace, the traditionalists came to him to persuade him to change his mind; he was also told to buy some ritual elements including kolanuts and yam for *imule* (oath-taking). Moreover, a 22-man delegation was sent to him in 2003 to persuade him to provide money to buy ritual materials for it rain as the town was experiencing drought. He refused their demand but assured them that the God he served would bring rainfall. According to him, he invited some Christians in the town who organised a rally and offered prayers to God; rain fell! It was recorded that the harvest of that year was greater than the previous years.

The second major power contestation was the Ogun festival which was perhaps the major festival of the town and where the *Oba* was the chief priest and celebrant. The seven-day festival was usually celebrated in August of every year, whereas he was enthroned in July. The headquarters of the shrine of Ogun was in the palace and two public Ogun shrines were usually used for the festival. As a town's festival, traditionalists and people of other religions were expected to participate. During this festival, hundreds of masquerades would be in attendance, processing through the street of Ayetoro, and halting vehicular movement. As the *Oba*, he had to provide for the essential rites to

---

[32] Banji Aluko, "Ayetoro Ekiti: Banished Born-Again King Converts Community, *Sunday Tribune*, 21 March 2010. http://www.tribune.com.ng/sun/index.php/church-features/596-ayetoro-ekiti-banished-born-again-king-converts-community.html

the ritual custodians; he was informed that the second in command to the *Oba* already contributed his own. The action was so intense such that *Oba* had to leave the town for an eleven-day prayer on another mountain in Oyo State. His prayer was "that evil should befall (the celebrants) in their shrine."[33] The *Oba* came back a day after the celebration.

When the *Oba* got to the town, he was greeted with unpleasant news. The carrier of the principal masquerade fell down several times on the way to the shrine. By tradition, it is considered a taboo to the carrier to fall down as that usually spells dooms and calamities for the participants and the entire community. To the traditionalists, the incident was in consequence of the decision of the *Oba* not to participate in the festival. Thus, led by a woman chief, the people grouped themselves together, chanting war songs and pronouncing *Oba*'s imminent demise. To the *Oba*, it was the answer to his 11-day prayer. Coincidentally, the leader of the protest dies shortly after.

The contest between *Oba* Samuel Ajayi and the traditionalist of Ayetoro represents the Yoruba attitude for power-relations and the superiority of power. It was claimed as testified to by subsequent events in Ayetoro that *Oba* Ajayi's religious experience had brought sporadic religious change, and social and political development to the town. For instance, while the palace shrine of Ogun has been taken over by a telecommunication mast, the two major shrines of Ogun had been pulled down. Not only that has the number of Christians in Ayetoro-Ekiti increased considerably, it has affected the traditional political institution as 90 percent of the traditionalists now jettison indigenous worship for church attendance. It is noteworthy that the Olowo-Awo (the chief priest of Awo cult) has become born again and even attended the Redeemed Christian Church of God's Holy Ghost service. The *Oba* also attributed certain developments including the construction of some notable roads (Ado-Otun-Omu Aran road, for example), building of more houses by indigenes, and appointment of some indigenes to political offices in Ekiti State to the divine encounter just imbibed by the indigenes.[34]

The situation with *Oba* (Dr.) Matthew Olayiwola Oyeyode Oyekale, *Adegbookun* III, the *Olaaresa* of Masifa-Ile, in Ejigbo Local Government of Osun State of Nigeria was another strong case of response to demystification of indigenous tradition. *Oba* Oyekale was born again before he was enthroned. As soon as he became king, the elders among the royal families in the town came to him to remind him that *"Oba ko l'esin"* (the *Oba* has no preferred religion). Hence, he needed to observe and actively participate in the various *òrìṣà* that were earlier mentioned to him. They even advised him to 'act like a chameleon' in the matter of religion for the sake peace and unity in the town.[35]

---

[33] Ibid.

[34] Ibid. He pointed out that in 2003, Honourable Adeola Alofe was appointed the Secretary to the State Government; in 2004 Honourable Friday Aderemi became the Speaker of the State House of Assembly. He noted that the number of houses build in one year of his reign was more than the number of the houses built in eleven years.

[35] Olaaresa of Masifa Ile-Ejigbo, Ejigbo Local Government.

There were threats to dethrone him for his rejection to participate in indigenous rituals. According to him, efforts were made to bewitch him and members of his family. They denied him of his rights such as refusal to accrue to him the money realized from the produce of palm tree plantations that were considered the right of the *Oba*. The traditionalists insisted that the revenue would be used to provide for the ritual ingredients which he had refused to involve in.

The Chiefs-in-Council boycotted the palace and announced to the town's people not to visit the *Oba* in the palace nor salute him '*Kabiyesi*' as this was a visible honour always acclaimed a traditional ruler whenever his subject sees his instruments of office or himself. According to him, rather than get disturbed by the utmost disrespect with which he was treated, he was comforted by the Holy Spirit. The *Oba* drew his consolation and empowered himself with the words of Scriptures, particularly Matthew 28:20 and always recited Psalm 23:1-4 thus:

> Because the Lord is my Shepherd, I have everything I need
> Even though when walking through the dark valley of death
> I will not be afraid;
> For you are close beside me,
> Guarding, guiding all the way (The Living Bible)

The *Oba* and members of his family would pray and sing praises unto God for one or two hours every night. This response to the intimidation was however surprising to the persecutors.

There were other specific cases of responses. For instance, there was a Sango priest who came to the *Oba*'s palace, threatening to harm him. After he had prepared himself outside with some incantations and invocations that would cast spell on sighting the *Oba*. Disappointedly, the *Oba* refused to see him, the action which infuriated him and which made him determine to inflict danger on the *Oba*. This was so believed by the indigenes that they were perplexed and horrified. The *Oba* was advised to call the Sango priests in the town in order to inquire of the implications of the visit of the Sango priest, and possibly entreat them. Instead, the response of the *Oba* was a biblical passage: "No weapon that is fashioned against me shall prosper" (Isaiah 54:17). It was to the people's dismay, according to the *Oba* that he was alive years after the Sango priest came to the palace, and in fact it was reported that the Sango priest was nowhere to be found after the incident.

Demand to be initiated into Ogboni cult was another challenge for *Oba* Oyekale. The *Oba* stated that the *Apena* of Ogboni in Ikire who was also a member of the royal council, requested him secretly and in public, by tradition, to get initiated into the cult from the first day he ascended the throne. The *Oba* would himself react sharply that he would never. Other chiefs and others were amazed with the response of the *Oba* as this action was strange for a traditional ruler. The chiefs interpreted *Oba*'s reaction as too tough and revolutionary. The *Oba*, instead, claiming to be led by the Holy Spirit, invited the *Apena* and preached to him. The Apena however informed the *Oba* that there was truth in the message of the *Oba* but that those in the cult also included Christians and Muslims. After a lot of persuasion to become "born again'" as he himself, the *Apena* declined and left the *Oba*, not adhering to the message of the *Oba*.

Some years later, the *Apena* started roaming the street with excreta on his body. His children would look for him and take him back to his house. There were rumours that the *Apena* must have offended the *Oba*. To the *Oba*, God is a God of love, and that if it was true that such an incident was traceable to him, then the *Apena* must have attempted evil against the *Oba*, which punishment was from God. When the man finally died, it was reported that he must have been killed by the *Oba*. Though the *Apena* was already old, the interpretation of the near-insanity and death of the *Apena* was an indication that the God of *Oba* Oyekale was powerful than that of the *Apena*.

The encounter with the masquerades was another strong point of contestation of tradition. *Egungun* festival is one important festival that is universal among the Yoruba as this connects the human to the divine in ancestral ritual celebrations. For the Ejigbo people, *egungun* has its primordial importance and it is ritually connected to the *Oba*. Egungun festival takes several days. The seventh day climaxes the festival when the *Oba* sits in the midst of all the *egungun* at the market square. The *egungun* dance in turns for the traditional ruler. *Egungun* devotees, traditional chiefs and other elders protested against this since the *Oba* would participate in the festival, claiming that it is idol worshipping which is against his Christian faith.

Oba Oyekale narrated that there was a year when a masquerade came forcefully into the palace when he was out of the town. He attempted to enter through the main entrance but fell down two times. He entered the backyard; while attempting to get out, he fell down the third time, and he left. According to *Oba* Oyekale, the *egungun* could no longer see the light of the day again for several years as stated by the relative of the *egungun*.

The significance of *Ifa* and its varieties of expressions and activities is strong as it serves as the bedrock of all operations in Yorúbáland. One year after his enthronement, *Ifa* diviners and devotees informed *Oba* Oyekale of *Ifa* festival, the first day of which had to take place inside the palace. When he refused them, the traditional chiefs came and persuaded the *Oba* to allow them to perform the festival in front of the palace. It took place in the midnight. The festival was celebrated with heavy beating of drums and gongs, and singing of abusive songs directed particularly to the *Oba*. It was interspersed with incantations such as '*Asun-un-parada-ni-tigi-aja*' (rafter lays flat without shaking), which was chanted to cast spell on the *Oba* and his accomplices to die in their sleep. The *Oba* overheard them but according to him, he held on to certain biblical promises one of which was by Jesus that states: 'I will never leave you nor forsake you.' The *Oba* said the family and he woke up the second day without any harm. Moreover, the people had erected an image upon which they already poured blood on in front of the palace. They left their *Ifa* gongs beside the erected image.

Displeased, the *Oba* invoked the name of Jesus Christ and uprooted the 'idol' and threw it into a nearby bush. He threw the *Ifa* gongs into a pit latrine. It was a market day. This incident amazed the people of the town. People who had the courage inquired from the *Oba* what he did to those items and he told them how he had treated the materials. The priests and devotees of *Ifa* were however furious. This feat became a reference point of recognizing the higher and superior power between that of the *Oba* and those of the 'idol worshippers'. These 'idol worshippers' later caught the fancy of the *Oba*'s Christian faith, claiming as unbelievable that *Oba* had a physical contact with the dangerous image without a terrible consequence.

Some months later, some Christian youths organized a crusade in front of the palace at the market square. Unknowingly, and in response to the earlier disdainful treatment of indigenous practice by Christians, particularly the *Oba*, priests and devotees of *Ifa* planned a revenge attack. As the crusade started with praise and worship, they attackers emerged with *Ifa* gongs and drums to disturb and disrupt the programme. They came with different kinds of charms which they used to beat 'brethren', intending to inflict diseases on their victims, the wife of the *Oba* inclusive. The attackers however resorted to violence since the charms did not work on the victims. They threw stones; some people including the wife of the *Oba* were seriously injured. They also damaged the equipment used for the crusade. The violence was so intense that even when the *Oba* appealed to the attackers, they did not yield. The *Oba* ordered that the crusade be moved into the palace. The attackers would not go immediately. They prevented the Christians from continuing their programme.

According to the *Oba*'s narration, the young evangelist, an indigene of the town who headed the crusade sensed a terrible danger. He instructed the participants to continue to shout 'Jesus is Lord'. They chorused this continuously and heavy rain suddenly began to fall. This mysterious rain which came without any sign drove the attackers away. It was also reported that the ringleader of this attack fell from a roof not long after the incident. This were regarded as 'divine intervention' citing such biblical passages as 'If God be for us, who can be against us' (Rom. 8:31), in addition to Isaiah 54:17 already cited above.

For the Ode-Ekiti community, *Oba* Samuel Adara Aderiye, the Olode reigned for 13 years but he was finally banished. He was claimed to have been born again before he was installed the *Oba* of the town. It is important to state that he had made his position known about the contradiction of his Christian faith and rituals involved in kingship institution. In fact, he had refused to undergo certain important installation rites before ascending the throne. The kingmakers however thought that he would outgrow his spiritual 'adolescence' and come to reality after his installation as the father of the community and fulfil his divine-priest obligations of his new office as the representative of the deities and ancestors. Not only this, he was reported to have destroyed all the sacred objects in his palace. He declined to participate in traditional festivals and even drove out a group of old women in the town who visited and pleaded with him to "give unto Caesar what is Caesar's." The action of the *Oba* was interpreted as arrogance, disrespectful and insensitivity.

The event that led to the banishment of *Oba* Aderiye from the town was during the *Semuregede* festival in which, by tradition, he was required to perform seven rites and perhaps wear some paraphernalia relating to the performance. He performed only one and refused to wear the paraphernalia. The chief priest of the festival got out of the palace in annoyance. The *Oba* had been accused of causing much tragedy on the indigenes by desecrating important king-related rituals through his refusal to worship the deities and perform those rituals. It was alleged that this was responsible for the untimely death of prominent songs and daughters and mysterious killing of children by their parents.

The indigenes who were angered by the consequences of the action of the *Oba* came to the palace with cutlasses and expletives, singing war songs. They took him to the market square from where they ordered him out of the town. The youths went to the palace and demonstrated the death of the king symbolically by cutting cut down the trees around it. Thereafter, the traditional chiefs and the kingmakers sent a letter of deposition of the *Olode* of Ode to Ekiti State Government. It was reported that although there was an appeal for forgiveness by the *Oba* and intervention by the *Owa* of Egbe, the traditional ruler of a neighbouring town, such efforts turned to the deaf ears of the protesters, while his own ruling house also disowned him.

Contesting the old way, interpreting primordiality

We have so far examined, from different communities, how people responded to what they considered a demystification of indigenous traditions by traditional rulers who claimed to have found a new faith which, according to them, could not be compromised. Our case studies revealed that contest for power was fundamental to the actions, reactions and responses of both the traditionalists and the born again traditional rulers. Certain pertinent questions follow. What is the place of indigenous tradition within the contemporary religiously pluralistic context? How do the attitudes of the born again traditional rulers to be understood in relation to human rights? How do we relate indigenous tradition on the one hand, and the attitude of the born again traditional rulers on the other hand, to social development? What are the implications of the attitudes of born again traditional rulers on indigenous religious traditions? The questions bother on different interpretations of the primordiality of tradition and culture in relation to human existence.

To those who contest the attitude and actions of the born again traditional rulers, they hold to the static notion of tradition and culture. They hold that each community has its unique tradition and culture and that these should remain intact notwithstanding contacts from outside. Such people distinguish religion from tradition and culture; this is a functional understanding. In this regard, Christianity is one, and tradition and culture another. Thus, you can be a Christian and hold on to certain tradition as the structure of the society as well as its tradition and culture demands. Sometimes the tradition and culture are incorporated into the religion of the people. This view allows for compromise, tolerance and accommodation. To these people, it is an abomination and sacrilege for traditional rulers to refuse to participate in indigenous rituals and worship. Those who hold this view see nothing wrong in what is termed 'religious concubinage'. Thus, they participate in 'persecuting' the born again traditional rulers.[36]

The second position holds structural-functionalist view that Christianity, and tradition and culture are one and the same. This is the view of the 'born again' traditional rulers. It postulates an evolutionary stance of human existence and culture, and the dynamism of culture. To them, the primordiality of Oduduwa as the progenitor of Yoruba race should be understood as a process of human civilization and knowledge, but that the biblical narrative is the authentic one. This is expressed by *Oba* Adedapo Tejuoso, the *Osile* of Oke-Ona and *Oba* Adetoyese Odugbemi, the *Olufi* of Gbongan. Using the biblical narrative, *Oba* Odugbemi connected Christianity and kingship institution and that the institution of Obaship which was ordained by God must be guided by biblical principles and criteria as contained in Deuteronomy 17:14-19.[37] According to him,

> God gave the (Israelites) criteria for choosing a king. And if it was not ordained by God, it would not have been recorded in the Bible. So whoever thinks that Christianity and Obaship are different things or what they can put in a water-tight compartment, they do not understand the matter.... [God] gave the guideline for the choice and operation of the king.

The logic of the narrative of *Oba* Odugbemi is not in the correctness of the theology of the story and its contextual significance for the Yoruba, but on appealing to superior authority. His interest is to defend his Christian faith by preferring the primordiality of biblical story against Oduduwa myth and the worship of deities. He pontificated that

> Whether Oduduwa believes in the Bible or not does not remove the authenticity of that recording by God. People worship deities because of their ignorance, because everyone whether a king or any other human being is created by a superior Being ...[W]hen God created man, he made man the overall ruler of all things he crated. The deities they have and are worshipping are created by God. Therefore if Oduduwa believed that he must worship deities, it was because of his limited knowledge of God at that time. Like I always tell my people, I have not come to destroy the

---

[36] Interview with the Olokuku of Okuku, Olaoluwa Local Government. January 2008; Also, Interview with *Oba* Dr. Solomon Oyeno Ojo, Onifin of Ikonifin, Bode-Osi via Iwo, Ola-Oluwa Local Government, Osun State

[37] See "Why we formed association of Born Again Christian Obas."

system but I have come to expatiate and develop the system. If anybody makes deity his God, such fellow is making mistakes...To me it is like man demoting himself by worshipping deities. [38]

Furthermore, *Oba* Odugbemi stated that the reality of the *Òrìṣà* and indigenous worship could only be preserved in museum as "monuments to show us (and other people) what our past looked like"[39] and not to making the deities an object of worship.

In trying to understand how *Oba* Adedapo Tejuoso was able to negotiate his own born again faith with indigenous tradition in an uncontested manner in spite of the deep indigenous system of Egba community, some important factors could be noted. One, *Oba* Tejuoso's paternal and maternal as a Chief *Ifa* High Priest who confirmed the suitable of the Egba to settle in Abeokuta c. 1830 and as the first *Osile* of Oke-Ona Egba in Abeokuta in 1897 respectively place him on high level of recognition. Secondly, *Oba* Tejuoso's professional career as medical doctor is impressive; he had several degrees from reputable international institutions outside Nigeria. Third, the social networks of *Oba* Tejuoso are unsurpassed. For instance, besides being honoured with "Patron of Rotary" in Nigeria, he was given a global award in the association. Among his recognition as a sportsman, he was the first African to be elected a member of the International Badminton Federation (IBF), 1981-1987. He used this position to campaign against the apartheid regime in the then South Africa.

In politics, at the time Nigeria was at the brink of break-up after the 1993 election, he was nominated with the other 5 traditional rulers (one from each of the six geopolitical zones of Nigeria) as government delegate to the National Constitutional Conference of 1994/95 to assist in restoring confidence in the unity of Nigeria. In social and economic services, he has been instrumental to the award of scholarship to the needy students and the establishment of Oke-Ona Egba Community Bank, the first Community Bank in Egbaland. All of these could have endeared him to serve as an impetus for his acceptance beyond religious divide.

Furthermore, the association of *Oba* Adedapo Tejuoso as the chairman of the Governing Board of Prison Rehabilitation Mission International (PREMI), an NGO which Director General was Pastor Kayode Williams (a former armed robber and prisoner) devoted to the training of prison inmates and re-integration of ex-prisoners into the society. *Oba* Tejuoso collaborates with the Nigerian Prisons Service Authorities and PREMI to raise money for the reformation of ex-convicts. *Oba* Tejuoso himself has an evangelical outreach named *Oba* Karunwi III Evangelical Movement upon which platform he preaches the gospel to different parts of the country. It is noted that he had publicly destroyed *orisa Obatala* in Karunwi's compound at Ago-Oko in Abeokuta with the challenge that the *orisa* would never be able to kill him as

---

[38] Ibid.
[39] Ibid.

speculated. He had also built several churches in Surulere, Lagos; Ago-Oko in Abeokuta; and Ebute-Metta, Lagos.

It was perhaps his activities in social development overshadow religious sentiments he was in fact awarded as 'the Best *Oba* in the South West of Nigeria' in 2005 by Nigerian Royalty Award, and recently received the national honour of the Commander of the Order of the Niger (C.O.N.). Our understanding of this scenario is that *Oba* Tejuoso successfully contests the old way and reinforces his 'born again' through his social activities inspired by his religious commitment.[40]

Conclusion

The changing face of kingship institution through the 'born again' experience of some traditional rulers in Nigeria is a clear case of clash of culture, understanding culture to be the ways of life of a given people. Of course, this phenomenon has altered in a radical and drastic way indigenous religious institution since kingship institution in Nigeria embodies the tradition and culture of the people. In this age of globalization, can a culture claim to be hegemonic? However, in defence of cultural heterogeneity, most communities are aware of the social development and better life most made possible by education and openness to wider society and culture, there is need to understand what it takes to achieve advancement. We realize that in several of the case studies examined, the community desired advancement, and sometimes subtly or deceptively lured their would-be 'cultural bigots' into kingship hoping that such would come back to their senses in terms of reconsidering their Christian faith position for the ascribed status which turned out not to be the case. The issue may not be resolved after all. Traditional communities are still operating in secrecy and closeness that are now becoming obsolete and strange. The need perhaps would be to redefine our sense of kingship institution, reform aspects which may advance the communities socially, spiritually and politically. There are values in kingship institution that inspire Nigerian communality, instil orderliness and cooperation, and reinforce a sense of humanity and peaceful coexistence.

References

Adeboye, Olufunke,. "The 'Born-Again' *Oba*: Pentecostalism and Traditional Chieftaincy in Yorúbáland" *Lagos Historical Review: A Journal of the Department of History & Strategic Studies,* 2007, Vol. 7: 1-20

Adekanmbi, Dare. "Showcasing Nigeria's Female Traditional Rulers" *Nigeria Tribune,* 02 June 2010. Accessed 14 October, 2010

Adeyemi, Muyiwa, "Why We Formed Association of Born Again Christian Obas" http://www.onlinenigeria.com/chritianlinks/ad2.asp?blurb=54. Accessed

---

[40] *Oba* (King) *Oba* Dr. Adedapo Adewale Tejuoso CON, (M.A.; M.B.; CH.B; B.A.O.; D.T.M.&H.; D.P.H.; D.I.H., F.M.C.G.P.; F.W.A.C.P. Karunwi III, Oranmiyan, 8th Osile Oke-Ona, Egba, Ogun State

20/11/2010; http://groups.yahoo.com/group/Naija-news/message/2391.
Guardian News of Saturday, October 12, 2002. Accessed 17/02/2011

Akinfenwa, O.B. "Traditional Rulers and the Challenges of Democratization in Nigeria" in R.A. Akanmidu *et al.* (ed.), *Religion and Democracy in the 21st Century*, (Akungba, Nigeria: A Publication of the Nigerian Association for the Study of Religions) 2007: 1-10

Akinola, G.A.,. "Religion and the Obasanjo Administration" http://www.utexas.edu/conferences/africa/ads/1543.html Accessed March 1. 2008

Aluko, Banji, "Ayetoro Ekiti: Banished Born-Again King Converts Community *Sunday Tribune*, 21 March 2010. *http://www.tribune.com.ng/sun/index.php/church-features/596-ayetoro-ekiti-banished-born-again-king-converts-community.html*

Ariyibi, Gbenga, "Born-Again Traditional Ruler Dethroned in Ekiti" http://www.onlinenigeria.com (Thursday, July 24) 2003.

Asemota, Andy, "*Oba* Declares War on Ogboni, Witches" *Daily Sun*, November 25. 2006.

Babayemi S.O., "The Role of Traditional Rulers in Inter-Religious Dialogue in Nigeria" in Jacob K. Olupona (ed.), *Religion and Peace in Multi-Faith Nigeria* (Ile-Ife, Nigeria: Obafemi Awolowo University)1992, 197-200

Coffie-Gyamfi, Charles. 2006. "For Ogun Monarchs, Should It Be Burial By Faith Or Tradition?" http://www.guardiannewsngr.com/life-e_style/article13/030606

Dopamu, Abiola T. "The Place of Traditional Rulers in a Democratic System of Government in Yorúbáland" in Adam K. arap Chepkwony & Peter M.J. Hess (eds.), *Human Views on God: Variety Not Monotony: Essays in Honour of Ade P. Dopamu* (Eldoret: Moi University Press)*2010*, 53-61

Horton, Robin and J.D.Y. Peel. "Conversion and Confusion: A Rejoinder on Christianity in Eastern Nigeria" *Journal of African Studies,* 1976 Vol. 10: 481-497

Ifeka-Moller, C.,. "White Power: Social-Structural Factors in Conversion to Christianity, Eastern Nigeria, 1921-1966", *Canadian Journal of African Studies*, 1974 Vol. 8, No. 1: 55-72

Ikenga-Metuh, Emefie, "The Shattered Microcosm: A Critical Survey of Explanations of Conversion in Africa" in Kirsten Holst Peterson (ed.) *Religion, Development and African Identity* (Uppsala: Scandinavian Institute of African Studies) 1987: 11-27

Lois, Fuller. *African Traditional Religion.* Kaduna: Baraka Press. 2001

Ogungbile, David O, "Myth, Ritual and Identity in the Religious Traditions of the Osogbo People of Western Nigeria." PhD Dissertation, Obafemi Awolowo University, Ile-Ife, Nigeria. 2003.

Ogungbile, David O,. Islam and Cultural Identity in Nigeria: The Òşogbo-Yoruba Experience" *Orita: Ibadan Journal of Religious Studies*. 1998 Vol. XXX/1-2: 123-137.

Ogungbile, David, "Have You Been Born Again?" *The Eagle: The Magazine of Council Commercial School*, Vol. VIII, (Ilesha, Oyo State, Nigeria) 1977: 43-44

Ogungbile, David O. & Akintunde E. Akinade (eds.), *Creativity and Change in Nigerian Christianity* (Lagos, Nigeria: Malthouse: 2010)

Olomola, Isola, "Yoruba Monarchism in Transition: A Preliminary Survey" in Biodun Adediran (ed.) Cultural Studies in Ife. (Ile-Ife: Institute of Cultural Studies, Obafemi Awolowo University) 1995: 42-58.

Roth, Guenther & Claus Wittich (eds.). *Max Weber: Economy and Society*, Vols. 1 & 2, University of California Press, 1978 the Regents

Shittu H. and B. Inuwa, "Islam and Traditional Beliefs of the Obas in Yorubaland" R.A. Raji, A.P. Dopamu, et al (ed.) *Religion, Governance and Development in the 21st Century* (Ago-Iwoye, Ogun State: A Publication of the Nigerian Association for the Study of Religions2006.): 358-370

Tejuoso, *Oba* Dr. Adedapo Adewale (M.A.; M.B.; CH.B; B.A.O.; D.T.M.&H.; D.P.H.; D.I.H., F.M.C.G.P.; F.W.A.C.P, CON, Karunwi III, Oranmiyan, 8th Osile Oke-Ona, Egba, Ogun State

Thomas, Tunde, "Hypocrite! *Ifa* Priest Blasts *Oba* Tejuoso over Idol Worship Disclaimer" *Weekly Spectator,* (April 2006,):26

Thomas, Tunde,. "You're a Bigot: Bassey Ekpo Bassey Hits Obong of Calabar" *Weekly Spectator,* (April 16,2006):26

Turaki, Yusuf, *Foundations of African Traditional Religions and Worldview*. Nairobi, Kenya: International Bible Society Africa 2001

Personal Interviews, Interactions and Communications:
- *Oba* (Dr.) Matthew Olayiwola Oyeyode Oyekale, Adegbokun III, the Ola-Aresa of Masifa-Ile via Ejigbo, Osun State, (Graduate of Law, Obafemi Awolowo University, State Counsel in Oyo State Ministry of Justice, 1982-1984). January 2008.
- *Oba* Samuel Olufisan Ajayi, the Odundun Asodedero I, Alayetoro of Ayetoro Ekiti, Ido-Osi Local Government, Ekiti State (Graduate of Business Administration).
- *Oba* Samuel Adelegan Popoola, Ogboni of Ipole, Atakunmosa East Local Government, Osun State.
- *Oba* (Dr.) Solomon Oyeno Ojo, Onifin of Ikonifin, Bode-Osi via Iwo, OlaOluwa LG., Osun State
- *Oba* (Dr.) Adedapo Adewale Tejuoso, Osile of Oke-Ona, Egba, Ogun State, CON, (M.A.; M.B.; CH.B; B.A.O.; D.T.M.&H.; D.P.H.; D.I.H., F.M.C.G.P.; F.W.A.C.P. July, 2005
- *Oba* (Dr.) Adetoyese Oyeniyi Odugbemi, Olufi of Gbongan (PhD Agriculture), Osun State, January 2008.
- *Oba* Olatunde Falabi, Akire of Ikire, Irewole Local Government, Osun State. January 2008.
- *Oba* Olokuku of Okuku, OlaOluwa L.G.A., Osun State January 2008
- *Oba* Akinla of Erin, Osun State, November 1993

II

Knowledge, Power, Vitality and Representations

5

An epistemic critique of *Ifa* as a revelatory source of knowledge

- Yunusa Kehinde Salami

Introduction

Yoruba cosmology gives a position of repute to *Orunmila* and *Ifa* on the question of ultimate meaning and knowledge of the world and of the individual human beings. This chapter examines the epistemic role assigned *Ifa* divination in Yoruba epistemic system in order to ascertain the level of certainty and fallibility of *Ifa* as a source of revelatory knowledge.

Ifa as a religion and a source of revelatory knowledge

Ifa has been variously regarded as a religion and a repository of knowledge. In Yoruba culture both at home in Nigeria and in diaspora, *Ifa*, as represented by *Orunmila*, has been treated as a religion with its great number of worshippers and followership. Those involved in *Ifa* religious worship lay a lot of emphasis on the prowess of *Orunmila* as one of the deities of Olodumare, the supreme deity in Yoruba cosmology and spiritualism. *Ifa* involves a form of worship by the devotees. This worship includes a compendium of performances and praise singing by the *Babalawo*.

Wande Abimbola sees *Ifa* as a special divinity among the Yoruba. For him, "the Yoruba believe that it was *Olodumare* who sent *Ifa* forth from the heavens and who charged him to use his wisdom to repair the world. The wisdom, knowledge, and luminosity with which Olodumare endowed *Ifa* account for *Ifa*'s pre-eminence among divinities in Yoruba land." (Abimbola 1983:6) On the other hand, another *Ifa* scholar, William Bascom, sees *Ifa* as "a system of divination based on sixteen basic and 256 derivative figures (*odu*) obtained either by the manipulation of sixteen palm nuts (*ikin*) or by the toss of a chain (opele) of eight half seed shells." (William 1991:3)

Given Kola Abimbola's submission, it is possible to conceive *Ifa* in different mutually inclusive ways. For Kola Abimbola (2005:47),

> *Ifa* (also known as *Orunmila* or Orunla) is the name of the god of knowledge and wisdom; *Ifa* is used to refer to the divination process related to the god of knowledge and wisdom; there is a body of knowledge

also called *Ifa* (*Ifa* Literary Corpus). This body of knowledge is the Sacred Text of Yoruba Religion and all its denominations in Africa and the Diaspora...There are some special *Ifa* poems that function as incantations or powerful words. When uttered, believers think that the words can reveal truth in the sense that whatever they state will happen. These *Ifa* incantations are used mainly for medicinal purposes...

In the same respect, Wande Abimbola is of the view that; "the Yoruba people themselves regard *Ifa* as the great authority on their mythology, history and philosophy...." (1975: iii)

From the reading thus far, *Ifa* can be identified as one of the most important of the gods who was "sent by *Olodumare*, the supreme God, from on high, charged with the responsibility of using his God-given incomparable wisdom and capacity for omniscience to order the world aright, and to ensure that both it and its inhabitants do not spin out of their proper orbit. Hence, *Ifa*'s nickname, 'A-kere-finu-sogbon', which is an allusion to the fact that *Ifa* is reputed to be among the youngest gods, yet *Ifa* is endowed with unsurpassable knowledge." (Taiwo 2004:305)

This is gradually shifting us towards the revelatory capacity of *Ifa* as a means of divination. An ascription of godliness to *Ifa* and treating it as a divinity gives some credence to *Ifa* as a source of divination for the knowledge beyond immediate cognition. Makinde, in agreement with Wande Abimbola and some others, "identifies *Ifa* with *Orunmila*, the owner or possessor of wisdom and knowledge." (Makinde 2007:69) Makinde goes further to assert that *Orunmila*, through *Ifa*, brought to the world such knowledge that consists of such branches as "science of nature (physics), animals (biology), plants (botany), medicinal plants (herbalism), oral incantations (*ofo*), and all the sciences associated with healing diseases(medicine)..." (Makinde 2007:69)

Attempts are severally made to ascribe to *Ifa* the status of the unsurpassable repository of knowledge and wisdom. (W. Abimbola 1975, 1983; Taiwo 2004) *Ifa* is seen to be omniscient. It is regarded as a deity, which transcends the limits of human cognitive capacities, "has the capacity to know from several perspectives at the same time, and is not bound by the time-space constraints of human knowing." (Taiwo 2004:305) A critical look at the kind of epistemological assistances that people seek to get from *Ifa* reveals that they are such that requires knowing about a future that is beyond the ambience of the present scope of our senses. They include such request about what the future holds for individuals or groups. For instance, when a new child is born, there is the need to know what path the child will pass through to live his or her life. This in some places may be called the *akosejaye* (the planned passage) or the *ayanmo, ipin,* or *akunleyan* (the destiny), that the child brought to the worlds of the living.

In this respect, when a child is born, the elders around, especially those with filial relationship, would wish to know the dos and don'ts for the newborn child. This, as one can rightly perceived, may be to prevent the child and a later grown up human person from groping unnecessarily in the world before finding the right step to take. This will put the human person on the right path concerning what to do and what not to do with respect to the trade to learn, which space to occupy within a particular point in time, which wife or husband to marry and from where to marry. In another but very similar sense, when all precautions are taken and things still are not going well, individuals or groups of people may wish to seek the assistance of *Ifa* in knowing what the causes are. *Ifa* may also be contacted for explanation in cases when what is considered a favourable way of existence is up turned. The nexus between the kind of knowledge sought from *Ifa* and the ones through other mystical explanation for human beings and human existence is that they are usually such that are beyond the reach of the ordinary human capacities. Those mundane things of every day experiences are usually not thought to form part of the knowledge that deserves being taken to *Ifa* for divination or consultation. It is just those kinds of knowledge that human beings consider themselves incapable of penetrating. As observed earlier, this is relevant mostly because of the belief that the destiny of individuals or groups consists of many things about the success and failure, joy and sadness, health and ill health that such individuals may go through in life.

As this discussion suggests, *Ifa* seems to be more of

> a process of pursuit of knowledge about destiny, i.e. about the course of life...Because destiny is the sense of becoming endowed the individual by the human spiritual and rational nature, *Ifa* is, in fact, a process of attempting to understand...that quality in the human which makes him/her characteristically destined. (Eze 1988:174)

This is necessary to enable a human being realise the fullness and reality of self. The question of human destiny is one of the prominent areas in which *Ifa*'s epistemic prowess is mostly accorded recognition in Yoruba thought.

Yoruba account of predestination

In the Yoruba conception of human person (W. Abimbola 1971; Hallen 1989; Salami 1981; 2007), a human person is made of *ara, emi* and *ori*. *Ara* is body, *emi* is soul while *ori* is the inner head. *Ori* (the inner head) is regarded as the bearer of destiny. This account of human person emphasizes the importance of *ori* and by implication, makes destiny or predestination a necessary component of a human person. With this introduction of '*ori*', the third component, there is a challenge to the Cartesian dualist account of human person. This gives a tripartite conception of human person as against the dualist account of Descartes.

Yoruba generally refer to *ori* as the unconscious self, as inner head, as one's guardian spirit, and as the bearer of destiny. According to Gbadegesin, "...it is the *ori* that selects the destiny of the person before *Olodumare* (the

Supreme deity) who normally endorses such a choice." (Gbadegesin 1984:175) Another account of Yoruba concept of *ori* is given by Idowu, who claims that Yoruba regard *ori* as the personality Spirit. For Idowu, *ori* "is the very essence of personality...it is this *ori* that rules, controls, and guides the 'life' and activities of the person." (Idowu 1962) Going by Idowu and other available materials on *ori* and destiny, a person's destiny can be known as *ipin-ori* or shortened to be *iponri*. This can be translated as the *ori's* portion or lot. *Ipin* means portion, and *ori* means the inner head. So, *iponri* means *ori's portion or lot*.

The question, however, is about the status of *ori* vis-à-vis other causal agents. Can we regard *ori* as the antecedent cause of all other possible causes? In other words, do we see other causes as mere causal manifestations of one underlying cause - *ori*? If the answer is yes, then we can correctly argue that there is a connection between the Yoruba concept of *ori* and destiny. This takes us to the other related Yoruba notions of *ipin* (that which is allocated to someone), *ayanmo* (that which is affixed to someone), and *akunleyan* (that which is chosen kneeling). All of these concepts convey the idea of destiny, which, if critically examined, could be seen to convey some important differences. For Idowu, "...we have a trimophous conception of destiny." (Idowu 1962; Salami 1996:6)

Going by these related terms, a little clarification may be warranted. For instance, *ayanmo* and *ipin* imply something imposed on human persons, without any enquiry on whether they wanted it or not. *Ayanmo* and *ipin* are predominantly suggestive of the influence of an external factor against which we are powerless. Consequently, one may, it seems to me, argue that what becomes one's destiny is not within one's ability to choose. Given this account, the action one finds oneself performing here on earth, is independent of one's choice or wishes in this world. The account renders human beings as mere toys in the hands of the gods. On the other hand, *akunleyan* is suggestive of one's conscious choice, most probably, without any external compulsion. In spite of these differences in Yoruba conceptions of predestination, a person comes into the world with his destiny doubly sealed, and whatever a person does achieve, or whatever happens to him, is a precise working out of his destiny. (Idowu 1962:183; Morakinyo 1983)

The upshot of this is that in Yoruba universe, each human being is predestined to lead a kind of life and not others. That is, each human being while in *isalu orun* (heavenly abode), chose or found affixed on him or her, a particular kind of destiny which he or she is expected to actualise, unravel, or manifest in this *isalu aye* (earthly world). On this account, destiny represents the kind of choice or affixation in *isalu orun*, which will invariably determine the earthly success or failure. It is believed that the choice or affixation of a good *ori* ensures that the individual concerned would lead a successful and prosperous life on earth, while the choice or affixation of a bad *ori* condemns the individual concerned to a life of failure.

Ifa and the knowledge of human destiny

Going by the discussion thus far about the epistemic status of *Ifa* in relation to the question of ultimate reality of persons and communities, the point is highly emphasised with respect to the question of destiny. There is the assumption that while the lifeless bodies (*ara*) was picking its *ori*, the marker of destiny, in *isalu orun*, from Ajala's house, *Orunmila* was there watching the kind of *ori* that individuals were picking. On the point of this, he is regarded, in Yoruba cosmology, as the *eleri ipin*, the one who was present when individuals were picking their *ori* or destiny in *isalu orun*, heaven, and so he is regarded as the one who can enter the witness box between the ori, destiny, and the actual possessors of destiny.

The concept of *Ori* and destiny is well discussed in some chapters and verses of *Ifa*. The most aptly relevant verses can be found in *Ogunda Meji* and *Ogbegunda* or *Ogbeyonu*. (W. Abimbola 1976 :116-149; Idowu 1962:179-200). Relevant verses of *Ifa* give the idea that individual went as a whole person with a whole body and soul to pick *ori*. The verses tell of three friends, *Oriseeku*(the son of *Ogun*), *Orileemere* (the son of *Ija*) and *Afuwape* (the son of *Orunmila*) who were going from heaven to earth to settle down. The account involved sacrifices by *Afuwape* (the son of *Orunmila*) before going to pick his *ori*. As this account goes, this sacrifice aided *Afuwape's* choice of a good and durable *Ori* which withstood the hazards of the journey to earth and upon which *Afuwape* became a successful man on earth.

The initial problem is that it is already contained in the Yoruba account of predestination that the chooser of destiny in *isalu orun* (heaven) would have passed through or would have crossed the river of forgetfulness while coming to *ode-isalaye* (the human world) and so cannot remember or have a reflective memory of having ever picked an *Ori*.

The question from this is how to link a destiny to a man who never remembered anything or have been made to forget everything in connection with the destiny or the fact of picking it. If the destiny and its choice are to be of principal relevance to the life of a person, that person must be able to link himself or his life to the destiny and its choice.

It is generally assumed that the problem generated by the river of forgetfulness can be adequately taken care of by the Yoruba account according to which *Ifa* was present at the time when individuals were picking their individual *Ori*. Based on the supposed presence of *Ifa* oracle, it is believed that *Ifa divination* can help to reveal the sort of *Ori* which was chosen and, perhaps, what can be done to change a bad one for good.

The position assumes the authenticity of *Ifa* as a plausible means to the knowledge of the transcendent. If this is granted, then, we shall also grant the possibility of linking a person to his destiny through the revelatory knowledge of *Ifa oracle*. Given this account, it is assumed that anyone who wishes to have his destiny revealed to him would simply seek the assistance of *Ifa* oracle and its priest. This informs the practice in which the Yoruba consult *Ifa* at the birth of a new child to know the *akosejaye*; what the future has in stock for the child.

In spite of this reassuring support from the revelatory prowess of *Ifa* oracle, its capacity to give an adequate knowledge of what the future holds for individuals and groups can be challenged. For instance, the question of inter-subjective verifiability can be raised. A critic may object that *the modus operandi* of *Ifa* as a source of knowledge is not open to the empirical methodology of verification. It does not allow crosschecking of facts. In fact, two *Ifa* priests may differ or disagree on what *Ifa* says about the destiny of a particular individual. The critic may claim further that there is little likelihood, if any, for *Ifa* to provide the supposed missing link in the memory-phases of a person P1 at t1 who picked an *ori*, and by extension, destiny, and, the person P2 at t2 who unravels the destiny as encapsulated by the *ori*.

This critique of *Ifa* may be too hasty. The critic may not have sufficiently explored the potentialities or efficacy of *Ifa* as a means of knowing. The method of *Ifa* divination should be sufficiently explored. The possible variations that may occur about what *Ifa* reveals may be due to the variations in the levels of proficiency of different *Ifa* priests and not necessarily a product of the limitation of *ifa* oracle. Again, this introduces the problem of epistemic relativism. Relativism will amount to the position that what is true or amounts to knowledge for me is true or knowledge for me and what is so for you or any other person is also knowledge or true as such. In this case, knowledge becomes a mere conjecture.

If relativism is true, then, conflicting theories or modes of thought can be held together. This, according to the critics, is self-refuting, and so, relativism is self-stultifying. This possibility for different verdicts from different *Ifa* priests on the same puzzle makes *Ifa* divination not to offer an acceptable warrant for any judgment and so, acceptance of one verdict from *Ifa* divination rather than another is arbitrary. On this ground, appeals to evidence as a way of settling disputes will not work because any evidence can be interpreted in ways which are so different as to be incommensurable. This can be likened to Quine's thesis of indeterminacy of translation according to which the same data may yield different interpretations given different manuals of translation. (Quine 1964)

This lack of inter-subjective verifiability may also lead to the problem of authoritarianism. The fact that the result of *Ifa* divination concerning what the future holds in stock for an individual or groups of individuals cannot be interpersonally tested raises the question of subjectivity. It leaves us with a situation in which an individual assumes that what he deciphers from *Ifa* divination about the essence and totality of a person remains what the reality is for that person or persons.

In spite of some of these possible objections against the revelatory source of knowledge through *Ifa* divination, Philip Peek claims that "...divination sessions are not instances of arbitrary, idiosyncratic behaviour by diviners." (Peek 1998:172) Rather than being arbitrary or subjective, Eze sees *Ifa* divination as "...a system – or rather a 'way' – of interpretation and understanding inscribed in the religious-hermeneutic tradition of the Yoruba as well as many other African peoples...."(Eze 1988:173) Eze conceives Ifá as a practice of deep understanding, which is of philosophic nature "because it is a reflective process of seeking knowledge about human life and action- by way of established discernment and epistemological processes.

However, no matter what we may say, knowledge derived from *Ifa* divination remains a kind of knowledge which more often derives its source from other persons. We can always raise the problem of the moral character (*iwa*) of the mediator between *Ifa* and the inquirer. In other words, "their honesty, their reliability as sources of information – becomes a fundamental criterion to evaluating the reliability of second-hand information obtained from them." (Hallen 2004:301) This raises our attention to the possibility of mischief, fraud, and sheer incompetence on the part of *Ifa* priests. After all, there have been cases when clients were asked to carry out some sacrifices to actualise some desired effects in their lives and nothing actually is effected in turn. In addition to these, there may be the "epistemological problem of how chance and probability, on the one hand, and any supposed extra-empirical cognitive mechanisms, on the other, play out in the manipulation of the divination instruments." (Taiwo 2004:311)

Nevertheless, these objections may not necessarily prove the inefficacy of *Ifa* as a source of reliable knowledge. It may simply mean that further critical studies of *Ifa* as a source of knowledge should be made to discover reasons for the present fallibility state in *Ifa* divination to pave way for better and more epistemological understanding and manipulation of *Ifa* divination to achieve more reliable epistemic results.

Conclusion

In this chapter, an attempt has been made to examine the position of *Ifa* in Yoruba religious and epistemological worldview. The paper examines the status of *Ifá* as a deity, which attracts a lot of followership and worship among the Yoruba of Nigeria and the diaspora. As a deity, *Ifa* is seen, among the Yoruba, as the commissioner, from *Olodumare*, in charge of knowledge and wisdom. This belief accords *Ifa* the status of a repository of knowledge that has special knowledge of the destiny of individual human beings as well as that of the society. The paper identifies some epistemological limitations to the power of *Ifa* to give a kind of knowledge that may be infallible and indubitable. However, the paper observes that further critical studies of *Ifa*, as a source of knowledge, may pave way for better and more epistemological understanding and manipulation of *Ifa* divination to achieve more reliable epistemic results.

References

Abimbola, Kola, *Yoruba Culture: A Philosophical Account* (Birmingham: Iroko Academic Publishers) 2005
Abimbola Wande,. *Sixteen Great Poems of Ifa* (Niamey: UNESCO)1975

Abimbola, Wande, *Ifa: An Exposition of Ifa literary Corpus* (Ibadan: Oxford University Press) 1976: 116-149

Abimbola, Wande. "La notion de personne en Afrique Noire." *Centre National de la Recherche Scientifique,* , 1971, no. 544:73-89

Abimbola, Wande, *Ijinle Ohun Enu Ifa, Apa Kinni,* 2nd ed. (Oyo: AIM Press) 1983

Bascom, William, *Ifa Divination: Communication Between Gods and Men in West Africa* (Bloomington: Indiana University Press) 1991

Eze E.C.,. "The Problem of Knowledge in Divination: The Example of *Ifa,"* in E.C. Eze (ed.) *African Philosophy: An Anthology* (Oxford: Blackwell) 1988: 173-175

Eze, E.C. (ed.) *African Philosophy: An Anthology* (Massachusetts: Blackwell) 1988.

Gbadegesin, Olusegun, "Destiny, Personality, and the Ultimate Reality of Human existence: A Yoruba Perspective," *Ultimate Reality and Meaning,* 1984 Vol.7, No.3: 177-188

Hallen Barry, "Yoruba Moral Epistemology," in Kwasi Wiredu (ed.) *A Companion to African Philosophy* (Oxford: Blackwell) 2004: 296-303

Hallen, Barry, *"Eniyan: A Critical Analysis of the Yoruba Concepts of Person"* in C.S. Momoh (ed), *The Substance of African Philosophy* (Auchi: African Philosophy Projects) 1989: 328-354

Idowu, Bolaji, *Olodumare: God in Yoruba Belief* (London: Longman) 1989.

Makinde, M.A., *African Philosophy: The Demise of a Controversy* (Ile-Ife: Obafemi Awolowo University Press) 2007.

Morakinyo, Olufemi,. "The Ayanmo Myth and Mental Health Care in West Africa", in *Journal of Culture and Ideas* 1983, No.1: 68-73

Peek Philip M. "'Divination': A Way of Knowing?" in E.C. Eze (ed.) *African Philosophy: An Anthology* (Massachusetts: Blackwell) 1998: 171-172

Quine W.V.O., *From a Logical Point of View* (Cambridge: Harvard University Press) 1964.

Salami, Yunusa Kehinde. "Human Personality and Immortality in Traditional Yoruba Cosmology", *Africana Marburgensia* Vol.24, 1981, No.1:4-13

Salami, Yunusa Kehinde. "Predestination, Freedom, and Responsibility: A Case in Yoruba Moral Philosophy." *Research in Yoruba Language and Literatures,* No.7 (1996): 5-14

Salami, Yunusa Kehinde,. " Predestinacao e a metafisica da identidade: um estudo de caso ioruba." *Afro-Asia* No. 35, 2007: 263-280

Taiwo, Olufemi, *"Ifa*: An Account of a Divination System and Some Concluding Epistemological Questions" in Kwasi Wiredu (ed.), *A Companion to African Philosophy* (Oxford: Blackwell) 2004: 304-312

6

The drop of oil that puts out the fire: the *Orisa Sonponna,* moral knowledge and responsibility in the age of AIDS and biowarfare[1]

- Mei Mei Sanford

I

In 1971-1972, a little more than a decade after Independence, a public health poster appeared in Ibadan, which charged people: *"E gbe ogun ti Sonponna!"* The ostensible English meaning was: "Wage war against smallpox!" However, the poster failed as health measure because it made no Yoruba sense. The word "Sonponna" means not simply "smallpox" but the *orisa* (deity) of smallpox (and, more recently, HIV/AIDS) and healing.[2] This article reflects on ways Yoruba understandings of epidemic disease differ from the Western model. It attempts to answer the question of why the poster made no sense to most of its readers. It begins to explore what Sonponna religion tells us about the practical, moral, religious and ethical dimensions of smallpox, and of HIV/AIDS, a new domain of Sonponna. Finally, it explores the ethical choices and responsibilities that the religions of Sonponna and other *orisa* present.

II

The Yoruba *orisa* (deities or, more exactly, dimensions of power) each image and control an area of human experience with its gifts and dangers: *Osun*, a cup of water and a flood; Ogun, the contributions of technology and the cost of war. Sonponna, or Obaluaye, "Ruler of the World," as he is often called, is

---

[1] With thanks to Akinsola Akiwowo, Professor emeritus, Department of Sociology and Anthropology, Obafemi Awolowo University, and to Karen McCarthy Brown, Professor, Religion and Society, Caspersen Graduate School, Drew University. Dedicated to Adebola, the Iyalode Sonponna of Iragbiji of blessed memory. I appreciate the thoughtful responses of my colleagues at the Institute of Cultural Studies, Obafemi Awolowo University, especially the acting director, Prof. Wale Adeniran; of Prof. Aremu, H.O.D., Department of Fine Arts; and of the audience at the Institute lecture series where an earlier version of this article was presented.

[2] I thank *orisa* priestess Adedoyin Faniyi for the insight that epidemic diseases are Sonponna. Personal communication, October 2006, Osogbo. Not all diseases are Sonponna. As Jacob Kehinde Olupona has pointed out (personal communication, November 2003, Atlanta) leprosy is presently and historically distinct from Sonponna, and is attributed to the orisa Obatala. Contemporary practices and beliefs place HIV/AIDS, polio and malaria in Sonponna's sphere, as this paper attests. Historical work on the orisa attribution, if any, of polio and malaria would be very useful to these discussions.

both the source and healer of virulent disease: smallpox, malaria, and, more recently, AIDS and polio. The potency of Sonponna is multivalent. He appears in his praise poetry wearing many tiny gourds of *oogun*. *Oogun*, often translated as 'medicine' is more accurately rendered as effectuating substance. Hunters also wear gourds of *oogun* sewn into their shirts for protection and striking power. The British colonial administration made the charge that the Sonponna priesthood and its practices spread smallpox, and they attempted to obliterate the religion. Yoruba considered an outbreak of smallpox or other infectious disease to be Sonponna acting directly or through the agency of his *olorisa* (priestesses and priests) to call, chastise, or initiate.[3] These *olorisa* also developed and used techniques of inoculation. Infection and inoculation are the results of the same or similar substance put to different uses. Sonponna and his priests' *oogun* are capable of inflaming and of pacifying disease.

Sonponna's *oriki*, praise poetry, chanted by Adebola, the Iyalode Sonponna (chief priestess) of Iragbiji, Osun State, shows him to be a "strong and unwavering [warrior] on horseback."[4] *Oriki* collected by Bakare Gbadamosi and translated by Ulli Beier describes him as the "jingling horseman" from the river Niger "who settles his quarrels with a spear" (1970, 29). The spear (*oko*) is essential to Sonponna, but even more so is the spear's function: *gun*[h], "to pierce." Piercing infects and it inoculates. An incantation used to protect a person from Sonponna's dangers describes this piercing and its multivalent potency:

> One says that the leaves with which we poison arrows
> Are the same that we use to cure the wound of the arrow? (Verger 1995, 297)

In this last *oriki*, Sonponna the horseman is described as being from the north, where the river Niger touches Yorubaland. This is because he is Bariba-Tapa or Nupe. It is also because, as the *oriki* says: "The road is clouded with dust when you pursue your enemy." (Beier 1970) This dust, flying everywhere from the hooves of the rider's horse, is also the sand blown south from the Sahel in the harmattan winds of the dry season, winds that carry Sonponna and pierce and pit the skin with smallpox.

The imagery in these *oriki* and this *ofo* (incantation) is that of war. Akinsola Akiwowo derives the word *ogun* [mh] (war) from the root *gun*, "to pierce."[5] (Personal communication) War is piercing. Sonponna, the wielder of the lance, is war. Most people in Ibadan in 1971-1972 when they saw the poster that said "*E gbe ogun ti Sonponna!*" were unwilling or saw no point in waging war against War. They didn't like the odds.

---

[3] Presumably, other persons of ritual power also could invoke Sonponna's manifestation as the disease. Olalere Sulola contracted smallpox as a small boy when a masquerade cursed the town where he and his siblings were staying. Personal communication, November 2006, Ile-Ife.
[4] Interview, August 2003, Iragbiji.
[5] Akinsola Akiwoso, personal communication, October 2003, Alexandria, Virginia.

III

So how do Yoruba approach Sonponna and in what additional ways do they see him? The Sonponna priestesses of Iragbiji, Iyalode Sonponna, Omonile, and Adebola Ogunnike, address him as *"Kabiyesi"* (ruler) and as *"Baba"* (father). Iyalode's recitation of his *oriki* began, like the one Gbadamosi recorded, with many declarations of respect and appeals for help from other *orisa*, ancestors and other powers. She does not begin with evocation and invocation of his fearsome power, just as one does not enter immediately into *Kabiyesi*'s presence when one enters a palace, but travels through forecourts and greets elders and chiefs. Next, Iyalode sang the following song:

Olomoyoyo
E wa wo Baba olowo
Abomoyoyo
E wa wo Baba olowo
Olomoyoyo
E wa wo Baba olowo

The possessor of many, many different and distinct children,
Come and see the father of riches!
The one who always appears with many children,
Come and see the father of riches!
The possessor of many, many different and distinct children,
Come and see the father of riches!

Sonponna is addressed, intimately, as *"Baba,"* Father. He has many children of many different kinds of character, and he knows each one. It was in this mode that my friend Titilayo Sangoyoyin addressed Sonponna in Iragbiji in 1992. She was ill with malaria and enlisted me to drive her to get help. First we went to her sister-in-law, a nurse who gave her an injection. Next we went to the Sonponna shrine where she greeted Iya Sonponna, and gave her a gift of money for the *orisa*. Then Layo knelt down, her hands in a gesture of pleading and spoke urgently to Sonponna. *"Baba* mi (my father)," she said, "help me! I'm sick. I hurt!" Iya Sonponna divined for her and we returned home where she gathered leaves and brewed a healing tea. She got better.

Iya Sonponna is *Baba*'s child as a member of her lineage through which she inherited her priesthood and her title. Omonile and her *ikeji* are *Baba*'s - or, Olomoyoyo's - children in another, crucial, way. The parents of each of them had difficulty having children and asked Sonponna for help. In return, they promised to dedicate a child to his priesthood and in this way the two *onisonponna* became priestesses. One of the two experienced Sonponna as the giver of children in an additional way. As a young adult woman, she was plagued with *abiku* (children dying repeatedly in infancy). She appealed to *Baba* and was able to rear healthy children. As they told their stories to me, they spoke of their *Baba* with exuberance, pride, tenderness and joy, the same emotions I heard in Iya Sonponna's voice as she praised him in the song. All *orisa* give their devotees children and it is no accident that Samuel (God hears) is among the most popular Christian male names in Nigeria. The devotee's experience of Sonponna as father is primary. Sonponna is greeted first in his most intimate connection.

Although I am separating Sonponna's aspects for the purposes of this article, in reality they are never entirely separate. Akinsola Akiwowo suggests that Sonponna's children are, in addition to his devotees and his progeny, all the children at risk for the disease. He remembers that in Lagos in the 1940s, small children were most vulnerable to contracting the disease (Beier, 1970). After Iyalode sang the song, she moved to the two-line evocation discussed above of Sonponna in his terrifying and awesome aspect as piercer. She sang it very quickly and very softly and followed it immediately with prayer and evocation of Sonponna's delivering, protecting and healing power:

Agba eni lowo iku
Agba eni lowo arun
Agba eni lowo elenini
Elenini ile, elenini ode, elenini ofurufu
A ma gba eni lowo gbogbo won
Orun omo l'eru darigbo (dari s'igbo)

The one who delivers a person from death
The one who delivers a person from disease
The one who delivers a person from all enemies
Enemies at home, enemies outside, enemies in the air
The one who will deliver a person from all of them
The one who takes the child's burden and throws it into the bush.

In these lines, Sonponna's awesome power turns to protect his devotees.

While the Ibadan poster called for people to isolate and wage war on the disease, the Iragbiji priestesses of Sonponna engage him in his complexity. A ritual greeting before his altar is:

Ero pese ni t'igbin
Come softly, healingly, like a snail.

Ero is an antidote for poison, and a softener of anger, obduracy, and difficulty. The snail is the oldest being in the world, and its pace is temperate and calm. The liquid that lubricates the snail in its shell is one of the most powerful cooling and pacifying agents in Yoruba ritual. Ritual, praise poetry and story include detailed description of the climatic conditions (the dry harmattan season) favourable to the disease, and the disease's symptoms and processes in the body. For example, in Brazil, devotees wash with popcorn, as part of prayer, to cure or prevent the disease. The popped kernels image the exploded smallpox pustules. Washing with them inoculates, or precipitates the illness' crisis and brings on healing.

Every five days the Iragbiji priestesses make offerings to Sonponna and all the *orisa* at outdoor shrines and at crossroads throughout the city for the inhabitants' health and well-being. Akiwowo remembers that in Lagos in the 1940's that the Sonponna priests and priestesses would periodically cleanse the city with offerings of red palm oil, a ritually cooling substance, and cowries. While the public rituals on behalf of Iragbiji town are made every five days, the Iyalode Sonponna makes a private ceremony for Sonponna not less than every three days. This is a concerted and intense effort of gift, prayer, *oriki*, incantation and divination in which Iyalode Sonponna is in intimate dialogue with *Kabiyesi*, Obaluaye, the Ruler of the World. It is this responsiveness and responsibility that has averted the disease in Iragbiji in the past and continues to do so.

An *itan*, story, told about Sonponna and his younger brother Sango describes Sonponna as possessing the coolness, contained composure and command of an elder. He has here, as Obaluaye, the character most often desired of sovereignty: the ability to wield immense power with deliberation. Sango, the passionate, impetuous, imperial *orisa* of the Oyo Empire, and the owner of lightning, shows off his fiery powers to his brother. He spits fire from his tongue and ignites one fire, then another, then many fires. Obaluaye sits and watches quietly. Finally, Sango ignites a large fire, walks into it, emerges unburned, and stands proudly before his brother. Obaluaye rises, detaches a gourd of *oogun*, medicine, from his vest, and pours a single drop of oil on the nearest fire. Immediately all the fires are extinguished. And Sango falls at Obaluaye's feet and prostrates himself in humility.[6]

While in the earlier *oriki*, Sonponna is the embodiment of feverish heat itself, in this story, he exemplifies *tutu*, coolness, in contrast to Sango's rashness. His *oogun* extinguishes the fire as medicine cools a fever. Sango's power to ignite fire and to be unaffected by it pale beside Sonponna's power to put it out. This story and other stories, songs, *oriki* and incantations, heard together, maintain his complex nature. His devotees experience him whole, his aspects of sovereign, father, piercing warrior, protector, and healer inseparable from each other. In their particularity, stories like this one, and like those of Ogun in the works of Sandra Barnes and Karen McCarthy Brown, offer acute psychological description and offer an array of choices for human beings (Barnes 1980, 1997; Brown 1991, 1997). They reveal epidemic disease as an arena for human conduct and moral choice. How do we choose to handle the fire under the skin of epidemics, the piercing fire of the battlefield, and the biochemical fire that merges the two?

Iyalode Sonponna and the other priestesses, acting on behalf of the city of Iragbiji, have chosen to engage Sonponna with offerings and coolness, to hold

---

[6] Personal communication, Sango priest Adeleke Sangoyoyin, August 2003, Lagos. Sonponna's dominion over Sango in a story told by a Sango devotee is unexpected and intensifies the awe that surrounds Sonponna in this itan.

him and themselves to the ties of relationship, to refuse to attempt to deal with disease in isolation from him - as the Ibadan poster expected people to do. Sonponna conceptualizes and embodies the power of disease and of healing. The dualisms unavoidably present in the preceding English sentence--concept and body, spirit and matter, disease and healing, and in the Ibadan poster described at the start of this chapter, are joined in Sonponna, and are therefore met in a unified response in traditional Yoruba practice. The elements of ritual, medicines, knowledge (in the modes of *oriki*, *itan*, and *ofo*), and living relationship are multiple, as was Titilayo Sangoyoyin's response to having malaria, yet they are interrelated and work together.

IV

In the *orisa* religious system, the relationship between *orisa* and devotee is very important. So, too, are the actions and moral choices of the devotees. Ritual does not obviate choice, but is, itself, chosen action. The Iragbiji *onisonponna*, (priestesses and priests of Sonponna) intervene actively and repeatedly for the health of the city. Today, all of us have similar choices and responsibilities, with global implications. Do we preserve or destroy the remaining live smallpox now stored in a research bank? A leading researcher and activist has argued that it must be destroyed, that the risks of the re-emergence of smallpox are too great. In the present world, biological warfare capacities and the willingness to deploy them are increasing. Why add to the arsenal when one aggressive use could ignite the epidemic so painstakingly eradicated?

And yet, a 2003 study at George Mason University in Virginia found that smallpox vaccine may be useful in developing patient resistance to HIV. "Blood cells from people vaccinated against smallpox were four times less likely to become infected with HIV."[7] The biochemistry that these researchers are just beginning to understand links smallpox and HIV/AIDS as the ritual knowledge and practice of the Iragbiji *onisonponna* have evidenced for some time.

Orisa religion does not remove human choice, or, in Marxist terms, does not mystify human responsibility. Karen McCarthy Brown has described Haitian Vodu as delineating the spheres of power in the persons of its deities (evidenced in rituals, iconography, songs and stories) in a way that makes plain the varieties of choice about uses of that power. Similarly, Sandra Barnes in her case study of the Yoruba *orisa* Ogun sees Him as technology in both its creative and destructive capacities.

I believe that we can understand Sonponna similarly, and other *orisa* such as *Osun*, as well. In addition to the unseen and the material dimensions, they offer a range of possible human actions, responses and interventions. What decisions will we as individuals, groups and national policy makers make about nuclear power and weapons of mass destruction (the sphere of *Ogun*);

---

[7] *USA Today*, September 15, 2003, 7D.

smallpox reserves, germ warfare and HIV/AIDS prevention and treatment (the sphere of Sonponna); and universally available potable water, the biophagic healing properties of certain rivers, and the control of water transmitted diseases such as typhoid, cholera, amoebic dysentery, river blindness, and schistosomiasis (the sphere of *Osun*)?

V

Sonponna, *Ogun* and *Osun* and their *olorisa* have much to tell us about making these decisions, not only because they have modes of knowledge and action that complement the academic sciences, but because they reveal the larger embedded context of the problems we face, and remind us of our choices and responsibilities. It is necessary to see Sonponna wholly, as disease, healing and health together, accessible by multiple modes of understanding, ritual and academic scientific, and present internationally and locally. A final note: Some Yoruba friends of Akiwowo have expressed dismay at the proclivity of Americans for running off to Nigeria to find and make videotapes of the *orisa*. "Why," they say, "do *oyinbo* (foreigners) go to Nigeria to film *orisa*? Don't they know they are in America, too? Why don't they stay home and make offerings so that bad things don't happen in their own place?"[8] Point well taken. There is much to do for *alaafia* (peace and healing), religiously, ethically, academically, socially and politically on both sides of the ocean.

References

Barnes, Sandra, ed. . *Ogun: An Old God for a New Age.* Philadelphia: Institute for the Study of Human Issues. 1980
Barnes, Sandra, ed., *Africa's Ogun: Old World and New*, 2nd expanded edition. (Bloomington: Indiana University Press) 1997
Beier, Ulli, *Yoruba Poetry.* (Cambridge: Cambridge University Press) 1970
Brown, Karen McCarthy.. *Mama Lola: A Vodu Priestess in Brooklyn.*(Berkeley: University of California Press.) 1991
Brown, Karen McCarthy. "Systematic Remembering, Systematic Forgetting: Ogou in Haiti." In Sandra Barnes, *Africa's Ogun: Old World and New*, 2nd expanded edition.(Bloomington: Indiana University Press) 1997. 65-89
Verger, Pierre Fatumbi. *Ewe: The Use of Plants in Yoruba Society.* Sao Paulo: Editora Schwarcz, 1995

---

[8] Akinsola Akiwoso, personal communication, April 2003, Alexandria, Virginia.

7

Health, Healing, and Restoring

- Danoye Oguntola-Laguda

Introduction

The importance of a health care delivery system to humanity cannot be overemphasized, most especially in societies that are still in the throes of social, economic, political and cultural development. In Nigeria, a multi-religious society with its attendant pluralism, the problem of inadequate health care is one of many challenges facing the managers of the country polity. Other problems include poverty, ignorance, and illiteracy, among others. The main task in the health care sector, in Nigeria today is how to restore people's health to its original state before ailment ensues.

Western orthodox medicine, which is the main source of health care delivery, has not been able to adequately care for the needs of the people. Government investments in this regard have been poor. The situation has made traditional medicine popular among the people. In fact, the numbers of traditional medical centres in the country are now legion. They provide alternative medical services to the people at cheaper rate and within the traditional religion of their forbearers. The media is agog in Nigeria with advertisements on the efficacy of the traditional method of healing and the various products available for sale. These advertisements address diseases such as malaria fever, body pain, diabetes, infertility, fibroid, jaundice, and cough, among others. According to the practitioners, these drugs are procured from herbs, bark of trees, and animal and inanimate objects. It may involve the use of incantations as well as sacrifice to certain divinities. In spite of the contributions of traditional medicine to the health care sector of the Nigerian polity, it has continued to confront the challenges of relevance and efficacy, especially from non-adherents of traditional religion (mostly Christians and Muslims). The arguments of these groups often centre on the relationship and interaction between traditional medicine and the cults of the divinities and the ancestors prevalent in traditional religion. It has further been argued that traditional medicine is archaic, cannibalistic and ritualistic.

Our effort in this chapter is to examine the indigenous concept of healing, health and restoration of the body and soul to its original peaceful and holistic state before ailment by using the indigenous religious traditions of the people. We also seek to examine the methods of healing as well as the healers.

Because of its value and popularities in recent times, we shall examine developments in the traditional healing system and how this has been appropriated by people of other religious traditions such as Islam and Christianity in the country. It is also our intention to respond to the debate on relevance and efficacy of traditional health care system and medicaments to the overall health care system in the Nigeria. Although we shall discuss traditional health and medicine in Nigeria, in general, our focus will be on the Yoruba, one of the three major ethnic groups in the country.

Healing and health care delivery system in indigenous religions

A healthy person is someone in a state of absence of diseases. It is a state of well being which can engender productivity. On the contrary, an unhealthy person will suggest a personage that is affected by a disease or ailment, which has tampered with the harmony between the body and the soul. This kind of person cannot be expected to function properly and will need to be healed of the ailment(s) that assail him or her. This perhaps may have informed the opinion of Adeoye when he posits: "Diseases are detrimental to human productivity at all levels" (Dopamu 2003:18). He further claims that poverty and backwardness are inseparable allies of diseases in every clime.

In Nigerian indigenous religious thought and tradition, diseases and ailments are attached to the agency of supernatural entities. This will suggest that the health care delivery system should relate and interact with the religious beliefs of the people who practice traditional religion. The treatments of these diseases are procured within the people's belief in traditional medicine, which is only one part of a complex belief system. The major beliefs include; beliefs in one Supreme God, divinities, ancestors, spirits, magic and medicine. These beliefs are better taken and appreciated as a whole.

Medicine is an art, which seeks to restore and preserve health. It is curative as well as preventive because it builds up anti-bodies that help the body to resist infection by boosting its organs (Idowu 1996:177). According to Awolalu and Dopamu, medicine is a process of:

> ...using available forces of nature to prevent disease and to restore and preserve health. It is prophylactic and therapeutic (Awolalu and Dopamu 1979:240).

D.S. Shishima describes healing and health care as the core of medicinal practice. In traditional health care, it includes the use of drugs and herbs that cure and prevent diseases; as well as objects or recipes with magical effects, the purpose of which could be negative or positive (Shishima 1995:119). Douglas Guthrie further defines the traditional concept of medicine in Nigeria as "folks or domestic medicine, which are identified with early pre-historic man" (Guthrie 1982:823).

The healing process seeks to apply herbal formula to minor ailments such as cold, and constipation. However, more serious ailments with metaphysical dimensions are treated with adequate use of charms and amulets, incantations or sorcery (Guthrie 1982:823). All the above-mentioned scholars explain traditional medicine as a healing method for diseases and ailments with the objective of giving succour to people who are sick and to prevent them from being attacked by diseases. Also, this concept shows that medicine and its practice relate to magic and religion. Idowu and Dopamu have variously alluded to this in their conclusions on Yoruba traditional medicine. Idowu argues that the diviners and priests of traditional religion are the main agents that engage in the practice of traditional medicine (Idowu 1996:198). Dopamu also opines that Yoruba medicine is closely related to religion, especially in areas of rituals, taboos, divination and attachment to the cult of the divinities and ancestors. In this regard, *Osanyin* and *Ifa* are used as means for divination and diagnosis (Dopamu 2005:444). M. J. Field demonstrates in his submission cited by Idowu on the relation between medicine and religion among West Africans that:

> Magic or as it is more often called in West Africa, medicine always involves concrete apparatus...there is no activity in this life which cannot be assisted by medicine (Idowu 1996:199).

The opinion of Field suggests a symbiotic relationship among medicine, magic and religion. S. Nadel also discovers this interaction in the traditional medical thought of the Nupe people in Nigeria. He informs that medicine refer to both skills, often of the esoteric and miraculous kind, and to healing practices (Idowu 1996:199). This will suggest that magic and medicine depend on spiritual beliefs and supernatural beings.

In the indigenous thought of the Nigerian people, illness and sickness are products of the breakdown in the harmony between the human being and elemental (spiritual) forces as earlier stated. This harmony could be physiological, moral, spiritual as well as ontological. I share in the belief that health; ill health and healing in Nigerian indigenous religious thought rely greatly on magic and religion. This factor has greatly affected traditional health care delivery in relation to the treatment of diseases. For example, common cold, headaches, catarrh, are seen as a sign of the displeasure and anger of the Supreme Being, divinities and ancestors with human beings. It could also suggest a manifestation of attacks of evil spirits and evil machination of ones enemies.

The healing and restoration process in traditional medical practice is holistic. It treats the body, soul and spirit. In the opinion of Shishima, traditional medicine treats the whole human being in body and soul. On the other hand, magic could be classified into good and bad. The former is socially approved, because it has social benefits and the latter is rejected by the society because it often brings havoc on individuals, groups and communities

(Shishima 1995:119). This will imply that magic could be employed or deployed in the healing process.

Agencies in healing practice

The healers are experts in the art of medicine and magic. It is not gender exclusive. My investigations among the Yoruba, Efik, Ibibio, Idoma and Tiv people in Nigeria, have shown that some of the healers claimed to have inherited the practice from their forbearers. Some claimed that they were taught the art of medicine by divinities and other spiritual beings in dreams, trances or during spiritual meetings with spirits in the grove (Idowu 1996:200).

The traditional healer in the opinion of Geoffrey Parrinder is a scientist. He writes, *inter alia*, that:

> A medicine man (doctor) is a scientist in that he seeks to discover and use the laws of the universe, not only of nature but also spiritual forces ... believing there are hidden powers that can be tapped...in order to meet various ailments (Parrinder 1969:159).

The submission of Parrinder posits that the traditional healer is invested with or had acquired the power to heal all forms of diseases or ailments. He is a psychiatrist, physician, wonder healer and ritualist who, without a laboratory, carries out researches on the spiritual and medicinal powers of herbs and roots as well as their functions. Consequently, he employs this vast knowledge in the diagnosis and treatment of ailments. He recites incantations, remembers herbal formulas, concoctions to treat all kind of diseases with ease. Among the Yoruba, they are known as *Onisegun*, the Nupe refer to them as *Cigbeni* while the Tiv call them *Ortwer*. A *Dibia* among the Igbo is the traditional healer, the magician and the witchdoctor.

These healers provide all services found in a health care delivery system. They are the laboratory technologists, physicians, pharmacist as well as the gynaecologists and surgeon. In Yorubaland, we have three categories of professionals in the traditional health care service. These are *Onisegun, Elegbogi* and *Babalawo*. *Onisegun* is an expert in magic and metaphysical matters, he employs spiritual elements for his practice. He is also versed in herbal remedies, which do not fall primarily within his calling. In the opinion of Dopamu, the *Onisegun* is involved in *sise oogun* (preparing medicine), which is an art of engagement in the treatment of diseases. He informs that:

> The *Onisegun* (practitioner of Ogun) does not concern himself only with the treatment of diseases but also understands the nature and aetiology of disease or illness before embarking on treatment (Dopamu 2005:444).

The *Elegbogi* or *Elewe omo*, is an herbalist who is well versed and respected in herbal combinations that have requisite properties to cure ailments. *Elegbogi* is not often concerned with rituals or incantations attached to traditional medicine. He/she only sells leaves, bark of trees, animal skins and parts, birds, roots and other inanimate objects used by the *Onisegun*. The *Babalawo* is a diviner who consults divinities, especially *Osanyin* (divinity of diseases) and *Orunmila* (Wisdom Divinity) to diagnose disease(s) of their patients. This group of healers relies on sacrifice as a therapy for diseases.

Although, the functions of the three classes of healers in Yoruba traditional health care service are supposed to be inter-related and independent. However, it is common now in Yorùbáland to find the three functions vested in one person. This situation may have informed the position of Dopamu that all the three medical practitioners mentioned here should have a good knowledge of divination for diagnosis.

My interaction with the first two classes—*Onisegun* and *Elegbogi*—shows that they depend greatly on their knowledge of diseases and medicine to intervene in patient illness. It is not impossible for any of these two categories of healers to patronize the *Babalawo* (Diviners) to determine the cause of the ailment of their patient. This is often the case when the *Onisegun* suspects the ailment to have metaphysical dimensions. Therefore, divination and the knowledge of aetiology of diseases are used for diagnosis. Every healer is, therefore, not a diviner. Consequently, I wish to propose that even though divination is part of traditional health care delivery system among the Yoruba people, it is not compulsory for all practitioners to have knowledge of it for effective service delivery.

Yoruba traditional health care delivery methods

Traditional health providers adopt many methods in their effort to deliver health care. The operational technique is comparable to western medical practices. Except that the latter depend sometimes on laboratory test before therapy could commence. The healers listen to the complaint of their patient to determine the kind and extent of disease(s). They diagnose and make prescriptions based on experience and sometime on the directive(s) given by the oracle. Sacrifice could be prescribed with requisite medication. In Yorùbáland, the *Onisegun* gives concoctions or makes incisions (*gbere*) in the body of patients. He could also prescribe ritual bath and use of some concoctions for such bath at crossroads (*orita meta*). For diseases with spiritual causes, *Onisegun* may need to interact with the Babalawo in order to consult the oracle Ifa, to understand the dimension of the ailment and necessary therapy to adopt for the patient. *Elegbogi* takes the case history of the patient and based on his knowledge of the aetiology of diseases, prescribes herbal formula, which he believes has necessary therapeutic properties that can heal the disease and give succour to the patient.

The patient may be asked to perform some rituals, observe taboo (*ewo*) and sacrifice (*ebo*) animals or birds to the deities. He may also need to bury, eat, rub or wash his body with infusion, by putting objects under his pillow or carry it about in his pockets, reciting incantation after the concoction has been prepared before using it; in order to get the desired cure for his ailment (Dopamu 2005:444). In this process many things could be used as elemental part of the medicine. They include:

> Herbs, leaves, roots, barks, stems, seeds, flowers, fruits buds, sap or juices of trees and plants. Various births, their feather, beak, gizzard, head, foot, toes, bones, various animals, their skin, bones, skulls, head, gills, and excretions. Various reptiles like lizard, snakes Iguana, gecko, chameleon various insects like butterfly, ply, wasp, beetle, cricket, ants, bees, other inanimate objects such as gunpowder, iron, shell, sand, water, stone, sulphur, honey, salt, rum, palm oil, and other types of liquid (Dopamu 2000:8).

The medicine is often prepared by grinding or pounding (*gugun*), burning (*jijo*), boiling (*sise*), or squeezing juice (*gbigbo*) out of the materials. It could also be by cooking the ingredients or mixing them with soap for bath. Some may involve incantation (*ayajo, oro Ife, asan, epe*, etc.) before use.

A cure may be effected by the use of remedy resembling the diseases (telepathy). For example, in traditional gynaecology, a woman may be asked to eat the womb of a productive animal (*eku eda*) in order to cure her of infertility. In traditional orthopaedics, a specific animal's bones, especially the fowl animals or bird bones could be broken, just like in the patient's case. Healing could be achieved through this telepathy method. This is akin to magic. Incision (*gbere*) among the Yoruba traditional healers is common. This could be made in all parts of the body and rubbed with burnt powdered substances made from a combination of many of the elements earlier mentioned. The incisions could be made with razor blades, knives, axes, cutlasses, and needles, among other objects. Incantations and prayers could accompany it.

In time past, traditional healers used their residence as well as the groove as clinics. In some cases, the shrine of some divinities could be the hospital or maternity homes. However, in recent times however, they have erected offices, and employed attendants as assistants, some whom are trainees.

The efficacy of traditional health care delivery system cannot be overemphasized. In fact, patronage has increased tremendously. In Lagos (Yorùbáland) and Calabar (Efikland) pregnant women prefer to combine traditional antenatal with western orthodox medical antenatal. In Alimosho Local Government Area of Lagos State as at 2007, about 186 traditional antenatal were identified with commendable patronage. It was, however, discovered that women prefer to deliver their babies at the western orthodox maternity hospitals that are abound in the area.

Traditional medicine and other religions

The pluralistic nature of the Nigerian nation has made religious interaction and acculturation possible. In fact, some of the practices, doctrines and tenets of indigenous religions in the country have been appropriated by Islam and Christianity. These two religious traditions are now very popular among the Nigerian populace. It could be argued that it is the patronage of these religious traditions by Nigerians that has affected the acceptability of traditional religion vis-à-vis its health care system by this category of people. However, in the Christian tradition, especially among African Independent Churches in Nigeria, such as the Celestial Church of Christ, The Aladura Church, Christ Apostolic Church, among others, indigenous healing methods have been appropriated. The church leaders now engage in alternative medical practice, which involves the use of herbal formula, and in some cases, magic. This is often practiced under the guise of divine healing. Prayers are used as means of diagnosis and herbal prescriptions are made. It could involve ritual bath at a flowing river with burnt substances mixed with soap. Some members of the Celestial Church are made to do sacrifice (*Ipese*) as a therapy for ailments.

A.O. Dairo observes that some Pentecostals are also involved in these syncretic practices. This has led to suspicion with regard to their operations. In fact, according to Dairo, they combine "Africanness with the Bible" (Dairo 1995:9). It should be noted, however, that none of the leaders of these Christian groups agree that they are appropriating the traditional healing methods, but they obviously combine prayer and fasting with traditional paramedics. In the opinion of Dairo:

> It is difficult to ascertain the source of the healing power since man is susceptible to manipulation by some agencies other than the divine (Jesus Christ). One sometime doubt the forces behind some miracle healers because some healers could use the power of divinities and cults under the guise of Holy Spirit (Dairo 1995:8).

The implication of this situation for the Nigerian indigenous religious thought is that the traditional healers are now "*appropriating*" the tenets, doctrines, liturgies of imported religious traditions. However, behind this façade, they continue to use traditional healing methods. This is not to say that divine healing among Christians in Nigeria is not possible, but I wish to submit that there are lot of suspicions on the activities of the Christian healers especially within the fold of African Independent Churches and some Pentecostals.

Muslims are involved in this appropriation as well. In fact, there are Muslim from Nupeland, who now reside in Lagos that engage in full traditional healing making use of the traditional methods earlier described. These methods are combined with recitation of some chapters and verses of the Holy Quran. Writing about how Islam spread to Ede, a town in South

West Nigeria, M.O. Adeniyi informs that medicine, charms and amulets were used by Buremo, a local Muslim medicine man, in providing assistance to the Ede people in their war against Ibadan warriors (Adeniyi 1995:59).

Muslim clergy in Yorùbáland have taken traditional medicine as a vocation and healing as a profession. They combine, in this regard, both Islamic and traditional medicine to cure diseases. According to O.M. Ademola:

> Mallam (Muslim clerics) writes Quranic verses on a black slate using ink prepared from local tree *Oori* and washes it with water for drinking. They also use tree back (Epo Obo), leaves of plant (*birana*) kadura and at times alligator pepper, which are grinded and added to honey before drinking. This is known as *Gari Tira* (Ademola 1995:110).

Tira, a protection charm is given to patrons to hang in their houses or put on their persons as protection against evil machination of the enemies. The Muslim healers often demanded for animals and birds victims as elements of sacrifice. It is suspected that these sacrifices are for some divinities. They engage in divination through the sand or rosary, night vigils, fasting and praying with recitation of Qur'anic verses. These are some of their methodologies. They are now using the electronic and print media as outlet to advertise their products. The efficacy of these methods as a form of healing is not in doubt, but its syncretic nature and the deceit and exploitations associated with the practice leave much to desire.

Modern trend in Yoruba traditional health care delivery system

Traditional health and healing system has witnessed many changes as well as developments in recent times in Nigeria. In fact, the awareness about its efficacy has become known to all and sundry. Traditional healers have "westernized" their practices and have adopted the electronic and print media as a means of marketing their products and also creating awareness about their products' efficacy. Emphasis is no longer placed on sacrifices to the divinities, incantations or incisions. They now combine the western-orthodox diagnosis system and laboratory test to determine the ailments of their patients. At Yem Kem, a traditional healing "shop" in Lagos, there are resident doctors and laboratory technologists who diagnosis patients before prescribing one of many herbal formulas in its pharmacy. This is more vivid in the usage of scientific equipment. For example, in gynaecology, antenatal and maternity practice, ultra-sound scanning machine is used to determine the sex, position and the well being of the developing foetus. If surgery is needed, the doctors at Yem Kem refer patients to teaching hospitals for adequate attention and therapy.

We also observe that these modern trends and dynamics have not affected oracular diagnosis by the *babalawo*. This is because some ailments and diseases, as earlier discussed in this paper have metaphysical dimensions. For example, *magun* is a metaphysical means of checking the activities of adulterous women, and scientific diagnosis cannot detect it, neither can it give remedy for it cure. At the popular Oko Oloyun Healing Home in Lagos, traditional diagnosis is combined with western methods. The *Onisegun* and *Elegbogi* are still popular among the people. The latter are predominant at market places where people consult them on common and simple ailments such as cold, headache, malaria fever, typhoid fever, jaundice, body pain, sexually transmitted diseases (STDs), among other ailments devoid of metaphysical diagnosis. Our study has shown that the influence of the *Onisegun* has reduced considerably due to modernity and influx of foreign religious ideologies into Nigerian religious space.

There is now ample opportunity for non-conventional doctors with knowledge of traditional herbs to delve into the health care system. Bamidele Ogaga, Engr. Olowu (now late) and Akintunde Ayeni, agree that a traditional health care delivery system is necessary as a complement to western orthodox medicine. Ogaga is a western-trained doctor, who specializes in nutrition. Through his research, he has discovered that the nutritional values in fruits, leaves, barks, roots, etc., are capable of curing various diseases. Like the two other healers mentioned above, he suggests that government should invest in research into traditional medicine by importing laboratory equipment that could be used to further enhance the sector. This equipment could be used for the extraction of toxic elements inherent in some herbs or barks.

The enthusiasm generated by traditional medicine in Nigeria in recent times cannot be overemphasized. People with diseases and ailments that seem incurable to orthodox medicine take solace in the traditional therapy. In fact, traditional medical healers with considerable successes have handled ailments such as diabetes, high blood pressure, fibroid, low sperm count, etc. Christians and Muslims who hitherto are against the use of traditional medicine have come not only appropriating it into their divine healing system, but also found a basis for it in their scriptures. According to Ogaga, the Christian basis for herbal medicine is in Ezekiel 47:12 which states:

> And by the river upon the bark on this side, and on that side, shall grow all trees for meat, whose leaf shall not fade...Because their water they issue out of sanctuary...and the leaf therefore shall be for medicine.

The Pentecostal Christians, as well as Mission Church members, now patronize traditional medicine as a healing method.

Conclusion

In this chapter, we have discussed the importance and value of good health to Nigerians and the ailments that afflict the people. It is noted that in desperate situations, Nigerians have turned to traditional health care delivery system for succour. This chapter has also shown that there is a symbiotic relationship between religion and traditional medicine on the one hand and magic on the other hand. In Yoruba traditional health care system, *Onisegun, Elegbogi* and *Babalawo* are well versed in the art of magic as well as medicine that are given symbolic sacredness by indigenous religion of the people.

The efficacy of traditional health care delivery is not in doubt and practitioners have adopted the electronic and print media as channels for advancing their products. Importation of laboratory equipment and their usage has enhanced greatly the process of healing as the "doctors" can now with a degree of conviction, determine an ailment, its sources and what herbs or methods could be used for its cure or control. This could account for the growth in patronage and relevance of the healing methods as alternative and compliment to the western orthodox health care system. In fact some western orthodox medical practitioners are reported to have directed their patients to seek traditional medical services for ailments that seem mysterious or defile "medical" solutions. The appropriation of the traditional health care methods by Christians and Muslims as part of their divine healing process may point to the acculturation of the two religious traditions. It should be noted, however, that some traditional medical practitioners have adopted the Christians and Islamic approaches in order to gain acceptance and relevance from their patrons. We are convinced that traditional health care system has come to stay and its relevance can only be measured by its successes, which are not in doubt.

References

Ademola, O.M., 1995. "Attitude of Muslims Towards Traditional Medicine" in in Gbola Aderibigbe and Deji Ayegboyin (eds.), *Religion, Medicine, and Healing* (A Publication of the Nigerian Association for the Study of Religions and Education, NASRED): 109-112

Adeniyi, M.O., 1995. "Interaction Through Medicine, Charms and Amulets: Islam and the Yoruba Traditional Religion" in Gbola Aderibigbe and Deji Ayegboyin (eds.), *Religion, Medicine, and Healing* (A Publication of the Nigerian Association for the Study of Religions and Education, NASRED): 58-62

Aderibigbe Gbola and Deji Ayegboyin (eds.), 1995. *Religion, Medicine and Healing* (A Publication of the Nigerian Association for the Study of Religions and Education, NASRED)

Awolalu, J.O. and P.A. Dopamu, 1979. *West African Traditional Religion* (Ibadan: Onibonoje Press).

Buckley, A.D., 1985. *Yoruba Medicine* (Oxford: Clarendon Press).

Dairo, A.O., 1995. "Christianity and Healing: The Yoruba Experience" in Gbola Aderibigbe and Deji Ayegboyin (eds.), *Religion, Medicine and Healing* (A Publication of the Nigerian Association for the Study of Religions and Education, NASRED): 6-11

Dopamu, 2005

Dopamu, P. Ade, 2000. "Yoruba Traditional Medicine in Health Care Delivery," in Nike Lawal (ed.), *Yoruba Life and Culture* (St. Cloud State University): pp.8ff

Dopamu, P. A., 2003. *African Culture, Modern Science and Religious Thought* (Ilorin: ACRS).

Dopamu, P.A., 1979. "Yoruba Magic and Medicine and their Relevance for Today" *Religions: Journal of the Nigerian Association for the Study of Religions*, Vol. 4: 5-14.
Field, M.J., 1937, *Religion and Medicine of the Ga People* (London: Oxford University Press).
Guthrie, D. S. 1982,"Medicine: History of" *Encyclopedia Britannica* Vol.11: 823
Hallgren, Roland; "Religion and Health Among Traditional Yoruba" *Orita: Ibadan Journal of Religious Studies* Vol. xxiv/1-2, 1992: 67ff
Idowu, E.B., 1973. *African Traditional Religion: A Definition* (London: SCM Press).
Idowu, E.B., 1996. (Revised), *Olodumare: God in Yoruba Belief* (London: SCM Press).
Lawal, Nike (ed.), 2000. *Yoruba Life and Culture* (St. Cloud State University Press).
Nadel, S.F., 1954. *Nupe Religions* (London: Routledge and Kegan Paul Ltd).
Parrinder, E.G., (ed.), 1969. *West African Religion* (London: Eppworth Press).
Shishima, D.S., 1995. "The Whole Nature of African Traditional Medicine: The Tiv Experience" in in Gbola Aderibigbe and Deji Ayegboyin (eds.), *Religion, Medicine, and Healing* (A Publication of the Nigerian Association for the Study of Religions and Education, NASRED): 119-126
Taylor, J. V., 1969. *The Primal Vision* (London: SMC Press).

Personal Interviews

- Ogaga, Bamidele, 66 years, Lagos. Interviewed on 21st of August 2001.
- Olowu, A. Engineer, 68 years, Lagos. Interviewed on 20th of February, 2002 (died 2008).
- Ayeni, Akintunde, 56 years, Trained herbalist, has a supermarket of herbal drugs in Lagos and other parts of South-west of Nigeria. Interviewed at his Egbeda residence in Lagos on the 14th May 2006.

8

Shrines and sovereignty in religious life and experience

- Charles Obafemi Jegede

Introduction

There is not an issue that is puzzling to the minds as much as the reality of the divine. The issue is both epistemological and as well as ontological. Epistemological, because of an inherent push to accept or reject the reality, ontological because of the beingness, it raises question on whether the divine is or not. This question does not arise when the issue of matter or materiality is being discussed. The domain where the divine is regarded to be of relevance is the domain of religion as religion is virtually empty without the divine. Humans from time immemorial create shrines as practical devices through which the reality of the divine can be validated. The history of religion and religious practice has long been associated with the reality of the divine.

In Nigerian indigenous religious tradition, the spiritual/divine is as real as the material. In fact, there is an imposing and permeating presence of the divine. This is in sharp contrast with western cosmology where reality is enshrined mainly within the domain of physicality. This explains why in western cosmology the supernatural is relegated to the background. This is essentially true considering the western scientific paradigms, which are inherently naturalistic despite the apparent pervasive role of the supernatural even in the western science (Brenner 1985). The reality of the supernatural is not part of any debate, but the location, activation and substantiation for optimum benefits of the Nigerian. The divine is both immanent and transcendental and as a result, they are approachable, they can be experienced as indubitable reality. In Nigeria, gods or *Orisa* guide the affairs of most indigenous persons, families and communities. For this reason, from birth to death, the *Orisa* influence every aspect of their lives. This explains why atheism and agnosticism are inconceivable. At one point, or the other, most indigenous Nigerians have experienced a kind of hierophany, a divine disclosure or an appearance of divinity. By implication the divine is enshrined in the spiritual domain of Nigerian cosmology. In a bid to localize or situate the divine so as to have direct access to them, Nigerians naturally create shrines. A shrine therefore is the meeting place of the material human and the spiritual divine. The glaringly imperative questions are, when exactly does any object become a sacred object or when does a place become a shrine? Is it before the activation through the use of specialized ritual and behaviour? Why the differentiation between the "before activation and the after activation?" In the face of modernity and globalization, are shrines still important?

Fieldwork

In this chapter, I drew heavily on my experience as a researcher in African religion and medicine. I also carefully followed the Okija scenario in Anambra State of Nigeria. This chapter is a distillation of my observations of the practices of the *babalawo* (father of ancient wisdom) in Osogbo. My participation in several rituals including initiation rituals into Osun cult and divination sessions in the Osun Osogbo shrine during and after the festival period enriches my data. I drew from three major sources: the *Ifa* corpus, the legends of Osogbo, and my interpretation of events in Okija. The Osogbo legend is the most "pounded" issue regarding the founding of Osogbo and the myth in *Ifa*, which is of tremendous revelation and is often neglected and unexplored. My keen interest in the Okija saga aided me in arriving at an objective understanding of shrines in Igbo land of Eastern Nigeria. Also, my close observation of the symbolic relevance of what is regarded as simple, insignificant and negligible objects and how these are activated through the use of plants, invocation and incantation and songs, thereby making these objects immediately become sacred, transcendental or supernatural. I observed closely some forms of synergy of herbs with the spiritual object or symbols and the synchronisation of material objects to bring out the spiritual component to invoke awe and wonder. The process is systemic and it is an evocation and invocation of spiritual component in matter. Materiality therefore has no foundation in the philosophy and religion of Nigerian indigenous religious tradition. Through the activation of material objects, they are symbolically showcasing the immanence of the divine, and as well validating the fact that the divine influences every activity.

Issues in perspectives

Too many misconceptions regarding shrines in Nigerian indigenous religious tradition have thrived for so long. When the word shrine is mentioned, what immediately leap into the imagination are grisly images. What the picture foreshadows is that of a disgusting image of backwardness, totally offensive to cultured personalities. It creates fear and conjures the meaning of a place where ritual killings are done for money making, and all forms of evil with which the Nigerian society is suffused. In such shrines, human parts such as hand, head, genitals and others are said to be found for the purpose of money-making rituals. To the modern elitist, Christian or Muslim minds, shrines will imply primitivism, dirtiness, idolatry and fetishism. The modern mind for example sees palm oil on the top of *Esu* (one of the principle divinities of the Yoruba) in *Esu* shrine as irritating and filthy, sees conjured spirits and forces in Sango shrine as occultism and the preservation of forest for ritual purposes and as shrine for the *Orisa* as wastage and primitivism. The questions that are begging to be answered are what is the true meaning and concept of shrine in Nigerian Indigenous Religious Tradition? Are shrines really meant for evil?

In Nigerian indigenous religious traditions, shrines function as the spot that binds the community together, and also to the divine—it is a uniting energy. In practically all ethnic groups and communities in Nigeria, there are shrines. Most of these shrines are created with adequate support of the traditional authority in which they exist to serve general and specific functions. Even the shrines in Okija, Anambra State, Nigeria which were portrayed in a negative light have been known for over a hundred years to serve as some sort of traditional jurisprudence guided by taboos under the supreme authority of the Okija gods. There are many activities of Okija shrine that are positive in nature, and therefore serve the interest of the Okija community as well as a larger interest of the Igbo people. Many shrines among the Igbo, in many respects have reputation for justice in the settlement of disputes especially land and family disputes. In doing this, oaths are taken and are considered binding in the presence of the divine. A native of Okija claims that the shrine was consistently patronized by politicians and by big business men and women from many parts of Igbo land, when they felt cheated. They sought redress through the Okija shrines. This is because it is crucial that the divine witnesses the sessions so as to serve as agent of judgment.

The main business is oath-taking, and traditional oath-taking is a common feature of resolving disputes in Africa. It can also be used in detecting criminals (Edu 2004). According to Abdulmumini Oba (2008), traditional oaths play decisive roles in customary law arbitration and are recognised and accorded due respect by the courts. Among the Igbo and particularly in Okija shrines, various disagreements were settled by oath-taking at the shrine. The priests, for example, claim they were not doing anything illegal. Indeed, the shrines are run by a legally registered cultural body, thereby legitimizing their activities. In effect, several eminent Igbo personalities supported them. It also helped to generate taboos that guide the moral and spiritual lives of the people. When oaths are taken and a covenant made in the shrine, it is binding on all the parties concerned. Okija shrines instil on Okija community and adherents of the shrine the need for trust and respect for neighbours; it also serves as an agent of judgment and nemesis thereby inculcating discipline.

Many shrines, especially those that are named after mountains, rivers and forests, in Nigerian Indigenous Religious Tradition are meant for the preservation of the ecosystem. In a community, there can be a taboo that prevents fishing from a particular river principally to preserve the fish in the river for collective advantage. Stan Stevens (1992, 2) notes that traditional religion and practices are veritable means by which the indigenous societies preserve their ecosystem and biodiversity. It has been revealed that many traditional practices do not damage the environment but enhance it.

Most of the cultures in Nigeria have rich folk and religious traditions on the conservation of biodiversity and sustainable use of natural resources.

Studies on sacred grooves reveal that they are priceless treasure of great ecological, biological, religious and historical values. In the evolution of religions, sacred grooves, mountains, rivers and trees once played a vital role. This accounts for the reasons why the Nigerians have established several natural places and have protected them from destruction since time immemorial. Access to these sites is usually restricted by taboos and management codes designed to regulate particular activities. These sacred places are regarded as inviolate from ordinary use and set apart, dedicated and consecrated for religious use and observance. These areas of unblemished nature are also sanctuaries for the *Orisa*. Most of them left great history and mysteries behind them. The shrines provide for them a ceremonial home and the sculptures embody their myths. Strangely, such practices are becoming extinct in most parts of Nigeria due to changes in religion, and in recent times, industrialization. This has resulted in desecration and desacralization of not only the shrine but the entirety of Nigerian cosmology. A case in point was that of Odo shrine, an ancestral shrine of the Abor community in Ojebiogene Area Development Council of Enugu State where some Christian youths in the area destroyed the Odo masquerade shrine. The reason was because it was suspected that some diabolical persons in the community use juju (witchcraft) under the cover of the Odo shrine to harm their opponent and other innocent people. The question that enters the mind is, is it the shrine that must be destroyed? Much of the sacredness in nature has been rejected creating disharmony bringing about an emergence and re-emergence of new diseases in people and communities. Human history is littered with the ruins of socio-cultural matrices that rose to dominance and power, and then receded to obscurity (Field 1999). There is the need to protect shrines in Nigeria from threat.

Sacred sites also serve as ethnic identity and play a key role in the indigenous and traditional people's culture and life styles. Among the Remo people of Ogun State Nigeria, Oro shrine, an ancestral shrine among the Yoruba of Nigeria and Benin republic, was in 1999-2000 used to eliminate thieves and robbers in the land. Oro is an indispensable divinity that is used to douse tension in the land so as to bring about equilibrium especially during crisis period. During political, economic, ecological crises and even war, people take recourse in the shrine. For example during the June 12, 1993 saga, there was going to be a great disturbance. In the midst of the talk of war, the Oba of Benin was reported to have led his priests to the Olokun shrine where sacrifices were offered on behalf of the nation. It was also reported in 2005 that Ekiadolor community Edo State recently had witnessed a traditional ritual during which Oba's representatives led traditional chiefs in placing a curse on all those who are involved in bloody cultism in Ekiadolor College of Education. The *Oba* of Benin Omo N'Oba Erediauwa has said of recent that he is currently tackling the scourge of high crime rate in Edo State by going to the shrine of the ancestors to invoke their energy.

Before the advent of western medicine and especially during an epidemic of small pox, *Obaluaye*'s shrine was the hiding place for the people of Epe in

Lagos state of Nigeria. Sacrifices were offered to this divinity and the epidemic would stop. Shrines in many parts of Nigeria can be used to serve the selfish interest of priests, priestesses and adherent of the gods. For example, experience shows that fraudulent individuals do come to Osun shrine to deceive victims and to perpetrate their evil intentions. Shrine officials can manipulate their divinities for personal enrichment and vendetta. This is in fact a deplorable use of what should serve the collective good. Nevertheless, shrines among the indigenous people of Nigeria serve as centres of cohesion, symbols of unity of intention and goals. Therefore, it is not the destruction of the shrine that would solve the problem as such amounts to desecration, but rather dealing with guilty individuals as the shrines are not guilty of the evil perpetrated by the shrine officials.

Shrine, which can be translated as *ojubo* or *oju ibo* (the centre or the eye of worship) in Yoruba is also a place where worship and sacrifices are offered to the divine. The revelation of the divine is a sacred revelation of spiritual beings. It showcases the inherent nature of humans to participate in spiritual beingness so as to live the sacred life. According to a respondent who is also the Aseda of Osogbo, divinities are not just Orisa or divine beings, but also energies in the cosmos which must be propitiated with ritual. Shrine therefore is the place where the divine is identified and are offered necessary sacrifices. It is also the physicalization and domestication of spiritual realities for easy access. It is the place where an individual, family, group of people or community gather for worship and prayers.

Shrine can either be personal (Ottenberg 1970) or corporate; a personal shrine is a shrine owned by individuals and these shrines can be found in personal rooms, parlour, farm or any other place where the owners may deem fit. All the divinities (*Orisa*) belong to the individual as well as to the community, and their shrines are found in many communities so as to serve communal advantages. Although the indigenous people in Nigeria are communalistic, there is nevertheless the individualistic dimension. As there are communal shrines, there are also shrines for families and individuals. None of the divinities worshipped at these shrines are solely to serve personal or collective advantages.

In Nigerian Indigenous Religious Tradition, the reality of the existence of the divinity is validated with the reality of the existence of natural phenomena. This explains why all the divinities by virtue of their extraordinariness are invisible and so, they are represented and associated with natural objects. For example, Ogun is associated with iron or stone, while Osun is associated with a spring or flowing river and *Obatala* with purity.

Sacred/Profane dichotomy

In view of the imperative of the physical in the validation of spiritual realities, the sacred/profane dichotomy and the formation of shrines deserves critical analysis. The issue has always been concerned with an existence of two worlds which have nothing in common. It is about the categorization of object in place, space and time into the sacred and profane categories. The sacred implies that which is holy, separated, special and uncommon. This is what the Yoruba refer to as *òwò* (that which deserve special honour and careful handling and is also guided by taboos). The profane category is regarded to be those things which are general, common or mundane. This is what can be referred to as *sakala* (that which is of no spiritual essence or special relevance and can be handled anyhow and is not guided by taboo). The assumption is that the sacred/profane opposition is absolute, that it is systematically pervasive, and that it refers to things totally not aspectual.

The general understanding of scholars such as Mircea Eliade, Tylor, Frazer *et al.* writing on the distinction between the sacred and the profane is the basis for the phenomenology of religion. The conceptual blur becomes apparent given the problems of differentiation and categorization of phenomena into the sacred and profane domains. As Matthew Evans (2003) argues, the sacred is the key concept in the sociology of religion. Despite its importance and long pedigree, the concept remains under-conceptualized and the use of the sacred obscures meaning. Emile Durkheim in his *Elementary Forms of Religion* stressed the total otherness of the sacred and the profane and specifically denied that there is a continuum between the sacred and worldly evaluation.

What this implies is that the two realms are totally different orders. This assumption within the context of Nigerian Indigenous Religious Tradition is at best questionable. It is my thesis in this paper that in Nigerian indigenous religious traditions, the concept of the distinction between the profane and the sacred does not arise. I argue that the Nigeria universe is mainly sacred, therefore every place is a shrine and that every object has a material and spiritual reality and that there are no criteria with which the religious and nonreligious phenomena can be separated. To regard and categorize the universe into the sacred and profane is tantamount to reductionism which is alien to African cosmology. According to Evans (2003:36), we could probably blame the problem of sacred profane dichotomy on over-precision or simply on the vagaries of language. Within the context of Nigerian indigenous religious tradition, I propose in this chapter that what the priests and priestesses do is just to activate the objects and that the sacredness is already imbued in every object in space before the activation through specific cultural behaviour and ritual. I mean that, there is the non-tangible attributes of every object or space and the activation of the non-tangible attributes of objects on a landscape or space is what makes a place or an object a shrine. The activated "non-tangibles" in the attributes of natural objects is what can be referred to as life, energy, power, the divine or gods as the case may be. This is what makes it possible that a shrine can serve the role of intermediary, and provides access to the divine (Stephen Mellor 1992:10).

Humanity exists universally in a physical medium. The physical objects which are regarded as profane are means by which one may ritually come to terms with and control the spiritual forces of nature by creating and validating the divine world within the "real" world. Opposition does not imply "absolute heterogeneity" but on the contrary designate a particular kind of relation by virtue of which the two extremes are encompassed as a kind of totality, as the same order of facts (Evans 2003). Although some anthropologists have argued that the sacred/profane opposition as it derives from Durkheim is analytically unsound and overtly ethnocentric. One of the difficulties is that unlike the right/left presupposition the sacred/profane distinction is not always explicit.

At the beginning of the sacred and profane, Eliade makes the following assertion: the first possible definition of the sacred is that it is the opposite of the profane. In his description of the sacred space, he claims that it is an "irruption," a "break" in the homogeneity of the space - a revelation of Reality. Sacred space involves the discovery of a "fixed point" a centre patterned after mythic paradigm. By contrast profane space is neutral homogenous and a "relative" even "chaotic" and non-real. It is the meaningless vastness of the temporal domain, devoid of any true order or ontological orientation, and always threatened by "non-being." In this passage, Eliade constructs a model of the sacred/profane opposition, which reflects the cosmology of many traditional societies, yet it will be mistaken to take precisely this form of presupposition as universal archetype.

Physical, spiritual and the formation of shrine

Despite the apparently pervasive presence of the mysterious in all physical objects and space, the reality of the spiritual and the interconnectedness between the spiritual and physical is still a subject of debate in academic discourse. The ontological and epistemological issue regarding the debate on the reality of the spiritual does not pose any puzzle in Nigerian Indigenous Religious Tradition. The spiritual cannot exist *in vacuo* of the physical. What I mean by this is, if the physical does not exist, the spiritual cannot be conceived. So in the formation of a shrine, the physical objects are coupled with music, invocation and incantation so much that the divine or spiritual assumes the physical and a shrine is formed. By inference, it is logical that unlike Eliade's assertion spiritual reality also belongs to our world. The process and movement of the transformation of the physical "profane" to the spiritual sacred is what I call the liminal stage. The question that is compelling here is what is the status of the shrine objects before the sacralization or before it becomes sacred. To attempt an answer to this question, it moves us into a difficult and conceptual domain. That is the problem of language as means of differentiation. It could have been for the sake of convenience of language that differences are made between the shrines' objects and space before they are sacralized. Sacralization, in this chapter, I regard as metaphysical awakening of matter, which is a process of bringing the gods into physical reality. So, reality itself is the fusion of physical and the spiritual. Suzanne Wenger captures it this way:

> The modern physicists' symbolic approach to the mystery of being manifest itself in their formula of the equivalence of mass and energy or the

equivalence of gravitation and inertia, which are subatomic phenomenon. (1983:84)

Whatever is physical as space and material objects in the shrine have the double attributes of being divine and physical. Though they are symbolic, they are also expressions of spiritual reality. The symbols themselves touch and exhilarate centres of life beyond the reach of vocabularies of reason and coercion.

Osun and Osogbo, Nigeria

Osogbo, Osun Osogbo and Osun shrine are almost synonymous. According to Yoruba tradition as in *Ifa* Ose'tura:

Kohunkoro Awo Ewi nle Ado
Orun mu dede kanle Awo ode Ijesa
Alakan ni nbe lodo ni n te iye aakara pepepe
Awon ni nwon difa fun igba Irunmole ojukotun
A bu fun igba Irunmole Ojukosi

Kohunkoro the diviner of the King of Ado
Orun mu dede kanle the diviner of Ijesa town
It was crabs that were inside the river
And were mark as if they are doing divination
Performed *Ifa* divination for 200 divinities of Ojukotun town.
And another 200 divinities of Ojukosi town.

The life of the gods became miserable and their authority was broken down because of the neglect of *Osun*, but their authority was restored when Osun was admitted into their council. Thus, *Osun* possesses so much power that she positively influences the activities of the gods. She is therefore indispensable in the day to day activities of the divinities in heaven and on earth. Among all the divinities, *Osun* is the Iyalode representing the potent but hidden power of womanhood in the control of the Yoruba universe.
The holy *odu Ogunda 'se* establishes this:

Kube kube oke Ijero
Ajalu winwin
Eni a gbola fun lola nye
A dia fun Osun seegesi oniko olorun
Kubekube oke Ijero
Ajalu winwin

Whoever is given honour deserves it
Performed *Ifa* divination for *Osun seegesi*
Who has entourage from heaven.

According to this odu, in *Osun* dwells the energy of femininity, beauty and fecundity. She is symbolized in *Omi* (water), which is life, *Ota Osun* (small and strong stone from Osun river), *Ide* (brass), and *Edan* (symbol of authority in Yoruba theocratic system). She does not go out alone; she goes with *Iko* (entourage) which signifies her kingly position. Hence for everywhere she goes, she goes with *Edan*; her symbol of authority. *Edan* can be regarded as maze; it is the symbol of sovereignty of a king. This explains why for every Osun festival, there is always *Edan* which serves as insight to the authority of Osun in Osogbo land. The king of the city, *Ataoja*, as in all Yoruba community of south-western Nigeria is the *Alase ekeji Orisa* which means representative of the gods, or one whose authority is derived from the gods. The testimony of the Iya Osun lends credence to this. She claims that the supreme ruler in Osogbo is Osun and that the *Ataoja* is the Deputy. The *Ataoja* derives his authority from Osun. By implication the gods are the rulers of the people while the kings are representatives of the gods. Olupona (2001) captures this succinctly in his assertion that the sacred kingship in Osogbo derives its source from *Orisa Osun* as exemplified in the Osun festival drummers' rhythm that Osun is the king and the eldest.

According to the Odu Ogbe Alara, it was *Osun* who rescued the people of Osogbo when their lives became miserable. In the dangerous times of tribal wars, Osogbo gave a home to refugees from every direction. When the Fulani war was coming from Ilorin, it is believed that it was *Osun* who stopped the war from entering Osogbo. This is the basis for which the people of Osogbo handed over their lives to Osun as a precondition for them to enjoy the privilege of her blessing, protection and peace. This is how the annual Osun festival was instituted. It is impossible to conceive of a year when the Osun festival will not be celebrated in Osogbo. Respondents reinforced this position by claiming that it was *Osun* who helped Osogbo to become the capital of Osun State. The development that Osogbo is experiencing today has been attributed to the benevolence of *Osun*:

> *Panduku oju ina*
> *A benu gbooro*
> *Lo difa fun Osun*
> *Ti n lo re e tun Ilu Osogbo se*
> *Ni'jo ti ilu Osogbo fo bi igba*
> *To ya peere bi aso*
>
> *Panduku oju ina*
> *A benu gbooro*
> Performed *Ifa* divination for Osun
> When she was going to reform Osogbo town
> When Osogbo broke like calabash
> When it tore like cloth

This can be adduced as the reason why it is not surprising to find a close connection between Osun shrine and the rulership of the people of Osogbo. The *Aworo Osun* asserted that the shrine is itself a palace and in fact, it is the first palace. The isolation of secular activities from religious ones makes little or no sense in a place where spirits' shrines are central to most activities of community life and the separation of the secular.

Osun shrine

It was observed that Osun shrine is the traditional religious and political centre as well as the cathedral of traditional religion in Osogbo, the capital of Osun State, South Western Nigeria. It is a well structured, clearly delimited space regarded as the concentration of the reality of *Osun* and other divinities. Though the shrine is in Osogbo land, the people do not claim that it is their personal property. Devotees of all states and nationalities come to Osun Osogbo shrine for religious pilgrimage and for meditation. It also serves as a sight for private as well as public rituals. The area where the shrine is located houses many of the Yoruba *Orisa* such as *Ogun, Egbe, Sango, Obaluaye, Iya Moopo* and many others. Osun shrine, therefore, embodies many of the *Orisa*. The theme that runs through the book *Osun Across the Waters* that although *Osun*'s shrine is located in Osogbo and as one of the most important pilgrimage centres of all *Osun* devotees and adherents of traditional religion, the Osun river flows round many parts of the world in her own way. Rowland Abiodun (2001:10) in his contribution to the same book made this explicit. The Osun water flows from Igede Ekiti to Ijesa land and to Osogbo and many other parts of Yoruba land to the Caribbean, Latin America and North America. The question that is imperative in the sacred/profane dichotomy is, was Osun sacred or did the river, groove and the surroundings posses the sacred and spiritual qualities only after the experience of Laroye and Timehin, the first progenitors of Osogbo land?

To clarify this pertinent question and issue, it is important for us to state the antecedent of the shrine. It was the shortage of water at Ipole, few kilometres from Osogbo that led Laroye, Timehin and their hunting cohort to the holy land. When they got to the holy land, they saw the need to settle there awhile as they needed to pitch their tent where there would be enough water. They did not recognize the sacredness of the spot. They fell a huge tree and the noise was very disturbing (Beier 1975) and the ghosts in the forest were displeased and they started to complain bitterly thus: *Oso igbo n binu o, gbogbo ikoko aro o mi le ti fo tan* (the forces in the forest are angry, you have broken all my pots for indigo dyeing). The *oso*, forces or ghost, were already in the forest before Laroye and Timehin got there. By implication, there was already sacredness in the forest as the place was already a place of awe and wonder before their infiltration. All venerable mountains, rivers, forests, stone, trees and other shrines in Nigeria were already shrines before humans encounter them.

Everything in nature and space symbolizes support and in fact the symbol of true humanness is expressed thus: *eniyan lasoo mi* (humans are my cloth). From pounded yam to land, farm, trees, the sky, mountains and rocks to land *ile ogere a foko yeri* (land ogere which uses hoes to decorate its head) are themselves objects used for a shrine, junctions, entrances and others are shrines and objects of shrine in their own right since they all have the "otherness." Broom is one of the important paraphernalia in *Obaluaye*'s shrine; this is because *Obaluaye* which western scholarship refers to as god of small pox is also the god of cleanliness. The fact that pounded yam is the king of all foods and that it is white in colour makes it a true symbol of *Obatala*. This is because *Obatala* is regarded as the supreme *Orisa* and the true symbol of all purity. According to Suzanne Wenger (1983:89), "white is the sacred sum of all colours in light."

The unusual noise of owl, mouse, cat and barking of dog strikes the Nigerian person as divine directive or divine information. For example, among the Yoruba, if a dog cries especially at night, it is sounding the warning of impending death. If somebody is sick and a cat is carried close to him/her, and the cat does not run away, the cat is giving message that the person will soon be well and he will not die as a result of the sickness. If the cat should run away, it means the person will die. Lightening, storm and wind, when a river overflows its bound, if a big tree suddenly fell or dried up, all give impression of the reality of the spiritual within the physical and the reality is one and the same. This is what Henry Sawyer (1968:150) refers to as "presence of presences within Nature." Similarly trees which are unusually big and difficult to cut and rocks of peculiar shapes and sizes, high mountain, yam and other farm produce in Nigerian indigenous religious traditions are vivid evidences of the presence of the spiritual and the physical which constitute reality. Seideltz (2002:44) quoting Larson, Sawyer, and McCollough (1998:30) in his attempt to define the sacred claims that it is a socially influenced perception of either some divine being or some sense of the ultimate reality of truth. This is what James (1992:152) calls "religious experience." Thus shrine is a landscape, which embodies the reality of the supernatural because of the inherent spiritual reality in the physical reality. This is what Suzanne Wenger (1983:62) refers to as "metaphysical awakening of matter." This goes a long way to prove the fact that shrine embody the fusion of the natural and the supernatural. A shrine, therefore, is a place where objects in nature or in space are combined in a systemic manner, to express the reality of the divine in nature, accord the divine their deserved veneration and seek the faces of the divine for guidance and control. This reinforces more vigorously the fact that the reality of the physical is the reality of the spiritual and that they interact. It can also be deduced here that the active forces in everything in nature and in space are within, and these active forces are the divine, spirits or gods. There is the transcendental dimension of all earthly being and matter. There is also the transformation of physical to spiritual and the spiritual to physical, this is continuity and eternity in Nigerian Indigenous Religious Tradition.

It is therefore acceptable to say that everywhere is a shrine within the context of Nigerian indigenous religious tradition. Given the name *oju-ibo*, it implies that everything in land and space are venerable. Since people will not worship everything at the same time, some things in nature which are representational of other things not combined are combined in a systematic manner. A centre is landscaped in a community, a place is earmarked in a room, parlour or compound where the people offer sacrifice, venerate the divine and seek its face for favour. It was observed during the course of my investigation that one of the factors responsible for this is the inherent eagerness of humans to identify with the divine through the stimulation of human spiritual components.

From the indigenous religious paradigms, at every junction and entrance of a town, there is supposed to be a shrine for *Esu* and *Obaluaye* as they help to ward off evil as well as war and diseases. At the entrance, outskirt and four corners of most cities, villages and community centre of a compound, and in fact, houses rooms and parlour in Nigeria, especially the Yoruba of South-western Nigeria, there are always shrines. According to a respondent in Osogbo, it implies that every object in space is sacred and every place is a shrine. This explains why the name for collective name gods, *Orisa* or that which inhabit Nigerian universe is *Irunmole* (the innumerable beings that inhabit the universe). This explains why it is not possible to conceive of any place or object in Nigerian indigenous religious tradition as simply profane or mundane.

References

Colpe and Casten, "Sacred and the Profane," translated from German by Reussel M. Stockman. In *The Encyclopaedia of Religion*, ed. Mircea Eliade. XI-XII 1993: 511-526.

Dike, Tony, "Tension in Enugu As Youth Destroy Shrine," *Vanguard*, January 5. 2005

Durkheim, Emile.. *The Elementary Forms of Religious Life*. New York: Free Press. 1965

Edu, O.K. "The Effect of Customary Arbitral Award on Substantive Litigation. Setting Matter Straight," *Journal of Private and Property Law* 25 (2004)

Eliade, Mircea. *The Sacred and Profane*. Translated by William Trask. New York: Harcourt Bruce & Co. 1959.

Evans, Matthew T. "The Sacred: Differentiating, Clarifying and Extending Concept." *Review of Religious Research* 45 (1) . (2003): 32-47.

Field, David N., "Ecology, Modernity and the New South African: Theology of Eco-justice." *Journal of Christian Thought* 2 (1) 199: 44-48.

Laduke, Betty. "Susanne Wenger and Nigeria's Sacred Osun Grove." *Women's Arts Journal* 10 (1) (1989): 7-21.

Masuzawa, Tomoko. "The Sacred Differences in the Elementary Form: On Durkheim last Quest." *Representation*, No . 23 (1988):25-50.

Mellon, Stephen P. "The Exhibition and Conservation of African Objects: Considering the Nontangibles." *Journal of the American Institute for conservation* 31 (1) (1992): 1-8.

Milner Jr., Murray. "Status and Sacredness: Worship and Salvation as Forms of Status Transformation." *Journal of the Scientific Study of Religion* 33 (2) 1994 : .99-109.

Oba, Abdulmumini A. "Juju Oaths in Customary Law Arbitration and Their Legal Validity in Nigerian Courts." *Journal of African Law* 52 (1) 2008, : 138-158.

Olupona J.K.. "Orisa Osun: Yoruba Sacred kingship and Civil Religion in Osogbo, Nigeria." In *Osun Across the Waters: A Yoruba Goddess in Africa and the Americas*, eds. Joseph M. Murphy and Mei-Mei Sanford, Bloomington: Indiana University Press:): 46-67.

Parish, Jane. "Antiwitchcraft Shrine Among the Akan: Possession and the Gathering." *African Studies Review* 46 (3) 2003,: 17-34.

Ray, Benjamin. "Sacred Space and Royal Shrines in Bugunda." *History of Religion* 16 (4):1977.: 363-373.: Rowland, Abiodun "Hidden Power: Osun the Seventeenth Odu." In *Osun Across the Waters: A Yoruba Goddess in Africa and the Americas*, eds. Joseph M. Murphy and Mei-Mei Sanford(Bloomington: Indiana University Press) 2001: 10-24..

Sawyer, Harry. The Practice of the Presence. *Numen* 15 1968. : 142-161.

Seidlitz, Larry et al.. "Development of the Spiritual Transcendent Index." *Journal for the Scientific Study of Religion* 41(3) 2002:: 439–453.

Shinner, Larry E. "Sacred Space, Profane Space, Human Space." *Journal of the American Academy of Religion* 40 (4) 1972.: 425-436.

Simon Ottenberg. "Personal Shrine at Afikpo." *Ethnology* 9 (1) (1970): 26-51.

Stark, Rodney and Roger Finke.. *Acts of Faith: Explaining the Human Side of Religion* (Berkeley: University of California Press) 2000

Stark, Rodney and William Bainbridge. *A Theory of Religion*.(New Brunswick, NJ: Rutgers University) 1996.

Steven, Stanley, ed.. *Conservation Through Cultural Survival: Indigenous People and Protected Area*. Washington, DC: Island Press) 1997

Ulli, Beier.. *The Return of the Gods: The Sacred Arts of Susanne Wenger* (Cambridge: Cambridge University Press) 1975

Uwakwe, Abugu.. "Benin Monarch Invokes the Gods Against Crime in Edo." *Daily Independent*, September 23. 2005

Wenger, Susanne and Gert Chesi.. *The Sacred Grove of Osogbo* Korneuburg, (Austria: Ueberreuter Offserbruck Korneuburg) 1990

Wenger, Susanne and Gert Chesi.. *A Life with the Gods in their Yoruba Homeland*. Worgl, Austria: Perlinger, 1985

William, James. *Varieties of Religious Experience: A Study in Human Nature*. 9 New York: Penguin Book) 1982.

Wolff, Norma H. and Michael Warren, The Agbeni Shango Shrine in Ibadan: A Century of Continuity. *African Arts* vol. 31 (3)(1998): 36-49, 94.

9

Power, secret knowledge, and secret societies

- Ibigbolade Simon Aderibigbe & Danoye Oguntola-Laguda

Introduction

The importance and relevance of secret societies in the socio-political and economic culture of Nigerian indigenous religious traditions cannot be overemphasized. These societies are exclusive and restricted to initiates who seek esoteric knowledge of the mundane and transcendental world. In practical terms, it could be said that the way of the secret society is a way of life that reflects one invisible tradition that has existed on earth for years. In the search for knowledge, secret societies become imperative, and through the use of acquired knowledge, members seek power so as to influence the social economic and political situations in their environment. The source of power in African philosophy is not exercised only through politics, but also through esoteric means that have transcendental value. In the opinion of Stephen Ellis and Gerrie ter Haar "the belief that real effective power is exercised in secret is particularly strong" (2005: 84). This will suggest that membership of secret societies in Nigerian religious space has direct relationship to the acquisition and exercise of power.

There are various types of secret societies ranging from indigenous to imported. There are also reformed groups who are "*refined*" models of the aboriginal groups. This chapter will mainly examine the relation between power and secret societies in Nigeria in general and Yorùbáland in particular. We shall further attempt a typology and classification of the types of secret societies in relation to their functions and relevance to the social dynamics of religious, political, and economic power sharing in the Nigerian society.

Power and secret societies

Power and the struggle towards acquiring it, has become intensely global. This quest for power is primarily because of the urge in man to seek to control his environment and the resources therein. Also the value attached to power and the use to which it is often put has made it "*compelling*". Millions of people are reported to have been killed, maimed or assassinated by those struggling to acquire power in Nigeria, Kenya, Sudan, Liberia, and Iraq, to name just a few.

Bertrand Russell regarded power as "the fundamental concept in social science, in the same sense in which energy is a fundamental concept in physics" (1938, 1). Max Weber also describes power and the struggle for its acquisition as:

> The probability that one actor within a social relationship will be in a position to carry out his own despite resistance; regardless of the basis on which this probability rest. (1968, 406)

The definitions of Russell and Weber suggest that power is a necessity in the society. However, to acquire power man must go beyond himself and seek interaction with his *"neighbours"* and transcendental realities. In politics for example, the struggle for power has made it imperative for those in leadership to make interaction with the constituents. Burns explains power as a process. He writes:

> Power is a process in which power holders possessing certain motives and goals have the capacity to secure changes in the behaviour of a respondent (human or animal and in the environment) by utilizing including factors of skill, relative to the target of their power wielding and necessary to secure changes. (1978, 120)

From Burns's explanation we observe that the motive of the power seeker gives impetus to the interaction between him/her and the source of power. These motives could include: wielding power, recognition, prestige, pride, glory, social control, spiritual control and economic relevance.

Writing about the Yoruba people in Nigeria, Bolaji Idowu opines that Ogboni, a major secret society, is formed in all probability to protect the indigenous institutions of the people from annihilation: "It must have been originally an exclusive organization limited to the original owners of the land" (1996, 22). J.O. Awolalu and P. A. Dopamu claim that the secret societies earned their name because of the toga of secrecy. The memberships are restricted and the groups engage in mysterious activities (Awolalu and Dopamu 2005, 243). Since the memberships of secret societies are restricted, their activities are subject to speculations. While some claim that their activities have positive impact on the growth and development of the society, others claim that their functions are evil and retrogressive.

In the opinion of Laguda, a secret society refers to an association or organization, which has element of mysteries and secrecy in its operations (2003:120). These groups enter into pacts to cooperate through thick and thin for the achievement of their purposes and to make sure that no members betray each other (Idowu 1996, 157). Social lives of members are governed by the tenets and ethical codes of these groups. In Nigeria, most secret societies have religious origin and background whence they acquire their reverence, relevance and values. As we shall see later, there are secret societies in Nigeria that only seek knowledge about the transcendental world promising their member esoteric acquisition of knowledge that will engender power. Ellis and ter Haar observe that secret societies in Nigerian religious landscape are very popular even among political and educated elites. The members get initiated in search of knowledge and power by keeping information within a small-circle of people with a good quantum of spirituality and spiritual flavour. Some of these groups like the Rosicrucian, ARMOC, Freemason, Sheperdhill are imported, while others like Ogboni, Amukala, Mmuo, Ekpe are indigenous (Ellis and ter Haar 2005, 76). They further posit that some members of secret societies are also Christians and Muslims. Former Head of State, Olusegun Obasanjo (1999-2007) is a Christian of Baptist Mission (denomination) and also a rumoured member of Ogboni and Osugbo in his hometown, Abeokuta. Bola Ige, a former Minister of Justice during Obasanjo's first term (1999-2003) was a member of Rosicrucian, the same group, to which his mentor and one of the prominent Nigerian political nationalists, Obafemi Awolowo, also belonged.

The members, apart from the search for knowledge and power, also seek to deploy the acquired knowledge and power. This arguably is best done in secret. As earlier mentioned, Ellis and ter Haar are strong advocates of the thesis that effective power is exercised in secret. They relied on the theory of Weber that "all powers are more effectively exercised in secret than in public (1954, 334). These authors underscored the importance and value of secrecy also quoted George Simmel. He writes that:

> The secret offers the possibility of a second world alongside the manifest world...and it is perhaps one of man's greatest achievements. (1996, 330)

From the theories of Weber and Simmel, Ellis and ter Haar posit that power is always related to the control and restriction of information. Thus, the concept of secrecy implies exclusive control over types of knowledge that are not to be shared by all and sundry (Ellis and ter Haar 2004, 84). R.J. Gehman also states, that mystical powers are beyond our mundane comprehension. They are powers from unseen and unexplained sources. These are the powers of witchcraft, magic and sorcery (Gehman 2001, 43). Therefore, the relationship between religion and power and secrecy as embedded in the nature and scope of secret societies cannot be over-emphasized.

Our discussion so far has shown that the search for power and esoteric knowledge may be the major factors responsible for the quest for membership of secret societies in Nigerian religious landscape. As we mentioned earlier, membership of these groups cut across all religious traditions. In Nigerian Indigenous Religious Tradition, they are more prominent. The Yoruba, Igbo, Efik, Ibibio, Nupe, Ijaw, Idoma and Tiv have various secret societies, which have specific social, political, economic and cultural functions. These groups are not anti-social. They essentially partake in traditional religious rites and rituals as part of societal dynamics for the well being of members and, arguably the general society.

Types of secret societies

Types of secret societies in Nigerian religious space could be broadly categorized into two: the indigenous and the imported groups. The former are of traditional origin and they are backed by spiritual and mystical power inherent in the traditional religion of the people. The latter are Western and Asiatic in orientation. They open initiates to new knowledge, power and influence that transcend the mundane. In fact those that belong to the former group are prone to the use of magic, medicine and sorcery.

Awolalu and Dopamu identified three types of secret societies among the people of West Africa. The first and major one is *religious secret societies*. These societies are attached to the worship of a divinity or spirit. They are also concerned with the cult of the dead-masquerades (these groups are common in Nigeria, among the Yoruba, Efik, Ibibio, Nupe, Ijaw as well as the Igbo). Because of their affinity to the cult of the ancestor, they feature prominently at funerals and memorial ceremonies. They also emphasize the use of magic and medicine associated with traditional healing. For example, the religious secret societies in Yorubaland like *Eyo, Egungun, Gelede Agemo* are attached to socio-cultural festivals, which are occasions for rejoicing when masked "spirits" come out from the spiritual world to perform rituals. The second type identified by Awolalu and Dopamu are the secret societies with socio-cultural functions. These could also be found in Yorubaland and Efik, located in the *Osugbo* and *Ekpe* societies, respectively. In fact these two groups played prominent roles when the king and his lieutenants were crowned. Some like Ogboni in Egbaland are attached to puberty rites for male child. Such children are initiated when they reach puberty (between ages 10 to 12 years). Members are initiated and trained in tribal customs, religion, morality, and endurance, among other virtues. The rituals attached to the initiation are mainly to prepare the initiates for the rigour of adulthood and social responsibility.

The last groups are those referred to as anti-social groups. They are considered to be highly cannibalistic. Not much is known about their activities, but they are held in awe by members of the society (Awolalu and Dopamu 2006, 245-247). The group includes societies of witches and wizards. They are classified in Yoruba traditional society as possessing esoteric power that can wreak havoc on the society and perceived enemies.

The classification by Awolalu and Dopamu creates some questions. These include the issue of cannibalism, which is often assumed. In fact it is often said that the Oro (the Oro secret society, usually regarded as traditional cultic police, is found in different forms in most parts of Yoruba land)[1] group in

---

[1] The cultic activities are performed in the middle of the night and are forbidden to be witnessed by women and the non-initiates.

Yorubaland kill and consume their victims, who are mostly non-initiates that refuse to abide by the restrictions placed on the society and community during socio-cultural, political and economic rituals and festivals. There is a popular dictum among Yoruba people that *a kii ri ajeku Oro* (we do not see the victims of Oro). This does not imply that the Oro groups are carnivorous or cannibalistic. On the contrary the Oro group sentences their victims to death with the authority of political leadership, the king. This classification of Awolalu and Dopamu only points to the traditional religious based secret societies. There are as identified by Ellis and ter Haar imported secret societies like the Rosicrucian, AMORC, as well as freemason among others. Our study of the secret societies among the Yoruba Efik and Igbo of Nigeria has shown that the broad categorization could further be subdivided. It is in pursuance of this proposition that we propose the following classifications.

Classification of Secret Societies among Yoruba, Efik and Igbo

Traditional Groups	Imported Groups	Syncretic Groups
Amukala Awo opa Eyo Egungun Igunko Gelede Osugbo Ogboni Ekpe – (Efik and Ibibio) Mmuo – (Igbo) Maun – (Igbo)	Freemason Rosicrucian AMORC Temple Solaitre Sheperdhill	Eckankar Reformed Ogboni Fraternity (ROF) Ijo Orunmila Godianism (Igbo)

The three broad categories are not enough to appreciate the dynamics of secret societies among the people. There is need for a sub-categorization that will demonstrate the functions of the groups. Within the traditional groups we have social cultural, socio-political, and religious groups. Their functions and relevance could be interwoven but they could be mutually exclusive.

Traditional groups

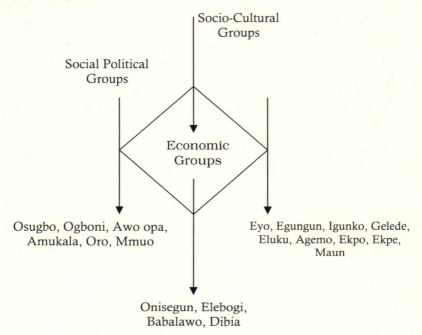

From the diagram above, all the subgroups are religious and lay claim to sacredness. In fact, they adopt one deity as the group divinity. The Ogboni group adopts *Onile* as their deity. This is represented symbolically, by bronze carving with male and female face in both sides known as *Edan*. The worship of *Onile* is akin to the worship of *Orunmila* in Yoruba pantheon. The Osugbo carries, during public procession, what is known as *Ogbo*. This is the object of worship of this group. All the groups engage in the worship of *Ogun* (god of iron), *Orunmila* (wisdom divinity), *Obatala* (arch divinity), Esu (bailiff of god) and *Ile* (mother-earth). All these, are primordial divinities in Yoruba pantheon. The socio-political groups are engaged in the traditional politics of the land. In fact, in Egbaland, Lagos, Ijebuland a well as Ile-Ife, the *Osugbo* play significant roles in the selection and coronation process of a king. They also constitute spiritual advisers to the king.

The socio-cultural groups are attached to festivals. These festivals could be annual or bi-monthly. Some are even weekly. The Egungun festival among the Yoruba is often celebrated annually. During *Ojo ose* (the first day of the week) prayers are offered for the well being of members, and the community as a whole after the prayers in *Igbale* (*Egungun* shrine) one masquerade will be masked and go round the town as a mark of celebration. The *Eyo* festival in Lagos is not fixed for any time but it is attached to the funeral and burial rituals of kings and other prominent indigenes of the town. Therefore the masquerades, which are masked in, white robes, *Opambata* (a staff) and beautiful head dresses go about town for ritual purposes. It should be noted that many of the traditional groups, discussed above are sometimes interconnected and may carry out activities that mutually benefit members, although rivalry and struggle for supremacy may sometimes jeopardize comradeship and set off bitter inter group 'warfare.' In fact individuals can belong to as many groups as possible. This is considered to be a mark of respect and honour. The religious groups are not many. In fact, Oro group is the most prominent of the groups (Laguda 2003: 123). However, all the traditional groups have religious orientation and are considered sacred.

The imported secret societies are highly civil and have the attributes and nature of Gnosticism in their quest for esoteric knowledge and power, which are beyond the immediate comprehension of man. The syncretic groups are purely reformative. In fact, they tend to modernize the tenets and ethics of the traditional and some imported groups. A typical example is Reformed Ogboni Fraternity (ROF), which is a blend of the tenets, beliefs and ethics of the Ogboni and the freemasons. In the opinion of Bolaji Idowu (1996:157), "ROF started in order to reform the masquerading exterior of the Ogboni (Osugbo)." The word 'reformed' was adopted as a prefix to remove the often-vexed opinion that all Yoruba cultic groups are agents of the devil. *Ijo Orunmila*, and Godianism are admixtures of Yoruba traditional religion and Christianity, and Gnosticism and Christianity respectively.

We observe in the course of this research that all the secret societies bind their members to secrecy through an oath and covenant relationship with a particular divinity. Death and hardship are often proposed as punishment for divulging the secrets of the group to non-initiates that seek such information. Thus, the secret societies give room for rumour to thrive about their activities since they are not open to investigation and research.

Functions of secret societies

Secret societies in Nigeria generally set out to preserve and protect the indigenous institutions of the land from annihilation (Idowu 1996, 22). This function seems to be the paramount socio-cultural function of the group, especially the traditional groups. They determine ritual behaviour and regulate social attitude. Therefore, they protect the sacredness of the religion of their forbearers. Also they protect and support the political leaders in the land. In Yorubaland members of Osugbo/Ogboni take active role in the administration of the kingdom (Laguda 2003:120) because they are the custodian of ancestry, ancient civilization and liturgy as well as theology of the people. Therefore, administration of justice, formulation of legislation and execution of judicial pronouncements are part of their duties.

At the individual level, membership of a secret society boosts the psychological well being of initiates. Being a member increases social status and value of members. In fact among the Efik and Ibibio to belong to Ekpe and Ekpo societies is considered elitist and it could be a license to secure government favour in relation to business and economic gratification. In Yorubaland, membership of Osugbo enhances the social status of individuals. Our study has shown that in Yorubaland, you could belong to as many secret societies as possible; the more the number, the better the social and traditional relevance of the individual in the society.

Secret societies give ethical trainings to initiates. In fact, they teach social sympathy, communal existence, courage and marital responsibilities. This is common among the Efik and Ibibio. The ladies are initiated into the "fattening room," an exclusive group for women. In Egbaland (Yoruba) a boy of 10 years old must be initiated into the Osugbo society to show that he has come of age.

The introduction of imported secret societies into Nigerian religious space has changed the attitude of the people towards membership and initiation to traditional secret societies. The imported societies came with the promise of esoteric knowledge and mysterious power that are beyond the ordinary, thereby making membership a privilege for those of superior intelligence. Memberships are open initially to educated elites in the society. Therefore, members occupy prominent and viable offices in economy, politics, social and judicial institutions. Therefore, members of same group(s) are favoured in making decisions and also in judicial judgments and pronouncements. This situation encourages many people in the country to secure initiation into secret societies. Also the claim that secret societies give opportunity for spiritual development and acquisition of magical power(s) has also been a driving force towards increase in membership. In the traditional group, we observed it was evident that members are knowledgeable in the art of magic and healing process. They use this knowledge to assist new initiates and also to introduce them to the art. This forms a sort of employment opportunity especially with the growing value of traditional medicine(s) both herbal and metaphysical. They claim to be capable of preparing charms, which could be worn to interviews to secure jobs. Also some forms of liquids may be prepared and given to the client to lick so that whatever words spoken become potent and the addressed would act as directed. In addition charms are prepared for businessmen and woman to promote extraordinary dividends in trade flow or securing of contracts. While it may be difficult to subject these claims to empirical verification, the fact of the sheer number of people who believe in them and therefore become willing members attest to the visibility and popularity of the practices.

From the above functions of secret societies in Nigeria, the impact of the group(s) on the psyche, empowerment, social security and upward mobility is significantly indicative. Membership of secret societies is a major boost to social and economic status of individuals. In fact political appointment could be secured through this means. Initiates also feel secured in terms of social security based on the new "power" acquisition in magic and herbs. As for justice and equity, secret societies' membership does not guarantee this, but provide bias latitude for members to violate judicial process with the belief that the judgment will always be in their favour. There was a time (1950-1979) when law enforcement officers and judicial officers in Nigeria were "mostly" members of secret societies. Although with government pronouncement against it in the latter part of this period, there has been a preserved reduction in the membership and influence(s) of secrete societies-at least publicly

Final reflections

Our preoccupation in this paper has been to establish the inter-play between secret societies in Nigerian religious space and the quest for and use of power by individuals through the agency of group dynamics. In this regard, we observe that apart from social, religious, political and economic motives for wanting to be initiated into secret societies, Nigerians also wish to obtain power with esoteric values. This power is often used in secrecy. This perhaps makes the secret societies not only a source of power but also an avenue for exercising such power. In the early days of Nigerian Independence, it was a popular claim that all decisions and policies of government were first discussed in meeting place(s) of secret societies before they were made known to the populace. In fact indigenous, imported as well as the reformed secret societies became very paramount during this period. Membership was a source of pride and formed a basic key to political relevance, economic success and social status.

It should be noted however that in recent times the role of secret societies has witnessed a downturn. Nigerians now embrace imported religions (Christianity and Islam) to the detriment of the indigenous religion of their forbears. These religions have condemned the activities and membership of secret societies. Thus, their adherents who are still members cannot boast of it. Apart from this, government pronouncement on the ban on secret societies among civil servants dealt a major blow to the growth and relevance of the secret societies. Further, the traditional institutions, such as Obaship and Chieftaincy have become subservient to civil authority. Thus the importance of the role secret societies play in such institutions has been reduced drastically. However, our study among the Yoruba, Efik and Ibibio has shown that secret societies are still in existence and their relevance acknowledged even though their functions have been reduced. The state government must approve some socio-cultural festivals such as *Eyo*, *Egungun* and *Igunko* among the Yoruba before they can be staged. Although the approval is mere academic as state governors have made it a "normal" procedure to invest public funds on sponsoring these festivals. The last Eyo festival staged in Lagos in August 2003, cost the Lagos state government about 20 million naira (Laguda 2003:8). The significance of this expenditure is the clear demonstration that secret societies engendered by our indigenous religious traditions are still relevant in the education and spiritual development as well as the sustenance of our cultural and spiritual values.

References

Awolalu J.O. and P.A. Dopamu, *West African Traditional Religion*, Revised Edition (Lagos: Macmillan). 2005.

Burns, J.M., *Leadership* (New York: Harper Torch Books) 1978.

Ellis S. and G. ter Haar, *Worlds of Power: Religious Thought and Political Practice in Africa* (London: Hurst and Company). 2004.

Gehman, R.J., *African Traditional Religion In The Light Of The Bible*. Bukuru, Plateau State, Nigeria: Africa Christian Textbooks. 2001.

Idowu, B., *Olodumare: God in Yoruba Belief* (Lagos: Longman) Revised and Enlarged Edition. 1996.

Laguda, Danoye-Oguntola , *Journal of Religious Studies* 4 (1) , 2003.

Rheinstein, M. (ed.). *Max Weber on Law in Economy and Society* (Cambridge, M.A Harvard University, Press) 1954

Russell, B., *Power: A New Social Analysis* (New York, Norton) 1938.

Simmel, G., *The Sociology of George Simmel* (New York: The Free Press)1964.

Weber M., *The Theory Of Social And Economic Organization* (New York: Macmillan).1968,

10

Vestiges of indigenous spirituality in the lives and experiences of Christian and Muslim religious founders and leaders

- Dorcas Olubanke Akintunde

Introduction

Christianity was brought into most of sub-Saharan Africa by missionaries from Western Europe and North America, especially in the nineteenth century. These missionaries generally tried to set up local congregations and church organisations along the lines of those they were familiar with in their home countries, but by the end of the nineteenth century many African Christians had formed independent denominations. Some tended to follow the pattern of church organization bequeathed to them by the missionaries, and their desire for independence of control by foreign missionaries was a reaction against the racism that came to the fore in the age of the new imperialism—roughly between 1870 and the beginning of the First World War (Cox 2001).

Most of the expansion of Christianity in Africa in the twentieth century, especially the latter half of the century, has been the result of the missionary efforts of the African Independent Churches (sometimes called African Instituted Churches, African Indigenous Churches, African Initiated Churches or African International Churches) (Anderson 2000:8). These sprouted out of the mainline Churches due to various factors, which will be highlighted in this work. What made them 'indigenous', 'independent', and 'African'? Analysing this question is the thrust of this chapter.

Missionary activities and African religion

Colonialism did not create space for the African culture. Western missionaries were largely negative about African culture and Africans were alienated from the gospel dressed up in European garb. The 'colonisers' did not recognise that African culture had its own wisdom, insights and values that informed the lives of Africans. Thus, the missionaries approach to Christianise Africans was based on coercion. They required Africans to renounce everything related to their religious beliefs to be a 'proper' Christian. Everything African in their perspective was evil, paganistic and heathen. The missionaries demonised most African beliefs and practices. Not only in this respect were Africans deprived of leadership opportunities in Christianity. This and other 'evil' towards African beliefs is succinctly described by Ezra Chitando:

> The demonisation of most African beliefs and practices by the missionaries also encouraged Africans to seek alternative havens of belonging. Lack of leadership opportunities, personal ambitions, theological controversies and other factors resulted in the rapid multiplication of AICs. (2004:117)

Chitando's submission is apt for other African countries generally and Nigeria in particular, that is, what operates in southern part of Africa, is relevant to the Nigerian situation. In some mainline churches in South Africa, Africans experienced racism, while many white Christians discriminated against blacks, and treated them as junior brothers or sisters (Chitando 2004:120). As a result of these experiences, they broke away from the mainline churches and developed a theology, which took into cognisance the African culture, and practices. In essence, they adapted Christian teaching and liturgy to indigenous cosmology and ways of worship, and they stressed expressive and emotional phenomena and cater to the strong fears of witchcraft among Africans. Thus, many founders of AICs appropriate indigenous traditions in their movements. They never abandoned their particular practices; they simply stopped practicing them within the boundaries of the missionary churches. They were forced to live with a dichotomy of minds and souls, which was the result of the attempt to supplant the core of their values of existence and beliefs with foreign ones. Chitando states further on this,

Africans by the 1920s had taken it upon themselves to couch the Christian message in African idiom. Rejecting the verdict of most foreign missionaries that African culture was heathen and in need of cleansing by the gospel, many founders of AICs actively sought to appropriate indigenous traditions in their movements. (Chitando 2004:120)

Despite the fact that most of these founders had little formal education, they succeeded in creative adaptation of African Traditional Religion, and the Christian message was radically transformed and interpreted. Some of these founders included Oshitelu,[1] Moses Orimolade (Cherubim and Seraphim),[2] Joseph Ayo Babalola and the Precious Stone Society (The Christ Apostolic Church),[3] Ijo Orile Ede Adulawo Ti Kristi (National Church of Christ) founded in 1919 by the Reverend Adeniran Oke in Ibadan (Ogungbile 2001). These founders cropped up as a natural development of the meeting of Christian

---

[1] Jehu-Appiah, Jerisdan H., An overview of indigenous African churches in Britain: an approach through the historical survey of African Pentecostalism. http://www.pctii.org/wcc/jehu95.html
[2] Cherubim & Seraphim Movement Church. http://www.csmovementchurchusa.org/
[3] Christ Apostolic Church Worldwide Network. History of Christ Apostolic Church. http://www.cacworldwide.net/history.asp

message with the cultures of the African people. And their preaching was basically on two themes: complete trust, dependence and reliance upon God; and the abandonment of fetish relics and practices. They preached that the fetishes were no longer necessary for a relationship with God, and in order to petition God. All that the deities were believed to do God could do for them, and do it better if people trusted in him only and avoided the double life they were used to as members of the historic churches. The wind of 'schism' also blew on these AICs some years after and another group evolved—the New Pentecostal Churches. What makes this group different from the AICs?

The new Pentecostal churches

In the early 1980s there was another splinter group from the AICs—the 'New Pentecostal Churches. While, AICs (Anderson 1992) have historical, theological and liturgical links with western Pentecostalism, this splinter group has none. It is necessary to distinguish between AICs and "new pentecostal" AICs. Like the AICs, they vary from small independent house churches to rapidly growing and vast church organisations. These are exemplified in the Deeper Life Church in Nigeria under William F. Kumuyi (Ojo 1992:135), Christ Life Church headed by Bishop Wale Oke, Winners Chapel, led by Bishop Oyedepo[4] and the Redeemed Christian Church of God, (RCCG) headed by Dr. Adeboye[5] among others. Membership of these churches is from both the European mission-founded churches and from the AICs, and this is sometimes a source of tension. There is a strong western Pentecostal influence in many of these churches both in liturgy and in leadership patterns, and North American neo-pentecostal evangelists are often promoted. The difference between these churches and churches of western Pentecostal origin is mainly in church government, which is entirely black and is more of a local, autonomous nature with no organisational links with Pentecostal denominations outside Africa. Founders are charismatic, younger men who are respected for their preaching and leadership abilities, and who are relatively well educated, though not necessarily in theology. The membership tends to consist of younger, more affluent and better-educated people. For example, Pastor Adeboye was a lecturer of applied mathematics at the University of Lagos, while Bishop Wale Oke is an alumnus of the University of Ibadan. These churches tend to oppose some traditional African practices as well as those of older AICs. They ban alcohol and tobacco, polygyny, the ancestor cult, the use of symbolic objects in healing rituals and the wearing of church uniforms. They are today probably the fastest growing expression of Christianity in Africa generally and Nigeria in particular and have exploded on the African religious scene in the past two decades. This is corroborated by Daniel Jordan Smith:

---

[4] David Oyedepo Ministries International Inc. http://www.davidoyedepoministries.org/
[5] The Redeemed Christian Church of God. http://www.rccg.org/

Pentecostalism is the religious denomination with the most adherence in the region, and it is evident everywhere. In the South it is rare to take a taxi, ride a bus, read a billboard, or buy a snack on the street, without coming upon a religious reference or proselytizing. (Paris 2006)

Religious specialists and the use of indigenous mediums

It is gratifying to note that despite the total reference to the Bible by both the AICs and the new pentecostal movements, there are elements of traditional practices in their worship and liturgy. Aylward Shorter vividly describes the indigenisation of the Christian Eucharist among the Beti people in Cameroon. This was the Ndzon Melen Eucharistic Rite, devised by Fr. P. C. Ngumu and Fr. P. Abega in 1969. According to him, the whole celebration was African in flavour and inspiration. It was very far from being a western celebration of the Roman rite, with a few African elements inserted. This was ensured, among other things, by continuous dance and African instrumental and vocal music. Many feast days, in all AICs including Sunday, function in this manner.

Bernard Mangematin used a form of traditional praise prayer known as *oriki* as a form of catechesis in the school curriculum (Shorter). The *oriki* is a form of prayer by which the Yoruba praise their gods in a manner that is in complete conformity with the culture. It is a poetic hymn, chanted in honour of an *orisa*, or divinity, or of an important person. It can be addressed to a divinity either in the privacy of an early morning offering or in regular cult meetings and festivals. It is a series of epithets or appellations addressed to the subject by the devotee, which is both expressive and efficacious. Not only does it encapsulate the essence of the subject, but also it enhances its presence. It empowers, it propitiates, and it augments the reputation of the subject. It strengthens the bond between praise-singer and subject and it spreads healing and harmony in the community.

The *oriki* is essentially oral, spontaneous and imaginative. It recruits ideas and images from a wide spectrum of sources, and appeals as much to the emotions as to the intellect. The *oriki* tradition is an aspect of the Yoruba cultural heritage, which unites Christians of every denomination, thus, the different *oriki* of God in worship, as exemplified in the wordings of a song by Prophetess Bola Are of the Christ Apostolic Church, Nigeria:

Baba, ku ise o, Baba,
Apata ayeraye,
Alade Wura,
Alagbara giga,
O gbe nu Wundia s'ola,
A ja kari aye,
Oba to n w'ese wa nu,
Oba to n gbe nii ga,
Oba to n wo igba arun,
Awogba arun ma gbe'je,
Olorun ayeraye,

Olorun Babalola
Kabiyesi, Olorun Orun,

Father, we appreciate you,
Eternal Rock of ages,
With the crown of Gold,
The Mighty One,
Who dwells in the womb of the Virgin,
Who reigns in all the earth,
He who cleanse us from sins,
The King who exalts,
The King who heals,
The King who heals without fulfilment of vows,
The Almighty,
The God of Babalola,
The King, and the God of Heaven.

In both the AICs and new Pentecostal assemblies, substantial time is devoted to worship session to exalt, adore and worship God. In African Traditional Religion, in the worship of the *orisas*, exaltation similarly precedes prayers of supplication. In addition to this, David Ogungbile notes the incorporation of indigenous elements in worship in the National Church of Christ in Nigeria:

> The Church accepts the use of traditional elements such as the kola nut, bitter kola, alligator pepper, salt, honey, and water for naming and marriage ceremonies. As a theocentric and sacred cosmos, the Yoruba consider these items to be sacred and ritual objects. In some other Churches there exists the separation of traditional and Church ceremonies. During the traditional ceremonies that precede Church ceremonies, the items can be used in the celebrants' homes. Ijo Adulawo combines the two, and members are made to include the items to be used for consecrating newborn babies and solemnizing marriages in the church itself (2001: 74).

The use of water in healing

Ogungbile, while alluding to the relevance of indigenous objects to healing in some AICs, makes the following statement concerning the use of water:

> This includes the drinking of consecrated water to cure certain ailments and diseases, sprinkling of holy water on certain places to bring fortune and prosperity, and the use of streams for ritual bath with soap and sponges as prescribed by the prophets and prophetesses. It should however, be stated that none of these methods is exclusive of the others. (1997: 99)

Healing by the religious leaders of the AICs also include "laying on hands" or prayer for the sick, this is usually accompanied by the use of various symbolic objects such ropes, staffs, papers, ash, blessed oil, candles, Easter palm branches, incense, scapula, medals, etc. These are thought to possess magical power that can affect an immediate cure or offer protection from evil spirits just like amulets from a traditional healer. The Christ Apostolic Church, however, rely on holy or blessed water, hence, the appellation, "*Ijo olomi tutu.*" Most of the songs are composed in line with this belief:

Jesu Olomi Iye re, o, Omi iye,
Oso mu ni be o ka sororo,
Aje mu nibe o ka sororo,
Emere mu nibe, o ka sororo,
Jesu Olomi iye re o, omi iye

Here comes Jesus, the One who heals with water of life,
People with familiar spirits (witches, wizards), etc., drink out of the water,
And they confess instantly.

The position of women

It is women who constitute the majority of members within AICs, new Pentecostal and they have been central in the emergence of the mission churches. Significantly, women participated freely in leading many of the rituals just like in African Traditional Religion, specifically in the worship of *Yemoja*, *Osun* and other goddesses. In most churches and ministries, women are viewed as valuable workers, as they often do the majority of the overall ministry. Yet not all agree on women's roles. Women are often restricted from certain areas of ministry within the church that have to do with speaking and leadership specifically in the AICs. However, the new Pentecostals allow for female pastors, and women teach and are not restricted from speaking at all during church services. Women sit in the governing bodies at the ward, state and general levels. Women influence the development of policy and curricula. The arguments of the AICs are based on the various interpretations of Paul's words regarding women's roles found in 1 Cor. 14:34-35 and 1 Tim. 2:11-3:7. The exegesis of these texts is not our focus in this work. In both the AICs and the new Pentecostals, children, youth and adults are taught every Sunday by women. They are taught gospel principles, scripture stories, values and morals. Women prophesied in the church assembly, and therefore probably also taught there. 1 Cor. 11:5 mention women praying and prophesying in public assembly, this is evidently the reference point for the churches.

Divination is the practice of foreseeing future events or discovering hidden knowledge through supernatural means. Today diviners use the method of questioning their patients, encouraging them to agree with him or her in deciphering the cause of illness and the hope of healing. This is not far fetched from the practices in AICs. These churches enjoy large patronage because of the issue of prophecy. Fear of the unknown always draws Africans generally, and Nigerians in particular, to search for God and to know what the future holds. Traditional healers are believed to heal their patients through the mediation of ancestors. They are said to depend on the promptings or revelations of the ancestors. It is believed that some illnesses are sent by the ancestors. Such ritual illnesses can only be cured by ritual performance. During the ritual performance, the use of the drum is said to be of utmost importance because the drum is seen as a medium of communication per excellence between the healer and the ancestors. Jesus as the healer par excellence is the core of the practices of AICs. The ability to see visions, to interpret dreams, and to heal is the major factors for the proliferation and spread of AICs.

Some AICs believe that some traditional objects aid the healing process. This is peculiar to the Cherubim and Seraphim and the Celestial Church of God as noted by Ogungbile. According to him, sponges/soap wash off misfortunes, while palm fronds are used to avert danger. Fruit, are prescribed in healing as communal sacrifices, as well as means of inviting blessings. Such fruits are coconut, orange, pawpaw, mango, banana, etc. Salt, honey, roasted ground corn, etc., are thought to invoke happiness and sweetness. Animals like hen, goat, sheep, etc., are sacrificed to cure extreme diseases (Ogungbile 1997).

In the past, the tearing of the skin of the drum was a symbol of conversion to Christianity. This was based on the belief that the drum was a medium of communication between the traditional healer and the ancestors. The sound of the drum is believed to arouse the ancestral spirits. It is believed that through the sound of the drum together with the accompanying rhythmic dancing and the clapping of hands, the traditional healer can bring about the presence of the ancestral spirits. It is believed that in the context of a healing ritual, dancing soothes the pain. It restores the lost equilibrium. It is therefore seen as a physiological therapy. The use of drums as a means of communicating with the ancestral spirits remains valid at a symbolic level. It is an intentional invitation to the spirits to heed the requests of the supplicants. It also has the effect of summoning the applicants to be attentive. It is for this reason that in some African cultures drums are being used during consecration not only to create an appropriate spiritual disposition but also to acknowledge the divine presence after the words of consecration have been pronounced. Drumming, clapping and dancing are characteristics of the AICs and the new Pentecostal churches. In the Christ Apostolic Church for example, the Holy Spirit is invoked to participate in the worship with deafening drumming, clapping, dancing and singing:

Wa, Wa, Wa, Emi Mimo,
Wa Wa, Wa, Alagbara; Wa o, Wa o, Wa o.

Come down, Holy Spirit,
Come down the Mighty One, Come.

Also,

Atewo ni mo fi a mo, bi o ba moore,
Ijo jijo ni mo fi a mo bi o ba moore.

If you are appreciative of the Lord's goodness, your clapping will so indicate

Another is,

Ogun oso gbogbo, atepa, ogun aje gbogbo, atepa
All the powers of witches and wizards are trampled upon.

Elaborate and colourful feasts

The Igbo of the Eastern part of Nigeria and Roman Catholic Church easily comes to mind here. Catholic missionaries used this considerably to their advantage as they made their acts of public worship (liturgy) as elaborate and colourful as possible. During religious feasts, especially the Mass and various devotions to the Blessed Eucharist and the saints, altars were beautifully decorated with flowers, lighted candles, incense and colourful vestments were used. Statues of saints as well as the crucifix were displayed at strategic places. Organ music always accompanies the choir, which sang hymns in Latin and Vernacular. Such well-dramatised celebrations made significant impact in the minds of people, and not infrequently helped conversion. National Church of Christ in Nigeria in his research gave a vivid description of such an occasion specifically when the missionaries came to Onitsha on August 28, 1887 on the feast of Most Holy Heart of Mary:

> Fair weather allows a good crowd of Onitsha people to assist our divine service today, which are (sic) celebrated with exceptional solemnity. Palm branches behind the statues of the Blessed Virgin and St. Joseph are studded with flowers. Papers, variously coloured are fixed to the windows by Father Superior; a splendid garniture, made perfectly by one of our girls, enhances the spell of our sanctuary, already shining with a great number of marvellous branches of flowers gathered on the altar and around the statues, with a beautiful background of harmonious green, tastely set out. (Obi 1985:382)

Similarly, there was some resemblance of aspects of Igbo indigenous religious worship and certain features of the Roman liturgy. One clear example was the similarity between the awe and dominant sense of mystery that largely characterised the Pius V Roman Liturgy in vogue in the pre-Vatican II era on the one hand, and the dense ritual symbolism, aura and mystically-oriented nature of Igbo indigenous religion. This is exemplified in the elaborate ritual paraphernalia and drama that generally accompany the procession of ritual officiants, or the movement of physical symbols of a deity by Igbo traditional religionists, and the rite of Benediction to the Blessed Sacrament or the Corpus Christi celebration of Roman Catholics (Uzukwu 2005).

Rite of renewal/purification

This is the ritual of the first fruits and it is prominent in the Eastern part of Nigeria. While it is difficult to envisage such a ritual in the urban area where vegetables are available throughout ceremonially consumed at the chief's place. These are exemplified in the annual harvest feasts in the AICs and other mainline churches. In the Celestial Church of Christ (CCC) and Cherubim and Seraphim (C & S), it is not an uncommon feature to have various types of fruits displayed not only during festivals, but at every Sunday service to signify divine provision, and fruitfulness in the various assemblies.

Language of worship, objects, music and titles in the churches

It can be argued that though the level and degree of influence of language, music and art may not be even, yet, the overall impact of Igbo language, music and art on the Catholic Church, particularly since Vatican II, is huge and highly significant. Serious commitment on the part of the local church since 1970 to the use of Igbo language in the administration of the sacraments and sacramental, including bearing of Igbo names by candidates at baptism, has brought about the greater influence of the indigenous language in the church. The initial objection and protest that formed part of the novel practice in the 1970s quickly died down. Thus, Igbo language gradually has since become accepted as the ordinary language of liturgical worship and sacramental administration in the Catholic Church in Igboland. The successful translation of basic religious texts into the indigenous language, especially the entire Bible, the Roman Missal and sacramental rites, is very positive and relevant. The greater usage of Igbo language in the Church's liturgy naturally brings with it the employment of many indigenous religious concepts, idioms, and expressions into the lexicon of the Roman Catholic Church in Igboland. This, in turn, brings into the Catholic tradition certain orientation in spirituality and moral attitude from the Igbo indigenous religious and cultural background (Van Binsbergen 2003).

The influence of the indigenous religion on the church's liturgical music in the post-Vatican II era is equally significant; this is mainly attributed to the Diocesan and inter-Diocesan Liturgical Music Commissions. Through their effort, the Catholic Church in Igboland has been able to mobilise and encourage talented individuals to use their skills in order to blend indigenous rhythms, tunes and motifs into the Church's musical ensemble. This is evident in rhythmic appeal and gusto of many contemporary musical pieces for specific aspects of the liturgy in the Igbo Church today specifically songs for Offertory, Holy Communion, and Free Choruses. The indigenous religious culture has a rich tradition of joyful rituals and thanksgiving to ancestral and other benevolent spirits, special offering and dedication of animals and things, to patron deities and nature forces.[6] The indigenous religious culture is partly responsible, therefore, for the emerging rich collection of soul-stirring liturgical pieces (Ejizu).

In the field of art, gifted Igbo carvers, sculptors and other art-creators have been able to employ local materials as well as indigenous religio-cultural ideas, symbols and motifs to express some important Christian themes and values. Some churches in Igbo land are adorned with beautifully carved doors rich in indigenous art-forms and other religious ritual symbols today adorn several churches and Catholic religious centres in Igboland (Kalu 1998). The use of the Rosary by Catholics can be linked to the divination object (*opele*) of the *Ifa* worshippers in the indigenous religion of the Yoruba (Abimbola 2005). The Priest in *Ifa* worship however, is the only one to divine using the rosary, while the 'petitioner' makes request with the rosary in addition with some cowries shells or some coins in contemporary society.

The traditional age-grade system has also left its impact on the Church. In some cases, the titles and practices have been adopted wholesale into the Church, while in some others there have been varying degrees of modification, especially where religious rituals are involved. Examples are in the knighthood, it is becoming acceptable to the people who are versed in the indigenous background or cultural institutions like secret society and prestige clubs, e.g. *Otu-Odu, Ekwe/Lolo, Ekpe, Okonko, Odo* (Onwu 2002). In the area of social and human organisation within the Church, the influence of the indigenous culture has been significant as well. The Roman Catholic Church, as well as the Nigerian Baptist Convention have drawn inspiration, from the indigenous cultural patterns as the age-grade system among the Igbo in associations like the Catholic Men's Organisation (CMO), Catholic Women's Organisation (CWO), Catholic Boys' (CBO), and Catholic Girls Organisation (CGO), at the station, parish, deanery, diocesan and inter-diocesan levels. The Nigerian Baptist Convention's categorisation falls between Royal Auxiliary, Lydia's Society and Women Missionary Union.[7] The Offertory dance of young maidens, which is gradually gaining ground in several dioceses, has direct link to the indigenous dance of young virgin girls at shrines of local deities during the *Isi-ebili* festival in parts of Igboland (Kalu 1988).

---

[6] Some examples cited by Ejizu include: the *Ikwuaru* festival in the Nnewi-Ozubulu area during which fat bulls are purchased, paraded and offered to honour local patron arch-deities, the practice of commissioning *Mbari* art gallery in the south-central zone, or artfully-decorated *Ikenga* sculptures in the Anambara sub-culture area, the performance of special musical lyrics and dance by minstrels, and/or prestigious and highly decorated masquerade like *Ijere, Oka-nga, Ozo-Ebunu, Ikpirikpi Ogu/Iri-agha*, by adult males, etc. See also http://www.afrikaworld.net/afrel/ejizu-atrcath.htm

[7] Oral Interview at Camp Young, Ede, January 2006, at the annual anniversary of the Lydia's Society of the Nigerian Baptist Convention; Oral interview with Rev. Akanji, a Baptist Priest at the Divinity School, University of Edinburgh, May 2, 2008.

Islam

Having highlighted the 'Africanness' in Christendom, can Islam be absolved? Are their vestiges of traditional religion in the way Islam is practised in Africa generally and Nigeria in particular? As with Christianity, a multiplicity of sects has emerged within the Islamic faith. The prominent sects include the *Izalatul-Bid'ah Wa Igamat al' Sunnah*, abbreviated as the *Yan Izala*, founded by Mallam Ismaila Idris. Another prominent sect is *Izala*, a strong reformist group favoured by Islamic intellectuals (Neo-Libertarian). Others are the Sunni Islam, the Wahhabism (Salafism), the Shi'I Islam, the Alawis, Khariji and the Sufis. However, two main Islamic denominations are practised in Nigeria: Tijaniyya and Quadiriyya, with Tijaniyya practised more widely. The majority of northern Muslims, especially the commoners (*talakawa*), embraced Tijaniyya in both the urban centres and rural areas. Quadiriyya has more elitist adherents who are predominantly among the aristocratic Fulani ruling houses and the privileged members of their society (Uzoma 2004:4).

Islam teaches that there is one God, Allah, and this is purely an African (Yoruba) concept of *Olodumare*. The Islamic sayings: *laila, ila, lahu*...that is, there is only one God attests to this.

The idea of predestination originated from the traditional belief of Nigerians, and has been taken over by Islam. It is termed *'kadara'* or *'ayanmo'*. Thus, like in traditional religion, Muslims offer prayers to 'change' *kadara* (cf. Jabez in 1 Chronicles 4:9-11). Like the indigenous religion of Africans, Islam maintains a positive disposition toward the well being of human beings. Islam also centres greatly on social and familial roles, like the indigenous religion. There are many rules in the Koran and Sunna on what to do and what not to do in everyday life, examples abound in some *Odu Ifa*. e. g. In theory, *Ifa* priests as representative of all *Ifa* worshippers should be ethical practitioners, and are bound to heed the word of *Ifa* and *Ifa*'s code of ethics as prescribed in many *Odu*, which is another safe guard in their use. We see this oath in the holy Odu Iwori Meji:

Iwori teju mo ohun ti nse ni
Bi o ba te Ifa tan
Ki o tun iye e re te
Iwori teju mo ohun ti nse ni
Awo, ma fi eja igba gun ope
Iwori teju mo ohun ti nse ni
Awo, ma fi aimowe wo odo
Iwori teju mo ohun ti nse ni
Awo, ma fi ibinu yo obe
Iwori teju mo ohun ti nse ni
Awo, ma fi kanjukanju jaye
Iwori teju mo ohun ti nse ni
Awo, ma fi warawara mkun ola
Iwori teju mo ohun ti nse ni
Awo, maseke, sodale

Iwori teju mo ohun ti nse ni
Awo, ma puro jaye
Iwori teju mo ohun ti nse ni
Awo, ma se igberaga si agba
Iwori teju mo ohun ti nse ni
Awo, ma so ireti nu
Iwori teju mo ohun ti nse ni
Awo, ma san bante Awo
Iwori teju mo ohun ti nse ni
Awo, bi o ba tefa tan
Ki o tun iye e re te o
Iwori teju mo ohun ti nse ni

Iwori take a critical look at what affects you
If you undergo *Ifa* initiation (Itelodu)
Endeavour to use your wisdom and intelligence
Iwori take a critical look at what affects you
Awo, do not use a broken rope to climb a palm-tree
Iwori take a critical look at what affects you
Awo, do no enter into the river without knowing how to swim
Iwori take a critical look at what affects you
Awo, do not draw a knife in anger
Iwori take a critical look at what affects you
Awo, do not be in haste to enjoy your life
Iwori take a critical look at what affects you
Awo, do not be in a hurry to acquire wealth
Iwori take a critical look at what affects you
Awo, do not lie, do not be treacherous
Iwori take a critical look at what affects you
Awo, do not deceive in order to enjoy your life
Iwori take a critical look at what affects you
Awo, do not be arrogant to elders
Iwori take a critical look at what affects you
Awo, do not lose hope
Iwori take a critical look at what affects you
Awo, do not make love to your colleague's spouse
Iwori take a critical look at what affects you
Awo, when you have been given *Ifa* initiation
Initiate yourself again by using your wisdom and intelligence
Iwori take a critical look at what affects you. (Sanchez 2008)

Islam includes heaven and hell, and one's earthly actions determine to which one will go after judgment. Muslims think that human good works alone can qualify a person for heaven. This is also a crucial teaching in the indigenous religion:

S'o tito, se rere,
Eni ba s'otito; nii mole e gbe.

Say the truth, do good,
In order to find the favour of God.

A Muslim cannot be assured of entering into Paradise after death without living as a Muslim. Most Muslims will not claim they are assured entrance to paradise. Islam has a Judgment Day upon which all dead are reawakened to be either condemned or allowed to enter Paradise. The indigenous religion's belief in the judgement day goes thus,

> E maa sika laye o, tori a o rorun,
> Ta baa de bode a o rojo
>
> Do not be involved in wickedness while you are alive, because heaven is the ultimate destination;
> An account will be required of everybody at the gate of heaven.

Islam does not, of course, reject as false every aspect of belief and practice found in indigenous religion. It accepts a spirit world, and the Qur'an sanctions the belief in mystical powers. In consequence it has been able to accommodate itself to many of the spirit forces found within the primal religions of West Africa. Moreover a number of other important traditional practices, like divination, or magic accepted as *sihr*, are with qualification and modification recognised by Islam as legitimate.

Healing in Islam

In the practice of Islamic religion is the application of water for healing just like with the AICs. Contemporary Nigerian Muslims hold night vigils and attend services with bottle of water for healing purposes. Ogungbile establishes this fact in his research on the Fadillullah Muslim Mission, Osogbo, Nigeria (2004). He states further about the use of indigenous objects and practices in this assembly,

> The Mission has a stream very close to the mosque which is used for clients who receive prescriptions for ritual bath...a client might decide to go to her or his own stream or river of choice for prescribed ritual bath. (2004)

As already discussed with the use of the Rosary among Roman Catholics and *Ifa* priests, Muslims make use of the rosary, or *tira* in divination. This does not exclude divination with 'sand' that is '*yanrin tite*,' which is the practice among of the indigenous religion.

Polygamy

This is not exclusive of Islam and traditional religion as some Christians are polygamous. However, while the Old Testament is replete of various polygamous unions, the New Testament teaching emphasizes monogamy. In Matt. 19:8-9 and Mark 10:1-12: Jesus replied, "Moses permitted you to divorce your wives because your hearts were hard. But it was not this way from the beginning. I tell you that anyone who divorces his wife, except for marital unfaithfulness, and marries another woman commits adultery." Islamic injunction is however similar to the Old Testament feature where polygamy is now frowned upon, as in Holy Qu'ran 4:3.

In conclusion, it is apparent that both Christianity and Islam as they are being practised in contemporary society cannot be divorced from some elements of the indigenous religion. These are manifested in the liturgy, dressing, worship, arts and prayers in the two imported religions generally, and AICs in particular. In all, both Christians and Muslims cannot but sing:

A wa o soro ile wa o,
A wa o soro ile wa o.
Esin kan o pe ....
O yee,
Esin kan o pe,
Ka wa ma soro.
A wa o soro ile wa o.
Eni to ba fe,
Ko ki wa.
Eeyan ti o si fe,
Ko yan wa lodi!
A wa o soro ile wa o.

We are going to worship our ancestral religions.
We are going to worship our ancestral religions.
No religion can say ...
O yes,
No religion can say,
That we should not worship our ancestral gods.
Anyone who likes,
Can continue greet us.
Anyone who dislikes,
May greet us no more!
We will worship the gods of our ancestors.

References

Abimbola, Wande, 2005. Assessing Dialogue. Paper presented at World Council of Churches conference "Critical moment in interreligious dialogue," Geneva. http://www.oikoumene.org/en/resources/documents/wcc-programmes/interreligious-dialogue-and-cooperation/interreligious-trust-and-respect/geneva-june-2005-documents/prof-wande-abimbola-plenary-presentation-7-june-2005.html

Anderson, A., 1992. *Bazalwane: African Pentecostals in South Africa*. Pretoria: Unisa Press: 28–31.

Anderson, A., 1997. Pluriformity and Contextuality in African Initiated Churches. http://artsweb.bham.ac.uk/aanderson/Publications/pluriformity_and_contextuality_i.htm

Anderson, A., 2000. *Zion and Pentecost: The Spirituality and Experience of Pentecostal and Zionist/Apostolic Churches*, Pretoria, UNISA Press, 2000.

Cherubim & Seraphim Movement Church. http://www.csmovementchurchusa.org/

Chitando, Ezra, 2004. African Instituted Churches in Southern Africa: Paragons of Regional Integration?' in *African Journal of International Affairs* 7 (1 & 2): 117–132.

Christ Apostolic Church Worldwide Network. History of Christ Apostolic Church. http://www.cacworldwide.net/history.asp

Cox, H. 2001. Fire from Heaven. The Rise of Pentecostal Spirituality and the Reshaping of Religion in the 21st Century. Reading, MA: Addison–Wesley.

David Oyedepo Ministries International Inc. http://www.davidoyedepoministries.org/

Ejizu, Christopher I. The Influence of African Indigenous Religions on Roman Catholicism, the Igbo Example. http://www.afrikaworld.net/afrel/ejizu-atrcath.htm.

Hastings, Adrian, 1994. The Church in Africa: 1450-1950. Oxford: Clarendon Press.

Isichei, Elizabeth, 1995. *A History of Christianity in Africa from Antiquity to the Present*. London: Wm. B. Eerdmans Publishing.

Jehu-Appiah, Jerisdan H. An overview of indigenous African churches in Britain: an approach through the historical survey of African Pentecostalism. http://www.pctii.org/wcc/jehu95.html.

Kalu, O.U., 1988. Under the Eyes of the Gods: Sacralization and Control of Social Order in Igboland. Ahiajoku Lecture Series. http://ahiajoku.igbonet.com/1988/

Neo-Libertarian. http://www.neo-libertarian.com/muslimsects.html

Obi, C. A. 1985. A Hundred Years of the Catholic Church in Eastern Nigeria, 1885–1985. Onitsha: Africana-FEB Publishers.

Ogungbile, D. O., 1997. Meeting Point of Culture and Health: The Case of the Aladura Churches in Nigeria. *Nordic Journal of African Studies* 6(1): 98–111.

Ogungbile, D. O., 2001. The Dynamics of Language in Cultural Revolution and African Spirituality: The Case of Ijo Orile-Ede Adulawo Ti Kristi (National Church of Christ) in Nigeria. *Nordic Journal of African Studies*, 10 (1) 66–79.

Ogungbile, D. O., 2004. Religion Experience and Women Leadership in Nigerian Islam. *Jenda: a Journal of Culture and African Women Studies* 6. http://www.iiav.nl/ezines/web/JENda/2005/No6/jendajournal/ogungbile.html

Ojo, Matthews A. 1992. Deeper Life Bible Church of Nigeria. In *New Dimensions in African Christianity*, ed. Paul Gifford. Nairobi: All Africa Conference of Churches.

Onwu, E. N. 2002. Towards an Understanding of Igbo Traditional Religious Life and Philosophy. Ahiajoku Lecture Series. http://ahiajoku.igbonet.com/2002/

Paris, Liana. 2006. Pentecostal Churches in Nigeria Wage Religious Battle against HIV/AIDS. The Watson Institute for International Studies. http://www.watsoninstitute.org/news_detail.cfm?id=497

Sancheze, Ifalola. 2008. *Ifa* Yesterday, *Ifa* Today, *Ifa* Tomorrow: *Ifa* thoughts and Philosophy. http://ifalolablospot.com

Shorter, Aylward. Inculturation of African Traditional Religious Values in Christianity—How far? http://www.afrikaworld.net/afrel/shorter.htm

Turner, H.W. 1967. The History of an African Independent Church (Church of the Lord (Aladura)). Oxford: Clarendon Press.

Uzoma, Rose. 2004. Religious Pluralism, Cultural Differences, and Social Stability in Nigeria. *Brigham Young Law Review* 2: 651–664

Uzukwu, E. 2005. Mission Theology: Biblical and Historical Perspectives. Teachings of the Church, Miltown Dublin.

Van Binsbergen, Wim. 2003. African spirituality: an approach from intercultural philosophy. *Forum for Intercultural Philosophy* 4: 1–45.

World Council of Churches. 1995. Presentations on Black Majority Churches in Britain. http://www.pctii.org/wcc/reports95.html

11

Indigenous voices in music performances of contemporary Christian and Muslim Missions

- Yomi Daramola

Introduction

Islam and Christianity have become prominent religions among the Yoruba. They both had far-reaching effects on the political, social, economic and religious situations of the Yoruba people. Among the two religions, Islam was the first to be noticed. The roles played by these religions in the socio-political life of the Yoruba were both negative and positive. While Islam brought about forces that eroded the authority of Yoruba rulers, Christianity carried with it forces that paved the way for European domination. Positively, both religions, apart from the fact that they co-operated with and aided the British Administration in Lagos in the task of ending fratricidal civil wars among the Yoruba towards the end of the nineteenth century (Atanda 1980:42), they also encouraged learning and produced new crop of elites that served as potent forces of change in Yorubaland. While the Muslims introduced and favoured literacy in Arabic through the many Quranic schools established, the Christians introduced and promoted Western education through the establishment of mission schools.

The effect of the two foreign religions on Yoruba politics and society was still on the increase when another factor emerged which had a greater effect on the society than that produced by these two religions. This was colonialism, that is, the domination of the country by foreigners, which in this case were the Europeans. The influences of the two religions according to Vidal (1987:446) may be described as transculturation for they involved the transplantation of foreign institutions and values into the Nigerian indigenous ones or their total eradication where they constituted an obstacle to the foreign ones.

Yorubaland had its contact with Islam around the seventeenth century. Though the date of its entry cannot be fixed with precision, mention was made of Muslims in Yorubaland around that time. According to Gbadamosi (1978:4), the introduction of Islam was unannounced and unplanned. He went further to say that the percolation of Islam into Yorubaland did not result from the direction of any organized evangelization movement, or under the warrant of any Islamized political authority. Although Johnson (1969:26), claims that "Mohammedanism" (Islam) was introduced to Yorubaland towards the close of the eighteenth century, historical findings show that the introduction of the religion was earlier than that time. For example, Crowder (1978:91) observed that Islam had made its influence felt in Oyo Empire before eighteenth century.

The contact was through link with the Islamized areas during the time of war and peace. The varied contact meant some intermingling which facilitated the infiltration of Islam into Yorubaland most especially the north-western part of the Yorubaland. Before the period of 1840s, almost all the important canters of Islam in Yorubaland were based in the Oyo Empire and by the early 1840s, there had been a considerable pronouncement of Islamic activities in places like Owu (before its destruction in 1825) and Badagry (Gbadamosi 1978).

The main currents of Islam reached old Oyo from Nupeland (Balogun 1978:18) through trade routes which connected present-day northern Nigeria with Yorubaland in the southwest. From old Oyo, Islam spread through Muslim traders and itinerant scholars and preachers to Ilorin, Kuwo, Iseyin, Ogbomoso, Iwo and other places in the Yorubaland (Balogun 1978:18). The pioneers of this religion in Yorubaland penetrated into the land selling their wares and spreading their faith into the bargain. At that initial stage, Islam was essentially a religion of alien merchants who settled in separate Muslim quarters in the major urban and commercial centres where they practiced their religion and its attendant musical activities.

In Lagos, historical records show that Islam was already in the city during the time of Adele I (c.1775-80 and 1832-34) (Balogun 1978). The traditional ruler permitted the practice of the religion at the expense of his throne in 1780 and by the time he came back to his throne in 1832, the traditional ruler not only supported the free practice of the religion, but also saw to it that it was firmly planted in his court in Lagos. In fact, Muslims in and outside the court enjoyed his patronage.

The acceptance of Islam in Yorubaland was also, in some cases, due to the fact that the religion did not attempt to destroy indigenous religion in Yoruba land. There were many shrines among the people. Although Yoruba people were polytheists, they acknowledged the existence of a supreme God who was usually referred to as God of the sky and who was believed to be assisted by a pantheon of gods and spirits. Thus, Muslim introduction of the worship of Allah must have seemed unobjectionable.

Although Islam did not pave way for making sacrifices to local gods, oracular consultation, nor approve of religious 'magic,' the traditional cults recognized its rituals as worship, which could be interpreted by the uninitiated in terms of local occult practices. For instance, the Muslim prayer ritual, fasting, and in due course the building of impressive mosques could be accepted as the peculiar but distinguishing features of a new cult (Stride & Ifeka 1971:139).

A number of other positive but mainly non-religious factors that contributed to the acceptance and spread of Islam among the Yoruba includes the emergence of economic potency, military prowess, population movement most especially of the nomadic Fulani, the acceptance of the religion by most traditional rulers, and of course, the fratricidal wars in Yorubaland towards the end of eighteenth century at the time Islam was becoming more powerful a religion among the people.

The penetration of Christianity into Yorubaland is premised on three major events which were of historical significance. The events, which occurred in Europe, paved way for the introduction of Christianity in the West African and eventually in Yorubaland. These events are the evangelical revival of the 18th century, the formation of Christian Missionary Societies and the abolition of the slave trade (Opeloye 1998:139-148). After the abolition of the slave trade the British government founded the colony of Sierra Leone in order to re-settle the freed slaves there. The colony was soon transformed into a Christian population through the missionary activities of the C.M.S., which first established their mission work among the liberated slaves (Opeloye 1998:143). Its introduction in Yorubaland was in the second half of the 19th century. The dual aim of the missions was to encourage 'lawful' trade between the Europeans and Africans as a replacement for slave trade and to convert the indigenes to Christianity. This was well hatched, if not in all sphere, at least in bringing missionaries in the country and the Yoruba had their own share of it. Badagry became the first city where a mission was established in 1842 by the first missionaries from the Methodist mission. The efforts of the Methodists to Christianize the people were reinforced by the Church Missionary Society (CMS) under the leadership of Henry Townsend, Samuel Ajayi Crowther and others who participated vigorously to evangelize Abeokuta from where Christianity spread to other parts of the Yorubaland. Other Christian missions followed suit and Christianity became well entrenched into the peoples' consciousness and religious experience. African Independent Churches (Aladura/White garment churches) emerged much later with the intention to infuse the indigenous experience and materials into Christianity.

In the contemporary times, Islam and Christianity have become firmly rooted along with the traditional religion in Yorubaland. Most of the time, these three religions interact though each of them has its tradition and culture within the context of which its adherent operates. Most often also, there is the tendency of syncretism in the ways and manners adherents practice their religions. This is evident in one of the Yoruba traditional ditties that run thus:

> *Awa o soro ile wa o, Awa o soro ile wa o,*
> *Igbagbo/Imale o pe o ye*
> *Igbagbo/Imale o pe k'awa ma soro,*
> *Awa o soro ile wa o*

> We are going to celebrate our indigenous rite (2ce)
> Christianity/Islam could not
> Christianity/Islam could not prevent us from celebrating it
> We are going to celebrate our indigenous rite

From this song, it became evident that it is not uncommon to find Muslims and Christians participating, most of the time actively, in indigenous religious rites and cultural ceremonies. In spite of this however, the practitioners of the two foreign religions—Islam and Christianity have not relented in their efforts to bring people closer to God through what Christians refer to as evangelism and what Muslims refer to as *'da'wah'*. This paper hopes to explore into the role music plays in the evangelistic efforts of the two religions and ascertain the level at which indigenous concepts and ideas are used as materials for musical expressions in the two religions. This is premised on a theory that musical materials are used to ascertain the possibility of cultural contact among widely separated peoples.

Islam and Christianity: the issue of evangelism

The concept of evangelism is most synonymous with Christian religion though the interpretation of the word transcends utopian application. To evangelize is to try to persuade other people to share enthusiasm for specific beliefs and ideas either religious or otherwise.

The concept of evangelism in Islam is what is known as *da'wah*. One of the major tasks of Muslims is to engage in the propagation of Islamic faith (*da'wah*). This has been ordered by Almighty Allah as stated in the Holy Quran (3:104; 9:122). It is like a disobedience to holy order for a Muslim not to participate fully in the *da'wah* activities. The obedience to the order may be performed through giving money, knowledge, power, strength, and influence to its realization and promotion. In consciousness of the order of *da'wah*, the early Muslims engaged themselves in the spread of the faith across the globe within the limit of their knowledge, wealth, strength and power. Today, Islam is a religion with a wide acceptability throughout the African continent. Its spread has always been linked with both warfare and trade along with series of *da'wah* efforts.

Evangelism through music

Throughout the Yorubaland today, Christianity and Islam have been found dominant in the use of music for the propagation of the faiths. By the middle of the nineteenth century, Christian music had become a household name among the people. At the initial stage, it was used to consolidate the ideals and concepts of the European masters through songs, litany and lyrics which were used during worship and socio-religious activities. During church service, the vogue was usually British liturgical music or European classical music especially, during special occasion like harvest, Christmas and Easter celebrations. In missionary schools, it was European based ditties and drumming on the band-set. At every possible opportunity, music was used to promote the culture and ideals of the foreign pioneers of the religion on the shores of the Yorubaland.

Later, this became interpolated by musical elements from the traditions and cultures of the people. By the end of the 19th century, there had emerged

Yoruba music nationalists who championed the fight for the acceptability of the Yoruba traditional musical elements as part of liturgical and socio-religious music. Some of these nationalists include Robert Arungbaolu Coker, Rev. T. Ola Olude, Rev. J.J. Ransome Kuti, Akin George, Dayo Dedeke, Thomas Ekundayo Philips, Ayo Bankole, Ben Oriere, Olaolu Omideyi (Omojola 2001, 83) and a host of others. From this trend began the traditions of Yoruba Church and Gospel music for evangelism and propagation of Christian faith. A lot of musicians grew out of this breakthrough as choir masters and choristers. Some of them are today prominent in Nigerian popular music while a lot remained Gospel music artistes and band owners.

In Islam, the use of the word "music" to describe musical activities is usually with some reservations and caution. This is because of the negative attitudes of the Islamic law givers towards music. This has generated a lot of argument about the permissibility of music in the religion and different schools of thought have developed each with its own opinion and submission about the permissibility of music in Islam and each substantiating its position with Quranic verses. The use of music in Islamic liturgy is not common. Even when the liturgical activity is musical, it is not regarded as music. However, the use of music in Islamic socio-religious activities among the Yoruba is very common. Unlike in the Christian faith where music has been part of what was given to the Yoruba converts, the use of music for *da'wah* purpose is an opinion formed by Yoruba Muslims as a stereotype of what is practiced in Christianity to increase the chances of gaining more converts and retaining the already converted most especially the youths. The use of music as part of *da'wah* activities among the Yoruba started at Quranic schools where music was used to teach specific Quranic verses to newly converted Muslims for them to be able to read recite and understand Arabic and Quranic languages as part of their obligations to the newly accepted religion. This not only became the practice among the early Muslim clerics among the Yoruba, it eventually became a taste by which *omo-ile kewu* (Quranic school pupils) are attracted and fascinated (Daramola 2008:139-140). This served as a point of cue to many Yoruba Muslim musicians. Some of them today are renown musicians of Yoruba Islamized popular music types such as *apala, fuji, waka* and *senwele* while some remained in the mainstream musical practice of the *Alasalatu*[1] which is noted for core Islamic socio-religious music.

The two musical cultures of our discourse have influenced and being influenced by the traditional cultures of the people. As the acceptance of the faith in the two religions is held to imply belief in certain philosophies, so are the musical practices in them for evangelistic purposes. Such philosophies include the Uniqueness of God interpreted in the music as *Olodumare*,

---

[1] Though the word Alasalatu is synonymous to Yoruba Muslim women, the word is now generally used to describe the musicians (male and female) who not only perform solely at Islamic religious activities, but who are also mindful of Islamic injunctions about music-making. Unlike their Muslim counterparts who play their music for commercial purposes, the Alasalatu musicians follow strictly the restrictions given for the performance of music for the purpose of *da'wah* even though they also make some money from music-making.

Olorun, Olohun and Oluwa; efficacy of prayer; sanctity of the religious books; creation; resurrection; death and eternity etc. However, there are a lot of indigenous concepts and ideas that are expressed in and through these philosophies. Culture is a way of life. The musicians of these musical cultures expressed the indigenous ways of life as they perceived it either in a negative or a positive way or even in an ambivalent manner. For example, the description of the Yoruba deities (gods) by the musicians of the two musical cultures is usually in a negative term. The following excerpts describe how some of the traditional religious concepts are perceived:

> *Jesu n kigbe, O ni e wa gb'Oun gbo*
> *Orisa te gbe kale te gbe sile,*
> *Alenu ma le fohunm te gbojule*
> *Jesu n kigbe O ni e wa gb'Oun gbo*
>
> Jesus is calling out to you people to come and accept Him
> The gods that are made by you and worshipped by you
> They have mouth but cannot talk
> Jesus is calling out to you people to come and accept Him

The lyric above is one of the oldest lyrics used during Christian evangelism and became popular with the roving evangelists. The impression being made through this lyric is that the gods do not perform any spiritual or practical act themselves and therefore are not as relevant in the affairs of man as Jesus Christ:

> *A o l'eni taa le ke si*
> *A o l'eni taa le sa ba*
> *To koja Olohun Sati Ramonu*
> *A o l'eni taa le sa ba*
> *Orisa kan o si to le gb'eda la*
> *A o l'eni taa le sa ba*
>
> There is non else to be called upon
> There is none else to run to
> Besides the everlasting God
> There is none else to run to
> There is no other deity that can save human beings
> There is none else to run to
> Or:
> *Je-su lo to ni I gba*
> *Ko s'orisa*
> *Orisa kan ko le gba ni la*
> *Ko s'orisa*
>
> It is Jesus only that can save
> No deity (idol)
> No deity (idol) can save man
> No deity (idol)

The lyrics above express the Yoruba Christians and Muslims belief that only Allah (the Supreme Being) and Jesus Christ can provide salvation. Salvation in this context is all encompassing. It means total protection from all evils, provision in all ramifications and prevention from falling into evil alliances and thoughts. Even though they recognize the existence of the deities, but it is believed that they cannot be brought to the issues of total salvation:[2]

Esu ko le kole ti Jesu
Bo kole a o wo
Esu kole kole ti Jesu

Satan[3] cannot pitch his tent beside that of Jesus
If he does, we shall demolish it
Satan cannot pitch his ten beside that of Jesus

Or:

Ko ni raaye lodede mi
Asitani eni eko
Ko ni raaye lodede mi

He shall not have a place in my abode
Satan the rejected
He shall not have a place in my abode

In the excerpts cited above, Satan, which is misinterpreted as "*Esu*" is usually portrayed in the two religions as evil carrier and is always prayed against in all the endeavours of the worshippers. This misconception is used most often to prevent converts from backsliding (going back to their former religions). Also, the fierceness of some Yoruba deities in judgements is also found prominent in some lyrics of the two religions. For example,

Olorun ko gbeja mi gbami lowo okunkun,
Bi won ba ran Sango o, k'Olorun o gbeja
Bi won ba gbe afose, ki wo ran oro,
Bombu ni o yin si won bi won ba n tafa
Ko maa ro gbamu lagbolee won

God fight my battle save me from the darkness[4]
If Sango is contracted, God should be on the defence
If *afose* (the instrument of enchantment) is used, God should use His word
Send explosives to them if they tried to shoot their arrows
Let it explode sporadically in their compounds

---

[2] Salvation in this context differs from that which is expressed in Christian religion.
[3] The concept of *Esu* among the Yoruba is not the same thing as the Biblical Satan though it is so interpreted in Islamic and Christian religions.
[4] Darkness in this context means cultic doings and enchantments.

Just like *Esu, Sango* is highly dreaded by the Yoruba because of his fierceness in carrying out his judgments on culprits. It is the belief of the worshippers in the two religions of our discourse that only the Supreme Being can curb these fierce deities when they are contacted to wrath evil on people either justly or unjustly.

Furthermore, the recognition of the power of strange forces and enemies also sometimes forms concepts upon which the lyrics of music in both Christian and Islamic religions among the Yoruba are premised. These strange forces include that of *oso, aje, emere, agude,* and *agudegude.* These forces are believed to be capable of causing misfortunes to their victims and they are usually regarded as enemies of mankind. Each of these strange forces is a spirit which inhibits human beings to function. Though it is also believed that they are sometimes benevolent most especially to their members, when it comes to performing their functions on the malevolent note, they do not have regards for anybody even members of their families. Examples of songs that reflect on the recognition of these forces include:

Ba mi gberu mi baba o, k'emi le r'ona gbegba
Oso t'oloun o pa mi iro nla
Emere to loun o pa mi iro,
Aje to loun o pa mi iron la
Agudegude to loun o pa mi iro nla

Bear my burden for me oh father, please make a way for me
Make any wizardry against me a nullity
Make every move of familiar spirits against me a nullity
Make any witchcraft against me a nullity
Make every combined enchantment against me a nullity

Or:

Bami f'oju otaa mi ko fo tan
Bami f'oju otaa mi ko fo tan
Oso to ba ni n ma ma gberi
Aje to ba ni n ma ma goke
Bami f'oju otaa mi ko fo tan

Give my enemies a total blindness
Give my enemies a total blindness
The wizard who says I should not rise
The witch who says I should not rise up
Give my enemies a total blindness

Or:

Baba ta l'ofa
Baba ta l'ofa oloro
Oso ti ko je n gbadun
Baba ta l'ofa oloro

Aje ti ko je n gbadun
Baba ta l'ofa oloro

Father, shoot him/her an arrow
Father, shoot him/her a poisonous arrow
The wizard who will not allow me to rest
Father, shoot him/her a poisonous arrow
The witch who will not allow me to rest
Father, shoot him/her a poisonous arrow

One of the traditional ways of obtaining good and sound health among the Yoruba was by taking herbs and concoctions from leaves and plants roots. This remained principally the vogue before the emergence of the two foreign religions by which converts were discouraged from participating in the use of herbs as preventive and curative measures for diseases. This is because the traditional practice was regarded by the pioneers of these religions as fetish. This also is represented in the music performed during evangelistic endeavour during Islamic *da'wah* or Christian crusades. Such lyrics include:

Mase doju adura (adua) timi
Mase doju adura (adua) timi
Iwo lo ni n ma ma ja'we
Iwo lo ni n ma ma wa 'gbo
Lai j'awo o, lai wa'gbo
Mase doju adura (adua) timi

Don't let me be ashamed of my trust in the efficacy of prayers
Don't let me be ashamed of my trust in the efficacy of prayers
You have warned me no longer to pluck leaves
You have warned me no longer to dig roots
By obeying these injunctions
Don't let me be ashamed of my trust in the efficacy of prayers

Celebrations during annual festivals and commemoration of deities and ancestors usually attract communal participation. Today, while some ardent Yoruba Christians and Muslims loathe participation of members in such communal activities because such participation, they believed, will negate the objectives and tenets of their religions, some are just lethargic about it. This viewpoint is noticed in lyrics such as:

B'elegungun n s'egungun,
B'oloro n s'oro
Ko seyi to kan mi n be
Mo ya ba Mohamodu lo

During the masquerade festivals
At the commemoration ceremony for the spirits
I am less concerned
I have followed Mohammed

And

Emi ti mo se Islaamu
T'emi ba mi niyen
Iwo ti o ko too se
Tie ba e niyen

My decision to be in Islamic religion
By this decision mine has come upon me
You that renounce the religion
Yours has come upon you

On the other hand, some of the people believed that adopting any of these religions does not mean abandonment of traditional ways of life and this is represented in songs such as:

Igbagbo o
Imale o
Esin abalaye o
Olorun lo m'esin a se la o

Christianity,
Islam or
Traditional religion
One only needs God's approval of ones worship to be saved

Or

Belegungun n se
Ma ba won se
B'oloro n soro
Ma ba won se
Ilu o besin je
Ijo o le besin je o
E ma ba wa l'asa je

When it is time for *egungun* festival
I will participate
When it is time to celebrate the spirits
I am available
Drumming does not defile a religion
Dancing can by no means defile a religion
Let nobody defile our culture

These lyrics emphasize the concept of communality, which is the hallmark of the concept of family (*ebi*) among the Yoruba. In a single *ebi* you can find a reasonable number of people representing each of the religions found in the society. That is, in every Yoruba family you will find groups of Christians, Muslims and traditionalists. Being a member of any religious group does not remove you from the family. In fact, it is impossible for anybody to renounce his or her family because of anything including religion. It is the family that can renounce anyone that is found wanting either because of criminal activity or misdemeanour. To these groups of people, most especially the traditional musicians either Christians or Muslims, communality and the concept of *ebi* is culture bound and should not be neglected based on religious inclinations.

The issue of life after death in Yoruba traditional religion which is referred to in the Christian and Islamic religions among the Yoruba as resurrection (*ajinde* and *agbende* in paradise and *al-quiyama* respectively), is usually talked about when there is the need to admonish members of the two religions to refrain from evil doings. This view is the cornerstone in the two religions though it is shared in other religions. It is always emphasized and expressed in all aspects of the religions while music/songs have been an important medium for achieving this. Examples of such songs include:

Bo dara bi o da, o d'Al-Qiyamah
Bo dara bi o da, o d'Al- Qiyamah
Iyawo oniyawo o kere ni palo
Bo dara bi o da, o d'Al- Qiyamah

If it is good or not, heaven surely will tell
If it is good or not, heaven surely will tell
Another man's wife dragged into your (room) parlor
If it is good or not, heaven surely will tell

Or

Ajinde, Ajinde,
Ajinde dara nikehin onigbagbo
Jesu Oluwa je ki n joba peluu Re

Resurrection, resurrection,
To resurrect is the best for Christians in the last days
Jesus, Lord grant me to reign with you

Conclusion

This chapter has tried to open up some vistas about the contemporary outlook of how Yoruba Muslims and Christians in the contemporary times evangelize through music and how the music reflects on some indigenous concepts and ideas. It is established through lyric excerpts discussed in this paper that most of the time the music is based on spiritual warfare, exorcism and protection of the fundamentals of each of the foreign religions. Most of the performance of the music portrays indigenous ways of life as fetish and sacrilege. However, there are some points in time when the musicians remain ambivalent in their attitude towards traditional culture and values.

In the final analysis, it has been found that music has become a veritable tool for evangelism in Christian and Islamic religions among the Yoruba especially now that the music industry has become a very good channel for evangelistic ideologies. In this trend however, traditional concepts always serve as thematic and inspirational sources for composing songs and lyrics for the sensitization of the converts.

At this juncture, it can be concluded that as long as the culture remains the source of interpretation of customs, values, and the logic of behaviour in any given society, the expression of cultural ideas through music of the people, irrespective of what religious inclination is being propagated, will remain the metronome on which the rhythm of life in terms of change and continuity in religious atmosphere is maintained.

References

Atanda, J.A. (1980), *An Introduction to Yoruba History*. Caxton Press (West Africa) Limited, Ibadan.

Balogun, S.A. (1978), "Introduction and Spread of Islam in West Africa before the Nineteenth Century: A Reassessment." *Odu: A Journal of West African Studies*, n.s., No. 18, Ile-Ife: 1-24.

Crowder, Michael (1978), *The Story of Nigeria*. London, Faber & Faber

Daramola, Yomi (2008), "Education and Aesthetic Values in Yoruba Islamic Music" *JANIM: Journal of the Association of Nigerian Musicologists*, (Special Edition): 139-150.

Gbadamosi, T.G.O. (1978), *The Growth of Islam among the Yoruba 1841-1908*. London: Longman.

Johnson, S.O. (1969), *The History of the Yorubas*. Lagos: C.M.S.

Olupona, J.K. (1992), "The Dynamics of Religion and Interfaith Dialogue in Nigeria." In J.K. Olupona (ed.) *Religion and Peace in Multifaith Nigeria*, Ile-Ife: Obafemi Awolowo University Press: 1-9.

Omojola Bode, 2001, "African Music in Christian Liturgy: The Yoruba Tradition," *Nigerian Music Review*, Vol. 2 (Special Edition): 83.

Opeloye, M.O. 1998, "Evolution of Religious Culture Among the Yoruba," in Deji Ogunremi & Biodun Adediran (eds.) *Culture and Society in Yorubaland*: 139-148.

Stride & Ifeka., 1971, *Peoples and Empires of West Africa: West Africa in History, 1000-1800*, Nigeria: Thomas Nelson (Nigeria) Ltd.

Vidal Tunji, (1987), "Foreign Impact on Music," in Toyin Falola and G.O. Oguntomisin (eds.) *The History of Nigeria*, Vol. II: 44

12

Portrayal of indigenous religions and *Ifa* divination in Ola Rotimi's *Gods are not to blame*

- Victoria O. Adeniyi

Introduction

Ifa is a religious practice employed in solving human socio-biological problems among the Yoruba of south-western Nigeria. The Yoruba explore into *Ifa* divination with the intention of extracting from it the information that can be used as solution to man's problems. Thus, *Ifa* divination is regarded as an indigenous cultural health care system that is used to fill in the gaps believed to be created by the inadequacy of the conventional healthcare system in African societies.

It is an indubitable fact that the Yoruba are endowed with diversity of divinities and *Ifa* is undoubtedly the most important of these numerous divinities of the Yoruba people. He was one of the four hundred and one (401) divinities sent by *Olodumare* (God) to this world (Abimbola 1977:1) with specific assignments through *Orunmila*. *Orunmila* is regarded as the father of *Ifa*. This is why the *Ifa* system is connected with the god, *Orunmila*. "*Orunmila*" is said to be a contraction of the word "*orun-lo-mo-ati-la*", meaning only "Heaven can effect deliverance", *Orunmila*, as a god, is seen as the chief consultant and adviser in matters pertaining to all knowledge.

Ifa is believed to have lived between 600 AD and 1660 AD at Ile-Ife, which is considered as the cradle of Yoruba civilization (Shaw 1978). It is believed that green and yellow are his colours. Yellow indicates warmth, that is, his humility and hospitality, while green suggests an evocation of healing. The two colours, therefore, imply the healing and protective nature of *Ifa*. In traditional Yoruba society, the life of everyman, from birth to death is dominated and regulated by *Ifa*. No one takes any important step without consulting *Ifa*, the god of wisdom. All the important rites of passage have to be sanctioned and authenticated by *Ifa*, the voice of the divinities and the wisdom of the ancestors (Abimbola 1997:1).

Ifa was put in charge of divination because of his wisdom, which he acquired from *Olodumare*. He knew all the secrets of the universe. This is why he is regarded as the possessor of knowledge of matters affecting the fate of man, predicting the future and prescribing remedies of sacrifice, which will change or enhance one's fate. *Ifa* tells his supplicants how to evade unfortunate fate or how to maintain a favourable one.

This chapter is an effort to show that fate, which is a universal concept, still differs from one culture to another on the conception of its unalterability. By extension, it is an attempt to show that the Yoruba's conception of fate implies that man's efforts have significant effects on the participation of the supernatural powers in the affairs of man. To resign oneself to fate is to be crippled fast (Rotimi 1979).

The necessity for this chapter is, therefore, to show to what extent Ola Rotimi has gone Greek in his conception of fate, and to what extent his conception of this term differs from the Yoruba conception of it, considering the Yoruba cultural background of the play. This chapter also attempts to unveil the Yoruba understanding of the concept of fate and the role of *Ifa* divination in its alterability among the Yoruba.

The concept of Fate: definitions

The concept of fate has been interchangeably used as destiny or fatalism. It, as defined by *Oxford Advanced Learners' Dictionary*, implies "power believed to control all events in a way that cannot be resisted." Thus, we can infer that fate implies some measure of interference or participation of the gods or supernatural powers in the affairs of man. In shedding more light on the concept of fate, Steven Cahn (1969:4) argues that if it is true that an event will occur, then it is left to man to do anything that can prevent the occurrence of the event. If he does the action, the occurrence of the event will not take place. On the other hand, if he fails to do anything, then the event will occur.

Many great philosophers, however, seem to hold contradictory opinion about the concept of fate. For instance, Morgenbesier and Walsh (1962:1) claim that fate does not allow man to prevent the occurrence of any event from occurring. In other words, if a person is fated to die in 1970, then he will die in 1970 whether or not he attempts suicide in 1968. A.J. Ayer (1963:238) also believes that fate implies that the future is unalterable. For him, the effect our actions have on the future is what fate denies. It is not correct to assert that fate implies that things would not change irrespective of one's action. Fate affirms that an event will occur, but this is not to say that the occurrence of the event will take place no matter what anyone does. Adolf Grunbaum's point (1953: 772) is similar to that of Ayer. To him, fate implies that if one goes into combat and if some bullet has one's name on it, one will be killed even if one were to wear an impenetrable bulletproof suit of armour in battle.

The University of California Associates interpretation of fate is in support of Grunbaum's point. To them, fate implies that "man's will is no match for the decrees of fate. It is futile to take measures for his welfare, his health and his safety, for man is powerless to escape his fate" (1949: 614). This should not be so because if it is fated that one will die by drowning, it is not futile to learn how to swim since that knowledge may prevent one from drowning. If one's ability to swim then saves one from drowning, then according to fate, it was fated that one's ability to swim would save one from drowning.

H. Van Remsselaer Wilson, like his counterparts, is pessimistic about the concept of fate. As he puts it:

> The typical fatalist contends that human wisdom, human skill, even human stupidity, have no causal continuity with the future. The same future will occur, according to the fatalist, no matter what we human beings know or don't know, do or don't do, seek or shun... (1955:70)

It is fallacy to claim that human actions do not make any difference in the long run. As Steven Cahn puts it, human actions "do make a difference. Indeed, they are fated to make a difference. But this means that no one can prevent their making a difference, it does not mean that they make no difference" (1969:23).

Thus, fate can be seen as a term, which implies some measures of interference or participation of the gods or supernatural powers in the affairs of man, but this is not to say that man's efforts have no effects on the participation of supernatural powers in man's affairs. With this understanding, it is of paramount importance to examine the concept within the Nigerian context with particular reference to the Yoruba.

The Yoruba conception of fate and the role of *Ifa* divination

The Yoruba are a deeply religious people who have a strong belief in the existence of supernatural powers. It is believed that such powers affect the everyday life of man for good or evil. The Yoruba are so strong in their belief in the supernatural that they hold fate in high esteem and believe that the success or failure of a man depends on the choice he made in heaven. Although, human efforts cannot be ruled out for success or failure, the greater part of it is being played by fate. In other words, both head (*ori*—viewed as the home of fate) and one's efforts matter to achieve success in life. As Idowu asserts:

> If one is predestined to succeed by the choice of a good *ori*, one cannot actually achieve success without the use of one's *ese* (leg) the symbol of activity and power. (Idowu 1982:148)

Fate, among the Yoruba, is known as *ayanmo* (choice) or *ipin* (portion) or *kadara* (divine share for man) or *iponri* (the *ori*'s portion). All these names are associated with *ori* (the inner head). A man's success or failure is ascribed to the type of head he chose in heaven.

To the Yoruba, *ori* means the "inner person," and it is also the name for the soul (the personality soul). Although, *ori* is the word for the physical "head," to the Yoruba, the physical *ori* is a symbol for "*ori-inu*" (the internal head or the inner person). This is what makes a man. It is this *ori* that kneels down and chooses its destiny, and comes into the world to fulfil its chosen destiny. The Yoruba believe that whatever the *ori* chooses must come to be fulfilled in the world.

It is believed that the end for which a person is made is inextricably bound up with his destiny. The Yoruba are of the belief that a person retains his destiny in one of three ways: he kneels down and chooses his destiny (*Akunle-yan*); or he kneels down and receives his destiny (*Akunle-gba*); or he kneels down and his destiny is affixed to him (*Ayanmo*). The main idea behind the three-way conception of destiny within the Nigerian context, with particular reference to the Yoruba, is that the person who is coming into the world must kneel down before *Olodumare* for its conferment, which is believed to be unalterable.

The Yoruba oral traditions claim that it is *ori* that kneels down before *Olodumare* to choose, receive or have the destiny affixed to it. Having chosen or received the destiny, he embarks on his journey into the world. Arriving at the gates between heaven and earth, he encounters "the Gate-keeper" (*Onibode*) to whom he must answer some questions like "Where are you going?", "What are you going to do?" etc. After saying what he is going to do in the world, whatever he says is double-sealed, and he passes to the world where he forgets at once what has happened to him in heaven and what his destiny is all about.

The act of double-sealing whatever *ori* speaks out at the gates between heaven and earth is an indication, so it is claimed, that the destiny is unalterable and there is nothing anybody can do about it thenceforth. This is why the Yoruba usually say that whatever one chooses while kneeling before *Olodumare* is what is fulfilled upon arriving to the world.

However, the conception of the inalterability of destiny is considerably modified. The Yoruba believe that a person's destiny can be altered positively through the aid of *Orunmila*, who is known as the custodian of the destinies of both divinities and men. Oral tradition holds that he is fully knowledgeable in the affairs of man's destiny because he was present when man was created and his destiny sealed. And because he knows all the secrets of man's being, he can predict what the future has for man or prescribe remedies against any unhappy event. He is referred to as "the witness" or "advocate of destiny" (*Eleri-ipin*).

The Yoruba believe that *Orunmila* can reveal the future to his priests through *Ifa*, the geomantic form of divination that is connected with the cult of *Orunmila*. The *Ifa* culture is so important among the Yoruba that *Ifa* is consulted for guidance and assurance before a Yoruba man attempts to take any step in life. Man's destiny, therefore, becomes positively alterable through the consultation with the agency of this *Orunmila*.

The Yoruba worship and propitiate *Orunmila* for good health because he is believed to control traditional healthcare system. This system of healing in *Ifa* is effected through divination. *Orunmila* automatically becomes one's personal divinity so that good health may be ensured by sending messages to the supplicant through *Ifa*, and receiving sacrifices from the supplicant. This is why *Ifa* divination is considered to be an important factor in the life of every Yoruba person.

Ifa divination is made of Yoruba oral poetry, which "is an impressive preliterate academic system" (Abimbola 1975:2). It consists of sixteen main *odu* (signs), which can further produce 256 *odu* when combined randomly. The content of each *odu* is analyzed in form of story and experiences are related in form of fable stories. It is seen as a means of communication between the gods and human beings in African societies, with particular reference to the Yoruba societies of Nigeria. This supports Bascom's (1969) assertion that *Ifa* divination helps the *Ifa* priests to know what is hidden to ordinary human beings. It helps them to see into the unknown world and interpret what they see for human beings in the physical world.

The Yoruba believe that *Orunmila* was the first person to practice the art of indigenous medicine in the Yoruba kingdom. It is believed that God, *Olodumare*, who sent him to the world to find solutions to human socio-biological problems, vested him with the knowledge of *Ifa* divination. This made him travel from one Yoruba community to another, fulfilling this mission. He would divine the problems of his clients to find out the exact problem, the causes of the problem, and the likely solutions to the problem.

In contemporary Yorubaland, *Ifa* priests are still using *Ifa* divination to help individuals, and search for solution to their problems. As the *Ifa* priest divines and explores the *Ifa* verse that appears, he interprets it to know the nature and causes of the problems of the patient. It is his interpretation of the *Ifa odu* that leads to the solution or the steps to take to solve the problems of the client.

Ifa divination plays an important role in the social activities of the Yoruba. They are very curious to know what the future holds for them. They, therefore, consult an *Ifa* priest before a marriage, at birth of a child, before the appointment of a king, when a person is sick, etc. The *Ifa* priest takes his tool of divination, divines, and interprets whatever he sees on the divination tray. The *odu* might then say that the client should go and sacrifice to his *ori*.

To make an offering to the *ori*, the physical *ori* is the emblem with kolanut or fish stuck on it, while the blood of the fowl or animal is smeared on it. Offerings are made to one's *ori* as well as one's parents' *ori*. The emblem for the father's *ori* is the big toe of the right foot, while that for the mother's *ori* is the big toe of the left foot.

The Yoruba people also believe that the *omo araye* (sadistic foes) can also alter a person's fate negatively. These are personified in witches, wizards, secret cults and anybody with evil intention. These can spoil every opportunity of people's success by debarring *ori* from carrying out its destiny. Hence, people say, "*K'aye ma pa kadara mi da* (may the sadistic foes not change my good destiny)."

It is also believed that an individual's character can negatively affect his fate. In other words, a man's failure or happiness may be his own responsibility. Idowu asserts: The Yoruba believe that a good destiny unsupported by character is worthless. Destiny can also be spoilt by one's action, especially by acts of rashness and impatience. People are especially warned against impatience, as by it a person may easily forfeit the good fortune which is in store for him (1982:179).

A person needs to cooperate to make his good destiny a reality by acquiring patience and practicing good character. A person's bad destiny may be rectified if it can be ascertained. For example, if after the birth of a child, the oracle consulted reveals that the child has a bad destiny, things to be done to rectify it are told by *Ifa* upon consultation. A substitutionary sacrifice is made as a remedy to forestall an unhappy fulfilment.

In summary, the Yoruba generally believe that anybody coming into the world is predestined by *Olodumare*, double-sealed by "the Gate Keeper," and his destiny thereafter becomes unalterable. The conception of the inalterability can, however, be controlled with the making of certain sacrifices to maintain a happy destiny or to rectify an unhappy one. By extension, it is believed that anybody who has chosen a good destiny and is aided by the supernatural powers and his ability to work hard will become successful in life. Anybody who has chosen a bad destiny has the chance of rectifying it by performing sufficient sacrifice.

Although the concept of fate implies the participation of the supernatural powers in the affairs of man, this is not to say that all things will turn out as they will regardless of man's effort to retain the good fortune or to rectify the bad fortune. The moral behind the Yoruba conception of fate is to practice caution and patience in life, while at the same time avoiding a life of total inaction.

With our understanding of the concept of fate as it is universally believed along side with the Yoruba conception of it, we would examine the concept as it applies to Rotimi's *The Gods Are Not To Blame,* paying particular attention to its reality among the Yoruba as evidenced in *Ifa* divination culture.

The conception of Fate in *The Gods Are Not To Blame*

Ola Rotimi's *The Gods Are Not To Blame* is an adaptation of the tragic drama, Sophocle's *King Oedipus,* from Greece into the African soil under the veils of the Yoruba cultural background. The play centres on the tragedy of a man trying to escape his fate, which has been decreed at this birth. In the Greek tragedy, we learn of the curse on the house of Cadmus, the Theban king. The latest in the lineage was King Laius whose wife was Jocasta. They had a baby boy who was said to have had a curse on him as he was destined to kill his father and marry his mother. Out of human sympathy, the baby with feet pierced was given to a shepherd. The shepherd gave the baby to the king of Corinth for adoption, as he had no issue.

This baby was named Oedipus (i.e. pierced foot). He grew up and was aware of the curse. He decided to leave Corinth and later killed a man who happened to be his unknown father. He fled to Theban at a time the state needed a saviour from the attack of a beast known as Sphinx. He killed the beast and was made king. As custom demanded, he had to take Jocasta as wife. This served to fulfil the prophecy. Later as events unfold themselves, he is discovered to have been the murderer of King Laius and that the woman with whom he now has four children is his mother. It is this Greek tragedy that Rotimi has transposed into the story of *Odewale*. The only socio-cultural difference is that the story now takes place in Yorubaland and has Yoruba characters and culture.

Rotimi also departs structurally from the Sophoclean version by introducing a narrator in his prologue. The narrator tells us about the birth of *Odewale* (the hero), to king *Adetusa* and his wife *Ojuola*. As custom demands, *Odewale* is taken to Ogun shrine, which is expected to reveal what the boy's future is going to be. *Odewale* is said to have brought a bad mission as he has been destined to kill his father and marry his mother. To prevent this, the Ogun priest ties the ill-fated child's feet with strings of cowries and gives him to *Gbonka*, the king special messenger, to be destroyed in the evil grove. But as fate would have it, *Gbonka* does not destroy the baby, but he gives him to *Ogundele*, a hunter from *Ijekun Yemoja* who was with *Alaka*, his young assistant. Thirty-two years later, *Odewale* meets his unknown father and the two quarrel over a piece of land. The man calls *Odewale* "a man from a bush tribe" and this makes *Odewale* hit the man with a hoe, thereby killing his unknown father.

The people of *Ikolu*, taking advantage of the death in the palace, attack the people of *Kutuje*. *Odewale* comes to the land of *Kutuje* at this moment, gathers the people of *Kutuje* under his power and, consequently attacks the people of *Ikolu* with the people of *Kutuje* behind him. He frees the people of *Kutuje* and seizes the land of *Ikolu*. This makes the people of *Kutuje*, in their joy, break tradition and make *Odewale* king without consulting the *Ifa* oracle. As custom demands, *Ojuola*, the motherly Queen of the former King *Adetusa*, is given to *Odewale* as wife with whom he has four children, thus, fulfilling the prophecy.

In this play, Rotimi's fatalistic worldview has been structured along that of the Greek. It is the tragedy of an individual born with a curse on him. The central issue in the play can thus be seen as tragic inevitability of man's helplessness before his fate. This is to say that one cannot change one's fate, and that any attempt to change one's fate becomes a catapult to speed one's step to one's fatalistic destination.

It is this universal message, which has inspired Ola Rotimi to transplant the ancient Greek story of King Oedipus into African soil. This message, as V.U. Ola remarks, "continues to be less awesome, necessary and elevating today as it was to the Greek of the 5th century B.C." (1982: 23). As the message reads:

> We too need to be told that man is a limited and contingent creature, subject to sudden disrupting forces. Success is not finally to be measured by fame or material prosperity. Human greatness consists ultimately in nobly accepting the responsibility of being what we are, human freedom, in the personal working out of our fate in terms appropriate to ourselves. Though we may be innocent, we are all potentially guilty because of the germ of self-sufficiency and arrogance in our nature. (Paul Roche 1954:4)

To the Greeks, man is a helpless victim before whatever forces that oppress him, and he has no other choice than to have a sense of endurance with which he faces whatever suffering he comes in contact with. Within the Greek context, king Oedipus, in his innocence, has become the ethnical archetype of Greek tragedy as it is reflected in the lines of King Lear: "As flies to wanton boys, are we to the gods. They kill us for their sport" (William Shakespeare 1958). Wole Soyinka in his reaction to the above pessimistic view of life says:

> Like the Yoruba deities, but to a thousand fold degree, the Greek gods also commit serious infractions against mortal well-being. The Greek catalogue is one of list, greed, sadism, megalomania and sheer cursedness. But the morality of reparation appears totally alien to the ethical concepts of the ancient Greeks. Punishments, when the offence happens to encroach on the mortal, preserves of another deity and that deity is stronger or successfully appeals to father Zeus, the greatest reprobate of all. (1976:14)

Rotimi was influenced by the psychological base of tragedy flaw of the hero, which has its origin in Aristotle's "Poetics." Sophocle's representation of Oedipus as being destroyed, though innocent, would be out of order to the African audience whose moral bias and understanding of the relationship between man and god is one of complementarity.

Rotimi in his attempt not to sound Greek in his worldview, which is contradictory to the Yoruba worldview, took recourse to the Aristotelian concept of the tragic hero, but this only led him to another difficulty. Aristotle's theory of tragedy, being basically humanistic, rarely takes into consideration the existence of religious drama or "recognizes the fact that the gods could be capricious" (Ola 1982:24).

Aristotle finds unmerited suffering revolting and that the divine background of Oedipus' suffering is of little or no significance to the philosopher. Rotimi makes a blend of these two ideas together. *Odewale*'s curse that he should kill his father and marry his mother and his quick temper are strong indications of fate. The latter is so strong that we too can say at the end of the play that "The gods are not to blame," even when we know that they are to blame within the play's context.

The gods found it easy to fulfil their prophecy on *Odewale* largely because of his hot-temper with which he has been imbued by the playwright. This has been confirmed by Baba Fakunle as he tells *Odewale*: "Your hot-temper, like a disease from birth, is the curse that has brought you trouble" (29). It has also been supported by Queen *Ojuola* as she pleads with king *Odewale*: "My Lord, pray, cool your anger" (35). Later on, she fearfully asserts: "My Lord is so angry that I cannot even think" (54).

Baba Alaka, the old man to whom *Odewale* was handed over as a baby, has also corroborated this fact by saying: "I am glad to see that your youthful hot-temper is still with you, my brother, scorpion!" (61). *Odewale* himself confirms his hot-temper as he says, "Plead with him or I shall loose my temper" (20). Also, when he prays before the household shrine for some of his wife's patience:

> God! What a woman. Give me some of her patience, I pray you…some of her cool heart. Let her cool spirit enter my body, and cool the hot, hot, hotness in my blood—the hot blood of gorilla! Cool me, Ogun, cool me. The touch of palm oil is cool to the body. Cool me. The blood is hot (39).

Odewale only prays here, but there is more to it than praying. The Yoruba believe that *eni to ba dake tara re aba dake* (He who is not vocal about his situation, suffers being denied the needed assistance). *Odewale* should have consulted the *Ifa* oracle to know what sacrifices he should have offered to be cured of this birth disease, his hot-temper.

In addition, *Odewale*'s realization of his hot-temper was too late. By this time, he had unknowingly killed his father out of hot-temper over the issue of a piece of land. He had subsequently inherited his mother as a wife to match his new status as the new king of *Kutuje*. Thus, at the end of the play, he informs the audience that he has contributed to his tragedy. As he puts it:

> …Do not blame the gods. Let no one blame the powers. My people learn from my fall. The powers would have failed if I did not let them use me. They knew my weaknesses…(p. 71)

With this understanding, it could be seen that much as Rotimi has tried to universalize the theme of tragic inevitability, one discovers that what has been the inexorability of fate in *King Oedipus* has now become the issue of personal culpability in Rotimi's play (Etherton, 1982:119). Etherton remarks on the contradiction between the non-reconciliatory position of the Greek and the Yoruba gods:

> The traditional Yoruba concept of fate is only superficially the same as the Greek concept expressed in *King Oedipus*… Yoruba traditionally believe that your fate is your own doing. You kneel down and receive it as a gift from *Olodumare* before being born. It is intrinsic to Yoruba cosmology that a person's fate is never irreversible and that it can be changed from evil to good by appropriate sacrifices…(1982:103)

He further observes that unlike the Greek Olympian pantheon, the Yoruba gods are not capricious, least of all, Ogun. But in Rotimi's play, Ogun can be invoked as *Odewale* uses his name and instrument, the hoe, to kill king *Adetusa*, his unknown father.

Secondly, the fatalistic worldview is not allowed to work on its own. It has largely been realized through the inherent weaknesses especially the hot-tempter, in the character of *Odewale*. As Ola observes:

> Propelled by destiny and his own flaws, his search for the killer of his father became one with the search for, and eventual discovery of his own identity. In the process, his arrogance and sense of self-sufficiency are revealed (1982:30).

Conclusion

Ola Rotimi's conception of fate in *The Gods Are Not To Blame* is one of a divine punishment. Although Rotimi has explored the concept of fate in the drama, his approach to it differs from the Yoruba conception of it. His play, which is a transposition of the Greek tragedy, uses the Greek mythology. His theoretical misconception is that he fails to distinguish between the Greek and Yoruba cosmologies. The Yoruba gods are not as capricious as he painted them in the play. They can be appeased.

In conclusion, although the play carries the universal message that one cannot change one's fate, one discovers that in Yoruba mythology, it is believed that the gods can be appeased with appropriate sacrifices through the *Ifa* oracle to rectify any bad fate. Thus, the curse on *Odewale* is not as convincing as that on King Oedipus simply because *Odewale*'s curse is not a family curse. Despite Rotimi's efforts to separate the two, the concept of fate mirrored in the drama is more of the Greek worldview than of the Yoruba. The significant role of *Ifa* divination culture among the Yoruba is played down upon.

References

Abimbola, Wande, 1975. *Sixteen Great Poems of Ifa,* Paris: UNESCO.
Abimbola, Wande, 1977. *Ifa Divination Poetry.* New York: NOK Publishers Ltd.
Ayer, A.J. 1963. *The Concept of a Person and Other Essays,* London: Macmillan.
Bascom, W. 1969. *Ifa Divination: Communication between Gods and Men in West Africa.* London: Indian University Press.
Cahn, S.M. 1969. *Fate, Logic and Time.* London: Yale University Press.
Etherton, Michael. 1982. *The Development of African Drama.* London: Hutchinson & Co Publishers.
Grunbaum, Adolf. 1953. Causality and the Science of Human Behaviour. In *Readings in the Philosophy of Science,* ed. Herbert Feigl and May Brodbeck, 766–78. New York: Appleton-Century-Crofts.
Hornby, A.S., ed. 1989. *Oxford Advanced Learner's Dictionary of Current English,* 4th

ed. London: Oxford University Press.
Idowu, E.B. 1982. *Olodumare: God in Yoruba Belief*. Nigeria: Longman.
Morgenbesier, S. and T. Walsh, eds. 1962. *Free Will*. New Jersey: Englewood Cliffs.
Ola, V.U. 1982. The Concept of Tragedy in Ola Rotimi's The Gods Are Not To Blame. *Okike: An African Journal of New Writing* 22: 23–31.
Rotimi, Ola.1979. *The Gods Are Not To Blame*. London: Oxford University Press.
Shakespeare, William. 1958. *King Lear*. Baltimore: Penguin Books.
Shaw, T. 1978. *Nigeria: Its Archaeology and Medicine in Early History*. London: Thames and Hudson.
Sophocles. 1958. *The Oedipus Plays of Sophocles: Oedipus the King; Oedipus at Colonus; Antigone*. Trans. Paul Roche. New York: New American Literary.
Sophocles. 1974. *The Theban Plays of Sophocles*. Trans. E.F. Watling. Harmondsworth: Penguin.
Soyinka, Wole.1976. *Myth, Literature and the African World*. London: Cambridge University Press.
University of California Associates .1949. "The Freedom of the Will." In *Reading in Philosophical Analysis*, ed. Herbert Feigl and Wilfred Sellars, 594-615. New York: Appleton-Century-Crofts, Inc.
Wilson, H.V.R. 1955, Causal Discontinuity in Fatalism and Indeterminism, *The Journal of Philosophy*, 52: 134-158.

III

Rites, Rituals and Festivals

13

Comparative studies of rites of passages among the Ngas, Mupun and Mwaghavul of the Jos Plateau in central Nigeria

- Umar Habila Dadem Danfulani

Introduction

This work examines rites of passages in the traditional religions of three ethnic groups living on the Jos Plateau in Nigeria. They are the Ngas, Mupun and Mwaghavul Chadic-speakers of the Jos Plateau. They are found on the eastern part of the Jos Plateau, approximately located in the centre of Nigeria. The study belongs largely to the period from circa 1600 – 1850 CE; that is, from the settlement of the Chadic-speakers on the Jos Plateau, after their migration from their traditional homeland in the Borno-Chad basin (between C.1000 and 1600 AD), to 1935, reckoned to be the beginning of modern times in the area (Datok, 1983; Isichei, 1981; Danfulani, 1995 and Wambutda, 1991). These culturally distinguished ethnic groups were pacified (conquered) by the West African Royal Frontier Force (WARFF) of the British Constabulary between 1907 and 1914.

Prior to this period, their only contact with the outside world was through two major interactions with the Hausa. The first contact was peaceful. This was initiated through various trading or settlement *amana*, pacts, trust, treaty or covenant making rites between some Hausa persons or individuals and a number of communities of Jos Plateau. Goshit (1980:59; Jos Prof. 275/132) recorded one such pact between a group of Hausa and the Ngas polity of Per or Amper, which means water gushing from a stone aquiver, which the Hausa Muslims named Chika.

Defining rites of passages

In examining rites of passages, it is imperative that the contribution throws light on the categories that constitutes the rites of passages of these three ethnic groups. This includes three categories of rites of passages. This is based on the typology provided by Cox (1998: x), when he asserts that rituals should be categorized according to the function they perform for the community that produce and possess them. His taxonomy of rituals includes *calendrical* rituals, *life cycle* rituals and *crisis* rituals.

The first are rites of passages of temporary cycle or calendrical rituals, which the Ngas, Mupun and Mwghavul regard as their ethnic national festivals. The rites of passages of temporary cycle affect and involve all the communities of the three ethnic groups. They are known by various names and are usually performed or celebrated from one polity to the other. The passage rites of temporary cycle or calendrical rites are focused on national and communal ritual activities. I thus refer to them as calendrical rituals or rites of passages of temporary cycle because they are used for marking time within the year since they occur yearly, with the exception of *bwenene*, the festival of the dead, which is celebrated among the Mupun every fourteenth year.

The second category is life cycle or life crisis rituals, which constitute another rich area of ceremonies and dramatic performance in the lives of the Ngas, Mupun and Mwaghavul. Life cycle rituals are focused or centred on the life of an individual and cover the important landmarks in the life of a single individual because of the dignity and worth of human life as a whole, biologically, spiritually, politically, economically, socially and politically. As we will later see below, the French anthropologist, Arnold van Gennep refers to a ritual process shared by these first two categories, though he clearly differentiated between the two.

The third category is made up of crisis rituals. These rituals mark the passage of communities through perilous, difficult and troublesome times in their shared or corporate life. Such times are marked by events beyond ordinary human control bordering on the matter of life and death. The British anthropologist, Victor W. Turner (1969) refers to them as 'rituals of affliction' and incorporates them into rites of passage.

Mwaghavul rites of passages of temporary cycle or calendrical rituals

In examining 'Rites of Passages', Arnold van Gennep, whose book *The Rites of Passages*, first appeared in 1908, stimulated interest in the study of these set of rituals. Van Gennep asserts that:

> The universe itself is governed by a periodicity, which has repercussions on human life, with stages and transitions, movements forward, and periods of relative inactivity. We should therefore include among ceremonies of human passage those rites occasioned by celestial changes, such as the change over from month to month from season to season and 'from year to year' (1960:3).

Rites of passages of temporary cycle or calendrical rituals celebrate the passage of time or events such as New Year, New Moon, planting/cropping season, harvest festivals and national liberation or independence.

These rites of passages of temporary cycle or calendrical rituals are otherwise referred to as cultural festivals. Cultural festivals play prominent roles in the Mwaghavul society. It is pertinent to note that although the Mwaghavul people are a linguistic group, they claim different places of origin (for example Pushit and Panyam claim to have come from Ngung while Kombun claim Vet). There is no record of warfare between the Mwaghavul polities and no one can assert that one polity feared any of the other polities. The Mwaghavul were however feared by their non-Mwaghavul neighbours in pre-modern times. For example the Mwaghavul of Pushit greatly influenced their non-Mwaghavul neighbours such as the Pyem, Fier, the Kadung and the Mupun.

Cultural festivals served as means of interaction among the Mwaghavul people and with their non-Mwaghavul neighbours. Each Mwaghavul polity had its cultural festival celebrated during the time of leisure, that is, after the harvest period. These festivals were connected with hunting, horse racing and dances. The development of these festivals is obscure but one thing is clear and that is, they were celebrated in the places mentioned below many years ago and in that strict order. Both Bulus (1986) and Haggai (1986) independently pointed out that these festivals and places of celebration were as follows:

Festival	**Place**
Wus	Panyam
Riyem	Pushit
Tidiu	Komben
Dileng	Bwai
Kopshu	Mpang
Bwangzuhum	Kerang

Added to these festivals were *alogholam* of Alogham and *Mugo* of Mangu. These festivals are still being annually celebrated today in the places mentioned. These festivals were highly cherished by the Mwaghavul people and despite the presence of agencies of change, they have continued unabated into the contemporary period. Since these festivals carried different names and were celebrated in different places, their patterns of celebration differ one from the other. However the main features that characterized the festivals were horseracing and dances such as *velang* (cornstalk fluting festival), *bel* (reed flute dance), *pwaghal* (victory war dance) and *ceer* (old and young women's dance).

Kwat: hunting festival

Kwat, hunting followed immediately after the festivals and lasted till the rainy season when farming commenced. During hunting, those who killed a game (wild animal) took part of the meat to the *Miskaham* (chief) to show their appreciation. The killing of large wild animals such as leopards (*lushim*), lions (*bwor*) and elephants (*nii*) was celebrated for several days by the village and the killer celebrated as hero and was carried shoulder-high during dance for the celebration. Bulus (1986, 1990) has clearly highlighted the hunting festival in Mwaghavul land. The hunting season commenced with the secret performance of some rituals by *kum* traditional or indigenous religious chief priests. The priest responsible knows the time to contact a diviner (*ngu-kos-pah*) for favour. The diviner gave a day on which to perform the ritual. On the set day, the chief priest, some members of the clan or village rode to the spot on horses. There, the priests made fire from wood (*feel*) and reed (*buu*) through friction (*piyaghar wus*) and set it on the bush. According to (Bulus 1986, 1990) in some communities like Bwai/Ruf in Kombun district, the old women shaved their hair. The rite of bush burning by the priest signalled the commencement of the hunting period.

After three days of the commencement, a festival was held to mark horseracing (*sogho*). Horse riders from different communities came to help that community celebrate the day. The hunting festivals were called by different names in different polities. These festivals lasted from the month of December to April each year. This period was usually a festive period throughout Mwaghavul land. Other festivals include *Luwet* held in Mangun (Bulus 1986, 1990). It was a kind of wrestling festival in which young men made ropes from jute fibre and whipped each other. These ropes gave snappy sounds and could hit hard. This festival was held to test manhood and endurance. Brave young men could win love/hands of girls that might lead to marriage. The *luwet* festival of Mangun was actually a harvest festival similar to the Ngas harvest festival of *mos tar*, beer festival of the shooting of the moon. The young men beat themselves in both festivals indicative of the joy that comes with harvest. It is a jesting way of saying "the harvest is already here, I am strong and healthy, I will surely partake in it; no magnitude of beating will stop me from partaking in it. Just beat me, just beat me!" In Mangun, this festival was followed by marriage of girls to their suitors.

The celebration of the festivals served as a meeting point for boys and girls where the best dancers attracted suitors and girls or boys were likely to choose marriage partners from there. The festivals were celebrated with a lavish abundance of the local three-day beer *mos*, usually brewed from sorghum or guinea-corn *suwa naan* and/or bush rush millet *kas*. These festivals were strong binding forces between the Mwaghavul polities.

Age-grades and age-set organizations

A prominent feature of the pre-colonial Mwaghavul society was the division of the population into age-spans according to period of birth. Chagu (1985) stated that the Mwaghavul society was divided into three broad age sets. These were elders (*dikam mo*) whose approximate age ranged from fifty-five (55) and above. Following this group was the *nan-mo* or the middle aged that were in the range of thirty five to fifty-five. These were followed by the youth (*zilang mo* for males and *jirap mo* for females). The youth according to him were further divided into two-the older youth (*zilang mo*) and younger youth from ten years to twenty-one years. All those below ten years were regarded as children (*jep mo*).

The *dikam mo* were in their retiring stage and took less active part in any work demanding the vigorous use of the body such as farming and warfare. They were highly respected in society for their age, wisdom and life experience (*erlebnis*). They were regarded as wise men in the society and took decisions on family, clan and village matters. They acted as advisers to the younger generation and settled disputes at the various levels. When women reached this age and were post-menopausal, they became highly respected and no longer ran away from the masquerades as they had already become men.

The *nan-mo* ages set were the warriors and farmers who constituted the arrow head and bulk of the labour force and carried out most of the serious activities in society. They did these duties alongside the *zilang mo* as a form of training for the *zilang mo*. They trained them in warfare and all work demanding physical strength like farming, harvesting and threshing, house roofing, wood-curving, granary building, spear/arrow making, procurement and mixing of potent poisons for spear/arrows heads and the digging graves, among many other such activities. The *jep zilang mo*, were mainly engaged in farming activities, weeding, and harvesting, among many other chores. These they did mainly through age set communal work force called *wuk* in which they took turns in working for each other as a group. The female of this age group also engaged in a kind of celebrating friendship in the group called *gwom shar*. They would, all in the group of about 10 to twenty members, contribute special local beans called *kwakil* and ingredients and millet to cook food and *war* (gruel) in the compound of one of the members so chosen and celebrate their friendship for a day or two. This was done during the hunting season. Girls who were old enough for marriage ate the *gwom shar* meal for the last time because after *bwanzuhum*, which was the last festival in the year, these girls were kidnapped or waylaid and captured through snatching or wife-theft to become wives of their suitors. Wife-theft was the preferred method of marriage in traditional Mwaghavul society. The *jep mo* especially the older ones from eight to eleven years ran errands and looked after livestock. Age grade is also determined amongst Mwaghavul men through *can/pun* male circumcision and puberty rites as each set of boys went through the experience together, while the girls determine their age grades through *gwom shar* friendship meals.

Rites of passages of temporary cycle/calendrical rituals

Jos Plateau communities, especially the Mupun and Mwaghavul use religious calendrical festivals or rites of passages of temporary cycle to reckon the passage of time and the years. Bwenene festival of the dead comes up among the Mupun after every fourteen years. This necessitated many years of preparations that assume a gigantic scale in the last two to three years before the event. Vwan/pun or chan comes up every four to five years. Thus age in traditional times is determined according to how many *vwan/pun* life cycle rituals or *bwenene* festival of the dead one has witnessed in life. How do Jos Plateau communities reckon or keep time? They recognize a twelve month lunar year each counted as one moon, *tar*, roughly corresponding to the lunation of the moon. They kept strict records with:

The high priest and his several assistants, in order that their manifold rites may be correctly adjusted to the appropriate times of the year, used a calendar in which each year consisted of twelve lunation or lunar months. The high priest was aware that after three lunar years, he would have fallen behind the civil calendar by one lunar month. Every three years, therefore, he applied a corrective to this by a month's alteration in the calendar date of rituals (Berthoud 1969:46, cf. Neiers, 1979).

The high priest (*mishkom kum*) is able to maintain an accurate counting of the months by stowing away stalks of a particular grass in the rafters, thatch or roof of his hut-shrine at the end of every month or with the passage of every month. Months/moons are reckoned according to the activities that predominated each month. Thus we have *tar byang maar*, the month for the start of cultivation, *tar kop*, the month in which sowing starts, *tar per maar*, the month for cultivating digitalis elixir (*fonio, accha or kusuk*), *tar saak maar*, the month for the cultivation of sorghum or maize (*kop shwa*), *tar ka shwa* the month for transplanting sorghum, *tar shwa/ka kas*, the month for transplanting millet, *tar gwom/le yil* the month for second ridging, *tar dyip shwa mbulwu* month for harvesting maize, *tar dyip shwa naan* the month for harvesting sorghum, *tar chan kusuk*, the month for harvesting *digitalis elixir* and so forth.

Though *tar* is rendered moon/month, it is dynamically used more like a season. The Mupun and Mwaghavul would thus talk of the moon or season of a particular festival, while the Ngas talk about *tar mos Bwir*, the mean the month/season of the beer festival of Kabwir village, *tar mostar*, the month/season of the beer festival of the shooting of the moon, and *tar mos lun*, the dry season beer festival of the ancestors (Wambutda 1991:90 and Danfulani 1995:30). The Mwaghavul talk of the season of their festivals which must begin annually from Dikibin, to Npang (Ampang West) and then to the other polities in this strict order: Kerang, Kopaal, Kumbun, Pianiya (Panyam), Sulwa, Ruf, Bwai, Pushit, then Bungha and Mangu, with Chakfem and Jipal performing their festivals separately (Bulus 1986:67 and Danfulani 1995:30). The Mupun celebrated their seasons according to the flute horn dance of the ancestors (*fer nji*), hunting season *tar kwat* and in accordance with other types of flute, drums and other instruments used.

Life cycle or Life crisis rituals

Most of the materials used for the Mwaghavul case study are from the well-researched and very rich works of Bulus (1986, 1990), and a piece written on the subject by Pauline Lere (1995), supported greatly by empirical fieldwork and observations of the author, including a great deal of cross references from the works of Danfulani (2003).

Ontological and social dimensions of life crisis rituals

The human being in African society is defined in terms of life crisis, rituals and symbolism both ontologically and socially. Ontologically, s/he is a life-force in vital relationship with other life forces both horizontally and vertically. This is why Ikenga-Metuh asserts:

> Man ontologically is best viewed as a living force in active communion with other living forces in the world. Every person is a nexus of interacting elements of the self and of the world which determines and is determined by his behaviour. Thus the true concept of man is lost if he is considered in isolation [as it is done in the Western world]. He is all the time interacting with other beings in the universe to which he is linked by a network of relationships. Man in African Religious philosophy therefore is best studied as a life force in the midst of other life-forces. This is very clearly seen in the African doctrine of man (1987: 171, 185).

Sociologically, the human being is defined in reference to his/her position in the different groups to which s/he belongs. As s/he grows biologically, and assumes more responsibilities in society, his/her social position and status may also change. In many African societies, including that of the Mwaghavul, this transition or change from one state of being to another, ontologically, biologically and socially, is accompanied by a set of ritual performances which have come to be recognized and called *life crisis rituals* (Ikenga-Metuh, 1987: 185).

Thus life crisis rituals form a special category of *rites of passages* that are unique or peculiar in their application to human beings. These rituals are performed to mark transition into different crucial phases of human life like pregnancy and birth, naming, social and biological puberty or manhood and womanhood, marriage, fatherhood and motherhood, title taking or advancement to a higher social class, occupational specialization/call to a socio-political or religious office and death and burial (Ikenga-Metuh, 1987: 185). Though these rituals are found in all societies but they tend to reach their maximum expression in small-scale societies, relatively stable and cyclical societies, where change is bound up with biological and meteorological rhythms and reoccurrences rather than with technological innovations. In consequence, though these crisis rituals are concerned with and centred on individuals, they in addition mark changes in relationships of all the peoples connected with them by ties of kinship (blood), conjugal (marriage) and other social linkages, political and economic associations, and spiritual and religious ties such as covenant making, sacrifice, priestly functions, divination and mantic sciences, among others (cf. Ikenga-Metuh 1987: 186). Thus the "big moments" in the lives of individuals, such as *can* or *pun*, that is, puberty or manhood circumcision/initiation rites for a single Mwaghavul boy or novice becomes the "big moments" for others as well. This is because the maternal and paternal uncles of a Mwaghavul neophyte or candidate celebrate the event with the boy, even in opposing units as they engage in a mock fight against each other at a high point during the festival. The "big moments" are the important indices of life crisis rituals as identified by Victor Turner (1970: 7). The Mwaghavul are not left behind in this philosophical task.

Arnold van Gennep, however, drew the attention of scholars to the reality that life crisis rituals can be differentiated from other rites of passages, such as calendrical rituals or rites of passages of temporary cycle. According to him, when the activities associated with life crisis rituals are examined, in terms of their order and content, it is possible to distinguish precisely three distinct phases and characteristics, celebrating three distinct stages, which others do not have. These three phases and characteristics are encapsulated in the reality that life crisis rituals celebrate the rites of *separation, transition,* and *incorporation* (Van Gennep, 1960, 11-12).

Van Gennep, however, pronounces two cautions to scholars over the three phases that are characteristics of life crisis rituals. Firstly, van Gennep warns that although a theoretically complete life crisis ritual includes *rites of separation, rites of transition* and *rites of incorporation*, yet in specific instances, these three aspects are not always equally important or equally elaborated, nor are they found developed to the same extent by all peoples or in specific ceremonial pattern. For example, rites of separation are prominent in funeral ceremonies, while rites of incorporation appear strongly in marriage, and transition rites play important roles in pregnancy, betrothal and puberty/initiation rites (van Gennep, 1960: 11-12, cf. Ikenga-Metuh, 1987: 187-188).

The second caution pertain life crisis rites such as birth, initiation and marriage or death that have other objectives, besides the life crisis rituals they are associated with. For example, marriage ceremonies may include fertility rites and rituals of longevity, while initiation may include propitiation and oath rites, birth ceremonies may include protection rites and consultation with diviners and oracles, while funeral rites may include defensive and reversal of spiritual attacks rites (cf. Ikenga-Metuh 1987:188).

These characteristics should be borne in mind in the interpretation of African life crisis rituals and in any attempt of arriving at a correct hermeneutics of Mwaghavul life crisis rituals described in this chapter. Four major categories of Mwaghavul life crisis rituals have been examined in the work. These are pregnancy and birth, boys' initiation and puberty rites, marriage, and death and burial rites.

Mupun and Mwaghavul life cycle or life crisis rituals
Pregnancy and birth

After a few months of marriage, elderly women would be watching out for signs of pregnancy in the *mat po* (a bride or newly married woman). If it was noticed that she was pregnant, her husband's family were delighted, especially her mother-in-law who would soon be expecting a grandchild. The women would usually exclaim *tar del ra*, meaning, "the moon has passed her by" implying that she did not experience any menstrual flow during her last menstrual cycle. The expectation of pregnancy soon after marriage is so high that her husband's close relatives would ask during greeting "how is she?" If she has started showing signs of pregnancy, the reply was *"ra ret na"* meaning "she is good to look at", or "she is good looking"; the implication being that it could not be said of a human being that "s/he is good to look at" or "good looking" or "beginning to look good" without incurring the charge of *ke* witchcraft accusations. This is because while an animal may look good for food, the same could not be said of a human being, except in the case of the pregnant woman.

The Mwaghavul recognized sexual intercourse (*kwaam*) as necessary for conception. The belief was that the semen (*ndugal*) gave the life of the child while the mother's blood (*aas*, egg/ovum) gave the body (Bulus, 1986, 1990). According to Bulus (1986, 1990), when a woman was conceiving for the first time, she would undergo some rituals. These rituals separated her and set her aside in preparation for motherhood. She was thus hedged around with rituals and taboos that were aimed at protecting her in her pregnant and condition, together with her unborn baby—the new life she was bearing—until she carried the pregnancy to term.

First was the ritual of *tughunpas* to prevent abortion. Pieces of calabash were nailed to the woman's door with an arrow so that when she entered where the arrows were kept, no harm would befall the foetus. The *tughunpas* ritual was done in the early stage of pregnancy. Rituals that follow this first one move the pregnant woman who has been set aside and separated from other women into the threshold or transitory period of her pregnancy. Henceforth she is semi-sacred, a taboo and people around her try their best to please her because she is carrying new life.

Next was the *vwang mulam* ritual, which was performed when the pregnancy was four to six months—*vwang mulam* literary means washing away the slippery (*spirogiara*). The ritual took place at the stream or river in the company of some women. A kind of weed was fetched in the stream signifying the washing away of all the guilty acts the woman committed before marriage. A chicken provided for the ritual was waived (*shoor*) over the woman to further take away any punishment that should have followed the breach of any societal lore, laws and taboos in the past.

Following this ritual was the ritual of *tok shiri* (ritual of sacred places). This was done to prevent miscarriage and once this ritual was performed, the woman could go to the stream or river without fear of miscarriage. This ritual prevented the pregnant woman from riding a horse, climbing a rock, or a tree and carrying heavy things. *Tok shiri* ritual of sacred places permitted the pregnant woman to breach taboos usually associated with prohibitions imposed on sacred places. For instance, men, woman and children were prohibited from resting under the cool sheds of sacred trees (*ting waar*), open bush shrines (*pe waar*) and within the premises of closed or house shrines (*lu kum*). Since the pregnant woman was believed to be carrying one of the late ancestors, she was permitted in her pregnant condition to rest in any of these places if she so wished out of tiredness. The ritual was therefore meant to protect the woman and ensure save delivery. Bulus (1986, 1990) recorded that among the Mangun community, the ritual of *kum kihpuk*, was performed for the woman's first pregnancy only as well as the *kumbish or kumbang* ritual.

Where a woman frequently experienced miscarriage, the ritual of *nang aak* was performed for the woman by a diviner (*gu-kos-pa*) or priest (who was also an herbalist). A calabash crossed with charcoal was brought and the pregnant woman sat on it to the extent that her clothing covered it. The diviner or herbalist took leaves in his hands, shook them and enquired from the pregnancy she was carrying. If the calabash broke in the process of the enquiry, it meant that the woman had been responsible for her miscarriages (alluding to breaches ranging from infidelity to witchcraft). However, if the calabash did not break, if meant her hands were clean and other factors would be held responsible. In both cases, further enquiries were made by the diviner to ascertain the major aetiology/cause and also to enable the diviners and other herbal healers proffer the correct solution(s) to the problem at hand (Danfulani, 1995).

When a woman remained childless (that suffered from the matter of the dry tree—*jyer*) after marriage for sometimes, the husband married another wife (or other wives). In Mwaghavul society, having many children, especially sons was a sign of wealth, prestige and sure way of the man's name continuing in that society. Childlessness was attributed to the anger of parents or ancestors. Childlessness was believed to block the rebirth or reincarnation (*ta wong*) of the spirits of the ancestors.

A pregnant woman could give birth anywhere, anytime and Mwaghavul names depict where one was born, for example, *Dabong/Nabong* (a male/female child born on the farm or in the band where crops are kept), *Da ar/Na ar* (a male/female child born by the road side), or when one was born, for example *Pusmut* (evening), or circumstances at birth for example *Dyelchin* (given by justice), *Kyesyen* (exhausting medicine, indicating the child was sickly as an infant) and *Molfwang* (the maternal uncles have preserved or done something good).

Indoors for seven days

No matter where the woman delivered, the placenta (*jirem*) and other birth debris (blood and other dirt) were collected in a pot and buried. The pot containing all these birth dirts was buried in an upside position with portions of protruding into the surface. It was then broken to show that the child was no longer in the womb but it had been born. Henceforth, it bound the child to family, the earth (where the ancestors lived) and the land, to which s/he belonged and for which the child must be willing to die in its defence.

After delivery, the nursing mother was expected to stay indoors with the baby for seven days or till the umbilical cord dropped. This was known as *luu paar* and the woman was known as *mat paar*. This does not, however, mean that she never went outside the compound! In reality the *zai* - that is, the adjoining wall between two huts - is temporarily broken down to allow her access into the outside wall. This is because of the belief that she was in a temporary state of ritual pollution and thus cannot enter the compound through the *po bong* gate, which will render all medicines, deities, and ancestral spirits guarding the compound powerless. Moreover, this indoor stay was to prevent the spirits from getting the baby back. So when a baby was born, the traditional priests (*nyem kum mo*) would look for a spider and place it on the child's head with the assumption that when he or she dies, she or he would be taken to heaven because according to Mwaghavul belief, God (*Naan*) sent human beings down to earth on a spider web (Bulus, 1986, 1990).

During this time, the woman was taken care of by elderly women in the family, especially her mother-in-law or elder sisters of the husband who gave her hot water bath everyday, massages her stomach with hot water, and kept both baby and mother warm. The mother received special treatment during this time in terms of food. The midwives (elderly women in the family) ensured the woman took only hot liquid and food. Neighbours and relatives brought gifts of food to the woman. It was specially prepared local beans or *fonio* (digitalis exilir) known as *gwom paar*. Immediately a woman delivered, a massage would be sent to her parents and usually the mother or a close elderly female relative of her father would come and minister during the period of staying indoors.

Pun Laa ritual (child education) and *Put Tol* (coming-out) rites as rituals of incorporation of mother and child

After the seven days of being indoors, an elaborate ritual was performed to release the woman to go outside and be incorporated into society and thus regain her freedom to go anywhere she wanted. The requirements for this ritual were: the presence of all children in the community, cooked millet (*shool*), chicken (*kwe*), gruel (*waar*), olive oil (*mwor paat*), gourd (*been*), a winnower (*kutut*), local beniseed (*kudul*) and a hoe (*cyan*). The officiating priest went down to the stream where the community fetched drinking water along with the children and a chicken. At the stream, the priest spread powdered medicine and asked the children to search for three spiders (*lu naan*). The spiders were trapped by droppings of olive oil and then picked up. One of these must be picked on the way to where the chicken was to be roasted. Water was fetched in a gourd and carried away by an uncircumcised boy appointed for the ritual.

The chicken was then slaughtered and roasted and eaten by the priest and the children. After eating the roasted chicken, the priest and those who went down to the stream went back home for the purification rites. On arrival in the home, the priest called the mother of the child three times before she answered. She was asked to come to the door and to put her right foot out. The priest closed the upper part of the door with the winnower (*kutut*) and poured the water from the gourd from the top of the door. He brushed the winnower down to her foot, telling her to remove her foot before the rain falls (referring to the water from the gourd). The same process was repeated with her left leg. After this, she was asked to sit down on the door step and then he placed the winnower on her head and stirred it round with the fresh grass (*tar*) collected from the stream to cover the water in the gourd (*been*).

This was followed by the ritual of integration. The officiating priest gave some cooked millet (*shool*) to the mother and the appointed or leading boy (*laa pun*) of the ritual. This was offered to them first on their left palms, which they exchanged and ate. Next, they were served on their right palms, which they exchanged and passed on to the boys who had gone down to the stream and others who were waiting to eat. This signified the reintegration and incorporation of the woman back into the society.

Next, the officiating priest poured gruel into a calabash, put some powdered medicine in it and shot porcupine strand (*pas kiyek*) to stand erect in the calabash. The mother and the leading ritual boy (*la pun*) were asked to drink jointly from the calabash at the same time (*mu bal or mu kaat*); first from the left and then to the right.

After this, the baby was brought out into the open for the very first time amidst shouts, smiles, jubilation and great joy. The three spiders brought back from the outing to the river by the priest and children were soaked in olive oil. The first one was placed on what the Mwaghavul refer to as the "breathing spot" or fontanel (*pelbyab*), that is the centre of the head of the child; the second one was placed on the chest or the collar bone of the baby, and the third was placed on the mother's collar bone. The officiating priest took the baby (with smiles and happiness), lifted him or her towards the sky, that is, towards *Naan* (God), (and actually throws the child towards the sky and catches him/her several times), saying continuously: *Na Naan, yi naa bina, a we cin yi ye*? This means: "Mother Goddess [God in Mwaghavul is feminine], see my [precious] thing, who will give you?" This, ironically, was the rite of presenting the child to *Naan* God the giver. Then he took a hoe and beat it at the entrance of the compound indicating that the woman was free to go out from then. The ritual was immediately followed by eating and drinking the cooked millet (*shool*) and the gruel (*waar*) and sending some to neighbours so that they too could bless the child. No name was given to the child on that day, until he or she was weaned. Male children were circumcised when they reached 8 to 14 years old.

A few weeks or months after the birth, the woman's mother along with some close relatives would arrange to go and see the child. They brought specially prepared local beans seasoned with *kudul* (a local seasoning) and chicken meat also dressed in or coated with *kudul*. It was a special occasion and got the attention of the woman's husband who also prepared to receive his in-laws to see the child by making gruel and food. After the visit, the in-laws were sent back with gifts, especially of *kas* bull rush millet and fonio, that is, *digitalic exilir* (*kusuk*).

Childhood

Childhood lasted from about eight to fourteen years when the child was initiated into manhood or womanhood by the observation of the respective maturation or puberty rites. Between birth and three years when children were weaned, the child was most of the time with the mother who carried him/her along wherever she went. Mothers backed their children with skin/leather prepared in such a way that the woman could back the baby by fastening the straps of the skin to her waist and the chest or abdomen area immediately above her stomach. This skin was known as *shim luhut laa*, which means the leather or skin used for backing a baby. The child was breastfed until weaning at about three years.

Weaning started with the gradual introduction of gruel (*waar*) from 6-9 months, followed gradually by solid food. After weaning, children were kept most of the time with their grandparents or great-grand parents while the mother went to the farm, fetched firewood from the bush, fetched water from the stream or attended to any domestic or family chores/duties. As the children reached about six to eight years of age, they looked after sheep or goats under the supervision of the grandparents. Children were active and kept themselves busy by engaging in play and games such as sliding on the smooth surface of rocks, swinging from trees (*zere*) and jumping with ropes woven from different types of grasses (such as *pil* the spear grass and *pitem* raffia palm) among other games.

During the dry season, boys engaged themselves in hunting lizards (*tibilak*) and rats (*jios*), cutting grass for thatching, fetching firewood from further and deeper into the bush, and making flutes of various sizes in preparation for dance festivals, among other activities. While the girls were engaged mainly in household chores especially looking after younger siblings, drying grains on flat rocks to dry, grinding or milling grains on the traditional millstone, pounding *fonio*, (*digitalis exilir*), washing cooking utensils and fetching water from the village stream or water point among other tasks.

Boys' puberty rites: circumcision

Circumcision, called *can* was intricately interwoven with the religious festival of *pun nji*. *Nji* among the Mwaghavul people was regarded as the spirits or cult of the ancestors. It was customary for the spirits of the ancestors, *nji* to be called back to earth *pun* by a lot of rituals to partake in a festival with the living in which a great deal of the three-day beer mos is brewed and assorted foods are prepared. During the *pun nji* festival, a lot of food, a special traditional bean called *kwakil* coated with fried beniseed *kudul* and other favourite foods of known ancestors were prepared for the celebration.

The rites of *can* circumcision were conducted every four years for boys from seven to eleven years (Haggai 1986 and Bulus 1986, 1990). The circumcision ceremony also served as the initiation ceremony in the life of the boy as it marked his acceptance into the social structure of adult world. After the initiation, those initiated were allowed to participate in all social and religious duties and ceremonies of the society.

Circumcision was the physical removal of the foreskin or natural covering on boys' penis. Some scholars have thus referred to it as male genital mutilation (MGM). *Can* boys' circumcision amongst the Mwaghavul was ritually performed in a sacred or circumcision grove, *bong can*, recognised for the purpose by priests. At the circumcision grove (*bong can*) a prayer seeking the blessing of the ancestors (*nji*) and deities (*kum*) was said by the surgeon before the operation. No pain relieving drugs were administered before the circumcision. Bulus (1986, 1990) described the process as follows:

> During the circumcision, boys were held in sitting position with their faces covered to prevent them from seeing the bare knife...the foreskin is cut off, removing the 'low, dirty' feminine-like part of the boy. The bloody objects were buried secretly.

The circumcision wounds were covered with soft leaves and then later in the day, or the next day, they were dressed in hemp-like sisal leaves called *lijam*. The *lijam* was grown in the grove exclusively for the purpose of circumcision. The circumcised boys remained in the circumcision grove (*bong can*) from dusk to dawn. Their circumcision wound dressing (*lijam*) was called *yang* because it was kept in position by neatly arranged stalk and the wound was dressed in the circumcision grove until the wound was completely healed. The wounds were dressed with herbs from *ting tohol* or *mawe* (herbs). During this period of nursing their wounds, the circumcised boys were called *jep-midang* (tail boys). The tail here referred to the extra string used in holding the woven frame (*yang*) which kept the circumcised penis in place. It hanged at the back of the waist as tail.

While their wounds were healing, the parents of the circumcised boys made arrangements for their new cloths, which were triangular pants, known as *fwat* (or *bante* in Hausa) This was a local hand woven loom from cotton. Before the invention of *bante*, a penis sheath called *tilong* or *nimwet* was made from a palm frond. The wearing of *bante* or *tilong* marked the rite of incorporation after the wound has been healed.

The coming back home of the circumcised boys after the wounds were healed was herald with jubilation and congratulation by their women relatives like aunts who brought gifts of chickens and or well prepared local beans (*kwakil*) seasoned with special tasty scenting fried seed known as *kudul*. Others brought *fonio* dough, *digitalis exilir* or food cooked from hungry rice (*gwon kusuk*) dressed with stock and meat on top. This gift of special food to the boys that were circumcised was known as *gwom midang* (food for newly circumcised boys). Before the official coming back home, it was religiously a taboo for a woman to see boys still nursing circumcision wound. The age of a child in Mwaghavul society depended on when he was circumcised and how many circumcision festivals he has witnessed. The year a child was circumcised was used as reference points for events in the life of the individual. For example in making reference to say the death of any member of the family, they would say he or she died in the year so and so was circumcised or a year or two after. Circumcision commence with the ritual of the 'stealing of the boys' from their homes to the circumcision grove known as *wat (waat) laa* or *wat jep*. This is because the boys are usually stolen without the knowledge of their mothers, the other women, and other children in society. This marked the beginning of their separation from the rest of society. *Waat jep/waat laa* sets them aside from other children in society. With *waat jep/waat laa*, the separation phase in boy's puberty rites has begun.

Puberty

Puberty for boys commenced with initiation (*punji*) which might have coincided with circumcision or after the circumcision (as described above). Initiation was done every four years. In some Mwaghavul polities, this was performed together with circumcision as it is the case in Pushit (Haggai: 1986) but in some Mwaghavul communities, the circumcision (*can*) was done every year while the initiation was done every four years, such as in Bwonpe (Chagu 1985).

During the initiation, every clan head (*sakan*) presented boys in his clan to the chief priest (*Miskaham kum*) for the initiation and the elders in each clan were also represented or went along with the boys to prevent them from being swallowed by the *nji* (ancestral spirits). The boys to be initiated were warned not to eat meat, go into their mothers' mud ceiling granary (*durum*), touch cooking pots or go into their mothers' room as a kind of preparation. Mothers of initiates provided new baskets (*kichik*) for fishing, new pots for brewing and keeping the three-day beer (*mwos*) and a new string sachet for keeping fish.

During the threshold or liminal stage of initiation/puberty rites, the neophytes went through a great deal of physical, emotional and psychological tests of pain, torture, endurance, and hardships that brought changes, which transformed them into men. The main events during the initiation were fishing (*tu pupwap*) the presentation to *nji*, target practice with the bow and arrows at the shooting range (*tu gurum*), the symbolic swallowing and vomiting by the *nji* ancestors and introduction to *nji*. Chagu (1985) and Bulus

(1986, 1990) have elaborately described the initiation rites of boys in Mwaghavul land.

The initiates and the priest in charge of the initiation gathered in the chief priests' compound. The chief priest would then inquire from other priests if there was any foul or goat that year for the initiation. The answer was usually positive. A pot of three-day beer was brought and poured into the calabash for drinking, while some is poured into a gourd to be taken the river where the fishing is billed to take place. To proceed to the river, one of the initiation priests took the lead to pave the way with a branch of tree. The initiates followed each with his basket and sachet *(shang)* and another priest followed behind, closing the rank. At the river the boys were sent to hunt for the wild peanut *(tunghus)* which was poured and mixed with the wine in the gourd. Thereafter, an initiation priest *(gu can)* positioned himself in the water while another priest sits on the bank. The initiation priest held the gourd and prayed to the spirits of the river *(yem dung mo)* for success. The prayer was followed by three drops of wine from the gourd (the number of drops differed from one community to another). After this, the leading initiate was asked to step into the river first, followed by the others.

The fishing started and the first catch by any boy was given to the priest who cut into two and put it back into the river. This was dedicating it to the river spirits as a form of sacrifice. The fish caught were given to the *nji* priest at the bank who skewed them on pieces of sticks to number seven to be taken for the chief priest for sacrifice.

After the sacrifice, the initiation priest did something mysterious by making the water level to be rising and at the same time shout to the boys to rush out of the water to escape being drowned. The slowest boy could get drowned. The water could rise to the initiating priests' knee level. The priest asked the boys to go back into the river which by this time was subsiding to its normal level. The process of rising water level and subsiding back to normal level was repeated three times at intervals during the fishing ritual

At the end of the fishing ritual, the initiating priest put back some of the fish (alive) into the river, telling the river spirits to take those so that they may find fish again when next they came for the fishing ritual. Before leaving the river, the initiates were asked to touch the river with their feet *(lop shii dung)* and run to the hill where the priest warned them to leave behind everything they had taken from the river. The contingent moved back to the chief priest's compound who welcomed them back with a fishing ritual dance, saying and reciting parables *(tam pupwap)* those with *nji nineen* introduced their initiates to it the following day. The dance continued to their respective homes till day break.

After the fishing ritual was the ritual of presenting the initiates to *nji*. The initiates wore penis sheath *(tilong)* made of palm front. In the absence of this, the boys dressed in *yang* (stalk). They were presented to *nji* in a shrine garden *(bong can)* or *nji* shrine. They were all made to sit in a single file as made, each with his spear in front of him. They sat according to their clans. The initiates were then presented to the *nji*. Paternal uncles represented the boys to *nji* while maternal uncles protected the child from being snatched by the *nji*. This ritual was known as *daar kaa laa*. It used to be a fierce battle between the two sides. Any advance by the *nji* party to snatch the initiate was met with a shout of *wura mang kwe, wur mang kwe* meaning "she snatches, she snatches" and the defence party (maternal uncles) responded repulsively *a we cin yi ye, a we cin yi ye?*, meaning, "who will give you? Who will give you?" It was a kind of mock but fierce wrestling match where the wrestlers drank the three-day beer *mos* at intervals but the initiates were not allowed to eat anything till evening. It fact, the mock fight was so fierce that some men or even the children could sustain mild wounds and on some rare occasions, a person may accidentally be mortally wounded or even get killed.

The major event of this presentation to *nji* took place in the afternoon. The chief priest accompanied by his lieutenants went round with wine mixed with human liver in a calabash sewn with a skinned human skull each initiate sips the wine and spews up in the air. This action received the praise of *ko gwa! ko gwa!* meaning: "good boy! Good boy!" or "well done boy! Well done boy!" It was highly tempting to swallow the sip since the initiates had stayed without food since morning. But it was a test of endurance and manhood.

The boys proceeded to shooting range with spears after this. It is noteworthy that those who went to the shooting range were those who had successfully been defended from the terror of *nji* (*bar poo nji*). The shooting range was called *tu gurum* or *pus kop*. A tree representing human being (*ron*) as the target was shot by each boy. In going to shoot, each initiate shouted the place of origin of his clan as he moved swiftly to shoot. For example, some of the clans came from Gung, Difiri, Muduhulut, Tokshel, Bure, Paal, etc., shouted *woo kop o, kop o, a gung o, a kat me mat a ar be ra ku kum del di o* (meaning, any "My spear, my spear, put on your best show and try, if there is a woman on the way, she should give way for deity to pass"). Bulus (1986, 1990) said that at the end of this shooting, each initiate was taken on shoulders by his defence team (maternal uncles) amidst jubilation. With an air of success in defending the child, the uncles sat to drink the three-day beer *mos* from preserved pot of beer called *tughul nighin* (mother's pot). The final initiation rite was the presentation to *nji* for swallowing. The initiates left home very early before dawn to the chief priests' yard. Throughout that day, they would not eat anything to show that they were being swallowed by *nji*. The mother of every initiate prepared very delicious local bean (*kwakil*) or food from *fonio*, covered with oil and pieces of grass added to it which will hook or choke the *nji* to vomit her son. If a mother does not prepare that food, her son would remain in the *nji's* belly and the belly of the *nji* was so large that it could contain all the initiates. Any 'bad' child was drowned by a big pool of water, symbolizing the stomach of the nji, which is located in the initiating place. From there they were led blind-folded to go and see the spot from where the *nji* emits. The spot was covered with broken pieces of pot (*ghir*). This is the ritual of *Naa Nji* "seeing the ancestors" or "introducing the initiates to the ancestors" and it marks the last ritual that officially closes *pun* boys' puberty rites. It is the last ritual which both introduces the initiates to communion with the *nji* ancestors and to other ritual *Kum* deities of the clan.

The boys were sternly warned not to reveal the secret of what they saw or went through to anybody. To legitimize this, the oath of secrecy was administered when they boys were taken to an old woman with a hoe on her head. This was the rite of showing their faces to an old post-menopausal woman to see (*chin yit nin mat naa*). By touching the hoe on her head, they had taken the oath of secrecy, indicating that they had sworn to keep all their experiences a secret and also to defend their clans and land with their lives if the need arose. This was the beginning of the incorporation phase.

When the entire process of initiation was over with the secrecy oath administered, the total process of incorporation rites was prosecuted in earnest. The boys were dressed up with strip-cloth (*zaal*), skin bag (*kuluk*), leather skin (*nar*) and a triangular waist band (*fwat* or *banti/bante*). They were shaved and they wore bangles (*kim*) on their hands. Before they were shouldered home, they showed their faces to one elderly woman-mother of the child (*nighin laa*). The next day, the women celebrated the return of the initiates with *cheer* dance. The women danced this particular dance from one particular compound to another of the initiates who had successfully returned home. They got gifts of salt and meat from the family of the initiates.

There were lessons for the initiates to learn during the whole process of the initiation rites. Initiation itself was training in manhood and endurance (bravery). At the fishing ritual, boys were trained to be smart when faced with danger, at the wrestling; they were exposed to violence so that they could take part in war as men. Therefore, initiation prepared the boy for manhood responsibilities including marriage.

Inheritance

The property of a deceased man especially his land asset was divided among his surviving sons and his dead son who was survived by sons. For instance if a man had five sons and four were living at the time of his death, the property was divided among the four living sons, but if the dead sons had children, the property was divided into five because the children of the dead man inherited him. Where the sons were too young to be on their own the brother of the deceased took over the assets of the deceased and took over the upbringing of the children until he married for them. In the case where the sons were grown up, the farms, livestock and other personal property of the deceased were shared among them. Where the deceased was a chief (*Miskagham*), the eldest son inherited him. Among the Mwaghavul, the youngest son inherited the house/compound that belonged to the dead man while the older sons were expected to establish or build house for their families nearby in the vicinity of the main family compound.

Inheritance was patrilineal; therefore daughters of a deceased man had no share in assets. If the deceased had only one wife, and had three sons from that one wife, then his property was shared equally among all of them. But if the deceased had two or three wives, with each wife having a son or sons, then the property was divided into two or three according to the number of wives provided each woman had a son. The asset was shared equally among the wives, the number of their sons notwithstanding. Therefore, the wife who had four sons had equal share of the property of her husband with her mate who had one son. The sons would in turn share the portion of the assets given to their mother equally and the woman and the woman who had one son, her portion will be given to the son all by himself (Chagu: 1985).

In Mwaghavul culture, widowhood inheritance was practiced. Widows were inherited by one of the brothers of the deceased. Tradition states that the widow had considerable say in whoever inherited her and she also had the choice of returning to her parents and remarry elsewhere. Most widows choose to remain in their deceased husband's family in order to cater for their children.

The property of a deceased woman was inherited by her husband and children. The significance of inheritance among the Mwaghavul lay in the necessity to perpetuate the name of the family and continuity of its membership as a corporate group.

Marriage

The oral sources are unanimous that everyone got married and marriage was the most important event in the life of an individual (Haggai 1986 and Chagu 1985). Marriage (*dyik*) was the union between a man and woman from two different clans or villages who were known not to have any close blood ties. It was a means of raising a family and bringing unity and peace amongst the in-laws. Marriage was so central in Mwaghavul culture that there was hardly any normal person who did not get married. However a few cases of abnormality such as serious disability and insanity could prevent one from marriage. The main purpose of marriage was procreation. This explains the reason for adding other wives when the first wife was childless. Marriage ceased to be meaningful where there were no children. Marriage (*dyik*, which means "to build") between villages and clans fostered unity and the clans and villages became interrelated because of marriage. A man who found it difficult to secure a wife near his own locality would travel to a distant village and pick a wife. The family, clan or village from which one married became his *sihiir* (in-laws) and so you could not wage any war with them. Dispute between such families, clans or villages were quickly resolved by the elders (*nyem nan mo*) before it degenerated into open conflict. There were three major ways of securing a wife. These were: childhood betrothal, elopement and widow inheritance.

Childhood betrothal

Here parents were actively involved in contracting marriage between their son and a girl from a good family tradition, record or history. The parents of a boy had the responsibility of choosing a wife for him. This they did when the children were quite young from about 8-9 years (Haggai 1986). When a parent became interested in a girl in another family somewhere, he would visit the family and verbally indicate interest in the girl to marry his son, marking the beginning of the separation phase. Most often this choice was done without the consent of either the boy or girl.

When both parents agree, they kept it as a covenant between themselves and the father of the boy visited the house of the girl's parents regularly to serve as assurance to her parents that she had been set aside for the purpose of marriage that is still in the distant future. Thus in this type of marriage, the transition or threshold phase was quite lengthy. With the commencement of puberty, the boy's parents gave her a metal bangle called *Khim*. Its acceptance by the girl simultaneously showed her willingness to marry the boy and love for him. Anyone who saw her with the *Khim* knew that she had been betrothed and from then, the payment of bride price started and continued gradually until marriage. Before the putting of the *khim* on the girl, formal consent of the girl and the parents for marriage was sought through a middleman (*gu'ar*). Everything given to the parents of the girl as bride wealth (*mbi kwaam*) went through the middleman who kept detail record of all submissions of dowry items by the parents of the boy through him. The bride price included a hoe (*girik*), salt, grain (millet and *fonio* or *digitalis exilir—kusuk*), and livestock (*long*) which could either be sheep or goat depending on which ever was given and accepted by the girl's parents. Among the wealth, horse (*bring kwaat*) was one of the items that must be given before a girls bride price was considered paid. Chagu (1985) pointed out that the horse could be given after the marriage. In pre-colonial Mwaghavul society, the significance of the bride price was not so much its economic value as was the type of cultural obligations, which the union created between the families. One of these obligations was agricultural labour service to the in-laws called *mar mat*. He also gave gifts and presents and it was an obligation to be of good conduct to his in-laws.

One of the most significant traditions in the courtship and preparation for marriage was the taking of grain and animal usually sheep or goat to the parents of the girl so that they can prepare the three-day beer (*mwos/mos*) and food and invite all members of their clans to formally notify them that their daughter had got a suitor. This was called *se reep*. This was done twice over an interval as could be afforded by the boy's parents.

Before the girl got married, the maternal parents and family (extended family of the girls' mother or mother's brothers) were notified through the drinking three-day beer (*mwos/mos*) and the eating goat meat or mutton provided by the suitor. The suitor of the girl brought a bag of bull rush millet (*kas*) and goat for the mother of the girl to brew the three-day beer (*mos/mwos*) and cook the meat, respectively, in her own parents' house and invite the extended relations to drink and eat as notification of the marriage. This was done to get the blessing and support of the maternal parents of the girl for the marriage. Danfulani (2003) has identified the stages of childhood betrothal as follows:

Step one – Making inquiries – the parents of a boy make inquiries about the family of the girl they are interested in marrying for their son. This might involve *paa* (divination) to get proper guidance to the right girl.

Step two – Choosing the *gu'ar* (middleman or go-between). The family of the boy now looks for a man of good reputation acceptable to the girl's family as a go-between the two families in all issues relating to the marriage negotiation. The first visit was to seek the formal consent of the girl and her family. Thereafter all bride price were given to the girl's family through the middleman.

Step three – First visit to the girl's parents led by the *gu'ar* (middleman). The *gu'ar* informed the girl's family in advance about the intended visit. The male relations of the girl's father would meet in the girl's compound to receive the august visitors. After declaring their intentions as to which girl in the family they have come to ask her hand in marriage, the girl will be called and asked whether she knew those who have come. Acceptance of salt from the visiting would-be-in-law meant consent. If the salt is rejected, it indicated rejection of the suitor.

Step four – Heart to heart talk – (*Tong Chin*). This is a close mutual talk between the two families and was done in a form of a feast where relations contributed materially and through representatives to this heart-to-heart talk between the families.

Step five – *Se reep* (public notification of girl's relations through drinking and eating). This was in three rounds. First, *Naa pun* was the father's pot(s) of three-day beer (*mos*). The boy's parents brought liquor and goats or sheep meat to the girl's father to invite the key decision-makers of his family to meet with the boy's relations. During this visit, all the bride wealth items (*bi kwaam*) agreed upon earlier were presented to the girl's family. This may include salt (*kiin*), a bag of millet (*tip kas*), a bag of fonio (*tip kusuk*), a hoe (*cyan girik*), four goats, bangles (*khim*) and a horse (*biring*).

Secondly *Mos* (or *mwos*) *kin* – This was a drinking and eating party, where the three-day beer mos and fonio (*kusuk*) meal including plenty meat were consumed, in the family of the girl's maternal uncles (parents) as notification that the daughter of their own daughter was getting married. By this time the marriage (that is the period when the groom may arrange for the kidnapping or stealing of his wife) was near and could take place anytime.

Marriage under the childhood betrothal took two forms. First when the bride wealth (*mbi kwaam*) and the necessary obligations were done, the middleman would ask for the girl to be given to her husband. The family of the girl would then arrange a time and the *lamat* would escort her to her marital home. She would be adorned with ornaments and local powder (ochre) known as *lip*. This brought to an end the rather long period of courtship and transition and started the last phase of incorporation. The family of the groom would receive her with jubilation and celebration. She would usually be very shy and always try to hide herself or cover herself and be very loyal to her husband, parent in-laws and members of the husband's extended family. This rite incorporated and rehabilitated the new bride in her marital and conjugal home. This more formal type of marriage was however rare.

The second and more popular mode of marriage saw the suitor's friends or male family members forcefully snatching, stealing or kidnapping the bride to be. They way laid the girl when she was alone or with little children while on her way to or from the river fetching water, fetching firewood or the bush where she had gone to relief herself. She would usually struggle to resist by screaming or shouting but the men would over power her and carry her to a close relation to the husband or to the husband's house directly. This was called *ya mat* and most of the marriages were done like that. *Ya mat*, literally the "catching of a wife", "kidnapping of a wife" took place in the dry season and not during the rainy or farming season. This was performed either while the bride wealth was being settled, or afterwards; and some brides actively connive with their would-be kidnappers. However, in other instances, wife theft may occur without prior knowledge of the bride's parents or even the bride herself. In such cases, the family of the bride may raise a great deal of dust. There are known instances where the frantic struggles and cries of a would-be-bride led to her rescue by the members of her family, clan or village. Thus this mode of marriage ritual does not allow for academic analysis of life crisis using the approach of Arnold van Gennep that observes three phases of *separation, transition* and *incorporation* as examined at the beginning of this chapter.

Elopement

Elopement was the second method through which young men secured wives. Here a man and woman planned secretly to get married. At an arranged time, the girl would follow friends or relations arranged by the man when she was returning from fetching water, firewood, at a grinding/milling stone or the market. This usually took place with little resistance from the girl. She would be taken not straight to the man's house but to a home of a close relative who lived some distance away to hide her there (*zok mat*). Most young men will consummate the wedding before the rite of *zok mat*. After a few days, the man would mobilize his relations, usually paternal uncles to visit the parents of the girl and disclose the whereabouts of their daughter. They would tell the parents of the 'missing' girl in a "pleading and wailing voice" (*maap*) that their daughter was not killed by a wild animal but that she is in their custody. Thereafter, they would begin to pay the bride wealth according to Mwaghavul tradition. The girl moved to the house of the man after the revelation. Sometimes the girl would have been engaged to another man. The bride wealth was taken from the husband in custody of the girl and returned to the man who had betrothed her. Elopement was very often a course of conflict. In an attempt to elope or seize a girl by her husband's friends or relations, the girl's relations put up strong resistance through fighting to get her back. Elopement in Mwaghvaul tradition also does not allow scholars to apply Arnold van Gennep's theory of *separation, transition* and *incorporation* to the study of life crisis rituals. It is interesting to know that the early Christians accepted the elopement method as a legitimate way of marrying girls from the Mwaghavul traditional religious background since their parents would not willingly allow young Christian boys to marry their daughters. After both bride and groom to be had agreed, the groom-to-be would arrange with his Christian friends to way lay and kidnap and willing bride and run with her to the mission station. They would follow the traditional customs of announcing her disappearance and pay both the "goat of assuaging anger" (*long dor*) and the bride wealth to her parents, while the girl stays in hiding at the mission compound. After all these, the bride wealth will be settled (See Danfulani 2003).

Widowhood inheritance

The brother or a relation of a deceased man inherited his wife (*fwan mat*). This was usually in addition to the wife (wives) he already had. Sometimes too, an unmarried man would inherit the widow of his brother or relation. This is because the widow (*mat ka*) was asked to choose a man who would look after her and her children from amongst the male relations of her late husband. Marriage through widowhood inheritance enabled the woman to remain in the family especially where she was of good conduct and hard working. It also enabled her to take care of her children. Since the society was a polygamous society this practice did not create much problem in the family even though rivalry or jealousy may develop between the wives as in most polygamous families. The widow (*mat ka*), however, had the option of re-marrying outside the family if she so wished.

Residence for the newly married couple was patrilocal where the wife went to live with her husband and his family. His home became her home after marriage. Parents of the groom were actively involved in the marriage of the first wife but after that the man could marry other wives too. Subsequent wives were the sole responsibility of the man himself without parental involvement. The common Mwaghavul family in the pre-colonial period was therefore a polygamous family. The traditional household consisted of a man, his wives and their children, his parents and even grandparents, his unmarried brothers and sisters. Where his children grow up and marry their wives and children also became members of the household.

Chastity was greatly upheld in marriage and adultery was severely punished. Adultery was taken as offense against ancestral spirits (*Nji*) and to appease the wrath that would follow, both the man and woman were to bring goat or chicken to be offered as sacrifice by religious priest on their behalf to avert calamity befalling the man or woman.

The stability of the marriage depended on a number of factors the most important being children. To die childless especially without a male child who would ensure the continuity of the family name was a curse and shame to the Mwaghavul man. Childlessness or bearing only female children by the first wife was a major factor that contributed to polygamy because there would be so much pressure on the man to marry again to have children or male children.

Divorce was rare even though it could happen where the woman did not have children or male children. Divorce was obtained by refunding the bride wealth and where there were children they remain with the husband as the children belonged to him. Divorced women could remarry other men of their choice. Women everywhere amongst Jos Plateau polities were very free as has been exemplified in the work of Rev. Sister Maria de Paul Neiers (1979). A woman could leave her husband and remarry another man of her choice at any time. This became even compelling especially where starvation was a feature in the family of the husband. Starvation was common in the months of June and July when the new crops were not ready and this was a major cause of women leaving their husbands. A woman could go to the market, a festival dance and/or any public occasion and never return to her husband because she had taken off with another man (Danfulani 2003).

Funeral rites

Death is the inevitable end of every human being. To the Mwaghavul, death was a transition from the world of a human being to the world of the spirits. They believed that at death, the personality of the soul which is the spiritual substance, the essential person separated from the physical body. The physical was buried and decayed while the soul went to *yil nji* by the absence of the shadow of the body that the Mwaghavul believe is the soul and has departed to *yil nji*. Death was painful, especially that of young people. The physical departure was painful but the Mwaghavul believed that life continued in the next world. Bulus (1986, 1990) reports that the Mwaghavul believed that at death, the soul went to *cibeling* a good place away beyond the hills on the eastern horizon, somewhere in the vicinity of the sunrise. Naturally, everyone hopes to reach the place but on the way, there is a bad place – a kind of underworld called *wongohor* into which might fall as the journey to *cibeling* was difficult and only good people reach there. Once an individual fell into *wongohor,* there was no escape.

The dead man/woman was dressed in strip-cloth (*zaal*) just around the waist and carried for burial either on the back or on reed plated or woven mat (*kiram*). This was done on the same day of death or a day after. Some Mwaghavul communities buried their dead in a sitting position facing the east (*cibeling*) and some in a lying position. Chief priests, priests and very old people were highly honoured during burial. After sitting or laying the dead body in the grave, the grave was covered with wood, thorns and cactus to keep away hyenas which robbed graves at night. This was the separation phase of the dead from the living. In death and burial rites, transition rites began with separation rites, since the latter was rather very short, starting with the cessation of human life.

Three days after the burial of the dead body, some few priests from the paternal family went to the grave and opened it up to examine it using traditional methods to determine both the character of the deceased while s/he was alive and the cause of death (Danfulani 2003). This ritual was called *naa kiciir* (examining the contents of the grave) and it was very significant as it revealed the true character of the deceased and the cause of death. One major reason often given for cause of bad character was involvement in witchcraft activities (*sohot*), while the major cause of death in many cases was witchcraft (*sohot*) and seldomly sorcery (*lohom*) and breach of taboos, among others. Others were hidden or unconfessed sins such as adultery, theft or stealing. The transition, threshold or liminal phase of life had started and the soul will remain in limbo or in betwixt and between for the next one year or so.

Not all deaths received proper funeral rites (Bulus, 1986, 1990). According to Bulus, deaths caused by thunder (*yindek*), small pox and leprosy were bad deaths. Such bodies were buried in shallow graves in a swampy area (*wum duwang*). The death of a thief, witch, sorcerer and slaves also did not receive proper funeral rites as they could just be thrown in grooves and gorges. However, those who died of leprosy, small pox and thunder could become *nji* ancestors after 7 years. Bulus (1986, 1990) reported that they could be received in half of 7 years but broken pots must be heaped as a sign that they have not completed the circle of their purification. However, a witch was never allowed the luxury of rebirth as s/he was either killed by sizzling through witch hunting and burning or the contents of his/her grave was usually evacuated and totally burnt to ashes to prevent rebirth/reincarnation (*ta wong*).

One year after burial, dead ancestors were deified as *nji* ancestral spirits in a ritual of second burial known as "the beer festival of taking/removing the head/skull" (*mwos mangkaa*). This ritual involved several rites of incorporation of the ancestral spirit into the cult of ancestors (the *nji*) and secret society of masquerades (*wong*). It is of great importance to note that this important ritual was performed by the maternal uncles—the mother's brothers. The skull of the dead man was removed from the grave and examined in the scientific art of traditional craniology. This ritual terminated the transition rites and started the final phase of incorporation of the soul of the deceased as an ancestor. *Mwos* (locally brewed alcohol) and special gruel from *fonio* known as *war lubang* were used for the ritual. The gruel was poured on the skull and when it ran through the expected cracks, it was declared normal (*kaa ni shwaa waar*—"the head/skull has drunk gruel"). The ancestor would then be honoured by keeping his skull in the shrine (*lu kum*). But if the gruel did not run through the expected cracks, the skull was thrown away as worthless because the deceased was thus proven to have lived and led a bad life because of his bad character. Henceforth, he was suspected of involving himself in witchcraft activities.

The final phase of incorporation rituals was deification rituals to honour a dead ancestor. This was known as *lop-kop* or *le-kop* meaning planting a base. It took place several years after the death of the ancestor, usually seven to ten years. It depended on the readiness of the relatives of the ancestor to conduct the ritual which usually lasted about a month. It involved a lot of cooking and drinking. The deification was done in one chosen compound where all those deifying their ancestors in the community gathered. Relatives and well wishers contributed towards the ceremony. After this ritual, the ancestors could be called upon to intervene during sacrifice, prayer or offering. Amongst the Mupun, this was called bwenene, which occurred every fourteenth year in the societies (Danfulani, 2003).

Bulus (1986, 1990) described two ways through which ancestors were deified in pre-colonial Mwaghavul society. The ritual requirements consisted of blood and liver; *mwos* or *mos* (locally brewed beer) and loose fonio meal or food (*gwom fwon*), that is, made from *digitalis exilir*. These were presented to ancestors to come and eat in a cycle of seven rounds. In the case of an informant, Dikam Vombok of Mangun, the ancestors were represented by seven flat stones, arranged in a cycle, where they were fed, with food and libations poured on each stone as observed by Bulus and Danfulani during field work in 1985.

The consumption of the food by brown ants (*kamkaghas*) meant the honouring of the ritual and its acceptance by the *Nji*. According to Pofi Dangshwahar, an informant of Bulus (1986), that was interviewed in 1985 from Bwai, the spirits of the *Nji* ancestor are invisible and since they are not human beings, they are said to change or metamorphose into brown giant ants called *kamkaghas* to consume any sacrificial meal/food. The ritual symbolic requirements consisted of jaw bones and a heap of loose fonio meal/food (*gwom fwon*). The jaw bones came from the animals brought for the ritual. They represented ancestors to be deified. These were held standing by the food. Any jaw bone that fell indicated unworthiness for honour by, protection and posterity of the community, clan or polity. During the trial, the jawbones were said to move round.

Mwaghavul people strongly believed in rebirth or reincarnation, while the whole gamut of death and all that it represented was merely seen as a transition. They believed that the living-dead reincarnated to be reborn as new babies within the family. This was known as *ta wong*. Sometimes children did certain things that proved that they were indeed reincarnated ancestor. For example, it was common for a child to go and show a spot in the ground where he had hidden treasure or revealed certain mysteries that were done only by ancestors that lived long ago. Dead people also visited loved ones through dreams and visions and could offer help to the living, especially widows. *Ta wong* rebirth or reincarnation terminated the state of ancestorship after the soul of the deceased had been reborn in several children. The child was reborn through the shooting star (*zar dang* or tail possessing star).

Mupun and Mwaghavul crisis rituals

Mupun and Mwaghavul traditional societies usually put on the toga during the period of crisis. This is usually occasioned by the urgent invitation of the requisite religious functionaries to handle the emergent at hand through the performance of the adequate rituals. Crisis is said to have occurred when a particular clan, village or ethnic group declare war on another either during the time of peace or during war time. Crisis is also occasioned by the experience of drought (*puus chyan*) or too much rain (*fwan*), a plague of quella birds, locust invasion (*chibel*), caterpillar (*nambur*) or other invasion of crops by other insects, the emergence of a strange illness, mass deaths due to witchcraft attacks (*sot*), the appearance of a ghost (*shon*) in the society and epidemics such as cholera, small pox (*muut bin*), chicken pox (*ndisuk*), influenza or any illness/situation that threatens communal life or the lives of individuals living within a community.

The approach to crisis rituals among the Mupun and Mwaghavul is usually urgent as delay may lead to a considerable lost of human lives. In the case of war, all the men folk do not only constitute themselves into an army of soldiers armed with shields, bows, arrows, machetes and spears, but they immediately constitute themselves into the body of masquerades (*nwong*). This would usually scare the womenfolk into taking refuge in doors, while the men now turned into masquerades are left out doors to face the danger ahead. The men then performed the ritual of dressing in war garb including the rubbing of ritual red ochre (*lip*) on their bodies. In the case of drought, a full ritual of rain making is called for (see Danfulani and Haruna 1998 and 1999 for details).

Conclusion

The rites of passages being performed today among the Ngas, Mupun and Mwaghavul are different from the way they were performed in olden or ancient times. For instance, today calendrical rituals are no longer staged in their traditional seasonal epochs, but they are rather performed annually in line with Christmas and the Easter periods. As for life cycle or crisis rituals, most of the traditional rites associated with them during ancient times have died out completely because of the impact of the processes of modernization, urbanization, Islamization and hausanization, Christianization and westernization, the introduction of the poll tax, western economic system and coinage, and industrialization (especially the tin mining), generally, aside from the sweeping winds of globalization that have encroached drastically upon the process of glocalization, which should be robust enough to withstand the onslaught of change being brought from outside. For the Ngas, Mupun and Mwaghavul, the thesis proposed by Ogbu Kalu (1996) and Emefie Ikenga-Metuh (1981) and other scholars concerning the flight or retreat of the gods is true in many respects. This is indeed the case concerning the rites of passages concerning life cycle/crisis rituals. The remnants are very few and these continue to survive in the form of some bride wealth items usually paid as part of standard marriage contract recognized by the Church, insisting of the need for *ngu'ar*, a go between in matters of marriage and the provision of traditional names for children, which though in the native tongues of the respective ethnic groups continue to reflect Christian values, among very few others.

Concerning the traditional religions of the Jos Plateau people, most of the cultural and ritual practices have disappeared, even though the art of *nwong* masquerading have enjoyed a higher level of survival than most other aspects if the traditional religions. This is despite the fact that a number of the masquerades have disappeared aside from the whole gamut of the cult of the ancestors, which curiously enough is usually associated with masquerading. The survival of the art of masquerading is largely the case not because they are used any longer for maintaining law and order or as the depositories of history, but because masquerades are associated with festivals that are still merely performed more as vestiges of revivalism and tourism.

Thus the attempts at revivalism within the traditional religions of the Ngas, Mupun and Mwaghavul that started in the wake of structural adjustment programme (SAP) of the mid-eighties that birthed tough economic crunch has not taken the direction of returning to the religions of the forefathers among these ethnic groups. The attempts at revivalism taking place today has ended with very novel, romantic and nostalgic renewal of cultural festivals, annual cropping, harvesting and hunting festivals, a return to the use of traditional cultural items such as knives, spears, staffs, and the revival and creation of new political titles.

Meanwhile, the stages observed by Arnold Van Gennep, viz: separation, transition (threshold or luminal) and incorporation stages in life cycle or crisis rituals remain unchanged notwithstanding whether they are staged within African traditional religious traditions, or within Christian, Islamic, Buddhist and Hindu traditions. However, the agents and impact of change have greatly eroded away the various stages of life cycle/crisis rituals. In fact this is true of the various aspects of Ngas, Mupun and Mwaghavul traditional religions. The vast majority of these ethnic groups have become Christian en-mass with very few Muslims among them.

References

Berthoud, Jacques A. (1969). *The Sole Function*, South Africa: University of Natal Press.

Bulus, Linus Yaktal C (1986). *Mwaghavul Traditional Religion and Its Cultural Hybrids*. Unpublished BA Long Essay, Department of Religious Studies, Jos.

Bulus, Linus Yaktal C (1990). *The Religious Significance of Mwaghavul Puberty and Manhood Rites*. Unpublished MA. Diss, Department of Religious Studies, Jos.

Cox, James L (1998). "Introduction: Ritual, Rites of Passage and the Interaction between Christian and Traditional Religions". In *Rites of Passage in Contemporary Africa*, RCAS, Religion in Contemporary Africa Series, Cardiff, GB: Cardiff Academic Press.

Danfulani, U.H.D. and Andrew Haruna (1998). "Redressing Drought: Rituals of Rain-making among the Guruntun and Mupun people of Nigeria". In *Africana Marburgensia*, Marburg University, Germany, 31(1&2)20-36.

Danfulani, U.H.D. and Andrew Haruna (1999). "Rituals of Rain-making among the Gurumtum and Mupun People". *Studies of the Department of African Languages and Cultures*, 26(28)23-45, Institute of Oriental Studies, Warsaw University.

Danfulani, Umar H.D (1995). *Pebbles and Deities: Pa Divination among the Ngas, Mupun and Mwaghavul in Nigeria* (1994 Uppsala Diss.). Frankfurt am Main, Bern, Berlin, New York: Peter Lang.

Danfulani, Umar Habila Dadem (2003). *Understanding Nyam: studies in the history and culture of the Ngas, Mupun and Mwaghavul in Nigeria*, Koln: Köppe.

Datok, Polycarp F. (1983). *A Short History of Sura (Panyam): C (1730-1981)*, Jos, Nigeria: Nigeria Bible Translation Trust.

Goshit, Zacharia Damina (1980). "A Hundred Years of Religious Change in Ngasland," BA Long Essay, History Department, University of Jos, Nigeria

Haggai, John Edmund (1986). *Lead on!: Leadership that Endures in a Changing World*, Waco, Tx. : Word Books.

Ikenga-Metuh, Emefie (1981). *God and Man in African Religion*. London & Sydney: Geoffrey Chapman.

Isichei, Elizabeth (1981). *Junior History of Nigeria*, London: Macmillan Education.

Kalu, U. Ogbu (1996). *The Embattled Gods: Christianization of Igboland, 1841-1991* Lagos, London: MINAJ Publishers

Lere, Pauline Mark, (1996). *Rev. Dr. David O.V. Lot: His Life and Church Development on the Jos Plateau*, Jos, Nigeria: Jos University Press.

Neiers, Marie de Paul (1979). *The Peoples of the Jos Plateau, Nigeria (European University Studies)*, Frankfurt: Peter Lang GmbH

Turner, Victor W. (1969). The Ritual Process: Structure and Anti-Structure. Harmondsworth: Penguin Books.

Turner, W. Victor (1970). *The Forest of Symbols* (first published in 1967) Ithaca: Cornell University Press.

Uka, Kalu (1985). *Colonel Ben Brim*, Enugu: Fourth Dimension Publishers.

van Gennep, Arnold (1960). *The Rites of Passage* (1st published, 1908). Translated from the French by Monika B. Vizedom and Gabrielle L. Caffee. London: Routledge and Kegan Paul.

Wambutda, D. Nimcir (1991). *A Study of Conversion Among the Angas of Plateau State of Nigeria, with Emphasis on Christianity*. Frankfurt am Main, Bern, Berlin and New York: Peter Lang.

14

Burial rites and reincarnation in the indigenous tradition of the Ikwerre people of Upper Niger Delta

- Wellington O. Wotogbe-Weneka

Introduction

The Ikwerre who address themselves as the *Iwhoroha*[1] constitute one of the major ethnic groups which makeup the present Rivers State of Nigeria. On the whole, the geographical location designated Ikwerre spreads over four local government areas of Rivers State of Nigeria, namely, the Port Harcourt, Ikwerre, Obio/Akpor and Emohua local government areas. Socio-linguistically, Ikwerre is also divided into four sub-groups - of Reo, Esila, Ishimbam and Opa, being the easier labels often used by Ogbakor Ikwerre[2] to identify people of the same dialect, the various dialectal differences notwithstanding, just as it is the case with other African communities in terms of language.

---

[1] The word *Iwhereoha* (also spelt Iwhoroha) explains a traditional ruler (Chief S. N. Wali-Eze Oha Apara), though now merely seen as an alternative word for the 'Ikwerre' of our study is in fact the original and real name of the people. The word has two syllables-viz *'Iwhere'* and 'Oha.' *'Iwhere'* is a corruption of the syllable *'Iwhuru'* which means, actual, proper, or simply indigenous as opposed to the present syllable *'Iwhere'* which means 'shamefulness' in one context and shyness in another. On the other hand, *'Oha'* stands for 'town' or 'village' or 'native', most appropriately 'native.' A combination of the two syllables *'Iwhuru'* and *'Oha'* will render the meaning of *'Iwhereoha'* as proper or actual native. The name served to distinguish the people from infiltrators, particularly their Ibo neighbours whose superimposing influence on the indigenous people in the earlier times was beginning to pose a threat to the survival of the people. The Ibo phrase *'Ikwere'* means 'you agree.' *Ihe agwara gi I kwere* also means 'whatever they tell you, you agree;' which seems to suggest that the *Iwhereoha* people easily give to the Ibo whatever they asked from them, especially 'land' for their enterprising establishment at the time. It then sounds surprising and calls for a thorough investigation as to why this word 'Ikwerre' has now become the term with which to describe the people of this ethnicity, except one is satisfied with the explanation that the Ibo at that time and up until the era of Eastern Nigerian government dominated every sphere of life in the area in administrative, educational, ecclesiastical and above all political set ups. On the other hand the term *Iwhereoha* is also a mark of contentment for among the people, there is a feeling of pride and elation when addressed as an *Iwhereoha* which some people interpret to depict the people as civilized, well fed, and superior unlike their immediate neighbours.

[2] This is the premier cultural association of the Ikwerre Ethu Nationality other branches of this association include Ikwerre Development Association and Ikwerre Research Committee (to which the present writer belongs).

Ikwerre is naturally blessed with a vast expanse of land for agricultural purposes and several streams and creeks for fishing. This geographical condition places the Ikwerre in an advantageous position of benefiting from an amphibious environment. Thus, in addition to supplying the entire Rivers State of Nigeria with major food stuffs particularly garri, plantain and yam; Ikwerre towns and villages within the saline waters such as the Ogbakiri, Emqhua and Rumuolumeni engage in fishing occupation on a comparable degree with their Ijo neighbours.

With their *Eregbu* or *Oduma* and *Owu ama* dances coupled with *Egelege* (wrestling) matches and other numerous ritualistic festivals and festivities, life is full of enjoyment among the traditional Ikwerre. The Ikwerre are overwhelmingly religious. Of the three recognized religions[3] in Nigeria, the indigenous religious system seems the most penetrating of the three as evidenced from the people's ways of life and the basic traditional belief systems such as their belief in reincarnation, which is our focus in this paper. In short, like the words of Idowu about the Yoruba "in all things they are religious. Religion forms the foundation and the all-governing principles of life for them." (Idowu 1962:5)

One of the cardinal hallmarks of the indigenous religious belief system of the Ikwerre is the belief in reincarnation. While some religions[4] tended to have denied or marginalized the belief (at least Christianity recognizes the possibility of the resurrection of the body), African communities of which the Ikwerre, our area study is a part, see the belief in reincarnation as a guide in interpreting people's activities in their everyday life. For as Ogbu Kalu once observed, "Reincarnation is crucial in understanding the African perception of man and life." (Ogbu Kalu 1978:14) Indeed, there are divergent opinions in various literature as to this religious and highly philosophical concept called 'Reincarnation,' but we need not bother about such detail now, at this juncture, we will analyse the significance of the belief among the Ikwerre of Upper Niger Delta.

Reincarnation among the Ikwerre

Among the Ikwerre of our study, the belief in reincarnation is a matter of certainty. Those who expressed their doubt as to practicability of the belief have often been told right in their faces the very ancestral spirit that incarnated them. One can unequivocally assert that it is their strong belief in reincarnation that serves as the conceptual paradigm through which their elaborate rituals associated with birth, puberty, death and burial can be comprehended. In which case, it can be argued that in Ikwerre, as in most African societies, the birth of a child is a process, which begins long before the child arrives in this world and continues long there after.[5]

At the birth of a new baby the traditional Ikwerre will require the services

---

[3] These are African Traditional or Indigenous Religion, Islam and Christianity.
[4] Christianity and Islam are best examples here.
[5] See also Mbiti, *African Religion and Philosophy*, p. 110.

of a reputable diviner[6] to know the very ancestor that has reincarnated in the new baby. Birth rites or ceremonies are then aimed at receiving the ancestral spirit that has "come back" to where "he" rightly belongs, particularly the ancestral spirit of close relatives. Again, if such ceremonies are not performed, or poorly performed as the belief goes, the reincarnated spirit begins to feel rejected or poorly accepted by a people he manifested his love and regard for, by "coming back" into their midst.[7] Sequel to this, the new baby begins to withdraw, by being sickly and ultimately dying. During naming ceremonies following the divination, native names given to children are always in strict conformity with whom by their understanding and belief has reincarnated in the child being named. This also explains why such names which are post-fixed *ndha* (father), *nnhe* (mother) and those prefixed *nwene* (brother or sister) feature prominently in Ikwerre vocabulary.[8] A few examples of such names here will be relevant: *Nnenda* (her father's mother); *Nnwerenda* (Her father's wife); *Woyinda* (Her father's girl friend); *Didia* (His father, for some parts of Ikwerre whose name for father is *Didi*); *Enyinda* (His father's boy friend); *lhunda* (his or her father's face, by way of, facial resemblance); and *Nnennea* (her mother's mother) etc.

Death to the Ikwerre, just as in most African communities, is seen as a transitory stage in the continuous cycle rather than an annihilation of life. Various elaborate death rites are performed on and for the dead at the instance of death among the Ikwerre though with little or significant variations in the rites, depending on the ages of the deceased and the nature of death that has befallen one. Usually, corpses are washed and dressed properly before interment. It is believed that this would prevent repulsive odour and give the dead a sense of decency respectively during his rebirth or reincarnation. However, such corpses are never interred with shoes. The belief is that this would prevent their being reborn without toes (Arinze 1970:17).

Rites of "mouth cleansing" or washing are also performed with local palm gin, *kaikai,* to guard against mouth odour and teeth decay during the next incarnation. On the whole, utmost care is taken among the Ikwerre to make the deceased look decent as a result of the belief that if one is buried carelessly, one might not be accepted in the ancestral world. The view of Arinze is apt when he said, "without these ceremonies, the restless ghost of the deceased would return to haunt and harass his merciless relatives..."[9] It is also to be noted that these elaborate rituals are only applicable to those who die natural death. Those who die of swollen stomach, suicides, lunatics and such other unnatural deaths, signifying that they had lived bad lives are not given such respectable treatment, and are ultimately not buried, but thrown into the evil forest, except in a few cases, after propitiatory ritual cleansing sacrifices must have been performed.

---

[6] Interview with Moses Amaewhule of Omeketu on 1/11/88 Aged 67 years.
[7] Interview with Wagbara Ichem of Agubia on I2/16/87 Aged 75 Years.
[8] Interview with Moses Amaewhule of Omeketu.
[9] Interview with Friday Okpabi of AgwaWirie on 12/26/87 Aged 70 Years.

On the other hand, in the case of the death of a "changeling" or "the born to die" *(Ogbanje* among the Ibo or *Abiku* among the *Yoruba),* the body is deliberately made indecent by burying it or at times giving it some wounds all aimed at making the "changeling" feel badly treated and therefore refuse to come again into the family, to die before maturity (more will be noted on this as we progress). Burial and funeral rites are observed with varying details from place to place in Ikwerre but the underlying motifs as well as the general routine are the same. Usually there are two kinds of burial ceremonies and they go with different rites. One is the first burial ceremony.

This is held for all deaths, irrespective of age and title, though those of the elderly people are usually more elaborate. In a typical traditional burial of the deceased in Ikwerre, especially the aged, activities and rites ranging from the slaughtering of the cow usually by the first son, to some other minor rites are performed by friends and distant relations. Significantly, these rites are intended to dignify the dead and make him go into the ancestral plane blissfully. Here, the grave side oration also comes in. Opportunities are created for friends and relations to stand by the side of the grave when the body is set for burial to make some good will speeches or requests for protection from the spirit of the dead. During the burial also, some objects are buried with the body. Symbolically, this could be explained by the fact that it is believed among the Ikwerre that the journey to the hereafter is hectic and tiring, hence such objects like food, drinks, water, money (for transport etc are in some cases put into the coffin for the deceased to use on his way 'home')

The second burial is usually associated with only those who attained some standard of maturity in their lifetime. This is a consummation of the burial rites. It is generally believed among the people to be instrumental in enabling the departed to have a completed articulation with the ancestors in the ancestral domain. Other minor rites follow like the killing of a cow and those performed by members of the different cults and societies to which the deceased belonged during his lifetime.[10]

Ikwerre's belief in reincarnation and the "changeling"

In various tribes of Nigeria, the belief in the existence of 'changeling' (born to die) children is widespread. Though there could be a point of disagreement within these tribes as to the nature, causes and mission of these unique children, the various tribes have names with which they identify these children. Among the Ibo, they are called *Ogbanje*. The Yoruba call them *Abiku* while the Ikwerre of our study call them *Nwonnheowa (Omunnheowa* for plural).[11] These children are generally believed to have made pacts from the spirit world, to visit the earth briefly. And as such they initially please their earthly parents by their rapid growth, beauty, intelligence or cleverness, only to die prematurely when they would be of use to their parents; without any

---

[10] See also Obiandu, Concept of Reincarnation in Ikwerre, p. 20.
[11] Interview with Friday Okpabi of Agwawirie.

sign of ill health. However, it is also believed that these ill-fated children can also be stabilized in time. The name *nwonnheowa* as indicated earlier means "the child of the spirit world mother." These children of common but ill-fated destiny are seen from two facets among the Ikwerre people. That is, *Omuebiri* (meaning age group) and *Omuoke* (meaning group associated with a particular period of creation or reincarnation). In the former *Omuebiri,* they are believed to be a set or age group of friends who had made pacts in the spirit world to make brief visits to the earth and to die at an appointed and generally accepted time by their *ebiri* (age group). To give potency to this pact, this group is believed to have collectively buried the seals of this agreement in the various compounds into which each of them would be reborn, in their palm and foreheads for identification purposes in case the pact is not kept to by any of them. It follows therefore that if a new born child is identified through divination to be a "changeling" it is these buried identification seals or marks in the compounds and those in the palms and foreheads that the medicine men search for; and bring out, and then proceed to destroy them, thereby rendering the pact partners incapable of discovering the seal which would have enabled them to recognize him and subsequently recall or kill. The later, *Omuoke* is believed by the people to be a group of children not necessarily friends or age group, but coming under control of a common "mother" in the spirit world. According to this concept, these children are released into the world or earth at different times and are also recalled at the wish of their "spirit world mother." This systematic "sending out" to the earth and "recalling back" to the spirit world of children by the process of birth and death respectively, keep on repeating for as many times as their "spirit world mistress" or "mother" may wish. And in each instance of reincarnation, there are usually serious resemblances with the previous reincarnation. This system thus becomes incessant until the very families into which such children are often, "born" and often "recalled" realize the state of affairs and then send for the medicine men.

If in the process the phenomenon becomes unveiled to the parents, at the death of such "changelings," the parents proceed to cremate the corpse or give it some indelible knife-cuts or even rub the face with mud or charcoal, just to stop him from 're-coming.' In some parts of Ikwerre land, oil bean seeds are added in the coffin (if at all a coffin would be used) before burial. Here again, it will be seen that while the cremation and other such ill-treatments meted out to the corpse aim at giving the child the impression that it was badly treated and force it to refuse reincarnating into that very family again even when the "spirit world mother dictates so, the oil bean seeds symbolize dispersion of the spirit of that changeling to the unknown destination" (Parrinder 1976:84).

On the other hand, if the phenomenon becomes revealed in the lifetime or at the birth of the baby, the parents would consult a specialist medicine man who would in their usual skilful manner leave some slight physical deformity on the body of the child to disguise him from the "mother" in the spirit world. For instance, this could involve cutting off one of the child's toes or fingers most preferably the last and on the left side, and or indicating some tribal marks on the face to make the child look confusing or unidentifiable to the "spirit world mother." Which ever course a family adopts, it must be coupled with some ritual sacrifice by a medicine man. These beliefs and practices, bizarre as they sound to an outsider, are no doubt of significant importance to the traditional Ikwerre. This is because with it, the people believe that they can be saved from those shocks often experienced by the sudden unexpected death of their bright looking children.

Kinds of reincarnation in Ikwerre

From the foregoing, it can now be seen that the Ikwerre believe in reincarnation, which can especially be derived from the significance of the various rites that becloud the life cycle of the people of Ikwerre. There is also the conception among the people that reincarnation has some ramifications. In other words, the Ikwerre believe that the soul of the dead can be reborn into either human or animal forms, depending largely on the moral rectitude and social acceptability of the person in his previous lifetime. This belief parallels in other cultures. For instance, Parrinder tells us "India's belief has a moral concomitant, the Karma brings one back to a higher or lower destiny in the next life. He may rise to the level of a priest or sink to that of an animal, the soul may be reborn as male or female and in any family" (1976:85). Thus, among the Ikwerre even though it is generally believed that all souls reincarnate but not all reincarnate into human form. For a soul to reincarnate into human form, the prerequisite of having lived its previous life in a good and acceptable manner must have been satisfied. This therefore confirms their belief that the social and moral life of man, to a large extent, affects the reincarnation of the man after death. As a result, many people being conscious of this condition strive very hard to live a morally and socially acceptable life so as to earn them a human reincarnation. A clear proof of this is seen when a good person dies through natural death. Here, relatives begin to wish that he reincarnates into their midst, definitely not in the form of a beast or a tree but that of a human being. After such human reincarnation, diviners are still invited to determine which of the ancestors has 'returned.' This is, if they lacked reasonable evidence to understand the soul that has returned without the aid of a diviner. It is also noteworthy that such human reincarnation as it is believed among the people could vary in terms of sex. Though rare, in some cases dead male are believed to be capable of reincarnating in female forms, and vice versa.

Conversely, there is the belief in Ikwerre that the bad ones who lived extremely bad lives in their life times would reincarnate into non-human forms. However, not all categories of bad lives attract the punishment of reincarnating in non-human forms, because those whose life patterns were fairly satisfactory could reincarnate in human form but certainly into an undesirable level of human being. For example, they could reincarnate having some physical deformities, servile status or destitute. There is yet other non-human aspect of reincarnation among the Ikwerre. This may be seen as a sort of transmigration of the soul or metempsychosis by some observers. This is different from the first because it involves a voluntary change into animal forms or tree forms.

Generally speaking, one can say that this Ikwerre belief rests on the principle that the inescapable punishment for those whose lives were extremely badly spent is that instead of enjoying a human rebirth, their souls reincarnate in either beast or tree forms. The above circumstance may be doubted by an outsider, but then it becomes quite obviously convincing when tales are told and vivid examples given about such trees that "bleed" each time they receive knife-cuts. Nevertheless, no one has scientifically tested the blood-like sap to give credence to the belief. But certainly this understanding has made it a commonplace practice among the people of Ikwerre to curse one to reincarnate in the forest or in form of a tree for one bad act or another. Again, much as the belief in the issue of some souls reincarnating in animal form is widespread, it does not seem to hold water as examples that could substantiate such beliefs are significantly lacking. In Ikwerre, all animals are edible except totemic species, or as a result of one's taste and interest.

Also among the Ikwerre especially in Omagwa and Isiokpo areas, there existed a certain belief, which cannot be near separated from witchcraft. The belief is that some indigenous "highly spirited daughters," traditionally called *Oke Omurinya,* possess powers that enable their spirit to escape from their bodies and turn into animals such as lions, pigs etc. to haunt or do mischief to their enemies, especially destroying their farm crops. This is believed to happen only in the night when the bodies would be asleep. This, as we were made to understand, does not mean the same thing as reincarnation, because the spirit later re-enters the bodies for the sleeping person to awaken.

Multiple reincarnations in Ikwerre

No discussion of the concept of reincarnation among the Ikwerre would be complete without an attempt to take an in-depth look into the enigmatic and probably paradoxical concept of multiple reincarnation. Generally speaking, the Ikwerre believe that there is no limit to the number of times the dead can reincarnate. Devoid of common logic as the concept or belief looks, it is tenaciously held to by the people. Thus, the people believe that for those who grew old before their death, that their hands, legs, and other prominent parts of their bodies reincarnate into full bodies, resembling the dead in a few areas, while the incarnates of the real soul or heart bear greater resemblance with the deceased. This no doubt sounds paradoxical to the earlier dimension, but Parrinder seems to have succinctly explained the phenomenon thus:

> That a dead person may be reborn in several descendants has suggested to some writers that Africans are not logical in their thinking or are pre-logical, but in fact this agrees quite well with the philosophy of power, for power for one force can strengthen or weaken another or several. (1976:85)

Significance of reincarnation in Ikwerre

The Ikwerre concept of reincarnation and its puzzling mechanics no doubt have some far-reaching significance. This becomes more obvious when the extent to which man's reincarnation depends on the personal morality of the man in the previous lifetime comes into focus. Thus, one can identify the religious, social and psychological significance of this all-important concept for the people.

In its religious significance, reincarnation is not generally simple doctrine. It includes theories of the effect of personal morality on the rebirth or reincarnation process. The belief obviously has a tremendous effect on the individual's present life in so far as the kind of life he would reincarnate into is determined by his present life. Since all are anxious to have a happy reincarnation every body makes strenuous efforts to live morally blameless life. This belief is therefore another great incentive for the people of Ikwerre to live a very high standard of morality at all levels, but especially among those playing leading role in the society such as the village or clan heads who are looked upon as spiritual leaders of exemplary character. However, this is given, more credence when one realizes that the traditional religious beliefs of the people of Ikwerre emphasize the importance of morals in practice and insist that such morals must extend into all areas of life for the welfare of the individual and society at large.

In social sphere, the concept of reincarnation has quite a lot to offer to mankind in Ikwerre setting. For instance, it is the belief that the soul reincarnates and it is not only in an attempt to manifest this belief in practice but also in a bid to create conditions necessary for reincarnation that the people of Ikwerre evolved the numerous ceremonies and rites that surround life in Ikwerre land. These rites which range from birth, naming, death to burial rites in addition to the manifestations they make and the ideal conditions they tend to create for reincarnation to take place also create opportunities and forums for traditional dances performed during ritualistic festivals. These are understood to be important elements of diversion and relaxation as well as means of social interactions. Such festive life perpetuates certain rules of the traditional society and even guarantees their survival. During such ritualistic festivals, the Ikwerre people truly celebrate their cohesiveness and affirm their basic belief system. This is particularly characteristic of those rites that require elaborate celebrations such as the birth rites and some burial rites. Therefore those rites dictated by the desires of the people of Ikwerre to manifest their belief in reincarnation and also create necessary conditions for it, have a concomitant social aim that really makes for a social regeneration among the people.

It is also noteworthy that in Ikwerre, differences of character and status are explained with reference to the reincarnating spirit. So the concept is also significant for providing explanation to the differences in social hierarchy.

From the psychological view point, some of the significant features of reincarnation are traceable to the fact that emotional acceptance of reincarnation doctrine involves considerable, modification of one's general philosophy. This is more so when it is realized that the belief in reincarnation tends to counteract such negative traits as racial prejudice, national or sexual chauvinism and a host of other response patterns based on the erroneous notion that you are what you are, and have not been anything else. The belief that certain illnesses, physical and psychiatric, have their, roots in a past reincarnation is rife, and without the knowledge of the reincarnation they can be very difficult to cure. The conception of the Ikwerre man about reincarnation gives him an idea of the previous life of the affected and therefore renders his hospitalization less difficult. It could also be argued that during the festivals that surround the many rites that becloud life in Ikwerre as the people get aesthetically carried away, the spiritual dimension of man becomes accessible to the unseen powers. This obviously promotes concord and harmony between the worshippers and the worshipped in the community.

Some final remarks

From the discussion so far, we have seen that in the traditional belief of the Ikwerre, the doctrine of reincarnation is more of an article of faith requiring no further investigation, than mere conjecture. This firm belief of the people in the cyclical movement of human beings and their souls in the Cosmos confirms the other belief of the people that death is not, and has never been an annihilation of life, but a transitory stage. At this concluding stage, one can suggest that in the general life pattern of Ikwerre people, there is an apparent awareness of the relationship between the present life of the people on earth and their fate in the hereafter, which in some ways affect their life in their next incarnation. This awareness has injected into the feelings and sensibilities of people of Ikwerre the desirability of an appreciable mode reincarnation. As a result, moral rectitude, an inescapable corollary of such feelings, has up to some extent been identified as the people's watchword. In all probabilities, reincarnation in all its ramifications is an axiom among Ikwerre people. Death to them merely separates the carcass from the real essence of man, which later assumes a new body by the process of rebirth or reincarnation. Although a greater part of this study tended to have emphasized the pros of this reincarnational belief of the Ikwerre, a necessary critical assessment of this belief will no doubt reveal some of its detestable consequences on the economic and social life of the people. For instance, the belief that people's status in their contemporary time was predetermined by their lives in the previous lifetime, has unconsciously brought about some measure of laxity and abdication of responsibility. Thus, these attitudinal failures have much doom to spell on the societal prospects.

In Ikwerre, it is common for people who are faced with difficulties that could be momentary to see those difficulties as being their destiny for this lifetime, and then to hope that they would be compensated very well in their next incarnation. This situation does not make for personal effort, industry and resourcefulness.

Again, it has been observed among the Ikwerre that their belief in reincarnation creates unnecessary inferiority complex. For instance, a reincarnate of one who did not live up to expectation in his previous life time, would always be reminded of the short coming that beset him in the past lifetime. This sort of irrational association makes some young men and women of the area feel inferior and do not participate to their best in most of the social activities.

The belief in reincarnation also brings about some avoidable vendetta among tribes or members of families. This happens when one grows up to be told that in one's previous incarnation that a man from a neighbouring clan, tribe or family caused one's death probably by poisoning or association. In such a case, the young man begins to be unnecessarily careful about the named people or person. In addition, the tendency had always been that he would cast some revengeful eyes on them, with the aim of revenging his untimely demise in the previous incarnation as it is widely believed by the people.

On a general note, if this concept of reincarnation, especially as it is held by the Ikwerre is subjected to a strict scrutiny, it would be observed that the belief is capable of having some concomitant effects that could be limitlessly devastating on the intellectual, sociological and economic characters of the various localities through Ikwerre land.

References

Arinze, F. A., *Sacrifice in Ibo Religion*. Ibadan: Ibadan University Press, 1970
Idowu, E. Bolaji, *Olodumare: God in Yoruba Belief*. London: Longmans, 1962
Kalu, Ogbu, ed., *Readings in African Cultural Development*. Enugu: Fourth Dimension Publishing Coy Ltd, 1978
Mbiti, J. S., *African Religion and Philosophy*. London: HEB, 1969
Obiandu, M. F., *Concept of Reincarnation in Ikwerre*. NCE Long Essay. Port-Harcourt: College of Education, 1983
Parrinder, E. G., *Africa's Three Religions*. London: Sheldon Press, 1976

15

Igue Festival among the Benin people: response and resilience of indigenous religion

- Wilson E. Ehianu & Mercy I. Idumwonyi

Introduction

James Frazer in his book, *The Golden Bough,* argues that religion grew out of magic and then human beings tried to control their own lives and environment by imitating what they saw happening in nature; this therefore led to the use of rituals, spells and magical objects in many areas of life. But the failure of these gave birth to placation and beseeching the help of supernatural powers, instead of trying to control them. These rituals and incantations became sacrifices and prayers, which thereafter formed a major part of religious festivals. During festivals, 'a propitiation or conciliation of power superior to man' is enabled so that today festivals now occupy an integral part in most religions of the world. The subject of festival is an important aspect in Nigerian indigenous religious traditions; their significance lies in the fact that they illustrate among other things historical events, coming of age, harvesting of crops and appeasement of various gods for protection against enemies, evil or epidemic disease. The following features and beliefs underlie most festivals. In the first place, they are occasions to venerate the ancestors upon whom the security of the kingdom is believed to rest. Through their observance, religious ideas are perpetuated and passed on to the next generation. Festivals are accorded high premium because of their leavening and unifying influence on the community. Most festivals illustrate and re-enact historical events and are occasions to mollify deities believed to be liable for protection against enemies, evil or epidemic disease (Oduyoye 1983, 50). Festivals as Oduyoye has observed provides recurrent opportunities for communal re-creation and social revival. If creation is a special province of God, it is in recreation that men revitalize God's creation so that it does not become ancient history but a present reality. The recreation of history (natural or social history) aspect of festivals makes the participation of the king and chiefs obligatory in the drama of festivals (152).

Some festivals are family/village based; others are embraced in the entire kingdom. *Igue* festival in Benin kingdom belongs to the latter category. In spite of the onslaught of Christianity and other transformative agents, *Igue* festival, which has existed for well over six hundred years, remains largely undiminished. This perspective of traditional beliefs and practices, Ezeanya calls "the endurance of conviction."[1] Roman Catholicism in Benin remains skin-deep in the religious fabric of the people even after over a hundred and fifty years of the church's presence in the area. The consensus is that for the church to be firmly rooted in Benin, inculturation efforts must not only be seen as necessary but urgent.

This study undertakes an in-depth investigation of *Igue* festival in Benin. It further highlights attempts by the Roman Catholic missionaries to extirpate or super-impose Roman Catholicism on the people. Elements of *Igue* festival which are dear to the people and which have no bearing with idolatry are identified for possible assimilation into Catholic liturgy and practitioners. Challenges in this regard are highlighted and the entire study is concluded.

The Benin Kingdom

The kingdom was one of the earliest kingdoms to emerge in the coastal region and was already a powerful state by early 1400AD. Unlike most of their neighbours, the Beninese succeeded in creating a highly developed system of centralized government, which survived almost unchanged until the conquest of Benin by the British in 1897 (Thatcher 1974, 20). In the sphere of religion, the people subscribe to their indigenous religion, which entails the belief in the existence of a Supreme Being called *Osa-no-buwa* (the creator of the universe); they also venerate *Ebo* (Spirit powers). Some of these spirits powers were said to be benevolent while others were malevolent. The belief in the existence and power of the ancestors, reincarnation, charm, medicine, witchcraft, sacrifice, festivals and so on, form an integral part of the religion which serves such functions as explaining and predicting space time events. These are believed to ensure order, security and prosperity in the kingdom (Ehianu 1998, 1).

Mbiti's observation that Africans like to celebrate life is applicable to the Benin people. Festivals in Benin kingdom are significant in many ways. In the first place, they are occasions to venerate the ancestors upon whom the security of the kingdom is believed to rest. Through their observance, religious ideas are perpetuated and passed on to the next generation. Festivals are also accorded high premium because of their leavening and unifying influence on the community. Some festivals such as *Ekaaba, ikpoleki, ema gh' roh,* etc are family and/or village based; others embrace the entire kingdom and *Igue* festival belongs to the latter category (Mbiti 1995, 19). *Igue* is a feast organized to commemorate the remarkable deliverance from the intrigues of the old year and also an opportunity to request for the God(s) beneficence in the New Year.

---

[1] Bigard Memorial Seminary, *Bigard Theological Studies* 19, no. 2 (1999): p. 1.

Igue Festival

The cultural excellence of the Beninese finds crystallization in *Igue* festival. Of all the festivals in Benin kingdom, *Igue* is the most acclaimed because it cuts across every strata of the community as the monarch (*Oba*), members of the palace societies and the entire Benin community is actively involved. A commencing celebration takes place at the *Oba*'s Palace, as the *Oba* is the spiritual and political head of the kingdom, and ends with the natives within the kingdom.

The Origin of Igue Festival and the Myth of Ubi, *Ewẹrẹ* and *Ȯyọyọ*

Oral tradition situates the origin of *Igue* festival in 1440AD, during the reign of *Oba* Ewuare the great. Since then, it has subsisted as an annual festival in the kingdom. It has been acknowledged that certain practices, which are associated with *Igue* festival, deserve attention given their historical significance.

In 1440 AD, there lived on the Benin-*Ughoton* Road a Chief (*Ogieka*) in a village called *Ėkạ* who had three beautiful daughters, *Ubi, Ewẹrẹ* and *Ȯyọyọ*. The news of the beauty of these three sisters constantly reached the *Oba* in the palace. Consequently, *Ewuare* requested that this chief in *Ėkạ* give him the eldest of the three daughters in marriage but the Chief objected to the *Oba*'s request on the ground that his eldest daughter *Ubi* was shrewd, disobedient and disrespectful. At the *Oba* persistence, the chief reluctantly sent his eldest daughter, *Ubi*, to the *Oba* not minding whether she was willing or not. *Ubi* however refused any connection with the *Oba* and was unfriendly to all the women and the maids in the harem. She was reputed to be inclined to all imaginable forms of atrocity. To aggravate the situation, *Ubi* began to bed-wet and urinate within the house, an act which was inflexibly forbidden and considered spiritually unhealthy and contrary to Benin custom. The *Oba* tried in vain to get his bride to turn a new leaf and ordered *Ubi* to be sent away from the harem. She was accordingly sent away by the maids and *Ihogbe* (palace societies) who struck her with fire-brands, sticks, brooms, etc chanting the refrain, *Ubi-rie*, which means *Ubi*, the naughty one go (Obadigie 1985:51; Egharevba 2005:19-21).

Three days later, *Oba* Ewuare asked the Chief in *Ėkạ* to send his second daughter to him as a replacement for *Ubi* and *Ogieka* agreed. On the advice of the oracle, *Ėwẹrẹ* (*Ogieka's* second daughter) was received into the palace amidst pomp and pageantry. The *Oba* ordered the *Ihogbe* to escort her and to be received by the *Osuma* as an honour for her entry into the palace. And as she entered the palace the women in the harem, dancing for joy sang the following in Benin:

Ėwẹrẹ de, kie n' Ėwẹrẹ

Ėwẹrẹ is coming, open for *Ėwẹrẹ*

They also encouraged everyone to pay tribute as a mark of respect to the new bride with the song

Gha kie o, Odibo gha kia za

Open the storehouse ... steward, open the storehouse

So that gifts of all kind were poured on the *Oba* and *Ėwęrę* from all parts of the kingdom in the weeks that followed the marriage.

Unlike *Ubi*, *Ėwęrę* acted humbly, respectfully and honorably. Peace, love, concord, health and prosperity prevailed in the harem, and the entire kingdom. Not too long after *Ėwęrę* entered the harem, she became homesick as she often desired to see her younger sister - *Òyọyọ*, and so she cried daily. The pathetic situation was made known by the *Oba* to *Ogieka* who resultantly released *Òyọyọ* to visit *Ėwęrę* at the royal harem. At *Òyọyọ*' entry into the harem the women and maids began to sing the following song:

A rhi Ėwęrę gi Omo vb'ugha o,
Ewere gh' Òyoyo
Ėwęrę gh'ovbi-erha, Ewere gh' Òyọyọ
Ėwęręgh'ovbi-iy'ue, Ewere gh' Òyọyọ
Ėwęrę, Ėwęrę, Gh' Òyọyọ
Ėwęrę, Ėwęrę, Gh' Òyọyọ

Ėwęrę has been taken to the *Oba* in the palace,
Ėwęrę, look at Òyọyọ
Ėwęrę, look at your father's child
Ėwęrę, look at Òyọyọ
Ėwęrę, look at your mother's child
Ėwęrę, look at Òyọyọ

Ėwęrę was very pleased with her sister as they chatted and laughed together. It became evident that *Ėwęrę* was very unwilling to let her sister return home so that the *Oba* eventually married *Òyọyọ* as well; and this was how two sisters, *Ėwęrę* and *Òyọyọ* become wives of the same *Oba*.

Sacrificial/Ritual Dimension of *Igue* Festival

Thereafter annually, throughout his reign, *Ewuare* in a bid to mark the peace and prosperity that prevailed in the kingdom by reason of his marriage to *Ėwęrę* celebrated the *Ugie Ėwęrę* in honour of his cherished wife; this *Ugie* (festival) became the anniversary of his happy and prosperous marriage to *Ėwęrę* and was tagged the *Ugie Igue* (*Igue* festival). Items for sacrifice include cock (*okporu*), guinea fowl (*oronmwen*), pigeon (*elekhukhu*), and in some instances animals of higher status such as goat (*ewe*), cow (*emila*), leopard (*ekpen*), etc are used. Other items include kola-nuts (*evbe*), white native chalk (*Orhue*), coconuts (*kokodia/ivin ebo*) and drinks (*ayon*). All these items, which symbolically have their varying functions, are used for the worship of the *head*. The *head*, which characteristically represent the God(s) that is not visible is believed, would bring about good luck and fortune. The blood of these ritual animals are shed in exchange for human life; kola-nut embodies long life and whoever presents it is believed to have brought life while the native chalk signify tranquillity and the coconut denotes peace and reassurance. The drinks are poured on the earth as libation for the God(s) and ancestors.

The *Ihogbe* (one of the palace societies) present the symbolic leaves designated *Ẹwẹrẹ* leaves and the *orhue*. The *orhue*'s symbolism derives from its white colour. There are three colours in Benin colour syndrome—white, black and red. The symbolic values invested in these colours determine the choice of ritual objects—white pigeon, charcoal, roasted yam; a parrot's red tail, red piece of cloth, animal blood for red. Generally, white is the symbol of peace, joy, good health, good luck, purity, fertility, etc. (Oduyoye 1983:203). Some days after, everyone would celebrate his own *Igue* in his own house with his immediate and/or extended family according to their capacity. Ugie *Ẹwẹrẹ* while being marked at the palace, the *Ihogbe* (palace societies) present the symbolic leaves designated as *Ẹwẹrẹ* leaves to the *Oba*.

At this Ugie (festival), members of the community, in a manner reminiscent of the beneficence of *Ẹwẹrẹ* would dance with *ebe- Ẹwẹrẹ* — *Ẹwẹrẹ* fortune leaves. In remembrance of the ejection of *Ubi*, the disrespectful and sacrilegious wife would beat the earth with sticks urging *Ubi* who has acquired the connotation of all that is evil and distasteful to depart from the community (Obadigie 1985:51). And since that time, it has been the prayer of the Beninese not to make a journey on *Ubi*' day, but only on Ewere' day; so that the journey might be as happy and prosperous as that of Ewere, *Okhien-Ewere*, as it is often said to a sojourner.

The *Igue* Festival calendar

Igue festival like the Jewish feast of booths is a holy convocation that runs annually anytime between seven to fourteen days. Usually its observation coincides with the last month of the standard calendar of modern usage, December, it takes place in the second half of the month and could end in the first week of the first month, January of the New Year; but in accordance to the Benin native calendar as determined by lunar calculation as well as the authority of the *oba*.

This is an occasion for socio-political and religio-cultural activities as it is a period set aside to commemorate the remarkable deliverance from the intrigues of the old year and also call on the God(s) and ancestors to bless them in the New Year. Every bit of the program is carried out with utmost caution because of its theological significance for the living and the ancestors who are believed to be in attendance. J. Marquet's postulation about mankind holds for the Beninese. For by means of certain words, certain gestures and certain objects, man believes that he can acquire a larger share of the power that permeates the universe and can use it for his own ends. These words, gestures and objects are effective because they are charged with power (Omijeh 1983:195).

Ritual performance and celebration of *Igue* Festival

The festival starts with the *Ugie 'roba*, the ceremony of the *Oba*'s father or ancestral worship. This is observed in two parts, on one hand, the chiefs come for *Otue ugie'roba* (greetings for the ancestors), and the *Oba* welcomes them with an offer of kola-nuts (*evbe*) and drinks (*ayon*), which are received appropriately. The following day, members of the *Ihogbe* along with important Benin chieftains come to the palace in ceremonial dance procession with the '*eben*' (royal scepter which are symbol of authority) for the *Ugie 'roba* to pay homage to the *Oba*. In traditional parlance, they are said to come to '*gbe 'ben.*' It is a day for '*ayee*,' remembrance of the ancestors. The *Oba* prays with the *evbe* and life animals for the palace and the kingdom and thereafter, the different animals used for the '*ayee*' are slaughtered and shared to all the chiefs and people present. This is a day of feasting and gladness and the celebration goes from dusk till dawn in the palace.

This affords members of the various palace societies and the general public the opportunity to entertain the *Oba* with a number of dances. The *Oba* himself takes part in the dances, while surrounded by his *ada* and *eben*. These are held aloft by *omuada* (royal attendants). The *ada*, which is the equivalent of *ofo* in Igboland (Eastern Nigeria) are emblems of political and religious authority. It symbolizes the truthfulness and righteousness expected to proceed out of the mouth of judges, priests and kings. The *Oba* usually confers or confirms titles on this day.

On the second day, the *Ugie ogun* (festival of irons) and *Otue Igue* (felicitation visits) are observed. On this day, the *Oba* is gaily dressed in a heavy ivory-beaded garment, which is rarely worn (Oduyoye 1983:203).

This is a day set aside for the commemoration of the victories of the *Oba* since creation of the dynasty in 1200 AD till 1914 AD. It is on record that the institution of kingship had witnessed various oppositions. First, it was Chief Ogiamen who opposed Eweka (I) until the score was settled in favor of the *Oba* at the *Ekiokpagha* (Okpagha market square). Another was Agho Obaseki who attempted to take advantage of *Oba Ovaramwen's* deportation to Calabar by the British Colonial invaders in 1897. He however submitted to the authority of *Oba* Eweka (II) in 1914. A further confrontation came from the *Uzama Ni hiron*, the seven king makers, who wielded so much power during the reign of *Oba* Ewedo and did not take kindly to the relocation of the seat of government from *Usama* to the present location and again during *Oba* Esigie's reign in a physical confrontation, they invited *Oba* Esigie to a battle, in their defeat, they were made to retake an oath of allegiance to the *Oba*.

These confrontations and victories are no mean feat; they became commemorative at the end of each year since Esigie's reign. The mock re-enactment of this event is significant for two reasons. One, it recreates the supremacy of the *Oba* over the *Uzamas* and secondly, it serves as a reminder of the oath of total allegiance by the kingmakers to the authority of the *Oba*. This drama is the annual ritual of *Ugie ogun* and is part of the celebrations in the *Igue* festival.

After the mock re-enactment, the *Oba* sits at the *ogiukpo* (royal chambers), flanked by his wives and children. He gets sanctified by the *Ogi' Efa,* the chief priests. While incanting, a sacrificial animal's blood is smeared on the *Oba*'s forehead; thereafter he offers prayers and gives the sacrificial items to the *Isekhure* (a hereditary title-holder) who in turn offers prayers and hands the animal to Chief *Ihama* (the head of the *Ihogbe,* the official relatives of the *Oba*). After the sacrifice, the chiefs dance before the *Oba* and his family with the *Eben,* symbolizing loyalty. It should here be noted that the *Ada* is the superior emblem and it takes precedence, wherever it appears, over the *eben*. All titled chiefs could possess the *eben* but only a chosen few are conferred with the right to possess the *ada,* which must however not be flaunted before the *Oba*. The *oba* in time past usually orders the execution of any one who defaults and flaunts the *ada* before him (Ehianu 2007:12).

This is followed by the occasion of the *Igue Oba*. It is a day for the *Oba* to worship the God(s) symbolized in his head for enabling him see the end of the year and the beginning of another one. Every eligible chief holding the *eben* comes to rejoice with the *Oba* at the palace in ceremonial dance processions from their various homes with their well-wishers (Musa 1996:7). This event again, spells the *Oba's* supremacy and serves as a reminder of the subjects' loyalty. The symbolic *Ute* (village) masquerade, *ekoko n'Ute,* is usually on hand to perform to the *Oba*'s admiration.

Two days after the *Igue Oba,* is the day for the *Ugie Emobo* (making of hand). It is the last rite in the series of the *Oba's Igue* ceremony. On this occasion, the *Oba* comes out to the palace gates to a camp (*eko*) specially built at the main entrance to the palace. It is at this camp that the *Oba* worships the *edion-edo* (Edo Ancestors). He approaches the *edion* with a special *ukhure* (staff of authority) and *eben*; he declares to the ancestors that he has successfully performed the cleansing, purification or appeasement rites on behalf of the Edos and decrees that any evil yet to vamoose is seized and sent to *Udo*. After this, the *Oba's Igue* rites come to an end. The *Igue Ivbioba* (*Oba*'s children Igue) is held on the same day the *Oba* ends his own *Igue* rites on the *Igue Emobo* day. Every child fixes his own time.

The next part is referred to as *Igue Edo hia' (Igue* for all the Edos) comes up two days after the *Igue Ivbioba*. It is *Igue* of mass participation. At night, the head of each family gathers his family members for the '*uhun*' (head) ceremony. Items for the '*uhun*' are not different from what was aforementioned. A male who must not be the eldest is called to '*gue uhunmwun,*' pray with the coconut and a live bird, holding it to the head of those present at the occasion one after the other. The first person to have his head worshipped is the eldest of the family and thereafter the head of every other person present is touched. Here, the head (*uhun*) is addressed as the God(s) that have seen them throughout the old year and also blessed them so much. The sacrificial animal is thereafter slaughtered and the blood is prayerfully smeared on the people's forehead while the coconut water that was preserved is given to everyone present. The ceremony is followed by the *Ugie Ewẹrẹ* the next day. For the proximity, the *Ugie Ėwẹrẹ* is regarded as an integral part of the *Igue Edohia*.

The prayer could go thus:

vbe ni ma du gie ukpona,
Ukponode, ma vbe dia rue

As we celebrate this year' festival
May we be alive to celebrate yet another

Natural phenomena in *Igue* Festival

Following the *head (uhun) worship* ceremony is the *ugie Ėwẹrẹ*. Here a symbolic act to chase away *Ubi that* has been embodied as evil spirits within the kingdom is done. At dawn before the cock crows, the youths in their various locations set to usher in *Ėwẹrẹ* prepares for the customary '*l'ubi* fire' ceremony. As the night recedes, and dawn approaches the youths make fire with sticks and pieces of wood. At an agreed upon time, they remove the sticks made into firebrands in their hands, and sometimes cudgels, broomsticks, etc. And they start to chant *l'ubi-rie, l'ubi-rie, l'ubi-rie* (go with cleansing), while stamping their feet on the earth they make straight to the moat[1] to discard the firebrands and other dangerous items. From there, they make straight to the hill top where the shrub (bush) is searched for *ebe ėwẹrẹ*. As they find the leaf, incantations and prayers are made; the remaining firebrands and the supposed weapons are thrown away. They get enough leaves and with good speed excitedly dance back to town, moving from house to house, giving the leaves to people who eventually paste the piece on their fore-head while singing:

Ėwẹrẹ de, kie ne, ewere
Ėwẹrẹ erha mwen, kie ne ewere
Ėwẹrẹ iye mwen, kie ne ewere
Ėwẹrẹ , ewere n' oyoyo.
Ukodo ewere, ore mwan na

Ėwẹrẹ is coming, open for Ėwẹrẹ
my father's ewere, open for Ėwẹrẹ
my mother's ewere, open for Ėwẹrẹ
Ėwẹrẹ that is full of life
the earthen pot of Ėwẹrẹ is here

---

[1] There are three main moats or (very deep) ditches (*Iya*) surrounding the city. The first and second moats were dug by *Oba* Oguola in about 1280AD and 1290 AD respectively, to serve as barriers to keep off the invaders in time of wars against Akpanigiakon, the Duke of Udo who was then harassing the City. By the order of *Oba* Oguola, all the important towns and villages in Benin copied the example and dug similar moats or ditches round their villages as fortifications against enemies. The third moat which is in the heart of the city was dug by *Oba* Ewuare in about 1460 AD when the City was depopulating as a result of his inhuman mourning laws over the death of his two sons, Kuoboyuwa the Edaiken (Crown Prince) and Ezuwarha the Onogie (Duke) of Iyowa, who poisoned each other and both died on the same day.

The excited youths, while giving out pieces of leaves from their bunch, pray and prophesy blessing upon the recipients. The recipients in turn rewards the youth in monetary terms. This continues till the early morning sunsets. It should be noted that this day is the beginning of a New Year for all Beninese. On this day, the slaughtered animal used for the *ugie Igue* the night before is made into food for everybody's merriment.

Several times there are some natural occurrences that inform the people of the kingdom and create a belief that the God(s) had heard their prayers and accepted their appeasement. This natural occurrence could come in the form of light showers on the early hours of the *ugie Ėwẹrẹ* day so that the people believe that the God(s) have sent the rain to wash off *Ubi* or the weather would be so cool and nobody complains of heat and the people say, 'we foresee a peaceful year ahead and it shall be well as this day is in this new year.'

The *ėwẹrẹ* leaf ceremony is first played in the palace where Chief Osuma (a senior titled chieftain and a member of the *Eghaevbo n'ore*, the Executive Council) presents the *Oba* with *ebe Ėwẹrẹ* in a gaiety procession, dancing and singing melodious traditional songs about *Ėwẹrẹ*. As the palace activity is ongoing, the youth within the kingdom dance from house to house and along the street, ensuring every person in the kingdom is reached with the leaves; the people delightfully cut a piece from the bunch of *ebe Ėwẹrẹ* and paste it on their forehead as a mark of blessing and good luck for the approaching year.

The present *Oba, Uku-Akpolokpolo Omo N' Oba Erediawa*, the 38th *Oba* of Benin introduced some modifications to the observance of *Igue* festival. Presently, the festival climaxes with a thanksgiving service at the traditional places of worship in *Aruosa* in *Ogboka*, *Aruosa* at *Erie* Street and finally at Holy *Aruosa* Cathedral along A*kpakpava* Street, Benin City (Musa 1996: 9).

Significance of *Igue* Festival in Benin

The *Igue* festival as an annual event in Benin is an occasion for elaborate cultural re-enactment and display (Airen 2008, 10). Apart from being the tourist destination, it is a time for spiritual re-awakening and revival at the levels of the individual and the community. It is a period traditionally set aside to thank the God(s) and the ancestors for the life, blessings and prosperity for the *Oba*, his harem and subjects and particularly for the kingdom at large; ritual appeasement to expunge evil from the land is done and merriment for witnessing the birth of another year is very elaborate. While the Roman Catholic Church uses incense for purification, the *orhue* serves the same purpose in Benin religious life.

At *Ugie Igue*, ancestral gods, sacred places and relics are given their due veneration, purification or deification respectively. The beauty, glamour and excellence of the kingdom symbolized by the *Oba* is brought to the fore and celebrated. The *Igue* dance at which the *Oba* participates with his chiefs with the display of *Eben* (symbol of authority) and sundry regalia and insignia of office is beauty and culture to behold. The movement of the dance is ritualized and the streams of superstitions flow through the dance, which are many and varied. The researcher on African philosophy, culture and cosmology will find attendance to *Igue* festival a rewarding exercise. Still at the *Igue* festival, the *Oba* may confirm and/or confer titles on well deserving citizens though this could be done at such other times as the *Oba* deems fit.

During *Igue* festival, the *Ogiefa*, Chief Priest—like the high priest of Old Testament times—on behalf of the *Oba* atones for the transgression of the kingdom and any evil spirits are symbolically excommunicated from it with the chant *l'ubi-rie,* that is, cry of rejection and wish for cleansing; and *Ewẹrẹ* (blessing) invoked on every family within the entire kingdom. Thus, Benin's abhorrence for evil is confirmed. The exchange of gifts and goodwill messages amongst friends and families on one hand and between the *Oba* and his subjects on the other hand serve to promote social cohesion between individual and families, and renews the social contract between the *Oba* and his subjects, and amongst the people, as important developmental issues meant for the benefit of the people are tabled.

The annual celebration of *Igue* has helped to foster peace, unity and revitalized the culture. At this gathering, young ones are taught the precepts of Benin kingdom and sustaining factors, here also the historical facts are taught so that the kingdom and what *Igue* stands for is kept alive.

Gender dimension in cultural and religious life

One then asks where the women in the kingdom are, do they make contributory roles, if so, what are they? Women are the least known and represented segment of the kingdom in the royal court art of Benin. They seldom appear among the rich panoply of *Obas*, Chiefs, attendant, local rulers, historical figures and events that are cast in bronze and other artwork. Kaplan (2007:141-149) is of the view that when they appear in art their presence is either subtly conveyed or reserved for display in domains set apart for women. As a result women are missing from nearly all that is seen as 'art' by the West. As a warrior people, the male ethos was pervasive, exulting in deeds and display. Women were to attend quietly to reproducing society—a function of female sexuality in the human experience. As is often the case in a warrior society, women's visibility and independence were severely limited and controlled and they were valued primarily as mothers.

It was until not *Oba* Esigie's (c. 1504-1550) reign, in his bid to acknowledge the mother for her role towards the protection and expansion of the kingdom, the *Iyoba* title was instituted. This was meant to extol the high standards for women and for men in the society to honour their mothers. The *Iyoba Idia* continues to be remembered and rewarded to this day by her presence at *Igue*, the major annual court rituals. Thus the first queen mother, *Idia*, attained title, fame, name and visibility in art—the most desired and rare privileges accorded to women in Benin. *Oba Esigie* consequently set a precedent for honouring women in Benin. In like manner, *Ewẹrẹ* and *Ọyọyọ* are remembered annually for their significant roles in ensuring the restoration of peace to the kingdom.

It is for this reason that the spiritual, social, economic value and influence of women during the *Ugie Igue* cannot be downplayed. Being in a joyous mood during the festival they help to supply traditional songs to the *Oba* and to the chieftains who come to pay tribute to the *Oba* using *ukuse* (maraca) to give rhythm to the songs. And while the young women join other members of the kingdom to dance from house to house and along the streets sharing the *ebe ewere*, the older women are at home ensuring the animals used in worshipping the *uhun*, (the head, which is God personified) are cooked for everyone to eat.

It should however be noted that her role is still very secondary even though many like *Obas* Ewuare and Esigie honour their mothers and wives for the varying roles played in communal development. Yet in contemporary times as it has always been, no matter the woman' status, she cannot say prayers using any of the sacrificial paraphernalia nor could she smear the blood of a slaughtered animal used for the rites on the forehead of anyone. Her consent was never sought for in any issue, as was pictured in *Ubi*'s marriage to the *Oba* and her eventual ejection from the harem. Today, many wives who could not have children in their marriages are given physical assaults that sometimes drive them crazy, leading them to pack out of their matrimonial homes. The prejudice and discriminatory practices against women are evidently deep-rooted in social-cultural and religious ideologies in Benin.

Christian missions in Benin Kingdom

The sprawling kingdom of Benin was the target of and host to Christian missioners of diverse denominations. Christianity as preached by the Roman Catholic Church gained foothold in Benin kingdom in the mid-nineteenth century after two unsuccessful attempts. The success recorded at the third attempt was largely because some of the initial problems which included, communication barrier, conditional acceptance of Christianity by the reigning *Oba*, inter-tribal wars, refusal of the missionaries to adapt the religion to Beninese culture, shortage of funds and personnel, etc. had either fizzled out with time or had been addressed by the missionaries. For instance, schools and health centres were established to take care of the educational and health needs of the people. Added to this was the fact that the increasing commercial contact between Benin and the Europeans enhanced the worldview of both parties to the effect that the missionaries were accorded better reception (Abhuere 2002:18). The above factors coupled with the disillusionment that greeted the conquest of Benin kingdom by the British in 1897, the soil was thus prepared for Christianity to flourish in the area. The Beninese came to realize that their deities and the *Oba*, on whom the security of the kingdom rested, were not invincible and so some of them were ready to give their conqueror's "god" a try.

The success of the catholic missionaries was an impetus to other missionary organizations. In 1902, the Church Missionary Society (CMS) under the leadership of Rt. Rev. James Johnson began evangelical work in

Warri, Sapele, Eme-ora and Benin. Rev. James Johnson, like the biblical Moses was assisted in this task by individuals like J.A. Oyesile, an Ora man, Madam Arokunbo Ovonranmwen an early Christian convert and wife of *Oba* Ovonranmwen who after spending three years with her deposed husband in Calabar returned permanently to Benin in 1900 resolved to be a committed Christian. She donated her late father's house to the CMS through Mr. J.A Oyesile. This was rebuilt on the present site of the Cathedral as the first CMS church in Benin City. Bishop Johnson, who dedicated the church on 2nd November, 1902 named it St. Mathew Anglican Church. The Church became the nerve center, and fountain of the CMS from which other CMS churches in Benin Kingdom sprang (Oviasu 2002:v-vii).

Next to the CMS in the chronology of churches in Benin Kingdom came the Baptist church. History records indicate that in 1852, Bowen and his wife arrived at Ijaiye for mission work. They were cordially received and given land on which to build. Work began in earnest and in 1854, Baptist Chapel, the first ever in Nigeria was built in Ijaiye. From here, missionaries (whites and blacks) were commissioned to evangelize other parts of the country, Benin inclusive. Another version says that in January 1921, a sermon that was preached by the CMS Minister annoyed certain members to the extent that they lost interest in the CMS church. These people, driven by a common interest, wrote to the Baptist mission headquarters in Lagos for the establishment of a Baptist church in Benin.

The church building work started almost immediately and by the end of 1923, the auditorium located at Ugbague was completed and dedicated. Branches of the church were established at Uhi, Igieduma, Ekenwan, Iboro, Gelegele, Ofunoma and Igiuovbiobo to mention but a few (Uwagboe 2000:9-11).

Missionary's attitude to Beninese religio-cultural milieu and *Igue* resilience

A common feature of the aforementioned mission churches in Benin as in most African societies was their uncompromising attitude to the religions and cultural heritage of their host. Beliefs in witchcraft were regarded as figment of the imagination, while ancestral veneration was attributed to primitive thinking and ignorance (Okolugbo 1984, 68). Missionary contempt and iconoclasm on Benin culture produced results, which were many and varied. Ehianu's observation among the Ika is applicable to the situation in Benin. With education and the threat of sanctions, which the churches imposed on their members, four categories of people emerged. The first abandoned such practices that were condemned by the churches, the second indulged clandestinely, another indulged by proxy, and the fourth group withdrew from the church (Ehianu 2005:124). In Benin the situation was much more volatile. Apart from the impetus that was given to the formation of indigenous churches, it led to the secession or transfer of allegiance from one missionary body to another. For instance, as a result of the insistence of the First Baptist

Church, later Benin United Baptist Church that polygamy must be tolerated, some who stressed monogamy as the ideal Christian marriage left the church to found the Central Baptist Church, Kings Square Benin City, a parallel Baptist Church which not only subsists till date but also has established branches in Uzebu, New Benin, Ologbo, Ugbekun, Ugbowo amongst others (Uwagboe 2000:15-16).

The evangelical revival of the twentieth century, which left in its wake, the Pentecostal movement with records of unbridled proliferation and attitudinal arrogance serves to complicate an already tense situation. These groups, apart from discrediting extant churches in Benin as elsewhere, targeted the Benin religious and cultural practices for unprovoked assault. The denial by the churches of the Benin traditional values, mores and aspirations without satisfactory substitute or explanation left much to be desired and sparked off criticism not only from the non-believing population but also from Benin Christians themselves.

Speaking about the Akan who had a problem similar to that of the Beninese, Okolugbo cites Dr. Busia as saying:

> For the conversion to the Christian faith to be more than superficial, the Christian church must come to grips with traditional beliefs and practices; and with the worldview that these beliefs and practices imply... failure to do that will place the new converts between two worlds, the old tradition and custom of his culture which he is striving to leave behind; and the new beliefs and practices to which he is still a stranger. (Okolugbo 1984:94)

The predicament of the church in Benin today is that it has failed to root itself in Benin's life in spite of the seemingly overwhelming presence of the gospel. Instead of displacing the traditional religion in the lives of its adherents, Christianity remains an appendix to indigenous beliefs and practices. During life crises, recourse is made to traditional practices— divination, and observance of sacrifices, rites and festivals. Christianity should not detach itself from everything traditional simply because it wants to assert its unique position. There are certainly good elements in traditional religion which will surely enrich the gospel message. We shall limit our focus to those elements in *Igue* festival which will not only nourish the Christian faith and promote religious tolerance but also make the religion more at home with the people and consequently enhance the task of evangelism in the area.

Contextual relevance in Inculturation Theology

Igue festival began as an anniversary to commemorate a royal marriage, which ushered in peace, unity and progress in Benin kingdom. With the passage of time, the festival acquired or incorporated traditional religious practices such as ancestor veneration, worship of deities and exorcism, which were not part of the festival *ab initio*. This is understandable given the fact that Africans take a holistic view of religion. Life undertakings are meaningless until they are coloured with religion. Care must therefore be taken not to throw the baby away with the bath water. There are good principles in African religion and indeed *Igue* festival, which the Beninese cherish irrespective of religious affiliation. These include religious tolerance, respect for ancestors, priests and constituted authorities.

The Roman Catholic Church, the Anglican (CMS) Church, the Cherubim and Seraphim churches and numerous others have periods set aside to remember their saints and/or heroes. It will go down well with the Benin Christians if their past heroes, some of whom laid down their lives on account of the gospel or in defence of the Benin kingdom, are recognized and celebrations and/or prayers instituted for them. Prejudice unintended, it stands proper and opposite to mention *Oba* Ewuare (believed to be the first Benin convert to Christianity), Queen Arokun Ovonramwen (a foremost Anglican convert, bequeathed her late father's house to be used for church services), Queen Idia (led the Benin kingdom to war), Queen Iden (offered herself to be scarified to restore the lost glory of the palace) and a host of others (Aisien 2001:68).

An ongoing phenomenon in church liturgy is the inculturation of traditional songs, usages and prayer patterns. Though this is more noticeable in the indigenous, charismatic and Pentecostal churches, orthodox denominations have not been unaffected. It started in the early 1980s when gospel music took Nigerian music industry by storm. A common feature of these songs is that the attributes of the Christian God, Jesus and the Holy Spirit substitutes the deities, ancestors, great personalities and spirits. A few examples of these songs will suffice:

Ogbe ma vbe diaru 2ce
Ise logbe e evbo
Ise logbe e
Ise logbe e
Evbo[1]

This celebration of
(New year) we've
come for. It shall be
a blessing to all of us.
Amen.

This folk song rendered during *Igue* festival has found its way into the liturgy of most churches. Where *Igue* was hitherto mentioned, Christian festivals – Christmas, New Year, Easter and Harvest (which ever applies) is injected.

We take another song:

---

[1] G. Obahiagbon, interview by author, January 7th, 2004.

Oba ma kponmwe
Ima n' ivbue hia rrie
Urho Mwe nue
Oba n' okpolo
Baba ma kponmwen O!
Ma n'ivbue hia riu urho mwe re
So rie kponmwen mwan[1]

O King, we thank you
we your subjects give you praise
the great King
father we thank you
We your children bring praise to you.
come and receive our thanks

This song is rendered when various families in Benin kingdom goes to wish the *Oba* long life during his coronation/*Igue* festival. In this song, such epithets earlier ascribed to the *Oba*, now goes to *Osanobuwa*, the Supreme Being that is believed to have created the universe. Such a move is commendable as the practice of the Christian faith becomes rooted in Benin traditional spirituality.

Igue festival promotes and encourages the communal and communitarian spirit propagated by the early Christians.[2] Every stratum of the society is involved, the freeborn and the slave alike. The seven to fourteen days long celebration of *Igue* provides an auspicious opportunity for the churches in Benin Kingdom to appraise their performance in the area of charity with regards to the orphans, widows, destitute, victims of calamities, refugees (if any), jobless and such other persons in the kingdom. In addition to presenting gifts to the Monarch, observers of *Igue* festival are encouraged to extend similar gestures to the less privileged in their midst.[3]

Igue festival climaxes with an exorcism. Evil spirits are symbolically chased out with *Ubi* and blessings invoked on the community. Exorcism as a special ministry in Christendom should be intensified to complement efforts made by adherents of other religions. True, the methods may differ but the principles and goals remain the same. Anointing is another integral part of the *Igue* festival. The *Oba* and sacred places are sanctified with the blood of animals; this is again replicated in Christianity. While the bloods of animals are used during *Igue* festival, olive oil or some other ointments are used in churches and prayer homes. The assertion of Chief Nosakhare Isekhure is illuminating here as he espouses the striking similarity of purpose, which exists between anointing in African religion and Christianity. He speaks:

---

[1] Ibid.

[2] B. Okoro, interview by author, November 11th, 2003.

[3] V. Inagbor, interview by author, December 1st, 2003.

Igue is anointing. As in all anointing, it is the spirit personality that is sanctified, not any object outside or different. The head is the main focus because it represents the totality of human existence.[1]

Anointing rite as a religious ritual antedates Christianity in Benin Kingdom. As with traditional religion, anointing in Christendom is believed on one hand to ward off malevolent spirits, which are perceived to inflict untold calamities on people and on the other hand, it is believed that it could bestow good fortune and healing on recipient.

It would be recalled that the Christian Bible has an account of how sin and redemption came into the world through Eve and Mary respectively. Also the Benin traditional account of *Ubi* and *Ewẹrẹ* are not different as *Ewẹrẹ* is believed to have brought redemption to the kingdom so that today her memory is sweet and celebrated with the intention of purging the land of evil and ushering in good luck for the coming year. In general term, "*Ewẹrẹ*" means peace in Benin. It further signifies harmony, prosperity and progress as the entrance of *Ewẹrẹ* into the palace signified peace for the *Oba*. In some churches especially the orthodox denominations, a day, often referred to as "Mothering Sunday" is set aside to recognize and to celebrate womanhood. Children present gift items to their mothers as token of appreciation and re-enactment of their love for the mothers. In the same vein, a day is usually set aside by various churches for couples to reflect and celebrate their marital union as traditionally exemplified by *Oba* Ewuare. It is a day set aside to renew marital vows and show remorse for shortcomings. Gift items may be exchanged and special thanks given to God for the joy of home and marriage. This no doubt will make Christianity more rooted in Benin culture.

The successful translation of the Holy Bible into Benin language remains a landmark in the quest for inculturation of the gospel in Benin. Further to this, the teaching of the native dialect should be promoted in schools and seminaries while copies of the Benin Bible should be made available in libraries and churches. In addition to strengthening the office of church interpreters, church liturgy should be interspersed with Benin language so that worshippers can understand and practice the Christian religion in their indigenous language.

Conclusion

Igue festival is an annual event in Benin which is observed by the *Oba* and all Beninese to mark the end of a year and to celebrate the beginning of another according to their native calendar as determined by the lunar calculation as well as the authority of the *Oba* (*Edo National* Vol.1, No.2, 2004:11). The festival apart from enhancing the communal and communitarian spirit of the celebrants and the kingdom, showcases the cultural richness and world view of the Beninese people.

---

[1] N. Isekhure, interview by author, December 1st, 2003.

With the advent of the Christian missionaries and the subsequent unfolding of the so-called civilizing programmes (referred to by many as a Pandora of sorts), the religious and social life of the people was irretrievably affected. The Benin converts to Christianity found themselves at a crossroad, wistful and unable to return to their indigenous religion and at the same time at sea with the new religion wherein they were baptized. Thus, Christianity became the religion at such times when all was well, while recourse was made to the native religion in times of life crises. This paper decries this situation and seeks to suggest possible ways by which the Christian religion can be rooted in Benin culture and be nourished by it. Until and unless these suggestions are taken seriously, the Christian religion and Benin culture will remain mutually exclusive with the former remaining merely skin deep in the lives of the people.

Reference

Abhuere, P., 2002. The Roman Catholic Church and Mission in Bini Land: (1810-1950). Unpublished Long Essay, University of Benin.

Airen, M., 2008. Culture, Society and the People's Heritage: Igue Festival as an All-time Covenant in Benin Cultural History. A Term Paper submitted to the Department of Sociology, and Anthropology, College of Arts and Social Sciences, Igbinedion University, Okada.

Aisien, E., 2001. *The Benin City Pilgrim Stations,* Benin City: Aisien Publications

Edokpaigbe, I., (2004) "The Relevance of Igue Festival in Contemporary Era" *in Edo National* Vol.1, No.2: 11- 18

Egharevba, J. U., 2005. *A Short History of Benin.* Benin: Fortune and Temperance Publishing Coy.

Ehianu, W.E., 1998. The Church and Human Development: A Case Study of Owa Land, 1900-1970. MA. Thesis, Edo State University, Ekpoma.

Ehianu, W.E., 2005. "The Ika People and the Quest for Long Life." *EPHA: Ekpoma Journal of Religious Studies* 5 (2): 124-135.

Ehianu, W.E., 2007. Ecumenism in Benin and Environs in the Light of Vatican II's Unitatis Redintegratio 1962–2005. PhD Dissertation, Ambrose Alli University, Ekpoma.

Ezeanya, E., 1999. "Traditional Values in Iboland" in *Bigard Memorial Seminary,* Enugu, Vol.19 No.1: 1-10

Frazer, J., 1994. *The Golden Bough.* London: Oxford University Press.

Kaplan, F.E.S., 2007. "Women in Benin Society and Art." In Barbara Plankensteiner (ed.) *Benin Kings and Rituals: Court Arts from Nigeria,* The Art Institute of Chicago: Snoeck Publishers: 141–149

Mbiti, J.S., 1995. *Introduction to African Religion.* London: Heinemann.

Musa, A.J., 1996/97. "Let Us Forge Ahead" *The Voice* 35: 1-15

Obadigie, J.O., (1985) "Igue Festival" in A. Omoruyi (ed.) *Benin Series* Vol.13: 47 - 51.

Oduyoye, M., 1983. "Festivals: The Cultivation of Nature and the Celebration of History." In E.A.A. Adegbola (ed.) *West Africa Traditional Religion,* Ibadan: Daystar Press: 150-169

Oduyoye, M., 1983. "Potent Speech." In E.A.A. Adegbola (ed.) *West African Traditional Religion,* Ibadan: Daystar Press: 203-232

Okolugbo, E., 1984. *A Short History of Christianity in Nigeria: The Ndosumili and the Ukwuani.* Ibadan: Daystar Press.

Omijeh, M., 1983. "The Significance of Orhue in Benin Symbolism," in E.A.A. Adegbola (ed.) *Traditional Religion in West Africa*, Ibadan: Daystar Press: 195-197

Oviasu, V.O., 2002. *The Centenary of Christianity, Anglican Communion in the Diocese of Benin, 1902-2002*. Benin City: Anglican Diocese of Benin City.

Thatcher, P., 1974. *West African History*. London: Longman Ltd.

Uwagboe, O.J., 2000. *The Baptist Mission and the Educational Development of Benin City*. B.A. Thesis, University of Benin.

16

Celebrating indigeneity in the shadow of heritage: another version of the *Osun* Osogbo Festival in Nigeria

- Peter Probst

I

One of the main themes in Jacob Olupona's oeuvre is the persistence of Indigenous African Religions.[1] As he writes, far from being just "little traditions" as Robert Redfield (1956) once put it, "indigenous religious traditions are entirely relevant to the modernity project. Indigenous tradition and cultures continue to play important roles in forming and refashioning world cultures, beliefs, and identities" (Olupona 2003: xv).

A vivid expression of this persistence is the popularity of the notion of cultural heritage and indigeneity. In the course of the last two decades the cultural dynamics of globalization has led to new experiences of locality and belonging of which these developments are part of. Yet, as several authors have stressed, the relationship between heritage and indigenous religions is a difficult one.[2] While the former tends to protect the latter and thus enabling indigenous religions to survive, the internal heterogeneity of indigenous religions equally tends to become curtailed and reshaped once these religions become the object of heritage projects.

In the following, I want to discuss these issues in view of the annual *Osun* festival in Osogbo, Nigeria.[3] *Osun* is a Yoruba river deity associated with notions of fertility, femininity, motherhood, sexuality, wealth, wisdom, knowledge, healing, beauty, art, and power. In fact, *Osun* has different identities, resulting out of the various conditions under which people have lent meaning to her. In her homestead Osogbo, she is revered as the city's guardian deity. Each year in August a twelve-day long festival is carried out to celebrate the specific relationship between the deity and the people of Osogbo. Over the past decades the event has become one of the most prominent cultural festivals in Nigeria. Due to the declaration of the *Osun* grove as a

---

[1] See Olupona (2003, 2008).
[2] See for instance the work of Lowenthal (1998) and Werbner (1998).
[3] The following analysis is based on my own research on art and heritage politics in Osogbo. See Probst (2004, 2007, forthcoming).

UNESCO world heritage site in July 2005, the festival has experienced additional popularity.

In a lucid analysis Olupona (2001) has focused on the importance of the festival as a "civil religion" in terms of both generating and combining feelings of religious belonging and political identity. The (American) debate on religious revitalization on which the model of "civil religion" is based upon was well suited for the volume in which Olupona's piece appeared. Entitled *Osun across The Waters* (Murphy and Sanford 2001), the book addressed the various ways how the Yoruba river goddess *Osun* has left her original homestead in Osogbo and has crossed the "Black Atlantic." As a result, nowadays the *Osun* festival is celebrated not only in Nigeria but also in England, the USA, Latin America, the Caribbean and many other places of the world wherever people have received the call to serve and follow the deity.

Surely, the concrete realization and performance of the festival varies from place to place. Yet there is a general consensus that the celebration is modelled after the original festival in *Osun*'s hometown Osogbo. Here the popular understanding of the festival focuses on a series of oral traditions explaining the migration of Osogbo's pair of ancestors Timehin and Laaroye into the present settlement area. According to these traditions it was Osogbo's first ruler, Laaroye ,who is said to have established a pact of mutual protection with the spiritual authority of the region *Osun*. Just as *Osun* promised to protect Larooye and his people, the latter promised to honour and respect *Osun*. As a result *Osun* became Osogbo's guardian deity and the annual *Osun* festival the ritual platform on which the primal pact is ritually renewed every year.

The above narrative stands in the centre of the brochures published by the Osogbo Heritage Council. Besides the official version, however, one finds numerous other versions giving a different account of what has happened in the past. It is on one specific aspect of these unofficial traditions I want to focus on in this essay. Neither the publications of the Heritage Council nor the scholarly literature make any reference to it.[4] Following this version means to start the discussion of the *Osun* festival not with what is taking place in August but in December, the time of the so-called image festival (*òdun ere*).

II

Taking place at the end of the dry season, the image festival (*òdun ere*) belongs to the minor events in the ritual calendar of Osogbo. According to Adejumo (1994) the origin of the festival goes back to a small-pox epidemic which led to a special festival in honour of Obaluaye, the Yoruba deity of sickness, suffering, anger and heat. During the festival *Osun*, *Obatala* and other 'cool' deities are therefore asked to plead with Obaluaye to remain calm, not to strike them with anger and spare the people of pain and pestilences.

---

[4] Exceptions are two short references made by Wenger (Chesi 1983) and Ofugha's (2005). Both passages remain remarks in passing. No attempt is made to follow the story further.

On the eve of the festival a night vigil is observed on the premises of the *Osun* shrine. Inside the shrine a series of wooden sculptures associated with the various Yoruba deities present in Osogbo are kept. The eulogies of each single deity are uttered and small sacrifices are made. At dawn drummers come in and the praise continues with more singing and dancing. In the morning a ram, sponsored by the *Ataoja* (king of Osogbo), is brought into the shrine together with money and schnapps. The animal is slaughtered by the *Osun* chief priest (*àwòrò*) in front of the figures with blood sprinkled on them. While the ram is then cooked and prepared for a big feast, the sculptures are brought out for display. During the next hours people arrive, participate in the feasting and present gifts to the sculptures associates with the deities residing in Osogbo. The *Osun* chief priestess offers sacrifices to the sculptures asking for help and assistance. To see if the sacrifice has been accepted the *Osun* chief priestess casts kola nuts. In the past, the positive answer marked the beginning of a public procession during which the sculptures were carried on the head of female devotees around the town visiting the sacred site (*ibú*) of each deity ending with a joint dance together with the *Ataoja* before the palace shrine. Due to reservations among the Muslim majority in town and in the palace, the procession has been reduced to march across the street to the market and back again.

The decoration of the sculptures, their public display, the singing of their songs, the utterance of their eulogies, the dancing in their rhythm, and the dressing with their attributes is not only an act of bodily remembrance in the sense of the Yoruba word for image (*àwòrán*); it is essentially also a collective act of (re)activating or recharging Osogbo's spiritual force field with the new energy (*ase*) that was infused into that of the newly decorated sculptures. While the image festival recharges or reloads both Osogbo's ritual landscape and the people living in it with new energy, it also prepares the ground for the biggest ritual event of the year, the *Osun* festival. In fact, the two festivals go together. Thus, the redecoration of images at the palace shrine provides not only the ritual frame for the new initiates into *Osun*, it is also the platform for the presentation of the votary maid (*Arugbá*), the key figure in the forthcoming *Osun* festival.

The maid has to be a virgin, chosen by *Ifa* from the members of the royal family providing the ruling *Ataoja*. Interestingly, the washing of a new ritual object is the same as the washing of an initiate. Thus, the washing and decoration of the carvings during the image festival coincides with the washing and subsequent public presentation of a newly selected *Arugba* at the last day of the image festival. For this the washing is done by the chief *Osun* priestess, the former *Arugba* and the priestesses of the other deities within which the *Arugba* is going to be initiated. Water is taken from the *Ataoja*'s private brook (*ibú òkánlà*) and poured over the body of the novice. With every gush the eulogy of a deity is chanted and asked to help very much the same as in the washing of the carvings described above. Comparing then the washing of the images with the washing of the *Arugba* it becomes apparent that "washing" (*we*) refers to a particular procedure by which persons become images just as images become persons. That is, both objects and persons change their status by being washed with particular herbs and addressed with certain incantations. The aim of these activities is to imbue the object or the person with the energy of the deity. Only through the animation of images the latter can come into being. If done properly and approached in the right way, the deity will then appear before the 'inner eye' (*ojú inú*) of the beholder who is then able to communicate with the deity.

Given this context, preparations for the *Osun* festival begin immediately after the image festival with the so-called stone festival (*odún ota*). Nine days after Osogbo's ritual forcefield has been recharged, the *Osun* chief priest together with the *Arugba* and other male devotees leave the palace and go to the grove. Behind the river shrine, at a place called *ibú Láròóyè* the priest dives into the river to bring out new sacred stones (*ota*). After the gathering of the stones they are put in a calabash (*igbá*) and carried by the *Arugba* to the palace. Here she is welcomed by the *Ataoja* who takes out the stones from the calabash and puts them into his own private vessel (*àwo*) filled with his own private part of *Osun*'s liquid body.

III

What happens during the dry season sets the stage for the biggest ritual in Osogbo. In August each year, roughly half a year after the Image festival in December, the *Osun* festival takes place.[5]

The opening of the festival is called *ìwó pópó*, ("coming down *Pópó Street*") and begins with a public procession of the *Ataoja* and his wives to a certain junction in the city centre where he receives gifts and demonstrations of allegiance. The purpose of the event is two-fold. On the one hand it serves to ensure the safety of the festival participants and the effectiveness of their ritual actions. On the other hand it certifies relations of seniority and juniority between the various groups within Osogbo as well as between Osogbo and its ties with the neighbouring Yoruba kingdoms. Accordingly the main event takes places at a junction in the city centre where the major roads to Ilesa, Ede, Ilorin and Ilobu converge.

Throughout the next two days, Tuesday and Wednesday, individuals and groups come to the palace and offer gifts to the *Ataoja* and the *Osun* chief priestess and priest. It's a possibility to express concerns, ask for help, show thankfulness and hear the advice of *Osun* and the ancestors.

On the fourth day, a Thursday, all activities are centred on the lightning and dancing around the sixteen point lamp (*àtùpà olójúmérindínlogún*). The lamp is a simple metal construction with sixteen sockets placed vertically along a pole. It is said to have belonged to Osanyin, the deity of herbal medicine, but was later conquered by Timehin/Larooye upon their arrival in the area. Accordingly, the ceremonial dance around the lamp in the evening

---

[5] Since the festival has been discussed in numerous publications (Ajibade 2005, Beier 1956, Farotimi 1990, Kayode 2006, Olupona 2001, Ogungbile 2002) the following description is brief and focuses on the main points only.

basically re-enacts that primal conquest story. *Ifa* drums (*àràn*) are played, songs of the hunter's guild are sung and rifles are shot. *Osun* officials, *Ifa* priests, *Ogun* devotees, kingmakers, and many others get up and dance around the lamp. Most important, however, is the dance of the *Ataoja*. Three dances around the lamp are required. The first two take place shortly after the lighting of the lamp; the last one happens early in the morning and includes a dance around the Ogun shrine of Timehin at the market opposite the palace. When the group returns to the palace the fire is extinguished and the lamp is removed, a sign indicating the victory over Osanyin, the medicine, herbs and bush, defeated by *Ogun/Timehin*, deity of war and iron.

The three days after the dance around the sixteen point lamp—Friday, Saturday and Sunday—are filled with the reception of visitors, a big feast at the palace, and short appearances of the *Ataoja* and his entourage. Slowly bending the body back and forth in this way resembling the rhythmic flows of the *Osun* river, the group dances from the palace to the market and back again. Sacrifices and divination continue as more people arrive. Some are *Osun* devotees from other towns on a regular pilgrimage to *Osun*'s homestead. Others are fulfilling their promise to return to *Osun* after having once attended the festival and received help from goddess.

The eighth day, a Monday, is devoted to *ibori iboadé*, literally, the "sacrifice for the head and crown." Yoruba aesthetics and cosmology conceive the head as the seat or container of an "inner head" (*orí inú*) that acts as an independent deity with its own wishes, temperament and character.[6] The *Ataoja*'s 'inner head' is symbolized by two sorts of heavily beaded objects: a conical shaped container (*ìbòrì*) as the house of the *Ataoja*'s inner head and his crowns (*adé*). The beaded regalia objects stand in the centre of the main ceremony of the day. In contrast to the other two previous events the ceremony is not open to the public. Only the *Ataoja*, his relatives, and the main *Osun* officials are taking part in it. One by one the eulogies of the past Ataojas are sung and their help and assistance is requested. After the divination for the incumbent *Ataoja* the latter makes a libation to the crowns in front of him and addresses those present. Greeting the various parties assembled, he stresses the importance of the annual festival, goes into naming off the various ancestors and ends with a general blessing of the assembly not without reminding its members to be pure in their hearts, forget any grudges, and show love and goodness. As a kind of oath to *Osun*, a bowl of honey, one of *Osun*'s favourite dishes, is passed around for the assembly to taste.

The next two days, Tuesday and Wednesday, are filled again with the reception of visitors. The activities of the eleventh day—a Thursday—concentrate solely on the events scheduled for the following day. In the house of the most senior member of the lineage that provides the incumbent of the *Ataoja*, members of Ogboni gather. The chief priest (*olúwo*) of Ogboni presides over the meeting. Also present is the *Ataoja*. Indebted to the earth deity and mediating between the *Ataoja* and his people, Ogboni offers its

---

[6] See Lawal (1985, 2001).

support for the *Ataoja*. At the same time, *Osun* devotees escort the *Arugba*, that is the votary maid, to the former compound of the current *Ataoja*. Here *Ifa* and *Osun* are consulted, sacrifices are offered, and measures are taken to strengthen the *Arugba* for the task ahead.

The twelfth day of the festival—a Friday—marks the climax of the events. Early in the morning the *Alare*, the head of Ogboni's most secret branch (*orò*) leads a procession of elderly men and women of his own lineage to the *orò* meeting place in the *Osun* grove to make a sacrifice of atonement to *ohúntóto*, an ancient divinity associated with the earth. Meanwhile at the *Osun* palace shrine, *Osun* officials have prepared *Osun*'s wooden calabash (*igbá òsun*) and filled it with emblems of Ogboni and *Osun* which the *Arugba* will carry today to the river side. The calabash itself is then put on the head of the *Arugba* who is dressed with bead strings and brass bangles, her head covered with a coloured and cowries-decorated cloth (*ofi*) so that the content and the face of the *Arugba* remain hidden. After having received final blessings from the *Ataoja* at the grave of his ancestors she then enters the palace courtyard where she is greeted by an excited crowd. Led by the chief *Osun* priestess and protected by a ring of policemen, *Osun* devotees, and ensembles of *dùndún* and *gángan* drum ensembles, she slowly walks towards the grove followed— in due distance—by the *Ataoja* and his entourage. Having reached the grove the *Arugba* branches off through her own gate and disappears in the river shrine while the crowd proceeds further to the main entrance towards the river bank. Speeches by the *Ataoja* and representatives of the state are given followed by performances and pledges of allegiance to the *Ataoja* from the various factions of the public. After the *Ataoja* has received the greetings, he retreats to a place at the river called *ibú láàró*. It is here where Larooye is said to have received the fish from *Osun* as the sign of acceptance for the sacrifice. Shielded by the thick bush the *Ataoja* puts on the veiled royal crown (*adé*). Now dressed in full regalia he enters the river shrine where he sits on a cowrie adorned stone where Larooye is believed to have sat and communicated with *Osun*. The *Osun* chief priestess consults the oracle asking for blessings and *Osun*'s continued assistance. Eventually the *Osun* chief priestess and a group of male *Osun* devotees get up and carry a big wooden calabash filled with all the sacrificial food items people have brought from the shrine to the river. The moment they appear at the shrine entrance, a hectic commotion sets in and the large crowd having waited outside moves to the river side. After having fought their way through the crowd, the devotees stop at the river bank where the *Osun* chief priest addresses the deity with a few words of gratitude and respect. Under the jubilating applause of the bystanders the content of the bowl is then thrown into the water. With the sacrifice performed, the water is now charged with ritual power and as such acts as an effective concoction (*àgbo*) that can heal, give strength and wash away evil. While the sacrifices are slowly floating down river, people are eager to fill the river water in plastic containers and to wash their faces and those of their children. In the afternoon, while the public is still busy fetching water, the *Ataoja* and his entourage go back to the palace. The *Arugba* and some of the *Osun* devotees stay behind in the river shrine where she receives presents and congratulations from the public. Eventually the *Arugba* and her troupe leave the shrine too. Instead of following the main road, however, she takes a shortcut and proceeds to the market opposite the palace. At the Timehin shrine (*ògún Timéhìn*) shrine she offers a sacrifice to *Ogun* thanking him for the support and asking for continued assistance. She then proceeds home to the palace. Touching the calabash on the *Arugba*'s head three times the *Ataoja* thanks her for the work she has done. Afterwards she enters the *Osun* shrine at the palace where she foretells the future of the city. With the disappearance of the *Arugba* the festival is officially concluded.

IV

While the publications of the Osogbo Heritage Council explain the festival as a "remembrance festival" which aims to memorialize the primal pact of mutual protection between Laaroye and *Osun*, other versions—murmurs of memory as it were—favour different interpretations. One version has it that initially *Osun* and Larooye were lovers. Both had children together. Angered about the constant intrusion of Larooye's people into her territory, however, *Osun* got furious and 'stole' the common children. Larooye pleaded to release the children but in vain. Finally, *Osun* gave in but only after Larooye had performed a sacrifice. It is this story, so it is claimed, which informs the 'real' meaning of the festival.

Reading the ritual events from this perspective a different narrative emerges. To explicate it means to link it with another alternative narrative focusing on the office of the *Osun* chief priest (*àwòrò*). In olden times, so it is said, the office of the *Ataoja* and that of the *Osun* chief priest were one. Being the owner of the *Osun* cult the *Ataoja* was also the cult's primary male ritual official. A split between the two offices happened only during the reign of Latona II from 1933 to 1944. Latona II was Osogbo's first Christian ruler. His conversion to Christianity made it difficult for him to combine his ritual tasks as *Osun*'s chief priest with his public status as a Christian. His effort to find a way out eventually resulted in filling the office of the *Osun* chief priest with a person different from himself. The incumbent of the *Osun* chief priest is therefore a relatively new modification within the *Osun* cult. What it conceals is the close relationship between the *Arugba*, the *Osun* chief priestess and his male counterpart. As the recruitment rules for all three offices show, both metaphorically and physically all three are closely related to one another. Thus the *Arugba* is recruited from the house of the ruling *Ataoja* while the *Osun* priestess is usually chosen from the widows of a former *Ataoja* who used to be also the *Osun* chief priest.

Following this relationship the ritual acts performed at the very end of the image festival appear in a different light. As mentioned above the stone festival marks the end of the image festival. The main protagonist is the *Osun* chief priest who dives into *Osun*'s liquid body, the *Osun* river, from where he brings out the river pebbles (*ota*), which the *Ataoja* has to keep in the palace. The pebbles are considered to be both containers of *Osun*'s energy as well as children of *Osun*. Accordingly, one of the many names *Osun* is referred to is *Òsun Olómoyoyo*, meaning "*Osun* the one who possesses and bestows uncountable children." Given this characterization, the diving of the *Osun* chief priest into the river can be seen as alluding to the love affair *Osun* had with Larooye. That is, the diving of the *Osun* chief priest (who used to be identical with the *Ataoja*) into the water may symbolize Larooye's primal impregnation of *Osun* with the pebbles the priest brings out from the river representing the children resulting from that action. Following this line of interpretation, what happens during the *Osun* festival can be understood as a re-enactment of the events which led to *Osun*'s break with Larooye and Larooye's subsequent attempt to fix the relationship. The former refers to the intrusion of Larooye's people and the conquest of the sixteen point lamp, the latter to Larooye's making of a sacrifice to *Osun* at the river.

The sacrifice marks the climax of the festival. As shown above, the main figure that day is the *Arugba*. She carries the calabash (*igbá*) with the symbols of rulership specific to Osogbo to the river, i.e. *Osun*. All three—the *Arugba*, the calabash and *Osun*—belong together. As the daughter of the relationship between *Osun* and Larooye she has come out of the womb of *Osun* represented by the calabash.[7] In the midst of people accompanying her she proceeds to the river. When reaching the grove, however, she slips away from the crowd and enters her own gate, an event, which can be related to *Osun*'s anger and her 'stealing' or rather reclaiming the children she has with Larooye. Accordingly, the *Arugba* reappears only after a sacrifice has been made. Carrying the calabash back to the palace symbolizes the regaining of fertility of the town as the result of the 'repaired' relationship between *Osun* and the *Ataoja*.

V

As tempting as it is to see the above interpretation of the *Osun* festival as a "counter narrative" to the official version supported by the palace, one should not forget Olupona's emphasis that the *Osun* festival is a "civil religion". That is, civil religions are—just as the public sphere in which they exist—heterogeneous by nature. The collective religious identity they strive to achieve is reached by negotiation not by confrontation. Surely, in the case of Osogbo it can be debated to what extent this element of negotiation really holds true. Fact is, however, that a binary approach does not do justice to the way the participants perceive and experience the festival. Even in the framing of identity by notions of heritage and indigeneity a multiplicity of voices exists. Neither of them is absolute for sense and meaning is generated in the process of performance rather than by following a 'text'. As a result, multiple meanings prevail. Seen in this light the purpose of the contribution was to

---

[7] The interpretation of the calabash as a womb and sign for fertility is a prominent theme in Yoruba iconography, see Apter (1992), Abiodun (1989) and Witte (1986). Visual reference to this interpretation can also be seen in the vaginal shape of the entrances and passages which mark a distinctive feature of the architectures erected by Susanne Wenger and collaborators in the *Osun* grove.

focus on a version of the festival, which does not live outside the realm of heritage but rather in the shadow of it.

References

Abiodun, Rowland. 1989. Woman in Yoruba Religious Images. *African Languages and Cultures* 2 (1): 1-18.
Adejumo, Ademola. 1994. Osogbo Festival of Images. An Insight into some Aspects of Yoruba Art and History. In *African Art. Definitions, Forms and Styles*, ed Ron Kalilu, 63-74. Ogbomoso: Ladoke Akintola University.
Ajibade, Olusola. 2005. Negotiating Performance. *Osun* in the Verbal and Visual metaphors. http://opus.ub.uni-bayreuth.de/volltexte/2005/188/
Apter, Andrew. 1992. *Black Critics and Kings. The Hermeneutics of Power in Yoruba Society*. Chicago: Chicago University Press.
Beier, Ulli. 1956. Oshun Festival. *Nigeria Magazine* 53: 170-187.
Chesi, Gerd. 1983. *Susanne Wenger. A Life with the Gods in their Yoruba Hinterland*. Wörgl: Perlinger Verlag.
Farotimi, David. 1990. *The Osun Festival in the History of Osogbo*. Lagos: Facelift.
Kayode, Afolabi. 2006. *The Osun Osogbo Festival of Nigeria*. (DVD) j Frontline Television.
Lawal, Babatunde. 1985. Ori. On the Significance of the Head in Yoruba Sculpture. *Journal of Anthropological Research* 41: 91-103.
Lawal, Babatunde. 2001. Aworan: Representing the Self and Its Metaphysical Other in Yoruba Art. *Art Bulletin* 83 (3): 498-526.
Lowenthal, David. 1998. Fabricating Heritage. *Memory and History*, 10 (1): 5-24.
Murphy, Joseph & Mei Mei Sanford, eds. 2001. *Osun Across the Waters: A Yoruba Goddess in Africa and the Americas*. Bloomington: Indiana University Press.
Ofugha, Omosimuna. 2005. *Osun* Osogbo Opens Tourism Mines in Nigeria. In *The Capitol*, 1 (2): 10-17.
Ogungbile, David. 2003. *Myth, Ritual and Identity in the Religious Traditions of the Osogbo People of Western Nigeria*. Unpublished PhD diss., Department of Religious Studies, Obafemi Awolowo University, Ile-Ife, Nigeria.
Olupona, Jacob. 2001. Orisa *Osun*. Yoruba Sacred Kingship and Civil Religion in Osogbo, Nigeria. In *Osun Across the Waters. A Yoruba Goddess in Africa and the Americas*, ed. Joseph Murphy and Mei-Mei Sanford, Bloomington: Indiana University Press: 46-67.
Olupona, Jacob, ed. 2003. *Beyond Primitivism. Indigenous Religious Traditions and Modernity*. London: Routledge.
Olupona, Jacob, ed. 2008. *Orisa Devotion as World Religion. The Globalization of Yoruba Religious Culture*. Madison: University of Wisconsin Press.
Probst, Peter. 2004. Keeping the Goddess Alive. Marketing Culture and Remembering the Past in Osogbo. *Social Analysis* 48 (1): 33-54.
Probst, Peter. 2007. Picturing the Past. Heritage, Photography and the Politics of Appearance in a Yoruba City. In *Reclaiming Heritage: Alternative Imaginaries in West Africa*, ed. Michael Rowlands and Ferdinand De Jong, San Francisco: LeftCoast Press: 99-125.
Probst, Peter. Forthcoming. *Producing Presence. The Art of Heritage in a Yoruba City*. Bloomington: Indiana University Press.
Redfield, Robert. 1956. *Little Communities*. Chicago: Chicago University Press.
Werbner, Richard, ed. 1998. *Memory in the Postcolony*. London: Zed Press.

Witte, Hans. 1986. The Invisible Mothers. Female Power in Yoruba Iconography. In *Visible Religion*, V-VI, Institute of Religious Iconography, State University Groningen. Leiden: E.J. Brill: 301-325.

17

Drama, poetry and ritual in Zangbeto Festival of the Ògù people of Badagry

- George Olusola Ajibade

Introduction

This chapter discusses the fusion of poetic, religious and dramatic elements in Zangbeto cultural festival of the Ògù people of Badagry, Lagos state. It is an ethnographical study drawing data from both oral literature and the performance of the festival. The analysis of data benefits from both hermeneutic and sociology of religion to explicate the religious and social function of Zangbeto among the Ògù people of Badagry. This ethnographic study identifies a shift of traditional theatre from ritual into entertainment among the people. It concludes that Zangbeto as a form of theatre is being employed by the Ògù community people as a form of signification and communication through which they reaffirm the beliefs that nourish their community.

Drama, poetry and ritual: interface in indigenous religiosity

Drama has always existed in one form or the other in Nigerian societies, having its foundation in festivals and religious rituals. Yorùbá drama exists both in unwritten and written forms. It is a slice of real life with the intensity of a play that contains mimic and repletion aiming at performing various functions. Friesen (2005) has commented on Young (1914 and 1933) that he has 'proposed the theory that individuals involved with planning religious liturgy made a conscious choice to develop characters, costumes, dialogue and stage directions to perform the most perplexing element of Christian doctrine: the resurrection implied by the empty tomb on Easter' (Friesen, 2005: 8).

The elements of drama in Yorùbá traditional festivals cannot be overlooked because dramatic performances and plays are replete in Yorùbá traditional rituals. In other words, performance as an aspect of drama has always been a major aspect of traditional poetry of the Yorùbá people and poetry is inseparable from drama. Oral poetry is usually composed during performance but that the degree of composition varies from genre to genre and from tradition to tradition; it is nil in some while in others, the totality of the poem being rendered is that of the artist performing it (Finnegan, 1970). The Yorùbá traditional poetry is delimited into various genres, each genre being associated with a particular performance mode.

The specific origin of Nigerian theatre and drama are speculative but there is the existence, in many Nigerian societies, of a robust theatrical tradition (Ogunbiyi 1981). The primitive root of that tradition can be traced to and seen in the numerous religious rituals and festivals that exist in many Nigerian communities. As an expression of the relationship between man, society and nature, drama arose out of fundamental human needs in the dawn of human civilization and has continued to express those needs ever since. With reference to ritual drama, DeGraft (1976:6) opines that:

> The participants seek such desired effects as social solidarity, or through which they attempt to reaffirm, keep alive, or commemorate such facts, beliefs, relationships, and attitudes as the community considers vital to its sanity and continued healthy existence.

The observation of DeGraft above shows that both secular drama and sacred drama are not only interwoven, they 'have concomitant objectives that aim at providing the human community with alternate forms of release from its fears, and a vehicle for its aspiration of control over its destiny' (Badejo 1996: 135). Critically examined, one will agree that this objective is one of the principal reasons for people to engage in religious activities.

One of the central tenets of religion is the principle of imitation. In other words, there is a mimetic principle in religion. Likewise, there is mimetic principle in drama. Expression of theatrical need and religious impulses through mimesis also necessitates the production of poetry in diverse forms. This is done by heightening of speech, in an orderly manner to make it expressive and memorable. Thus, the language of religion is poetic when one considers the functionality and utility of poetry in different religious contexts and traditions, especially in Africa. However closely related poetry and religion are, there is the need to circumspectly demarcate between sacred and secular poetry, although both are product of imaginations. Sacred poetry might be revelatory and transcendental while secular poetry might be, although inspirational, but artistic inspiration that is sheer play of language. Sacred poetry should not be seen as an ornamental way or as a provider of an appealing guise in which to clothe social commentary on instruction in matters of morality, even though it can in addition to spiritual perform this role. The point of emphasis at this juncture is that drama, poetry and religion are intertwined.

Adédèjì's studies (1969, 1971, 1973 and 1981) are central for his elucidation and foremost attempt to identify the specific period of transition of traditional theatre from ritual into entertainment, with reference to Yorùbá theatre. Drawing extensively from historical audience, Adédèjì (1981: 223) demonstrates how *Sàngó*, who reigned as Aláàfin of Òyó, "probably about the fourteenth century, is thought to have introduced the phenomenon of the ancestor-worship called *bàbá* (father) or later, *egúngún* (masquerade)". He maintains that by the middle of the sixteenth century the institution had become formalized into a kind of festival through which various lineages specialize in one dance-display or the other, mainly in commemorating their departed souls. The refinement and perfection of those aspects, ostensibly for purely entertainment purposes, marked, by 1700 the birth of professional Yorùbá theatre. The view of Chambers (1903) tallies with scholars' view on the origin of drama among the Yorùbá people. The position of this paradigm is that the ancient and medieval cultures developed highly significant folk festivals to celebrate meaningful events that are theatrical. It has been noted that 'there is hardly any Yoruba community without one or more traditional festivals' (Danmole (2008: 207).These festivals 'partly serve to re-enact the establishment of various Yoruba communities (Ogunba 1991:51). The above observations are true of the Ogu people of Badagry, Lagos state especially in regards to Zangbeto festival.

The Ògù people of Badagry

Badagry, founded around 1425 A.D., is populated by the Ògù (erroneously called Egùn by the Yorùbá) immigrants from Gold Coast (modern Ghana), Dahomey (modern Benin Republic), Togo and the Awori, a Yórùbá speaking race. This makes the town a heterogonous and a bilingual community. In view of its strategic location, Badagry has at different times played different roles of socio-economic importance in the course of its history. It was a major market, a trading entrepot and a commercial centre serving the Àjá and Yorùbá countries. It was a frontier state sharing borders with the ancient kingdom of Dahomey and Port Novo before the creation of International boundaries. It was an important southern terminus during the trans-Saharan trade and also a famous harbour for the ignominious trans-Atlantic slave trade.

As a coastal town, it was the main port serving the Yorùbá hinterland up to the second half of the nineteenth century. Badagry, the land of the Ògù people is noted for historic events. The First Storey Building in Nigeria was constructed in Badagry town in 1845 by Rev. C.A. Gollmer of the Church Missionary Society (CMS) and the English bible was translated into the Yoruba language by a free slave boy for Bishop Samuel Ajayi Crowther in 1846. Likewise, the site of the Agia Tree Monument is where Christianity was first preached in Nigeria by Thomas Birch Freeman and Henry Townsend who arrived at Badagry town on 24th September 1842. Hence, Badagry was the first base of the Christian missionaries in modern Nigeria as well as the first point of call of the explorers and the colonial imperialists. All these made the town to be of great importance to the historical development of Nigerian hinterland. Even today, in spite of its proximity to Lagos, it still maintains a recognizable position.

The ancient town of Badagry gained prominence during the villainous Trans-Atlantic slave trade that swept through the whole of West Africa between sixteenth and eighteenth centuries. Apart from serving as the major exit point for millions of African slaves on their journey to the offshore, Badagry has recorded many fists in the Nigerian history. The Ògù people of Badagry are part of the Yorùbá/Popo sub-group who migrated from the ancient Kétu kingdom in the present day Benin Republic. According to an oral source, the Ògù people moved first from Ilé-Ifè in the late thirteenth century into the Dahomey Empire. A band led by Akran Gbagoe, moved Eastwards along the Porto-Novo and Yewa creeks (Now Badagry) settling along the Keveme coastline and creeks to Ologe Lagoon to form the chain of Ògù communities with Badagry encompasses the Island and mainland communities of Kweme, Wesere, Iworo, Ajido, Topo, Ale, Aradagun, Akarakumo, Ibereko, Itoga, Agbalata, Seme, Kankon, Ajara, etc. The claim that the people originated from Ile-Ife is doubtful considering the gap between the Yorùbá dialect of Ife and Badagry people. Also, the name of the progenitor and other names of the people in this area have no resemblance in meaning and phonology.

Badagry came into existence in the pre-colonial period with a legendary personage Agbethe, cultivating a vegetable farm in the Island town. This farm land assumed prominence with the reference Agbethegreme meaning (the farm of Agbethe) with which the thriving farming community was referred to this Badagry, the centre of Ògù people derived its name 'Agbadaigi' from Agbagreme, which was corrupted into Badagry at the advent of the Europeans in the sixteenth century.

Badagry like other Yorùbá states had established the institution of divine kingship (*De Wheno Aholu*). The stool had produced 17 *Akrans* of Badagry starting from the earliest *De whenue Aholu Akran Gbafoe* to the present (2010) *De Whenu Aholu Menu-Toyi I* who is the paramount ruler of Ògùland and Chairman of the Badagry Divisional chieftaincy committee. As a part of the Lagos socio-cultural region and lying on the ECOWAS Trans-African route, the Ògù people are highly hospitable and very receptive to new ideas. The prevalence of marine resources and water swamps resulted in the eating of crabs, fishes, lobsters and snails and their main occupations are fishing and farming.

What is Zangbeto?

The etymology of the word Zangbeto is (*Zan*-night; *gbeto*-person/people) but the origin of the organization is shrouded in mystery. Oral tradition puts it that Zangbeto is a sea spirit that people used to visit before going to the sea but at a stage he came out of the sea clad in raffia. On the advice of the Ifá Oracle he was lured out of his domain into the palace and has since then been residing there. Zangbeto has no symbol other than the raffia costume with some masks. Sacrifices are, however, offered to him on the beach and elders are said to constantly consult him when necessary. Zangbeto is the vigilante raffia masquerade which is highly valued by the Ògù people for its capability to assume different forms during performance. Though it is one of the ancestral cults of the Ògù people of Badagry and environs, it is usually performed to commemorate state functions and to sanitize the community of miscreants and dangers, thus serving as a form of law enforcement mechanism in the community. Besides, as most of the festivals among the Yoruba are used to honour ancestors (Olupona 1991:32) Zangbeto performs this function too. The Zangbeto masquerade is celebrated in Badagry every year (usually between July and August) and the duration is for nine days, during which many of the indigenous Badagry people make merry and do not work. For example, this year (2010) was celebrated between 30th July and 7th August 2010. Although the cult is mainly male but the festival includes males and some females who have passed child-bearing age. The Zangbeto serves as a socio-political and religious cult and members of the group are said to have magical powers that enhance the performance of their roles in the society. They dress in raffia and the costume usually has scary masks of horns of animals with various designs at the region of the head. The Zangbetos form a secret society and have their own temple from which they usually emerge to perform their patrolling duties or ritual dance during the festivals. It performs the role of night-watchmen patrolling the streets of the village and dispensing justice. Hence, they serve as the traditional Police to the people of Badagry to solve disputes and ensure that the law takes its course. The attendant (Atókùn) accompanies the Zangbeto and acts both as a crowd controller (during day-time festivals) and as an interpreter. Also, there are other cult members who follow Zangbeto during performances.

Normally, the community people can arrange guards that will institute peace and harmony in their town but, the people recourse to Zangbeto whom they believed is loaded with supernatural powers that can help them sanitize their community. The Zangbeto performs the ritual drama at the market square, or the chief's compound or the front of the king or village chief's house. The performances of Zangbeto is not for any monetary gain it is the belief of this group that they are part of the community or the society and that they owe the society a duty and responsibility. For this reason, they identify bad acts or behaviours of a person or group of people in the society and reveal these acts to the people through their performances for amendments. Thus, they are regarded as sanitizers of the community. One of the duties of the Zangbeto is to search for perpetrators of evils especially those who use darkness to perpetrate evil. Beside the vigilante duties of Zangbeto, it is the Ògù people's equivalent of Eégún Alárìnjo among the Oyo Yorùbá that engages in acrobatic display to entertain and amuse the audience. Zangbeto has a lot of tricks, acrobatics, and pantomime, to say nothing of dance, song and sacred overtones. Zangbeto has its own brand of poetry without which an outing or performance is incomplete. The lyrics go along with the whole performance.

A constant feature of the coast dwellers is the need to effectively defend their settlements against external aggressors from the overseas and hinterland neighbours. They have to be warlike because of the unique position they occupy on trade routes. The Egba and their neighbouring Egun coast dwellers fought bitterly during the nineteenth and the early part of twentieth centuries while the Ijaw mounted series of raids on Ìjèbú Ẹrè (Ijebu coast dwellers) during the same period. Faced with this situation, each group of coast dwellers set up various organizations and devised various techniques to effectively combat and forge aggressions. 'Okoso', a special boat mounted by spear and javelin bearers among Ìjèbú Ẹrè and Zangbeto (the Night Guards/night watch Lord), among the Ògù, are some of the men that aided war adventures.

Most of the devices and the adventures for which they were forged have, over the peaceful years, become ceremonial, Zangbeto, however, still retain most of its traditional and religious functions. Each Egun quarter and every settlement has its Zangbeto, in fact, every Ògù community, whether in Togo or Benin Republic has its Zangbeto. Zangbeto has therefore become the identity of the Egun people. The cult played a leading role during the Yorùbá inter-tribal wars of late nineteenth and early twentieth centuries. Zangbeto in raffia was used to frighten enemies away from the battlefield; such opponents took Zangbeto to be 'Òrò' (i.e. fairy) and it was used to scout for enemies both at the war camps and their settlements. The raffia costume served as camouflage to the soldiers in the bush while the belief that Zangbeto imbibes his subjects with supernatural power must have instilled psychological confidence in the warriors of that time.

The organizational structure of Zangbeto cult is simple and pyramidal. The authority comes from the apex which is occupied by *Agboadasi,* the executive head, whose authority is required on all acts, spiritual and ordinary. In the past, the occupant of that post played significant role at the battlefield. All cases of criminal acts detected are reported to him, he fixes the date of the Zagbeto festival and makes the required sacrifice. He is directly responsible to the Ọba who is the ceremonial head of the cult. Next to *Agboadasi* is the *Zangan*, the district head. In the past he was an army commander of a section in the war field but today he takes care of the Zangbeto under his command in the district (i.e. in the quarter). He is directly responsible to Agboadasi. Next to Zangan is 'Kogan' the sectional head who takes care of a batch of about ten cult members and next to him is the 'Kisonyito', the messenger. In the past, those holding the office of the messenger were the detective agents of the Zangbeto cult. Today, two officers have been added, that of *'Iyalode'* (Women Patron) and secretary.

The chain of command is, till today, strictly from Kisonyito through Kogan to Zangan and ultimately to Agboadasi. Membership of the cult is open to all male Egun who are above reproach in character. Oral test is conducted for every applicant and only a few are admitted on oath into the cult. Discipline is severe and strictly enforced, any member of the public can report malpractices by a Zangbeto to any of the officers who rigorously monitor the activities of their subordinates and maintain proper discipline within the cult.

Zangbeto in contemporary Ògù Society

Days of inter-tribal wars are over and, besides, modern organized armed forces take care of external aggression or internal subversion. The Police Forces were also set up to combat crimes; it is therefore surprising to find a traditional organization like Zangbeto actively performing some of the functions ascribed to the organs set up by the government.[1] Festivals are held once a year and sacrifices are offered to commemorate the activities of the olden days. Apart from dancing and feasting, the war organizations in those two communities and many others are moribund. Although, the traditional roles of Zangbeto have changed in a way; the cult still performs the functions of maintaining law and order as it was centuries ago, but not exactly. Zangbeto now directs its attacks mostly on criminal operating in urban areas instead of the opposing army on the battlefield. Means of effecting law and order have similarly not undergone much change; sticks, cutlasses, gong flutes and charms are the tools of Zangbeto as they have been over a hundred years ago.

Zangbeto maintains law and order in Badagry up till today in diverse forms. Zangbeto preserves properties by placing symbolic and charmed objects on them. For example, charms are tied round fruit trees like kola nut and maize as scare crow to prevent thieves from stealing in such farms.[2] Many indigenes of Ògù strongly believe that whoever steals from the farm where they put charm is doomed; hence they keep off. Zangbeto also engages in environmental sanitation by displaying dry banana leaves on spots where refuse should no longer be dumped and most of those acquainted with it comply for the fear of being inflicted by Zangbeto. Correspondingly, the members of Zangbeto cult use sacrifices and rituals to ward off evils in the community during the outbreak of epidemics to appease the bane forces that the people believe are responsible for such occurrences. On the sixth day of Zangbeto festival, prayers are offered and a pig is slaughtered at the beach as a sacrifice for peace and harmony. Another function of Zangbeto is to satirize the criminals in the society. The job entails triple actions of deterrence, discovery and prosecution. During the day, the members of the Kisonyito group of the cult go to market places, bar and restaurants, hotels and motor parks. They watch the movements and listen to the speech of people. If necessary, a Zangbeto trails the movement of an individual suspected of having criminal intentions. Any criminal act detected during this time will be promptly reported to Kogán, the sectional head of the cult. If the need be, an arrest could be effected otherwise the final resting place of the suspect is closely watched at night. The group also watches what an individual says; the

---

[1] Among the Ijaw and Ijebu Ere, for example, all the war organizations and devices have become ceremonial. The famous '*Egungun*' and '*Oro*' cults among the Yorùbá no longer do not arrest witches nor do they execute criminals. *Egúngún* and *Oro*, the once dreaded cults, have become mere entertaining fads.

[2] This is similar to *aakè*, the scare crow objects among the Yoruba people of the southwestern region of Nigeria. Various objects that have deeper semiotic meanings are placed on valuable materials to prevent them from stolen by thieves.

aim of this is to nip rumour mongering at the bud and give necessary feedback to the traditional rulers-Ọba and chiefs. In this regard, Zangbeto performs social, religious and political functions in the community.

Zangbeto also imposes curfew on the town from 12 midnight to 5 a.m. during this period, road blocks are mounted at strategic places in the town. Those entering or leaving the town are periodically checked. Visitors with genuine intentions may be escorted to their destinations while those suspected to be criminals are arrested after interrogations. Apart from this, patrol on foot is mounted in the town. The cult members on duty at night make use of various instruments to carry out their duty. The flute is particularly useful requesting the help of other Zangbeto. Communication on information about suspected criminals are conveyed through the flute. For example, whenever the flute is blown vigorously and continuously it is a signal for help. Other styles of whistling are restricted to the members of Zangbeto cult. Whenever they need the help of people outside the cult this is made known and people, especially male adults who are armed will come out to join their force. In a situation like this, the police are usually contacted. Due to the activities of Zangbeto and even the youths who are not members, Badagry is one of the relatively crime-free zones of Lagos State.

It is mostly during the night that prosecution and punishment are meted by the Zangbeto. Criminals caught during the day and the suspects are *arrayed* for prosecutions at night. Those caught at night are also tried before day break. Zangan, the district head handles most of the cases. After interrogation, the accused may be pronounced guilty on the weight of the evidence presented, and a fine is imposed; the fine varies with the severity of the offence. The venue of the judgment depends on the location of the Zangan at the time the accused was caught. Except those caught or suspected during the day, Zangbeto institutes instant justice. As for the accused person resident in Badagry, Zangbeto could evade his compound and order him out to defend himself against the allegation made. Most of the cult members interviewed admitted that because of the constant harassment by the Police on Zangbeto many of those caught are now transferred to police stations.

Zangbeto enforces his judgment through blackmail and curses. Thus, an accused found guilty is given a period within which to pay the fine. If he fails to act according to the judgment and within the stipulated period, Zangbeto's costume will be deposited in his residence with a posse of Zangbeto. If the culprit is adamant, he will be blackmailed throughout the area in which he resides; his crime will be made known to the public and he will become a detestable person in the community. If it is an intractable case the person will be taken to the beach to be cursed. The Badagry people believe in the potency and efficacy of Zangbeto's curses and this instils a kind of fear in the hearts of the people and makes them to avoid being cursed by Zangbeto. The above shows the role of Zangbeto cult in maintaining law and order in the community. Zangbeto is still relevant among the Ògù people of Badagry, although they enter into occasional conflict with the modern law enforcement agents-mainly, the policemen. The main reason for their relevance in the jury sector of the society is nothing other than ineffectiveness of the constituted law enforcement agent in Nigeria. Crime is at the alarming rate and the community people felt that they are not adequately protected; hence they have to improvise their self means of protection of life and properties. A vigilante group like Zangbeto definitely has a role to play and it is actively playing it. It has been observed that in many localities in Nigeria there are various vigilante groups that have sprung up over the years who are out to defend the fundamental human rights of their people.

There is a vital spiritual entity that pervades the organization. Zangbeto, as far as the people are concerned, is a spirit possessed with mysterious powers capable of destroying an individual. This belief is firmly held by members of the Zangbeto and most members from Ògù community in general. In fact, members of the cult strongly believe that they are imbibed with the spirit and if they misuse it they are doomed. This belief has, no doubt, contributed to the respect accorded to the cult members by the community people. It was clearly shown by many of our respondents that this belief is still being upheld by many members of the community; although many expressed contrary view and said that it will be eroded away as the society becomes more scientifically and technologically oriented. This latter view is most likely to hold to an extent. The 2010 edition of carnival in Badagry showed the fusion of many traditional heritages being performed during the Zangbeto's festival. It was a parade of an array of cultural display that lasted for about a week, which included the Zangbeto masquerade display in its awesome colour; the next day was devoted to the exciting and impressing spirit dance from the Vothum masquerade and the Gbenepo royal procession accompanied by the town's monarch and his royal court in a communal royal felicitation.[3] The activity was concluded with a Gala Nite held at the Marine Beach Park being built to further enhance tourism potentials in the town. This shows that communal participation in this festival is more of tourism than spirituality. However, the Zangbeto masquerade display at Ajido community represents the spirits of the ancestors returning to commune with the living in a harmonious relationship.

Zangbeto's poetic performance

The Zangbeto, or the people of the night, is the spirit of an ancestor who protects the community from evil and drives out evil spirits and witches and they dispense justice in the village. In the ceremony the Zangbeto is represented as a colourful haystack, wildly spinning around in a field accompanied by drums and assisted by human spiritual interpreters and guides. After a while the Zangbeto stops and starts to shake and is then tipped over to show the audience that there is no human inside. The spirit has instead left a figure or taken the shape of any object such as a turtle. Then the Zangbeto is turned back and starts immediately to spin again. The human caretaker directing the Zangbeto acts as a middleman in the day to day life,

---

[3] The full account of 2010 Badagry carnival was reported by Mary Ekah (2010) "Reinventing Badagry's Cultural Past," *This Day Live*, http://www.thisdaylive.com/articles, August 13, 2010.

keeping order in the community. The Zangbeto mask's explosive character evokes a power that inhabited the earth long before the appearance of man and remains a source of wisdom and continuity for the Ogu people of Badagry. They are men in a costume that resembles a haystack but are in a trance which enables their bodies to be inhabited by spirits who have special knowledge of the actions of people.

Every time the Zangbeto wants to perform, the body movement, the dance steps, and the oral poetry by his followers are always repeated. Zangbeto and his followers believes that doing exactly how it was done before their time makes their acts potent and even they are immune to the other forces that aims at grousing them. The oral poetry performed during Zangbeto festival make the heart of his followers merry and reassures them that they have a god that resides among them. Also, during their performances, the display of many magical powers is a form of drama to the audience. The Zangbeto changes into different forms. Turning into fishes is the climax of the performance because according to the Ògù history Zangbeto is from the sea. When he changes into the fish, the people know that the performance has come to an end. This symbolizes the departure of Zangbeto into his original abode.

By the time Zangbeto changes into these various forms his followers will be singing. Zangbeto will be dancing to the melodies of the lyrics and the drum called Hungan which is about five feet tall. The singers too dance around the drum. The drumming, dancing and singing are done annually during the festival and they are dramatic. Below are some of the songs Zangbeto's followers sing while he does almost all the dancing.[4]

The first song below is usually rendered at the beginning of Zangbeto's performances. The song is sung by the followers of Zangbeto to show their faith and fate in this deity. He is regarded as their god; the only one they owe allegiance to, and the provider of their needs. It also shows their determination to devote their lives unto Zangbeto because of his benefits to them. The song reveals the origin and abode of Zangbeto. According to the history of the Ògù people as said earlier, Zangbeto resides in the sea and the people believe that he provides for the needs of the community. It is their belief that whenever he appears he brings drinks and fishes for the people. This shows their belief that he cares for his people.

Zangbeto we yin miton	Zangbeto is our own
Zangbeto we yin oodun	Zangbeto is our own god
Ewo minna sen	It is he we will worship
Min na do oodun awe	We have no other god

---

[4] Although, the oral history has it that the Tgù people of Badagry migrated from Ile-Ife we have no linguistic evidence to support this view. The poetic performance of Zangbeto, the most revered and significant communal festival and deity of the Tgù, shows clearly that the Ògù people are distinct. Also, the presence and annual similar performance of Zangbeto in Benin Republic, formerly Dahomey, is evidence that they migrated from that region prior and after the Trans-Atlantic slave trade. There are also varieties of dialects within the Tgù dialect which include Thevi, whla, Seto and Toli among others.

Zangbeto we yo miton	Zangbeto is our own
N do èyí wa	If he goes to the sea
Ena na eh weri go na mi	He always bring fishes for us
Ewo we min na sen	It is him we will worship
Zangbeto we min na sen	It is Zangbeto we will worship
Zangbeto we yin miton	Zangbeto is our own
Zangbeto we yin odun miton	Zangbeto is our own god
Ewo mi na sen	It is him we will worship
Min ma do vodun awe	We have no other god
Zangbeto we yin miton	Zangbeto is our own

The last two lines of the above song are used to reinforce and reaffirm the followers' position on their commitment to Zangbeto.

The second song below also reveals the providence power of Zangbeto just like the first song.

Lead:	Zangan we jehen	Zangan bought drinks for us[5]
Chorus:	Zangan	Zangan
Lead:	Gbeto we jehan bon a ni nu eh eh	Gbeto brought drinks for us
Chorus:	Gbeto	Gbeto
Lead:	Zangbeto we ho meul wan a eh	But it is Zangbeto who brings fishes for us
Chorus:	Zangbeto	Zangbeto

The third song shows that the Ògù community people pride themselves in Zangbeto. He is regarded as their civil responsibility and duty that cannot and must not be neglected. This song is in line with the first song:

Lead:	Azon miton we	It is our work
Chorus:	Ye mape mile ji	They cannot remove him from us
Lead:	Ònú minton we	It is our heritage
Chorus:	Ye mape mile ji	They cannot remove him from us
Lead:	Zangan minton we	Zangan is our heritage
Chorus:	Ye mape mile ji	They cannot remove him from us
Lead:	Baalè minton we	Baale is our heritage
Chorus:	Ye mape minton ji	They cannot remove him from us
Lead:	Zanni minton we	Zanni is our heritage
Chorus:	Ye mape mile ji	They cannot remove him from us
Lead:	Gbangbalago minton we	They cannot remove him from us
Lead:	Gbajo minton we	Gbajo is our heritage
Chorus:	Ye mape mile ji	They cannot remove him from us
Lead:	Vodun minton we	Vodun is our own,
Chorus:	Ye mape mili ji	They cannot remove him from us
Lead:	Zangbeto minton we	Zangbeto is our own
Chorus:	Ye mape mile ji	They cannot remove him from us.

---

[5] Zangan is used here synonymous to Zangbeto.

The next song rendered by the Zangbeto cult functionaries shows how the people link this deity to the reigning traditional leader and the patriarchs:

Lead:	*Zanvi le sí baba lo di ye*	He is a father to Zanvi
Chorus:	*Baba! Oh Baba lo di ye oh*	BabaFather! This is the father
Lead:	*Otona le si baba lo di ye*	He is the father of the town
Chorus:	*Baba! Oh Baba lo di ye oh*	BabaFather! This is the father
Lead:	*Baale we Baba me ton be*	The village chief is our father
Chorus:	*Baba! Oh Baba lo di ye oh*	BabaFather! This is our father
Lead:	*Zangan we Baba me ton be*	Zangan is our father
Chorus:	*Baba! Oh Baba lo di ye oh*	BabaFather! This is our father

This reinforces their social ties and genealogy grandeur. One of the great ancestors of the Ogu people is Zanvi. Referring to Zangbeto as the father to Zanvi is the indication that, to them, Zangbeto is not distant from the people; he takes part in the day-to-day administration of the community. The above poetry is a form of oríkì of the deity as the father of all members of the community, and this is performed annually. This is concomitant to Finnegan (1970: 120) who proves that, "among the Yorùbá, the praises of the king, with the complete list of predecessors and their praises must be recited once a year in the public". The song also shows verbal veneration to the traditional political authority by the Zangbeto cult group. This sort of verbal veneration usually performs two main functions in this kind of social context. The first is that it shows the commitment of the Zangbeto group to the course of the traditional political authority in the community to reiterate their support for his administration. Secondly, it is a form of appeal to the traditional political authority to gain his support as well whenever they take any step against any suspect within the community. Therefore, the king or better put the village head serves as the executive arm of the community's administration while the Zangbeto (using the spiritual prowess) serves as the judicial arm of the administration within the community.

Hailing the deity repeatedly as seen above has the effect of focusing attention on the deity as personally present with them as father who is present with his children. Therefore, with the dancing gestures and the repetition of these festivals, the people are always impressed. In order that the members of the community may not be bored, some elements of entertainment are now introduced into the festival performance and as a matter of this scene, a dramatic situation is created. This reinforces the idea that drama evolved from festival, mainly ritual drama.

The last song below reinforces unity and oneness as thrusts and pillars of development in any given community:

Lead: *Gbemi tona po e nanyon*	If your voices are lifted up as one
Chorus: *Hen eh*	Yes
Lead: *E sona mu e nanyon*	If it is so, it will be good
Chorus: *Hen eh*	Yes
Lead: *Gbemi tona po e nanyon*	If your voice are lifted up as one

Mini do hen a gun eegoo	To unite the group
Chorus: *Gbemi tona po e nanyon*	If your voices are lifted up as one
Gbemi tona po e nanyon	If your voices are lifted up as one
Gbemi tona po e nanyon	If your voices are lifted up as one
Mini do hen a gìn eegoo	To unite the group

As seen from the first line to the end, it is only when voices of the community people, especially that of the Zangbeto cult group are lifted up as one that good thing can be done. 'Lifting up voices' within its proper context connotes that the cult people should be united in fighting against all forms of agents of disunity and threats that are inimical to the progress of their community.

One can see from the song that conflicts and disorderliness that might find their ways into the community through disunity find redress in the dialectic of Zangbeto's poetic performance. Clamour for unity and oneness is a necessity to development in any organization and community. Division is a great threat to their job, security of the community. When the appeal is made to the people especially the members of Zangbeto cult group, the audience becomes involved in the ritual drama and the Zangbeto's voices are well respected as someone who is vested with power to challenge the chthonic realm on behalf of the whole community. The observation of Soyinka (1976: 2-3) on ritual drama is very useful and applicable here when he maintains that:

> A chthonic realm, a storehouse for creative and destructive essences, it required a challenger, a human representative to breach it periodically on behalf of the well-being of the community. The stage, the ritual arena of confrontation, came to represent the symbolic chthonic space and presence of the challenger within.

The Ògù people opine that there are forces behind various misdemeanours exhibits by the people and that both physical and spiritual means are needed to ensure peaceful existence in the community. Hence, there is the need for someone to challenge the chthonic realm.

In all, the praise chanters moves freely among the three phases of the divinity's existence: the mythical past when the *òrìṣà* lived among men on earth; his present divine involvement in nature and human affairs; the continuing worship offered to him by his devotees in which he is mystically encountered (Lindom 1990: 208).

Conclusion

The Zangbeto festival of the Ògù people of Badagry is a ritual drama that envelopes various elements such as force of recreation, communality, sanitization, and peaceful existence. This civil deity occupies a central space in every sphere of people's lives. It serves various purposes ranging from religious, political to social. Through singing and dancing, they dramatize the philosophical meaning of the festival as secular interwoven with the sacred symbolic elements. There is also a demonstration of these philosophical meanings and essence in the rendering of oral poetry. The Zangbeto cult group members and the audience through verbal artistry impersonate the characteristics of the earthly representative of Zangbeto; revealing all benefits derivable from him. Although, various religious beliefs of the people are seen, most especially in the oral poetry of Zangbeto, it is highly evident that there is a shift of traditional theatre from ritual into entertainment among the people. The entertainment part of this ritual drama surpasses the religious connotation. It must also necessary to state that this traditional festival of the people is witnessing tremendous changes. Although, it still functions as a law enforcement traditional institution within the community but its roles are contingent upon the statutory law enforcement agent of the state.

References

Adedeji, J.A. 1969. "The Alarinjo Theatre: The Study of a Yoruba Theatrical Art from its earliest Beginnings to the Present Times", Unpublished Ph.D. Thesis, University of Ibadan.

Adedeji, J.A. 1971. "Oral Tradition and the Contemporary Theatre in Nigeria", *Research in African Literatures*, 2 (2): 134-149.

Adedeji, J.A. 1973. "Trends in the Content and Form of the Opening Glee in Yoruba Drama", *Research in African Literatures*, 4 (1): 32-47.

Adedeji, J.A. 1981. "Alarinjo: The Traditional Yoruba Travelling Theatre", In: *Drama and Theatre in Nigeria: A Critical Source Book*, (ed.) Yemi Ogunbiyi, Lagos: Nigerian Magazine: 221-248.

Badejo, Diedre. 1996. *ÒṢUN ṢÈÈGÈSÍ: The Elegant Deity of Wealth, Power and Femininity*, Trenton, New Jersey: Africa World Press.

Chambers, E.K. 1903. *The Medieval Stage*, Oxford: Oxford University Press.

Danmole, H.O. 2008. "Religious Encounter in Southwestern Nigeria: The Domestication of Islam among the Yoruba." In: Olupona J.K. and Terry Ray (eds.) *Orisa Devotion as World Religion: The Globalization of Yoruba Religious Culture*, The University of Wisconsin Press. Page 202-221.

DeGraft, J.C. 1976. "Roots of African Drama and Theatre", *African Literature Today*, (8): 1-25.

Ekah, Mary. (2010) "Reinventing Badagry's Cultural Past," *This Day Live*, http://www.thisdaylive.com/articles, August 13, 2010

Friesen, Lauren. 2005. "Drama and Religion: the Search for a New Paradigm," *The Journal of Religion and Theatre*, 4 (1): 8-15.

Lindom, Thomas. 1990. "Oriki Orişa: The Yoruba Prayer of Praise," *Journal of Religion in Africa*, 20, (2): 205-224.

Ogunba, Oyin. 1991. "Hegemonic Festivals in Yorubaland." Ife: *Annals of the Institute of Cultural Studies*, Ile-Ife: Obafemi Awolowo University.

Ogunbiyi, Yemi. 1979. Drama and Theatre in Nigeria: A Critical Source Book.

Olupona, K. Jacob. 1991. "Contemporary Religious Terrain." In: *Religion and Society in Nigeria*, eds. Olupona J. K. and Toyin Falola. Ibadan: Spectrum Books.

Soyinka, Wole. 1976. *Myth, Literature, and the African World*. Cambridge: Cambridge University Press.

Young, Karl. 1914. "The Origin of the Easter Play", In: *Publications of the Modern Language Association of America*, (ed.) Howard, W.G., Vol. XXIX: 1-59.

Young, Karl. 1933. *The Drama of the Medieval Church*, Oxford: Clarendon Press.

IV

Ethics, Women and Indigenous Spirituality

18

Eto: a retributive principle in Owhe society

- S.G.A. Oseovo Onibere

Introduction

Eto is regarded in Owhe community[1] as a retributive principle which ensures that the evil-doer does not go unpunished.[2] It is in this sense that justice can be predicated of its operations. In what follows attempts will be made to demonstrate how this thesis finds development in the analysis of Owhe concept of *eto*.

Etymologically *eto* as a medicinal preparation, and *eto* as chewing-sticks have the same spelling and tone-marks. However, both must be clearly distinguished in our present consideration. It is possible to include *eto*, chewing-sticks, in the preparation of the former; but not necessarily so. The implication is that when *eto*, chewing-sticks, have been ritually treated by the attachment of other medicinal items upon which invocations have been made, everything becomes *eto* as a cultic object.

The role of the *obueva*, diviner, in the preparation of *eto* must be given its proper emphasis. It is he who identifies the tree that can be used as part of the *eto* assembly. Other items in the *eto* cluster include a parrot's feathers, bones and fingernails of certain animals, cowrie shells, snails' shells, coconut shell, a beak of a duck, etc. after the ritual treatment of all these they are tied into a bundle and placed in a basket woven for the purposes.[3] The basket together with the *eto* is housed in the shrine of the operator since no efforts are made to separate this phenomenon from the owner's divinity where there is one. An operator is permitted to have more than one *eto* as their strengths are in gradations. However, it is to be observed that one man one *eto* is a much more common occurrence. It is also in evidenced that *eto* can be prepared and sold to anyone who needs it. But it does appear that many operators have it through paternal inheritance.[4]

---

[1] The Owhe community is to be located among the Isoko of the Niger Delta of Nigeria. See O. Ikime, *The Isoko People: A History Survey* (Ibadan: University Press, 1972), p. xxii

[2] Cf. J. O. Awolalu, *Yoruba Beliefs and Sacrificial Rites* (London: Longman, 1979), pp. 33 et passim.

[3] It is noteworthy that a fishing-basket (uge) can perform the same function.

[4] One of the informants did not allow me to see his *eto* if the sum of N20.00 was not paid. According to him, the *eto* was inherited and so very powerful and important. Many of the *eto* I saw were obtained through inheritance.

II

When the Owhe say:
Whe o no o rowo ome uvinye avo iso etoto owhe oma ha
Koo me no o rowo owhe inwe avo ivrinwe ere toto oma?

You did not nauseate when you bit my anus with its faeces
Why should I nauseate when I bit your nose with its phlegm?

They are in effect indicating that any person responsible for upsetting the balance of society through an antisocial act must not escape the retributive principle. That the people are not concerned with punishing the offender from wrong motives is demonstrated by another saying: *Orukeje o re ru owho kpo agba ho ure*, "Retaliation brings disastrous consequences."[5] It is thus evident that witches, sorcerers, murderers, thieves, etc. are sure to incur the displeasure of the community. One of the ways of dealing effectively with such persons is to have recourse to *eto*.[6] This retributive principle, it is true, can be directed against an individual or a group of persons who have committed an antisocial act. Two stories will presently be told to show how this has happened in practice.

There was an individual in Owhe community who went to Orogun, a town in Urhoboland,[7] to make a living. He was married with children. But he was apparently not satisfied with his wife since he made away with another man's wife from Erowha-Owhe. The dispossessed man was in much confusion. Eventually he settled on a plan to use *eto* against the adulterer in the hope that he would retrace his steps after the chastisement. He consulted an *eto* operator at once, told him his story and requested that the adulterer be made to suffer for his misconduct.

On the basis of this operator-client agreement, *eto* was sent into immediate action, reached where the offender was and inflicted him with the malady of body heat. Consequently he was restless as he was experiencing heat in every point of his body. It was not difficult for him to know what was responsible for his affliction for he saw signs of *eto*'s presence. Guilty conscience immediately convinced him that the source of the trouble was none other than the woman he was unlawfully keeping in his possession. He at once took a trip to Erowha-Owhe, his home village, to plead for mercy. He met the dispossessed man who was not ready for reconciliation because he wanted the adulterer to suffer much longer for his malpractice. He however agreed later after much pleading; whereupon he asked the victim to purchase the following: three goats, two sheep, two dogs and a substantial number of fowls. He was to pay one hundred naira in addition. It was not easy for the adulterer to fulfil this demand judging from his economic level of existence. But he had no choice.

---

[5] The dictum engenders the idea that anyone who retaliates will surely be paid back in excess to his surprise.
[6] Other phenomena, such as *eha* and *ovo* approximate their functions to that of *eto*.
[7] The Urhobo are among the contiguous neighbours of the Isoko.

He made strenuous efforts to procure the enumerated items which he presented to the aggrieved man. The latter consulted the operator to neutralize the effects of the *eto*. This was done and in a split second the victim regained his health. The wife of the aggrieved man was returned to him and full reconciliation was thus effected.[8]

The other story[9] tells of how *eto* was recently invoked against a group of persons in Owhe community. At Otibio-Owhe some unknown individuals decided on the mischievous plan of catching fish from a pond which belongs to the whole village. The fishing was done in such a way as to virtually empty the fish-pond of its fish contents. This naturally induced sentiments of anger in the inhabitants who resorted to *eto* in order to give the culprits their just deserts. Up till the time of the writer's interview the result of the *eto* consultation was still unknown. Things may become clear later on. The inhabitants are however confident that the source of the malpractice will not remain too long hidden. What is important for our purpose is that there is an instance of a whole community rising to the challenge of corporate misconduct.

III

It is certainly of significance to substantiate the forerunning stories by describing the precise operation mode of *eto*, having now detailed the circumstances for its invocation. This is likely to enable us understand its various ramifications so as to better appraise its role in Owhe society.

Once it is established that an offence, say stealing, has been committed, the offended individual consults an *eto* operator and lodges his complaint. A day is appointed for the operation. In the night of the expected day, the client repairs to the house of the operator and pays the prescribed fee. Where there is a prior understanding between the client and the operator, say on the ground of consanguine relationship, the fee may be waved. At this point the stage is really prepared for the ritual to commence in earnest.

The *eto* is taken from the shrine of the operator and placed on the ground outside the house with a piece of firebrand resting on it. It should be noted that no congregation is expected since it is solely a client-operator undertaking. The operator then raises the *eto* and makes the following invocation:

Ekuowa ibri, ekuowa ibri
Oja nana whe ovo osai ki e ke ome
Owho no o tho oware me na
Eto nya who kpa era ku ei
O whu o kpo! O whu o kpo!
Eme o ru ome eto, eme o ru ome eto
Ko o kpo ewo, ko othethe oro ye ei

---

[8] Interview with Mr. E. Ogo, aged 80, at Erawha-Owhe, 4th April, 1980
[9] Ibid.

Ko o ro eva uwou ko o gbe nya oma obo rie
Ko o gbe so ese wo – o o
Te kie oja ke ome, te kie oja ke ome
Ekuowa ibri! Ekuowa ibri! (note of invocation)

You are the only one to solve this problem
The person who is responsible for stealing my property
Eto, proceed to shower fire on him
Let him die at once, let him die at once
Eto is worrying me, *eto* is worrying me
If he goes to farm let a snake bite him
If he is at home let him cut himself
Let some trouble come to him
Come and help me out, come and help me out.

At the end of this invocation the *eto* is placed on the ground again, the firebrand is taken from it, the operator uses it in describing a circle over his head and throws it towards the direction the *eto* is facing. If the firebrand falls longitudinally, it is an omen that the *eto* is on its journey to the desired destination. On the contrary, if the firebrand falls latitudinally, then the *eto* is clearly indicating its unwillingness to undertake the task. The operator ensures that the firebrand is thrown three times before consulting the diviner (*obueva*) to unveil the reason for refusal to take off. Some of the reasons why this usually happens are as follows. The weather may not be conducive to a smooth take off of the *eto*. For instance, in the event of rainfall the *eto* will not be encouraged to fulfil its assignment. In fact there may be no resort to divination to know this; it is one of the ritual interdictions surrounding its operation. Another reason for its unwillingness to undertake the mission is associated with the countering medicine (*ifue*) of the evildoer. The offender, knowing that repercussions will attend his malicious act, may decide to arm himself against such with a protective medicine. Further, some persons naturally enjoy immunity from *eto*'s punitive measures as incorporated in their destiny (*otatha*).

However, when no hindrance occurs, the *eto* speeds on its way. One of the most mysterious aspects of the phenomenon is that the *eto* and the firebrand do not leave where the ritual has taken place. Yet any observant eye can see the firebrand shooting through the sky and sparking as it goes.[10] A fascinating point in the journey is that when the *eto* arrives at the town or village where the offender is, a silk-cotton tree (*ahe*) arrests its further advance for interrogation:

Bove who re nya?
Ono who be woe mo bru?

---

[10] The present writer had a personal experience of *eto* in 1961 when he was in the Secondary Grammar School at Emevor, Isoko Division. He was petrified to see the *eto* shooting through the sky.

Eme ohwo na o ru?
Eme o wha oware uyoma na ze?

Where are you going?
To whom is your punitive expedition directed?
What offence has he committed?
And what were the circumstances?

The *eto* is only allowed to proceed upon receiving satisfactory answers to this barrel of questions. Should it fail to justify its mission, it may have to be turned back from there. The name of the victim may be (and usually is) unknown; but that does not constitute any obstacle to *eto* from whom no secrets are hidden. What is more, no distance is beyond its compass of action.

On its arrival at its destination, it enters the house of the victim where its luminous light is visible only to the offender. Occasionally too the *eto* can set the victim's house on fire, making neighbours assume that some has been careless with fire, unless the *eto* is see before it lands on the house. But what is sure to happen in any *eto* errand is that the offender having noticed its presence, experiences heat all over his body. In some cases this may even extend to members of his family. If it is the intention of the *eto* to have the victim liquidated, he falls down, shouts loudly and then passes away. At times the victim may not die instantly. He may take ill and after a short time undergoes a transition to the hereafter. There are some victims who may be afflicted with insanity. The *eto* can decide to do whatever it likes with the victim; the business of the offended is simply to send it to requite the victim. In some cases the offender may not be aware of *eto*'s presence; and so when malady strikes the priest-diviner is consulted for a solution. Having traced the source to *eto* the remedial line of action is to approach the offended party who will contact the operator to recall the punitive expedition of his *eto*. This is on the assumption that reconciliatory measures have been taken by the victim and the offended party. Worthy of note, however, is the fact that the offender can neutralize the effects of *eto* without any reference to the client-operator agreement. He simply consults another obo (medicine-man) who is versed in counteracting the disastrous effects of *eto*. There are occasions when the *eto* is not even allowed to enter the compound of the victim, let alone to afflict him with sickness. Does this mean that the success of *eto* cannot be guaranteed in every instance? The answer to this will soon become evident as the inquiry develops.

Whatever the case, the *eto* flies back to its owner without the usual sparking. The sparking, our sources maintain, enables the *eto* to know its route to its destination. Once this is known, the sparking becomes superfluous for its return journey. Moreover, the *eto* is expected to finish its operation and be back the same day. On its return it informs the operator directly or through the medium of dream. It is only then that the operator will be able to know whether the mission undertaken was successful or not.

Another version of the *eto* operation which induces corporate action, exists among the Owhe people. According to this (and the reader is here reminded of the story of the fish-pond narrated above), a whole community may be interested in punishing a person or a group of persons who have committed an offence against it. We shall briefly describe how this operates, emphasizing the areas of difference between it and the earlier one described.

The whole community, including men and women, assembles in the compound of the high priest of the town or village involved in the matter. Every man comes with his *eto* just as every woman comes with her disused broom.[11] While all the women stand by their heap of brooms; each man stands by his *eto*. Invocations are made by all simultaneously. At the end of this each man throws his firebrand which is expected to set off in the manner already discussed. As for the womenfolk, no firebrands accompany their invocations. When the exercise has been concluded the men take their *eto* home; whereas the womenfolk never take back their brooms. The corporate *eto* action is said to be very efficacious in dealing with an offence involving the entire community.

IV

The description of *eto* operation automatically raises a number of difficulties which will naturally cry for solutions at this point. One of such is the failure of *eto* to take off owing to poor weather. One would have thought that a potent phenomenon such as *eto* should not be handicapped in its operations by physical hazards.[12] After all *eto* does successfully defy natural laws when it shoots through the sky, is suspended in motion by the silk-cotton tree, enters the house of the victim with all doors barred and can even set the house on fire. Certainly it seems odd and incredible that after all these supernatural accomplishments, rainfall can prevent *eto* from proceeding on its course. A relief to this problem can be probably found in the view already expressed that poor weather is one of the ritual interdictions that govern its operations. The reason for this interdiction is conceivably beyond the ken of contemporary votaries since it is hidden in antiquity.

A second problem that needs some investigation is the interrogation of the *eto* by the silkcotton tree. From all that has been said hitherto, *eto* is an instrument of justice. But it is to be simultaneously observed that *eto* can be manipulated in such a way as to serve the malicious intentions of the client or victim.[13] Evidently where such occurs the integrity of the *eto* falls into disrepute. It is probably in recognition of this fact that the *ahe* has been admitted into the system to ensure that justices is done to both parties in the

---

[11] The brooms mentioned here must be regarded as very old and no more used for the purpose of sweeping. In fact they have become so worn out that they can no longer function effectively.

[12] Interview with Chief Ojaide, Chief priest of Igbozue divinity, aged 75 years, at Otibio-Owhe, 6th April 1980. It is even maintained that an *eto* can hide under a heap of grass after rainfall should it be sent on an errand.

[13] We are here recalled to the fact of counteracting medicine (*ifue*) which can act irrespective of the ethical basis of the case.

offence. To be sure, there are occasions when an offence may be committed in inadvertence or out of a compelling necessity. The issue becomes more compounded where the wrongdoer does not even know to whom he should make reparations. Such situations demand, in view of Owhe ethics, that the offences be overlooked. Conversely, cases of deliberate wrongdoing must be attended by repercussions. However this may be, what makes the justice of the silkcotton tree (*ahe*) most indisputable is the fact that it is not subject to any negative influence, terrestrial or celestial. One is therefore not surprised that Deity himself is regarded as the source of the silkcotton tree. This belief finds sustenance in the view that God is the only impartial judge of all. It is this consideration that makes us liken the silkcotton tree to the Supreme Court of Appeal where absolute justice is supposed to reside.

There is the third problem and this has to do with the silkcotton tree. With justice guaranteed from the silkcotton tree's interrogation, one would have been led to assume that no further injustice would be evidenced in *eto*'s operation. And yet on arrival at its destination *eto* can be prevented from fulfilling its purpose already sanctioned as just by the silkcotton tree. As already indicated earlier, there are occasions when the offender may even prevent the *eto* from taking off by means of a protective medicine (*ifue*). A thief who has stolen under inexcusable circumstances can thus conveniently avert the consequences of his misconduct. Evidently this cannot be said to be in the interest of justice. In effect, it is an encouragement to engage in wrongdoing with attendant undermining of societal stability. Nor should we charge this to the importance of the silk cotton tree because cases do not reach it for screening. The justice of a high court judge cannot be impeached until he has mismanaged a case brought before him. So it is with the silkcotton tree.

It is however gratifying to note that this problem is not intractable on the basis of the following discussion. Many types of *eto* exist, all differing in their strengths. Some are so strong that the mere mockery of them can bring their displeasure on the mocker. A story[14] is told to a man whose father was preparing to send his *eto* on an errand (*vi eto uwou*). To this man his father's *eto* was an obvious irrelevance. Consequently he ridiculed the *eto* saying

Eme enana esai rue?
Enana esai kpe ohwo?
Eware no a ro obo ru esai siwi ohwo ho
Ahwo akpo a laye oma rai kehe
Wha tolo no me rue ude

What can this do?
Can this kill a person?
The works of men's hands cannot save.
People simply engage themselves in fruitless labour
Take this useless thing from my presence.

---

[14] Interview with Mr. S. Umukoro, c.70 years, a devotee of Owise-Owhe, at Oto-Owhe, 10th June, 1980.

He could hardly conclude this utterance when the *eto* dashed him to the floor and plunged him into a state of fainting. He foamed at the mouth with his whole body covered with sweat. The whole family was thrown into trepidation. Water was poured on him to no effect. The father knowing the root cause quickly divined to know the precise ritual for bringing the situation under control. The *eto* demanded a cock. This was provided, sacrificed on to the *eto* and the son's health was instantly restored. This story no doubt illustrated that some *eto* are very potent in dealing with offenders. In a circumstance where an offender has armed himself with a protective medicine such a powerful *eto* will have no problem in achieving its mission. We are reminded of the corporate *eto* action by the entire community which breaks no confrontation from any offender. (Moreover, our sources emphatically claim that some *eto* have no counteracting medicine (*ifue*) whatsoever). Where a weak *eto* is overpowered by the offender's *ifue*, it is possible to send a much more powerful *eto* to overshadow the potency of the protective medicine.[15] As a matter of fact, a not-too-potent *eto* can achieve its mission if the offender is taken unawares, making it too late for him to take precautionary measures – granted that he has no permanent *ifue* with him.

All this coupled with the screening exercise of the silkcotton tree compels the conclusion that *eto* is indubitably an instrument of justice, externalizing deities judgmental attribute among the Owhe people.[16]

References

Awolalu, J. O., *Yoruba Beliefs and Sacrificial Rites* (London: Longman, 1979)

Ikime, O., *The Isoko People: A Historical Survey* (Ibadan: University Press, 1972)

---

[15] There are occasions when a victim's *otatha* can render the operation of *eto* ineffective. At any rate, the victim does still suffer some repercussions though he cannot be killed.

[16] Cf. J. O. Awolalu, *Yoruba Beliefs and Sacrificial Rites*, pp. 33ff

19

Egbo: Gating spiritual security and morality in the Igbo context

- Obododimma Oha

Introduction

Nna anyi egbo o! Nna anyi egbo o![1] This is an alert, a warning, a speech act which spectators normally perform when the *mmanwu* (or *mmonwu*, 'masked spirit') is chasing someone who has run through a space where an *egbo* (a ritual gate) has been mounted. At one level of interpretation, the speech act is assumed to be performed in the interest of the *mmanwu*, to save it from the unpleasant consequences of violating a cultural code of conduct.[2] At another level, too, the speech act may be performed with the intent of protecting the person being pursued from coming to harm. Indeed, sometimes, spectators may perform the speech act when there is no *egbo* in sight; in this case as a way of deceiving the *mmanwu*, bringing the chase to a sudden end, and saving the person being pursued. A clear case of using discourse to try to save both the *patient* and the *agent* from trouble at the same time, the speech act shows how the culture revises the subjectivity of the spectator, empowering the latter discursively to control the behaviour of the *mmanwu*. The *egbo* call thus enters into an ancient Igbo mechanism for power balancing and conflict management. And in this case, a culturally shared system of representation provides the possibility of disarming the assailant and also offers solace to the

---

[1] *Nna anyi egbo o!* means: "Our Father (look out) (there is) an *egbo*." The masquerade is addressed in the familial term as "father" because it is seen as the manifestation of the dead ancestor. It is also a term invested with affection and respect, which shows how the masked spirit is accepted in the culture, even if it enacts violence. Often the violence is seen as a means of correcting and teaching an erring "child" a lesson.

[2] That *mmanwu* does not chase someone frontally through an *egbo* is but one of the laws governing *mmanwu* cultic practice. It is not only the *egbo* that *mmanwu* is forbidden from chasing someone through; in some Igbo communities, *mmanwu* is also forbidden from chasing someone into a farm where yams grow. Perhaps one reason for this is that the yam is considered a sacred crop and its farm a sacred space. Other *iwu mmanwu* (*mmanwu* laws) that seem to be directed toward checking the excesses of the *mmanwu* include: (1) *mmanwu* should not chase someone into a house or living room; (2) *mmanwu* should not pursue an elderly woman or cane her; (3) *mmanwu* should not enter a woman's room or house (Ubesie 2006, 105–106). There are also laws, which differ from community to community, concerning how *mmanwu* should not be treated. But generally, all *mmanwu* laws forbid disrespect for the masked spirit.

one in danger. In fact, very often, individuals who are being chased by the *mmanwu* would look out for such cultural location of refuge, based on the presupposition that the *mmanwu* can read spatiality and know where to halt its aggression. A *mmanwu* that passes through an *egbo* with the front has spiritually destroyed itself, which is why all *mmanwu* (the type treated as ancestral spirits) must turn and enter an *egbo* backwards, at the same time bowing. *Mmanwu* would normally not chase somebody through an *egbo*. But even if it is necessary for it to pass through an *egbo*, it has to enter backwards (in other words, it has to *back in*, instead of *backing off*!). Naturally, the *mmanwu* does the chasing; the individual person does the running.[3] Nnabuenyi Ugonna, commenting on this chase (which he refers to as 'dramatic chase') states:

> Intermittently any mask, but in particular the *akakpo*, instils fear into the spectators by giving them what may be called "dramatic" chase. The initiated deferentially move back while the non-initiates flee. No human would allow himself to be approached closely by a spirit because of the sacredness of the *mmọnwụ* character. (1984: 110)

But the "dramatic" chase as a symbolic or communicative behaviour in *mmanwu* performance is constrained by the larger semiotic in which case the chaser as an actor must submit to the presence and meaning of other cultural forms of control like the *egbo*.

This article explores the semiotics of the *egbo* in Igbo culture and traditional religious philosophy, and tries to identify its relevance to conflict management and ethical re-orientation in the contemporary Igbo society.

The system of spiritual security in Igbo culture

Given that the *egbo* is part of the system of spiritual security in Igbo culture, it is necessary to explore this system briefly, as a way of properly situating the *egbo* iconography and philosophy in the present discourse. The Igbo believe that there are malevolent forces and individuals that may want to harm other

---

[3] It would be an abomination to stand up to the *mmanw* as the presence of the ancestors. Unfortunately, one of the ways through which early (and even modern) Christian converts in Igbo societies (have) tried to demonstrate their strong Christian convictions was/has been to resist the *mmanw*; to fight, or abuse the *mmanw*; which is symbolically referred to as *itikwe isi mm* ·or *kp·nt m*. Considered a big crime, it is what Enoch actualizes in Chinua Achebe's *Things Fall Apart*, which forces the Mother Spirit to emerge—something that rarely happens—to roam the night and mourn her murdered son. And all the *mmanw*· throughout the land also emerge (one of them called "Ekwensu" came from Uli), according to Achebe, to teach the Christians a lesson. We find a similar representation of confrontation with the *mmanw* in Pete Edochie's film on St. Tansi, called *Avenge Me, Iwene My Son*. The saint is portrayed in the film as physically confronting the local *mmanw*·that were preventing his parishioners from moving about freely to attend to their Christian religious obligations. Both priest and ancestral spirit—each costumed according to the variety of his spirituality (the priest in priestly vestment and the masquerade in smoked raffia skirt) engage in what looked like a wrestling match. Of course, from another perspective, one could see the wrestling as not just being physical but also spiritual, with the Priest Saint no longer satisfied with the doctrine of turning the other cheek, but opting for spiritual violence against the traditional religious system.

people—the ancient struggle between Good and Evil— and so make efforts to act proactively; in this case, individuals or groups take measures to protect themselves.

Such measures include the use of charms and amulets, which are either worn on the body or kept on or inside a particular property they want protected. Soldiers who went to war against neighbouring communities in the past had to wear these protective charms (or *ọgwụ*), which suggests recruiting spiritual defensive forces on their own side. Since such spiritual forms of security were used on both sides of the war, it was simply a matter of which spiritual reinforcement was stronger than the other. It also indicated that the indigenous people saw war as something that also happens at the spiritual level, and so the human participant needed to be properly fortified.

Narratives of spiritualized indigenous Igbo warfare in the past presented cases such as sending thunder and lightning to kill the enemy; sending bees to sting and kill the enemy, or to cause disorder among the enemy forces; sending poisonous snakes to bite and destroy the enemy; sending soldier ants to drive away the enemy from their camps or houses, etc. Some narratives were also about soldiers becoming invisible to the enemy forces, or being invulnerable (through serious rituals of transmogrification). Thus each army always had to hire very powerful medicine men, sometimes from faraway lands, to ensure that they won the war. Sometimes, too, they depended on their oracles or deities, which were under some obligation to protect them or to fight on their own side. Chinua Achebe presents the case of the destruction of one of such deities by the people of Mbanta when the deity failed to fulfil its own part of the bargain. The very people who installed it to fight for them and protect them had to destroy it since it had proved useless or incapable of doing what it was created by them to do.

Apart from war, wrestling and masquerading were other serious engagements that often called for the creation of spiritual security. Wrestlers needed spiritual support to display extraordinary skills and to gain an upper hand in the contest. Just as in the case of warfare, they would be seen to be wrestling physically but within that physical struggle, a very dangerous spiritual contest was taking place. Wrestlers were also seen as representing their communities, and so the wrestling was, metaphorically speaking, a kind of "war" in which what was at stake was the supremacy of one community over another. Some wrestlers also featured in heroic narratives of the clan as having wrestled with powerful spirits and such narratives always indicated how charms or other spiritual protection served such heroes. One case in Igbo folklore that illustrates this very well is that of Ojaadịlị, the legendary hero who defeated all humans in wrestling matches in his community and had to go to the land of the spirits to challenge them too. One version of the legend tells us that in the land of the spirits, Ojaadịlị, indeed, defeated many spirit-wrestlers, but his victories made him arrogant and too blind to realize that smallness was not a sign of inferiority or weakness. Thus his own *Chi* (personal god) was fielded by the spirits to wrestle with him. He derogated his *Chi*, which was small in spiritual manifestation, and spoke scornfully to it. His

Chi was infuriated and not only defeated him outright, but also took his life. Which is the basis for the Igbo saying, "*Mmadụ anaghị echere chi ya aka mgba*" (One does not challenge one's personal god to a wrestling match). C.P. Ohia describes *Chi* in Igbo metaphysics as,

> ...God's representative in man (sic). It protects and guides man (sic) through the dangers and snares of the world. It is worried when man (sic) is in danger of any sort...The decisions of *Chi* are unalterable and cannot be challenged. (2006: 148-149).

Wrestling with one's *Chi*, obviously, is a great risk. More than a mere physical struggle, wrestling with one's *Chi* is an attempt to change one's destiny, a struggle that may even exist in the form of two clashing ideas or directions of thinking on one's mind.

In the context of *iti mmanwụ* (masquerade performance), the need for spiritual security was also considered very vital. The *mmanwụ* tested their skills and supremacy in some dangerous ways. One *mmanwụ* could cause another *mmanwụ* to be transfixed (what was called *ikọ ọgwụ*), to lose the ability to perform its songs, to shrink, etc. Individuals could also be harmed spiritually by the *mmanwụ* in the context of the performance, for instance if they looked so intently and directly at the *mmanwụ* (as it was believed). Tony Ubesie has observed that charms are means through which the *mmanwụ* deal with those who treat them with disdain (*ụzọ ha si na-emesi onye na-elelị ha ike bụ site n'ịkọ onye ahụ ọgwụ*) and for this reason people—especially non-initiates—have to keep a healthy and respectful distance from the *mmanwụ* (2006:99).

Of course, it was not every *mmanwụ* that was considered to be dangerous. There were particular grades of *mmanwụ*, performed on rare occasions that were dreaded. Among these were Ikwe of Ohakpu and Ekwensu of Uri (mentioned by Chinua Achebe in *Things Fall Apart*, now no longer performed). Individuals who desired to watch those dangerous *mmanwụ* (excluding women and children) had to make sure that they were spiritually fortified. Pregnant women were particularly discouraged from watching the *mmanwụ* and this was based on the belief that the pregnancy could be affected adversely, as in the case of baby malformation. Pregnancy, in the indigenous thought, has spiritual dimensions; it is principally the incarnation and return of a soul. Thus it is believed that a dangerous and malevolent spirit may replace/displace the incarnating soul. In other words, a pregnant woman is spiritually vulnerable (not just physically vulnerable) and is discouraged from exposing herself and her pregnancy to danger, as in the case of going to watch the *mmanwụ*. This raises the question of where we draw the line between entertainment and harm or violence in masquerade performances. The point is that what is considered violent and harmful was, ironically, part of the thrill to the performer and the audience. Risk taking was and is still a means of proving one's worth in the presence of others in Igbo thought.

Homesteads are spaces that are sometimes under attack, as in the case of robbery, or even malevolent spiritual intrusions. Thus, in the indigenous Igbo context, a family could seek a spiritual protection from a powerful medicine man, and bury their protective charms within the family space. Charms may be made to strike robbers with blindness, to make them become confused when they enter the homestead, to make them begin to quarrel and turn their weapons against themselves, etc. In addition to the charms, a family erects an *egbo* at the entrance to the homestead, to ward off evil forces.

Generally, these domestic, personal, and communal charms have overtly become abandoned by many people in the Igbo society, given the massive Christian impact on the society. Christian evangelists try to make people understand that only God (or Jesus Christ) can truly protect them, and that these charms are deceptive instruments of the devil. There was massive destruction of family and community deities and charms in the 80s and 90s during the community crusades of Rev. Father Ede. Stories spread that if any family or person refused to bring out their charms to the venue of the Christian revival before the arrival of the catholic priest, such people stood the risk of dying instantly or experiencing calamities as the priest prayed and called on the name of Jesus Christ in the community he was visiting. Thus, before the arrival of the priest at the venue of the revival, individuals brought out their charms secretly at night and dumped them at the venue of the revival. The people believed that dumping the charms at any other place could have incurred the wrath of the disgraced spirits in them, but handing them over to Father Ede ensured that their wrath was ineffectual.

It needs to be observed that in spite of the Christian revivals and attempts at discouraging Christians from seeking the indigenous spiritual solutions to their problems, there are still some who use charms secretly to protect themselves and their property. Sometimes, the miracles and evidence of protection they are promised in their churches do not seem to materialize and so they look for secret solutions. There have also been cases of people using Christian objects and sacraments as forms of spiritual protection (i.e., as substitutes for the local charms they are prevented from using). Some individuals hang rosaries, bottles of holy water, crosses, etc., in their vehicles, houses, farms, etc. Even bottles of holy water and car stickers obtained at the Father Ede crusades have been used for this purpose too. The practice essentially derives from, and is a continuation of, *ido iyi* or *ido arusi* (installing an icon of a deity/spirit to guard/protect something) in Igbo culture. Although it might be argued that some of these objects like the cross and the rosary are means of identifying the faith of the owner of the property (a kind of visual shibboleth), they are also viewed by those who use them as means of warding off satanic forces. In other words, they are comparable to the local *egbo* that is believed to ward off evil forces.

The point then is that the practice of *ihie egbo* (the act of making and dedicating the *egbo*) is located in the cultural and religious philosophy of installing a spiritual protector over something. In the next section, we examine briefly the philosophy of the *egbo* in Igbo culture.

The philosophy of the *Egbo*

Formed from the root morpheme '*gbo*' (which means 'prevent,' 'forestall,' and 'separate' - as in the case of separating two people that are fighting), *egbo* semiotically offers us an insight into the indigenous Igbo philosophy on the discursive dimension to conflict and conflict management. The sign, thus, is presented as not just a site of conflict, but a tool and mechanism for managing it. The *egbo* is a construction in the Igbo culture to stop evil, to save a helpless victim, to control the invading force (even if that force is culturally endowed with some authority, as in the case of the *mmanwu*), to reassure citizens about their protection in the society (i.e., that the cultural order also has made provision for their security needs, just as it has granted the power of interpellation and control to the *mmanwu*). This is interesting because it tends to reveal that even the elevated ancestral system is also under the cultural order and not above it. Even the *mmanwu*, as powerful as it is as police officer, ancestor, etc., is not above the law. In fact, it is being told that it cannot be above the system that has created and installed it.

The *egbo* thus is a special portal that is protective and defensive. Similar in shape to a goal post (without the net), it is constructed with the trunks of perennial plants (preferably the *ogirisi*) for the posts, and another trunk (sometimes bamboo stems) connecting the two posts. This connective trunk is wrapped with ritual leaves — *akoro*, *izizi*, and *okpoto*. These ritual leaves/plants are believed to have the power to resist evil forces. Often *akoro* and *izizi* are used in ritually dissociating oneself with evil and in cleansing, as for instance when an animal that is the totem of a deity has being accidentally killed or harmed.[4] The ritual leaves are therefore a strong presence in the *egbo* semiotic. Sometimes, too, the *okpoto* stem is merely placed across the entrance to the homestead or across the road,[5] to serve the same purpose of signifying 'STOP' to evil.

The Igbo, in placing the *egbo* at the entrance of a homestead, demonstrate awareness that human beings do not just have security needs, but that such security needs might be spiritual, or that physical security problems that

---

[4] In Uli clan, anyone in the traditional religion who sees a dead *eke* the royal python (maybe run over by a vehicle), would symbolically absolve self from blame (or dissociate self from the *ar*) by plucking some *ak r* and *izizi*, rubbing it across the eyes and whispering his or her innocence to the goddess whose totem is the snake. To leave the scene with showing some deep feelings of commiseration, or to rejoice at the fate of the *eke*, is believed to arouse the wrath of the goddess.

[5] The *egbo* is not constructed by just anybody. It is often done by the traditional priest or an *z*-titled person and dedicated by them too. This is because the *z*-tilted man is seen as a holy person in the Igbo culture. The same perception applies to the priest, even though this reverence has been abused greatly in modern times. Further, women do not tie or dedicate the *egbo*; it is a purely masculine affair. This may have to do with the predominant patriarchal nature of the society and the assumption that the man is the spiritual gate-keeper in the community and the family. But even if women do not tie or dedicate the *egbo*, they nevertheless have and do perform other important spiritual roles in the community.

people have may have spiritual backgrounds or dimensions. They believe that the spiritual and the physical worlds of the human being interact, and that to ignore the spiritual side is to move about blindly.

In many Igbo communities, it is the ọzọ-titled individuals that can put up an *egbo* at the entrances of their compounds (in which case, the *egbo* indicates to every passer-by that the compound belongs to an ọzọ-titled man). One reason for this is that the ọzọ-titled individual is considered a very holy person in Igbo culture, and so the *egbo* marks off his compound as a sacred space. Normally, some ways that the ọzọ-titled man's holiness is signified and protected include: the fireplace where food is being prepared for him is cordoned off with *omu nkwu* (tender palm frond) or *okpoto*; women who are menstruating are not allowed to go near where food is being prepared for the ọzọ-titled man or even cook for him; no one is allowed to physically attack or abuse him; he must not eat at the market-place; etc. The ọzọ-titled man must not tell lies or align with injustice and falsehood. He must not get drunk. He must not commit adultery or encourage it. He must not steal. He must not be involved in using charms or other spiritual diabolical means to harm people. These are ideal attributes and expectations which, unfortunately, have been undermined by the rapid transformation of the Igbo society and erosion of the moral fabric of the society. The ọzọ-titled person was a model of the desirable citizen: upright, peace-loving, and resourceful. Tony Ubesie writes that: "*Na mmadụ chiri ọzọ n'ala Igbo egosịla na onye ahụ dị ọcha n'ime mmụọ; na ọ bụ onye kwesịrị ntụkwasị obi, na ọ na-akwụwa aka ya ọtọ, bụrụkwa onye a gaghị enyo enyo*" (That a person has taken the ọzọ title shows that he is pure in heart; that he is dependable; that he is upright and is not a dubious character) (2006:119). It is therefore not surprising that the entrance to the compound of an ọzọ-titled man has an *egbo*, which warns those entering that they are about to enter a sacred place and must do away with all objectionable conduct.

Egbo may be for an individual/family (as in the case of the ọzọ-titled man) or for a community. The family *egbo* is placed at the entrance to the homestead, while the community *egbo* is placed at the entry points to the community (the roads that lead to the communal spaces). This type of *egbo* narrates a collective search for security in the community. At a time when the sense of community appears to have diminished in African societies, one can rightly argue that the community *egbo* is an important representation of the fact that the survival of the individual and that of the community are inextricably linked. Unfortunately, the alienation and pursuit of selfish interests in politics, religion, commerce, etc occasioned by modernity in the postcolonial African society has seriously undermined this sense of community. As people retreat into their personal worlds of capital accumulation, those ties that bind them together begin to snap. Indeed, one begins to see clearly the lived side of the collapse of community as imagined by Chinua Achebe in *Things Fall Apart*. It is, as a matter of fact, human beings that fall apart, as they neglect or refuse to service their communal relationships, working together to provide social services.

The representation of the individual as an *egbo* of course has some support in the cultural linkage of the ọzọ-titled man, a holy person, with the *egbo* itself. Indeed, the identification of the sacred *egbo* with the holy person is a symbolic statement that combating evil in a community or family involves a human pursuit of living above blame, living the ideal selfhood that makes society safe and orderly. An ọzọ-titled man is, metaphorically speaking, considered an egbo in his family and community. And, as all citizens of the community are culturally invited to rise to the holiness and resourcefulness of the ọzọ-titled person, they are, by implication, reminded that they have to be the *egbo* of their families and community as a whole.

Re-imagining the citizen as an *egbo*

One's personal spiritual security is located in the spiritual security of one's community, which is why if an individual commits an *arụ* (abomination), such a person is understood as having caused spiritual disharmony both within the self and the community and must set things right by performing the required atonement (*at-one-ment*, playfully put) and cleansing ritual. In such a case, the individual is also perceived *as an entrance to the whole community* and needs to be guarded spiritually. Through one individual, evil could enter the whole community, an analogical relation to the Biblical Fall of Adam and Eve. I would, in this regard, draw attention to how woman, in Igbo philosophy, is perceived as an important kind of *egbo* that needs to guard the self properly. The very fact that a woman gives birth to another human being suggests her being a kind of gate through which the community is populated. The human being she brings into the community also has a spiritual selfhood, in fact begins as a spirit and manifests in the flesh through conception. And conception in Igbo thought is a decision to come and live in a given family and given community. Sometimes, such a decision is made to punish, or in atonement for misdeeds of former life, which is one reason behind the ọgbanje phenomenon. A woman that does not guard herself well (both sexually and morally), may end up being the source through which an evil force would be born into the family or community. This also applies to men, since women are not the only actors in this human-spirit traffic. As a well-dedicated *egbo*, the individual watches out to ward off unwanted spiritual guests in the family and community.

Also, the cultural role of the woman as the teacher of morality in the family and the community in Africa (Suda 1999:72) makes her a kind of *egbo* that wards of unethical and immoral conduct. It is partly because of this cultural role that the woman is considered both the gate to the future and a source of goodness that stands in symbolic relation with the sacred *Ala*, the Earth Goddess. In this regard, being a woman is not a disadvantage as masculinist discourses tend to make us believe. It is rather a highly challenging identity and individual failure to live up to that sacred role does not make womanhood itself lose its ontological meaning. In fact, it is in this light that the indigenous Igbo would describe someone who lives a well-ordered, sane, and productive life as *nwunnye mmadụ* (female person), whether that person is a man or a woman. It is the *nwunye mmadụ* that individuals generally desire in marriage, leadership, etc. The *nwunye mmadụ* is the typical human *egbo* in the Igbo society.

As the mobile *egbo* of the community, the individual is given the responsibility of defending and protecting the community from spiritual corruption. And this is sometimes made clearer in the *ịgba ndụ* (covenant) in which members of the community or group vow not to allow evil to come to their fellow community members, or plan evil against them. That was one way the Igbo traditional religious system prevented conflicts in the community, for every participant in the *ịgba ndụ* would not want to place personal wellbeing at risk through violating the covenant.

It is just not enough to construct and put up an *egbo*; the person that puts it up has invariably subscribed to uprightness, to not being an agent of evil, for to be otherwise is to cancel out the symbolic statement being made through the *egbo*, and indeed to render the *egbo* powerless. It is to say that one cannot hold a faith and deny its power by doing what is contrary to what that faith represents. To put up an *egbo* and still go on to live an immoral life, or to plan to harm others, is to weaken one's spiritual security greatly, for the person who puts up the *egbo* would no longer know how vulnerable he is! Indeed, given the nature of the human being, some people do put up their *egbo*, with elaborate rituals and decorations, yet harbour evil, or plan evil against others; in other words, putting up the *egbo* becomes a mere deception strategy. But in such cases, the *egbo* turns from being a source of protection and defence to being a curse and an invitation to evil.

With the massive Christianization of the Igbo society, only very few *egbo* are constructed by the remaining adherents of Igbo traditional religions. This means that the community *egbo* is collapsing or has virtually collapsed, and the collapse means disharmony and vulnerability of the community. It means that the *egbo* now present in the lives of the members of the community speak divergently and are already conflict-oriented. One finds situations where the substitute *egbo* currently present in Igbo communities do not just clash in their forms and meanings, but tend to destroy the sense of community.

Another consequence is that the *nnukwu mmanwụ* (the big masked spirits) (as rich and important people are metaphorically referred to in the contemporary Igbo society) no longer watch out or listen to warning calls about the presence of some *egbo*. Of course, some of these *nnukwu mmanwụ* seek spiritual security, sometimes engaging in secret human sacrifice in the hope of obtaining this security. But what they obtain is not an *egbo* that protects and defends against evil. In fact, what they obtain is not an *egbo* at all. What they obtain is a curse for their families and communities.

The *Egbo* and the project of ethical re-orientation

Emeka George Ekwuru has drawn attention to the collapse of cultural and ethical framework in the contemporary Igbo society, stating as follows:

> The entire cultural sphere has lost its basic structural equilibrium and stability. There is socio-political turmoil, religious disorientation, and a high rate of moral degeneracy. The vital statistics are nothing but a litany of woes and shame on all fronts of cultural life. The major preoccupation is the fact that this situation of anomie is constituting itself into a new cultural way of life. People seem to be adjusting quickly to the abnormal ways and seem to get along very well. (1999:85)

Given this orientation to the abnormal, the ritual of the *ihie egbo* and its meaning are either lost or becoming lost to the contemporary Igbo. As Ekwuru has argued quite rightly, "Many villages and towns ... have stopped performing their annual rituals of regeneration. And where it (sic) is still done, it (sic) is bereft of its (sic) original meaning and intention" (5). With the absence of cultural icons and practices that help to invite citizens to differentiate between good and bad, to choose good and not bad, the modern Igbo person faces a danger of a "crisis of sense" in which truth suffers, as well as an ethical crisis in which individuals may seek to interpret ethical principles differently (even in the same community) and not bother how they achieve their materialistic goals.

In the context of this ethical crisis in the contemporary Igbo society, it becomes necessary to consider the intellectual and cultural significance of the *egbo* in the project of self-management and re-engineering of community. Perhaps an important starting point is the recognition of indigenous African systems of thought. One unfortunate thing about contemporary Igbo embrace of modernity and Western frameworks of thought—often confused with the so-called "receptivity to change" (Oguejiofor 1996:25)—is that the Igbo person cannot reconcile them with relationships and values in their local community. Unfortunately, too, they tend to disregard indigenous systems of thought, which they could revise and apply in some fruitful ways to their contemporary needs.

Perhaps one difficulty is that the Igbo society has transformed beyond the system and pattern of relationship that made the practice of the *ihie egbo* possible. With the greater looseness of the Igbo society occasioned by Western-style democracy and pursuit of individual freedom, Christian emphasis on keeping distance with indigenous practices considered "pagan", and general decline in the spirit of community, the *egbo* seems to have acquired some obsolescence in the contemporary Igbo imagination. Ironically, what seems to be replacing it is the icon of feudal power and indeed fearful subjectivity. Many *nouveau riche* and tilted men in many parts of Igboland now architecturally display this substitution of *egbo* with the tiger or lion-head design of the gates or entrances to their mansions or palaces. In this case, entering through the lion-headed gate to the rich person's or chief's compound/mansion is analogous to entering into the belly of the beast. Indeed, the wealth and social status of the owner of the house or mansion is assumed to determine the way the owner would be treated or regarded, even if the owner is a dubious character or has committed what is clearly a crime. The members of the community are thus drowned in the culture of silence and/or collusion with an objectionable conduct. The fact that ethics, morality, and justice have become casualties in the context of neo-Igbo worship of material wealth is signified in the modern Igbo saying, "*Ego na-ekwu*" (Money speaks).

Some concluding remarks

As we have seen in this essay, the *egbo* in Igbo culture provides an insight—it is indeed a paradigm—for conflict prevention, ethics and self-management, as well as community engineering. Representing the symbolic linkage of the individual and a cultural icon, the *egbo* provides a system of control whereby everyone, including the *mmanwụ*, are required to discard objectionable conduct. The ethically sound and law-abiding individual is culturally reinvented as an *egbo* that forestalls evil. The citizen is not just a passive observer of events but an actor that must be held accountable for what the society becomes. In this regard, a post-colonial African society that is wrestling with its *Chi* cannot afford to dispense with its forms of indigenous knowledge, for, in fact, understanding and using such indigenous knowledge is a demonstration of that commitment to be an *egbo* in a fast-changing world.

References

Achebe, Chinua. 1981. *Things Fall Apart*. Ibadan: Heinemann.
Ekwuru, Emeka George. 1999. *The Pangs of an African Culture in Travail*. Owerri: TOTAN Publishers.
Oguejiofor, Obi J. 1996. *The Influence of Igbo Traditional Religion on the Socio-political Character of the Igbo*. Nsukka: Fulladu Publishing Company.
Ohia, C.P. Chi-na-Eke. 2006. *Eke-na-Egwurugwu: The Causal Principles of Unity, Individuation, Multiplicity, and Differentiation in Igbo Metaphysics*. Owerri: Springfield.
Suda, Collette. 1996. The Centrality of Women in the Moral Teachings in African Society. *Nordic Journal of African Studies* 5 (2): 71–82.
Ubesie, Tony. 2006. *Odinala Ndi Igbo*. Ibadan: Ibadan University Press.
Ugonna, Nnabuenyi. 1984. *Mmonwu: A Dramatic Tradition of the Igbo*. Lagos: Lagos University Press.
Avenge Me, Iwene My Son. Film.

20

Indigenous spirituality, business ethics and contemporary challenges among the Igbo

- Celestina Omoso Isiramen

Introduction

The Igbo are one of the three largest ethnic groups in Nigeria, numbering about 15 million people. Although they are scattered all over the country, and in different parts of the world, they are basically located in Abia, Anambra, Ebonyi, Enugu and Imo states of Nigeria. These five Igbo states form the South East geographical zone in contemporary Nigeria. Their language is Igbo.

In the pre-colonial era, the Igbo political structure took the form of a "quasi democratic" republican system of government which guaranteed equality of the citizenry. The Igbo cultural life-style is a "manifestation of the aesthetic, the philosophical, the historical, the human and the divine milieu in the midst of human creativity."[1]

Although there are some Igbo who work with government, a vast majority of them are engaged in private business. They are into buying and selling and these activities constitute the bulk of Nigerian informal economy. The trading profession of the Igbo is said to have divine origin. It is said, in the traditional creation myth, that eight people (four men and four women) were originally created by God. These first original ancestors of Igbo chose a "Destiny of Wealth" for the people and they made it clear before the gods and goddesses that the Igbo people chose to make wealth through trading. These eight ancestors had opportunity to watch how the gods and goddesses related with each other as equals and how they traded with each other and how they all made profit. The people learnt the laws of social and economic relation based on social equality and personal freedom, and personal freedom after which the eight ancestors chose a Destiny to become a wealthy nation based on family values and trade. To that effect, *Igwe* (the God of rain) drew up the contract termed "articles of faith" thus:
1. The great Creator, *Chineke*, created the universe and all therein using parts of Him-Her-self; and is known as the God of Wealth.

---

[1] F. Ike and N. Edozien, "Understanding African Traditional Legal Reasoning, Jurisprudence and Justice in Igboland," *Catholic Institution for Development, Justice and Peace IDJAP,* (2001), 185.

2. The major members of the Holy family; those that concern people consist of *Ala, Igwe, Anyanwu, Amadioha, Ekwemsu*, and the Goddess of mysteries (the moon Goddess), who *Chineke* bonded together with laws of Social Equality and personal freedom.
3. *Chineke*, the Great Creator, created Human Spirit who is given a personal chosen Destiny; this Spirit-Destiny is called a person's CHI.
4. The Earth goddess and rain God, *Ala* and *Igwe* are husband and wife and people are their created children.
5. Ancestor worship is the guide in building a nation.
6. Divine manners of kinship and Trade are the guide in life.
7. Negotiation, based on this contract is the path-way to spiritual and Economic success; Wealth.[2]

While today, most Igbo profess Christianity, the indigenous ancient Igbo religion is known as *Odinani*. Every aspect of their indigenous existence including business ethics is religiously interpreted as has been highlighted above, such that the most fundamental characteristic of the culture of the Igbo is that it has its root in religion. It is thus difficult to differentiate between the sacred and the profane in the culture of Igbo.

However, the influence of foreign religions and foreign cultures which began with the incursion into Igbo land by the British in 1870s, have had a serious impact on their indigenous business ethics.[3] The most glaring examples are the present replacement of their indigenous religion with Christianity and a community life of individualism. These examples point to a dangerous trend for a business conscious people like the Igbo. What is required in contemporary times is a sound business ethics for a people whose fundamental idea of wealth is justice and fair play.

This chapter tries to examine the impact of indigenous religion on Igbo traditional business ethics in relation to modern business transactions. It is observed that reverence for the gods and the human person in business relations is waning fast and business transactions now mimic a rat race. As a by-product of the modern times, there seems to be a sharp separation between religious ethical considerations and that of business. In this sense, Brunner says that "all man-centred ethical systems are deemed to fail. Only what God does and wills is good and all that opposes God is bad."[4] Deriving from the Igbo experience, this chapter recommends the incorporation of spirituality and consciousness of human dignity as basis for sound business ethics in modern commerce.

---

[2] Ben and Bertha Benjamin, Ancient Igbo, htt// afrosacred star. Com/igbi. Htm,6
[3] C. Achebe, *Things Fall Apart*, London, 1958, V
[4] E. Brunner, *the Divine Imperative: A study of the Christian Ethics*, trans, (Wyon Philadelphia, Westminster, 1947), 53.

Indigenous spirituality and business ethics among the Igbo

Like other Africans, traditional Igbo possess the basic instinct of gregariousness. There is an intense common sharing of life. The individual is in the first place a member of his community. The Igbo is a man defined by his community. This is exemplified in the existence of community farmlands, economic trees, barns, markets, stream, shrines, masquerades, ritual objects and festivals among others. The understanding of the traditional Igbo about the community is that it is "a unity of the visible and invisible; the world of the physical living on the one hand and the world of the ancestors, divinities and the souls of children yet to be born to the individual kins-group."[5]

The Igbo recognize the superiority of the ancestors and spiritual beings and they acknowledge and honour their presence in the community. These spiritual beings are also considered to be benevolent and powerful representatives of the community in the spiritual world. Thus, among the Igbo, there is no dividing line between religion and culture. Their total worldview can be summed up in the words of A. Leonard that:

> They are in the strict and natural sense of the word, a firmly and deeply religious people of whom it can be said, as it has been said of the Hindus; they eat religiously and sin religiously. In a few words, the religion of these natives...is their existence and existence is their religion."[6]

Thus, several taboos found among the Igbo direct attention to the reality and the presence of the spiritual members of the community. As already noted, the Igbo trading acumen is divinely ordained. Drawn from the agreement reached by the Igbo and their eight original ancestors, there are taboos that prohibit cheating and exploitation in business. Business agreements are sealed by oaths to the *Ofo,* the symbol of truth and justice believed to kill any perjurers before the entire community. The *Ofo* symbol is pre-eminent in winning the favour and goodwill of the divinities in the promotion of peace and solidarity of the *Umunna* (community). Mythically, the *Ofo* is a compound. Among the Igbo, the *Ofo* is revered as a sacred object which mediates mysteriously the cosmic power, justice, truth and moral uprightness of God, divinities, and the ancestors.[7] To introduce the *Ofo* into any setting is to proclaim that nothing short of truth, justice and moral uprightness is demanded of the audience. To fail to uphold these values is to

---

[5] C. Ejizu, "African Traditional Religion and the Promotion of Community Living" Http: 11 www.africaworld.net/afrel/community. Html,2003
[6] A. Leonard, *The lower Niger and its Tribes,* (London, Frank Cass, 1968), 29
[7] C. Ejizu, *Ofo-Igbo Ritual Symbol,* (Nigeria, Fourth Dimension Publishing Co. Ltd, 1986), 131

provoke the wrath of, and destructive potency associated with *Ofo*."[8] C. Ejizu categorizes the various uses of the *Ofo* into the following:

Religious Context:
1. Medium of communication
2. In ritual sacrifices
3. In cleansing of taboos and abominations
4. Different rites of Initiation like into masquerade societies.

In contexts, which are largely socio-political, the ritual stick is utilized for:
1. Traditional Naming ceremony
2. Different title-taking
3. Covenant relationships including marriage.

In socio-ethical contexts, the *Ofo* is used as a sacred sanction in:
1. Attesting to the truth,
2. Affirming one's innocence and sincerity,
3. Serious oath-taking
4. Punishing of offending members of the group through cursing, disinheriting, ostracizing and expulsion.[9]

It is this last category that we are concerned with in this chapter.

In many Igbo communities, swearing on *Ofo* is the greatest form of oath-taking. O. Arungwa presents a typical oath-taking ritual with the *Ofo* symbol from Ngwaland:

> *Ofo a m asimgi gbuo nwoko*
> *ma o bu mwaanyi mere ihe a*
> *onwu burukwa nke ya*
> *mwoko ma o bu mwaanyi mere ihe a*
> *Na-ago ago kugbaokwa ya*
> *Eghu ya abadilu uba,*
> *ya alodila uwa na mmadu*
> *ya fuokwa ohia*
>
> *Nnu nna anyiha*
> *Unu gererekwa nti*
> *Una ekwedila onye ugha na*
> *Onye aruruala di ndu,*
> *N'aala una nyere anyi*

This *Ofo* I ask you to kill any man or woman who did this. Let him die. Man or woman who did this and denies, do kill him/her off. May his goats not increase and may he not re-incarnate. Let him miss his way. Our ancestors

---

[8] Eastern Nigerian art from the Toby and Barry Hecht collection from E. Belter "Life as an Artistic Process: Igbo *Ikenga and Ofo*", *African Arts*, (1988),21,2:66-71.
[9] C. Ejizu, Ofo-Igbo Ritual Symbol, 132-133

do hear. Allow not a liar to escape, nor an evil doer to live in the land you bequeathed to us.[10]

A violation of business agreement can also be punished through impoverishment, ostracization or incurable sickness that can be visited on the offender by the gods of the land as often revealed through *'Afa'* divination which is done by the *dibia* (Diviner). The *dibia* is an individual who wins the special favour and goodness of the divinities and the spirits toward the promotion of solidarity and peace of the Igbo community. The calling of the *dibia* is said to be derived from the divinity *Agwu* whose duty it is, to reveal to the diviner, secrets of the visible and invisible world for the community's welfare.

For the Igbo, the community is assured of happiness and prosperity only when equilibrium between the visible world and the invisible world is maintained. Indigenous religion provides the significance and meaning for the ethical dimension of business and forms the basis for business ethics. The traditional leaders make moral laws and invoke divine sanctions on anyone who dares to disobey. Thus, the traditional priest, individual deities and ancestral spirits, who are agents of divinities, actively participate in the execution of business ethics.[11] They bear the responsibilities to invoke sanctions and fines on defaulters.

Significantly in control of morality is the earth goddess *Ala* who "provides the sanction of the moral code, presiding over the peace and punishment of offenders."[12] Offences of criminal acts in business are offences against *Ala*. It is enunciated in the Igbo popular equivalent of the Biblical golden rule: *egbe bere ugo bere nko si ibe ya ebela nku kwaaya* (let the kit as well as the eagle perch (on the bench), and a curse (a broken wing) on whoever denies that right to the other."[13] As a co-creator with *Igwe* (the god of rain), *Ala* "makes rules of moral conduct; especially as related to the earth, called the laws of the land."[14] The protector of this law is ensured by *Ala*, and serious infringements are regarded as abomination, requiring ritual cleansing which go beyond the individual offender to the community whose well-being is thus threatened. In addition, "the Igbo mercantilism; trade and industry develop on the strong ethics of the numerous Ogwugwu shrine."[15] It is against this background that the import of the Okija shrine (which is widely misunderstood as a place of

---

[10] O. Arungwa. "The Ofo in the Traditional Religion of the Igbo People With Special Reference to Ugwaland." (unpublished B.A Thesis, Nsukka, 1972); 6-9

[11] C. Isiramen, " The African Traditional Religion's Ethics: A Paradigm for spirituality in the Global business Ethical standard" in N. Capaldi (ed.) *Business and Religion: A clash of civilization?* (Salem city: M&M Scribner press, 2005), 390.

[12] T. Okere, "The Poverty of Christian Individualism, Morality and an Africa Alternative". Htt;//www.crp.org/book/series 02/11-13/chapter Vii htm, 1.

[13] I. Umejesi, "The Golden rule and Religious Tolerance: A Case for Comparative Religion in Nigerian Schools" in *Journal of Academics:* Vol. 2, No.2 (April, 2007), 118-130.

[14] Ben and Bertha Benjamin, Ancient Igbo, http://afrosacred star.Com/igbi. Htm.6

[15] O. Chidoka "Okija: Not a show of shame http;//www.biafranigeria.com/archive '2004/Sep/01/102. html.

"decomposing corpses, deception and fraud") can be understood as an abode of oath taking in the honest sealing of business agreements. For instance, sanity is ensured in trading at the large and ever busy Onitsha market through the "traditional process of oath-taking represented by *ogwugwu haba* in Agule and Oji in *Odekpe*."[16]

There exist for the purpose of justice in business, several Ogwugwu shrines in Igbo land. There are many deities (*Arus*) in Okija. Some of them are "*Ogwugwu Isiula, Ogwugwu Akpu, Ihenemere-Idigbo, Ogwugwu mmiri*."[17]

Report has it that the Okija shrines have been in existence for over 200 years. It is said to be a tradition passed on to the people by their fore-fathers. The Okija Royal cabinet represented by Igwe-elect said that:

> the tradition of the worship of these deities is that the eldest person in the village...becomes the Chief Priest. People go to the shrine for settlement of their cases because of the immediate and constant justice they received from the shrines... If after the settlement of a case, the culprit finally dies; it is reported to the Chief Priest who allows the corpse to be brought and thrown into the shrine forest... Some of the skulls...in the shrine are older than all those who are now the Priests of the shrines.[18]

People go voluntarily to take oath at the shrine and anyone found guilty at the end is dealt with by the gods and such bodies are deposited at the Okija shrines as sacrifices to the gods. The attention of the Nigerian public was recently drawn to the deposited corpse in Okija shrine.

The Okija episode began to generate ripples in mid-2004, when the Nigeria Inspector General of Police, Mr. Tafa Balogun ordered the State Police Command to cordon off the *Ogwugwu* shrine in Okija community of Anambra state following a tip-off from one Obed Igwe.[19] About eighty decomposing corpses were found in various *Ogwugwu shrines* in the community. The majority of the priests in the shrines, which numbered about 40, were arrested for murder. The lawyer for the arrested priests, Stanley Malizu, however denied the allegation of murder levelled against the priests; rather he says, "there...have been deaths arising from violations and in such situations, families of the deceased voluntarily hand over bodies to the shrines in line with culture."[20] At the end of several court sessions, the priests were discharged and acquitted.

Business ethics among the Igbo is an arena where the transcendent teachings of holiness and spirituality confront the often negative business of money making and the rat race conditions that confront the market place. To the traditional Igbo, good business is to share in a society that encourages cooperative production and common consumption as a norm. Thus, the

---

[16] O. Chidoka, ibid.
[17] Quotation by Akpan Blessing, *The Age*, August 2004
[18] Okija Royal Cabinet, Quoted by Anayo Okili, *Vanguard*, August 23,2004.
[19] S. Malizu, in Geoffrey Anyanwu, *Daily Sun*, August 19, 2004.
[20] O. Chidoka, *op. cit.*

chosen items to be sold were such that put into consideration the moral, physical and spiritual growth of the human being and reverence for the Creator. However, with the clash of civilizations as experienced with the incursion of foreign religions, civilization and education, the Igbo indigenous religion began to be regarded with derision. Its laudable spiritual values are gradually being eroded. The effect on business is better described as unethical business sphere, where businessmen and women can do anything including destroying one another to make money.

The modern Igbo business sphere

The modern Igbo market exemplifies business devoid of spirituality. In modern Igbo business sphere, Igbo traditional religious ethics is struggling to justify its existence. This is exemplified in the continuous existence and patronage of the various shrines of *Ogwugwu* by the people in this modern era, against all odds. Ostracization and death still remain the major Igbo response to betrayal, swearing false oaths or resistance to communal decision. "The ultimate Igbo punishment that brings shame to the family is the depositing of the corpse of a relation at the evil forest (*Ajo ofia*)."[21] This means that the person is not worthy to be committed to earth. Every Igbo person tries to avoid this punishment and according to Chidoka, this is the origin of the corpses at Okija shrine.[22] These corpses are rejects that have desecrated the land.[23] Therefore, the interpretation of the activities at Okija shrine as a 'show of shame' is a modern misconception. And if there are infiltrations of the shrines by fraudulent individuals who parade as priests only to accumulate wealth by 'hook or crook' (as being speculated), it only appears to be a by-product of the modern era of 'get rich quick' without the fear of God and respect for human dignity.

The foreign influences occasioned by commerce, colonialism and foreign religions among the Igbo have affected reverence for community life and the spiritual beings in business matters. Some Igbo who have embraced Christianity distance themselves from indigenous religion, and castigate those that have remained faithful to the indigenous religion has people destined for hell. The story of Enoch in Chinua Achebe's *Things Fall Apart* illustrates how some Igbo began to turn against their culture in apparent response and agreement to the new civilization. Enoch was under suspicion of killing and eating the sacred python. He went further to desecrate and unmask the *Ogwugwu* in public.[24] The disregard for the community and disrespect for its ethics became the order of the day. In the borrowed words of W. Yeats, Chinua Achebe, described the situation thus:

---

[21] O. Chidoka, *op. cit.*
[22] O. Chidoka, *op. cit.*
[23] O. Chidoka, *op. cit.*
[24] C. Achebe, *op. cit.*

Turning and turning in a widening gyre. The falcon cannot hear the falconer; things fall apart the centre cannot hold, mere anarchy is loosed upon the world.[25]

Missionaries even established 'Christian villages' in some Igbo communities like Aguleri in Anambra state, thereby separating Christian converts from the other members of the community. This has had adverse impact on the unity of the people in the community. Events in the business sphere have, thus, taken a different turn. The indigenous religion has lost its exclusive control and dominance over the lives of the people. Consequently, the prevailing economic dispositions have lost every sense of spiritual discipline.

Furthermore, modernity has introduced urbanization. Urbanization ushered into Igbo community what A. Shorter described as "four tragedies of Africa:" pollution impoverishment, disorientation and secularization. The aftermath of urbanization in Africa is moral and cultural disorientation and an ultimate undermining of the traditional communities.[26] Apart from questioning traditional norms, new mores have been introduced through urbanization and modernization and these have led to one of the greatest problems of Igbo communalism. Urbanization and money economy have given rise to new ideals, new ethics, new patterns of living and new socio-economic possibilities.[27] The enviable tradition of community before individuals has metamorphosed into ungodly philosophies such as individualism, humanism, and materialism, "consumerism and the prioritization of wealth over persons have become its hallmark."[28] Mutual antagonism has created a situation that has transformed the ideals of 'all' to 'oneself,' and an increasing 'jungle mentality' where the only governing principle is to 'survive by all means.' Consequently, survival replaces reason. It is only against this background that one can possibly explain the ritual killings now prevalent in Igbo community. For instance, seven years ago, the indigenes of Ikeduru in Owerri, an Igbo community woke up to unfortunate news that an 11-year old boy has been murdered in a hotel. It was later discovered that the boy was 'only a victim in a long list of young people murdered by the Otokoto family crime syndicate.' The Otokoto family was killing and harvesting people's organs for sale to "foreign organ buyers..."[29] They were caught when they severed the head of Ikechukwu, a teenage bread seller in Owerri 7 years ago. After a long period of trial, the culprits were found guilty and sentenced to death.

This is alien to traditional Igbo sense of money making. In the light of the above, business philosophy in contemporary Igbo community is increasingly

---

[25] A. Shorter, "Urbanization: Today's Missionary Reality in Africa" in *AFER*, 1990, 290-300
[26] A. Shorter, "Urbanization: Today's Missionary Reality in Africa" in *AFER*, 1990, 290-300
[27] J. Njoku, "Conflicts and Transmutation in African Communalism" http://www.hollerafrica.com/showarticle ... Php? Art/d in *Business, Society and Culture Journal,*3
[28] J. Njoku, ibid.
[29] C. Isiramen, *op. cit.*

moving into the unexplored and potentially dehumanizing realms. NAFDAC (National Agency for Food, Drug Administration and Control) has been finding it a Herculean task to curb these excesses in modern business transactions in Nigeria especially in the business sphere dominated by the Igbo. Just like it is in the larger Nigerian society, the modern Igbo business sphere exemplifies "advanced fee fraud (419), drugs peddling, cheating, embezzlement of public funds and many others."[30] The craze for wealth has become neurotically insatiable and the concept of co-responsibility and co-operation has undergone considerable strain.

A paradigm for modern business ethics

The question that arises is whether the driving principle of profit-making in the modern market is incompatible with the ethical stipulations of the traditional Igbo. Can indigenous spirituality not be incorporated into modern commerce? No doubt, the naïve conception of modern human development based solely on material achievements has intensified the problem of incorporating spirituality into ethics. The aftermath as earlier noted has been devastating. This explains the endemic corruption in the Nigerian society.

We suggest a modernization of Igbo indigenous business ethical standards for modern business purposes. The positive impact of spirituality in modern Igbo business sphere must be emphasized. This involves the incorporation of gregariousness, communalism and spirituality into modern business ethics. Rather than relying on the long process of the Nigerian legal system these basic criteria emphasized by the Igbo indigenous religion and tradition in business transactions should be synchronized with those similar to the ethical teachings of Christianity and Islam towards the creation of spirituality and reverence for human dignity as guiding force for sound contemporary business ethics. The three religions emphasize love and reciprocity in human relations. The use of these religious principles as instant sanctions in the modern business sphere can be signed into law by the Nigerian legislators to give it legal authenticity. Any business ethics devoid of spirituality and without a focus on the authentic development of the human person is bound to fail. So, rather than religious exclusivism, disunity and segregation as exemplified by the various religions presently practised in the Nigerian society, a unity of purpose grounded in spirituality remains a paradigm for sound modern business ethics.

In this sense, civilization has to be embraced as a product of an optimistic ethical spiritual conception of the world. What is needed is to recover, re-establish and re-enact the indigenous religion of the Igbo people which encourages business transactions devoid of deontological and utilitarian extremes, and synchronize this with those aspects of the foreign religions which teach similar ideals in business. Corporate bodies and market unions must be legally empowered to enact and implement laws along religious lines

---

[30] S. Gregg, "Globalization: Insight from Catholic Social teachings," in N. Capaldi (ed.) *Business and Religion. A Clash of Civilization?* (Salem City, M&M Scribner Press, 2005), 426

as an exercise of control over the activities of their members. If at all times, the state must be called upon for legal actions against violation of business laws, then business ethics would be dysfunctional and reasonable commerce would grind to a halt. Self-enforcement is the hallmark of the indigenous religion, for which the enforcer is no other but the divinity. Christianity and Islam should find a way of making their members to face immediate punishment or judgment such as that which happened to the Biblical Ananias and Saphira who were struck dead for telling lies at the pronouncement of Apostle Peter.

Conclusion

It is obvious that in modern Nigeria, civilization appears to have been misunderstood to be advancement in wealth, knowledge and power without a place for spirituality. Apart from the development in modern Igbo business sphere, we must reflect on the danger in global business to which the world is presently being exposed. As has been experienced by the Igbo, it is dangerous to surrender to a naive satisfaction of individualistic material achievements which subsists on incredibly superficial conceptions of wealth and its accumulations. It suffices to say that the Igbo's "chosen destiny" as reflected above, is that everyone in the nation must work hard and become wealthy; and wealth is a sign of being divine because *Chineke* is wealthy. This again means that the belief and practice of social equality and personal freedom are the rudiments of fulfilling their chosen destiny of making money and becoming wealthy. This means that the Igbo are traders by religious conviction.

Be that as it may, our study in this chapter among Igbo justifies our submission that the ideals of the indigenous cultural business conception remain a veritable panacea to engender sanity in modern business endeavours. Since Nigeria is religiously plural, the ideals in other religions practiced in the country that are akin to that of the indigenous Igbo religion such as the love for one's neighbours, the importance of life after death and the principle of live and let live must be emphasized, re-enacted, legalized and enforced as a basis for the Nigerian business ethics. Individualism and other deontological tendencies must, therefore, be down-played. At the moment, the Nigerian business ethics is enforced through the long process of the legal court. It has been established that 'justice delayed is justice denied.' The Nigerian law should provide room for immediate sanctions in business misdemeanours along religious lines, such that communities and religious associations could be empowered to enforce immediate sanctions. This is already being practiced among the Igbo trade unions. Members are still made to swear to oath in various traditional shrines. A legal backing is however, required to avoid modern castigations. Our emphasis is the recognition of spiritual regulation and respect for human dignity as the basis for sound business ethics. Samuel Gregg's admonition in relation to Christianity and business in modern society is quite instructive here. He says:

The expansion of the free trade and of institutions such as the rule of law and private property throughout the world present us with tremendous opportunities for helping the developing world to raise its living standards. But the challenge of Catholicism in the midst of a globalizing world is to make sure that in the midst of ever increasing change that the great dignity of the human person, the only creature who God made for his own sake is not loss sight of... It is this Christian humanism that shows respect for the rich variety of cultures...principles that speak forever about the innate dignity of man and at all times and places express the spiritual grandeur of the human person.[31]

In addition, Imad-ad-Dean Ahmad says: "While we are on this earth, we should take care of everything: our bodies, our property, our friends and family and our mind and spirit." This is summed up in the Muslim proverb attributed to the prophet's cousin Al Ibn Talib:

...work for the next life as though you would die tomorrow... Good salesmanship requires recognition of spiritual and religious heritage and its links to the principle and history of the development of the market...[32]

The position of this essay is that recognition of God and the respect for human persons as a panacea for the corruption of good business ethics in the modern era.

References

Achebe, C, *Things Fall Apart*, London, 1958
Arungwa, O., "The *Ofo* in the Traditional Religion of the Igbo People with Special Reference to Ugwaland," Unpublished B.A Thesis, Nsukka, 1972
Benjamin, Ben & Bertha, Ancient Igbo, http://afrosacredater.com/igbo.htm.
Brunner, E, *The Divine Imperative: A study of the Christian Ethics,* trans. Wyon, Philadelpha Westminister, 1947
Chidoka O., "Okija, not a show of shame, http://www.biafranigeria.com/archixe' 2004/Sep/01/102 html
Daily Sun , August, 2004
Eastern Nigerian Art from Toby and Barry Hecht, collection from E. Benter "Life as an Artistic Process: Igbo *Ikenga* and *Ofo.*, *African Arts* 1988
Ejizu, C, "African Traditional Religion and the Promotion of Community Living" http://www.africanworld.net/afrel/community.html.
Ejizu, C. *Ofo: Igbo Ritual Symbol*, Nigeria, Fourth Dimension Publishing Co. Ltd; 1986
Ike, F., and Edozien, N., Catholic Institute for Development, justice and peace, *DJAP*, 2001
Isiramen C., in N. Calpadi (ed.) *Business and Religion: A clash of civilization?*, Salem City, M&M Scrinner Press, 2005

---

[31] Quoted by Imad-ad-Dean Ahmad, "Islam, Commerce and Business Ethics" in N. Capaldi, 212.
[32] Imad-ad-Dean Ahmad

Leonard, A. *The Lower Niger and its Tribes,* London, Frank Cass, 1968.
Njoku, J " Conflicts and Transmutations in African Communalism" in *Business, Society and Culture Journal,3,* http://www.hollerafrica.com/showarticle
Okere, J., "The Poverty of Christian Individualism, Morality and an African Alternative",http://www.crp.org/book/series/02/11-13
Shorter, A, "Urbanization: Today's Missionary Reality in Africa," in *AFER*, 1990. *Vanguard*, August 23, 2004
Umejesi I. "The Golden Rule and Religious Tolerance: A Case for Comparative Religion in Nigerian Schools" in *Journal of Academics:*, Vol. 2, No, 2, April, 2007.

21

Women in Yoruba and Igbo indigenous spirituality

- Oyeronke Olademo

Introduction

The social grouping called women, all of whose members are the same, feel the same, and experience the same degree of influence from different phenomena is to say the least illusive. No longer could it be assumed that a unique characteristic of sameness mark a group of people called women. Whereas it is true that biological components of the sexes are predominantly viewed as the prime category for being a woman, recent research work has proven the possibility of other qualifications for this grouping. The premise that women differ in their identities and experiences would be recognized in this chapter, nonetheless the term women will be employed for convenience sake rather than as a mark of sameness.

Religion has been variously defined depending on the priority of the person defining the phenomenon. Hence psychological, sociological, and theological definitions of religion may be given. In Nigeria, the concept of God-Supreme Being is a mark of religion in all cultures and the interaction of people with this Supreme Being often constitutes religion, either directly or indirectly. This interaction of the mortal with the immortal often involves rituals, liturgy and sacrifice. Many religions now occupy the landscape of Nigeria but the major ones are the Indigenous religions (Yoruba, Igbo, Tiv, Nupe, Ibibio, Tiv, Kanuri), Christianity (Orthodox, African Independent, Pentecostal/Charismatic/Zionist, Neo-Pentecostals), Islam (Tijaniyyah, Quadriyah, NASFAT, Qureeb), Asian religions (Hare Krisna, Buddhism, Taoism), New Age (Bahaism, Grail, Rosicrucian, Guru Maharaji). Both Christianity and Islam have been successfully domesticated by Nigerians (African Christianity). This chapter will focus on some indigenous religious spirituality in Nigeria.

Identity is a concept marked by different elements that are nonetheless interconnected. Identities are historically and discursively constructed and exist at different levels. For instance, just as individuals have identities, group identities could also be cited. Culture plays an important role in issues of identity and may be manipulated for different agendas by individuals and groups. Identity may also be described as a form of boundary construction for the people concerned. In other words, identity seems to say-this is me, in breath, length and depth—referring to a totality of experiences for the individual in a continuum. Religion is a significant component of identity (de)construction in all Nigerian cultures, especially for women who represent the sustaining factor in these religions. Consequently issues of identity constantly feature in our discourse on women and indigenous spiritualities in Nigeria.

Methodology for this chapter includes participant observation, historical analysis and feminist paradigm.

Theoretical background

Of basic importance to our discussions on women in Nigerian indigenous religions is the theory of identity politics. Identity politics refer to forces organizing and appealing to a group that is defined by specific characteristics and mobilizing this group identity as a means of gaining access to power. Identity politics could also manifest at the individual level with the individual attempting to gain access to power based on the components of personal identity, such as religious affiliation, ethnicity or class. A process of manipulation is inherent in identity politics and this is informed mainly by competing loyalties, which may be manipulated by the state and sometimes by social forces. Because identities are historically and discursively constructed, a significant role is ascribed to culture in the prescriptive and social influences of identities. Culture prescribes roles and often guards the moral boundaries of the individual as well as the collective. Consequently, women's identities and the challenges that attend them may to a large extent be located in cultural stipulations. Culture as a dynamic concept combines universal elements with the local and this proffers some implications for the place and role of women in identity politics. For instance, religion is crucial and integral to women's identity construction in Africa but at the same time, religious injunctions are not always friendly to women, specifically in the bid to gain access to power and structures of authority.

Further, the manifestation of group identity, which is a component of identity politics in the political realm almost always affects women negatively. As has been rightly noted, "an individual identity is especially problematic for women because a woman's life is filled with periods of changes" (Moghadam 1994); as a result of this, women are given symbolic identities as a group representing the soul and moral gauge of the society. This stance is often linked with the woman's biological capabilities for recreation thereby making women's reproductive activities a central issue. This puts a heavy burden on the women because their individual actions are now construed as representation the community rather than being informed by personal preferences as individuals in the society. A symbolic representation of women is a direct violation of women's identity because it is reinforced by restrictions in choices and mobility. Different experiences of different communities contribute to the features and impact of identity politics on women's lot. An example is the impact of colonization in communities that experienced it and the implication of this on women's roles and status. One of the impacts of the colonial experience in some African communities is the "transformation of state power to male-gender power which was accomplished at one level by the exclusion of women from state structures" (Oyewumi 1999). Also, colonization in Africa destabilized the duality of gender structures and divergent African female identities (Sudarkasa 1986, Amadiume 1987, Barber 1991, Olupona 1991, Oduyoye 1992, Ogundipe-Leslie 1994, Oyewumi 1999, Olajubu 2003). Furthermore, an important blow to the identity politics in African communities was the introduction of paid wage labour for the men, which resulted in the creation of a public space from which women were excluded.

To a certain extent in some contexts, limitations may be discerned for identity politics. For instance, an assumed feature of identity politics is harmony and a unified front among a group of people but sometimes divisions could occur within or in direct opposition to the idea of a unified front, thus the group's identity becomes contested. Such a situation is often directly proportional to the level of awareness and critical analysis existing among the group. The agenda and *modus operandi* of feminism at the onset, which assumes a common platform for all women and thus a common ground on which liberation from various types of oppression may be sought is no longer tenable. This position has been given a problematic twist by scholars that it is becoming clear that it is probable that no group with sameness in identity called "women" exist anywhere (Butler 1990). Thus examples of women who are opposed to the agenda and practices of feminism may be cited. Thus, identity politics is a dynamic theory that needs careful consideration as concerns women's spirituality in indigenous religions in Nigeria.

The word symbol is from the Greek verb *"symballein"* meaning "to throw or bring together." Theories on symbolism also have salient bearing on our discourse in this chapter. Symbols are forms of expressing meaning and coded means of communication. Usually, symbols point beyond themselves to something else. According to Livingston (1989), symbols could be representational or presentational. Representational symbols tie together based on conventions, i.e. agreed ways of doing things, habitual practice or customs. The meaning of such symbols is prescribed by their cultural context and use; hence embedded in them is an ample amount of flexibility. A symbol may mean different things in different cultural context depending on a people's habitual practice. Furthermore, presentational symbols often present an icon or an image and they are similar to that which they symbolize. Whereas there is no direct link between the representational symbol and that which it symbolizes, the opposite is true of the presentational symbol. An example of a presentational symbol is the map and the geographical areas represented on it.

Religious symbols are usually presentational; they are powerful transmitters of religious meaning and may not be easily changed or eradicated. Examples include blood, which is a symbol of sacrifice and water, which symbolizes life and cleansing. According to Kunin (2006) sacred objects and entities are symbols in religion. Moreover, symbolic activities in religion constitute a cultural system and the ritual space is the venue per excellence for the display of symbols. Worthy of mention also is Durkheim's observation that "there is a close integration of the system of religious symbols of a society and the patterns sanctioned by the common moral sentiments of the members of a community." Accordingly, religious symbols cannot be understood independently of their historical relations with the society. Women's spirituality in indigenous religions in Nigeria is replete with symbols in acts and sacred objects, which are all linked to the people's identity and history.

Another theory that could facilitate our discourse is the theory of the interpretation of texts in religion. It seems an agreeable fact that there is a distinction between the interpretation of a text and the text itself (Wadud 1999). In the first instance, every text is a product of specific historical, cultural and social setting. Invariably then, a level of politics is embedded in any given text. The situation of the religious text is however compounded because in addition to the point noted above, its interpretation is also dynamic. The interpretation of a text is subject to diverse agendas of the interpreters in different historical and social settings. The prescriptions of rights and obligations in some sacred scriptures illustrate this observation. The Bible and the Qur'an do not provide distinct rights for women and men as concerns spirituality but the reality in the practices of these religions is a different story. The interpretation of texts in religion has been in the custody of men predominantly. Recent examples of women in the field of archaeology and religion and linguistics may be cited but these are minimal. This explains why until few decades ago, the interpretation of texts in religion have been largely patriarchal. The interpretation of texts in religion results in the provision of normative paradigm for social relations and often bears links with issues of power and authority beyond the religious realm.

Lastly, of relevance to this chapter is the theory of capitalism, which is a broad theory but for our engagement here, the aspect that asserts that "religion is the spirit of capitalism and the link between religion and capitalism" (Ritzer 1983) would be considered. Specifically, the theory submits that Protestantism succeeded in turning the pursuit of profit into a moral crusade and backing the moral system that led to the unprecedented expansion of profit seeking and ultimately to the capitalist system. More importantly is the assertion of the theory that "capitalism is today an immense cosmos into which the individual is born" and how it "forces the individual in so far as she or he is involved in the system market relationships, to conform to capitalist rules of action" (Ritzer 1983). Invariably, that which sustains capitalism is religion; hence economics could utilize religion as a tool to achieve its aims. Conversely religion in the contemporary African setting employs capitalist systems in its daily activities. Thus is it plausible to speak of a mutual dependence between capitalism and religion in Africa? These theoretical backgrounds are to assist our explication of women's spirituality in Nigerian indigenous religions. Also, these theories should facilitate possible projections on trends that may yet unfold in this regard.

Women in Yoruba indigenous spirituality

Women's roles in Indigenous Yoruba religion hinge on religious narratives, especially the cosmological accounts of the people. These cosmological accounts prescribe and entrench social roles and status for women in Africa. The ritual space constitutes a significant arena for the display of women's spirituality among the Yoruba. These include leadership roles, healing, spirit possession, fertility rites, goddess worship, and divination knowledge.

African gender relationships are usually marked by mutual respect and complementary relations. Thus, women leadership is readily accepted and benefited from such leadership roles like the office of the priestess of various religious groups, diviners, herbalists, and female chiefs found in the society. These women lead in these capacities and serve as role models for the young girls. It should be noted that leadership was construed in traditional African societies as a trust that must be accounted for by the one in authority, whether male or female. Also, advanced age is generally regarded as a pointer to wisdom hence women leaders in African religions are wise and were before the recent times, often old. Women's spirituality in indigenous Nigerian religions often reflects notions of group identity and identity politics. For instance, characteristics and identity of women may be utilized as a means to gain access to power; usually this revolves around biological processes. These identities and characteristics are historically and discursively constructed as manifested in the age-old institution of motherhood. Though a disparity in individual inclinations among women is a reality, yet, it is possible to speak of women group identity due to the assumed common subscription to motherhood. For some ethnic groups in Africa, such as the Yoruba, motherhood is not a privilege limited to women who physically bear children; all women are mothers. The Yoruba adopts the child of a sibling of a barren woman to stay with her with the belief that *"ori omo lo n pe omo w'aye,"* i.e. "it is the personality soul of a child that attracts another child." In other words, a barren woman with a child (of whatever parentage) in the house stands a better chance of getting pregnant than one staying alone. On the other hand, all adult females are mothers to all children in the community; hence the Yoruba say, *"enikan ni n bi omo, gbogbo aye ni n ba nii wo,"* i.e. "only one person gives birth to a child, but the entire community involves in its training." Consequently, motherhood is a platform for group identity in Yorùbáland. This group identity exhibits strong links with rituals in the indigenous religion as explicated in the mysteries of motherhood, which binds women in the *Iya Mi* cult (witches). These women occupy positions of leadership in the polity and play important roles in the maintenance of order in the Yoruba society. Further, women's spirituality also manifest in the roles of female cultic functionaries, like the *Iyanifa*, and *Iya Osun*. Works on the personality, qualities and duties of the *Iya Osun* and *Iyanifa* may are available. However, the significant thing to note for this chapter is the changes attending qualifications of women leaders in Yoruba religion and the dynamic modes of operations that are constantly being negotiated in the ritual space by these women.

Issues pertaining to blood in the ritual space have been and remain controversial across religions worldwide and Yoruba religion is not exempted. Research however shows that rather than emanating from an understanding of menstrual blood as conterminous, the ban on menstrual blood in Yoruba ritual space is due to respect. In some religions, menstrual blood is construed as depleting power from the sacred space but the ban in Yoruba religion is because menstrual blood is perceived as conveyor of life and power, thus it is banned to avoid a clash of powers. A recent example seems apposite here; during the recent clash between the Modakeke and Ife peoples in Osun State Nigeria in August, 1997, women in Modakeke, I was reliably informed, obliged the community with their menstrual pads as one of the needed ingredients to prepare potent medicine (*oogun*) for the victory of the Modakeke warriors. Another issue worth mentioning is the assumed qualification for female leaders in indigenous religions as pertains to age. Before now, female leaders in Yoruba land were elderly and usually past menstruating stage but this is no more the case. Research confirms that some female leaders in Yoruba religion are within childbearing stages and only observe certain restrictions during their menstrual period. The implication of this stance is that Yoruba religion now has agile, sharp and versatile female leaders who can compete with their counterparts in other religions comfortably.

African indigenous religions ascribe to women and the female principle the ability to heal. Oftentimes a link is identified between the maternal principle and healing aptitudes with specific reference to procreation ability in women. This could be assumed for individual women who are called, trained, or both in the act of healing or it could be attributed to a group of women whose focus rest on healing of diseases. The assumption that healing powers belong to women's spirituality in African indigenous religions could be traced to African cosmological narratives many of which identify goddesses as sources of healing attributes. Such goddesses are also often times credited with the ability to bestow wealth. Yoruba goddesses are usually linked with water bodies like rivers, streams and oceans. In addition, symbolic attributes that are assumed for water are also ascribed to the feminine. These include peace, coolness, gentleness and soothing abilities. Goddess worship displays women's spirituality in Yoruba religion and the source of goddess worship among the Yoruba is the cosmological accounts. The Supreme Being has female and male assistants in the Yoruba belief system. These are known as the *orisa*, they are assistants who serve as intermediaries between *Olodumare* and human beings. Examples include *Yemanja, Olokun, Osun, Oba* and *Otin*. Healing is a female precinct in Yoruba religion. Yoruba goddesses specialize and are consulted on diverse healing matters, especially gynaecology and paediatrics. Likewise, there are many female healers who are trained in many methods of attaining healing including the use of herbs and special incantations and preparations. A principal element in notions of healing among the Yoruba is water and this in informed by the Yoruba belief in the intrinsic value of water. In addition to water, healers also utilize herbs and roots to effect healing. Closely linked to issues of healing among the Yoruba are those on fertility. Fertility rites concern the well-being of women and the society at large. In the first instance, procreation is of tremendous importance in every African society the Yoruba inclusive, because it guarantees collective immortality, thus everything is done to safeguard both mother and child. But beyond this, the fertility of the land is also significant because the people's survival depends on it. In many African societies there is a recognizable link between women's fertility and the fertility of the land. Rites are performed to sustain and safeguard all issues pertaining to fertility in Yoruba religion. The Yoruba celebrate the annual *Gelede* festival to appease the maternal principle and ensure fertility in the land. It is a celebration that involves music, dance and the use of different types of masks.

Spirit possession is another avenue through which women's spirituality in African religions is extensively displayed. It is an agreeable fact that through spirit-possession, women gain access to temporary respect and authority but sometimes this becomes permanent and positively affects the status of women in the society. Different theories have been propounded on spirit possession in African religions, ranging from alternative/compensatory source of power and recognition in the face of a male hegemony to emotional let off of tension by women. The important thing is that as mediums of the divine, these women when under spirit-possession, must be respected and their instructions obeyed. Among the Yoruba, a large percentage of devotees who undergo spirit possession are women. A salient feature of spirit possession in Yoruba religion is the display of the people's notion of mutual dependence of both genders. Hence, gods may possess either female or male devotees and the same is true for the goddesses. Also, the devotee under spirit possession exhibits characteristics of the deity in charge. For example, Sango is the Yoruba god of thunder and is characterized as being aggressive and volatile. Similarly, when Sango possesses a woman, she becomes aggressive and volatile. Furthermore, cross-dressing of genders is a feature of spirit possession, this explains the plaiting of hair by some male priests among the Yoruba; an example is the Sango priest. He plaits his hair in the *suku* style, and wears a skirt and blouse.

Women in African religions also have access to the science of divination. These are oracles that serve as compass for direction to the Africans in the journey of life. A prominent one is the *Ifa* Oracle among the Yoruba. Whereas the male priest of *Ifa* is known as the *Babalawo*, the priestess is called the Iyanifa. Training for both remains the same though the mode of graduation varies. The Iyanifa are versatile in the display of their spirituality, which by training enables them to be operative in diverse sectors of the polity including economics, aesthetics, politics and health. The contemporary relevance of this versatility cannot be overemphasized due to the dynamic nature of global influences presently. In sum, women's spirituality in Yoruba religion is rich, abundant and versatile. A clear pointer to this fact is the indelible influence of this spirituality on the role and status of women in Christianity and Islam in contemporary Africa.

Women in Igbo indigenous spirituality

The spiritual system of the Igbo people of Nigeria is one of the oldest on earth. The foundation of Igbo spirituality is the concept of *'chi,'* which is also the basis of creation. The popular names for the creator in Igbo land are *Chukwu* and *Chineke*; both of which display a close affinity to *'chi.'* Everyone and everything among the Igbo has a *'chi.'* Whereas the male aspect is called *'chi,'* the female dimension is known as *'eke.'* For the Igbo people, a combination of the female and male is essential to attaining success in any enterprise. The Igbo thus subscribe to complementary gender relations as recorded in the people's oral genres.

Ani, the earth goddess is the most important force of nature in Igboland. She is often referred to as the mother goddess, the great mother, or the queen of the underworld. She is the most loved deity in Igbo land and the closest to the people. Public morality and ethical codes are important aspects of her jurisprudence. Usually, sacred art depict her as a mother with a child in her arms or on her knees with a sword in hand. The Yam festival is the most important festival among the Igbo and it is held in her honour. In Umegw-Okpuala, a village in Abia State, Nigeria for instance, Ala is regarded as the wife of *Chineke*. She is often depicted as wearing many bangles, i.e. "*ezi nwanyi gbaola*" meaning "the woman with many bangles." She is seen as the mother and protector of the villagers. She is a giver of children, long life, wealth, peace and guidance. In this village, her festival-the new yam festival-occur every November and last for eight days.

Ani or *Ala*, the earth goddess thus provides the model for female spirituality among the Igbo. Just as she occupies an important place in the pantheon of gods, so also women feature prominently in Indigenous Igbo spirituality. Women perform many roles in Igbo indigenous religion. For instance, priesthood is open to male and female. The journey to attaining priesthood begins with a call by the deity concerned. Oftentimes, this involves spirit possession but the call may be refused. After series of trials in form of sicknesses of different kinds, indebtedness despite hard work and other types of difficult situations, the woman with the call eventually accepts the call of the deity concerned. Once the call is accepted, the priestess begins her training, which encompasses the acquisition of knowledge in the properties and use of herbs, roots and other medicinal preparations in the service of the deity. Also included in the training of the priestess are instructions on the laws, taboos, dances, food and songs of the deity to be served. The priestess possesses high social status in the community and is usually consulted for advice by those in authority.

Igbo women also function as mediums and diviners and by these they facilitate communication between mortals and the immortal. They reveal secrets through the science of divination and help chart useful course during crisis periods in the community. Again, women's spirituality manifests during rites of passage in Igbo land. From birth rituals to girl's nobility rites, to marriage and burial rites, women are active participants. A pregnant woman at the time of delivery is attended by other women among the Igbo. It is only at crisis period that men show up at the delivery of a pregnant woman. Women are the principal officiates at the puberty rites for girls as well. On widowhood rites, women have tremendous power in Igbo land, especially the Umu-Ada (daughters of a lineage). In sum, it may be asserted, that women's spirituality is marked by dynamism and complementary gender relations among the Igbo of Nigeria.

Conclusion

This chapter has attempted an analysis of women's spirituality in Yoruba and Igbo religions in Nigeria. Our illustrations were drawn from women's roles as leaders, cultic functionaries and members of guilds in Yorubaland, the place of women in the indigenous Igbo religion also engaged our attention. It came to fore during the discourse that women's spirituality is a crucial component of their identity construction and that this is constantly negotiated. We observed that women's spirituality faces different challenges that are negotiated, especially issues on blood in religion. In sum, we may assert that religion constitutes an important ingredient in women's identity construction in Nigeria and within each religion; women assess and prioritize balance as they seek to construct a dynamic identity in the continuously changing setting in the religious landscape of Nigeria.

References

Amadiume, Ifi, 1987. *Male Daughters, Female Husbands: Gender and Sex in an African Society*. London: Zed Books.

Barber, Karin, 1991. *I Could Speak Till Tomorrow: Oriki, Women, and the Past in a Yoruba Town*. Edinburgh: Edinburgh University Press.

Butler, Judith, 1990. *Gender Trouble: Feminism & the Subversion of Identity*. New York: Routledge.

Chhachhi, Amrita. 1990. Religious Fundamentalism and Women. *WAF Journal* 1: 14-15.

Christensen, Martin K.I. Worldwide Guide to Women in Leadership, http://www.guide2womenleaders.com

Crumbley, Deidre, 1992. Impurity and Power: Women in Aladura Churches. *Africa* 62 (4): 505-522.

Culture Kitchen. http://www.culturekitchen.com

Daly, Mary, 1973. *Beyond God the Father: Towards a Philosophy of Women's Liberation*. Boston: Beacon Press.

Johnson, Elizabeth A., 1992. *She Who Is: The Mystery of God in Feminist Theological Discourse*. New York: Crossroad Publishing Company.

Moghadam, Valentine M., ed. 1994. *Identity Politics and Women: Cultural Reassertions and Feminisms in International Perspective*. Oxford: Westview Press.

Ogundipe-Leslie, 'Molara, 1994. *Re-Creating Ourselves: African Women and Critical Transformations*. New Jersey: African World Press Inc.

Olajubu, Oyeronke, 2002 Reconnecting with the Waters: John 9. I-II. In *The Earth Story in the New Testament*, Vol. 5, ed. C. Habel & V. Bala Banski, 108-121.

London: Sheffield Academic Press.
Olajubu, Oyeronke, 2003. *Women in the Yoruba Religious Sphere*. New York: SUNY Press.
Olajubu, Oyeronke, 2005. Gender and Religion: Gender and African Religious Traditions. In *Encyclopedia of Religion, 2nd Edition*, ed. Lindsay Jones. New York: Thomson Gale: 3400-3406
Olupona, Jacob K., ed. 1991. *African Traditional Religion in Contemporary Society*. Minnesota: Paragon House.
Oyewumi, Oyeronke, 1999. *The Invention of Women*. Minneapolis: University of Minnesota Press.
Ray, Benjamin C., 2000. *African Religions 2nd edition*. New Jersey: Prentice Hall.
Ritzer, George, 1983. *Sociological Theory 2nd Edition*. New York: Alfred A. Knopf
Sudarkasa, Niara, 1986. The Status of Women in Indigenous African Society. *Feminist Studies*. Vol. 12(1): 91-103.
The Talking Drum Collective. Assata Shakur Speaks! http://www.assatashakur.org

22

Politics in an African Royal Harem: women and seclusion at the Royal Court of Benin, Nigeria

- Flora Edouwaye S. Kaplan

Introduction

Indigenous royal harems in Nigeria are little known beyond those that are part of Muslim emirates established in the north. The harem and practice of secluding of royal wives, however, has been known at the court of Benin in southwest Nigeria since the late fifteenth century, following first European contacts by Portuguese explorers; and it is still being practised in the twenty-first century. This chapter is based on the unique access to the harem and his wives granted me by the thirty-eighth *Oba* of Benin, the indigenous ruler, *Oba* Erediauwa (1979 - present). My ethnographic research began in 1983 and is ongoing. The initial purpose of my research was to study the harem and the political aspects of the roles played by royal wives. To that purpose, how women were and are recruited into the harem at court is relevant. I also sought to identify sources of power and influence available to royal women, and to assess what impact, if any, royal women had on the lives of ordinary women and men beyond the walls of the harem. The results of this study shed light on these issues and why seclusion of the *Oba's* wives persists in association with polygamy and the harem as a social institution. It reveals as well how the *Oba*'s wives, while rarely seen, contribute to the continuity of the court and its traditions in the contemporary Federal Republic of Nigeria.

This study is the first, based on direct observation and participation in the *Oba*'s harem at the Benin royal court by the author. What has been known is episodic, derived from oral tradition and information collected second-hand by colonial officials, historians, ethnographers, traders, and visitors who invariably were men – talking to other men about women, and then written down by men. In this respect Benin resembles many early accounts of palace women in the Middle East, China, India, and elsewhere that harems were found up to the twentieth century. Nineteenth century personal accounts of harem women in seclusion, such as the letters of Lady Mary Wortley Montagu, from Turkey (1804); and the book by Anna Leonowens, an English governess at the royal court, at Bangkok, Siam (1870) are among the rare glimpses of harems witnessed by women in western writings.[1]

"Politics" in this African harem is broadly defined to mean observable decision making and makers acting in public arenas with regard to control and distribution of resources perceived as scarce. It is not limited to offices held in a system of governance. "Resources" may be tangible in the form of lands, prestige and luxury goods, food staples, houses, and people, etc.; and they may be intangible in the form of spiritual powers, knowledge, skills, and the like. Power is defined here as the ability to implement and enforce decisions taken by royal wives; and influence as the ability through persuasion, personality, and/or by example to affect the decisions and actions of others. This study finds the political aspects of their decision making and their example reverberate throughout the larger society economically and socially.

Oral tradition suggests Benin royal women may not have been secluded earlier, but played a more overt political and public role during an earlier, more egalitarian period, said to be ruled by "sky kings," *Ogisos,* in the tenth to twelfth centuries. Little is known of that period to date, as it is undocumented by archaeology. When *Ogiso* rule ended, the current dynasty of *Obas* began. What is known of their beginnings was collected as oral tradition in the 1920s from people who were adults in 1897, when a major British military assault on Benin City ended native rule.[2] The names of thirty-one *Ogisos* were remembered, including a few women (princes and princesses were said to have ruled).[3]

With coming of the *Obas* at the end of the twelfth century, a male ethos prevailed, and royal women no longer held high political office, but played subordinate sex roles as wives and mothers. A Benin oral tradition justifies women's exclusion: Princess Edelayo (a daughter of *Oba* Ewuare, "The Great" (Ca. 1440- 1473 A.D.), was almost as rich and powerful as the *Oba.* But "...owing to a feminine indisposition," she was proscribed from becoming the *Oba* as she was about to be crowned. Thereafter, "...it was enacted that women should not be allowed to reign in Benin any more." No other women are mentioned in the succession of *Obas,* either before Princess Edelayo's missed opportunity, or after her, up the end of the nineteenth century, when Oba Ovonramwen (Ca. 1888-1914 A.D.) the last independent king to rule came to the throne. (See "Figure 1," a list of thirty-six *Obas,* reconstructed from oral tradition by Egharevba). In his classic text, *A Short History of Benin (1960),* Egharevba noted some princesses, *uvbi,* royal daughters of *Obas,* were

---

[1] There have been more studies of women by women (and some men) in the mid-to-early twentieth century, e.g., Thoko Ginindza, a Swazi woman, writing about an important Queen Mother in Swaziland, and Beverly Mack on women in the harem of the Emir of Kano. See Kaplan (1997) for the aforementioned chapters, and others in an important collection with reference to women of power.

[2] The interviews were initiated by Chief Jacob U. Egharevba, the first self-taught Benin historian, writing in English in the early decades of British colonial rule (1897-1960). Most of his work was printed privately as pamphlets and booklets from the 1930s on.

[3] Egharevba 1960, p. 76

remembered for their beauty and wealth; and other princesses remembered for the services they rendered to their fathers and brothers who ruled Benin. Among the royal wives, however, the only one who achieves lasting memory is the one who gives birth to the next *Oba*. She is shown in court art and memorialized in association with her son. The title of *Iyoba*, "Mother of the *Oba*," was created for *Idia*, the first Queen Mother of Benin, by her son, Oba Esigie (Ca. 1504-1550 A.D.).

Historical background

From medieval times the Benin kingdom dominated much of southern Nigeria. The *Obas* who followed the *Ogisos* at the end of the twelfth century were warrior kings. They raided their neighbours to the west and east, and warred against their enemies to the north. In the next seven hundred years, they exacted tribute at different times, from different ethnic groups in dispersed villages or towns and city states among the Yoruba, Igbo, Itsekiri, Urhobo, Nupe, Igala, etc., up to the end of the nineteenth century. The *Oba*, who stood at the apex of a ranked and hierarchical state society, combined temporal and spiritual power in his person. He could raise and field armies of five thousand and even ten thousand men to conquer others and to defend themselves as needed. He also extended, developed, and maintained Benin City, the urban heart of the kingdom, calling up large details of young adult males to work on major civic projects through dense tropical rainforest, like the more than ten miles of Benin City's walls, and the ninety or more miles of dump ramparts beyond the city and reached heights of forty to sixty feet.[4]

In 1897 the British, long engaged in colonial trade and expansion in Nigeria, and long frustrated by the Benin *Oba*'s control of inland trade in the south, used the excuse of a "massacre" to mount a heavy military assault against Benin City. A few months earlier, an uninvited and decidedly *un*diplomatic party, led by Acting Consul Captain James R. Phillips, had attempted to visit Benin City against the expressed wishes of the *Oba*. Their ambush and deaths triggered the assault the British titled a "Punitive Expedition," in 1897. It ended in the executions of a number of important chiefs, the exile of the reigning *Oba Ovonramwen* to Old Calabar, in eastern

---

[4] The pre-mechanical construction of Benin's earthen forest walls were "four to five times longer than the "Great Wall of China" and had moved over a hundred times more earth than the Great Pyramid of Cheops, in Egypt ..." (Darling, 1984 vols. I & II: 6). According to Connah the innermost Benin City walls could have been erected in a single dry season by 5,000 men, working ten hours a day (1975:103). But they were likely built over a longer period, and partially re-done following each rainy season. It also is likely the walls were built by different Obas, and oral tradition tells us exactly that: *"There are three main moats or ditches (iya) surrounding the city ... [the first two] dug by Oba Oguola" as a defensive measure. The third moat (ditch/iya) in the heart of the city was dug by Oba Ewuare about 1460 A. D.* (Egharevba 1960: 85). These tangible city (and forest) walls support the chronology of Benin *obas*, based on archaeology done thus far and dated. However the Benin walls are compared and the construction calculated the city walls and those in the rainforest represent a monumental achievement as well as an architectural one: they demanded extraordinary organization and community effort. The walls were and remain remarkable monuments to an indigenous state and urban civilization – that were maintained and remained in place for more than seven hundred years.

Nigeria, and the destruction of his palace and that of his mother, *Iyoba* Iheya (or Iha II*)*. The British expedition against Benin ended independent indigenous rule and ushered in an interregnum that lasted from 1897, to the *Oba's* passing in the east around the turn of the New Year in 1914. The British then found it expedient to officially restore the monarchy in Benin City. *Oba* Ovonramwen's first son and legitimate heir to the throne, Prince Aguobasimwin, took the title Oba Eweka II. [5]

The *Oba*'s Palace

Oba Eweka II (1914-1933) found the palace severely damaged by fires and shelling by cannon after the five days of fierce fighting in 1897. Many sections of the walls also had been deliberately levelled to prevent further resistance by Benin warriors. The harem at one end of the main building complex in the centre of the compound was badly damaged, emptied of its shrines and contents, the queens sent away. With limited resources Oba Eweka II slowly started to restore the palace, replacing the burnt thatched and shingled roofs with galvanized tin and iron sheeting, and walling in the compound now less than half its previous size. The *Oba* soon filled his harem, and was widely reputed to have had "100 wives", but no record of them remains. His many descendants acknowledge most were "outside wives" who did not live in the harem at court. Oba Eweka II who was not allowed by the British to name his mother, *Iyoba*, or to send her to *Uselu*, the traditional area for Queen Mothers outside the city, kept her close in a palace nearby, but in keeping with tradition, apart from his own.[6]

Oba Akenzua II (1933-1978), like his father before him continued to restore the palace. He established a Benin museum on land belonging to the pre-1897 compound and slowly began to revive rituals at the palace. He made use of photography to record important events and visits; and he allowed the public presence of his wives and children, and himself, to be recorded at *Igue*, an important annual festival at the palace. In actively using photography Oba Akenzua II was extending the traditional practice of archiving Benin history in bronze and ivory. At the same time, he was innovating in permitting images of himself and his living wives and children to appear on film, whereas they were not recorded at all in the past.

The *Oba*'s post-1897 compound covers more than 25 acres today in the centre of Benin City. It includes dozens of buildings, interior courtyards, stables, garages, storage facilities, and offices on the property. The size of his home sets it apart from the houses and compounds of other "big" men (and women) in the city. Up to the early decades of the twentieth century, the *Oba*'s palace had the highest walls and roofs, and most elaborately decorated buildings in Benin. Some roofs had added turrets decorated with

---

[5] Egharevba 1965, p. 28

[6] After Oba Akenzua II came to the throne in 1933, he gave his own mother (who was deceased), and his grandmother, who had not been allowed to reign as Iyoba, their titles.

monumental brass castings. Among them the most striking and ominous up to *Oba* Ovonramwen's time, were the large articulated brass castings of sinuous snakes, whose heads with toothed jaws hung open above the entrances to main buildings. Besides monumental brass castings, other rare and costly palace building materials were used: wood shingles, and *repoussé* brass sheathing over carved wood doors, lintels. Other buildings displayed polished clay, decorative panels with large snakes and leopards carved in relief.

The palace houses hundreds of people and daily receives hundreds more who come to the palace societies and guilds, as chiefs and priests, servants, attendants, and other classes of initiated persons. Each group has the exclusive use of their own section with many rooms set around the courtyards of different buildings. The palace is said to have "200" rooms, but "200" in Benin is a euphemism for infinite or "without number." No one knows how many rooms there are, actually The present palace is and has been a work-in-progress since the thirteenth century, with some rooms, service areas, wells, and buildings abandoned from time-to-time; and new rooms, courtyards, walls, offices, and spaces created and remodelled, redesigned, and reassigned. The *Oba's* palace, like the houses of "big men," as well as those of untitled men is and was the centre of an extended patrilineal (and polygamous) [royal] family. The continuity of the *Oba's* family assures the continuity of the Benin people, as he and they are one and the same. His ancestors are the collective ancestors of the state, the (former) kingdom, and all the Benin people. The royal palace is unique among the *Edo*–speaking peoples, however, in being the exclusive home of the sacred king, the *Oba*, who is at the centre of the Benin spiritual and cultural world, as well as its political and temporal one. As such the *Oba* and the palace today serve to locate and constitute Benin identity as an ethnic group in the modern nation-state of Nigeria.

The harem: seclusion as idea

Western notions of the harem are most often associated with seclusion in Islamic cultures. The word itself comes from the Arabic *hara-m,* meaning a forbidden, sacred place. The harem as a word and idea is more widely defined and applied to the space of a house reserved for the women of a family, private and secure; and it is not universally equated with seclusion. In Benin culture into the twentieth century, virtually all married women living in extended patrilineal families resided together in a harem, but they were neither forbidden to have necessary contact and transactions with men, nor were they secluded. Each woman in a harem had her own room or rooms for herself and her children; and she moved about outside the marital home to farm and trade locally. She could also visit her natal home and relations. Only the *Oba's* wives lived in the harem in strict seclusion.

Just when royal wives were first secluded in the *Oba's* palace is unclear. But archaeology strongly suggests royal women probably were living in seclusion at the palace by the early thirteenth century. Discoveries made in the early 1960s by Graham Connah, a South African archaeologist working in Benin City, revealed the bodies of some nineteen young women estimated to be between eighteen and twenty-five years of age. They were found at the bottom of a cistern in an abandoned courtyard of the pre-1897 palace site. The richness of their dress was represented by a few surviving scraps of the embroidered and drawn cloth they had worn. They also wore many bronze ornaments and rings that add to the interpretation they were royal women, possibly young wives of the *Oba*, who was regarded as a god-king on earth. Ethnography has it his favourite wives were buried with him when the *Oba* "went to meet his ancestors," a euphemism for his death. Fortunately, the rare and fragile materials associated with these young women and recovered by Connah, yielded important and early radiocarbon dates.[7] Therefore, it is evident human sacrifice and ritual burial associated with Benin culture were already being practised by the thirteenth century, and seclusion likely at the palace.

Seclusion of the *Oba*'s wives was and is a function of the *Oba*'s sacred nature and their bodily contact with him. His queens, the *iloi*, as a result may not be touched even accidentally by any man, including their own fathers, brothers, or close relatives, once married to the *Oba*. His person is *taboo*, and his wives who partake of his body also are taboo. The word "taboo" (*ta* – marking off, and *bu* – intensifying), signifies something forbidden, something that would be polluting or bring about misfortune, illness, or death as a result of contact. The *Oba*'s wives are secluded for their own safety and that of others.

The word taboo first entered western consciousness with the Polynesian word *tapu* (Tongan) or *kapu* (Hawaiian) in eighteenth century reports of Captain James Cook's voyages to the South Seas. A taboo is known to generate avoidance rules; and it identifies a person or class of persons (like a divine king, or mothers-in-law), or a thing in a culture (like certain foods), or in nature (like a totemic animal or class of animals) – that requires it be avoided. The late Queen Mother Aghahouwa of Benin, for example, was forbidden to eat deer; another family's members are forbidden to eat python, and so on. Each group is forbidden something in nature according to their lineage and their shared "family morning greeting" in Benin.

The concept of *mana* is related to taboo and defined as an extrasensory force that adheres to certain individuals. At the top of society the *Oba* of Benin, who is a sacred and divine king, is untouchable. But a *taboo* may also mark those at the bottom of a social hierarchy, like leather workers in Hindu society, who were classed as "untouchables." Slater noted in a discussion of *taboo* that the polar relationships between *mana* and *taboo* ("animatism") were considered a "minimal definition of religion" by R.T. Marrett in 1914. She found the study of *taboo* continues to be useful "at the point where the

---

[7] Connah 1975, p. 268

sociology of danger meets the psychology of aversion and the semiotics of order". [8]

The extraordinary way the *Oba* was regarded by his people, and the danger implicit in the power that adhered to him (what anthropologists call *mana*), were reported by European visitors to Benin City in the early nineteenth century. The French visitor Beauvois, in 1801, and the Englishman Adams, in 1823, reported "...the King [of Benin] could live without food or drink, subject to death, but destined to reappear on earth at the time of a definite period."[9] It is still widely believed in Benin that the *Oba* does not sleep, eat, or drink as ordinary people do; and that he never dies, but is reborn anew. Reincarnation is a concept integral to indigenous Benin religion, and clearly embodied in the person of the *Oba*. The Europeans described the *Oba* of Benin as "fetish." (The concepts of *taboo, mana, and* animatism, as they emerged in later nineteenth century anthropology, were not then in wide circulation.) The word, "fetish," from the Portuguese, *feitiço*, usually described an object, but in this case it described a person who was regarded with awe, and worshipped as embodying a potent spirit or deity: Captain Adams described it, thus:

> The Oba is ...fetiche, and the principal object of adoration in his dominions. He occupies a higher post here than the Pope does in Catholic Europe; for he is not only God's vice-regent upon earth, but a god himself, whose subjects both obey and adore him as such, although I believe their adoration to arise rather from fear than love; as cases of heresy, if proved, are followed by prompt decapitation." [10]

The harem: as place

The *Oba*'s harem is a world within the world of the vast palace - very much part of it, and at the same time, set apart. It is a sacred space only the *Oba* can enter and leave at will. As a place the harem is actually a series of interior buildings that, seen from the enclosed courtyard of its front entrance and massive wood door, appears to be separated from the main building of the palace that dominates the landscape. It is actually connected unseen at the rear through several secret doors. The large and spacious outer reception halls of the harem have high ceilings and coursed and smoothed, whitewashed mud walls. On occasion the queens enter the halls to meet distinguished visitors and women's groups at the outer door. Special groups such as the market women and their leaders who were (and are now) critically important to the stability, prosperity, and peace of the state (and former kingdom) are welcomed. Other women who are the wives and daughters of chiefs that serve

---

[8] Slater 1996, pp. 1279-1285
[9] Beauvois 1801
[10] Adams 1823, pp. 62-71

the *Oba* are both formally constituted and named groups.[11] They come to the harem on a regular basis to sing and dance with the wives in the outermost reception hall. They also constitute the eyes and ears of the queens and the links to a wide range of communities outside. They have access to pass and receive messages from the wives. These groups are an important presence at the palace, giving them public visibility in music and song with women's traditional instruments (netted calabashes, *ukuse*), a complement to the male guilds that drum, sing, and dance when there is a festival, a celebration, or special event. The women's groups "keep the palace warm," and make the wives happy when the *Oba* travels out to the national capital at Abuja, to meet with the country's President and other high government officials, or for tours and meetings with other traditional rulers in Nigeria.

The harem is the place where women's groups and visitors, together with a relatively open petitioning process, provide the queens with informal opportunities to play "political" roles outside as well as inside the *Oba*'s palace. They hear and respond to petitions and requests confided to them by women and men from different parts of Benin City and modern Edo State (formerly part of a more extensive former Benin kingdom). A wife considered influential inside the palace has more opportunity to attract followers outside the palace. She can also become knowledgeable of grassroots sentiments and issues that may not yet have reached the *Oba*. Such queens are rewarded personally by petitioners, increasing the capital and fund of intelligence available to her for further investment and material return. A queen can choose to use her influence on the outcome of disputes through her decision for action *or* inaction on the inside information she obtains – and compares across different sources. Queens have direct power in making decisions about their own property and its management, but they depend on their middlemen and women to carry out their orders and must be astute in choosing and using them. Queens, even those favoured by the *Oba*, can effect their decisions with regard to matters of importance to them, if they are judicious in what and when they choose to press a case. The *Oba*'s "favourites" are considered to have even more influence generally with others at the palace. Given that Benin women and men frequently operate in quite different spheres of action, their knowledge is seldom derived from the same sources. I suggest these dual streams of information coming from different but complementary sources potentially play important and political roles in the decision making of the *Oba*, and others beyond.

Close examination of activities of wives residing deep in the interior of the royal harem show they are and are not out of touch with the outside world. Rather, they are tied through their husband and their extended families (whose contacts are constantly widened by marriages) and linked to outside communities. A queen who is capable and has the skills can articulate a vital

---

[11] The present women's groups at the *Oba*'s Palace consist of the *Isikhuian*, the daughters and wives of chiefs; and a new one, *Ugwuaguwaba*, created for the mother of Oba Erediauwa (1979 – present); and the first Queen Mother to reign since the nineteenth century, Iyoba Aghahouwa (1981-1998).

and valuable network of people. Her choices are made to enhance her position in the harem, please the *Oba*, and maximize her possibilities for individual success. The latter is defined in terms of values and material goods (see the section on "Queens, *Iloi*" that follows).

Iloi: wives of the *Oba*

The royal wives or queens, *iloi*, as they are known in Benin, while rarely visible in public, have stood for traditional measures of success in marriage for women (and coincidentally for men). Success was and still is measured in number of children, followers, "name," proper burial, and remembrance. Polygamy, the marriage of one man to two or more wives increased a man's chances for success, especially in an agricultural society. Success for a woman in a traditional home meant a child or children raised to maturity, thus insuring her old age, a decent burial, and remembrance. Polygamy still flourishes not only at the royal court, but in Nigeria generally, where today it is paradoxically afforded by poor men as well as wealthy ones. The practice is usually masked by feigned ignorance, tolerated by the public, and often openly accepted. It is rarely challenged in the legal system that is based on *de jure* equality of the sexes and monogamy in marriage.

Each evening the queens in the royal harem retire to their separate quarters with their own children. Their servants (and in the past, slaves) also returned to the quarters they occupied adjacent to them. Periodically, queens move to special houses in the harem when they have their menses, and return to their own homes when the cycle is completed. During that time they neither cook nor engage in any activities inside or outside the harem. The queens will meet together under the aegis of the leader of the harem, the *Eson*, the *Oba*'s senior wife, in her home or in an open courtyard. They discuss issues of importance to them, plan for their role in festivals, watch young children together at play, and meet with older ones coming from school or from abroad with news to tell. They enjoy themselves and the children especially at storytelling under the stars when the *Oba* joins them in the harem. Many princesses mentioned to me such happy times they remembered as children that were shared with their father *Oba* Akenzua II.

Queens, otherwise conduct their affairs in private to the extent possible. Their affairs include managing their estates in other villages and towns, as well as businesses, houses, and other enterprises they either brought with them or acquired in the harem. In the old days their personal activities in the harem included trading (in cloth, beads, food stuffs, etc.) and creating domestic arts that generated income. In this regard they resembled most wives in harems across Benin, who were effectively, but more modestly (than royal wives) capitalized by their husbands with gifts or set-asides of land to be cultivated and animals to be raised. The proceeds wives receive from their enterprises are theirs to keep. In this way the *Oba*, as well as other husbands make their wives partially or fully self-sustaining; with leeway to demonstrate and profit by their individual initiative and abilities.

Men are forbidden to enter the harem. Audiences with them are conducted from a distance across the courtyard in front of the main harem entrance. Close female relatives of a queen or the wife of an important chief or civic leader may be admitted to one of the outer reception halls to greet the queens, to petition for someone else, to discuss a request, and to convey information. Today messages are usually conveyed in notes sent either through the Palace pages, *emuada,* who are celibate young males, or through the female servants who attend the queens. No one else is allowed to enter the harem itself. Visits by the queens outside the palace harem are still rare, and made only with the *Oba*'s permission.

The *Oba*'s wives, unlike a reigning Queen Mother, were and still are virtually invisible and largely unknown to the outside world. With few exceptions even their Palace names are not known to most people. A person wishing to refer to them (as I witnessed a number of times at festivals and on visits) often does so indirectly, referring to some observable quality, saying, "Ah, there is the *Yellow* Queen," or "See there is the *Black* Queen, etc." Even those who might have known of her or her family before she entered the Palace do not use their original given names: it is forbidden. Once the *Oba* gives you a name the old one is "forgotten" and never used again. At the palace and among those who either wish to or need to have contact them, the queen will be known and called by the name or names of their children, such as *Iye Ewere,* or *Iye Omoregbe,* for example, (respectively, meaning "Mother of Princess *Ewere,*" or "Mother of Prince *Omoregbe,*" and so on).

Among the rare descriptions of the *Oba*'s wives is an eye-witness account given by a British medical doctor, Dr. Felix N. Roth (M.R.C.S., and L.R.C.P.), who accompanied the 1897 "Benin Punitive Expedition." The occasion was the formal surrender of *Oba* Ovonramwen; the date the fifth of August, 1897. The *Oba* re-entered the city on that day, after six months of evading capture in the bush. He was richly dressed and heavily laden with coral beads. His Highness processed to his captors with an entourage of seven hundred or eight hundred persons including:

> Some twenty of his wives, who accompanied him, were of a very different class from those [women] seen previously. They had fine figures, with their hair worn in the European chignon style of some years ago, really wonderfully done in stuffed rows of hair, the head not being shaved on top like that of the lower classes, and they wore coral necklaces and ornaments and hairpins galore. [12]

On reaching Old Calabar, the British granted the *Oba*-in-exile his request that some of his wives be sent to join and comfort him. Two wives were sent initially, and two others joined him a little later. Their presence is made visible for the first time through nineteenth century photography.

---

[12] Ling Roth 1968 (1903), p. xiii

The harem: people in place

Among the *Oba*'s three main Palace societies the *Ibiwe* society had specific responsibility for the welfare of the *Oba*'s wives and children. The head of *Ibiwe*, the *Ine*, is the leader and looks after the royal household in general. The *Oshodin*, his second, is charged with looking after the harem in particular. He settles quarrels among wives that can not be settled by the *Eson*, the *Oba*'s senior wife. If there is too much conflict in the harem, the *Eson* calls on the *Oshodin* to intervene. He may enter the outer reception hall of the harem to conduct an inquiry among the parties involved. During such a query or on a visit, the *Oshodin* "sits down" on one of the polished red clay banquettes against the white wall of the large reception room, at a distance across from the women he meets and questions. Theoretically, this *Ibiwe* chief, the *Oshodin*, is empowered to settle any serious or unresolved problems even between the *Oba* and one or more of his wives. When asked how he would proceed, the *Oshodin* replied, "You must talk to each separately." Then with a smile he said, "Difficult to say...can you settle a tiger and a goat? If you want to cross a river with a tiger, do not take a goat along."

Among the queens it is the *Eson*, the *Oba*'s senior wife, who manages the harem day-to-day, and its wives and children. She is called, "The cock who crows the loudest," meaning she is to be heard and obeyed by all the other wives. The *Eson* is always the most senior wife in the harem, although she is not necessarily the *Oba*'s first wife. Other *Esons* may have left the harem, passed away, or been banished for cause. Whoever is the *Eson*, must see to it that order and harmony are preserved in the harem's domain if she is to retain the *Oba*'s favour. She has the most power and influence over the wives and their children by virtue of her position as the senior wife and leader of the harem. Every harem and polygamous household in Benin had its "*Eson*," who was its leader and senior wife. Younger wives who are "favourites" may use their influence in private, unbeknownst to her, to benefit themselves through his affections.

Eunuchs

The chief liaisons to the outside world of the royal harem in the old days were eunuchs, castrated or impaired males, who served the *Oba*'s wives into the early twentieth century. They constituted a separate group of persons who lived in the harem in their own quarters near the inner doors. It was the duty of eunuchs to "guard" the Queens in the harem, and they performed daily supervisory and other duties. They could mingle with the women and even touch the Queens. Eunuchs moved about freely within the harem itself, and between the harem's sacred space, and other parts of the compound of the *Oba*'s palace. They also moved about in the profane world outside the Palace. The profane world posed dangers of pollution to the wives through accidental or other contact, and threatened the lives of those who had touched them. A queen who befell that misfortune was expelled in disgrace from the Palace.

Eunuchs were much sought after outside the harem by those seeking interviews with and favours from the queens. They carried messages and took action on behalf of the queens in other parts of the Palace, in the city, into the countryside and beyond. Eunuchs greatly enriched themselves, thereby, and enjoyed autonomy and considerable discretion with regard to others, both inside and outside the harem. They used their power and influence among the wives and those petitioners who sought them out. The presence of eunuchs was noted by various European traders and visitors to Benin City, being remarked at other large towns that had local rulers from the sixteenth century on. The presence of eunuchs confirms the existence of royal harems in the contact period (and probably much earlier as I suggested in the previous section).

[Sir] Richard Burton, a peripatetic world traveller provided an eye witness description of a Palace eunuch in the mid-late nineteenth century: "*He was a little beardless old man, clad in a tremendous* petticoat ... [emphasis mine]." What Burton calls a "petticoat" (a woman's nineteenth century undergarment akin to our "slip"), was really more like a crinoline that *pouffs* out a wide gathered skirt or dress that was worn over it. The "petticoat" was actually a standard garment for Benin men, called a "wrapper," and tied in several styles. The wrapper's width or puffed out appearance was the result of a stiff woven fibre underskirt on formal occasions; and ordinarily the result of many layers of cloth on top, wrapped around a man's waist to achieve maximum width. The quality, quantity, and type of cloth as well as the overall bulk of a man's wrapper were key indicators of his wealth and status. Evidently, this eunuch was very important and successful.

Burton added the eunuch:

> "...assumed considerable dignity, speaking of the head Fiador [a major chief] as of a very common person." Burton observed, "The abominable institution is rare in Africa, and when found is borrowed from Asia. At Benin the habit of secluding the king's women has probably introduced their guardians of the harem."[13]

Palace pages

The last Palace eunuchs were remembered as a child by *Oba* Akenzua II's daughter, Princess Adesuwa, who married according to "native law and custom" in the harem, in 1959. There have been no eunuchs in the royal harem since the early 1940s and 1950s. Instead, the *Oba*'s youthful and celibate pages, *emuada,* carry messages to and from the queens, liaising with the *Oba* and others for them. They also carry notes and provide information from outsiders to the queens. But they can not touch them, nor do they live in the harem itself as the eunuchs once did. Their quarters are in another part of

---

[13] Ling Roth 1968 (1903), p. 40

the *Oba*'s palace. The senior *emuadas,* the *odionwere,* head pages, are the leaders of their group. They carry the *Oba's* swords of office, and act as special messengers. It is said there were also prepubescent female pages that belonged to the same palace societies (*Iweguae, Ibiwe*) as the male pages. The difference between the two groups was the girls left the palace once they reached puberty. The young men stayed past puberty until released by the *Oba* who used to give them a wife and land with which to start adult life. The girls are chosen to look very much alike, so no one can recognize them or tell them apart when they are acting as go-betweens and performing a service.

The Queen Mother

In historic sources and the literature on Benin there are few descriptions of the *Oba*'s wives. The woman most often mentioned by Europeans is the Queen Mother, who held the title of *Iyoba,* created by Oba Esigie (Ca. 1504-1550 A.D.) for his birth mother. *Idia* is the first woman to become *Iyoba,* and the Queen Mother of Benin. These women are the ones who may be mentioned after European contact in reports and diaries of visitors, traders, and explorers. She is also the woman most often represented in art in bronze, brass, and ivory. Her title, *Iyoba,* is literally translated as the (birth) mother of the *Oba.* Unlike queen mothers elsewhere she has no role in running of the *Oba*'s harem, in choosing his wives, or in conferring with her son face-to-face. Her palace, built for her by her son, is separate from his and situated at a distance. She never again enters his harem or palace once she is made *Iyoba.* Nevertheless, she continues to support him and keeps him apprised of the sentiments and actions in the larger outside community. As the *Iyoba,* she assumes a male gender role and functions as a senior male chief, hearing cases and settling disputes within her district and villages. [14]

Those *Iyobas* who came after the first Queen Mother *Idia,* held court at their own palaces, at *Uselu,* on the outskirts of Benin City, until the twentieth century. Those who were wealthy or powerful were noted in later periods of affluence in the mid- eighteenth to early nineteenth centuries. With economic decline and internal political turbulence in the late seventeenth century there were serious lapses of faith among indigenous Catholic converts in Benin City. Their lapses undoubtedly included resumption of human sacrifice, as well as "idolatry", and the "juju shrines" that were reported.[15] The Queen Mother (possibly *Iyoba Imarhiaede)* famously assisted the Portuguese Catholic missionaries fleeing Benin City at the end of the seventeenth century.

The recent reigning Queen Mother Aghahouwa (1981-1998), followed a traditional route to into the Palace. As a young girl, rumours of her beauty reached the Palace, and she was taken to the Palace. She was given to one of the trusted wives of *Oba* Eweka II (1914-1933) who raised her until she reached puberty. Then, *Oba* Eweka II married her to his first son who was later crowned and reigning as *Oba* Akenzua II (Ca. 1933-1978). As a young

---
[14] Kaplan, 1993, pp. 100-101
[15] Egharevba 1960, p. 37

bride the *Iyoba* told me she remembered wearing *bubu,* contemporary dress of the period and head tying cloth. She attended church, and afterwards was much admired by her husband and his friends who visited their home then outside the palace.

After Akenzua II came to the throne, however, they returned to the palace: she to the harem again, this time with the title of *Eson* the senior wife and leader of the harem. Then, she said, she wore a wrapper, the traditional dress, a sarong-like wrapping of cloth tucked in above the bosom and under the arms, and reaching to the ankles. The hairstyles she wore then were those reserved for queens, *iloi*; and modified according to her changing status with the birth of the future *Oba*, other children, and award of a title. The number and quality of the coral beads worn in her hair, and on her neck, wrists, and ankles, were a reflection of both her wealth and the favour she found in the *Oba's* eyes. The type and quality of cloth she wore were a statement of her importance and position. She wore imported brocades, hand woven Yoruba narrow strip- loom sewn cloths, *Ashoke,* "George", and later "lace" as it became prestigious. So, too, the dress of other wives reflected their means and relative status, as well as the favour they found with the *Oba*.

Where *Iyoba* Aghahouwa's path to and in the palace diverted from tradition was the decision of Oba Akenzua II, her husband, not to "put her away," after she gave birth to the first son, and future heir to the throne. She had other children for her husband after the future *Oba*. Later, she became the first Queen Mother to reign in nearly one hundred years (the last being Oba Ovonramwen 's mother, *Iheya* or *Iha* II, (Ca. 1888). Oba Erediauwa bestowed the title of *Iyoba* on his mother, the twenty-first of August 1981. Thereafter, *Iyoba* Aghahouwa, followed tradition by holding court at *Uselu* on certain days, hearing complaints, and receiving people from the community, as well as other visitors. Some came to greet her, others to have disputes heard and decided, and still others to have requests granted. She reigned until 1998 when, at age ninety-five, she went to meet her ancestors.

Recruitment and harem politics

The *Oba's* harem was viewed by young women with great fears and anxiety. Most of them were already well aware of the competition among wives in polygamous homes. At the Palace the stakes were higher to bear children, especially the first son and the first two daughters, and the consequences of inadvertently violating *taboos,* as well as the marriage oaths were more intimidating. Their fears were worsened by the isolation from supportive family members young women knew awaited them. An *Oba's* wife might never see her mother or family again. Whereas adultery was severely punished in Benin, in the past adultery with an *Oba's* wife was worse and resulted in both parties being killed. There is a saying (and a warning) about this to others: *"The tree where the leopard reposes [climbs] no other animals dare climb," Erhan n'Ekpen hin ri-Aramwen oha ovbe re hienren."* [16]

---

[16] Pers. Commun., *Enogie* of *Obazuwa-Iko,* Benin City, August 10th, 2001

Traditionally, the wives of the *Oba* were recruited into the palace harem in several ways: by a declaration, as a "gift," or by being "noticed." A young girl could be declared "an *Oba*'s wife," by her father or a close male relative, and had to be brought to the palace. In Benin, the declaration was viewed by women as something of a curse, since entry into the Palace harem meant the girl was thereafter separated from her family. Mothers were particularly reluctant to let daughters go, since that girl might be *her* only child (the case of a favourite queen who was chosen by *Oba* Akenzua II). Fathers were less reluctant, especially chiefs, since they usually had many children, at least a dozen, or up to thirty and more children. I know many chiefs and princes today who have children in comparable numbers.

A child, however, is the most precious "gift" a man could make to the *Oba*. Children were promised in fulfilment of a vow taken by a father (or at a mother's behest): for an illness cured, a misfortune avoided, good fortune realized, or the safe delivery of a baby after troubled pregnancies. A child could be given to curry favour with the palace, or to express gratitude for an honour or title received from the *Oba*. A budding young girl whose beauty was widely noted would be sent to the harem to be trained in Palace etiquette as a future royal wife. This was the case of Queen Mother Aghahouwa, who was brought up in the harem by a trusted Queen of *Oba* Eweka II.

Aside from gifts of young girls to the *Oba*, a young woman might catch the *Oba*'s attention or be "noticed" at a festival, on a visit to a town or village, while touring the kingdom, or when hearing a petition at the Palace. This is the case of one of the present *Oba*'s favourite wives. An official was sent to ask for her, and she, willingly, was brought to him. In the past not all girls given to the *Oba*, were married to him. Some were given out to chiefs and others the *Oba* wanted to reward for their service. In the old days the *Oba* could, on occasion, take a married Benin woman into his harem with impunity. Many *Obas* had liaisons with women outside the Palace, but there were no concubines in the royal harem. There were only wives and their children, wives-to-be, attendants, servants, and up to the late nineteenth century, female slaves taken in raids and wars. Those who proved reliable and trustworthy were rewarded, but they remained slaves, becoming neither concubines nor wives of the *Oba*. Queens were served by females only in the harem, except for pages and eunuchs in the old days. Oral traditions, like the one that tells the story how Queen Mother Idia's distinctive facial marks came to be made, on being "chosen" to marry Oba Ozolua *(Ca. 1481-1504 A.D.)*, speak to the personal anxieties a royal marriage engenders. [17]

Occasionally, a father would send a young girl who was considered incorrigible to the harem. There, she would be disciplined by the Queens. Isolation in the harem was itself a dreaded punishment; and when added to the hard work, withdrawal of food if stubborn, and other measures, the Queens usually produced the desired behaviour change. The wives also taught

---

[17] Kaplan, 1997/98, p. 91

by example, as their own behaviour was held to a high standard. The unruly child was soon reformed and returned to her family outside the Palace.

Despite the myriad ways that women were brought into the Palace, those the *Oba* wished to marry were carefully investigated beforehand. The girl's family had to be without stain and its members of good character and repute: wealth was not a criterion. Great care was taken there were no anomalies in the family of an intended wife or histories of physical or mental illness. In Benin, in general, marriage between members of the same lineage is forbidden, even at a distant degree.

Potentially the way to the palace was open to all women: there are no preferred lineages for marriage to the *Oba,* and no limit on the number of wives he could have. Those wives who came from the families of powerful chiefs came with considerable entourages of servants, slaves, and resources at their disposal, but that did not assure them status as a "favourite". It meant they had best chances of success in having relations with the *Oba* and at least producing a child or children. Some wives never had relations with the *Oba*; and others who did but never conceived. Those wives who came from more humble families relied on their attractiveness and demeanour to win his attention. Nonetheless, his wives provided links to families and communities throughout the *Oba*'s domain.

Of course, from time-to-time some wives and wives-to-be proved unable to adapt or were unsuited for life in the royal harem. These women were either sent away or looked for the chance to run away. [18] In those cases, they kept a low profile to avoid incurring the *Oba*'s anger and bringing harm to their extended family. Those wives who ran away tried to live quietly as far from the palace as possible. In early colonial days a runaway wife caused considerable problems for *Oba* Eweka II. He complained bitterly to a visiting British Resident of Ibadan about a policeman sent to dig in the palace, looking for a missing "wife" rumoured to have been sacrificed. [19] To dig in the ground at the palace, the abode of the ancestors in Benin, is an abomination. The missing woman (who may actually have been a servant in the Palace) was found to be alive and married, and living in a distant community. [20]

The *Oba* dispensed gifts among his wives and favourites, and provided staples virtually to all. Those who were good managers in administering their land or lands and houses acquired as a result of favour, or as gifts made to them by people seeking favours from the palace and the *Oba* could grow rich and comfortable in the harem. Each wife made decisions for herself and her offspring which enhanced their life chances, those of her family, and her community of origin. Certainly, there was intense competition among the wives, not only to have the first son, other sons, and daughters. Wives also competed to attract followers and to acquire resources from petitioners (conveyed through eunuchs in the past; and now by pages, and servants).

---

[18] Kaplan 1997/98, p.259
[19] Ward-Price, 1939, p. 238
[20] Pers. Commun. to the author, *Oba Erediauwa*, December 27th, 2004

Knowledge flowed to the Queens from their families, communities, and constituencies outside the palace. This intelligence was valuable to them, to the *Oba* and to others inside the palace. A wife's attractiveness to the *Oba* was balanced by her character and demeanour; and it was enhanced by the cleverness she showed in managing resources, including information, and in attracting followers. The wives' roles required "political" choices in the ways defined here.

Conclusions and comments

Entry into the harem opened the way for queens to develop client patronage, to obtain services from others, and to be rewarded materially. The *Oba*'s wives made decisions about the use and distribution of their resources in public arenas of action (e.g., in the harem, the palace, outside communities, villages, and the city). Visitors, petitioners, women's groups, chiefs, relations and others also laid the groundwork for development of personal networks. Each constitutes sources of influence and power that flows from and to the *Oba*'s wives. Together, they offer the queens on-going opportunity and flexibility within the ranked and structured hierarchy of the harem. That hierarchy includes a limited set of offices expressed in titles (*Ine, Osodin, Eson, Okaerie,* etc., and in categories of persons in positions of power. The *Oba* is the major source of power for the queens as he alone has the ability to award the only chiefly titles traditionally available to women who are his wives in the society. Award of a title to a queen is celebrated and her status (and influence) affirmed publicly, thereby increasing her personal capital.

The opportunity of royal women to rise in status, to choose and dispose, to garner and amass tangible, as well as intangible resources in the harem ultimately functions to make the harem an essentially open institution despite seclusion. It can be argued that seclusion and taboo actually enhance and cast a reflection of the *Oba's* power onto his wives. Further, that the *mana* that adheres to him as a sacred being, by its very nature, limits the access of others to him, and magnifies the roles of the queens. The joining of women from diverse levels of society in the royal harem ties the palace politically to the hinterland. It also projects centre stage the values and possibilities for women that were once pursued in all harems of the kingdom: a first son, children, a stable home, independent means, economic rewards, personal recognition, proper burial and remembrance. The restraints of the royal harem on personal mobility and visibility are compensated, even now, by those pursuits; and they are based on enduring Benin values: a "good head," individual initiative, service, personality, and cleverness. Thus, the harem with women in seclusion survives along with polygamy into the twenty-first century.

References

Adams, Captain John (1823) *Remarks on the Country Extending from Cape Palmas to the River Congo,* London: G. Woodfall.
Connah, Graham E. (1975) *The Archaeology of Benin,* Oxford: Clarendo.

Darling, P.J. (1984) *Archaeology and History in Southern Nigeria: The Ancient Linear Earthworks of Benin and Ishan*. Cambridge Monographs in African Archaeology 11, BAR International Series.
de Beauvois, Palisot (1801) *As to the Inhabitants of the Kingdom of Benin on the West Coast of the Tropical Africa*, Weimar: Industrie-Comptoirs
Egharevba, J.U, (1960) *A Short History of Benin*, Ibadan: Ibadan University Press
Egharevba, J.U, (1965) *Chronicles of Events in Benin*, Benin City: Kopin-Dogba Press.
Kaplan, Flora Edouwaye S. (1993) "Images of the Queen Mother in Benin Court Art", *African Arts* 26, 3
Kaplan, Flora Edouwaye S. (1997) "Iyoba, The Queen Mother of Benin: Images and Ambiguity in Gender and Sex Roles in Court Art" in Flora Edouwaye S. Kaplan (ed.), (1997/98) *Queens, Queen Mothers, Priestesses, and Power: Case Studies in African Gender*, vol. 810, New York: New York Academy of Sciences.
Kaplan, Flora Edouwaye S. (1997/98) *Queens, Queen Mothers, Priestesses, and Power: Case Studies in African Gender*, New York: New York Academy of Sciences.
Leonowens, Anna H., (1870) *The English Governess at Siamese Court: Being Recollections of Six Years in the Royal Palace at Bangkok*, London: Trubner.
Ling, Roth H. (1968) *Great Benin: Its Customs, Arts and Horrors*, London: Routledge and Kegan (originally published in 1903)
Montagu, Lady Mary Wortley (et *al.*), (1837) *The Letters and Works of Lady Mary Wortley Montagu*, New York: R. Bentley
Price, G. Ward (1939) *Year of Reckoning*, London: Cassell and Company, Limited
Slater, N. (1996) "Literacy and Old Comedy", in Worthington (ed.), *Voice into Text: Orality and Literacy in Ancient Greece*, Leiden: Brill

V

AIRTs in Diasporic Contexts

23

Orisha traditions in the West*

- Dianne M. Stewart Diakité

Pinpointing exactly where the *Orisha* chose to rest their pots in the Americas and the Caribbean is no easy task. They have danced and exchanged raffia with so many other gods commencing on Africa's soil and abiding across the Atlantic to slave settlements in the African diaspora.[1] Today, in the Black Atlantic world, beyond traditions claiming the *Orisha* appellative, we see traces of them in religious cultures such as *Vodou, Winti, Comfa, Kumina*, and Spiritualist and Sanctified Black Christian traditions. The *Orisha* can be examined as archetypes, principles, personalities, divinities, forces, energies, elements, and nature. In some senses, the *Orisha* are as old as time, encompassing and surpassing all of creation. From a cultural slant, the *Orisha* have come to rest in customs that comprise institutional religion and a spiritual orientation that now nurtures approximately thirty million people who pay homage to these illustrious and elusive entities. An estimated five million of these devotees make their homes in locations such as Salvador, Matanzas, Caracas, Tegucigalpa, Panama City, Port of Spain, Loiza, New York, South Carolina, Toronto, and Birmingham.[2]

Scholarly efforts to chronicle the dispersal of African religions throughout the Western Hemisphere unveil a tangled and enduring history of the multidirectional movement of African peoples across and around the Atlantic under circumstances as varied as diplomatic missions, global expeditions,

---

* (Reprinted from: *The Hope of Liberation in World Religions* (ed.) Miguel A. De La Torre (Waco Tx: Baylor University Press, 2008): Chapter 12: 239-256, 296-299

[1] See for example the works of Warner Lewis, *Guinea's Other Suns,* 1991, and Cabrera, *El Monte*, 1968, who interviewed devotees to African-derived religions in Cuba and Trinidad claiming mixed ethnic African heritages. Isabella Castellanos translated one such testimony from Cabrera's *El Monte*: "When I arrived from school, I would leave the 'Cristo ABC' ...[words that began the ... primer], and my father who was a Musunde mayombero [a Congo priest] and my mother who was an iyalocha [a Lucumi priestess] would wait for me with the other primer ... the one from over there, from Aku and Kunansia. ... at home I had to speak Yeza and Congo, and just as I would learn the catechism and the prayers, I would also learn how to pray, salute, and worship in lengua (an African language). ... one would master that which was proper here, but knowledge about 'over there' was also required" (996:44). Also see Barnes, *Africa's Ogun*, 1997.

[2] Extensive demographic data on devotees to African-derived religions are not readily available. These estimates were cited from http://www.adherents.com/Na/Na_671.html and might be grossly understated. See for example the homepage of the International Congress of Orisa Tradition and Culture at http://www.orisaworld.org which states that "Orisa Tradition and Culture [plays] a central role in the day-to-day lives of over 100 million people."

commercial ventures, human trafficking, indentured labour programmes, evangelical enterprises, military conscription, back-to-Africa emigration schemes, exiting-Africa immigration schemes, and Diaspora-inspired ancestral pilgrimages to the "Motherland".[3] Across these landscapes of encounter, the Yoruba-based *Orisha* tradition has mushroomed into present-day movements and spiritual families of *omorisa* (*Orisha* initiates). Although it would be premature and in some circumstances incorrect to conclude that *Orisha* traditions have roots as primitive as the auction blocks where the enslaved were portioned out to the highest bidders, at present, *Orisha* is arguably the most celebrated African-derived religion in the West. In some regions across the Black Atlantic, *Orisha* traditions have even furnished the wider society with defining cultural scripts, templates for African consciousness, and a meta-language for African spirituality: consider how the names of *Oshun* and *Yemaya*, feminine archetypes of beauty and power, ooze from the jazzed spoken word of Lorenz Tate on the *Love Jones* soundtrack;[4] cowrie shells mean something more than decorative adornment to Santeros in the streets of Havana; and the term *"ashe"* has almost replaced "amen" in countless sanctuaries across the Black World. *Orisha* traditions, like other mainstream religions, broker today not just the secularization of the spiritual but also the consecration of the profane.

If this is not enough to warrant a place for *Orisha* among the established "world religions," since the last decades of the twentieth century, *Orisha* devotees worldwide have embraced a global awareness of Yoruba civilization and its theological import across local communities in Africa and the African Diaspora. Organizing under the comprehensive umbrella of the International Congress of *Orisa* Tradition and Culture (*Orisa* World Congress), practitioners and scholars of African-derived religions, especially *Orisha*-inspired traditions, have been holding global meetings toward the formal recognition and official documentation of *Orisha* as a world religion.[5] As a result, efforts at centralization and institutionalization complement attempts to protect the legitimacy of local *Orisha* expressions across the globe.

This essay offers an elaboration of liberation theological motifs in *Orisha* traditions in the West and is indebted to the mounting literature in this area, much of which is conceptually framed by theories of African retention and religious syncretism. To begin such a task, we cannot attribute to African religion any foundational liberation theological agenda as we find for example

---

[3] See, for example, Schuler, *Alas, Alas, Kongo*, 1980; Sweet, *Recreating Africa*, 2003; Wilmore, *Black Religion and Black Radicalism*, 1972; Matory, "Surpassing 'Survival,'" 2001; and Kamari Clark, *Mapping Yoruba Networks*, 2004.

[4] The (spoken word) lyrics are as follows: "... Now do they call you daughter to the spinning pulsar / Or maybe queen of the two thousand moons / Sister to the distant yet rising star / Is your name Yemaya? Awe, hell no! It's got to be Oshun!" See track one, "Brother to the Night (A Blues for Nina)," written by Reginald Gibson, performed by Larenz Tate, *Love Jones* (audio CD), Sony, 1997.

[5] The Orisa World Congress was founded in 1981. For the most updated information on the Congress, see the official Web site at http://www.orisaworld.org.

in the protest theologies of African North America and Latin America.[6] African religion is not primarily oriented toward responding to social suffering. On the other hand, African religion has all the ingredients for liberation thought and praxis. In East Africa Nyabingi and Mau Mau rebels[7] shrouded their skins and political convictions with African religion and the latter "saved our country from white rule and exploitation," my Christian-identified Kenyan classmate once remarked with pride during a seminar discussion on African theology. We can consider a number of examples across Africa, from Queen Ya Asantewa's military protest against British colonial occupation of the Gold Coast, to the Igbo women's rebellion at Aba, to Kimpa Vita's campaign to reunite the Kongo kingdom. Was it even possible for Africans to hunt or go to war without accessing their gods, ancestors, oracles, medicines, and spiritual technologies? In the context of racial slavery, liberation praxis, if not theology, was axiomatic for countless Africans who must have asked Nana Peasant's question over and over of the exotic Christian fetishes- crucifixes, bibles, medallions of madonnas and saints- "dat protect ya?!" and who, like Lucy in *Sankofa*, had the impulse to tear the ropes holding images of the Virgin Mary from around their converted kinfolk's throats.[8]

For practitioners of African-derived religions, trans-generational racial slavery constituted the preliminary circumstance compelling individual and communal liberation praxis, a condition of primordial deprivation indeed for those born in the slave economies of the Americas and the Caribbean with iron around their necks. The Christian demonization of African religions went in tandem with this culture of involuntary servitude, providing divine justification for African bondage in the West and a new beginning for a new creation: the black race. Both forms of oppression are, at the very least, social oppressions that have deprived persons, families, communities, and civilizations of life, liberty, justice, and sovereignty - indeed all that the West has outlined as fundamental human rights.

In this type of inquiry African, African American, Latin American, and Caribbean theologies should each have some relevance to a liberation theological analysis of *Orisha* traditions in the West. This notwithstanding, my approach to liberation theology in this essay takes seriously the professional theological claim that authentic conceptual sources for liberation theology are situated where grassroots communities, inspired by religious convictions, struggle for justice. In other words, I resist here a top-down approach that principally acknowledges the conceptual formation of scholastic liberation theologies. I seek then to interrogate the orientations, beliefs, practices, and experiences that might inform a scholarly elaboration of

---

[6] Given the overlapping identities of persons of African Descent in the United States and Latin America, I will employ variations of the terms "African North America" and African U.S. Americans when referring to black people descended from Africans enslaved in the United States.

[7] See Nyabingi Movement, 1991; Weigert, *Traditional Religion and Guerrilla Warfare in Modern Africa*, 1995; Maloba, *Mau Mau and Kenya*, 1993; Rotberg and Mazrui, *Protest and Power in Black Africa*, 1970.

[8] Julie Dash, *Daughters of the Dust*, A Geechee Girls Production, 1991; Haile Gerima, *Sankofa*, Mypheduh Films Inc., 1993.

liberation theology in *Orisha* traditions, many of them "hidden transcripts"[9] offering alternative sources of meaning and power. Since there are infinite angles from which to approach the subject, I will begin with a limited discussion of widespread patterns and trends that indicate common beliefs, pre-occupations, and priorities of many *Orisha* devotees across the globe. In so doing, I will explore specific theological themes that address the question of liberation for *Orisha* practitioners. Through this exercise, I hope to underscore the implicit and explicit attention given to multiple oppressions within *Orisha* communities.

Foundational features of *Orisha* religion in the West

Orisha traditions in the West have their beginnings in the Yoruba and neighbouring religious cultures of West Africa. Following the integration of so many African cultures under conditions ripe for extinction, *Orisha* traditions have unfolded with some variation in the Americas and the Caribbean. Numerous studies providing extensive accounts of the shared and divergent *Orisha* sub-traditions are now widely available and their contents need not be repeated here.[10] Instead, I will present a concise outline of some of the foundational characteristics embraced across a wide spectrum of practicing communities.

The *Orisha* religion bears witness to the created order as dually contained. Distinct but interactive communities populate each world domain. The invisible domain is home to a community of deities (also called *Orisa*), spirits, ancestors, and other powers, while human, animal, and vegetative life forms, as well as elements and minerals, inhabit the visible domain. Much of *Orisha* religious practice is organized around individual devotees' affiliation with one or two of the 400+1 divinities.[11] Each *Orisha* is associated with an abundance of qualities, talents and skills, natural phenomena, departments of life, occupations, virtues and vices, human anatomy and physiology, flora and fauna, colours and temperaments, and other aspects of life and creation. To take the example of *Oshun*, Isabel Castellanos describes her many *caminos* (paths) for Cuban devotees:

> Ochún, the goddess of love. On the one hand, Ochún is Ochún Yeyé Moró (also called Yeyé Karí): a sensuous saint, all full of *joie de vivre*, knowledgeable in the art of lovemaking, fond of music, beautiful clothes, and dance. Together with Changó, she epitomizes the fullness of life. At the other end of the spectrum, Ochún is Ochún Kolé-Kolé (also called Ibú-

---

[9] See Scott, *Domination and the Arts of Resistance*, 1990.
[10] See, e.g., Brandon, *Santerнa from Africa to the New World*, 1993; De La Torre, *Santerнa*, 2004b; Harding, *A Refuge in Thunder*, 1995; Houk, *Spirits, Blood, and Drums*, 1993; and Lindsay, *Santerнa Aesthetics in Contemporary Latin American Art*, 1996.
[11] One often hears *Orisha* devotees claiming one *Orisha* as the owner of their head and a second as the owner of their feet or a maternal and a paternal *Orisha*. Although in theory there are 400+1 *Orisha*, most diasporic pantheons tend to acknowledge no more than 50 *Orisha*.

Kolú). Poor, owner of a single faded dress, this Ochún eats only what Mayimbe, the vulture, brings to her door. Another Ochún, Ochún Awé or Galadé ... is intimately related to death... at the centre of the continuum sits Ochún Ológodi or Olodí, who is very serious and domestic. She is not a dancer and, like Yumú, she is fond of sewing and keeping house. All the other Ochúns fall somewhere between the two ends of the continuum. (1996:45)

In addition to these intricate deities upon whom *omorisha* lavish their devotional energies and attention, *Orisha* communities recognize a representative high God, *Olodumare/Olorun/Olofin*, a remote, gender-neutral deity to which most of the created order is attributed.[12] The created order is also home to a class of 200+1 antigods, collectively called *Ajogun*, and is infused with a ubiquitous force (*ashe*) that energizes and empowers everything within creation. *Ashe* is commonly understood as "the power to make things happen."

Orisha devotees rely on ritual specialists and divination as well as their personal *ori* (inner divinity/soul complex) to navigate through life. Life is a journey, and while *Orisha* upholds a polydemonic concept of evil (the 200+1 antigods), good and evil are anything but essentialized categories. Agency is conceived as neutral, ambiguous, and contextually "good" or "evil." Because power is everywhere and can be accessed and deployed with constructive or destructive intentions, *Orisha* devotees seek to protect themselves against any malicious or antisocial forces that can potentially compromise their health, prosperity, and well-being. Toward this end, they make offerings and sacrifices to their ancestors and deities as they submit petitions of all sorts. These can range from prayers for good health and financial security to satisfaction in one's personal relationships and professional stability. Many of these *ebo*, as they are called, are prescribed through two major oracles: *Ifa* and *Merindinlogun/Eerindinglogun/Dinlogun*. Both divinatory systems are essentially sacred texts where the collective wisdom of the Yoruba heritage is recorded in the poetry, chants, and narratives of the lives of the *Orisha*. A less elaborate form of *obi* divination is also widely practised among *Orisha* devotees when circumstances might simply require affirmative or negative responses to basic questions.

Consultations with ritual specialists via divination readings begin even before a child is born and continue after death, for it is believed that the departed are still active beings who have only transitioned to the invisible domain to strengthen their *ashe*, to achieve an even higher status in the ontological order, and to be destined for familial reincarnation. *Orisha*

---

[12] *Olódùmarè* is often conceived of as male in diasporic *Orisha* lineages. *Olódùmarè* is also referred to as the Creator God, but that title is not exclusive; for other *Orisha* such as *Ogun* and *Obatala* are cited in the *Ifá* corpus as participating in the creation of humanity. For this reason, I accept Kola Abimbola's preference for the terminology "high" or "representative" god as a referent for *Olódùmarè*. See Abimbola, *Yoruba Culture*, 2006.

devotees maintain intimate relationships with their departed ancestors with confidence that they will continue to receive ancestral guidance and support.

Much of the ritual protocol and performance in the *Orisha* religion is punctuated with pageantry and symbolic paraphernalia. When Zora Neale Hurston opined that the Negro decorates the decoration, she must have had *Orisha* devotees somewhere in the back of her mind. Hurston could not have captured more poignantly the aesthetic mode of religious apprehension one comes to experience at the ritual centre of African-derived religions where "there can never be enough beauty, let alone too much" (1981:53). There are countless ceremonies surrounding various stages of initiation to the priesthood, anniversary celebrations for deities, priests, and ancestors, not to mention naming ceremonies, marriages, and funerals. The expectation at most ceremonial gatherings is that the *Orisha* will manifest through possession trance and fellowship with the visible community. *Orisha* ritual life displays talented and skilled specialists from consecrated drummers to those called to perform the ritual sacrifices of two- and four-legged animals. The repertoires of songs, dance and percussive ensembles, and tastes and dislikes connected with each *Orisha* known to any given community are exhaustive and continue to expand as *Orisha* practitioners travel and share experiences with fellow devotees in distant places.[13]

The institutional structure of the *Orisha* ritual house or *ile* preserves spiritual lineages where initiates are brought into the religion by apprenticing with a priest (*iyalorisha/babalorisha*) under the *ashe* of the patron *Orisha* for that spiritual family. In many areas of the Diaspora, devotees refer to their initiating priests as "godmothers" and "godfathers." The *ile* functions as the centre of ritual life and training. Most *ile* centres carry the name of a patron *Orisha* and house consecrated altars for a number of deities in the *Orisha* pantheon.

Orisha traditions illustrate that religion is ultimately a way of life and offers humans tools for managing life. To manage life well requires mastering the self. Self-mastery is facilitated by the development of *iwa pele* (gentle and noble character) and acceptance of one's *ita* (life purpose). By living in accordance with the collective wisdom of the ancestors and the ethical teachings of the tradition (acquired through divination and experience), *Orisha* devotees negotiate personal and communal life with the aim of overcoming misfortune, disease, and oppression in the here and now. Living a satisfying and abundant life, which includes sharing one's prosperity and good fortune with others, is encouraged by the promise of ancestorhood and reincarnation in the life to come.

Another long-standing goal of *Orisha* traditions in the West continues to be surviving the blight of religious persecution. This preoccupation cannot be overemphasized nor should it be taken for granted when one considers the abundance of time, monies, and energy expended by so many colonial state

---

[13] See Murphy, *Working the Spirit*, 1994; Brown, *Santerna Enthroned*, 2003; Lindsay, *Santerna Aesthetics in Contemporary Latin American Art*, 1996.

and church authorities to obliterate all traces of African religion in the New World. More subtly promoted today, yet no less vicious, this mandate remains a primary preoccupation of extremist Christian fundamentalist groups (Lopes, 2004:858). Subjected to incessant surveillance during and even after the slave era, *Orisha* communities, like all religious groups under attack, were compelled to prioritize the battles they would fight and the strategies they would deploy to overcome subjugation. Defending their gods against death and cultivating the courage to be had to take precedence. From this resistance praxis, which expressed *the conviction to remain African*, one can identify resources for the liberation of Christian theology and for an *Orisha* liberation theology. To approach this task, it is imperative to examine *Orisha* responses to the colonial denigration of African religion from the perspective of creative agency and theological licence.

Erasing African Religion: Afrophobia in the *Orisha* experience and an *Orisha* theology of inclusion

The different branches of liberation theology bear witness to suffering communities from diverse socio-cultural locations. For this reason we have seen bodies of thought giving primary consideration to the problem of race (Black theology), class (Latin American theology), and gender (white feminist theology). Women of colour have also performed intersectional analysis of race, class, gender, and culture in their theological treatments of the African U.S. American, Latin American, Caribbean, African, and Asian experience. Turning to the experiences of devotees to African-derived religions, the threat of religio-cultural genocide within Afrophobic slaveholding societies and the continued defamation of African-derived religions to this very day is a common denominator suffered by all.[14] In reflecting on the Cuban context, Philip Zwerling summarizes well this pervading ethos: "It is clear that in colonial Cuba, the Yorùbá religion was denigrated as little more than black magic, and afro Cuban culture was mocked as a part of the stereotypically primitive and uneducated 'negrito'" (2004:305).

Under conditions such as these, African encounters with Christianity became evident in the rituals of most *Orisha* expressions, especially Santeria traditions across Latin America. I am certainly not alone in arguing that the "christianisms" embedded within African-derived religions are evidence of African people's agency, resistance to colonial aggression, and spiritual dexterity.[15] With the theological backing of Christian missionaries, colonial slaveholding authorities saw to it that the concepts "African" and "religion" became intransigently fixed signifiers in the New World imagination for depraved savagery and white Christianity. Never the twain could meet, except

---

[14] For a fascinating and extensive analysis of the denigration of Vodoun in the American press/media see Bartkowski "Claims-Making and Typifications of Voodoo as a Deviant Religion," 1998.
[15] Stewart, *Three Eyes for the Journey,* 2005; Hucks and Stewart, "Authenticity and Authority in the Shaping of Trinidad *Orisha* Identity," 2003; McCarthy Brown, *Mama Lola,* 1991; Métreaux, Voodoo in Haiti, 1972; and Aiyejina and Gibbons, "Orisa (*Orisha*) Tradition in Trinidad," 1999.

in the innovations of African religious spaces and rituals, the *cabildos* and "feasts", where many devotees protected themselves and their spiritual inheritance by feigning conversion to the Catholic faith. Their appropriation of a tradition construed to stigmatize and condemn them was an assertion of theological dissent, challenging normative Christian theologies that either upheld or accommodated African enslavement and campaigns prohibiting the religious freedom of enslaved African communities. Far from creating a new syncretic religion, *Orisha* devotees adapted their religious inheritance to New World conditions and adopted "christianisms" most concordant with their foundational theological orientation.[16]

I would propose that, within *Orisha* traditions emerging from slave societies, we find blueprints for one of the principal claims of the liberation theology school. *Orisha* practitioners' inventive engagement with Christian traditions allowed for the earliest New World translations of Christianity on and in African terms. (Contextualization is the foundational task collectively affirmed by Christian liberation theologians.) Each Catholic saint adopted into the tradition, for example, was constructed to have the same tastes, powers, and proclivities as an analogous *Orisha*. The literature, songs, dances, offerings, and attributes associated with each power were, for the large part, furnished by the African traditions that came to comprise the various expressions of *Orisha* religion in the Americas and the Caribbean. These and other innovative developments undoubtedly protected *Orisha* traditions from extermination. As the colonial establishment attempted to erase African religion, *Orisha* devotees in the New World gave new spellings[17] not only to the names of African religions but also to the Christian name, contesting the mythology that Christianity was authentic religion and wholly other than the collection of "superstitions" and "barbaric" practices associated with "primitive" Africans. Through comparative theology and analogous reasoning, they asserted the sameness of Christianity and *Orisha* qua religion demonstrating, against the exclusive narrative of Christian revelation, multiple areas of compatibility between the two religious orientations.

Another dimension of *Orisha*'s liberation theology of inclusiveness pertains to a communal concept that Christians have labelled "the people of God" or the "elect". Even liberation theology reserves a space for divine election (God's chosen sufferers and those who struggle in solidarity with them). Sylvester Johnson's study of this phenomenon in North America identifies some of the most sinister uses of divine elections. When coupled with divine curses and a preoccupation with saving/othering the "heathen", the consequences have been crippling for the non-elect.[18] *Orisha* traditions

---

[16] Most treatments of *Orisha* traditions interpret them as New World syncretic religions forged from two Old World traditions. I see the logic for such an argument, but in the end I respectfully disagree with this conceptualization.

[17] Funso Aiyejina and Rawle Gibbons, "Orisa (*Orisha*) Tradition in Trinidad," 42.

[18] Johnson, *The Myth of Ham in Nineteenth-Century American*, 2004. For an earlier Native American treatment of biblical election and American Christianity see Warrior, "Canaanites, Cowboys, and Indians," 1989.

differ drastically on this point. There is no intrinsic script of "us versus them" in African religions and for much of the history of *Orisha* presence in the New World this basic fact seems to hold true. Police records, newspaper accounts, travelogues, and even sensationalized fiction bear witness to the fact that racial exclusion from white privilege did not encourage similar discriminatory practices in *Orisha* communities. Whether deliberately or not, African people, particularly in Latin American contexts, were successful in convincing many whites of the credibility of the *Orisha* religion. As João José Reis notes, "the history of Candomblé in nineteenth-century Bahia is the history of its creolization and *ethnic and racial mixing*" and by the latter part of the nineteenth century, "the sources so far available give the impression that all-African *terreiros* lived side by side with racially and ethnically mixed houses" (2001:129-31; emphasis in original).[19]

There is the invitation in black theology for privileged whites to become "ontologically black," and to express their "preferential option" for the poor and oppressed in Latin American theology. In *Orisha* traditions, the whites who spilled blood on the altars of the gods became African, at least spiritually and to some degree culturally, for there is no other way to practice this tradition without assenting to an African orientation and lifeworld. In this sense, *Orisha*, an African religion widely discredited in the Christian West, has managed to supplant Christianity as the grounding religious orientation for a sizeable number of phenotypic whites and mestizos in Latin America. This very fact is enough of an indictment of Christian arrogance and claims of universal relevance and it offers a fresh location for comparative theological dialogues intent on purging racist theological imaginations.

During the last quarter of the twentieth century, however, a new ideology and reformist theology began to take expression among black communities of *Orisha* devotees who, in some instances, questioned not only whether whites could partake of an African tradition but were also malcontented with how "white" the *Orisha* tradition had become. Concentrated expressions of this new black religious nationalism are evident among African U.S. American and Trinidadian converts to the *Orisha* religion.

Race-ing African Religion: Africa-centrism in the *Orisha* experience and Black Nationalist theologies of cultural reclamation

Under the *Orisha* umbrella we also find communities of black devotees dispensing with the christianisms that were adopted during periods of brutal censorship and repression. Racism and racial experience have encouraged a great proportion of phenotypically black devotees to claim the *Orisha* inheritance while appealing to African continental expressions of Yorùbá religion and culture as the most authentic and authoritative theological

---

[19] Also see Harding, *A Refuge in Thunder,* 1995; and Fandrich, "Defiant African Sisterhoods," 2005.

source. Many following this *Orisha* persuasion are professed black nationalists who see no promise of liberation for people of African descent in the Christianities currently claiming the hearts, souls, and minds of millions across Africa and the African diaspora. Tracey Hucks has argued that this "reclamation of Africa" through Yorùbá religion emerges time and again as an exercise of liberation theology and practice for personal, familial, and communal emancipation from the multidimensional oppression blacks have endured in the Christian West.[20]

By the 1960s, this theological platform became most pronounced in the United States within the discourse and praxis of a series of *Orisha*-based institutions, launched under the leadership of Oba Oseijeman Adefunmi I (1928-2005). Most definitive were the Yoruba Theological Archministry (New York City) and Oyotunji Village, which was founded in Sheldon, South Carolina, in 1972. The extent of Adefunmi's influence on African American and Caribbean converts to the *Orisha* religion has yet to be documented. His innovative Black Nationalist interpretation of the Yoruba religion offered a credible alternative for African U.S. Americans and others in the black Diaspora in search of African grammars of religious meaning. The introduction posted on the official website of the Oyotunji Village describes best the import of this movement for African U.S. Americans who, for the most part, had no tangibly accessible long-standing *Orisha* or African-derived religious institutions toward which their energies might be directed:

> 1959 is when the Gods and Goddesses of Africa were reclaimed by and for Africans in America. Before that time, to speak of Gods and Africa in the same breath was seen as blasphemy, hearsay or at least insanity. Until then, it had not been fully conceived or perceived that we: Africans in [America] or elsewhere were reflections of the divine energy which permeates the universe. After the deities return[ed] we could envision the heavens filled [with] African Goddesses and Gods and simultaneously see ourselves in the images of these divine entities. At last, the beginning of spiritual freedom. No longer are we dependent on the God of Palestine or Arabia for our salvation. Our Path to the heavens will be illuminated by Cultural Restoration![21]

Little did these black converts to the *Orisha* religion imagine that the struggle to "reclaim the African Gods and Goddesses" would not be unidirectionally aimed at severing all ties with mainstream Christian traditions. The struggle would likewise take place within the arena of *Orisha* theology and ritual practice as many white Cubans insisted on setting the parameters for recognition and official inclusion/initiation as well as

---

[20] See Tracey Hucks, "Approaching the African God: An Examination of African American Yoruba History from 1959 to the Present," PhD. Dissertation, Harvard University, 1998.
[21] Oyotunji Village, "About Us." See http://www.oyotunjiafricanvillage.org/about.htm.

ideological and aesthetic propriety. Appalled by the African-centred consciousness and perhaps threatened by the Black Nationalist orientation of fervent latecomers to a religion most of them had taken for granted since birth, more than a few Santeros resisted this encroachment upon their religious identity. This battle for *Orisha* terrain is certainly not exhaustive across the racial and ethnic divides of Latinos and African U.S. Americans, for there are countless examples of co-operation, empathy, and reciprocity between the two communities (Vega, 1995:201-6). Nevertheless, lingering tensions encouraged one anonymous African U.S. American devotee to tackle the issue in plain frankness with an essay entitled "A Debt Paid In Full: Latin and African-American Relations within the *Orisa* Community." Under the three most controversial subheadings "The Guilt Trip," "You Can't Keep Me out of My Own House," and "Living with the Black Stain," the author renders a fairly candid indictment of the exclusivity and ultimately racist demeanour exhibited by some Latino devotees toward African U.S. Americans and calls for honest and open dialogue in healing the rift between the two communities.[22]

Marta Vega sheds light on this moment in U.S. *Orisha* history as a period when "African Americans and Cuban Americans had to confront cultural barriers and racist attitudes before the *orishas* could encompass both communities." She goes on to write:

> The participation of the African American Community in Yoruba traditions increased *Orisha* exposure, but publicity made the Cuban traditional community uneasy, since many of its members were illegal aliens trying to maintain a low profile. The images of Catholic saints in Cuban/Puerto Rican Yoruba practice created another point of conflict between Latinos and African Americans, who wished to remove all images of Western European oppression from the tradition. These issues motivated African Americans to look increasingly towards Nigeria for their development of the *Orisha* traditional belief system. (1995:205)

An analogous situation has also unfolded within the *Orisha* community in Trinidad. Since the 1970s, Black Nationalist dissolution with all things white and Christian created elbowroom for new initiates within an already existent grassroots *Orisha* religious culture. The *Orisha* community has had to negotiate an ideological and theological divide that continues to generate both healthy and less salutary internal debate. In one camp we find devotees faithful to the ritual innovations absorbed by the tradition in earlier periods, and in another camp, those attempting to dispense with christianisms and other alien influences[23] toward the end of reforming the tradition in

---

[22] Roots and Rooted. "A Debt Paid in Full: Latin & African-American Relations within the *Orisa* Community." See http://rootsandrooted.org/afam-latin-relations.htm.

[23] Other traditions wielding influence over *Orisha* practice in Trinidad include rituals locally attributed to the "Kabbalah" tradition and Hinduism.

accordance with the rituals and theology of continental Yoruba religion. Through such growing pains, the Trinidadian *Orisha* tradition fared much better than Brazilian Candomblé in the discursive game of government "endorsement" and is positioned today among diasporic *Orisha* communities as perhaps the most organized and respectfully engaged in national public life and civic participation.[24]

However one views the broken *Orisha* calabash,[25] *Orisha*'s propensity for inclusion over exclusion is clearly an indispensable resource for internal dialogue not to mention its relevance to other established traditions such as Christianity and Islam. Today, difficult dialogues are certainly occurring across *Orisha* yards, speaking volumes about the theological health of the tradition. By the same token, equally important conversations about gender, class, and sexuality are muted within a number of communities on the ground and are just beginning to receive attention in the scholarly canon.[26]

In addition to an ethic of inclusion, another critical domain of *Orisha* ritual and thought should be prioritized in a discussion on liberation theology. The conception of the human in *Orisha* (and other African/African-derived religions) offers a theologically mature and affirmative portrait of *human becoming*. It also instinctively interrupts the Christian conception of human deprivation and the ontological inadequacy widely associated with blackness and African descendants in the Christian imagination.

There is no beginning and no ending to the story of humanity: the *Orisha* anthropological heritage

Underlying much of the discussion thus far is the *problem of the heathen*. This problem breathed new life into the twin projects of European expansion and Christendom. It goes without saying that Africans committed to the preservation of *Orisha* traditions would hardly find appealing a theological anthropology condemning them to double depravity, in need of redemption from original sin. Moreover, the nature of this sin is nothing other than being born into a world with the wrong colour, with the wrong culture, and pledging allegiance to false gods. Contesting this salvation history, where a white Christ is promised to return and rescue black/brown souls, is an implicit liberation theology in the logic of *Orisha* worship that prevailing scholastic liberation theologies have yet to interrogate.

---

[24] See Henry, *Reclaiming African Religions in Trinidad*, 2003. For critical commentary on the Brazilian government's racist appropriation of Candomble, Umbanda, and other African-derived Brazilian religions as a means of containing and depoliticizing the black masses, see Ferreira Da Silva, 2005:32-51; do Nascimento, *Brazil*, 1979; and Lopes, 2004: 838-60.

[25] Wande Abimbola has described the Yoruba/*Orisha* tradition as a broken calabash with scattered pieces across Africa and the African diaspora. See his *Ifa Will Mend Our Broken World* (Roxbury, Mass.: Aim, 1997).

[26] See Settles, 2006: 191-207; Clark, *Where Men Are Wives and Mothers Rule*, 2005; and Conner, 2005:143-66.

In *A Theology of Liberation*, Gustavo Gutiérrez attempted to characterize the new school of liberation theology noting that "today there is a greater sensitivity to the *anthropological aspects* of revelation" (1988:6-7); italics in original). This was and continues to be true of liberation theologians who have taken seriously the historical Jesus and his social location as an oppressed Jew under Roman imperial domination. For my purposes here, Gutiérrez's characterization invites comparative analysis of *Orisha* and Christian liberation thoughts on the question of theological anthropology. There are dimensions of *Orisha* belief and practice that, under mundane circumstances in pre-colonial Africa, had no intended social protest agenda. In the context of New World slave societies, the manifestation of deities in human form among *Orisha* devotees carried additional theological meanings. Each time God took on human flesh was a protest against the denial of humanity and humane treatment to enslaved Africans. And for what purpose does the Divine rest with and in humanity? Certainly not to redeem lost souls. Instead of embracing a theological anthropology of fallenness and the diminishment of Ham, *Orisha* ritual life centres on the performance of a theological anthropology that transmits humanity.

The "anthropological aspects of revelation" in the *Orisha* tradition allow humans to experience the Divine face to face, indeed to become Divine. We cannot underestimate how valuable this must have been to those obliged to labour under the curse of Canaan. Their bodies and souls knew that Genesis was *wrong* and their descendants relive this anthropological inheritance at every *bembe* celebration and sacred crossroads. In this theological schema we are compelled then to respect the cyclical understanding of the life process, and life experience – a *"livity"* (if I may borrow a term from the Rastafari tradition) which might be punctuated with all kinds of prophets and miracle workers but has no place for salvation history and the second coming of Christ. Even a liberationist Christ cannot replace the Communion of Ancestors and their responsibilities to those left behind. As indicated in the subsequent section, human struggles against injustice do not rest in the sole inspiration of one Messiah.

Liberation imperatives for articulating *Orisha* theologies

We know for certain that the "black church" in North America was not alone in providing institutional refuge to fugitive slaves.[27] The record of black resistance in Cuba tells us that "[h]istorically Santeria meetings had functioned in colonial times as covert gathering places [*quilombos*] to plan slave uprisings and anti-Spanish rebellions" (Zwerling, 2004:307). The Yoruba Cabildo, *Shango Tendum*, which sponsored a plot to topple the colonial regime in 1812 is one such example of many known and unknown spiritually inspired slave protests (Howard, 1998:11). Indeed "[a]s late as 1912,

---

[27] For sources on the African U.S. American independent church movement and abolitionist activism, see Wilmore, *Black Religion and Black Radicalism,* 1972; Cone, *For My People,* 1984; and Raboteau, *Slave Religion,* 2004.

an Afro Cuban revolt, joined by many santeros, was viciously suppressed by a Cuban government allied with the United States" (Zwerling, 2004:305). This pattern of resistance is repeated across the diaspora. And why wouldn't it be? Can any human being prostrate in chains before the altar of a foreign god, hungry for human sacrifices, neglect to seek refuge in her own? According to Brazilian historian, João José Reis:

> The sources insist that many candomblés of Bahia served as hideouts of fugitive slaves. Up until the middle of the century, newspaper and police reports expressed fear that African drumming served as rehearsals for slave uprisings. In 1826, a direct link can in fact be shown to have existed between a Candomblé house and a slave rebellion, involving a *quilombo* (runaway-slave community) on the outskirts of Salvador, where the police found a house containing several objects related to African religious rituals. (2001:130)

The absence of tangible evidence situating Candomblé at the spiritual and political root of a plethora of slave revolts[28] does not mean that the relationship between Candomblé liberation praxis and the 1826 rebellion should be counted as an aberrant occurrence in Brazilian slave history. Rather, it might suggest that Candomblé devotees were successful in covering their tracks, in eliminating the possibility of discovery as purveyors of socio-political resistance against the slaveholding regime. There is still much to discover about *Orisha* traditions and liberation praxis in Brazil and the wider African Diaspora. Apart from the conventional litmus test of religion-based slave revolts, Reis reminds us that:

> Candomble terreiros...became a major haven for runaway slaves, who sought them for religious obligations and other kinds of assistance, spiritual and secular. Slaves frequently looked for religious specialists to obtain herbs and concoctions to pacify their masters and to enlist the services of gods in obtaining the slaves' freedom. They often paid for consultations and services with goods stolen from masters (Reis, 2001:130).

Scholars and practitioners alike should do everything to publicize this suppressed narrative of African-derived liberation theology and praxis, a narrative that has not even made its way into the footnotes of Christian liberation theological texts. Grasping this historical picture of *Orisha* liberation praxis makes even more intelligible the contemporary interpretation of *Shango* as a deity of social justice requiring direct action

---

[28] Reis concedes that the 1826 revolt "provides ... the only explicit evidence of [the connection between African religion/Candomblй and slave uprisings] in a period when, conversely, Muslim slaves and libertos rebelled several times" (2001:130).

against systemic oppression.[29] The current literatures circulating in the *Orisha* community also convey a serious level of awareness about the role of religion in combating social oppressions. One Internet poll tallied responses from reported *Orisha* devotees on the "State of *Orisha* Community." Out of ten questions posed, five relate directly to the imperatives of liberation theology. To the question of whether "*Orisa' Ifa* worship has a role to play in the advancement of society," two hundred viewers responded of which 75 per cent strongly agreed and another 19 per cent agreed, with only 1 per cent strongly disagreeing. Of two hundred respondents, 52 per cent strongly agreed that "*Orisa* temples need to [be] more involved in feeding, clothing and housing poor and low-income families." This was followed by 23 per cent agreeing and 19 per cent mildly agreeing, with 1 per cent strongly disagreeing, 2 per cent disagreeing, and another 2 per cent mildly disagreeing.[30]

Taking nothing of the above for granted, if *Orisha* and other African-derived religions are ever to escape the discreditable verdict of worldwide condemnation, theologies delineating what *Orisha*/African religion is not are also imperative. As one Vodouisant remarked: "There is no such thing as Voodoo; it is a silly lie invented by you whites to injure us" (Seabrook, 1929: 27). The occasion to disrupt the automatic attribution of horrific antisocial rituals to African sacred traditions has long passed. This is not to deny that people of African descent, even some purporting spiritual allegiance to an African-derived religion, might readily engage in such dealings. It is to say though that the phenomenon of "evil sorcery" is neither sponsored by African religion nor by any other religion on the "primitive" side of the globe. Rather, it is a universal threat to the integrity of all religions. There is no doubt a conceptual understanding in African and other global religions that persons and invisible agents can deploy mystical power for harmful purposes. Still, no one would think of reducing Christianity to "Satanism" just because its conceptual framework contains the notion of "the devil," an agent who deploys mystical power toward harmful ends.[31] In the same poll noted above, 94 per cent of 199 respondents affirmed that "the *Orisa* community needs a legal defence fund to protect our right to practice," with 60 per cent of that number "strongly agreeing."[32] This issue has also been considered within umbrella organizations like the *Orisa* World Congress and the National

---

[29] Devotees in the Trinidadian *Orisha* community conspicuously embrace this image of *Shango*.
[30] Roots and Rooted. "Poll." http://www.rootsandrooted.org/poll001.htm.
[31] Daniele Mezzana identifies with precision the ideological bias at work in reductionistic representations of African Religion. According to Mezzana, "...there has always been a widespread tendency to interpret and assess African traditional religions starting from 'local,' or specific practices, which are then generalized without valid reason. This is the case with certain magical rites—which, incidentally, many such religions are opposed to—and of figures such as the feticheurs. Something no one would dream of doing with other religions; no one, for example, would define the essence of Christianity by the excessive devotional practices towards a given saint found in rural areas or—to mention a recent case—by the holy water jinx which the trainer of the Italian football team performed for the whole world to see on television. Nevertheless, this is what has happened, and continues to happen, with regard to African traditional religions." See Mezzana, *African Traditional Religion and Modernity: The End of a Stigma*, http://www.africansocieties.org/n3/eng_dic2002/religionitrad.htm, accessed August 4, 2007.
[32] Roots and Rooted. "Poll." http://www.rootsandrooted.org/poll001.htm.

African Religious Congress (NARC) and definitely presents an important theological focal point around which all *omorisha* can unite.

The imposed and internally generated tensions and silences under the *Orisha* umbrella position multiple sources for theological and ritual renewal at the centre of the debates and dialogues taking shape today in the community. African continental and diasporic *Orisha* lineages together offer a rich heritage for theological reflection and praxes of inclusion. We locate such angles of vision not only in longer standing *Orisha* communities that find religious meaning in Christianity and other traditions but also in novel trends and innovations. An important outcome of Black Nationalist attempts to approximate "authentic" Yoruba religion is the discovery of ancient African traditions that can actually challenge oppressive ideologies and practices within Diaspora lineages. For example, Black Nationalist legacies offer good reasons for the assumption that appeals to African sources for reconstructing Diaspora cultures entail absorbing more repressive gender patterns. But this after all may not be entirely true. A significant discovery gleaned from continental Yoruba contexts is that many of the male deities in the Diaspora pantheon were originally portrayed as feminine or gender-neutral in Africa.[33] What kind of feminist theologies of liberation might emerge from the image of a female hunter (*Ochosi*) to balance some of the stereotypical characterizations of femininity we find in the personages of *Oshun* and *Yemaya*? How might the diasporic bleaching of *Oshun* be challenged by more profound understandings of the beautiful in Yoruba philosophical thought?[34]

In the study of Yoruba history we also encounter a contested terrain of religious leadership and narratives of an extensive female priesthood that contravene diasporic trends of positioning the almost exclusively male *Ifa* priesthood at the apex of Yoruba knowledge and sacred science.[35] If not already underway, the potential to replace the Christian Bible and faith confession with an invented *Ifa* "Bible" and a form of Yoruba-*Ifa* evangelism exists in some circles. The continental Yoruba heritage, if engaged critically and thoroughly, offers as well as any other religious heritage platforms to dispute the masculinist project of aping God.

A final thought

Christian liberation theologies retain the privilege of having emerged within the same religious family as the "oppressor". This very fact ensured the production of a liberation theological voice that would conform to the methods and conventions of the western academy. If we examine earlier periods in Christian history, however, or in the history of any fragile religion

---

[33] Important examples from the most popular deities include *Olokun, Ochosi, Obatala and Olodùmarè*. See Abimbola, *Yoruba Culture*, 2006.
[34] See Settles, "The Sweet Fire of Honey," 2006. Also see De La Torre, "Ochun," 2001:837-61.
[35] See Peel, *Religious Encounter and the Making of the Yoruba*, 2001; Olupona, *Kingship, Religion and Rituals in a Nigerian Community*, 1991; Drewal, *Yoruba Ritual*, 1992; and Murphy and Sanford, *Osun Across the Waters*, 2001.

on the verge of extinction, protest material emerges as apocalyptic vision or in the silences of symbols and gestures. It is hoped that the coerced political quietude of operating underground will not frustrate the activation of liberation theologies among African religious communities in the New World. The task, however, begins with acceptance of alternative paths to liberation theology forged by communities still struggling with the category of "primitive religions." We cannot in all fairness expect of *Orisha* traditions that which no other could produce under similar constraints. The one looking over her shoulder is not preoccupied with the discipline required of the academician's pen. And then, the question should be asked, what kind of scholastic liberation theologies might *Orisha* communities produce? Perhaps the conversations here undertaken, not solely in this essay but in this very volume, can catalyze fragile religious traditions to contribute conceptual vistas to the liberation project. Most alluring for me, beyond the protest imperative, is the quest for the beautiful so melodramatically conveyed in *Orisha* and other African-derived religions. A different theological grammar emerges from this quest and might afford the children of the darker gods a new sense of the transmission of humanity (Stewart, 2005: xvii).

I think Frederich Schleiermacher was right about the essence of religion; but Hurston captured the point with the most compelling insights. Why does the Negro decorate the decoration after all? To remedy the tragic; to make life beautiful and extraordinary, and to feel deeply – deeply touched and transformed beyond ordinary self-limitations. There is an aesthetic orientation that keeps the old young and the weary strong. One must vibe with this aesthetic in the company of *Ibeji*.[36] Like the hums and chants of Negro spirituals and *Odu Ifa*, one must move in frequency with its polyrhythm, collapse into its coolness, and absences. This mode and its cadences (Hurston helped us to see) alert us to the sacred explosions that thrill, silence, and overwhelm us with unspeakable freedoms.

References

Abimbola, Kola, 2006. *Yoruba Culture: A Philosophical Account*. Birmingham, U.K.: Iroko Academic Publishers.

Abimbola, Wande, 1997. *Ifa Will Mend Our Broken World* (Roxbury, Mass.: Aim)

Aiyejina, Funso, and Rawle Gibbons. 1999. "Orisa (*Orisha*) Tradition in Trinidad." *Caribbean Quarterly* 45, no. 4 (December): (35-50)

Barnes, Sandra T., ed. 1997. *Africa's Ogun: Old World and New*. Bloomington: Indiana University Press

Bartkowski 1998. "Claims-Making and Typifications of Voodoo as a Deviant Religion: Hex, Lies and Videotape." *Journal for the Scientific Study of Religion* 37, no. 4 (1998): 559-79

Brandon, 1993. *Santería from Africa to the New World: The Dead Sell Memories*. Bloomington: Indiana University Press

Brown, David. 2003. *Santería Enthroned: Art, Ritual, and Innovation in an Afro-Cuban Religion,* Chicago: University of Chicago Press

---

[36] The *Orisha* Ibeji represents the phenomenon of twins/twinning.

Brown, Karen McCarthy. 1991. *Mama Lola: A Vodou Priestess in Brooklyn*. Berkeley: University of California Press.

Cabrera, Lydia. 1968. *El Monte: igbo, finda, ewe Orisha, vititi nfinda: notas sobre las religions, la magia, las supersticiones y el folklore de los negros criollos y el pueblo de Cuba*. Miami: Ediciones C.R.

Canstellanos, Isabella. 1996. "From Ulkumi to Lucumi: A Historical Overview of Religious Acculturation in Cuba." In *Santeria Aesthetics in Contemporary Latin American Art*. Ed. Arturo Lindsay Washington, D.C.: Smithsonian Institute Press: 39-50

Clark, Mary Ann. 2005. *Where Men Are Wives and Mothers Rule: Santeria Ritual Practices and Their Gender Implications*. Gainesville University Press of Florida.

Clarke, Kamari, M. 2004. *Mapping Yoruba Networks: Power and Agency in the Making of Transnational Communities*. Duke University Press

Cone, James H. 1984. *For My People: Black Theology and the Black Church. Where Have We Been and Where Are We Going?* Maryknoll, N.Y.: Orbis Books.

Conner, Randy P. 2005. "Rainbow's Children: Diversity of Gender and Sexuality in African-Diasporic Spiritual Traditions." In *Fragments of Bone: Neo African Religions in a New World*. Ed. By Patrick Bellegarde-Smith. Chicago: University of Illinois Press: 143-66

Dash, Julie, 1991. *Daughters of the Dust* (VHS). A Geechee Girl Production

De La Torre, Miguel A. 2001. "Ochun, [N]either the [M]other of All Cubans, [N]or the Bleached Virgin." *Journal of the American Academy of Religion* 69, no. 4: 837-61.

De La Torre, Miguel A. 2004b. *Santería: the Beliefs and Rituals of a Growing Religion in America*. Grand. Rapids: Eerdsmans

do Nascimento, Abdias. 1979. *Brazil: Mixture or Massacre: Essays in the Genocide of a Black People*. Dover, Mass.: Majority Press

Drewal, Margaret, 1992. *Yoruba Ritual: Performers, Play, Agency*. Bloomington: Indiana University Press

Fandrich, Ina J. 2005,"Defiant African Sisterhoods: The Voodoo Arrests of 1850s and 1860s in New Orleans."In *Fragments of Bones: New African Religions in a New world*. Ed. By Patrick Bellegarde-Smith. Chicago: University of Illinois Press (187-207)

Ferreira Da Silva, Denise. 2005 "Out of Africa? Umbanda and the 'Ordering' of the Modern Brazilian Space." In *Fragments of Bone: Neo African Religions in a New World*. Ed. By Patrick Bellegarde-Smith. Chicago: University of Illinois Press. 32-51

Gerima, Haile *Sankofu* (VHS), Mypheduh Films Inc., 1993

Gibson, Reginald. 1997. "Brother to the Night (A Blue for Nina)." In *Love Jones* (audio CD), Sony. Performed by Lorenz Tate.

Gutierrez, Gustavo, 1988 [1973]. *A Theology of Liberation: History, Politics, and Salvation*. Trans. and ed. by sister Caridad Inda and John Eagleson. Maryknoll, N.Y.: Orbis. Originally published in English by Orbis

Harding, Rachel. 1995. *A Refuge in Thunder: Candomblé and Alternative Spaces of Blackness*. Bloomington: Indiana University Press.

Henry, Frances. 2003. *Reclaiming African Religions in Trinidad: The Socio-Political Legitimization of the Orisha and Spiritual Baptist Faiths*. Port of Spain: UWI Press.

Houk, James. 1993. *Spirits, Blood, and Drums: The Orisha Religion in Trinidad*. Philadelphia: Temple University Press.

http://www.adherents.com/Na/Na_671.html

Hucks, Tracey and Dianne Stewart, 2003. "Authenticity and Authority in the Shaping of Trinidad *Orisha* Identity: Toward an African-Derived Religious Theory." *Western Journal of Black Studies*, Vol. 27, No. 3 (176-85)
Hucks, Tracey, 1998. "Approaching the African God: An Examination of African American Yoruba History from 1959 to the Present," Ph.D. Dissertation, Harvard University
Hurston, Zora Neale, 1981. *The Sanctified Church*. Berkeley: Turtle Island Foundation.
International Congress of Orisa Tradition and Culture at http://www.orisaworld.org
Johnson, Sylvester. 2004. *The Myth of Ham in Nineteenth-Century America: Race, Heathens and the People of God*. New York: Palgrave Macmillan.
Lindsay, Arturo, ed. 1996. *Santería Aesthetics in Contemporary Latin American Art*, Washington, D.C.: Smithsonian Institution Press.
Lopes, Nei. 2004. "African Religions in Brazil: Negotiation and Resistance: A Look From Within." *Journal of Black Studies* 34, no. 6 (838-60)
Maloba, Wunyabari O. 1993. *Mau Mau and Kenya: An Analysis of a Peasant Revolt*. Bloomington: Indiana University Press.
Matory, Lorand. 2001. "Surpassing 'Survival,': On the Urbanity of 'traditional Religion' in the Afro-Atlantic World." *The Black Scholar* 30, nos 3-4 (36-44)
Métreaux, Alfred. 1959. *Voodoo in Haiti*. Trans. by Hugo Charteris. London: Andre Deutsch.
Mezzana, Daniele *African Traditional Religion and Modernity: The End of a Stigma*, http://www.africansocieties.org/n3/eng_dic2002/religionitrad.htm.
Murphy Joseph M. and Mei-Mei Sanford (eds.), 2001. *Osun Across the Waters: A Yoruba Goddess in Africa and the Americas*. Bloomington, Indiana: Indiana University Press
Murphy, Joseph M. 1994. *Working the Spirit: Ceremonies of the African Diaspora*. Boston: Beacon.
Olupona, Jacob K. 1991. *Kingship, Religion and Rituals in a Nigerian Community: A Phenomenological Analysis of Ondo Yoruba Festivals*. Studies in Comparative Religion 28. Stockholm: Almqvist & Wiskell International.
Oyotunji Village, "About Us." See http://www.oyotunjiafricanvillage.org/about.htm.
Peel, J.D.Y., 2001. *Religious Encounter and the Making of the Yoruba*. Bloomington & Indianapolis: Indiana University Press
Raboteau, Albert. 2004. *Slave Religion: The "Invisible Institution" in the Antebellum South*. Oxford: Oxford University Press.
Reis, João José, 2001.Candomble in Nineteenth-Century Bahia: Priests, Followers, Clients." In *Rethinking the African Diaspora: The Making of a Black Atlantic World in the Bight of Benin and Brazil*. Ed. by Kristin Mann and Edna G. Bay. Portland, Ore.: Frank Cass (116-34)
"Roots and Rooted. A Debt Paid in Full: Latin & African-American Relations within the Orisa Community." http://rootsandrooted.org/afam-latin-relations.htm.
"Roots and Rooted. Poll." http://www.rootsandrooted.org/poll001.htm.
Rotberg Robert I., and Ali Mazuri (eds.). 1970. *Protest and Power in Black Africa*. New York: Oxford University Press.
Rutanga, M. 1991. *Nyabingi Movement: People's Anti-Colonial Struggles in Kigezi 1910-1930*. CRB Working Paper No. 18 Ctr. for Basic Research.
Schuler, Monica. 1980. " *Alas, Alas, Kongo: A Social History of Indentured African Immigration into Jamaica, 1841-1865*. Baltimore, MD: Johns Hopkins University Press.
Scott, James. 1990. *Domination and the Arts of Resistance: Hidden Transcripts*. New Haven: Yale University Press

Seabrook, William B. 1929. *The Magic Island*. New York: The Literary Guild of America. (Cited in Bartkowski, "Claims-Making and Typifications of Voodoo as a Deviant Religion" (559-79)
Settles, Shani. 2006. "The Sweet Fire of Honey: Womanist Visions of Osun as a Methodology of Emancipation," in *Deeper Shades of Purple: Womanism in Religion and Society*. Ed. By Stacey Floyd-Thompson. New York: New York University Press: (191-207)
Stewart, Dianne M. 2005. *Three Eyes for the Journey: African Dimensions of the Jamaican Religious Experience*. New York: Oxford University Press
Sweet, James. 2003. *Recreating Africa: Culture, Kinship, and Religion in the African-Portuguese World, 1440-1770*. Chapel Hill: University of North Carolina Press,
Vega, Marta. 1995. "The Yoruba *Orisha* Tradition Comes to New York." *African American Review* 29, no. 2 (201-6)

24

Dilemmas, controversies and challenges of African descendant *Ifa* priests and practitioners in the United States: some reflections

- Tony Menelik Van Der Meer (Awo Alakisa)

As we approach the second decade of the twenty-first century, the practice of *Ifa* continues to spread wider and deeper throughout the world—spreading from Yorùbáland of southwest Nigeria. The presence and manifestation of *Ifa* can be seen in Argentina, Brazil, Columbia, Cuba, Haiti, Mexico, Trinidad and Tobago, Venezuela and the United States (W. Abimbola 1997). *Ifa* is also spreading in many other places in the Caribbean, Latin and South America. In Cuba, Brazil and Trinidad—perhaps a more distinct cultural identity and unique national expression of *Ifa* practice exist within these various countries. In the United States—the question of a distinct cultural identity and its unique national expression is still evolving and developing among African descendant *Ifa* priests and practitioners.

In Cuba there are the *Lucumi* who have their own national expression of *Ifa/Orisa* practice; *Candomble* in Brazil and *Shango Baptist* in Trinidad. While one will find ethnic diversity between African descendants among priests and practitioners living and residing in the United States, there is also broader diversity of *Ifa/Orisa* practice based on national expression, i.e., *Lucumi, Candomble* and *Shango Baptist* living together in close proximity. All of these traditions are practised in the United States and in some cases side by side. While the sources of these practices are clearly Yorùbá, the songs, rituals and customs differ among the groups to some notable degree.

Ifa is the Yorùbá divinatory practice of casting *ikin* or throwing the *opele* chain by an *Ifa* priest to access the sacred knowledge/literature of *Odu* which contains stories of the *orisa*; it is the name of the divinity; and it is medicine and incantations (K. Abimbola 2005). In Brazil, the practice is primarily in the form of orisa. Trinidad also practices a form that is centred on the *orisa* (*Eerindinlogun*, 16-cowry shell divination), but is moving more in the direction centred on traditional *Ifa* divinatory practice. Cuba has a longer history that is more inclusive of all aspects of *Ifa*.

Over the past 20 years there have been a considerable number of African descendants in the United States, especially African Americans who have connected with master Nigerian *babalawos* and were initiated in various places of Nigeria in Ile-Ife, Osogbo, Oyo, Abeokuta, Ibadan and Lagos under different traditional *Ifa/Orisa* families. More recently, there are traditional *Ifa/Orisa* initiations occurring in the United States and Trinidad.

It is fair to state that the Cuban national expression of *Ifa/Orisa* practice in the United States have been an existing tradition for *Ifa* priest and practitioners since the 1950s (Brandon 1993). Among the growing Yorùbá influence over the 20 years—there is a growing shift—especially among African Americans identifying with an indigenous Nigerian expression of *Ifa/Orisa* practice. It is this shift and dynamic that has created *dilemmas, controversies* and *challenges* for African descendant *Ifa* priests and practitioners in the United States.

It is easy to note that there is a distinct set of common songs, dances, music, rituals, and customs as displayed among *Lucumi* or *Shango Baptist* practitioners during ceremonies, festivals or rituals. This display of traditional Nigerian *Ifa* practices among African descendants in the United States is not yet common as Brazil, Cuba and Trinidad. Why is this so, and if it will change, then how and when will it come about?

These practices among the *Lucumi, Shango Baptist* and *Candomble*, raise larger questions regarding the existence of the development of a national expression of African descendant *Ifa* priests and practitioners in the United States. Are there things in particular to the historical experiences and conditions of African descendants born in the United States that will emerge as some form of a national cultural identity that manifests or distinguishes itself within the practice of *Ifa*?

Background

My experience with *Ifa* began when I became aware of the practice in 1976 through Aukram Burton (*Ifatoojola*), then an African American Orisa-*Lucumi* practitioner, now an *Ifa* priest initiated in Oyo. In 1978, I had a reading done by Zaid Haynes (*Ifayomi*) of Jamaican roots, then an *Obataala* priest—initiated in the *Lucumi* tradition in the United States, now an *Ifa* priest initiated in Ibadan. Ifatoojola initially came out of the house of a Shango *santera* (priestess), Margie Baynes Quiniones (*Shangogumi*) who is believed to be the first African American priestess initiated in 1961 in New York, by Cuban priestess Leonore Dolme (Brandon 1993). While under the tutelage of Quiniones, Aukram received his *warriors* (Elegba, Ogun, Ochossi, and Osun (warrior orishas)) from Francisco (Pancho) Mora (*Iretegunda*), also believed to be the first Cuban *Ifa* priest who resided in the United States since 1946 (Brandon 1993). Ifatoojola eventually brought me to a *Centro* (a spiritual meeting) in Boston at the house of a Cuban *Yemaya* priest, Jorge Fandino. In 1983, I received my *warriors* from Jorge and eventually left his house sometime in 1992.

It was in 1994 when I participated in a workshop on Obi Abata that I met Afolabi Epega followed by classes by *Awise Agbaye* Wande Abimbola. After a series of classes and workshops with *Awise* Abimbola, he did a divination for me and eventually I received my one hand of *Ifa* (*Owo-Ifa-kan*) from him. *Awise* Abimbola conducted a four year program of *Ifa/Orisa* classes and workshops in the Boston area. He also did a series of classes in New York and Atlanta. I attended all of the *Awise's* classes and workshops during his time in Boston as well as assisted him with spiritual work. In 1999 I travelled with *Awise* Abimbola to Nigeria where I was initiated into *Ifa*. During that trip, Patricia McLeod (*Sangowumi*) from Trinidad was initiated to *Sango* and Marie Clark (*Osanlafunke*) from Miami was also initiated to *Obataala*.

In 2000 I travelled again to Nigeria with *Awise* Abimbola. During this particular trip there were 12 people who were initiated on his compound. Three of the initiates were *Awise's* sons. Four of the initiates were Latinos from Los Angeles, three men and one woman. There were also four African American males, one Haitian American woman and one European American male. During that trip to Nigeria, I also received a chieftaincy from the *babalawos* of Oyo along with James (Jim) Kunavich, a European American from Chicago, initiated in *Ifa* in the *Lucumi* tradition. Jim received the Title of *Erimi Awo Alaafin of Oyo* and I was given the Title of *Akogun Awo Alaafin of Oyo*.

Throughout the years, I continued to assist the *Awise* and attended many more of his classes and seminars, as well as regular *Ebi* (Orisa family) gatherings in Boston or Atlanta for those who were initiated in Oyo. Beginning in 2005, I visited Atlanta several times a year to continue studying with *Awise* Abimbola at the Atlanta *Ifa* Institute founded by him.

From 2001 to 2007, I visited Cuba on average twice a year, participating in numerous ceremonies and discussions with *Ifa/Orisa* priests and practitioners about the tradition and practice there. Through his travels to Nigeria and Cuba and studies and practice of *Ifa*, *Awise* Wande Abimbola is one of the few Master *Babalawos* who saw and continues to see the need for training *Ifa* practitioners throughout the Diaspora as well as emphasizing the importance of orality, understanding *Ifa* philosophical and spiritual principles, studying the literature of *Ifa* and learning the Yorùbá language. In *Awise* Abimbola's book, *Ifa Will Mend Our Broken World: Thoughts on Yorùbá Religion and Culture in Africa and the Diaspora*, he states,

> I have seen all of these problems, and I know the power of the United States in terms of communications. I know that if we are not careful, if we allow the situation ... go on for one generation, it may lead to the extinction of this religion, or create a new type of spirituality which is no longer to be regarded as Yorùbá. This is why I came here to educate people who I hope will commit themselves to training on a regular basis for a number of years. They will receive comprehensive information pertaining to the major divinities. They will become a new generation of priest and priestesses knowledgeable about Yorùbá culture and religion. They will know how to

divine competently, and recite the verses of *Ifa*, maybe in translation. They will know the chants of West Africa. Above all, I hope that they we will succeed in nurturing people who have Iwa pele (good character), which is the epitome of religion, Iwa lesin (Character is religion). (W. Abimbola 1997:26)

The work and focus that *Awise* Abimbola has set forth touch in many ways on the *dilemmas* of African descendant *Ifa* practitioners in the United States.

Dilemmas

From my own experiences, I see many dilemmas that exist for African descendant *Ifa* priests and practitioners in the United States; however, there are several major issues I will focus on here. Despite the dilemmas, *Ifa* priests of African descent in the United States (primarily African Americans) are on the cutting edge of bringing forth a viable spiritual practice to a broad population who would be receptive to the wisdom, philosophy and spirituality of *Ifa*.

Before the influence and emergence of contemporary Nigerian Yorùbá traditional *Ifa* divinatory practices in the United States, the Cuban influence was dominant and is still very influential. The Cubans are the ones outside of Nigeria who have preserved *Ifa* as a system. The Cuban *Ifa* tradition in the United States also has a system of which a culture of *Ifa* and *Orisa* (*Eerindinlogun*) priest exist. The Cuban system has common rituals, songs, dances and ceremonies that are practiced throughout the United States within Latino as well as in African American communities. Botanicas are common in these communities where spiritual items can be purchased for rituals, ceremonies and the propitiation of the divinities—even the local Bodegas (convenience stores) sell religious candles.

To a large extent, the Cuban tradition in the United States has an environment that supports its practice. Although the rituals and ceremonies are in Spanish, the Cuban system incorporates the Yorùbá language or what can be considered Spanish Yorùbá into their practice. They have adapted aspects of Yorùbá language within their own cultural linguistic context, even though they do not speak Yorùbá as a fluent language; they, however, do a great job in incorporating it in their practice ritually.

Some of these issues are dilemmas for African descendant *Ifa* priests and practitioners in the United States who practice contemporary Nigerian traditional *Ifa*. Unlike the Cubans and to some extent Trinidadians, African descendants in the United States have not been exposed to/or have a history of *Ifa/Orisa* practice as a system. What I mean by a system is common rituals, songs, chants, ceremonies that incorporate the language and exist within an environment that supports it as a culture.

A key dilemma for African descendant *Ifa* priests and practitioners in the United States is centred on the issue of environment. The African descendants who are initiated in Africa do so in an environment and culture that has centuries of people exposed to ritual and spiritual customs, ceremonies and festivals inherited in Yorùbá culture. The process of divination, *ebo* (sacrifice), *Owo-Ifa-kan*, *Te'fa*, conferring titles, Masqueraders; and the art and craft of making icons and ritual items and drums all have rich histories and rituals within themselves.

In Nigeria (as well as Cuba) there is an open culture of *Ifa/Orisa* priests that reinforces values, customs and standards for the community. There are structures and order for rituals, ceremonies, and festivals, along with specialist and divisions of labour. The environment of *Ifa/Orisa* practitioners in Yorùbáland also lends itself to sacred spaces—groves, shrines, rivers, forests, hills—as well as access to plants, palm nuts, kola nuts, chickens, goats, fish, etc.

African descendant *Ifa* priests and practitioners in the United States are virtually naked when it comes to this issue of an environment of practice. The question of an environment of practice makes the concern of orality, the application and practice of *Ifa/Orisa* as an oral tradition a very difficult proposition for African descendants in the United States. In the United States, there is a heavier reliance on reading verses in books of *Odu Ifa* than on those verses being committed to memory.

The environment of practice of a system supports what Peter B. Vaill in his book *Learning As A Way of Being*, addresses what he calls "continual learning,"

> In other words, it means continually exploring learning as a way of being as a *system*. Continual learning is nothing less than a developmental process of learning as a way of being. It is certainly never over or complete; a learner can never be sure that he or she has made hardly more than a start. The more fully a person achieves learning as a way of being, the more he or she will see that there is more to learn and will also see that the learning can be undertaken in the comfort of a fuller and fuller realization of the way of being (1996:80).

Learning as a way of being is about internalizing *Ifa* cultural practices into a functional system for African descendant priest and practitioners in the United States. This requires that an environment is created that simulates aspects of contemporary Nigerian traditional *Ifa* practice and is fused with the historical cultural narrative of African descendants in the United States. For many African descendants initiated in Nigeria who experience these rites of passage, do so in the context of their own experience, are, according to Jerome Bruner, "self-narrating...from the outside in as well as from the inside out. When circumstances ready us for change, we turn to others who have lived through one, become open to new trends and new ways of looking at ourselves in the world." (2002:84)

The point is that African descendants also have an experience and story to put on the table. The process of African descendants from the United States getting initiated to *Ifa* is about "self-examination and self interpretation" (Drewal 1992:63). This process is about one's transformation and selfhood. On this question of selfhood, Bruner again adds,

> One cannot resist the conclusion that the nature and shape of selfhood are indeed as much matters of cultural concern...as of individual concern. Or, to put it another way, selfhood involves a commitment to others as well as being "true to oneself." Selfhood without such commitment constitutes a form of sociopathy—the absence of a sense of responsibility to the requirements of social being." (2002: 69)

Perhaps the key to understanding Yorùbá culture and the deeper mysteries and philosophies of *Ifa* is in the language. Yorùbá language is a key dilemma for African descendant *Ifa* priest and practitioners in the United States. The use of Yorùbá language in rituals and ceremonies is very powerful and healing—it is a medicine in itself when used by priest on certain occasions. Chanting *Ifa* in Yorùbá is especially efficacious when completing *ebo*'s for supplicants.

The lack of knowledgeable African descendant *Ifa* priests and practitioners who have some proficiency of Yorùbá language only adds to the dilemma of our deeper learning of and engagement with *Odu Ifa* as well as deeper and more meaningful ways to give guidance to those who seek the wisdom of *Ifa*. Understanding the language allows African descendant *Ifa* priest to retrieve *Odu Ifa* verses from more primary sources of *Ifa* priest, while also learning from those priests' experiences and their understanding and nuances of those verses. Through Yorùbá language, the sacred knowledge of *Ifa* will be more accessible as *Awise* Abimbola points out, "Anybody who aspires to lead the community of one particular *Orisa* must be very knowledgeable about the mythology, history, the chants, the very character of that Orisa. This religion is based on knowledge" (W. Abimbola 1997:160).

It is also, by learning the Yorùbá language that African descendant priest will be able to learn *Ifa* verses faster as well as retain them. There is a key distinction between learning in Yorùbá how a verse is chanted by a credible *Ifa* priest and learning a verse from a book or on the internet.

Controversies

There are many controversies among African descendant *Ifa* practitioners in the United States and probably more controversy about them from priest and practitioners from other traditions of *Ifa/Orisa* practices. Three primary controversies would include the issue of *money* that is charged, as it relates to fees and services; *women* initiated in *Ifa*, and their roles; and the initiation of *European Americans* and their access to the sacred knowledge of *Ifa*. Class, gender and race are issues that need to be addressed in a forward and honest matter—it is not something to be silent or whisper about.

Ifa is not free. There is generally some exchange that takes place, be it barter or money. However, money is a big controversy for many reasons. One of the principles of *Iwa Pele* is humility (Kamara & Van Der Meer 2004). Those who are humble in material terms within the United States don't have much access to being initiated to the mysteries and sacred knowledge of *Ifa*. If one wants to be initiated in the Nigerian system in Nigeria, one is now looking at a minimum of $5,000. Initiations in the United States can double, tripled and even quadruple that amount. To receive one hand of *Ifa* in the United States, the fees range from $1,000 to $3,000 in some places. Is *Ifa* becoming commodified and gentrified to the point that it is out of reach to the poor and working class whose lives are in need of spiritual mending? Or will *Ifa* continue to be used to heal people's broken worlds and help rebuild our communities?

Women of African descent in the United States are in many ways on the cutting edge in terms of their initiation in *Ifa*. In many ways this is a new space for women and this is controversial not only among *Lucumi* practitioners but those of African descent who are initiated in the traditional Nigerian *Ifa* system. The idea of women initiated in *Ifa* is considered sacrilegious to some *Lucumi Babalawo* as well as those of African descent in the United States.

There are numerous *Ifa* verses that speak of women being included in the affairs with men. Is this controversy a case of sexism and or a lack of knowledge of *Ifa* sacred literature? Fasina Falade, an African descendant *Ifa* priest born in the United States and practising in Los Angeles, California points out in the *Odu, Ose Otura* how 400 of the divinities didn't recognize the contributions of Osun. As a result, their affairs did not turn out right. They eventually return to Olodumare and were ordered to return to earth and invite Osun into their deliberations. After including Osun, they began to have abundant blessings. "We can see how only one Deity successfully worked against the efforts of 400 other Deities simply because she was discriminated against on account of her sex. An *Ifa* follower must guard against entering into this kind of pitfall" (Falade 2002:242-244).

Chief Fama, a Nigerian Iyanfia (a woman *Ifa* priest) asks her Oluwo, Chief Fagbemi Ojo Alabi if there was an *Odu* that states that "a woman can or cannot be initiated to *Ifa*" (Adewale-Somadhi 1993:22). Chief Fagbemi's response was, "...there is no *Odu Ifa* that says a woman cannot TE IFA as there is no *Odu Ifa* that says only men can TE IFA. It is the same principle that guides a man into ITE FA that qualifies a woman to TE IFA" (22-23).

The initiation of women in *Ifa* in Cuba is also taking place. In personal conversations with Cuban *Babalawo* Victor Betacourt in 2006, he told me that 12 women have been initiated in Cuba since 2002.

The third controversy is the inclusion of Europeans in *Ifa* as priest and scholars who have access to this sacred knowledge. There is a strong feeling among some African descendant *Ifa* priests and practitioners in the United States who are against the idea of whites involved in the practice of *Ifa*. This feeling is rooted in a deep historical experience of the African slave trade, slavery and segregation in the Americas, as well as the current ugly practices of racism in the United States today. Because of African descendants' experience with the Black Holocaust (Anderson 1995), some African descendant *Ifa* priests feel that Europeans (whites) should not be involved. There are strong feelings that the children of those ancestors who raped, robbed, dehumanized and killed Africans—beginning with the slave trade—should not cohort with those offspring whose ancestors were wiped out by white supremacy.

Awise Wande Abimbola answered this controversial question of whites' involvement with *Ifa* over 10 years ago,

> One can easily understand why some people feel the way they do, based on their experience in the past, and to some extent their experience even now. But we would like to see this religion as a tool to heal all those wounds. This religion should not be a part of the racial problems of the Americas, or the world. This religion should be used as a bridge, as something to cure and heal those wounds, so that the future of the world will be one where there is no hate, where we can all live together irrespective of nationality, colour or creed. This is the way we envision this religion; we do not picture it in terms of excluding certain people. (W. Abimbola 1997:29)

Challenges

There are many significant challenges for African descendant *Ifa* priest and practitioners in the United States. Overcoming the dilemmas of *environment* and *language* are certainly chief among them. Key to the question of cultural environment in the United States is creating a culture of *Ifa* priest and practitioners. What is the environment of practice in the United States, and how are priests continuing to learn there? How do priests work together and how do they train novices? What are the ritual and ceremonial methodologies? How does the issue or question of culture in the United States reinforce the ability to create an environment that supports learning and developing Yorùbá language proficiency?

In my old *Santeria* days, things were hush-hush, very secretive and controlling by the godparents. Do we continue to conceal our practice, our beliefs and values or do we create an environment that comforts us and allows us to practice our faith openly and freely?

Should priests and practitioners be content with just being able to do a few Yorùbá greetings and songs along with saying *Ase* or do we deepen our acquisition of the language in order to understand Yorùbá culture and *Ifa* in a deeper way?

Awise Wande Abimbola accepted an award on behalf of the Nigerian government, a 2005 Proclamation by *UNESCO'S Intangible Cultural Heritage as Masterpieces of Oral and Intangible Heritage of Humanity*. The

Ifa divination system is an oral system and it is performed by a priest who begins with a short ritual chant before casting *Ifa* and declaring afterwards what *Ibo* accompanies the *Odu*. Once the *Odu* is identified, the priest chants verses of this *Odu* connecting *Ifa* narratives to the issues or concerns of the inquirer. To what degree do *Ifa* priests of African descent in the United States maintain orality? How is the art of *Ifa* divination carried out by African descendant priests in the United States and what are the learning methods used to develop and maintain this oral tradition? Even without incorporating Yorùbá language, are African descendant priests in the United States reciting *Odu* in English using the structure and narrative form as a central component of the divination process?

It is clear in my own experience and observations that orality is a major challenge for *Ifa* priest in the United States. Since orality is central to the traditional methods of learning the practice of *Ifa* in Nigeria, how can this tradition be carried out in the United States without the access and benefit of seasoned *babalawos* to pass this tradition on? With the absence of continued access to seasoned *babalawos*, what role can technology play in developing orality among *Ifa* Priest in the United States?

Another challenge for African descendant *Ifa* priests is the ecological aspect of the environment. How are we prescribing and disposing of *ebos*? There are things that *Ifa* priests can do that can be ecologically friendly to our environment. We should always remember the verse in *Osa meji—Osa The Bright Shining One* (W. Abimbola 1977:111) that warns us against sacrifice that enriches us while destroying the earth. The exploitation and abuse of the earth is threatening the survival of all living beings.

We must also remember that *ebo* is also a major part of feeding the family and community. In *Ifa: An Exposition of Ifa literary Corpus,* Abimbola shows us in the verse *Owonrin meji*, that the mouth is the father of sacrifices (*Olubobotiribo, baba ebo*):

> It is their mouths that we worship at Ife.
> I have given to those over here,
> I have given to those over there.
> There mouths.
> Their mouths can no longer fight against me.
> Their mouths cannot.
> I have given to those in my household,
> I have given to passers–by...(W. Abimbola 1977:39-40)

The most important current challenge for African American descendant *Ifa* practitioners in the United States is that of building community. There is a serious need for local, state, regional, national as well as international associations of *Ifa* practitioners. Through the local associations African descendant *Ifa* practitioners in United States initiated by different *Ifa/Orisa* families in Yorùbáland will be able to come together to develop, learn and function in a more cohesive and supportive environment. This will allow practitioners to adapt and change epistemologically to the shared experiences.

This process would allow practitioners to develop the needed trust and respect for one another and for the respective talents, skills and abilities each person brings. It would allow practitioners to develop a community of respected elders and priests whom the community has confidence in and whom they will seek for its guidance in personal and social matters. The process of building community will also help practitioners develop the unity it needs to take on the broader social issues plaguing our communities. It allows practitioners to build the kind of spirit in our families and communities that encourages African descendant *Ifa* practitioners in the United States to help lift up those who are down and celebrate those who are up.

The time has come for *Ifa* priest and practitioners from the African Diaspora to take up these *dilemmas, controversies* and *challenges* among themselves in a straightforward, honest and respectful way. The successful building of a culture of *Ifa* priests and practitioners and a creation of an environment and system in the United States that helps one to learn and internalize *Ifa* as a way of being depends on moving beyond these factors.

> Iwa la n wa, Iwa
>
> It is good character that we are looking for, good character.

References

Abimbola, Kola. *Yorùbá Culture: A Philosophical Account*. Birmingham, Iroko, 2005
Abimbola, Wande. *Ifa Divination Poetry*, NOK Publishers, New York, 1977.
Abimbola, Wande. *Ifa Will Mend Our Broken World*. Boston, AIM Books, 1997
Abimbola, Wande. *Ifa: An Exposition of Ifa Literary Corpus*, Oxford University Press, Ibadan, 1977.
Adewale-Somadhi, Farounbi Aina Mosunmola (Chief Fama). *Fundamental of the Yorùbá Religion (Orisa Worship)*. San Bernardino, Ile Orunmila Communications, 1993
Anderson, S. E. *The Black Holocaust for beginners*. New York, Writers and Readers, 1995
Brandon, George. *Santeria from African to the New World: The Dead Sell Memories*. Bloomington, Indiana University Press, 1993
Bruner, Jerome. *Making Stories: Law, Literature, Life*. Cambridge, Harvard University Press, 2002
Drewal, Margaret Thompson. *Yorùbá Ritual: Performers, Plays*, Agency. Bloomington, Indiana University Press, 1992
Falade, Fasina. *Ifa: The Key To Its Understanding*. Lynwood, Afa *Ifa* Publishing, 2002
Kamara, Jemadari , and Van Der Meer, T. Menelik (eds.). *State of the Race: Creating our 21st Century: Where Do We Go From Here*, Boston, Diaspora Press, 2004
Vaill, Peter B. *Learning As A Way of Being: Strategies for Survival in a World of Permanent White Water*. San Francisco, Jossy-Bass, 1996.

25

Separated by the Slave Trade: Nigerians and Cubans reunite through a shared cultural practice[1]

- Ivor L. Miller

Introduction

Throughout the twentieth century, scholars have debated the roles of West African cultural systems in the formation of societies in the Western Hemisphere. Many distinct models have been presented, some emphasizing 'absolute innovation' after a complete break with cultural systems in African source regions, others taking a romantic view of continuities despite a gauntlet of obstacles. Generalizations are hazardous, thanks to the wide variety of experiences during the period of the Atlantic slave trade; Africans left different regions, at different times, and entered vastly different colonial situations. This essay looks at a very specific African institution — the *Ékpè* leopard society — from a well-defined source region — the Cross River region of Nigeria and Cameroun, and its historically related Caribbean counterpart — the *Abakuá* society of Havana and Matanzas Cuba. Here I am not interested in proving either continuity or innovation, since living cultural practices are reinterpreted with each generation under any circumstances. The perspectives of culture bearers from either side of a trans-Atlantic tradition are rarely heard in the literature about their practices. Instead, we often read the work of anthropologists who come back from the field and write from their particular theoretical position.

This essay centres upon the views of leaders from both societies who have participated in recent meetings to display their traditions to each other in order to find common ground, whether in the confirmation of a shared symbolic vocabulary (called *Nsìbìdì* in West Africa) that includes a system of gestures, body masks, percussion ensembles, chants in a ritual language, geometric signs, and auditory vibrations from within an inner sanctum. Because they are responsible for the maintenance of these systems, and have

---

[1] Acknowledgements: Mayo Adediran, Sunday Adaka, Patrice Banchereau, Jill Cutler, Alex Jomaron, Victor Manfredi, David O. Ogungbile, Robert Farris Thompson, and all the Йкри and Abakuб members participating in the dialogue.

privileged access to information about their history and codes, their views should be of great interest to scholars.

Africans founded the *Abakuá* society in colonial Cuba in the 1800s. Today there are some 150 lodges and 20,000 members in the port cities of Matanzas and Havana. Since 2001, *Abakuá* leaders have participated in a series of meetings with representatives of their major source institution, the *Ékpè* (leopard) society of Nigeria and Cameroon. Since *Abakuá* and *Ékpè* do not speak the same colonial languages (Spanish and English), they have been communicating through the performance of *Nsìbìdì*. The process of these performances, including the selection of chants, body masks, and percussion, has presented new data useful in mapping the cultural history of this trans-Atlantic continuum.

Background

Decades ago, Cuban specialists foresaw the possibility of this unprecedented trans-Atlantic dialogue in what I am calling the '*Ékpè-Abakuá* continuum'.[2] Sixty years ago when concluding an essay about *Abakuá* performance as ritual theatre, Don Fernando Ortiz wrote,

> All evidence points to the remote antiquity of these esoteric afro-occidental fraternities. Undoubtedly, the detailed study of its Afro-Cuban survivals could partially rectify the ignorance, until now not dissipated, about the liturgical functions of the secret African fraternities . . . The scientific study of these secret fraternities of black provenance existing in America, particularly in Cuba, will without doubt help to better understand their African predecessors.[3]

Ortiz underscored the value of comparative research, but he may not have imagined the extent of the intimate involvement of *Abakuá* and *Ékpè* leaders themselves in the current process; the interest in communication is being generated by culture bearers on both sides who seek insight into the practices and symbols of their counterparts.

Additionally, after a lifetime studying the *Abakuá*, the eminent Cuban folklorist Lydia Cabrera pondered how future Africanists might use the data she had gathered. She refers to the African founders of *Abakuá* in Cuba as "Carabalí," since many embarked from the port city of Calabar:

---

[2] In a 1948 essay, North American anthropologist Melville Herskovits observed that since the study of cultural elements taught by Africans to members of American societies can help scholars better understand their African source regions, a trans-Atlantic dialogue can only be a win-win situation.

[3] Ortiz was also comparing ancient Greek ritual to Ékpè and Abakuá, thus the term "afro-occidental." "Todo lleva a pensar en la remota antigнedad de esas esotйricas fraternidades afrooccidentales. Indudablemente, el estudio minucioso de sus supervivencias afrocubanas podró suplir en parte el desconocimiento, hasta ahora no disipado, del funcionamiento litнrgico de las secretas fraternidades africanas . . . El estudio cientнfico de esas secretas fraternidades de troncalidad negra existentes en Амйrica, particularmente en Cuba, ayudara sin duda a la mejor comprensiyn de sus antecesoras de las naciones y tribus africanas." (Oritz 1950: 101).

Is it possible that the traditional narratives, the liturgy and the language conserved by the descendants of Carabalís in Cuba — the only slave society in which has developed this type of society emanated from the distant *Ékpè* — will be of interest to the study of the old societies that survive along the [African] coast, that are said to be threatened to the point of disappearing? Who knows if what has been lost there from foreign influences is still conserved in Cuba.[4]

Cabrera's questions illuminate two overarching questions discussed below by the culture bearers: to what extent do the immense narratives of *Abakuá* bear relation to the history of *Ékpè* in Africa, and to what extent does *Abakuá* retain ideas and teachings from there?

The recent 'summit meetings' between Nigerians and Cubans are drawing attention to a little known aspect of African-centred internationalism, since members of both groups are representatives of an indigenous government that emerged hundreds of years ago in the Calabar region of Nigeria and Cameroun. The Nigerian *Ékpè* (leopard), and the Cuban *Abakuá* both are hierarchically graded, with emblematic masked dance performance. The leaders of both groups believe their exchanges will strengthen both communities.

Before these meetings, neither the Nigerians nor the Cubans could confirm the existence of the other. The process began in 2000 when the Nigerians recognized words from their own language in a Cuban chant that identifies the port city of Calabar, Nigeria, as a source for *Abakuá*.[5] Specifically, the first Cuban lodge, Efí Kebutón, was named after Obutong, an Efik community in Calabar. With each meeting, as culture bearers on each side are studying the performance styles and language of the others, the communication has become more specific and therefore understood by a wider audience of initiates. As news of these encounters is being diffused on both sides of the Atlantic — through word-of-mouth, radio, television, the internet, newspapers, and scholarly literature — a cultural movement is developing as members of both groups organize themselves for future encounters.[6] This

---

[4] "¿Serнa posible que los relatos de tradiciones, la liturgia y el lenguaje que los descendientes de carabalнes conservaron en Cuba ъnico paнs esclavista en que este tipo de sociedad emanada de la lejana Ekppe se ha desarrollado, ofrecieran algъn interйs al estudio de las viejas sociedades que sobreviven en la Costa, ya amenazadas, segъn nos dicen de desaparecer? Quiйn sabe si lo que se ha perdido allб por influencias extracas aъn se conserva en Cuba. Y tambiйn pensamos en algъn futuro escudricador de nuestras cosas, interesado por estos apuntes, que armбndose de paciencia y con mayores facilidades para penetrar en el interior de la Potencia, cuyo acceso estб vedado a las mujeres, continъe en terreno poco explotado y rico aъn, las bъsquedas iniciadas a principios de siglo por el sociуlogo espacol Don Rafael Salillas, en un artнculo inconcluso publicado en Madrid, y luego por Don Fernando Ortiz." (Cabrera 1988: 10).

[5] A transcription of this chant published in Miller (2000) was the source for the Nigerians. This process is reviewed in Miller (2005).

[6] These items include: An Afropop Worldwide radio program "Voice of the Leopard" (available on the internet); televised interviews with the Cubans (2004), and with the author in Calabar (2004, 2005, 2008), several newspapers articles in Calabar and Cuba, the monograph "Voice of the Leopard" (2009). The webpage Afrocubaweb.com has posted some of the newspaper articles, and some information about general process.

essay documents the unfolding process from the perspectives of several participating culture bearers.

2001 Brooklyn, New York

In 2001, the first meeting between *Èkpè* and *Abakuá* occurred in New York City, when each group brought their masquerades, percussion and songs, and displayed them for the other.[7] The leader of the Cuban group was Mr. 'Román' Díaz, a professional percussionist from Havana, living in New York City since 1999. Díaz used inherited ritual chants to greet their Èfik hosts and to present the Cubans as linked to Calabar people through initiation lineages that have been continuous since their founding by Africans in Cuba. A man of few words, Mr. Díaz described his impressions of this encounter:

> The first impression came when we participated in the first encounter with the Èfiks in 2001 in Brooklyn. We assimilated the experience after the event by watching a video of our performance, when we saw that the Èfiks were able to recognize some of our words that came from their sources. And this gave us more security.

In other words, the Cubans selected materials from their inherited narratives to perform for Cross River peoples. Since the event was video-recorded, they were able to analyse the responses of their Èfik counterparts to their phrases, music, and dance, a method of comparative research.

2003 Michigan

Two years later, the organizers of the same Èfik National Association received another Cuban contingent at their annual meeting. 'Román' Diaz again participated, along with Mr. Ángel Guerrero, a master *Abakuá* chanter who had recently migrated from Havana. Díaz reported:

> Later in Michigan, we had the possibility of going with the maestro Ángel Guerrero, and the emotion was shared, since he is erudite in this material. While watching the Èfik performances, he could recognize all the liturgy that he has studied in Cuba through their dances, songs, as well as the comportment and treatment by the collective group of Èfiks in this event.

Both Cubans were moved by their interactions with the Èfik community, from their hospitable reception and private meeting with the *Obong* of Calabar, to the performances of traditional culture.[8]

2004 Calabar

---

[7] The events leading up to this encounter are described in Miller (2005).
[8] See Guerrero (2007) for his reflections upon this event.

Resulting from these encounters, in 2004, two Cuban *Abakuá* musicians travelled to Calabar, Nigeria to participate in the International *Ékpè* festival, at the invitation of the Governor of Cross River State. After observing their performances, one *Ékpè* leader, Engineer B.E. Bassey, wrote:

> The spontaneous reactions of the Cubans to *Ékpè*/Mgbè music, dance forms, acclamations and others, proved beyond doubt to the Cubans and *Ékpè*/Mgbè exponents that *Abakuá* and *Ékpè*/Mgbè are sister organizations with the same root. All are employing the same techniques to bring man into conscious contact with his psyche and enable him to know himself.[9]

If the Nigerians recognized the Cubans through their interactions with *Ékpè*, the Cubans were equally moved. Reflecting upon his performances in Calabar, 'Román' Díaz told me:

> The experience of being in Calabar was quite emotional, since the encounter with the land of an entire history known through the liturgy of the society or institution to which we belong, known as the *Abakuá*, gave us a sense of security, and filled us with respect towards all those persons who had made possible the survival of our institution, our religion, our lodges, however one might phrase it, through the onslaught of the years, based upon veracious acts conserved through the liturgy. Being in Calabar was also very emotional from the cultural point of view, of having the opportunity to visit these sacred places.

By "onslaught of the years," Díaz refers to the long history of oppression suffered by *Abakuá* in the colonial, republican, and revolutionary periods of Cuban history. As a political institution, a 'state within a state', *Abakuá* has by and large not been viewed kindly by the national authorities.[10] The experience of interacting with African counterparts in a celebratory event outside of the Cuban context no doubt contributed to some of the excitement from the Cubans.

As witness to the performance of the Cubans at the Calabar Cultural Centre, I was struck by the dramatic response of the public to the chanting and dancing of 'Román', and the lead drumming of Vicente Sánchez (for a detailed description, see Miller 2009). About this palpable connection with the Calabar people, Román remarked:

---

[9] Citation from Eng. Bassey's foreword to Miller (2009: xix).

[10] To name three examples, from the colonial, republican, and socialist periods, Cf. Trujillo y Monagas, D. Josŭ. 1882. *Los criminales de Cuba y D. Josŭ Trujillo: narraciyn de los servicios prestados en el cuerpo de policнa de La Habana*. Barcelona: Establecimiento Tipogrófico de Fidel Giro; Roche y Monteagudo, Rafael. 1908. *La policнa y sus misterios en Cuba; adicionada con 'La policia judicial', procedimientos, formularios, leyes, reglamentos, ordenanzas y disposiciones que conciernen a los cuerpos de seguriгad publica*. Primera ediciyn. La Habana: Imprenta 'La prueba'; "La sociedad secreta Abakuб (cбcigos)." 1969. *Revista Jurнdica Militar*. Ministerio de las FAR. Vol. 1. Pps. 13-24.

Being in Calabar, regarding the connection, I can't say that we searched this connection, as in: 'Ok, let's find the connection.' No. The connection was that through the previous years of study, through the entire liturgy that is the fundamental base of our information, we knew that this connection existed. Now, the act of being a participant filled us with satisfaction, and filled us with admiration and respect towards all those persons who had jealously guarded this information through the ritual, and by respecting sacred words or sacred acts, so that we have been able, through this language or liturgy, to be recognized by our brothers in Calabar.

Responses of *Ékpè* leaders to the Cubans in Calabar

For those present at the Cuban performance in Calabar, the experience had an immediate and lasting effect. Chief Ékpènyong Eyo Honesty Eyo II, an *Ékpè* title-holder in the Efe *Ékpè* Eyo Ema, commented upon the influence of the Cubans in Calabar:

I participated in the 2004 International *Ékpè* Festival when the Cuban *Abakuá* arrived. I hold them in a very high esteem; we thought that since their forefathers were taken to that place and died, we thought that was the end of the Cubans. My impression is that we should bring them again to Calabar; let people know that their great-great-grand-children are still existing. When the *Abakuá* sing their *Ékpè*, they start calling upon different owners of *Ékpè* here in Africa, and it has a very high meaning for me. When their forefathers left, the impression is that they disappeared forever, but now we know that they still have the *Ékpè* society in them, they hold that *Ékpè*, they did not forget it in spite of their torture. The message is that we here should educate our people, that those brothers who were taken away for slavery, that their children are still alive, and we should respect them, honour them, and be happy to see them.

The myriad obstacles facing *Ékpè* members in contemporary south-eastern Nigeria are such that the example of Cuban *Abakuá* is helping locals to reassess their practice and its values. Chief Ekon E. Imona, the Secretary of the Big Qua Clan Mgbè (*Ékpè*), describes how Cuban *Abakuá* has affected his own inherited practice of Mgbè:

At one time in my life, I did not associate myself with Mgbè, even though I was a title-holder. But the advent of the coming of the Cubans into Calabar for the International *Ékpè* festival in 2004 awakened a revival in my life. I asked myself: if the Cubans, who were taken from the soil of Africa to where they are today, could sustain Mgbè for over 200 years, why should we in Calabar allow Mgbè to die? There are a lot of things fighting Mgbè, wanting it to die, for instance the Churches around us here, they say Mgbè is 'fetish', and they preach against Mgbè. But if people who left here centuries ago, were able to keep Mgbè for so long, and they are still wanting it to exist, then there is something in Mgbè.

The Cuban example of faith in the value of inherited traditions with sources in the Calabar region is remarkable for the contemporary *Ékpè*, who are struggling with the legacy of British colonization that dismantled the power of jurisprudence that *Ékpè* embodied in the pre-colonial period.

Nigerian *Ékpè* organize for the Paris encounter

The 2004 visit of the Cubans to Calabar was well-documented on the internet. This resource drew the attention of 'culture brokers' in Paris, who arranged for an invitation through the prestigious Musée Quai Branly for representatives of *Ékpè* and *Abakuá* to meet onstage for a series of performances in 2007.[11] To prepare for this event, Calabar *Ékpè* leaders wisely created a multi-ethnic group in order to reflect the diversity of *Ékpè* traditions in the region, countering the dangerous 'ethnic nationalism' that has been used to divide historically related peoples.[12] The creation of Calabar Mgbè is a wonderful example of how the trans-Atlantic dialogue is useful in the local contexts of *Ékpè* in Nigeria. Precisely because the Cuban 'treaties' (mythic-histories) describe the creation of *Abakuá* through the contributions of each ethnic group in the Calabar region, the Cuban presence has helped local leaders insist on contemporary regional solidarity. Chief Ekon E. Imona, the President of Calabar Mgbè, explains:

> *Ékpè* in fact is an important vehicle to maintain peace in the region, and we have formed the Calabar Mgbè association in order to bring all *Ékpè* groups together. Since the Èfiks, the Efuts, and the Quas are always fighting each other, we felt that we could use *Ékpè* to bring unity between these groups. The birth of Calabar Mgbè is meant to unite these three ethnic groups in Calabar, because we have everything in common through *Ékpè*. And the rules in Mgbè, the laws, what happens in Qua land happens the same way in Èfik and Efut land. Forming this association is a means of bringing in peace which the Church cannot give us.

If on the one hand *Ékpè* represents for the Cubans a source for their practice, on the other hand, the Cubans represent for the Nigerians a proof of the value of their ancestral traditions. The *Iyamba* of Efe *Ékpè* Eyo Ema, Bassey Ekpo Bassey has recognized the potential of *Ékpè* — in an international perspective — as a political tool that can help mend divisions in the society. He spoke about the formation of Calabar Mgbè to foster international communication and regional peace:

---

[11] Special thanks to Alex Jomaron for his vision and efforts to make this event happen.
[12] For details, see Okwudiba Nnoli (*Ethnic politics in Nigeria*. Enugu, Nigeria: Fourth Dimension publishers, 1978).

Members of the Eyo Ema lodge invited the lodges of other ethnic areas, among the Èfik, Efut, Okonyong, Qua, and Umon, to join us in the formation of Calabar Mgbè in 2007. Until then, there was an altogether unacceptable situation in Calabar. The various ethnic areas were at daggers drawn against each other, and there was a real danger that the place might descend into episodic and miasmic violence, such as we have in the Niger Delta.

Ékpè was the culture of choice because it is practiced in each of these principalities or ethnic areas, where *Ékpè* is central to the traditional governance; *Ékpè* is the law, so to speak. Outside of the modern state system, *Ékpè* is the only social form that has authority and can organize. So we chose *Ékpè* and went to work with it.

If *Ékpè* was the traditional government in the Calabar region, it is now certainly not the official one. The contemporary power of *Ékpè* is in the cultural realm, where it is central to local identity. Calabar Mgbè was formed to represent the region culturally, as Iyamba B.E. Bassey continues to explain:

The real attraction for the participating lodges was an opportunity to share in the organization of the International *Ékpè* Festival which we had initiated in 2002 at the Eyo Ema lodge. We were ready to share it, in order to enlarge it, make it truly international, and place it at the disposal of the work of unity. The international *Ékpè* festival is now organized by the aggregate of *Ékpè* lodges of the Èfik, Efut, Okonyong, Qua, and Umon.

The festival became international in 2004 with the participation of Cuban *Abakuá*. Before that, we had the participation of Cameroon *Ékpè* members, but there was never a formalized participation from Cameroon; instead, members of the *Ékpè* society who were autochthonous to Cameroon, and who happened to be around, participated.

Ékpè has several provenances; there are many kinds of influences upon the Èfik *Ékpè*, from Balondo, Ekoi (Ejagham), Ìgbo, Qua, etc. We have these in the incantations, in the chants, even in the masquerades, to the extent that even royal British tradition is incorporated into *Ékpè*. So reaching out in the format of Calabar Mgbè affords us an opportunity of making direct contact with the sources of some of these influences that have made our *Ékpè* very eclectic.

Ékpè is called by different names in different places. By and large, it translates as leopard or lion. What puts all these leopard societies together is the centrality of the deity called Mboko. That is our Mother. Like the Great Mother Goddesses of other civilizations — Anat in Canaan, Inana in Sumeria, Ishtar in Babylon, Aphrodite in Greece, Isis in Egypt — in *Ékpè* communities, Mboko is our Mother.

Ékpè, to the extent that it expresses the sovereignty of a community, is for that reason rather isolate, and doesn't lend itself to corporation with *Ékpè* from other places. The only thing that made a difference to that kind of attitude in ancient times was the activity of Èfik traders, who took *Èkpè* wherever they went, and they were able to plant *Èkpè* in sundry places, and there was for that reason, some kind of flow in the culture. What we are doing now goes beyond the ambience created by trade. By bringing *Èkpè* from sundry places together, we reveal ourselves to each other, learn from each other, and we find that what comes out in terms of entertainment value, at least, is quite enchanting.

To prepare for the staged encounter with Cuban *Abakuá* in Paris, Calabar Mgbè selected an all-star group of performers. The members included chiefs and *abanékpè* (first-level initiates) who could drum, dance, sing, and perform *Nsìbìdì*, the esoteric form of *Èkpè* communication using gestures, percussion, and visual symbols. Bassey continues:

> The process of selecting the participants was very interesting. Everybody in Calabar Mgbè is technically competent in *Èkpè* matters, everybody is a chanter, the young people are all drummers; you have people practicing *Nsibidi* from the point of view of where they come from, even while certain *Nsibidi* forms are general. So it was quite interesting to put all these things together, to draw from all the participating ethnic groups with their differences, and then to wield them into a team that could perform together.

Participants reflecting upon the Paris encounters

In December of 2007 at the Musée Quai Branly in Paris, there were five staged performances, one of them recorded professionally. With only two days of rehearsal, no script, and no previous communication among the two groups, the events were exploratory and spontaneous. Among the Cubans, Angel Guerrero, a title-holder from the Itiá Mukandá Efó lodge, reflects:

> The encounter in Paris was very well organized and important. Aside from the informal encounter in 2001 with the Èfik National Association in Brooklyn, this was the first time that officially, members of both Cuban *Abakuá* and Nigerian *Èkpè* participated together in an activity of such magnitude in a place as important as the Musée Quai Branly of Paris. This was the first time in nearly 200 years that Cuban *Abakuá* and the representatives of their African ancestors had the possibility of sharing the same stage; this event had global repercussions as the first stage in a long path to follow in the process of reunification of both cultures.

> Our *Abakuá* music is a consequence of that music played in Calabar, of course it has suffered rhythmic transformations, but the encounter in Paris demonstrated that we could play together, and more importantly it proved that the legacy left by the first arrivals from Calabar who created and developed Cuban *Abakuá*, was genuine and authentic.

Guerrero's assessment demonstrates several complementary agendas in the process of communication with Calabar: to confirm the Calabar sources for Abakua traditions, to articulate the desire for increased contact, and to express the grandeur of *Ékpè* and *Abakuá* for the contemporary Cuban leadership.

Another Cuban performer, Pedro Martinez, an *abanékue* (first-level initiate) of the Ekueritonkó lodge in Havana, reflects upon his learning process and conclusions while in Paris:

> The experience in Paris with the Calabar Mgbè was quite moving, since there were so many similar things, and so many similar energies to those of the *Abakuá* ceremonies in Cuba. Also, we had many very positive interactions before the concerts. I went several times to the Calabar Mgbè dressing-room to observe their drums, how they were constructed; the conversations with them, and their reactions to our comportment towards them, was very beautiful. I had many moments with the Iyamba of Okoyong, and we had a good spiritual connection. We communicated through signs, energies, he through *Ékpè* symbols, and I through *Abakuá* symbols. And I had a very good connection with others in Calabar Mgbè.
>
> It was an historical meeting, because we came from *there*, and from there came the *Abakuá* religion that we profess in Cuba, that we have always tried to maintain by following the roots left by our ancestors many years ago. I feel very content to be part of this wonderful project.

By saying: "we came from there," Pedro signals how powerfully the Carabalí migrants affected the social identity of many Cuban communities into the present. The multi-layered interests of the Cubans in the Calabar group, from their social protocol, to their material culture, to the energy they emanated while performing indicate how meaningful this encounter was. Pedro continues:

> During these concerts there were many powerful moments when my hair stood on end, because — apart from the fact that were trying to represent what we do in Cuba, and they what they do in Calabar — for a concert it was quite close to ceremony, and we shared many beautiful moments of unity at the finale of each concert when we joined them to play together.
>
> It was a unique experience, being the first time I had the opportunity to play with an African group like this, interacting with them on stage, playing their instruments; it was good, truly a very emotional experience.
>
> Regarding their manner of playing and dancing, we share many things in common. Cuba is a place where people are always trying to update by using new ideas, adapting to the conditions of the time. In Calabar, I think that things were better conserved as they were in the past. For example in Cuba the dances are more virtuosic, using more stylistic movements, more exaggerated, with a wide repertory of movements that a soloist uses. Also,

in the *Abakuá* we have influences from many other African cultures that arrived to Cuba. The African Íreme [body mask], according to what I saw, dances more with movements like those of a cabildo [nation-group], like a procession or a march on Three King's Day, quite distinct from that of a soloist as such.

Pedro observed the overall feeling of communion and joy in the group experience, while explaining differences in terms of adaptation to different social contexts. His idea that the Calabar *Ékpè* perform like a 'nation-group' of the Cuban colonial period suggests that he sees the *Ékpè* performance as representing a past from which the *Abakuá* has transformed. In what follows, he uses several *Abauká* terms that are derived from Èfik, the lingua franca of the Calabar region:

> Regarding their masquerade costume, it's not far from ours at all! It has the same 'nkanika' [bell]; its 'ita muson' [hat disc] is a little bigger, but it seems to represent the same idea, the same message. About the music, I repeat that in Cuba there is a very large rhythmic repertory, but it was very easy to intertwine our two rhythmic traditions. Although their 'erikunde' [rattles] use a rhythmic pattern that we could not easily follow, the drums are indeed very similar, in terms of their sound, as well as construction. One distinction in the music is that the 'biankomeko' [drum ensemble] in Cuba has a larger solo drum, while the *Ékpè* solo drum was small. But in general I saw much similarity, as well as a very good connection between the Nigerians and us. I think that it was easier for us to learn their songs, than for them to learn ours. Also that it was harder for them to incorporate themselves to our playing, because of the complexity of our rhythms, of our language, and also because the manner in which we chant *Abakuá* is much more melodic and varied, while their melodies were repetitive. Even so, it's not too far from our tradition.

Whereas all the Cubans in Paris were professional musicians, the Calabar troupe, with two exceptions, were not professional performers. This factor affected the performances, and was observed by Pedro:

> I think that for Calabar Mgbè it was surprising to have left their land to participate in the Paris encounter. I think that they would have demonstrated many more details of their culture, like the gestures [*Nsibidi*] that speak through signs, but they were not very relaxed onstage. We Cubans are religious but at the same time we are artists, and we have one way of practising the religion away from the stage, and another way onstage. I think the next time they will feel much more comfortable and be freer. For example Bassey Jr., the son of the Iyamba of Ekoretonko, is a person with professional experience onstage; he helped out a lot, and there was a good connection with him too.
>
> I think that for us the encounter was even more moving, because the *Abakuá* didn't come from Cuba, it came from Calabar. For us the impact

was stronger, but since we are artists, we know how to control this emotion more than they who have not travelled as much; some had left Calabar for the first time. Myself, I was observing all the time, checking each one of them, their instruments, how they moved on the stage, how they sang, and developed their expression.

A fascinating aspect of Pedro's testimony is his awareness of the historic role the Cubans were playing. Communication with West African *Ékpè* has been a dream for many *Abakuá* leaders (as I learned from them over the years), yet the opportunity to travel was absent. This understanding forms part of the sensitivity of the Cubans towards their Calabar counterparts.

One of the common themes in the reflections of members of both groups, was their impression of the correct social protocol, of greeting, of respect, of acknowledgement, and communication through signs. Chief Ékpènyong É. Ekpo, the *Obong-Iyamba* of Okoyong, mentions this aspect:

> I am very happy about Paris, because of the way the Cubans mixed themselves with us. Very very happy! Even in the hotel and in the theatre, how they mix with us made me very happy! Some of them do not 'hear' English, very few of them speak English well, that was the only difficulty we had with them. But how they performed their *Ékpè*, I was shocked to see people who had left Africa or Nigeria for years, but yet they were still maintaining that culture. I was very happy. One very slight difference from their own *Ékpè* and our own here, is that we use raffia [netting for the Idem Ikwo masquerade], but they use cloth for their masquerade. I believe they could not get raffia where they live. From the drums, if you see the drums that they make by themselves, you will know that they are from here in Africa. I was happy to see those things. Even how they perform their dancing, singing, drumming, the rhythm of their drumming I was happy about it. Even up to the time we came back here, the socialism between ourselves and the Cubans shows that we have another set of relatives elsewhere. If you listen to most of the songs of the Cubans, you will hear our language. For instance, when they pronounce 'Mboko' [an *Ékpè* grade], though they don't pronounce it as we do, you will know that it is Mboko that they are singing. They mentioned the titles Obong Iyamba, they mentioned Dibo, they mentioned some of our villages here, like Obutong, and Usaghade.

Another member of Calabar Mgbè, Chief Hayford Solomon Edet is a leader of Mgbè ceremonies in Qua-Ejagham communities of Calabar Municipality. He led many songs in the Paris performances. Since the term *Abakuá* likely derives from the 'Àbàkpà' (or Qua-Ejagham) community of Calabar, Chief Edet has no hesitation in claiming the Cuban *Abakuá* as part of his own community:

> Every Qua Ejagham community we have here [in Calabar] has a counterpart in the Cameroons, because people migrated from there to here. We know that the Cuban *Abakuá* are Qua people, they are

Abakpa people. They are our own kith and kin, our brethren who travelled out from us. Everything that hovers in *Abakuá*, you can see the replica here. Particularly the *Nsibidi* signs, which we have here.

I recognized a lot our own traditions in what the Cubans did. In Calabar, in the Idagha [title-taking] time, in the early hours of the morning the young people will go out with the masquerade and inform the people in the community that something will happen. Christmas time, they also play, they perform with the masquerades, particularly there will be one drum used to talk to the masquerade when playing. The Cubans did this on stage in Paris. My impression is that we are waiting to receive them in Calabar any day, because we know that they are our brothers and sisters, and that they came from us.

The *Ékpè* and *Abakuá* musical structures are similar, both in the rhythms expressed, and in the approach to performance. Both begin with a vocal statement that introduces the performers, demonstrates their status, then greets the celestial bodies, the present members, and finally enters into the content of the song. Chief Edet comments upon this:

I noticed that the Cuban singing pattern is similar, when they start singing, there is a prelude, you don't just start singing straight in Mgbè. It's not permitted. You first do the chorusing, you sing a prelude before you start singing the actual song. When the masquerade recognizes you and greets you here, at the end we raise our shoulders in appreciation, they did that too! And our masquerades carry a staff to show their status, the Cuban masks also used staffs. And they still maintain their Ebongo masquerade with a straight head, erect. Their culture is very similar. They have a different approach to the use of the bell, but it's still a bell. I say Thank God for the Cubans, thank God they have maintained the culture they have brought from here, it's good!

We also noticed that when we merged and danced together at the show finale in Paris, their beats merged with ours, and they played very similar rhythms. During the finale of the last Paris show, we really felt the unity, it was a hallmark event. We were touched, and sharing that unity and fellowship again, there was so much affection and love, we felt that these are our people, and that there is a need to reunite.

I am interested in continuing to perform with the Cubans in festivals, because we need to propagate Mgbè, we want people to realize that Mgbè is a pillar in the world, that it has crossed the ocean, it is everywhere, and we want people to realize too that it can unite people very much, and we want to hold that unity and keep it for generations to come. Many of our people were taken to far away, and they still can come back and we can continue, so that nobody feels badly about what happened in the past.

> We are looking forward to that reunion with the Cubans one day, we have been praying for it. Others were selling our people, but the Quas did not run slave markets. Our people could be sent on an errand and captured, they were captured on their farms, or captured while fishing at sea. But we thank God that the Quas and Ejaghams did not engage in the slave trade. But we know that we lost quite a large chunk of our people. Those who did that, they know who they are, but we are looking forward to uniting with our Cuban family, that is the truth about it!

Chief Edet brings up the issue that the encounters with Cuban *Abakuá* will lead to reflections about Calabar history and the involvement of local leaders in the slave trade. Edet is quick to disassociate Qua ancestors from the mercantile aspect of *Ékpè*'s trans-Atlantic sojourn, an historical problem that is not fully settled.[13]

From an Efut community in Creek Town, Etim Ika is initiated into all the masquerade clubs of the Èfik Kingdom. He is highly trained in the inner-workings of *Ékpè*:

> Ever since we got to Paris, we joined the Cuban *Abakuá*, and they received us very well first with drinks, then with gifts, as it should be. We give thanks to the Cuban brothers, whose ancestors were taken away from us by the slave trade. In Paris we went to perform our own traditional *Ékpè*, and the Cubans also came with their own *Ékpè*, their own tradition. The way they played it was very nice, we loved it, and we danced together with them, and they danced together with us because they like the way we play our *Ékpè*. We shared the same hotel, the same dining table, we mixed up, and we enjoyed everything together, and we were very happy. By the grace of God, we will share together again, Enshalla.
>
> No matter that their masquerade was not like ours, the way they play, sing, and chant, convinced us that they really know something about *Ékpè*, because their chanting showed us that they were from this part of the country. They chanted in their own language, for example: "Ebonko Enyenisong", meaning "Ebonko from Èfikland" in Èfik, so these things made us understand that they are not novices in what they are doing, no matter that they don't chant as we do, but they gave us the impression that they are from here, because they chanted: "Efut Ibonda Enyenisong," a place here in Calabar. Maybe some of them are from Efut Ibonda. And the rest of them might have joined together to keep up this *Ékpè* in the way that

---

[13] Regarding Chief Edet's comment, historian David Northrup (2009 pers. com.) responded: "I think the Qua gentleman could be correct, if, by selling slaves, he means selling them directly to Europeans. As you know, the Efik were quite successful in monopolizing that part of the business along the Cross River Estuary. If he wishes to assert that the Qua had no subordinate role in the slave trade, I fear the weight of evidence stands against him."

they feel that it is good to maintain the culture of the Cross River region, where they come from.

The way they dance, no matter that they do not dance as we dance, but we recognize what they do as part of our own. Their drums are the same that we have in Calabar, no matter that the rhythmic patterns are not the same, but when they play we dance together with them very well.

Many Calabar Mgbè members emphasized their happiness in sharing their culture onstage with Cuban counterparts. Some comments about the distinctions in music and body mask performance, while too general for use in comparative analysis, demonstrate that all the participants are engaged in a process of critical dialogue, and comprehend its relevance for contemporary identity.

Inameti Orok Edet is a professional musician who played with the Calabar Cultural Centre ensemble for eight years. During the Paris encounter he played the lead 'talking' drum, and seems to have enjoyed the challenge to his talents provided by the Cubans:

> I felt very comfortable in Paris with the Cubans, who received us as friends and brothers. I appreciate them, for their drumming, and for their singing. They sang two types of music that I liked and I tried to memorize. Even till now I'm singing them here for myself. If someone asked me what the song means, I could not tell them, but I like it very much. Even if I don't know the meaning, their singing is very fine. Their drumming is different from ours, so I tried to learn from them, and even today I try to imitate the way they were drumming. If I had two months with them, I could learn it well.

> I felt very good in Paris, the experience was very challenging; I had to work hard to meet up with the Cubans. They were challenging me, so now I am training my own voice to improve. The man with dread-locks [Pedrito], he make me vex, that's why I drum very hard these days, to do my best. I like challenges, because they make me grow, and I want to learn more. By the time we left Paris, we made friends with the Cubans.

> I have worked professionally at the Calabar Cultural Centre for several years, and I can play 26 out of the 36 Nigerian cultural dances. I have had many good teachers, and I have surpassed them. I am very confident of myself, but in Paris, the Cubans made me sweat.

> But when it came to the masquerades, the Cubans could not surpass us, we 'xed' them out. Nigeria has so many masquerade styles, and our *Ékpè* is very colourful.

The sheer pleasure in meeting worthy competitors in an aesthetic 'battle' was part of Inameti's experience. Even the last comment about how the Calabar masquerades were more beautiful than those of Cuba is playful, in that 'they may have won over me in drumming, but we also won in masking.'

Ekpo Ekeng is the Chairman of the Youth Leaders of the Èfìk Kingdom. He joined the Calabar Mgbè team in Paris, to sing, play the *nkong* 'gong', and dance:

> Being in Paris with Calabar Mgbè was a wonderful experience; it was the first time I traveled abroad. The people of Paris were so caring, they were happy for the tradition of *Ékpè*, and *Ékpè* was exposed to the international world there.
>
> We did not know how to differentiate between the Cubans and Nigerians, because we interacted from the beginning to the end . . . In fact they felt like coming back to Nigeria. Some of them felt like they were Nigerians who were robbed of their own home, so they were supposed to go along with us. In fact we exchanged some gifts, and we promised to meet again. We are expecting to receive them in Nigeria because we know they are our brothers.

Some Cubans perceived the Nigerians as playing an ancient form of *Ékpè*; at the same time, some *Ékpè* perceived the Cubans as representing their past by evoking places in Calabar through chanting and performance style. Ekpo Ekeng continues:

> At the early stage of our program in Paris, we saw that it was an ancient *Ékpè* that they were playing, but as interaction went on day by day, we understood them very well. And what they were playing, we picked it up and understood it was the same *Ékpè* that we were playing, the rhythms the sounds, the signs of *Ékpè*, everything was the same; so we really understood and know that they were from Calabar, they were from Èfìk, Efut, Qua, and Umon; because whatever they did in their *Ékpè* was a reflection of our *Ékpè*. Even though we modernize it in an English way, if you look at it very well, you will see that it's the same thing. The costumes they used, though some of them were small [i.e., did not have the large raffia chest piece the *Ékpè* mask has], but they were the same masquerades of our modern *Ékpè*. So we find it accommodating, and we really believe that they are our brothers.

Responses of leaders in Calabar

Apart from the potential to use *Ékpè* and *Abakuá* performance for comparative analysis bearing upon historical relationships, the existence of a trans-Atlantic relationship is inspiring many Calabar leaders to think practically about their traditions in a global context. Since state and federal politicians in Nigeria have presented a festival-based tourism as an important project, *Ékpè* leaders are presenting the celebratory aspects of their traditions as ideal for festivals. The former Governor of Cross River State, Donald Duke, organized annual carnival celebrations during his tenure, an idea that has been followed in various parts of the country. Bassey Ekpo Bassey, the organizer of the International *Ékpè* Festival, and the Iyamba of *Efe Ékpè Eyo Ema*, presented the idea of the *Ékpè-Abakuá* continuum to a Nigerian tourism bureau, emphasizing the interests in Americans of African descent in participating:

> The aspect of *Ékpè* that concerns me is the culture. Because as a people we need self-identity. Black people in the Americas and Europe understand this much more than we do. Because people tend to look at them as not having any form of identity except that from the bush. So when they see a cultural form like *Ékpè*, they tend to cling to it, because it is self-identity for them; it is also proof that they did not come from the bush. Because *Ékpè* is a very high cultural form; it is religious, it embodies traditional philosophy, there are colourful celebratory aspects. So for them, *Ékpè* is proof that they had their own civilization.
>
> The first form of writing in sub-Saharan Africa is *Nsìbìdì*, which came from *Ékpè*, and survives in our *ukara* cloth and our inner temples. We have our own civilization, and as you study civilizations in ancient Egypt, China, Mesopotamia, Greece, etc., we also have our own civilization, which is embodied in *Ékpè*. So if you throw that away under the onslaught of Christianity, what is left? What is it that points to the fact that you have roots comparable to those of other peoples: white people, yellow people, and so forth. Because they look at Black people in the Americas, who answer to English names, practice the Christian religion, and wear European clothes.
>
> So the Cubans, who for over 200 years have clung onto this *Ékpè* cultural form, practiced it and deepened it, their hearts will bleed, if they come back here and see that Christianity has wiped *Ékpè* out from the base. In fact, people could then look at what they are presenting in Cuba as a fake, as something with no origins! As a people, there is no greater embodiment of our culture than *Ékpè*, which was and is a highly developed cultural form.[14]

Bassey exemplifies how *Ékpè* leaders are inserting the new awareness about *Abakuá* into a contemporary dialogue about tourism, in the hopes of sustaining international festivals centered upon *Ékpè*.[15]

In Uyo, Akwa Ibom State, Iberedem Fred Eno Essien built upon the momentum of the *Ékpè-Abakuá* encounters by organizing a group called Efe Nkomo Ibom (shrine of the great drum) in his own community. He identified the impact of Cuban *Abakuá* in local efforts to celebrate cultural history and achieve peace:

---

[14] Etubom Bassey (2005).
[15] Several other groups have responded with tourism projects that incorporate the Ékpè-Abakuá theme, particularly from Akwa Ibom State.

I have been on a crusade for the revival of our culture: As a tourism consultant, I have always been in favour of indigenous culture, which could be restructured and uplifted, projected to a stage that it would attract international interest, and bring in the benefits that are expected of a highly competitive tourism business. In Nigeria much of what we see these days are cultures grown from external influences, and in this part of the world — Akwa Ibom and Cross River States and into the Cameroons — one very outstanding indigenous cultural wealth that we have is the *Ékpè* society. But over time, interest in *Ékpè* has waned perhaps due to strong Christian religious influence and deep political manoeuvres of state, and so much has happened, they have cast aspersions upon the dignity, quality, and content of *Ékpè* that a lot of people have literally 'gone to church blindly', and have doubted the validity of holding on to that which is unequivocally theirs. This has not done well for us, because today, we have serious societal problems – we know that this would not have been so if *Ékpè* principles still held sway today.

Such problems as rape, robbery, murders, and general vandalism committed mostly by youths who are not properly in control because of low moral values. These are very worrying, and government today makes a lot of noise, uses a lot of money without getting expected results, and I know that because of the Christian religion, because of the manoeuvres of government, the elders who have an answer to these problems stand aside, they don't want to interfere, and things grow worse everyday. *Ékpè* is an instrument which is comfortable for use by the elders in controlling social problems. So one has always thought, 'can there ever be a way that these people could be empowered, energized into doing what we know they could do to put society back on track?' It has been a very difficult question to answer, and very little has been done about it, so *Ékpè* has been relegated to just the celebratory aspect of our cultural wealth that you see in local festivals, such as tourist events superficially enacted. It's a far cry from the deep philosophies manifested visible in the grandiose funerals exhibited by the monarchy of the passage of a king. It's very depressing to the psyche and dignity of our people.

We want to use the clear example from Cuba of the success of *Ékpè* as a societal block-building equipment, that could be used to put things in proper perspective, give full attention to worrisome issues from an all-encompassing strategy of nation-building at the rudimentary stage. When you want to treat society, you use moral issues; once the youth know that there are mechanisms of control in place, well established by our forebearers, then the capacity to control them is established. Cuba has shown us that what we believed in is alive and applicable today to solve problems. Cuba has shown us that we are not wrong about what we thought of our forebearers. Cuba has shown us that besides the Christian religion, there is a complementary alternative, because there is no conflict between *Ékpè* and Christianity. So these are two instruments that could be used together, with clear definition of areas of control. In fact the Native

Administration through the hierarchy of chiefdom, would be given a clear responsibility and therefore be seen as partners with government in controlling society for a balanced development.

Therefore our dream of working together for the emancipation of our people through the use of indigenous cultural policies will come to bear, now that we know that *we are not alone*. We are ever so happy and grateful to the Cuban *Abakuá* for bringing us back to our senses. Clearly the message is: 'Hey, you had it, we have it, it worked for us, we don't see why it won't work for you.' So we're going to embrace this resurgence, we are looking forward to a revival of our cultural systems through the leadership and moral principles of *Ékpè*. And we think that the development of an international platform linking three large groups: Cuban *Abakuá*, Calabar Mgbè (of Cross River State), and Efe Nkomo Ibom (of Akwa Ibom State) will generate that level of structure that we need to do things here.

We are ready to build an Afro-Cuban Friendship Forum, with a center in Akwa Ibom State. We want to see a situation where *Ékpè* lodges will be restructured to reflect the fact that we have satellite shrines in other areas of the world. I think that this center could be a rallying point for all peoples of the world of Ìbìbìò extraction and *Ékpè* lineage who want to come together.

We say in *Ékpè*: 'Àbàsì ikpaha, Afo ukpaha.' God will not die/ you will not die'. *Ékpè* is immortal.

How the myriad projects envisioned by *Ékpè* leaders progress remains to be seen; the important thing is that the trans-Atlantic dialogue is creating a renaissance, as Fred Essien put it, by opening up possibilities for educational, artistic, and economic production.

Ékpè leaders reassess the role of women in their practice

One of those possibilities has been a reassessment of the role of women in *Ékpè* practice. Being a society for males, in some communities women of royal lineages do become members but without access to the inner workings of the society. Since women have become very prominent in the many Christian denominations in southern Nigeria, *Ékpè* leaders are recognizing that for survival in the present requires their reassessment of the role of women in *Ékpè*. Chief Imona opines:

> If I had my way, we should modify Mgbè to bring in women, because they are the people sustaining the Churches today. Women have been made Bishops, and because of that people are going to church. But here, we are keeping Mgbè secrets away from women, and they are the mothers, they are the first teachers of the child, and the first teacher calling the child to say, 'look, my friend, that Mgbè you are going to is not good', and the child will follow the mother's advice.

I can remember even my wife when I was chanting in Mgbè, we say: 'Mbanma nsin owó, nsin ndi to', (meaning: I have reached the peak of Mgbè, I have initiated people, and also my own children into Mgbè), and my wife would say: 'go to orphanage, and look for the children you will carry and give', because they believe that when you say: 'Mbanma nsin owó', you are offering a child as a sacrifice to *Ékpè*. With this situation, if we have a way of bringing in women into Mgbè, you will see that nothing will happen to Mgbè in the near future.

Public Response from the Calabar Diaspora

Unexpected enthusiasm for the *Ékpè-Abakuá* encounters has been expressed by Cross River and Cuban people who have seen the performances, or who observed videos of them on the internet. Video footage posted on YouTube from the encounters in 2001, 2004, and 2007 has been receiving commentary in Èfik, English, *Abakuá* and Spanish, from viewers around the world. For example, some of the Paris footage received this message from an Èfik woman in England:

> This is my beautiful culture on display in Paris!
>
> 'Ndito Èfik! Sese *Ékpè* nyin ko ke Paris, ye ake Cuba!'
>
> Èfik children! Look at our *Ékpè* in Paris, and the Cuban one!
>
> 'Mmong ikemekendi sebe ndito eka! Yak ima odu ye kpukpru ebiet nyiñ tiede.'
>
> Water can't separate brothers! Let love dwell with us, wherever we are.
>
> I love my Èfik culture, and it's wonderful to see that slavery, distance, and time can't change a wonderful people and culture! 'Abasi Sosong-o!' God thank-you![16]

Spontaneous enthusiasm by enthusiasts demonstrates that these initiation societies are markers for the identity of the general population.

Asymmetrical access to information

The Cuban participants in the encounters with Nigerian *Ékpè* have so far been those living in the USA and in Europe. While we attempted to include *Abakuá* leaders living in Cuba, the difficulties of raising funding for such events in Nigeria, compounded with the difficulties of getting exit visas for some Cubans, has limited the pool of participants. The process has been further handicapped by the severe restrictions in communications, because those on the island have limited if no access to the internet and email. Not surprisingly,

---

[16] Vicky Otu, who lives in London and Nigeria, wrote this message in September 2008. She responded to my request by supplying translations of the Èfik phrases. (Otu 2008, pers. com.). See also <www.youtube.com/watch?v=i1udYdZXxEs&feature=related>

the lacuna in communications has resulted in some confusion among some *Abakuá* in Cuba who hear only rumours. Responding to this problem, Angel Guerrero, who lives in the USA but is well known to most *Abakuá* in Cuba, speaks about the effects of the unequal dissemination of information:

> Every historical processes has had followers and detractors, in this specific case I believe that ignorance and misinformation have played a fundamental role, because many in Cuba have not had direct access to news about this process and perhaps have viewed it with suspicion; it is also possible that some with bad intentions have conspired to confuse some *ekobios* [brothers], but none of these disputes along the way can impede a process as beautiful, healthy, and noble as this, that brings two related communities together. This is an irreversible process for the benefit of we Cuban *Abakuá* and the members of the *Ékpè* society of Nigeria.
>
> Eboémio Abasí bomé (thanks to the Supreme Being).

Cubans respond with a CD Project

Both Nigerians and Cubans are responding with creative projects that document and disseminate information about this process. After the 2004 event in Calabar, Etubom Bassey Ekpo Bassey and others made a documentary video program about the Festival while highlighting the Cuban participation. The Cuban participants in the Paris event who live in New York City are extending the conversation by recording a series of musical compositions with messages in the *Abakuá* language, in one case using the melody from a song performed by *Ékpè* in Paris. Like other performances in Caribbean popular culture, this project has multiple intentions: on the one hand the ritual phrases are directed to a large community of *Ékpè* and *Abakuá* members, on the other the jazz and funk inspired arrangements make the work accessible to a global community of Cuban music lovers.[17]

This trans-Atlantic dialogue began with a chant — in 2001 with "Okobio Enyenison" —has been sustained by the subsequent exchange of chants between both groups, and is now being extended through the creation of new chants based upon inherited materials. This process is consistent with the use of song in many West African contexts to record history.[18]

When I asked 'Román' Díaz to probe his experiences in Calabar and in Paris, he told me: "This conversation is a little difficult for me, because the acts speak for themselves . . . maybe I could create a poem where I could give you an explanation . . ." In fact, Roman's poetic response to the contemporary *Ékpè*, and to the corpus of *Abakuá* sacred texts, are an integral part of this CD project.

Pedro Martínez described this project and his vision for the future of this dialog:

---

[17] Cf Miller (2000) for a discussion of the multiple intentions of Caribbean performance.
[18] Herskovits (1967 vol. 2: 321).

> In response to our meeting with the Calabar Mgbè, we are recording a CD of innovative *Abakuá* music, and incorporating one of their melodies into our music.
>
> Thanks to this encounter and others that will come, I think that our two cultures will consolidate, will unite. I think that in Africa, *Ékpè* will become more united. Even within Cuba itself, the *Abakuá* will become much more united, because now there is a lot of competition between lodges, regarding questions of knowledge or jealousy. I think that the process of creating products, a book, a CD, with information about *Abakuá* and its links with Calabar, will go a long way toward uniting Cuba with Africa, as well as help to further unite the different lodges in Cuba.
>
> There are many people in Cuba who don't know that *Ékpè* is practiced in Africa today, or even that the sources of our *Abakuá* came from Calabar. Many young men don't know how it was born or from where, so this is a very good teaching. This knowledge gives us a lot of confidence, and it's a process. This kind of information cannot be channeled very quickly in Cuba. I can't say that tomorrow if the Iyamba of Èfik Obutong from Calabar visits Cuba that he would be allowed inside the 'butáme' [*Abakuá* temple]; this is a process that will not take months, nor a year, but I think it can and will occur. The process is one of ingesting all this information, so that the Cubans can interiorize, understand and accept all these changes.

This type of process has already commenced with another trans-Atlantic Diaspora in Cuba, that of the Yoruba *Ifá* divination system, a process that was activated when the *Ooni* of Ife made an official visit to Cuba in 1987.[19] The process ahead for the *Abakuá* is admittedly more difficult, since historically in Cuba, the Yoruba system has been stereotyped as 'more civilized', while the *Abakuá* have been stereotyped as criminals in many periods, partly because their high degree of organization and solidarity has been perceived as threatening by political leaders. This local problem partly explains why Cuban *Abakuá* have welcomed contact with Nigerian counterparts who offer historical legitimacy for their institution.

Angel Guerrero adds that the current CD project, like the event in Paris, could not have been possible without the long history of *Abakuá* artistic and ritual production in Cuba, particularly the history of recordings by the most stellar rumba groups of the island, as well as the most recent CD *Ibiono* — an *Abakuá* word meaning music with swing — performed by several *Abakuá* ritual chanters:

> The CD of *Abakuá* music that we are now creating with pride and professionalism is a consequence of the encounter in Paris that we all benefited from, the Cubans and Nigerians alike, since it allowed us to further consolidate our relations, and learn that many of the words and

---

[19] Cf. Abimbola & Miller (1997: 110-111).

chants used in our contemporary rites in Cuba are understood by our Nigerian brothers and vice versus, due to their common sources.

Ibiono [recorded in 2001] was an important part of this process of rapprochement with our African counterparts. This CD, being the first recorded in Cuba exclusively with *Abakuá* music and with a duration of more than 50 minutes, together with the contributions made by rumba groups like Los muñequitos de Matanzas, by AfroCuba of Matanzas, and by Yoruba Andabo, among others, opened the path in this process of cultural communication between communities separated by the miserable condition of slavery imposed by the European colonizers.[20] As clearly expressed by our Nigerian brothers in Paris, by listening to the *Ibiono* CD they learned that their culture, far from disappearing with those enslaved, had been well rooted in Cuba through the *Abakuá* society.

Conclusions

One of several trans-Atlantic African Diasporas, the *Ékpè-Abakuá* continuum with sources in the Cross River region of Nigeria and Cameroon has only recently received scholarly attention. Unlike the Yoruba-Nago Diaspora between West Africa and Brazil, there is so far no evidence of a historically continuous dialogue between *Ékpè* and *Abakuá* communities.[21] Instead, representatives of each group met for the first time in New York City in a performance context, a process ignited by the Nigerian interpretation of a Cuban chant that was recorded by professional musicians. It is instructive that in the 1950s, Cuban scholar Fernando Ortiz had correctly interpreted the same Cuban chant as identifying the Calabar community of Obutong, anticipating the same interpretation by Nigerian *Ékpè* in 2000, leading to the *Ékpè-Abakuá* encounters described here.[22] This essay documents and analyzes the reflections of Nigerian and Cuban participants in the incrementally dramatic series of encounters in the USA, Nigeria, and France, emphasizing the desire of all to build bridges across the Atlantic. This essay necessarily corrects the record in response to the mistaken view by recent scholars who argue that the process of dialogue within the *Ékpè-Abakuá* continuum is "politically dubious."[23] To the contrary, this process is an

---

[20] Cf. Guerrero (2008) for his reflections upon the process of creating *Ibiono* and its importance in the historiography of Cuban popular music.

[21] For an overview of this historical dialogue, see Matory (2005).

[22] Ortiz (1955: 254) wrote that the Cuban pronunciation of: "*Efн Butyn* or *Efiquebutyn* . . . in the pure language of the efik should be pronounced *Efik Obutyn*. . . . *Obutyn* was in Efнk the name of a great region of Calabar . . . and also of its ancient capital, today called Old Town by the English."
". . . el nombre de *Efн Butyn* o *Efiquebutyn*. Asн se pronuncia y escribe en Cuba; pero en pura lengua de los efik debiera decirse *Efik Obutyn*, o sea de los *Obutyn de Efik*. . . . *Obutyn* era en efik el nombre de una gran regiyn del Calabar, que comprendнa la cuarta parte del paнs, y tambiйn el de su antigua cuidad capital, hoy llamada por los ingleses Old Town" (Ortiz 1955: 254).

[23] Routon (2005: 371). "More recent scholarly efforts . . . take if for granted that initiates have a patently obvious interest in re-connecting with their putative transatlantic roots. These efforts suggest that the Abakuá's presumed nostalgia and desire to re-unite with their 'African' counterparts should be supported by scholars who can authenticate these transatlantic identifications. These kinds of joint

historical imperative according to *Abakuá* leaders, whose communities have been under siege throughout Cuban history as "obstacles to the progress of the nation," or as "criminal elements". What foreign scholars think about this problem is of little concern to the *Ékpè* and *Abakuá* participants, who have historically rejected the views expressed in the literature about their institutions as inaccurate and hostile. Instead, the example of Ortiz demonstrates that scholarship about trans-Atlantic communities will attain descriptive accuracy only when shared with the leadership of the groups being studied. Both Ortiz and his colleague Lydia Cabrera had earlier envisioned the use of their documentation of *Abakuá* for future comparisons with their African sources. In this essay, culture bearers who organized themselves for the series of performances with their trans-Atlantic counterparts reflect upon the process and its meanings. In the aftermath of a series of performances in Paris, *Ékpè* and *Abakuá* members are engaged in a series of creative activities, including the reorientation of their institutions to grapple with contemporary social problems, and the exploration of their cultural history through cultural festivals and commercial recordings. Thanks to the unprecedented openness from both *Ékpè* and *Abakuá* in discussing usually hidden facets of their traditions, scholars of the African Diaspora have rare opportunities to assess their historical relationship.

References

Abimbola, Wande & Ivor Miller. 1997. *Ifá Will Mend Our Broken World: Thoughts on Yorùbá Culture in West Africa and the Diaspora*. Roxbury, MA: AIM Books.

Bassey, Engineer Bassey Efiong. 2001. *Ékpè Efik: A Theosophical Perspective*. Victoria, B.C.: Trafford Publishing. [original 1998].

Bassey, Etubom Bassey Ekpo. 2005. Video-recorded statement made at the Tourism Bureau for Akwa Ibom State, Uyo. February.

Bassey, Etubom Bassey Ekpo. 2008. Audio-recorded interview with the author. Calabar. Bassey is the *Obong-Iyamba* (head) of Efe *Ékpè* Eyo Ema (the Eyo Ema *Ékpè* lodge) of the Ekoretonko Clan of Calabar. He was the National Deputy President of the Nigerian Union of Journalists, as well as the National Vice-Chairman of the Alliance for Democracy. February 25. Transcript revised by Bassey on March 3.

Cabrera, Lydia. 1988. *La Lengua Sagrada de los Ñañigos*. Miami: Colección del Chichereku en el exilio.

Díaz, 'Román'. 2008. Audio-recorded interview with the author in the home of Mr. Díaz 4. November 2008, Newark, New Jersey.

---

scholarly-native projects are not only marred by a number of theoretical conundrums but are also politically tendentious..." (Routon 2005: 376)

Anthropologist Kenneth Routon (2005: 371) recently challenged the trans-Atlantic dialog documented in this essay by asking: "Do they reflect a genuine desire of the Cuban Abakuá to reconnect with their purported cultural origins?... Could this be a case in which scholarly projects, such as the current vogue of research on transnational identities, overshadow the real interests of the groups they claim to have the ethnographic authority to represent?" The statements by Abakuá leaders in this essay are meant to dispel Routon's confusion in this matter.

Edet, Chief (Honorable) Hayford Solomon. 2008. Audio-recorded interview with the author, Calabar, Nigeria. Chief Edet belongs to Ekonib (Ikot Ansa Qua Clan), Ikpai Ohom Qua Clan, as well as Big Qua Clan, through various family ties. He is FCAI JP (Justice of the Peace). May 25. Revised by Chief H. S. Edet August 15.

Edet, Inameti Orok. 2008. Audio-recorded interview with the author. Calabar, Nigeria. Mr. Orok is a professional percussionist of traditional Nigerian music. He hails from Akpabuyo, a rural area that supplies Calabar with agricultural products. August 21.

Ekeng, Ekpo. 2008. Audio-recorded interview the author, Lagos, Nigeria. From Henshaw Town, Ekeng is the Chairman of the Youth Leaders for the entire Èfik Kingdom, capped by Edidem Nta Elijah Henshaw (the late Obong of Calabar). May 31. Revised by Mr. Ekeng, August 5.

Ekpo, Chief Ékpènyong Ékpènyong. 2008. I Audio-recorded interview with the author, Calabar, Nigeria. Chief Ekpo is the Obong-Iyamba of Okoyong. The Okoyong people migrated from the Mamfe region of Cameroon to Akampa, outside of Calabar Municipality, in the 19th century. He speaks both Èfik and Kion, the language of Okoyong people. His late father was a master of *Ékpè*; Chief Ekpo, in his 70s, is renown for his skills in singing and dancing *Ékpè*. He resides at Akampa Okoyong, the traditional headquarters of Okoyong. August 29.

Eyo, Chief Ernest Ékpènyong Eyo Honesty II. 2008. Audio-recorded interview with the author in Calabar. Chief Ékpènyong Eyo Honesty Eyo II, a native of Creek Town and Henshaw Town in Calabar, is a descendant of Eyo Honesty II, one of the great traders from Creek Town in the early nineteenth century. Chief Eyo holds the title of Mboko-mboko in Efe *Ékpè* Eyo Ema. He was a member of the Calabar Mgbè troupe in Paris, 2007. February.

Essien, (Sir) Fred. 2008. Audio-recorded interview with the author. Uyo, Akwa Ibom State, Nigeria. January 16. Transcription revised by Fred Essien January 21. Sir Essien held two honorific titles from Uruan and Ìbìbìò communities: 'Iberedem' and 'Ukai', both meaning 'one who is dependable'. He was an *Ékpè* leader from the Uruan community of Akwa Ibom State. Iberedem Fred Eno Essien passed away in December 2008.

Guerrero, Ángel. 2007. "'A father and son embrace': the significance of the encounter between *Abakuá* and *Ékpè*." Mr. Guerrero is the Aberiñán title-holder of the Itiá Mukandá Efól lodge of Havana. Posted in March at:
<http://afrocubaweb.com/abakwa/obongo3usvisit.htm#a%20father%20and%20s on%20embrace>

Guerrero, Ángel. 2008. "Ibiono." An essay in Spanish about the *Abakuá* music CD Ibiono, recorded in Havana. Posted in March at:
<http://afrocubaweb.com/abakwa/ibiono.htm>

Guerrero, Ángel. 2008b. Audio-recorded interview with the author in the home of Pedro Martínez, Union City, New Jersey. 3 November. Transcription revised by Mr. Guerrero 26 November, 2008.

Herskovits, Melville J. 1948. "The Contribution of Afroamerican Studies to Africanist Research." *American Anthropologist.* Vol. 50, no. 1 part 1 (January-March): 1-10.

Herskovits, Melville J.1967. *Dahomey: An Ancient West African Kingdom.* 2 vols. Evanston, IL: Northwestern UP.

Ika, Etim. 2008. Audio-recorded interview with the author, Calabar, Nigeria. August 6. Transcript revised by Prince Ika on August 13. Ika's father is the Muri (head) of the Efut Ifako Clan of Creek Town. His ancestors were Efuts (Balondos) who migrated from southwestern Cameroon.

Imona, Chief Ekon Effiong Ekon. 2008. Audio-recorded interview with the author, Big Qua Town, Calabar Municipality, Nigeria. Chief Imona holds the Mgbè title of Ntoe Mabo in Big Qua Town. He is the Secretary of the Big Qua Clan Mgbè, and the President of Calabar Mgbè. February 24. Transcription revised by Chief Imona in March.

Martínez, Pedro. 2008. Audio-recorded interview in the home of Pedro Martínez. 3 November, Union City, New Jersey. Transcript read and approved of by Mr. Martínez 17 November 2008.

Matory, J. Lorand. 2005. *Black Atlantic Religion: Tradition, Transnationalism, and Matriarchy in the Afro-Brazilian Candomblé*. Princeton UP.

Miller, Ivor. 2000. "Religious Symbolism in Cuban Political Performance." *TDR: A Journal of Performance Studies*. Vol. 44, no. 2 (T166): 30 - 55.

Miller, Ivor. 2005. "Cuban *Abakuá* chants: examining new evidence for the African Diaspora." *African Studies Review*. April. v. 48, n. 1: 23-58.

Miller, Ivor. 2009. *Voice of the Leopard: African Secret Societies and Cuba*. U P of Mississippi.

Nnoli, Okwudiba. 1978. *Ethnic politics in Nigeria*. Enugu, Nigeria: Fourth Dimension publishers.

Northrup, David. 2009. Email to the author regarding Qua participation in the trans-Atlantic slave trade. April 29.

Ortiz, Fernando. 1950. "La 'tragedia' de los ñáñigos." *Cuadernos Americanos*. Vol. LII, n. 4. (Julio-Agosto) México: 79-101.

Ortiz, Fernando. 1955. *Los instrumentos de la música afrocubana*, vol. 5. La Habana: Cárdenas y Cía.

Otu, Vicky. 2008. Email to the author. 6 December.

Routon, Kenneth. 2005. "Unimaginable Homelands? 'Africa' and the *Abakuá* Historical Imagination" *Journal of Latin American Anthropology*. Vol. 10, No. 2: 370-400.

Simmons, Donald C. 1956. "An Ethnographic Sketch of the Efik people"; "Notes on the Diary [of Antera Duke]." *Efik Traders of Old Calabar*. Daryll Forde, Ed. London: International African Institute: 1-26; 66-78.

Borderless Homeland: memory, identity and the spiritual experience of an African diaspora community

- David O. Ògúngbilé

Introduction

Diaspora discourse offers a wide range of interpretations and theorising for such disciplines as history, politics, economics, religious studies, sociology, anthropology, psychology, international relations, etc. Issues that have emerged from such discourse include immigrant, settler/indigene, centre/border, insider/outsider, and homeland/hostland. (Eck 2002; Sheffer 2003; Johnson 2007; Olupona 2007; Ogungbile 2010) The central focus however has been on the profound question of identity raises evolutionary concern for anthropologists and theologians. Barbara Sproul (1979: 1) puts it thus:

> The most profound human questions are ...Who are we? Why are we here? What is the purpose of our lives and our deaths? How should we understand our place in the world, in time and space? These are central questions of value and meaning...

Thinking about and acting out the perceived identity are reinforced by memory and imagination. In thinking and/or acting, however, the critical questions are: is identity imagined or real, for both an individual and the community? Community or identity is defined by Benedict Anderson as "an imagined political community." (Anderson 1993: 6)

Imagination provides the grammar for constructing and upholding the community or a nation through a process of routinization that transforms into a strong social and political unit. (Afolayan 2002: 14) As the community develops and expands, several other levels of identity are constructed and reinforced, defining some as host (owner of the territory) and others guests (visitors in a territory). Thus, in uniquely formal way, homeland is distinguished from hostland. Homeland/hostland identity is rehearsed and re-enacted through several means including retelling of myths and practice of rituals in defence of one's territory and in keeping others outside the fold.

It is however argued in this chapter that African Diaspora community in the Americas negotiates and forges a strong tie. This forging and negotiation help to recreate a homeland/hostland dichotomy through the principles that Hans Mol describes as myth, ritual and the processes of commitment and objectification. Such recreation thus fuses together individual members into a community that is 'borderless' and unrestricted by geographical boundary, colour or political ideology.

Engaging in Borderless Homeland discourse

The three major contacts I had with some groups of people of African descents and African-derived religious communities informed my inquiries and research into the phenomenon of the borderless homeland. First, sometime in 2000 during my graduate studies at Harvard University in Cambridge, I received a phone call from Professor Jacob Olupona, then of the University of California, Davis, California. He informed me of the desire by a group of people of African-descent in Boston area to hire a Yoruba instructor. I accepted the offer. The first meeting was scheduled in the apartment of one of the members who was, and still is, a devotee of *Ifá*.

By the time I arrived the venue, members were already seated, adorned in the paraphernalia of the different Òrìsà priests and priestesses depicting the Òrìsà they adored and worshipped. They were excited at my appearance. I also noticed on the divination tray placed by the shrine in the room, the signature of the Odu that was cast to ascertain the prospect of my intended engagement with them. We had the introductory meeting where each of them expressed their personal yearning for Yoruba language and tradition. I discovered immediately their passionate desire to deepen themselves in the knowledge and practice *of Òrìsà*. In addition to learning language, they requested me to teach and sing for them Òrìsà songs. This made me reorganize my Yoruba language lesson to incorporate teaching and singing of Òrìsà songs. At our meetings, members were always engrossed in singing and dancing to Òrìsà songs which they usually tape-recorded to aid their memory, learning and practice. The six-month intensive course lasted until I returned to Nigeria in September 2001.

My second experience came on Tuesday, March 20, 2001. I was invited by a group of devotees of African-derived religion to *Osun* festival in Boston, Massachusetts. The arrowheads of the festival were two African American ladies who claimed to be revitalizing Yoruba religion in Boston area and New York. Their adopted Yoruba-Òrìsà names were Osunkemi Olosun and Sangoyemi Osundiwura. Sangoyemi's given names were Barbara Easton who was at that time the interim General Secretary of Ebi Akinsilola Iroko.[1] The building where the festival was held housed *Osun* and *Sango* deities; a room each fully ornamented with respective paraphernalia of each deity was dedicated as shrine, adjacent to each other. Participants at this festival

---

[1] Personal communication: Barbara Sangoyemi Easton, Interim General Secretary, Ebi Akinsilola Iroko, 195 North Road, Hopkinton, Rhode Island 02833, USA, iyamopo@earthlink.net

included several persons of white American, African, African American, Cuban and Brazilian descents and a Jewess. The festival, declared opened by the Awise Wande Abimbola, was full of excitement with a lot of singing and dancing to Òrìsà, and food-sharing.

The third experience was in 2009 during my fellowship year at the Harvard Du Bois Institute for African and African American Research in Cambridge. I was invited again by the group that I taught Yoruba language and Òrìsà songs in 2001. At this time, learning Òrìsà songs was dominant in their desire. I discovered their deeper commitment and devotion to Òrìsà worship and a strong community that had been forged and strengthened. Most of them informed that they had visited Osogbo, Ife and Oyo, and had been initiated into the deities *Osun*, Sango, *Ifá*, etc. These contacts and interactions informed a more intense, deeper, and formal study of the community which is the fallout of this essay.

African Diaspora community in context

African Diaspora community is conceptually defined here in terms of political and spiritual dimensions. These two dimensions focus on the common narrative of the historical experience of slavery, commonly referred to as the middle passage, a forced migration from different parts and communities of African continent into the Americas. This experience which leads to cultural disconnection and social dislocation not only lingers on in the memory but also affects the present living experiences and reality of the people who are offspring of the slave experience. The inability to 'locate' their African 'root', the place of origin within Africa, is as discomforting, disorientating and distressful to them in their 'homeland' American community where they presently hold as their 'place of origin'.

Most popular descriptions of the people of African descent in the Americas are Black Americans, Negroes and later African Americans. While the distinction of 'blackness' and 'whiteness' has been noted to carry a pejorative meaning, African America emerged as a political identity that offers a somewhat psychological relief for the people. It need be mentioned that what I define as African Diaspora community is politically amorphous; the members draw from different geographical locations of African descent in the Americas including the Caribbean, Trinidad and Tobago, Jamaica, and Cuba. These people affirm and assert their common identity and community in 'spiritual' term as *'agbo ile'* (compound) which has its basis in the practice of African-derived religious traditions.

The following section presents and examines the autobiographies, self-narratives, of a few of the members of this African Diaspora community to illustrate my discussion of the 'borderless homeland'.

Short narratives of selected members of African Diaspora community

From our contacts and interactions, questions that could elicit information on the spiritual experience and practice of seven of the members of the group were drawn up to be answered in form of short narratives. They include:
- What are your names? Given name at birth, and the adopted names of Òrìsà
- How do you define yourself in terms of nativity?
- What was your religion(s)/denomination(s) prior to adopting Òrìsà?
- What were the factors responsible for the change of religion?
- What deity(ies) do you worship? How did you receive/adopt it? How do you worship the deity(ies)? Do you have altars/shrines? If yes, how did you construct the altars/shrines?
- What is your view of ancestor(s)?
- Do you have any connection(s) or personal contact with Africa?
- What are your personal life experiences? How have they informed and deepened your spirituality?
- What are your reactions to religions other than Òrìsà worship? What are your reactions to Africans who no longer practice indigenous religions?

The responses to these questions were used in constructing simple autobiographical narratives with editing including adding some words and statements for easy reading. The narratives, designed to focus on three aspects of the people's life, were thereafter analysed using Ninian Smart's "dimensions of the sacred" namely: the mythic, ritual, experiential, social, ethical, doctrinal, image/symbol) (Smart 1996).

(a) Birth and Family Background
(b) Religious Life and Formation: Experience and Practice
(c) Impressions about Other Religions and Africans

1. Anthony Van Der Meer (Akogun Awo)[2]

(a) Birth and Family Background
I am Anthony Van Der Meer, initiated as *Awo Alakisa* and given the title *Akogun Awo Alaafin* of Oyo. I am an African American. I never felt like an American.

(b) Religious Life and Formation: Experience and Practice
On my spiritual life, I had my first reading of *Ifa* in 1978, received *Esu, Ogun* and Eleke in 1983. I received one hand of *Ifa* in 1994 and was initiated to *Ifa* in 1999. I worship *Osun*, Obataala, *Ifa*, *Yemonja* and *Ogun*. I had contact with

---

[2] See his chapter for details of his personal religious life and experiences.

head priestess of *Osun* in 1990s. I worship *Esu, Ogun, Ifa, Ori* and *Ososi*. I sing *Osun* songs and offer sacrifices to her.

Some experiences that have deepened and informed my spirituality include a reconnection with my father after 32 years of separation. He was deported to Suriname and I lost all contact with him and my relatives in Suriname. It was through my practice that I was able to reunite with him. Ancestor is a central part of my spirituality. Primarily, it is the connection with my root in to Africa and those who died during the middle passage and those who were slaves and those who lived and fought segregation in this country, America.

I have visited Osogbo in Nigeria. I visited the *Osun* grove several times and have met with the priests and priestesses there. Also, I met with the artist of the grove, Susanne Wenger.

(c)   Impressions about Other Religions and Africans
The infiltration of Christianity and Islam into Yoruba religions has brought religious intolerance. This is really sad! Another sad issue is the contempt for African indigenous religions by Christians and Muslims. This shows how deep colonialism has impacted African people and their identity, and their sense of value for their own contributions to humanity. It is a rejection of one's self.

2.   Maria Clemencia Lee: Iyanifa Fatuma Sangoyemisi Atoke[3]

(a)   Birth and Family Background
Maria Clemencia Lee is my Catholic birth name. The name given to me in August 2003 in Oyo, Nigeria when I was initiated into *Ifá* as *Iyanifa* is Fatuma Sangoyemisi Atoke. My mother is Native American from Boyaca, Colombia, South America. My father is African-American from the slave plantation of General Robert E. Lee in Virginia. I am Afro (Latina) American.

(b)   Religious Life and Formation: Experience and Practice
The question about my spiritual transformation is very interesting. I resisted Catholicism because I felt a phoniness (fake) in the sincerity of humanity. My mother was terminally ill and my younger sister and I were in need of her fellow faith-folk to help us. They mocked us, especially when during Easter Sunday we didn't have new, clean clothes and they laughed us out of church. We later went to a foster/group home for children. There, our experience was different. The children were very nice, since we were all we had. My father later came back to Boston and brought us to the hospital where my mother was a patient. The hospital nurses wouldn't let us see our mother and we cried very loudly. My mother got out of her hospital bed to let us know she was alive and with tears from all of us we hugged. She had recently been operated on. The nurses were mad that she got out of bed when she heard us. My mother

---

[3] Clemencia is the wife of Anthony Van Deer Meer, the *Awo Alakisa*

later explained that she fought death to be with us. She had many stories about her time in her fight for life. She would mention she told death to "Get out of here!" This, to me showed me that the spirit is very powerful; not only for the individual but for those spirits she spoke to that she wasn't ready to die.

At the age of 38-39 I was her first child. Prior to me being born, doctors wanted to give her a hysterectomy (that is, take out her womb). She refused. She had my brother two years after me and had my sister the following two years. My brother later died at the age of three. I was five, my sister one. This was the beginning of my mother's health deterioration.

On my relationship with *Òrìsà*, and *Osun* in particular, *Osun* for me is an interesting *Òrìsà*. She represents at first the sensuality of femininity. Then as I listen more about her role with the other *Òrìsà*, she is priceless in the day-to-day business of life. I am connected with *Òrìsà* through studying *Ifá*. I basically started with getting divinations for problems, and then I learned that *Ifá* could also be used to answer any question. The *Òrìsà* would guide the story; *Osun* as well as *Sango* were predominant in my readings following *Orunmila* and *Esu*.

I don't practice or worship *Osun per se*. In my household we sing *Osun* songs. When she is in a divination she is fed yellow fruits and honey (*oyin*). I don't have an altar for *Osun*, but I do have a litre bottle of water and rocks from her river that I got in Nigeria. I have on my altar space a brass bracelet and a bell but I don't ring the bell religiously, as I should. When I feel good with my children or when I see happy people as yourself (referring to me), I praise *Osun* for having happy people. My deities include *Ifa*. I also have a shrine for my ancestors. I have *Sango* and *Esu*. I am also holding my nephews' *Ogun* and *Ifa*.

(c) Impressions about Other Religions and Africans: No comment

3. Kresna Brown 'Omilana'

(a) Birth and Family Background

My Name is Kresna Brown. I am an African, born on the Island of Jamaica. I have always considered myself an African. I have not taken a (*Òrìsà*) name. However, I was given a name upon 'being crowned' with *Yemonja*. I am not sure if the concept is the same in Africa or Nigeria (I have never been in Nigeria).

(b) Religious Life and Formation: Experience and Practice

The Lukumi system differs from how things are done in Nigeria. I was made aware that individuals are initiated into their family *Òrìsà*. However in the Diaspora under the Lukumi system out of Cuba, individuals receive their personal *Òrìsà* as their principal or primary *Òrìsà* and not that of the family. When one receives an *Òrìsà* in Lukumi tradition, he or she goes through a ceremony to get that *Òrìsà*. One's principal *Òrìsà* is received to one's head. It is tough to explain beyond that. *Ifa* divination tells one his/her principal *Òrìsà*. It can be determined through cowry shell divination also. But *Ifa* is the most reliable. But that is a whole other debate. The *Òrìsà* is placed on one's head and one now becomes a priest or priestess of that *Òrìsà*. This process is called 'crowning'.

An initiate receives various *Òrìsà*. All initiates however receive Olokun prior to going into initiation. In addition, also prior to initiation the candidate is required to have already received *Esu-Elegbara, Ogun, Ochoosi* and *Osun* staff of *Osanyin*, collectively known as the Warriors. The reception of the Warriors marks one's entrance into the religion. Prior to that, technically, one has no *Òrìsà* to worship. During the initiation, the initiate receives others. This differs from person to person.

Besides the principal *Òrìsà*, other *Òrìsà* received are not received to one's head as there is one already there and there can be only one. The others are called Adimu *Òrìsà*. They only give support to the initiate in various ways. To receive an *Òrìsà*, an individual must go through a ceremony irrespective of whether it is on your head or not.

In the Lukumi system, the religion is practiced in houses or *ile*. That is your entrance into the tradition and theoretically that is where you should stay. But theory does not always mesh well with practice. We live in a world of people; personalities do clash leading to separation and individuals establishing new relationships. One connects primarily with people in their *ile*. We come together to execute rituals and ceremonies that are too vast for one individual to accomplish. We all lend out support to get it done.

Participation is a learning experience. In every capacity in which we are performing rituals and ceremonies, we are learning. *Tambor* or *bembe*, ritual drumming for the *Òrìsà* are a learning experience also. Getting together to talk and discuss the tradition further our understanding. Some *ile* have classes where different aspects of the tradition are taught, from songs to dancing to divination.

Yemonja is my principal *Òrìsà*. I received *Obatala, Sango, Osun,* and *Ibeji*. All of these *Òrìsà* have formed an integral part of my worship. I may be called upon at any time to make offerings to them to ensure blessing and/or keep from harm, loss, and sickness. They continuously refer to each other if it is determined that I have some action outstanding with another.

I have an altar that houses all of my *Òrìsà*. I have a space for *Osun* on my altar; she resides there with other implements that I was instructed to give to her or that she requested of me. These implements include 5 jars of honey which surround her at all times and a small brass bell. However, since the *Òrìsà* are forces in nature, one can always make offerings to the sea, river, or other abodes where the *Òrìsà* resides. I am presently learning a set format for interacting with *Osun*. I propitiate her by offering her prayers, songs and food.

Ancestors are very central in the belief and worship of the Òrìsà. There is an Odu which reads:
> Baba Eni, Isese Eni,
> Iya Eni, Isese Eni,
> Ori Eni, Isese Eni,
> Ikin Eni, Isese Eni,
> Isese mo mo la ba bo kaa to bo Òrìsà.

Meaning,
> My Father is my root,
> My Mother is my root,
> My Ori is my root,
> *Ikin* (Palm kernel) is my root.
> It is my 'root' that I need to sacrifice to before Òrìsà.

Isese or *Asese* - I have translated here as 'root' - is the foundation of one's cultural practices given to us by our ancestors. Most of my negotiations in the religion are through my ancestors, who instruct me to offer such and such to these Òrìsà to achieve the goals that I am seeking. Ancestors are our foundation. With this in place, we can accomplish much. Without, it will be a tough going.

Some unique experiences have deepened my spirituality. Well, I recall returning to New York and had the most difficult time getting settled. No matter what I tried, nothing worked. After extensive searching, it was revealed that my *Ori* had imposed, so to speak, a period of barrenness, a period of trials. There was not much any of the Òrìsà could do as much as they would like. I was advised by Sango to offer sacrifice to *Olokun* as he would be able to help. After that, I stopped struggling and only waited. I accepted what was imposed upon me.

Approximately 8 weeks later, the doors began to be opened and my progress began. I learnt that being a devotee of the Òrìsà does not exempt us from trials. It however places all things into a context and helps us to negotiate life better. I grew to realize that not all things (unpleasant situations) can be avoided or sacrificed away. We must experience certain things (problems) to grow.

On another occasion, I was divining to my *Yemonja*. In the process, I asked if I was to do a particular favour for a friend. The response that I received was very ominous. I thought the answer was a strong 'no'. However when I cast (divined) again, the same response appeared. I inquired if the response pointed to death for my friend or myself. The answer was 'no.' I left it at that, being young and inexperienced at the time. Eight weeks later, my friend's father died. I realized that *Yemonja*'s responses were an attempt to get my attention and have me do further investigation: things I failed to see.

From another perspective, being an African is strong in me and has led me to this religion. Respect for the earth is spiritual. As African peoples, we must live and conduct ourselves as such and most importantly view the world as such which the *Ifa-Òrìsà* tradition has enabled me to do. Growing up in the island especially when one is from the countryside, there is a certain tie to the earth and respect for the earth. Many practice farming and this respect for the earth is cultivated into our being. While this experience may have provided us with some things, the *Ifa-Òrìsà* tradition has provided us with the remainder. Many cultural underpinnings to help us grow holistically were missing and we were unaware of this. *Ifa-Òrìsà* tradition has shaped this once-square-peg to fit into the round-hole of the universe.

(c) Impressions about Other Religions and Africans

My tolerance for such traditions as Christianity and Islam has waned. This is due mainly to their inability to believe that we can peacefully coexist. The civilizing mission of the Christians has continued unabated, from the time of the Crusades to the present; one sect after the other is carrying it on. After 1200 years of Islam and 2000 years of Christianity, what does Africans have to show for it?

I am firmly for the *Ifa-Òrìsà* tradition and I am for the removal and separation of ourselves from non-progressive traditions of which Christianity and Islam are a part. In the words of Jesus, we shall judge a tree by the fruits it bears. Collectively, Christianity and its followers have borne us bad fruits and Islam is no better. (These issues can be debated and hashed out.!) I am sure Africans may sight Ghana and Songhai and even state that they were Muslim States and we will debate. The religion of ruling elites is never that of the people. Many elites undertake conversion for political and economic expediency. Mansa Musa took the wealth of the people of Mali en route to Mecca in the name of hajj; what rubbish! (Again these issues are open to debate.) Islam and Christianity do not believe in peaceful co-existence and neither do I.

My aim is to solidify and consolidate the *Ifa-Òrìsà* tradition as a worldview to reshape the future of humanity. We have lived with 1200 years of Islam and 2000 years of Christianity; it is now time for something new. To that end we will draw upon our own cultural tradition and legacy and no one else. I call for Africans and the Yoruba who despise indigenous religions to wake up from the nightmare they have been living in before it is too late. The *Ifa-Òrìsà* tradition is not going anywhere. It will be accepted either by them or their children's children. It will be re-established greater than what it is.

4. Ann Marie Modeste George: Ola
(a) Birth and Family Background

Ann Marie Modeste is the name given to me at birth. This is written on my international passport. George was added when I got married in 1981. Ola was given to me by a friend in 1990 at the time we were interested in African names as a nickname and I have used that name to this day. I am called Ola George amongst my spiritual friends and family.

I was born in Trinidad West Indies. Trinidad is the larger of a twin island nation known as Trinidad and Tobago. I am an only child who was raised by my extended family, I was raised Seven Day Adventist. At least three/four generations of my maternal lineage are practitioners of that faith.

(b)   Religious Life and Formation: Experience and Practice
At age 16, I joined my mother in the United States. We attended the local Adventist Church in Cambridge. Several years later I was baptized into Adventism. I would attend church every Saturday but somehow I couldn't get involved in the various aspects of church life. I was asked to join the youth group to become an usher, but I was never able to give my all. The name 'Modeste' is well famous in the Adventist Church especially in the Caribbean. Therefore more was expected of me than I was willing and able to give. I was battling with my own personal faith having doubts and not feeling spiritually fulfilled. I eventually left the church.

In 1999, a Trinidadian man I knew from Cambridge/Trinidad community invited me to his church service, I was not aware that this man was a leader in the Spiritual/Shouter Baptist Faith, a faith of which I had no knowledge. I went to this church service with an open mind. The service was not like anything I had ever seen in my life. When I left the service I was certainly filled with something that I had never felt before. I began to research this faith; it was not easy getting information because I didn't know anyone from this religious background. At that time there wasn't much information I could acquire on the *Òrìsà* aspect of the Spiritual Baptist Faith of Trinidad.

I soon met and became acquainted with two practitioners of the faith, one is a Spiritual Baptist Mother, and the other was a member of the Shouter/*Òrìsà* religion for over thirty years. I later discovered that the *Òrìsà* religion is Trinidad's indigenous religion, having been brought to the Caribbean by slaves from West Africa.

I became drawn to *Òrìsà* tradition, in early 2000 when I was introduced to Baba Wande Abimbola by one of the two acquaintances I previously met at the church service. During this time, I was also introduced to the name *Ifa* by way of divination. Upon inquiry I was told that *Osun* was my *Òrìsà* and that there was strong ancestor presence with me and I needed to have an Ancestral Altar. All that information was a bit much for me and I didn't follow-up on *Ifa* until the end of 2000. I journeyed to Trinidad in August of 2000 to get initiated in the Shouter Faith. The events of that experience actually led me to *Ifa*.

The initiation process called 'mourning' was very intense; my first physical experience with *Òrìsà* was when *Ogun* possessed my spiritual brother while he was performing the rites and rituals on the three of us who were being initiated. My second experience was when I got a message from *Jakuta* 'appearing as a bright light/star coming down from the sky'. Upon telling my spiritual mother, she inquired as to who was *Jakuta* and nobody seemed to know. The next day she interpreted *Jakuta* to be St. Raphael. It was not until I became more involved with *Ifa* that I learned who *Jakuta* was 'the stone-thrower, affiliated with *Sango*.'

In 2002, I was spiritually prepared to set up my Ancestral Altar. In 2003, I received my first hand of *Ifa* and began preparing myself for initiation in Nigeria which took two-plus years to accomplish. My experience in Nigeria was breath-taking. I had no idea what to expect and I didn't know how this experience would transform my life. I was initiated to *Ifa*: my life unfolded before my eyes, a lot of things became crystal clear to me. I received *Esu Odara*, and later *Osun* who has been the spirit of healing in my life. I believe my first spiritual experience with *Osun* was when I entered the *Osun* grove in *Osogbo*. I was overwhelmed in this peaceful and quiet environment. At least that was how it was the day I was there!

(c)   Impressions about Other Religions and Africans
I am bothered about African people who imbibe Christianity and how they have no problem revering other people's ancestors and neglecting their own ancestors. Jews for the most part are faring very well in the world except for problems with Arabs and their war with Palestine. Jews have been doing very well especially in the United States. Thanks to all the Christians in the world who continue to give strength to the Jewish Ancestors of the Bible. It is very unfortunate that the Yoruba's despise indigenous religion, hopefully one day an inspiration will come to them that their ancestor should also be revered.

5.   Mojisola Osuntoki[4]

(a)   Birth and Family Background
My name is Osuntoki Mojisola. *Ijalu*, which I was told meant 'fighter' in the town, was given to me by *Oba* Efuntola Oseijeman Adefunmi I as my African name. A chief priestess of an *Òrìsà* in Ikoro-Ekiti gave me the name Osuntomilola while I was doing research there. I didn't state the Euro names. I don't think it is necessary at this time to go back into the dark and early days of mental slavery which my parents participated in unknowingly and unconsciously. I am a co-wife with Chief Priestess of *Sango, Iya Oni-Sango* of Oyotunji, Obabi Osadele.

(b)   Religious Life, Formation: Experience and Practice
My spirituality seems to be going through many levels within motherhood as mothers, and teachers of children and youths. My passion to reach the new age youth with old soul sensibilities engrossed me. I find out that children, the youths and their young parents are out of touch with the common sensibilities of who they are and what their relationship is and within the western world they are living in. They are out of touch with the understanding of their bodies and the powers of their mind and higher consciousness. So, I work to bring awareness and connection of their minds and bodies and their place in

---

[4] Mojisola refused to give her given name. I have done some editing, particularly I inserted English translations to the Yoruba words Osuntoki uses.

this world, from past to present, so we can have strong and intelligent youth to sustain and maintain a healthy world and society with the blessing and wisdom of the Elders. The connections need to be made so we can have intelligent mothers and fathers with children who are astute mentally, emotionally, and spiritually who respect and are cogent of Ancient wisdom and how to use it beneficially.

I have been worshipping *Yemonja* (which is water, *Osun*'s daughter). Over time I have received *Osun, Obatala, Yemonja, Olokun, Sango, Opa Osun Rere, Ori, Ifa*. This means I received the Awo of these *Irunmole* and *Òrìsà* - their power - their *Ase*. I give salutations to my shrines every day and give offerings weekly and as the *Irunmole/Òrìsà* may direct from *adifa* (diviners). I daily and regularly greet and feed *Osun*. My *Osun* and her items are placed on a mat, on the floor. *Osun*, as bodies of water (rivers, lakes, oceans, estuaries, lagoons), is usually seen in these manners (though she exists in other forms), lying on the earth and so this is how I have her displayed.

The shrine has brassware, brass jewellery, brass trays, brass bells, plants, mirror, *awon abela* (candles), etc. *Osun* descends as rain from the heavens, accumulates in pools and travels along the earth. So, she flows in me as in all and she is worshipped on a mat; the earth that we all stand on and this is how she represents her connection in nurturing or nursing the Earth with the breast milk of Her Life Waters.

An important occasion of spiritual significance occurred in my life. A man was visiting Oyotunji in South Carolina, its original land location before it moved to where it is now. He stayed in a motel one evening and left with a souvenir item from there. The police (*olopa*) wanted to arrest him and put him in their custody. He went to the Aafin (palace) to take refuge as in our traditional culture is, but the police arrested the Oba. But because we were very poor at that time, no one had enough money to release the Oba from the police cell. I had a few dollars which was enough for our Oba to be released.

In exchange, the Oba said he would initiate me. So, when the Oba asked before initiation who my *ori* should go to, *Osun* said she claimed me. Thus, I was initiated in 1971 and given the name Ijalu by my Godfather Oba Adefunmi I. So I am forever and beyond very grateful to him and forever and beyond honoured to serve the primordial energy of Life, *Osun*.

My spiritual journey which partly followed academic research has taken me to places in Nigeria namely Osogbo, Igbajo, Ife, Ondo, Ikoro-Ekiti and Ijero. I stayed in Ondo for a few days before going to Ikoro-Ekiti. I interviewed the Ajero and the chief priestess of *Ogun*. I visited *Obatala* compound in Ijero. In Osogbo, an artsy city, I interviewed a former Arugba Abimbola (I think her name is) and the former *Iya Osun* who was blind. I travelled to four different towns to research *Osun* for my Master's degree. I produced a video titled *Osun: Her Worship, Her Powers* that is used by some colleges and professors such as Dr. Badejo and Dr. Rowland Abiodun.

I would like in the future to document traditional religious dances and I am interested in the old architecture of the Aafin (palaces), shrines, especially those that were/are made of clay. I would like to video-document these historical landmarks, and also document some of the controversies of towns that are in conflict regarding different royal families who each say it is their turn to rule. I don't know; that might be too complicated.

Participating in African culture and worship is to find one's mind and the truth of who they are and to have self-understanding historically, culturally, in gender power, and all of this gives one to open roads to elevate the mind and know the better choices to make in the roads one must or needs to travel. In knowing the importance of my African culture and my indigenous Yoruba culture, it has opened levels of consciousness and knowledge. Realizing '*emi omo*' (I, a child of) Oduduwa and practicing the cultural concepts of my indigenous Yoruba culture, I am able to call upon (or draw upon) the powers and open the various doors and dimensions of knowledge of my Ancestors and to use them for the benefit of me, my family and friends, society.

In having this consciousness I realize that there are voices that talk to me; and I look to hear them in any way or form they may come. African culture and specifically for me, indigenous Yoruba culture has opened the doors for me to know, expect, and demand that my deities assist me in my judgment and life decisions.

(c)   Impressions about Other Religions and Africans: No comment

6.   Angela M. Herbert: Sangoronke Aina

(a)   Birth and Family Background

My birth name is Angela M. Herbert. My *Òrìsà* names are Sangoronke Ajike Egbetohun, Uhuanmen, Ojefunmike, Obidoyin Aina.

(b)   Religious Life and Formation: Experience and Practice

I was raised Catholic by my mother. My father did not go to church. I had a grandmother figure who was a bishop in the African Methodist Episcopal Church and who was also a spiritualist. Through her, I witnessed the experience of the spiritual transformations that occurred when our people of colour gathered to worship. It was here that I first heard the drum and saw the 'saints' lift their voices in songs; the drum caught their feet while listening to a language I did not recognize.

I grew up in a family of females and close family friends that were and are spiritually sensitive mediums and all with special gifts (i.e. third eye, healing, etc.). My own sister was born with the veil over her face. I was born with my umbilicus wrapped around my neck thrice. Hence I was named Aina. By the time I was 7 years old, my mother and aunties recognised that, unusually, I could see and hear what they could.

From that point on, I was constantly watched over. I was told to always walk in the light and not in the dark, and not to answer to voices in the dark. I understood that there was much more to our spirituality than what the Catholic Church was teaching us or would admit to. Thus, my childhood experiences led me to seek out and learn what our ancestors believed and practised that made our white slave captors torture and kill our people for maintaining our ancestral traditions.

My first introduction to traditional religion was through the Cuban lucumi houses. I read what I could and even went back to the Catholic Church after over 15 years. My spiritual sensitivities, as I call them, were increasing and I thought that if I had nowhere else to go, the church would suffice. But one day, they asked me to participate in a part of the service of 'call and response'. I tried to get out of it to no avail. My voice changed as if I manifested a deep voiced passionate Southern Baptist minister. I didn't know what I said, but when I came back (to my consciousness), the whole congregation was looking at me with their eyes popping out of their faces. I knew my time in the Catholic Church was done. So be it...

I finally met the person who would be my spiritual teacher and mentor in 1996, the *Awise*, Baba Ogunwande Abimbola. I went for a divination, and my spiritual journey began. This made sense; it spoke to my spirit and those of my ancestors. Things that I might have thought of being spooky were no longer. The first *bembe* spiritual celebration for *Esu* that I went to in 1997 landed me on the floor: I was knocked out. It was an *Olokun* priestess, my *iya* (mother) in *Olokun* practice that guided me and brought me back. Now I knew the *ase* of the drums, the praise songs of worship and the *ase* of the *Òrìsà*.

We were told that before one embarks upon anything in one's life, one must gain the support of one's ancestors. After series of divination, *ebo* (rituals) and talks, it was obvious that this was my calling, just like that of a church priest. I accepted this without question and began my preparations to travel to Nigeria. The ancestors smiled down upon me with bended ear! I was ready to submit to their will.

Due to my active participation in the *ile* (house) and the many experiences, my godmothers at the time were not sure which *Òrìsà* would claim my head: *Sango? Osun?* or *Egbe?* Why? Because at a celebration for *Osun*, she manifested to me in the company and stated that more than one *Òrìsà* was asking for my head. As I stated, I had already made the decision to submit to their will. Shortly thereafter, I was at the *ile*. My godmothers were in the shrine completing an *ebo*. I was sitting in the living room outside the shrine. There was another woman also sitting in the living room. She is a dancer by profession from Brazil and considered an *omo Osun* although not crowned. Beautiful manifestation of *Osun* when she dances, with the mirror and fan! That day, her spirit was down. She barely spoke or looked at me. She sat in the window staring out as if searching (for someone or something). Totally lost! I remember feeling so sad as if I wanted to cry for her. She looked as if she had given up and lost hope. I could not converse with her; I could only pick up these feelings.

The bell started to ring. The *ebo* was now prepared for *Yeye Osun*. It was a deliberate ring. It was heartfelt and penetrating. The energy shifted. The spirit was high. It touched me and enveloped me. I remember getting emotional. It was absolutely beautiful! And I felt my body responded like a soft, graceful and fluid sway as if water was flowing over me ever so gently. I became aware that the dancer was also taking in *Osun*'s pure love. I rose, or *Osun* lifted and raised me up and I danced with such fluidity and gracefulness.

When the dance ended and Angela (I) returned, the dancer sat me down and brought me some water. She said that I was absolutely beautiful, and that I had no idea that she had been questioning her faith and purpose. For her to have been abandoned and for *Osun* to have come before her at this time reinforced her faith and gave her the strength to carry on. We hugged both with tears in our eyes.

I realized my dream when I travelled to Nigeria in 2000. I was initiated by the *Elegun Sangodele*. I have no doubt in my mind that I have done what I was called to do. Because only two minutes after leaving the *igbodu*, Sango was marching with me. *Ase*! I was blessed have been able to travel to Osogbo, to *Osun* grove two days before being initiated. We sat in *Osun* shrine with the high priests, and they gave us water from her clay pot. They chanted, said prayers and sang to *Osun*. I was able to go back to Osogbo in 2005. We prayed with the high priests at her river, made offerings and I sang to her. The spirit was high!

I have a shrine for Sango and myself on which I always keep *oyin,* honey.

(c)   Impressions about Other Religions and Africans
I believe that we all have our destinies to fulfil. I have no problems with other religions as long as we are all striving for peace, love and respect for our ancestors, family, friends and community. It may take many roads to fulfil the destiny. I cannot sit in judgment of those who do not share my beliefs. Some of us are called to maintain the traditions of our ancestor. I am blessed that I was able to hear that call and heed it. *Ase*!

7.   Yvette M.[5]
(a)   Birth and Family Background
My name is very French from my father's side of the family who is from Martinique. My middle name was from my grandmother/father's mother, Marie. I was born and raised in Colon, Panama in Central America. I am of Jamaican, Barbados and Martinique grandparents who also have South Asian and Native Indian blood. I am an African from the Americas but not an American as it is defined in this country. I identify myself as Panamanian and Afro-Latina, woman of African descent.

(b)   Religious Life and Formation: Experience and Practice
I was raised very Catholic. My family is still Catholic and I still go to church with my father. As I became a practitioner (of *Òrìsà*) and went back to my family, I began saying 'that is not Catholic.' Everything was like hidden or

---

[5] M. is used for anonymous reason as requested by the informant. M. introduced her stories with the following statements to show her excitement at reflecting on her spiritual journey:
Thanks David for sharing this with me. I love your questions and they speak to me and my experience.... I think story telling is best when told and not only written. It was such a pleasure to stop and think of these things. I could go on and on .... Some of this is very personal.

related to Catholicism; but now I see it all came from Yoruba *Ifa*. I saw the similarities. However, I ask myself every time if I would have found *Ifa* if I was still home since my church at home is also very black including the priest. I felt very isolated there and things felt very white to me.

My identity has been important to me. I appreciate even more where I come from and being Panamanian. To me now, everything about being Panamanian is being black beyond just the country. I feel more beautiful in my skin now than ever because of what I feel inside not just how I may look outside. I feel more connected to other people of African descent since I began this spiritual journey and with *Ifa*. In this I see our connections and commonalities. Being a practitioner made me want to find out more about my ancestors, what country, etc. It made me learn more about Africa.

My spiritual experience has been reinforced by the community in Boston that has been created by Baba Awo Alakisa, a wonderful teacher who has guided me and allowed me to find my footing and answer the many questions I have. Through this, I have been given the opportunity of many travels in the US and Latin America, where I was able to see things first hand. This has now been part of my work career.

My spiritual transformation has been internal and external; internal in the way that I have found clarity in my purpose and direction in life. I continue to grow and find myself making a better sense of my world and the entire world I live in. I have been grieving my whole life, with *Ifá* in my life. I grieve in a different way. The twin-factor of dream and ancestor is the driving force of my life.

I have an absolute belief that the spirit of those we love walks with us on a daily basis. I sense that through dreams, smells, and sensing their presence. My mother died when I was young. I was in College. I grieve over her a lot. I don't get to touch her physically but I dream of her clearly. She sends me messages and tells me stories. She appears to me in my time of need. She lived in the US when she passed away. I was not present there. When she became ill, I struggled to be there but it wasn't possible; it was my sister who took care of her. The day she passed away, I dreamt of her taking me on a walk and asking me to wait for her.

I also had a dream recently when I felt the presence of my aunt who died a year ago. I could not sleep because I felt someone was present. The candle in my room was so bright it was like the fluorescent light. I finally fell asleep. The next morning I called and shared the dream with my sister. She said "Yes, I think it was Tia Norma." I knew it was her. In my country when you dream of someone, you buy their number. I bought the number and won money.

For me, it was not about the money; it was the fact that I never felt that she was there for me. It was more affirming to me than any words she could have said. Feeling their presence and winning that money was I think their way of saying: "I am here now with you, I am sorry." To dream of my mother and have her say: "here is my gypsy daughter," makes me so happy. To dream of my uncle who tells me to tell my cousin that she will be fine. When I called her, she said "your younger cousin has been put on bed rest for the rest of her pregnancy." Then I said to her: "Uncle told me to tell you she will be good." I write my dreams and they mean so much to me.

My mother, my aunt, my uncles are with me and I get to honour them through my offerings. I remember the things they liked to eat and drink and offer it to them. Ancestors sent me signs and placed me in situations that told me they were there with me and that they wanted me to tell the story.

Although I had many career choices, I have chosen with passion to create an organization to continue to tell the story of my ancestor to pick up from where they left off. I honour them on a daily basis because of the gift they gave me, to love self and community, unconditionally. I know that conflict is the order of the day but I deal with them differently. I see every difficulty as a learning moment. Many things continue to happen that say: "I am with you and you are going in the right direction."

I have not been initiated yet; but I hope to do so soon. I dream of my initiation. Although I see it as far away, I know it will happen. I am always told that I am *Osun* even though I received my hand in *Ogun* and *Egungun*. I find that they show when I need them most. I do feel I have a lot of *Osun* in me. How do I know I have a lot of *Osun* in me? My community work and my work with children are very important to me (this shows the connection). My friend in Nigeria tells me stories of *Osun*, and tells me to pray to her because she is in me. I have travelled to Latin America to Ecuador recently and they have a river called Chota. They also relate the river to the *Osun* river. When I arrived and looked at the river, I began crying. I felt it was a cleansing and that I had arrived home. *Olokun* comes up a lot for me. So do *Egungun* and *Ogun*. How?

It is because of my ancestors that I began to study more of *Ifá*. Ifa is not just a religion to me, it is a way of life, a way to see the world and navigate the world. I search for a place where I am accepted in my wholeness. I find great peace in my practice. For example, my divination for the New Year was the Òsun verse of "not being included and what that meant" (Odu Osetua). That verse speaks volume to me and how I do my work and not to fight about who invites me or not but to know that what I do is done with good intentions and for the betterment of the community.

My love for my people, black people, of the world is the *Osun* trait that I strongly hold. This verse is like a response to my feeling that my community work in Latin America and the US has been accepted but in Boston it is still somewhat rejected. Moreover, I become more conscious of things around me and activities that are performed. Colours mean more to me now and I pay more attention to what I say and how I say it.

African indigenous tradition is both interesting and imposing. I learned from Ify and other women I have met, that they might not be practitioners but when things go bad or they need something, people still turn to *Ifa*. But, I ask: "is this the product of colonialism that makes us turn away from what is authentically ours."

I have an altar for ancestors and many of the women in my life. Those who have passed are Òsun like to me.

(c) Impressions about Other Religions and Africans
I respect all religions and respect that different things speak to each of us. What upsets me is when folks come up to me and speak of one being more legitimate or powerful than the other. It is what it is for each individual. I still feel Catholic in many ways because it was how I was raised but I know I pray more and get down on my knees more now for *Ifa* than I ever did.

Crossing the border, building the homeland

In analysing the narratives of members of the African diaspora community, certain common and recurring elements that inform the spirituality which underline the formation of a homeland community that is not spatially or geographically bound are identified and discussed. This thus agrees in part with Johnson's claim that "In the homeland, the central ritual event brings into being through performance, the momentary fusion of kin, ancestors, and territory." (Johnson 2007: 146) I say in part because rather than being momentary, the fusion is permanent. I have also discovered some of these elements in the DVD documentary produced by an African American lady, Yeye Siju Osunyemi, who came to Nigeria to receive *Osun* initiation in Osogbo. (Osunyemi 2006)

(a) Orisa Practice: Finding Meaning, Space and Fulfilment

Orisa practice, for the African diaspora community, provides a way of building the bridge between the past and the present, and between the peoples of African descent in the Americas and those in African continent. The question of 'home' engages the search for the root. In the bid to build the bridge and reinforce the homeland, the practice of indigenous religion provides for the community a medium 'rebirth,' a reconnection to the real being and whole self, against the fragmented self, caused by the trauma of slavery. It is a means of spiritual stability. It helps to reclaim the real self and regain personal and communal identity.

Reading the stories of the new world practitioners of African religion makes us understand that the people believe that indigenous spirituality is the root of their real existence, being and beingness, and therefore their African identity. The practice of *orisa* for them gives unrestricted access to finding meaning, space and fulfilment in life through the mechanism of ritual. Besides telling the story of the slave experience, the myths of the several *orisa* in African pantheon, and ritual practices inspired by the myths strengthen the individual's personal and communal belief and worship. The practices of the *orisa* reveal that the *orisa* are at the basis of the worldview of the Africans as an individual and as a community. Those myths are also intricately linked with immense and intense ritual practices Most of these are taught and directed through *Ifa* corpus and divination.

Thus, myths and rituals are employed in understanding and organising human life and existence. Ritual activities are taken seriously. African Diaspora community imbues themselves with the energy derived from their practice of indigenous spirituality. The sense of commitment in and dedication to ritual practices including initiation and other performances empowers their personal and collective identity. As in indigenous African communities where no distinction is made between the sacred and the profane, material elements (such as water, colour, perfume, animals, earth, etc.) are objectified and interpreted in sacred term in otherwise American secular worldview and members now understand and accept those materials to carry spiritual significance.

In *Orisa* practice, the multiplicity of the *orisa*, the unrestricted access to *orisa* practice, the beauty, flexibility and openness of *orisa* worship and practice, and the fact that each person has an important place and identity in the scheme of the practice allure members to the religion. Members revealed that an individual usually has a principal *orisa* and could also be claimed by as many *orisa* as possible. One also has one's altar(s) for one's *orisa* to whom one offers sacrifices as one deems fit or as demanded by one's *orisa*.

Moreover, unlike in Christianity and Islam, the hierarchies in *orisa* worship and practices are not complex and not unnecessarily protected. Unrestricted freedom is guaranteed to members of whatever gender and status as the practice of *orisa* is inclusive of any willing practitioner. A member claimed that she enjoyed her acceptability by her *Orisa* community and that she enjoyed being able to dispense her gifts. Indigenous religious practice is a source of cultural renaissance for the people.

Joseph Murphy examines the devotion to African religion, particularly *Osun*, by the African Diaspora community:

> In the late eighteenth and early nineteenth centuries, Yorùbá men and women were enslaved in great number and taken across the Atlantic. In many areas, particularly in Brazil, Cuba, and Trinidad, they were able to maintain their devotion to Oshun and look to her for ways of coping with the dreadful challenges that faced them. (Murphy 2001: 225)

(b) Ancestor Worship: Connecting the living and the dead

To all members of the African Diaspora community, African ancestors are part of the community and lives of the people. The ancestors comprise the *orisa*, deceased Africans in African continent, people of African descent who passed through slavery as well as their deceased offspring in the Americas. Osunyemi defines and adores ancestors as "our family in the spirit world who have served as role models to us and our community. We are never alone, for we stand on the shoulders of those who have gone on before us. In this practice, we revere people who live exemplary lives." (2006: 12) Awo Alakisa states that "ancestors are a central part of my spirituality. It is the connection to Africa and those who died during the middle passage and those who were slaves and those who lived and fought segregation in this (America) country."

The practice of ancestor is intense and their worship provides a means of reconnecting with, and memorializing the past, and Africans of whatever generations regardless of their social milieux and geographical space they exist. It has been noted that most members of this community who were once Christians but now converted to *Orisa* practice feel worried that African Christians are not doing well in the treatment of their ancestors. They remark that Africans revere and honour Jewish ancestors and despise their own ancestors. Furthermore, most of our informants tell stories about their deceased close relatives, mother, father, aunt and brothers with whom they have intimate relationship and constantly interact in their dreams. Some of them narrate their dream experiences during which time their relatives communicate with them, and come to their aids at critical moments and in their times of despair and need.

(c) Hierophany, the Experiential and the Expressive: Aesthetics, Rhythm and Beauty

Hierophany, the manifestation of the sacred, reveals the rhythm, aesthetics and beauty in the living experiences of the African diaspora community. Members, through the narratives, reveal that they enjoy a great deal of experiential dimension through which their ways of life and life's decisions are ordered in *orisa* practice. This experiential dimension, including dreams, innate spiritual ability, charisma derived from the knowledge and practice of *orisa*, and initiation ritual play important role in their personal private and communal lives. Members make meanings from their dreams. To them, dream is spiritual and not psychological. It is a manifestation of spiritual beings including their ancestors.

Another mode of hierophanic experience is ecstasy, a product of rhythm, language, aesthetics and beauty, which an initiate encounters during ritual practice and/or drumming and singing. The practice of African-derived religion is highly expressive. The worldview of the people involves an interaction of the human, the spiritual and the natural. Practitioners engage in full-blown ritual practices, festival songs, and chants. These induce the possession by the spirit of their acclaimed and respective *orisa*.

Each *orisa* is identified with the paraphernalia, drum ensemble, orin (songs) and dance styles. Devotees learn, sing and dance to the expressive songs of *orisa*. These all produce important rhythms in language, aesthetics and beauty. The way the people ornament their shrines with natural elements (water, brass, eggs, honey, etc.), photos and abstract images of different colours reinforce their love for nature which is linked to aesthetics and beauty. Moreover, at initiation and some other times, a devotee openly puts on the paraphernalia of his or her adopted *orisa*, takes names that reflect the *orisa*.

(d) Personal Altar: Healing the Sick Soul, Liberating the Mind

The legacy and memory of the middle passage inscribed in the minds of the people in the Americas are always fresh, deep and intense. The community, through indigenous form of spirituality, inspires a sense of selfhood and self-esteem to respond to the effect of the social and political dislocation and imposed worthlessness in their geographical 'homeland' America.

The homeland identity constructed and reinforced through the worship of *Orisa* provides a creative way of healing the past in the present in order to empower the future. Thus, the borderless homeland provides a pragmatic means of resolving cultural, social, and political alienation and disconnection where 'òrìsà liberates the mind'.

The altar provides the space for the meeting of the spiritual and the humans. Each person has his or her altar(s) for his or her *orisa* to whom he or she offers sacrifices as a devotee deems fit or as demanded by *orisa*. Among the new world practitioners of indigenous religion, the processes of setting up of altars are simple and diversified according to the taste of the individuals. The flexibility, beauty and freedom involved in building personal altars are themselves self-liberating. Both genders are at liberty to construct and set up altars.

(e) Networking Relationship, Strengthening Spirituality and Community

Members of the African diaspora community express the feeling of homecoming into African continent through religious pilgrimage and initiation. Practitioners show the desire to visit the African homeland in order to draw from the spiritual energy of the 'source' and get deepened in the spirituality of the root. They go to indigenous communities such as Osogbo, Ife, and Oyo in Nigeria where the practice of *Orisa* still flourishes. The acclaimed *Osun* festival which has assumed an international posture also provides an opportunity for them to connect with their 'spiritual' members and express their spirituality. The main purpose of going to these African communities is to get initiation into some Yoruba *orisa*, notwithstanding the cost of the journey and exercise.

Most of the members of this community who come to Oyo undergo training in the general practice of indigenous spirituality in the school established by the Awise Ogunwande Abimbola, the *Ifa* exponent and an Oyo indigene, who functions as a major evangelist of indigenous religious traditions in the Americas. He it is who initiates members who are interested in *Ifa*. Some others come to *Ifa* Temple in Oke-Itase, Ile-Ife to be initiated under the *Araba Agbaye*. Osogbo is another place where some members go to receive initiation into *Osun*. Prince Atanda and other priests and priestesses of *Osun* deity are involved in the process.

It should be mentioned that several festival songs and initiation rituals have been documented in CDs and DVDs, while some are put on websites. There is also a huge production of books by devotees among the African religious practitioners to preserve the memory of Africa in places like Trinidad and Cuba. Hucks and Stewart observe that: "as the twenty-first century unfolds, *Orisha* (Yoruba) practitioners best symbolize this legacy of cultural and religious preservation" and reinforce Trinidad *Orisa* identity. "...[T]his process of preservation however is simultaneously a process of self-definition where *Òrìsà* leaders use ancient African ideals and principles to create new sources of religious meaning new paradigms of authority within the tradition." (2003)

Conclusion

Indigenous spirituality or religion does not only form a fundamental component of identity, it is central to self-definition and communal relationship. The homeland, as imagined and lived by the people, and as a point of reference, empowers, stabilizes and provides security, and encourages social and political networks where a member expresses him/herself without the fear of rejection or suppression. African Diaspora community perhaps enjoys this as the native or resident in African communities encourages their African Diaspora members to come home. As the borderless homeland becomes strengthened, a new sense of belonging and acceptance is forged, the terrible memory of rejection defuses, and a new and better identity is created. Noting that African indigenous religion has assumed a global status as demonstrated by the contributions in Olupona and Rey's *Orisa Devotion* (2008), I shall like to close with the remarks of Dwight Hopkins *et al.* that:

> For the majority of cultures around the world, religion thoroughly permeates and decisively affects the everyday rituals of survival and hope. Reflected in diverse spiritual customs, sacred symbols, and indigenous worship styles, global religions are permanent constituents of human life. ... [F]or most of the world's peoples, religion helps to construct the public realm ...[R]eligions embodied in disparate human cultures have served as the foundation ... for the resolution of hostility and the achievement of full humanity for those at the bottom of all societies...(2001: 1)

In conclusion, the identity of the African Diaspora community is cultural as it is spiritual. To them, the homeland is not restricted by geographical and political boundaries, but it is the space where the communion of the spiritual and the human is lived, enjoyed, and expressed in the eternal spirit of oneness and unity.

References

Afolayan, A. *Nationalism and the Nation-State* Ibadan: Hope Publications, 2002
Anderson, Benedict. *Imagined Communities*. London: Verso, 1993
Eck, Diana L. *A New Religious America: How a 'Christian Country' Has Become the World's Most Religiously Diverse Nation* New York: HarperCollins Publishers, 2002
Hopkins, Dwight N., Lois Ann Lorentzen, Eduardo Mendieta & David Batstone (eds.). *Religions/Globalizations: Theories and Cases* Durham and London: Duke University Press, 2001
Hucks, Tracey and Dianne Stewart. "Authenticity and Authority in the Shaping of Trinidad Orisha Identity: Toward an African-Derived Religious Theory" *Western Journal of Black Studies*, Vol. 27, No. 3 (2003): 176-85

Johnson, Paul Christopher. *Diaspora Conversions: Black Carib Religion and the Recovery of Africa* Berkeley, Los Angeles & London: University of California Press, 2007
Mol, Hans, *Identity and the Sacred: A Sketch for a New Social Scientific Theory of Religion*. Oxford: Blackwell or New York: Free Press, 1977
Murphy, Joseph M. & Mei-Mei Sanford (eds.). *Òsun Across the Waters: A Yorùbá Goddess in Africa and the Americas* Bloomington and Indianapolis: Indiana University Press, 2001
Murphy, Joseph M., "Oshun." In Stephen D. Glazier (ed.) *Encyclopaedia of African and African-American Religions* Routledge, 2001
Ogungbile, David O. "Faith Without Borders: Culture, Identity and Nigerian Immigrant Churches in Multicultural American Community." In D.O. Ogungbile & E. A. Akinade (eds.), *Creativity and Change in Nigerian Christianity* Lagos, Nigeria: Malthouse Press: 2010: 311-332
Olupona, Jacob K. & Regina Gemignani (eds.). *African Immigrant Religions in America* New York & London: New York University Press, 2007: 1-24
Olupona, Jacob K. and Terry Rey (eds.). *Orisa Devotion as World Religion: The Globalization of Yoruba Religious Culture* Madison, Wisconsin: the University of Wisconsin Press, 2008.
Osunyemi, Siju, *Priestess of Osun: My Practice*. Leicester, North Carolina, Zamani Productions, 2006
Sheffer, Gabriel. *Diaspora Politics: At Home Abroad* Cambridge: Cambridge University Press, 2003
Smart, Ninian. *Dimensions of the Sacred: An Anatomy of the World's Beliefs* Berkeley, Los Angeles: University of California Press, 1996
Sproul, Barbara. *Primal Myths: Creating the World* New York & London: Harper & Row, 1979

Postscript

Jacob Kehinde Olupona: a brief biography

- Ayodeji Ogunnaike

Jacob Kehinde Olupona, Professor of African Religious Traditions at the Divinity School and Professor of African and African American Studies in the Faculty of Arts and Sciences, Harvard University Cambridge, MA, USA is regarded as one of the foremost scholars working on religion in Africa and African religions. Born into an Anglican family of the Venerable and Mrs. Olupona, Prof. Olupona has always been deeply involved in the study of religion, culture, and society in Nigeria, and thus pursued a degree in religious studies at the University of Nigeria Nsukka.

Before leaving Nigeria to begin his graduate study, however, Professor Olupona completed his year of NYSC as a lecturer in Kwara College of Technology in Ilorin. He then joined Obafemi Awolowo University (formerly University of Ife) Ile-Ife in 1976 as a teaching fellow. Afterward, Professor Olupona continued on to Boston University to earn both his MA and PhD in the History of Religions in 1981 and 83 respectively. On his return to Nigeria, he proceeded to hold the positions of Lecturer and Senior Lecturer at OAU until 1995 in the Department of Religious Studies. It is often said that he is one of the very few major intellectuals specializing in the comparative study of religions, focusing on Islam, Christianity, and indigenous African religions. As a result Professor Olupona was recruited in 1995 by the University of California Davis where he served as a Professor in their African-American and African Studies department until 2006. While at UC Davis, he served as director of the African-American and African department studies for five years and Director of the Religious Studies Program for two years before that. It was after his time at UC Davis that Professor Olupona accepted an appointment at Harvard University to the faculty of the Divinity School as well as the Department of African and African American at the Faculty of Arts and Sciences where he has remained ever since.

On top of his joint-professorship, Professor Olupona wears several other hats here at Harvard, including his role as the Director of Graduate Studies in the African and African-American Studies Department since 2010. He has also served as the Chair of the Committee on African Studies from 2006-2009. He is a member of the committee on the study of religion, has served as the chair and member of the admission committees for graduate studies of both African and African American Studies and Harvard Divinity School, chairs the African and African American Religion course curriculum at the Harvard Divinity School, and directs the Nigeria and the World Seminar series for the Weatherhead Center for International Affairs to mention just a few.

Professor Olupona's accomplishments have been marked by several other institutions as well, as he has received honorary doctoral degrees from both the University of Edinburgh in 2000 and the University of Abuja, Nigeria in 2009. He has also garnered several major awards, grants, and fellowships from various organizations including, the Guggenheim Foundation, the American Philosophical Society, the Ford Foundation, the Davis Humanities Institute, the Rockefeller Foundation in Bellagio, Italy, the Wenner-Gren Foundation, and the Getty Foundation. In 2007 Professor Olupona was selected for the Nigerian National Merit Award, the highest academic distinction for Nigerian citizens.

Prof. Olupona's most recent book, *City of 201 Gods: Ile-Ife in Time, Space, and Imagination* just garnered him the illustrious Cabot Fellowship. The Cabot Fellowship was established in 1905 in honour of Walter Channing Cabot by his family, aims to award and encourage scholarly endeavours and academic distinction through the recognition of select Harvard faculty following significant publications and scholarly works that have made an impact in their fields. However, this is just one of an impressive list of 11 books, numerous chapters and articles, and countless speeches, seminars, and lectures delivered in the Americas, Africa, Asia, the Middle East, and Europe.

Select bibliography

A Toolkit: Peace Practice in Nigeria, Abuja; Published by Institute for Democracy in South Africa, (IDASA), 2004

Abdul, M.O.A. 1970. "Yoruba Divination and Islam." *Orita* 4.1 (June): 44-56

Abhuere, P. 2002. "The Roman Catholic Church and Mission in Bini Land, 1810-1950" Unpublished Long Essay, University of Benin.

Abimbola, Kola. 2005. *Yoruba Culture: A Philosophical Account*. Birmingham, U.K.: Iroko Academic Publishers.

Abimbola, Wande & Ivor Miller. 1997. *Ifá Will Mend Our Broken World: Thoughts on Yorùbá Culture in West Africa and the Diaspora*. Roxbury, MA: AIM Books.

Abimbola, Wande. 1971."La notion de personne en Afrique Noire." *Centre National de la Recherche Scientifique,* No. 544:73-89

Abimbola, Wande. 1975. *Sixteen Great Poems of Ifa*, Paris: UNESCO.

Abimbola, Wande. 1976. *Ifa: An Exposition of Ifa Literary Corpus* Ibadan: Oxford University Press

Abimbola, Wande. 1983 *Ijinle Ohun Enu Ifa, Apa Kinni* (2nd ed.) Oyo: AIM Press & Publishers

Abiodun, Rowland. 1989. "Woman in Yoruba Religious Images." *African Languages and Cultures* 2 (1): 1-18.

Achebe, Chinua. 1981 [1958]. *Things Fall Apart*. Ibadan: Heinemann.

Adams, Captain John. 1823. *Remarks on the Country Extending from Cape Palmas to the River Congo,* London: G. Woodfall.

Adeboye, Olufunke. 2007 "The 'Born-Again' Oba: Pentecostalism and Traditional Chieftaincy in Yorúbáland." *Lagos Historical Review: A Journal of the Department of History & Strategic Studies,* Vol. 7: 1-20

Adedeji, J.A. 1969. "The Alarinjo Theatre: The Study of a Yoruba Theatrical Art from its Earliest Beginnings to the Present Times." Unpublished Ph.D. Thesis, University of Ibadan.

Adedeji, J.A. 1971. "Oral Tradition and the Contemporary Theatre in Nigeria." *Research in African Literatures*, 2 (2): 134-149.

Adedeji, J.A. 1973. "Trends in the Content and Form of the Opening Glee in Yoruba Drama." *Research in African Literatures*, 4 (1): 32-47.

Adedeji, J.A. 1981. "Alarinjo: The Traditional Yoruba Travelling Theatre." In Yemi Ogunbiyi, *Drama and Theatre in Nigeria: A Critical Source Book* (ed.) Lagos: Nigerian Magazine: 221-248.

Adejumo, Ademola. 1994. Osogbo Festival of Images. An Insight into some Aspects of Yoruba Art and History. In Ron Kalilu (ed.) *African Art: Definitions, Forms and Styles*: 63-74. Ogbomoso: Ladoke Akintola University.

Adekanmbi Dare. 2010. "Showcasing Nigeria's Female Traditional Rulers" *Nigeria Tribune,* (02 June)

Aderibigbe Gbola & Deji Ayegboyin (eds.), 1995. *Religion, Medicine and Healing* A Publication of the Nigerian Association for the Study of Religions and Education
Adetugbo, Abiodun. 2001. *African Continuities in the Diaspora*. Lagos: Centre for Black and African Arts and Civilization
Adewale-Somadhi, Farounbi Aina Mosunmola (Chief Fama). 1993. *Fundamental of the Yorùbá Religion (Orisa Worship)*. San Bernardino: Ile Orunmila Communications
Afigbo, A.E. 1973. "The Missionaries and the Aro Expedition of 1901/02" *Journal of Religion in Africa* 5.2: 74-106
Afolayan, A. 2002. *Nationalism and the Nation-State* Ibadan: Hope Publications
Aisien, E. 2001. *The Benin City Pilgrim Stations,* Benin City: Aisien Publications
Aiyejina, Funso and Rawle Gibbons. 1999. "Orisa (Orisha) Tradition in Trinidad." *Caribbean Quarterly* 45, no. 4 (December): 35-50
Ajayi, J.F.A. 1965. *Christian Missions in Nigeria, 1841-1892: The Making of An Elite* London: Longman
Amadiume, Ifi. 1987. *Male Daughters, Female Husbands: Gender and Sex in an African Society*. London: Zed Books.
Amucheazi, E.C. 1974. "A Decade of Church Revolt in Eastern Nigeria, 1956-1966" *Odu* 10: 45-62.
Anderson, A., 1992. *Bazalwane: African Pentecostals in South Africa*. Pretoria: UNISA Press
Anderson, A., 2000. *Zion and Pentecost: The Spirituality and Experience of Pentecostal and Zionist/Apostolic Churches* Pretoria: UNISA Press
Anderson, Benedict. 1993. *Imagined Communities*. London: Verso
Anderson, S. E. 1995. *The Black Holocaust for beginners*. New York, Writers and Readers
Apter, Andrew. 1992. *Black Critics and Kings. The Hermeneutics of Power in Yoruba Society*. Chicago: Chicago University Press.
Arinze, F. A. 1970. *Sacrifice in Ibo Religion*. Ibadan: Ibadan University Press
Asemota, Andy. 2006. "Oba Declares War on Ogboni, Witches" *Daily Sun,* (November 25)
Atanda, J.A. 1980. *An Introduction to Yoruba History*. Ibadan: Caxton Press (West Africa) Limited
Awolalu J.O and P.A Dopamu. 2005 [1979].*West African Traditional Religion* (Revised Edition) Lagos: Macmillan
Awolalu, J. O. 1979. *Yoruba Beliefs and Sacrificial Rites* London: Longman, 1979
Ayandele, E.A. 1966. *The Missionary Impact on Modern Nigeria, 1842-1914* London: Longman
Ayandele, E.A. 1969. "Traditional Rulers and Missionaries in Pre-Colonial West Africa" *Tarikh* 31 (December): 23-37
Ayer, A.J. 1963. *The Concept of a Person and Other Essays* London: Macmillan.
Babayemi S.O. 1992. "The Role of Traditional Rulers in Inter-Religious Dialogue in Nigeria" In Jacob K. Olupona (ed.) *Religion and Peace in Multi-Faith Nigeria* Ile-Ife, Nigeria: Obafemi Awolowo University (197-200)
Badejo, Diedre. 1996. *ÒṢUN ṢÈÈGÈSÍ: The Elegant Deity of Wealth, Power and Femininity*, Trenton, New Jersey: Africa World Press.
Balogun, S.A. 1978. "Introduction and Spread of Islam in West Africa before the Nineteenth Century: A Reassessment." *Odu: A Journal of West African Studies*, n.s., No. 18, Ile-Ife: 1-24.
Barber, Karin, 1991. *I Could Speak Till Tomorrow: Oriki, Women, and the Past in a Yoruba Town*. Edinburgh: Edinburgh University Press.

Barnes, Sandra T. ed. 1997. *Africa's Ogun: Old World and New*. Bloomington: Indiana University Press
Barnes, Sandra, ed. 1980. *Ogun: An Old God for a New Age*. Philadelphia: Institute for the Study of Human Issues
Bartkowski 1998. "Claims-Making and Typifications of Voodoo as a Deviant Religion: Hex, Lies and Videotape." *Journal for the Scientific Study of Religion* 37, no. 4 (559-79)
Bascom, William. 1991 [1969]. *Ifa Divination: Communication between Gods and Men in West Africa*. Bloomington: Indiana University Press
Bassey, Engineer Bassey Efiong. 2001. (original 1998) *Ékpè Efik: A Theosophical Perspective*. Victoria, B.C.: Trafford Publishing
Beier, Ulli. 1956. "Oshun Festival." *Nigeria Magazine* 53: 170-187.
Beier, Ulli. 1970.*Yoruba Poetry*. Cambridge: Cambridge University Press
Berthoud, Jacques A. 1969. *The Sole Function*, South Africa: University of Natal Press.
Brandon, George. 1993. *Santería from Africa to the New World: The Dead Sell Memories*. Bloomington: Indiana University Press
Brown, David. 2003. *Santería Enthroned: Art, Ritual, and Innovation in an Afro-Cuban Religion*, Chicago: University of Chicago Press
Brown, Karen McCarthy.1997. "Systematic Remembering, Systematic Forgetting: Ogou in Haiti." In Sandra Barnes (ed.) *Africa's Ogun: Old World and New*, 2nd expanded edition.(Bloomington: Indiana University Press) (65-89)
Brown, Karen McCarthy. 1991. *Mama Lola: A Vodou Priestess in Brooklyn*. Berkeley: University of California Press.
Bruner, Jerome. 2002. *Making Stories: Law, Literature, Life*. Cambridge: Harvard University Press
Brunner, E. 1947 *The Divine Imperative: A study of the Christian Ethics*, trans. Wyon, Philadelpha Westminister
Buckley, A.D., 1985. *Yoruba Medicine* Oxford: Clarendon Press
Burns J.M. 1978. *Leadership* New York: Harper Torch Books
Butler, Judith, 1990. *Gender Trouble: Feminism & the Subversion of Identity*. New York: Routledge.
Cabrera, Lydia. 1968. *El Monte: igbo, finda, ewe Orisha, vititi nfinda: notas sobre las religions, la magia, las supersticiones y el folklore de los negros criollos y el pueblo de Cuba*. Miami: Ediciones C.R.
Cabrera, Lydia. 1988. *La Lengua Sagrada de los Ñañigos*. Miami: Colección del Chicherekú en el exilio.
Cahn, S.M. 1969. *Fate, Logic and Time*. London: Yale University Press.
Canstellanos, Isabella. 1996. "From Ulkumi to Lucumi: A Historical Overview of Religious Acculturation in Cuba." In *Santeria Aesthetics in Contemporary Latin American Art*. Ed. Arturo Lindsay Washington, D.C.: Smithsonian Institute Press: 39-50
Chambers, E.K. 1903. *The Medieval Stage*, Oxford: Oxford University Press.
Chesi, Gerd. 1983. *Susanne Wenger. A Life with the Gods in their Yoruba Hinterland*. Wörgl: Perlinger Verlag.
Chhachhi, Amrita. 1990. Religious Fundamentalism and Women. *WAF Journal* 1: 14-15.
Chitando, Ezra, 2004. African Instituted Churches in Southern Africa: Paragons of Regional Integration?' in *African Journal of International Affairs* 7 (1 & 2): 117–132.
Clark, Mary Ann. 2005. *Where Men Are Wives and Mothers Rule: Santeria Ritual Practices and Their Gender Implications*. Gainesville University Press of Florida.

Clarke, Kamari, M. 2004. *Mapping Yoruba Networks: Power and Agency in the Making of Transnational Communities*. Duke University Press

Clarke, P. B., 1982. *West Africa and Islam* London: Edward Arnold

Colpe and Casten. 1993. "Sacred and the Profane." Translated from German by Reussel M. Stockman. In *The Encyclopedia of Religion* (511-526)

Cone, James H. 1984. *For My People: Black Theology and the Black Church. Where Have We Been and Where Are We Going?* Maryknoll, N.Y.: Orbis *Books*.

Connah, Graham E. 1975. *The Archaeology of Benin* Oxford: Clarendo.

Conner, Randy P. 2005. "Rainbow's Children: Diversity of Gender and Sexuality in African-Diasporic Spiritual Traditions." In Patrick Bellegarde-Smith, ed. *Fragments* of *Bone: Neo African Religions in a New World*. Chicago: University of Illinois Press: 143-66

Cox, H. 2001. Fire from Heaven. The Rise of Pentecostal Spirituality and the Reshaping of Religion in the 21st Century. Reading, MA: Addison–Wesley.

Cox, James L (1998). "Introduction: Ritual, Rites of Passage and the Interaction between Christian and Traditional Religions". In *Rites of Passage in Contemporary Africa*, RCAS, Religion in Contemporary Africa Series, Cardiff, GB: Cardiff Academic Press.

Crampton, E.P.T., 1975. *Christianity in Northern Nigeria* (London: Geoffrey Chapman)

Crowder, Micheal. 1978. *The Story of Nigeria*. London: Faber & Faber

Crumbley, Deidre, 1992. Impurity and Power: Women in Aladura Churches. *Africa* 62 (4): 505-522.

Daly, Mary, 1973. *Beyond God the Father: Towards a Philosophy of Women's Liberation*. Boston: Beacon Press.

Danfulani, U.H.D. and Andrew Haruna. 1998. "Redressing Drought: Rituals of Rain-making among the Guruntun and Mupun people of Nigeria". In *Africana Marburgensia*, Marburg University, Germany, 31(1&2)20-36.

Danfulani, U.H.D. and Andrew Haruna. 1999. "Rituals of Rain-making among the Gurumtum and Mupun People". *Studies of the Department of African Languages and Cultures*, 26(28)23-45, Institute of Oriental Studies, Warsaw University.

Danfulani, Umar H.D 1995. *Pebbles and Deities: Pa Divination among the Ngas, Mupun and Mwaghavul in Nigeria* (1994 Uppsala Diss.) Frankfurt am Main, Bern, Berlin, New York: Peter Lang.

Danfulani, Umar Habila Dadem. 2003. *Understanding Nyam: studies in the history and culture of the Ngas, Mupun and Mwaghavul in Nigeria,* Koln: Köppe.

Danmole, H.O. 2008. "Religious Encounter in Southwestern Nigeria: The Domestication of Islam among the Yoruba." In: Olupona J.K. and Terry Ray (eds.) *Orisa Devotion as World Religion: The Globalization of Yoruba Religious Culture*, The University of Wisconsin Press.202-221.

Daramola, Yomi. 2008. "Education and Aesthetic Values in Yoruba Islamic Music" *JANIM: Journal of the Association of Nigerian Musicologists*, (Special Edition): 139-150.

Darling, P.J. 1984. *Archaeology and History in Southern Nigeria: The Ancient Linear Earthworks of Benin and Ishan*. Cambridge Monographs in African Archaeology 11, BAR International Series.

Dash, Julie 1991. *Daughters of the Dust* (VHS). A Geechee Girl Production

Datok, Polycarp F. 1983. *A Short History of Sura (Panyam): (C. 1730-1981)*, Jos, Nigeria: Nigeria Bible Translation Trust.

de Beauvois, Palisot. 1801. *As to the Inhabitants of the Kingdom of Benin on the West Coast of the Tropical Africa,* Weimar: Industrie-Comptoirs

De La Torre, Miguel A. 2001. "Ochun, [N]either the [M]other of All Cubans, [N]or the Bleached Virgin." *Journal of the American Academy of Religion* 69, no. 4: 837-61.
De La Torre, Miguel A. 2004. *Santería: the Beliefs and Rituals of a Growing Religion in America.* Grand. Rapids: Eerdsmans
DeGraft, J.C. 1976. "Roots of African Drama and Theatre", *African Literature Today*, (8): 1-25.
Dike, Tony. 2005. "Tension in Enugu As Youth Destroy Shrine," *Vanguard* (January 5)
do Nascimento, Abdias. 1979. *Brazil: Mixture or Massacre: Essays in the Genocide of a Black People.* Dover, Mass.: Majority Press
Dopamu, Abiola T. 2010. "The Place of Traditional Rulers in a Democratic System of Government in Yorúbáland" In Adam K. arap Chepkwony & Peter M.J. Hess (eds.), *Human Views on God: Variety Not Monotony: Essays in Honour of Ade P. Dopamu* (Eldoret: Moi University Press) (53-61)
Dopamu, P. A. (ed.). 2003. *African Culture, Modern Science and Religious Thought* (Ilorin: ACRS).
Dopamu, P. Ade, 2000. "Yoruba Traditional Medicine in Health Care Delivery" In Nike Lawal (ed.), *Yoruba Life and Culture* (St. Cloud State University)
Dopamu, P.A. 1979. "Yoruba Magic and Medicine and their Relevance for Today" *Religions: Journal of the Nigerian Association for the Study of Religions*, Vol. 4: 5-14.
Drewal, Margaret Thompson. 1992. *Yorùbá Ritual: Performers, Plays, Agency.* Bloomington, Indiana University Press
Durkheim, Emile. 1965. *The Elementary Forms of Religious Life.* New York: Free Press
Dzurgba, A. 1987. *Sociology of Religion,* Ibadan: A Publication of the Department of Adult Education, University of Ibadan
Eck, Diana L. 2002. *A New Religious America: How a 'Christian Country' Has Become the World's Most Religiously Diverse Nation* New York: HarperCollins Publishers
Edokpaigbe, I. 2004. "The Relevance of Igue Festival in Contemporary Era" *Edo National* Vol.1, No.2: 11- 18
Edu, O.K. 2004. "The Effect of Customary Arbitral Award on Substantive Litigation. Setting Matter Straight." *Journal of Private and Property Law* 25
Egharevba, J. U., 2005. *A Short History of Benin.* Benin: Fortune and Temperance Publishing Coy.
Egharevba, J.U. 1960. *A Short History of Benin,* Ibadan: Ibadan University Press
Egharevba, J.U. 1965. *Chronicles of Events in Benin,* Benin City: Kopin-Dogba Press.
Ehianu, W.E., 2005. "The Ika People and the Quest for Long Life." *EPHA: Ekpoma Journal of Religious Studies* 5 (2): 124-135.
Ejizu, C. 1986. *Ofo: Igbo Ritual Symbol,* Nigeria, Fourth Dimension Publishing Co. Ltd
Ekechi, Felix, 1972. *Missionary Enterprise and Rivalry in Igboland, 1857-1914* London: Frank Cass.
Ekwuru, Emeka George. 1999. *The Pangs of an African Culture in Travail.* Owerri: TOTAN Publishers.
Eliade, Mircea, 1958. *Patterns of Comparative Religion* London: 1958 English translation
Eliade, Mircea. 1959. *The Sacred and Profane.* Translated by William Trask. New York: Harcourt Bruce & Co.
Ellis S. and Gerrie ter Haar, 2004. *Worlds of Power: Religious Thought and Political Practice in Africa* London: Hurst and Company
Erivwo, S.U., 1973. "Christian Churches in Urhoboland", *Orita* 7.1 (June): 206-215

Etherton, Michael. 1982. *The Development of African Drama*. London: Hutchinson & Co Publishers.
Evans, Matthew T. 2003. "The Sacred: Differentiating, Clarifying and Extending Concept." *Review of Religious Research* 45 (1) : 32-47.
Evans-Pritchard, E.E. (ed.). ???? *Institutions of Primitive Society* Oxford: University Press
Evans-Pritchard, E.E. 1965. *Theories of Primitive Religion* Oxford: Clarendon Press
Eze, E.C. (ed.) 1988. *African Philosophy: An Anthology* Massachusetts: Blackwell
Ezeanya, E. 1999. "Traditional Values in Iboland" *Bigard Memorial Seminary,* Enugu, Vol.19 No.1: 1-10
Falade, Fasina. 2002. *Ifa: The Key To Its Understanding*. Lynwood: Afa Ifa Publishing
Fandrich, Ina J. 2005. "Defiant African Sisterhoods: The Voodoo Arrests of 1850s and 1860s in New Orleans."In Patrick Bellegarde-Smith (ed.) *Fragments of Bones: New African Religions in a New world*. Chicago: University of Illinois Press (187-207)
Ferreira Da Silva, Denise. 2005 "Out of Africa? Umbanda and the 'Ordering' of the Modern Brazilian Space." In *Fragments of Bone: Neo African Religions in a New World*. Ed. By Patrick Bellegarde-Smith. Chicago: University of Illinois Press. 32-51
Field, David N. "Ecology, Modernity and the New South African: Theology of Eco-justice." *Journal of Christian Thought* 2 (1) 199??: 44-48.
Field, M.J., 1937, *Religion and Medicine of the Ga People* London: Oxford University Press)
Frazer, J., 1994. *The Golden Bough*. London: Oxford University Press.
Friesen, Lauren. 2005. "Drama and Religion: the Search for a New Paradigm," *The Journal of Religion and Theatre*, 4 (1): 8-15.
Gbadamosi, T.G.O. 1978. *The Growth of Islam among the Yoruba 1841-1908*. London: Longman.
Gbadamosi, T.G.O. 1967. "The Establishment of Western education among Muslims in Nigeria" *JHSN* 4.1: 94ff
Gbadegesin, Olusegun. 1984. "Destiny, Personality, and the Ultimate Reality of Human existence: A Yoruba Perspective." *Ultimate Reality and Meaning* Vol.7, No.3: 177-188
Geertz, Clifford. 1973. "Thick Description: Toward an Interpretive Theory of Culture," in *The Interpretation of Cultures: Selected Essays by Clifford Geertz* New York: Basic Books
Gehman, R.J., 1989. *African Traditional Religion in Biblical Perspective* Kesho Publications, Kenya
Goshit, Zacharia Damina. 1980. "A Hundred Years of Religious Change in Ngasland." BA Long Essay, History Department, University of Jos, Nigeria
Grunbaum, Adolf. 1953. Causality and the Science of Human Behaviour. In *Readings in the Philosophy of Science*, ed. Herbert Feigl and May Brodbeck, 766–78. New York: Appleton-Century-Crofts.
Gutierrez, Gustavo, 1988 [1973]. *A Theology of Liberation: History, Politics, and Salvation*. Trans. and ed. by Sister Caridad Inda and John Eagleson. Maryknoll, N.Y.: Orbis
Haggai, John Edmund. 1986. *Lead on!: Leadership that Endures in a Changing World*, Waco, Tx. : Word Books.
Hallen, Barry. 2004. "Yoruba Moral Epistemology" in Kwasi Wiredu (ed.) *A Companion to African Philosophy* Oxford: Blackwell: 296-303

Hallen, Barry. 1989. *"Eniyan: A Critical Analysis of the Yoruba Concepts of Person"* in C.S. Momoh (ed), *The Substance of African Philosophy* Auchi: African Philosophy Projects: 328-354

Hallgren, Roland. 1992. "Religion and Health Among Traditional Yoruba" *Orita: Ibadan Journal of Religious Studies* Vol. xxiv/1-2: 67ff

Harding, Rachel. 1995. *A Refuge in Thunder: Candomblé and Alternative Spaces of Blackness*. Bloomington: Indiana University Press.

Hastings, Adrian, 1994. *The Church in Africa: 1450-1950*. Oxford: Clarendon Press.

Henry, Frances. 2003. *Reclaiming African Religions in Trinidad: The Socio-Political Legitimization of the Orisha and Spiritual Baptist Faiths*. Port of Spain: UWI Press.

Herskovits, Melville J. 1948. "The Contribution of Afroamerican Studies to Africanist Research." *American Anthropologist*. Vol. 50, no. 1 part 1 (January-March): 1-10.

Herskovits, Melville J.1967. *Dahomey: An Ancient West African Kingdom*. 2 vols. Evanston, IL: Northwestern UP.

Horton, Robin and J.D.Y. Peel. 1976. "Conversion and Confusion: A Rejoinder on Christianity in Eastern Nigeria" *Journal of African Studies* Vol. 10: 481-497

Horton, Robin, 1975. "On the Rationality of Conversion" *Africa* 45.3: 219-235; 45.4: 373-399

Houk, James. 1993. *Spirits, Blood, and Drums: The Orisha Religion in Trinidad*. Philadelphia: Temple University Press.

Hucks, Tracey and Dianne Stewart, 2003. "Authenticity and Authority in the Shaping of Trinidad Orisha Identity: Toward an African-Derived Religious Theory." *Western Journal of Black Studies*, Vol. 27, No. 3 (176-85)

Hucks, Tracey, 1998. "Approaching the African God: An Examination of African American Yoruba History from 1959 to the Present" Ph.D. Dissertation, Harvard University

Hurston, Zora Neale, 1981. *The Sanctified Church*. Berkeley: Turtle Island Foundation.

Idowu, E. Bolaji. 1973. *African Traditional Religion: A Definition* London: SCM Press

Idowu, E. Bolaji. 1996 [1962]. *Olodumare: God in Yoruba Belief* Lagos: Longman (Revised and Enlarged Edition)

Ifeka-Moller, C. 1974. "White Power: Social-Structural Factors in Conversion to Christianity, Eastern Nigeria, 1921-1966", *Canadian Journal of African Studies* Vol. 8, No. 1: 55-72

Ifemesia, C.C. 1962. "The Civilizing Mission of 1841", *JHSH*, 2.3 (December): 291-310

Ihekweazu, E. (ed.), 1985. *Traditional and Modern Culture* Enugu: Fourth Dimensions Publications

Ikime, Obaro. 1972. *The Isoko People: A Historical Survey* Ibadan: University Press

Ikime, Obaro. 1965. "The Coming of the C.M.S. to Itshekiri, Urhobo, and Isoko", *Nigeria Magazine*, 84 (September): 206-215;

International Congress of Orisa Tradition and Culture at http://www.orisaworld.org

Isichei, Elizabeth, 1995. *A History of Christianity in Africa from Antiquity to the Present*. London: Wm. B. Eerdmans Publishing.

Iwara, A.U. 2005. "Language and Communication in Conflict Resolution and Peace Building" *Perspectives on Peace and Conflicts in Africa: Essays in Honours of Gen (Dr) Abudusalami Abubakar*, Isaac Olawale Albert (ed.), Ibadan: Peace and Conflicts Studies, University of Ibadan & John Archer Publishers: 65-79 & 73-74.

Jensen, J. S. and L. H. Martin (eds.) 1997. *Rationality and the Study of Religion*, Aarhus Acta Jutlandica LXXII)

Johnson, Elizabeth A. 1992. *She Who Is: The Mystery of God in Feminist Theological Discourse*. New York: Crossroad Publishing Company.

Johnson, Paul Christopher. 2007. *Diaspora Conversions: Black Carib Religion and the Recovery of Africa* Berkeley, Los Angeles & London: University of California Press
Johnson, S.O. 1969. *The History of the Yorubas.* Lagos: C.M.S.
Johnson, Sylvester. 2004. *The Myth of Ham in Nineteenth-Century America: Race, Heathens and the People of God.* New York: Palgrave Macmillan.
Kalu, O. U. 1992. "Gods as Policemen: Religion and Social Control in Igboland", in J.K. Olupona (ed.) *Religious Plurality in Africa: Essays in Honour of J.S. Mbiti* (Berlin: Mouton)
Kalu, O.U. 1977. "Missionaries, Colonial Government and Secret Societies in S.E. Igboland" *JHSN:* 75-90
Kalu, O.U. 1977. "Waves from the Rivers: the Spread of Garrick Braide Movement in Igboland", *JHSN* 8.4
Kalu, O.U., 1978. "The Battle of the Gods: Christianization of Cross River Igboland", *JHSN* X.1: 1-18
Kalu, Ogbu, ed., *Readings in African Cultural Development.* Enugu: Fourth Dimension Publishing Coy Ltd, 1978
Kalu, U. Ogbu. 1996. *The Embattled Gods: Christianization of Igboland, 1841-1991* Lagos, London: MINAJ Publishers
Kamara, Jemadari , and Van Der Meer, T. Menelik (eds.). 2004. *State of the Race: Creating our 21st Century: Where Do We Go From Here,* Boston, Diaspora Press
Kaplan, F.E.S., 2007. "Women in Benin Society and Art" In Barbara Plankensteiner (ed.) *Benin Kings and Rituals: Court Arts from Nigeria,* The Art Institute of Chicago: Snoeck Publishers: 141–149
Kaplan, Flora Edouwaye S. 1993. "Images of the Queen Mother in Benin Court Art", *African Arts* 26, 3
Kaplan, Flora Edouwaye S. 1997/98. *Queens, Queen Mothers, Priestesses, and Power: Case Studies in African Gender,* New York: New York Academy of Sciences.
Knitter, Paul, 1984. "Roman Catholic Approaches to other Religions: Developments and Tensions" *International Bulletin of Missiological Research*, 8.2.
Kraemer, H. 1961 5th edition (1938). *The Christian Message in Non-Christian World* Grand Rapids: Kregel Publishers
Kurt Rudolph "Some Reflections on Approaches and Methodologies in the Study of Religions" In J. S. Jensen and L.H. Martin (eds.) *Secular Theories on Religion: Current Perspectives* University of Copenhagen: Museum Tusculanum Press, 2000: 231-247.
Laduke, Betty. 1989. "Susanne Wenger and Nigeria's Sacred Osun Grove." *Women's Arts Journal* 10 (1) (7-21).
Lawal, Babatunde. 2001. "Aworan: Representing the Self and Its Metaphysical Other in Yoruba Art." *Art Bulletin* 83 (3): 498-526.
Lawal, Babatunde. 1985. "Ori. On the Significance of the Head in Yoruba Sculpture." *Journal of Anthropological Research* 41: 91-103.
Lawal, Nike (ed.), 2000. *Yoruba Life and Culture* St. Cloud State University Press.
Leonard, A. 1968. *The Lower Niger and its Tribes,* London, Frank Cass, 1968
Leonowens, Anna H., (1870) *The English Governess at Siamese Court: Being Recollections of Six Years in the Royal Palace at Bangkok,* London: Trubner.
Lere, Pauline Mark, (1996). *Rev. Dr. David O.V. Lot: His Life and Church Development on the Jos Plateau,* Jos, Nigeria: Jos University Press.
Lincoln, Bruce, "Reflections on Theses on Method," in J. S. Jensen and L. H. Martin (eds.) *Secular Theories on Religion: Current Perspectives*, University of Copenhagen: Museum Tusculanum Press, 2000: 117-136.

Lindom, Thomas. 1990. "Oriki Orişa: The Yoruba Prayer of Praise," *Journal of Religion in Africa*, 20, (2): 205-224.
Lindsay, Arturo, ed. 1996. *Santería Aesthetics in Contemporary Latin American Art*, Washington, D.C.: Smithsonian Institution Press.
Ling, Roth H. (1968) *Great Benin: Its Customs, Arts and Horrors*, London: Routledge and Kegan (originally published in 1903)
Lois, Fuller. *African Traditional Religion*. Kaduna: Baraka Press. 2001
Lopes, Nei. 2004. "African Religions in Brazil: Negotiation and Resistance: A Look From Within." *Journal of Black Studies* 34, no. 6 (838-60)
Lowenthal, David. 1998. Fabricating Heritage. *Memory and History*, 10 (1): 5-24.
Makinde, M.A., *African Philosophy: The Demise of a Controversy* (Ile-Ife: Obafemi Awolowo University Press) 2007.
Maloba, Wunyabari O. 1993. *Mau Mau and Kenya: An Analysis of a Peasant Revolt*. Bloomington: Indiana University Press.
Masuzawa, Tomoko. "The Sacred Differences in the Elementary Form: On Durkheim last Quest." *Representation*, No . 23 (1988):25-50.
Matory, J. Lorand. 2005. *Black Atlantic Religion: Tradition, Transnationalism, and Matriarchy in the Afro-Brazilian Candomblé*. Princeton UP.
Matory, Lorand. 2001. "Surpassing 'Survival,': On the Urbanity of 'Traditional Religion' in the Afro-Atlantic World." *The Black Scholar* 30, nos 3-4 (36-44)
Mbiti, J. S., 1969. *African Religions and Philosophy*. London: Heinemann
Mbiti, J.S., 1995. *Introduction to African Religion*. London: Heinemann.
McCutcheon, Russell T., "How Do We Know What We Claim to Know?" In Russell T. McCutcheon (ed.) *The Insider /Outsider Problem in the Study of Religion: A Reader*, London: Cassell, 1999: 215-220
Mellon, Stephen P. "The Exhibition and Conservation of African Objects: Considering the Nontangibles." *Journal of the American Institute for conservation* 31 (1) (1992): 1-8.
Métreaux, Alfred. 1959. *Voodoo in Haiti*. Trans. by Hugo Charteris. London: Andre Deutsch.
Ikenga-Metuh, Emefie, 1987. "The Shattered Microcosm: A Critical Survey of Explanations of Conversion in Africa" in Kirsten Holst Peterson (ed.) *Religion, Development and African Identity* (Uppsala: Scandinavian Institute of African Studies) (11-27)
Ikenga-Metuh, Emefie. 1981. *God and Man in African Religion*. London & Sydney: Geoffrey Chapman.
Ikenga-Metuh, Emefie. 1985. *African Religions in Western Conceptual Schemes: The Problem of Interpretation (Studies in Igbo Religion)* Ibadan, Nigeria: Pastoral Institute
Ikenga-Metuh, Emefie. 1987. *Comparative Studies of African Traditional Religion* IMICO Publishers, Onitsha
Miller, Ivor. 2000. "Religious Symbolism in Cuban Political Performance." *TDR: A Journal of Performance Studies*. Vol. 44, no. 2 (T166): 30 - 55.
Miller, Ivor. 2005. "Cuban Abakuá chants: examining new evidence for the African Diaspora." *African Studies Review*. April. v. 48, n. 1: 23-58.
Miller, Ivor. 2009. *Voice of the Leopard: African Secret Societies and Cuba*. U P of Mississippi.
Milner Jr., Murray. "Status and Sacredness: Worship and Salvation as Forms of Status Transformation." *Journal of the Scientific Study of Religion* 33 (2) 1994 : .99-109.
Moghadam, Valentine M., ed. 1994. *Identity Politics and Women: Cultural Reassertions and Feminisms in International Perspective*. Oxford: Westview

Press.

Mol, Hans. 1977. *Identity and the Sacred: A Sketch for a New Social Scientific Theory of Religion.* Oxford: Blackwell or New York: Free Press

Montagu, Lady Mary Wortley (et al.). 1837. *The Letters and Works of Lady Mary Wortley Montagu,* New York: R. Bentley

Morakinyo, Olufemi. 1983. "The Ayanmo Myth and Mental Health Care in West Africa", in *Journal of Culture and Ideas* No.1 (68-73)

Morgenbesier, S. and T. Walsh, eds. 1962. *Free Will.* New Jersey: Englewood Cliffs.

Murphy, Joseph M. and Mei-Mei Sanford (eds.), 2001. *Osun Across the Waters: A Yoruba Goddess in Africa and the Americas.* Bloomington, Indiana: Indiana University Press

Murphy, Joseph M. 1994. *Working the Spirit: Ceremonies of the African Diaspora.* Boston: Beacon.

Murphy, Joseph M. 2001. "Oshun." In Stephen D. Glazier (ed.) *Encyclopaedia of African and African-American Religions* Routledge, 2001

Musa, A.J., 1996/97. "Let Us Forge Ahead" *The Voice* 35: 1-15

Nadel, S.F., 1954. *Nupe Religions* (London: Routledge and Kegan Paul Ltd).

Nasseef, Abdulla Omar, 1986. "Muslim-Christian Relations: Muslim Approach" *Current Dialogue 11* (December): 29-32.

Neiers, Marie de Paul (1979). *The Peoples of the Jos Plateau, Nigeria (European University Studies),* Frankfurt: Peter Lang GmbH

Nnoli, Okwudiba. 1978. *Ethnic politics in Nigeria.* Enugu, Nigeria: Fourth Dimension publishers.

Northrup, David. 2009. Email to the author regarding Qua participation in the trans-Atlantic slave trade. April 29.

Oba, Abdulmumini A. "Juju Oaths in Customary Law Arbitration and Their Legal Validity in Nigerian Courts." *Journal of African Law* 52 (1) 2008, : 138-158.

Obadigie, J.O., (1985) "Igue Festival" in A. Omoruyi (ed.) *Benin Series* Vol.13: 47 - 51.

Obi, C. A. 1985. A Hundred Years of the Catholic Church in Eastern Nigeria , 1885–1985. Onitsha: Africana-FEB Publishers.

Obiandu, M. F., *Concept of Reincarnation in Ikwerre.* NCE Long Essay. Port-Harcourt: College of Education, 1983

Oduyoye, M., 1983. "Festivals: The Cultivation of Nature and the Celebration of History." In E.A.A. Adegbola (ed.) *West Africa Traditional Religion*, Ibadan: Daystar Press: 150-169

Oduyoye, M., 1983. "Potent Speech." In E.A.A. Adegbola (ed.) *West African Traditional Religion,* Ibadan: Daystar Press: 203-232

Ofugha, Omosimuna. 2005. Osun Osogbo Opens Tourism Mines in Nigeria. In *The Capitol,* 1 (2): 10-17.

Oguejiofor, Obi J. 1996. *The Influence of Igbo Traditional Religion on the Socio-political Character of the Igbo.* Nsukka: Fulladu Publishing Company.

Ogunba, Oyin. 1991. "Hegemonic Festivals in Yorubaland." Ife: *Annals of the Institute of Cultural Studies*, Ile-Ife: Obafemi Awolowo University.

Ogunbiyi, Yemi. 1979. Drama and Theatre in Nigeria: A Critical Source Book.

Ogundipe-Leslie, 'Molara, 1994. *Re-Creating Ourselves: African Women and Critical Transformations.* New Jersey: African World Press Inc.

Ogungbile, David O. 1997. "Meeting Point of Culture and Health: The Case of the Aladura Churches in Nigeria." *Nordic Journal of African Studies* 6(1): (98–111)

Ogungbile, David O. 1998. "Islam and Cultural Identity in Nigeria: The Òşogbo-Yoruba Experience" *Orita: Ibadan Journal of Religious Studies.* Vol. XXX/1-2: (123-137)

Ogungbile, David O. 2001. "The Dynamics of Language in Cultural Revolution and African Spirituality: The Case of Ijo Orile-Ede Adulawo Ti Kristi (National Church of Christ) in Nigeria." *Nordic Journal of African Studies*, 10 (1) (66–79)

Ogungbile, David O. 2003 "Myth, Ritual and Identity in the Religious Traditions of the Osogbo People of Western Nigeria." PhD Dissertation, Obafemi Awolowo University, Ile-Ife, Nigeria.

Ogungbile, David O. 2004. Religion Experience and Women Leadership in Nigerian Islam. *Jenda: a Journal of Culture and African Women Studies* 6. http://www.iiav.nl/ezines/web/JENda/2005/No6/jendajournal/ogungbile.html

Ogungbile, David O. 2010. "Faith Without Borders: Culture, Identity and Nigerian Immigrant Churches in Multicultural American Community." In D.O. Ogungbile & E. A. Akinade (eds.), *Creativity and Change in Nigerian Christianity* Lagos, Nigeria: Malthouse Press (311-332)

Ogungbile, David O. and Akintunde E. Akinade (eds. 2010. *Creativity and Change in Nigerian Christianity* Lagos, Nigeria: Malthouse

Ohia, C.P. Chi-na-Eke. 2006. *Eke-na-Egwurugwu: The Causal Principles of Unity, Individuation, Multiplicity, and Differentiation in Igbo Metaphysics*. Owerri: Springfield.

Ojo, Matthews A. 1992. Deeper Life Bible Church of Nigeria. In *New Dimensions in African Christianity*, ed. Paul Gifford. Nairobi: All Africa Conference of Churches.

Okere, J. "The Poverty of Christian Individualism, Morality and an African Alternative",http://www.crp.org/book/series/02/11-13

Okolugbo, E., 1984. *A Short History of Christianity in Nigeria: The Ndosumili and the Ukwuani*. Ibadan: Daystar Press.

Ola, V.U. 1982. The Concept of Tragedy in Ola Rotimi's The Gods Are Not To Blame. *Okike: An African Journal of New Writing* 22: 23–31.

Olajubu, Oyeronke, 2002 Reconnecting with the Waters: John 9. I-II. In *The Earth Story in the New Testament,* Vol. 5, ed. C. Habel & V. BalaBanski, 108-121. London: Sheffield Academic Press.

Olajubu, Oyeronke, 2003. *Women in the Yoruba Religious Sphere*. New York: SUNY Press.

Olajubu, Oyeronke, 2005. Gender and Religion: Gender and African Religious Traditions. In *Encyclopedia of Religion, 2nd Edition*, ed. Lindsay Jones. New York: Thomson Gale: 3400-3406

Olomola, Isola, 1995. "Yoruba Monarchism in Transition: A Preliminary Survey" in Biodun Adediran (ed.) Cultural Studies in Ife. (Ile-Ife: Institute of Cultural Studies, Obafemi Awolowo University) (42-58)

Olupona, Jacob K. 1991. "Contemporary Religious Terrain." In: *Religion and Society in Nigeria*, eds. Olupona J. K. and Toyin Falola. Ibadan: Spectrum Books.

Olupona, Jacob K. 1991. *Kingship, Religion and Rituals in a Nigerian Community: A Phenomenological Study of the Ondo Yorùbá Festivals*. Stockholm Studies in Comparative Religion, 28. Almqvist & Wiksell International Stockholm, 1991

Olupona, Jacob K. 1992. "The Dynamics of Religion and Interfaith Dialogue in Nigeria" In J.K. Olupona (ed.) *Religion and Peace in Multifaith Nigeria*, Ile-Ife: Obafemi Awolowo University Press: 1-9.

Olupona, Jacob K. and Regina Gemignani (eds.) 2007. *African Immigrant Religions in America* New York & London: New York University Press: 1-24

Olupona, Jacob K. and Terry Rey (eds.),2008. *Orisa Devotion as World Religion: The Globalization of Yorùbá Religious Culture* Madison, Wisconsin: The University of Wisconsin Press

Olupona, Jacob K., ed. 1991. *African Traditional Religion in Contemporary Society*.

Minnesota: Paragon House.
Olupona, Jacob, ed. 2003. *Beyond Primitivism. Indigenous Religious Traditions and Modernity*. London: Routledge.
Olupona, Jacob. 2001. Orisa Osun. Yoruba Sacred Kingship and Civil Religion in Osogbo, Nigeria. In *Osun Across the Waters. A Yoruba Goddess in Africa and the Americas*, ed. Joseph Murphy and Mei-Mei Sanford, Bloomington: Indiana University Press: 46-67.
Omijeh, M., 1983. "The Significance of Orhue in Benin Symbolism." In E.A.A. Adegbola (ed.) *Traditional Religion in West Africa*, Ibadan: Daystar Press: 195-197
Omojola Bode, 2001, "African Music in Christian Liturgy: The Yoruba Tradition," *Nigerian Music Review*, Vol. 2 (Special Edition): 83.
Opeloye, M.O. 1998, "Evolution of Religious Culture Among the Yoruba". In Deji Ogunremi & Biodun Adediran (eds.) *Culture and Society in Yorubaland*: 139-148.
Opoku, Kofi Asare, 1978. *West African Traditional Religion* Accra: FEP International Private Limited
Ortiz, Fernando. 1950. "La 'tragedia' de los ñáñigos." *Cuadernos Americanos*. Vol. LII, n. 4. (Julio-Agosto) México: 79-101.
Ortiz, Fernando. 1955. *Los instrumentos de la música afrocubana*, vol. 5. La Habana: Cárdenas y Cía.
Osunyemi, Siju, *Priestess of Osun: My Practice*. Leicester, North Carolina, Zamani Productions, 2006
Oviasu, V.O., 2002. *The Centenary of Christianity, Anglican Communion in the Diocese of Benin, 1902-2002*. Benin City: Anglican Diocese of Benin City.
Oyewumi, Oyeronke, 1999. *The Invention of Women*. Minneapolis: University of Minnesota Press.
Parish, Jane. 2003. "Antiwitchcraft Shrine Among the Akan: Possession and the Gathering." *African Studies Review* 46 (3): 17-34.
Parrinder, E. G., *Africa's Three Religions*. London: Sheldon Press, 1976
Parrinder, E. Geoffrey, *African Traditional Religion* Sheldon Press, London, 1968
Parrinder, E.G., (ed.), 1969. *West African Religion* (London: Eppworth Press).
Peek Philip M. "'Divination': A Way of Knowing?" in E.C. Eze (ed.) *African Philosophy: An Anthology* (Massachusetts: Blackwell) 1998: 171-172
Peel, J.D.Y., 2001. *Religious Encounter and the Making of the Yoruba*. Bloomington & Indianapolis: Indiana University Press
Peter Donovan. 1999. "Neutrality in Religious Studies" In Russell T. McCutcheon (ed.) *The Insider/Outsider Problem in the Study of Religion: A Reader*, London: Cassell (235-247)
Price, G. Ward. 1939. *Year of Reckoning*, London: Cassell and Company, Limited
Probst, Peter. 2004. Keeping the Goddess Alive. Marketing Culture and Remembering the Past in Osogbo. *Social Analysis* 48 (1): 33-54.
Probst, Peter. 2007. Picturing the Past. Heritage, Photography and the Politics of Appearance in a Yoruba City. In *Reclaiming Heritage: Alternative Imaginaries in West Africa*, ed. Michael Rowlands and Ferdinand De Jong, San Francisco: LeftCoast Press: 99-125.
Probst, Peter. Forthcoming. *Producing Presence. The Art of Heritage in a Yoruba City*. Bloomington: Indiana University Press.
Pye, Michael, "The Study of Religions and Its Contribution to Problem-solving in a Plural World", *Marburg Journal of Religion*, Vol. ? No. ?, 2004: ???-???
Quine W.V.O. 1964. *From a Logical Point of View* Cambridge: Harvard University Press

Raboteau, Albert. 2004. *Slave Religion: The "Invisible Institution" in the Antebellum South*. Oxford: Oxford University Press.
Ranger, T. O. and I.N. Kimambo (eds.), 1972. *The Historical Study of African Religions* (Berkeley, California: University of California Press)
Ray, Benjamin C., 2000. *African Religions 2nd edition*. New Jersey: Prentice Hall.
Ray, Benjamin. 1977. "Sacred Space and Royal Shrines in Bugunda." *History of Religion* 16 (4): 363-373
Rowland, Abiodun. 2001. "Hidden Power: Osun the Seventeenth Odu." In Joseph M. Murphy and Mei-Mei Sanford (eds.). *Osun Across the Waters: A Yoruba Goddess in Africa and the Americas* Bloomington: Indiana University Press: 10-24
Redfield, Robert. 1956. *Little Communities*. Chicago: Chicago University Press.
Reis, João José, 2001.Candomble in Nineteenth-Century Bahia: Priests, Followers, Clients." In *Rethinking the African Diaspora: The Making of a Black Atlantic World in the Bight of Benin and Brazil*. Ed. by Kristin Mann and Edna G. Bay. Portland, Ore.: Frank Cass (116-34)
Rheinstein, M. (ed.). *Max Weber on Law in Economy and Society* (Cambridge, M.A Harvard University, Press) 1954
Ritzer, George, 2000 (1983). *Sociological Theory*, 4th edition, New York: McGraw-Hill International Editions
"Roots and Rooted. A Debt Paid in Full: Latin & African-American Relations within the Orisa Community." http://rootsandrooted.org/afam-latin-relations.htm.
Rotberg Robert I. and Ali Mazuri (eds.). 1970. *Protest and Power in Black Africa*. New York: Oxford University Press.
Roth, Guenther & Claus Wittich (eds.). *Max Weber: Economy and Society*, Vols. 1 & 2, University of California Press, 1978 the Regents
Rotimi, Ola.1979. *The Gods Are Not To Blame*. London: Oxford University Press.
Routon, Kenneth. 2005. "Unimaginable Homelands? 'Africa' and the Abakuá Historical Imagination" *Journal of Latin American Anthropology*. Vol. 10, No. 2: 370-400.
Russell, B., *Power: A New Social Analysis* (New York, Norton) 1938.
Rutanga, M. 1991. *Nyabingi Movement: People's Anti-Colonial Struggles in Kigezi 1910-1930*. CRB Working Paper No. 18 Ctr. for Basic Research.
Salami, Yunusa Kehinde. 1981. "Human Personality and Immortality in Traditional Yoruba Cosmology", *Africana Marburgensia* Vol.24, No.1:4-13
Salami, Yunusa Kehinde. 1996. "Predestination, Freedom, and Responsibility: A Case in Yoruba Moral Philosophy." *Research in Yoruba Language and Literatures*, No.7 (5-14)
Samartha, S.J., 1971. "Dialogue as a Continuing Christian Concern" in S.J. Samartha, *Living Faiths and the Ecumenical Movement* (Geneva: WCC Publications): 153-154
Sancheze, Ifalola. 2008. Ifa Yesterday, Ifa Today, Ifa Tomorrow: Ifa thoughts and Philosophy. http://ifalolablospot.com
Sanneh, Lamin, 1985. *Christianity in West Africa: A Religious Perspective* (Maryknoll, New York: Orbis Books)
Sawyer, Harry. 1968. The Practice of the Presence. *Numen* 15 (142-161)
Schuler, Monica. 1980. " *Alas, Alas, Kongo*: *A Social History of Indentured African Immigration into Jamaica, 1841-1865*. Baltimore, MD: Johns Hopkins University Press.
Scott, James. 1990. *Domination and the Arts of Resistance*: *Hidden Transcripts*. New Haven: Yale University Press

Seabrook, William B. 1929. *The Magic Island*. New York: The Literary Guild of America. (Cited in Bartkowski, "Claims-Making and Typifications of Voodoo as a Deviant Religion" (559-79)

Seidlitz, Larry et al.. "Development of the Spiritual Transcendent Index." *Journal for the Scientific Study of Religion* 41(3) 2002:: 439–453.

Settles, Shani. 2006. "The Sweet Fire of Honey: Womanist Visions of Osun as a Methodology of Emancipation." In *Deeper Shades of Purple: Womanism in Religion and Society*. Ed. By Stacey Floyd-Thompson. New York: New York University Press: (191-207)

Shakespeare, William. 1958. *King Lear*. Baltimore: Penguin Books.

Shaw, T. 1978. *Nigeria: Its Archaeology and Medicine in Early History*. London: Thames and Hudson.

Sheffer, Gabriel. 2003. *Diaspora Politics: At Home Abroad* Cambridge: Cambridge University Press

Shinner, Larry E.1972. "Sacred Space, Profane Space, Human Space." *Journal of the American Academy of Religion* 40 (4) (425-436)

Shishima, D.S., 1995. "The Whole Nature of African Traditional Medicine: The Tiv Experience" in in Gbola Aderibigbe and Deji Ayegboyin (eds.), *Religion, Medicine, and Healing* (A Publication of the Nigerian Association for the Study of Religions and Education, NASRED): 119-126

Shittu H. and B. Inuwa. 2006. "Islam and Traditional Beliefs of the Obas in Yorubaland" R.A. Raji, A.P. Dopamu, et al (ed.) *Religion, Governance and Development in the 21st Century* (Ago-Iwoye, Ogun State: A Publication of the Nigerian Association for the Study of Religions (358-370)

Shorter A. 2004. "Urbanization: Today's Missionary Reality in Africa," in *AFER*, 1990. *Vanguard*, August 23

Simmel, G. 1964. *The Sociology of George Simmel* (New York: The Free Press)1964.

Simmons, Donald C. 1956. "An Ethnographic Sketch of the Efik people"; "Notes on the Diary [of Antera Duke]." *Efik Traders of Old Calabar*. Daryll Forde, Ed. London: International African Institute: 1-26; 66-78.

Simon Ottenberg. 1970. "Personal Shrine at Afikpo." *Ethnology* 9 (1) (26-51)

Slater N. 1996. "Literacy and Old Comedy," in Worthington (ed.), *Voice into Text: Orality and Literacy in Ancient Greece*, Leiden: Brill

Smart, Ninian. 1969.*The Religious Experience of Mankind*. New York: Charles Scribner's Sons

Smart, Ninian. 1999. *Worldviews: Crosscultural Explorations of Human Beliefs* (3rd Edition) Prentice Hall

Smart, Ninian. 1996. *Dimensions of the Sacred: An Anatomy of the World's Beliefs* Berkeley, Los Angeles: University of California Press

Smith, A., 1970. "Some Considerations relating to the formation of States in Hausaland" *JHSN* 5.3 (December): 340

Sophocles. 1958. *The Oedipus Plays of Sophocles: Oedipus the King; Oedipus at Colonus; Antigone*. Trans. Paul Roche. New York: New American Literary.

Sophocles. 1974. *The Theban Plays of Sophocles*. Trans. E.F. Watling. Hardsmondworth: Penguin.

Soyinka, Wole.1976. *Myth, Literature and the African World*. London: Cambridge University Press.

Sproul, Barbara. 1979. *Primal Myths: Creating the World* New York & London: Harper & Row

Stark, Rodney and Roger Finke. 2000. *Acts of Faith: Explaining the Human Side of Religion* Berkeley: University of California Press

Stark, Rodney and William Bainbridge. 1996. *A Theory of Religion* New Brunswick, NJ: Rutgers University
Starkey, Peggy, 1985. "AGAPE: A Christian Criterion for Truth in the Other World Religions", *IRM* 74: 425-463
Steven, Stanley, ed.. *Conservation Through Cultural Survival: Indigenous People and Protected Area*. Washington, DC: Island Press) 1997
Stewart, Dianne M. 2005. *Three Eyes for the Journey: African Dimensions of the Jamaican Religious Experience*. New York: Oxford University Press
Stride & Ifeka., 1971, *Peoples and Empires of West Africa: West Africa in History, 1000-1800*, Nigeria: Thomas Nelson (Nigeria) Ltd.
Suda, Collette. 1996. The Centrality of Women in the Moral Teachings in African Society. *Nordic Journal of African Studies* 5 (2): 71–82.
Sudarkasa, Niara, 1986. The Status of Women in Indigenous African Society. *Feminist Studies*. Vol. 12(1): 91-103.
Sweet, James. 2003. *Recreating Africa: Culture, Kinship, and Religion in the African-Portuguese World, 1440-1770*. Chapel Hill: University of North Carolina Press,
Taiwo, Olufemi, "Ifa: An Account of a Divination System and Some Concluding Epistemological Questions" in Kwasi Wiredu (ed.), *A Companion to African Philosophy* (Oxford: Blackwell) 2004: 304-312
Tasie, G.O.M., 1976. *Christianity in the Niger Delta* (Leiden: E.J. Brill)
Taylor, J.V., 1969. *The Primal Vision* (London: SMC Press).
Thatcher, P., 1974. *West African History*. London: Longman Ltd.
Turaki, Yusuf, *Foundations of African Traditional Religions and Worldview*. Nairobi, Kenya: International Bible Society Africa 2001
Turner, H.W. 1967. *The History of an African Independent Church (Church of the Lord (Aladura))*. Oxford: Clarendon Press.
Turner, Victor W. (1969). *The Ritual Process: Structure and Anti-Structure*. Harmondsworth: Penguin Books.
Turner, W. Victor (1970). *The Forest of Symbols* (first published in 1967) Ithaca: Cornell University Press.
Ubah, C.N., 1976. "Problems of Christian Missionaries in the Muslim Emirates of Nigeria, 1900-1928" *Journal of African Studies* 3.3: 351-372
Ubah, C.N., 1985. "Islamic Culture and Nigerian Society" in E. Ihekweazu (ed.) *Traditional and Modern Culture* (Enugu: Fourth Dimensions Publ.): Chapter 16.
Ubesie, Tony. 2006. *Odinala Ndi Igbo*. Ibadan: Ibadan University Press.
Ugonna, Nnabuenyi. 1984. *Mmonwu: A Dramatic Tradition of the Igbo*. Lagos: Lagos University Press.
Uka, Kalu (1985). *Colonel Ben Brim*, Enugu: Fourth Dimension Publishers.
Ulli, Beier. 1975.*The Return of the Gods: The Sacred Arts of Susanne Wenger* Cambridge: Cambridge University Press
Umejesi I. "The Golden Rule and Religious Tolerance: A Case for Comparative Religion in Nigerian Schools" in *Journal of Academics:*, Vol. 2, No, 2, April, 2007.
Uwagboe, O.J., 2000. *The Baptist Mission and the Educational Development of Benin City*. B.A. Thesis, University of Benin.
Uwakwe, Abugu.. "Benin Monarch Invokes the Gods Against Crime in Edo." *Daily Independent*, September 23. 2005
Uzoma, Rose. 2004. Religious Pluralism, Cultural Differences, and Social Stability in Nigeria. *Brigham Young Law Review* 2: 651–664
Uzukwu, E. 2005. Mission Theology: Biblical and Historical Perspectives. Teachings of the Church, Miltown Dublin.

Vaill, Peter B. *Learning As A Way of Being: Strategies for Survival in a World of Permanent White Water*. San Francisco, Jossy-Bass, 1996.

Van Binsbergen, Wim. 2003. African spirituality: an approach from intercultural philosophy. *Forum for Intercultural Philosophy* 4: 1–45.

van Gennep, Arnold. 1960. *The Rites of Passage* (1st published, 1908). Translated from the French by Monika B. Vizedom and Gabrielle L. Caffee. London: Routledge and Kegan Paul.

Van Herik, Judith, "'Thick Description' and Psychology of Religion" in Robert L. Moore and Frank E. Reynolds (eds.) *Anthropology and the Study of Religion* Chicago, Illinois: Center for the Scientific Study of Religion, 1984

Vega, Marta. 1995. "The Yoruba Orisha Tradition Comes to New York." *African American Review* 29, no. 2 (201-6)

Verger, Pierre Fatumbi. *Ewe: The Use of Plants in Yoruba Society*. Sao Paulo: Editora Schwarcz, 1995

Vidal, Tunji. 1987. "Foreign Impact on Music", in Toyin Falola and G.O. Oguntomisin (eds.) *The History of Nigeria*, Vol. II: 44

Wambutda, D. Nimcir. 1991. *A Study of Conversion Among the Angas of Plateau State of Nigeria, with Emphasis on Christianity*. Frankfurt am Main, Bern, Berlin and New York: Peter Lang.

Weber M. 1968. *The Theory Of Social And Economic Organization* New York: Macmillan

Wenger, Susanne and Gert Chesi.. *A Life with the Gods in their Yoruba Homeland*. Worgl, Austria: Perlinger, 1985

Wenger, Susanne and Gert Chesi. 1990. *The Sacred Grove of Osogbo* Korneuburg Austria: Ueberreuter Offserbruck Korneuburg

Werbner, Richard, ed. 1998. *Memory in the Postcolony*. London: Zed Press.

Westerlund, David, *African religion in African Scholarship: A Preliminary Study of the Religious and Political Background,* Studies published by the Institute of Comparative Religion at the University of Stockholm 27. Stockholm: Almquist & Wiksell International, 1985

William, James. *Varieties of Religious Experience: A Study in Human Nature*. 9 New York: Penguin Book) 1982.

Wilson, H.V.R. 1955. Causal Discontinuity in Fatalism and Indeterminism. *The Journal of Philosophy*, 52: 134-158.

Witte, Hans. 1986. The Invisible Mothers. Female Power in Yoruba Iconography. In *Visible Religion*, V-VI, Institute of Religious Iconography, State University Groningen. Leiden: E.J. Brill: 301-325.

Wolff, Norma H. and Michael Warren The Agbeni Shango Shrine in Ibadan: A Century of Continuity. *African Arts* vol. 31 (3)(1998): 36-49, 94.

Young, Karl. 1933. *The Drama of the Medieval Church*, Oxford: Clarendon Press.

Index

Abdul, M.O.A.; 49, 66
Abega, Fr. P.; 150
Abhuere, P.; 237, 243
Abimbola, Kola; 95, 101, 333, 345, 349, 358
Abimbola, Wande & Miller, Ivor; 382
Abimbola, Wande; 95-97, 99, 101, 156, 160, 175, 179, 184, 340, 344, 345, 349, 351, 352, 354, 356-358, 380, 387, 394, 405
Abiodun, Rowland; 132, 135, 253
Academic bias and its ethical implications for inter-religious conflicts; 23
Achebe, Chinua; 280, 283, 287, 290, 295, 299
Adams, Captain John; 327
Adeboye, Dr. E.; 149
Adeboye, Olufunke; 76-78, 91
Adédèjì, J.A.; 256, 268
Adejumo, Ademola; 253
Adekanmbi, Dare; 70, 91
Ademola, O.M.; 118, 120
Adeniyi, M.O.; 118,120
Adeniyi, Victoria; 10, 175
Aderibigbe, Gbola & Ayegboyin, Deji; 120, 121
Aderibigbe, Gbola ; 8
Adetugbo, Abiodun; 2, 21
Adewale-Somadhi, Farounbi Aina Mosunmola; 358
Adeyemi, Muyiwa; 69, 80, 91
Afigbo, A.E.; 52, 66
Afolayan, A.; 385, 406

African Association for the Study of Religions (AASR); 1
African descendant *Ifa* priests and practitioners in the United States; 349
African Diaspora community in context; 387
African Independent Churches; 147
African indigenous religious traditions in Diasporic contexts; 16
African worldview, 42
Agbebi, Mojola ; 55
Agencies in healing practice; 114
Agia Tree Monument; 257
Airen, M.; 235, 243
Aisien, E.; 240, 243
Aiyejina, Funso & Gibbons, Rawle; 335, 336, 345
Ajayi, J.F.A.; 52, 54, 66
Ajibade, George O.; 12, 13, 248, 253, 255
Akanmidu, R.A.; 92
Akinfenwa, O.B.; 92
Akinola, G.A.; 78, 92
Akintunde, Dorcas; 9, 147
Akiwowo, Akinsola; 104, 106, 109
Al Ibn Talib; 299
Aládùrà Churches; 55, 58, 65, 117
Alawis; 157
Aluko, Banji; 92
Amadiume, Ifi; 303, 309
Amucheazi, Elochukwu C.; 57, 66
Anderson, Benedict A.; 149, 160, 161, 356, 358, 385, 406
Apter, Andrew; 253

Are, Prophetess Bola; 150
Arinze, F. A.; 219, 226
Ariyibi, Gbenga; 92
Arungwa, O.; 292, 293, 299
Asemota, Andy; 92
Association of Nigerian Christian Kings; 79
Association of the Born Again Christian Obas (AOBACO); 69, 70, 78-80
Atanda, A.A.; 163, 174
Awolalu, J.O. and Dopamu, P.A.; 4, 21, 23, 112, 120, 138, 140, 141, 146
Awolalu, J.O.; 66, 269, 276
Awolowo, Obafemi; 139
Awoniyi, Ropo; 6, 7, 69
Ayandele, E.A.; 40, 52-54, 66
Ayantayo, Jacob Kehinde; 5, 6, 23
Ayer, A.J.; 176, 184
Azuonye, C.; 39, 66
Babalola, Joseph Ayo; 148
Babayemi S.O.; 92
Badejo, Diedre; 256, 268
Balogun, S,A,; 164, 174
Bankole, Ayo; 167
Barber, Karin; 303, 309
Barnes, Sandra T.; 107-109, 329, 345
Bartkowski; 335, 345
Bascom, William; 95, 102, 179, 184
Bassey, Bassey Ekpo; 365, 375
Bassey, Engineer Bassey Efiong; 382
Bassey, Etubom Bassey Ekpo; 379, 382
Bassey, Iyamba B.E.; 366, 367
Batstone, David; 406
Beier, Ulli; 104, 109, 132, 248, 253
Benjamin, Ben & Bertha; 290, 293, 299
Berthoud, Jacques A; 192, 214
Bias and its manifestation in the contemporary religious studies scholarship; 26
Big Qua Clan Mgbè; 364
Blyden, Wilmot; 55, 65
Born Again phenomenon; 74
Born Again traditional rulers; 69

Brandon, George; 332, 345, 350, 358
Brown, David; 345
Brown, Karen McCarthy; 107-109, 346
Bruner, Jerome; 353, 354, 258
Brunner, E.; 290
Buckley, A.D.; 120
Bultman, Rudolf; 32
Bulus, Linus Yaktal C; 189, 190, 192, 193, 195-197, 200, 201, 211, 212
Burial rites and reincarnation in the indigenous tradition of the Ikwerre people; 217
Burns, J.M.; 138, 146
Butler, Judith; 309
Buxton, Fowell; 50
Cabrera, Lydia; 346, 360, 361, 382
Cahn, Steven M.; 176, 177, 184
Calabar Cultural Centre; 363
Campbell, J. G.; 55
Candomblé liberation; 342
Canstellanos, Isabella; 346
Capaldi, N.; 27, 293
Carr, Henry; 55
Casely-Hayford; 55
Catholic Boys' (CBO); 156
Catholic Girls Organisation (CGO); 156
Catholic Men's Organisation (CMO); 156
Catholic Women's Organisation (CWO); 156
Celestial Church of Christ; 117, 153, 155
Chagu; 191, 201, 205, 206
Chambers, E.K.; 257, 268
Cherubim and Seraphim; 148, 153, 155, 161, 240
Chesi, Gerd; 253
Chhachhi, Amrita; 309
Chidoka, O.; 293-295, 299
Chitando, Ezra; 148
Christ Apostolic Church; 76, 77, 82, 117, 148, 150, 152, 153, 161
Christ Life Church; 149
Christ Trumpeters' Church; 77
Christensen, Martin K.I.; 309

Church Missionary Society (CMS); 165, 237, 238, 240, 257
Clark, Mary Ann. 2005; 340, 346
Clarke P.B.; 48, 66
Clarke, Kamari, M.; 346
Classification of Secret Societies among Yoruba, Efik and Igbo; 141
Coffie-Gyamfi, Charles; 92
Colpe and Casten; 134
Comparative studies of rites of passages; 187
Cone, James H.; 346
Connah, Graham E.; 313, 316, 327
Conner, Randy P.; 346
Contemporary issues and current engagements in AIRTs; 2
Cox, H.; 147, 161, 187
Cox, James L; 214
Crampton, E.P.T.; 53, 66
Crowder, Michael; 164, 174
Crowther, Samuel Ajayi; 165, 257
Crumbley, Deidre; 309
Da Silva, Ferreira; 340
Dairo, A.O.; 117, 120
Daly, Mary; 309
Danfulani, Umar Habila Dadem; 11, 187, 192, 193, 196, 206, 209, 210, 212-215
Danmole, H.O.; 257, 268
Daramola, Yomi ; 9, 10, 163, 167, 174
Darling, P.J.; 313, 328, 328
Dash, Julie; 331
Datok, Polycarp F.; 87, 215
David Oyedepo Ministries International Inc.; 161
De Beauvois, Palisot; 328
De La Torre, Miguel A.; 329, 344, 346
Declaration of Helsinki; 34
Dedeke, Dayo; 167
Deeper Life Church; 149
DeGraft, J.C.; 256, 268
Diakité, Dianne M. Stewart; 329
Díaz, Román'; 363, 379, 382
Dike, K.O.; 52, 66

Dike, Tony; 134
Do Nascimento, Abdias; 346
Donovan, Peter; 33
Dopamu, Abiola T.; 92, 112-116, 120, 121
Drewal, Margaret; 344, 346, 354, 358
Dzurgba, A.; 29, 30, 36
Eck, Diana L; 385, 406
Eckankar; 59
Edet, Chief Hayford Solomon; 370-372, 383
Edet, Inameti Orok; 373, 374, 383
Edokpaigbe, I.; 243
Edu, K.O.; 125, 134
Egbo: Gating spiritual security and morality in the Igbo context; 277
Egharevba, J.U.; 229, 243, 312, 314, 322, 328
Egungun; 45
Ehianu, Wilson; 12, 227, 228, 233, 238, 243
Ejituwu, N.C.; 52
Ejizu, C.; 291, 292
Ejizu, Christopher I.; 156, 161, 299
Ekah, Mary; 263, 268
Ekechi, Felix; 52, 66
Ekeng, Ekpo; 374, 383
Ekpo, Chief Ékpènyong É.; 370, 371, 383
Ekwuru, Emeka George; 285-287
Eliade, Mircea; 29, 46, 66, 128, 129, 134
Ellis, Stephen & ter Haar, Gerrie; 137, 139, 141, 146
Epistemic critique of *Ifa* as a revelatory source of knowledge; 95
Erasing African religion; 335
Erivwo, S.U.; 52, 66
Essien, (Sir) Fred; 383
Etherton, Michael; 183, 184
Ethics, women and indigenous spirituality; 13
Eto: a retributive principle in Owhe society; 269
Evangelical Christian Renewal; 74
Evangelism in Christianity and Islam; 166

Evans, Matthew; 128, 129, 134
Evans-Pritchard, E.E.; 39, 41, 66
Eyo, Chief Ernest Ékpènyong Eyo Honesty II; 383
Eze, E.C.; 97, 100-102
Ezeanya; 228
Fadillullah Muslim Mission; 159
Fagunwa, Daniel; 10
Falade, Fasina; 355, 538
Falola, Toyin & Oguntomisin, G.O.; 174
Falola, Toyin; 268
Fandrich, Ina J.; 337, 346
Farotimi, David; 248, 253
Fate, concept of; 176
Ferreira Da Silva, Denise; 346
Field, David N.; 134
Field, M. J.; 113, 121, 126
Finnegan; 266
Frazer, J.; 243
Freeman, Thomas Birch; 257
Friesen Lauren; 255, 268
Full Gospel Businessmen's Fellowship (FGBMF); 79
Functions of secret societies; 143
Gbadamosi, Bakare; 104
Gbadamosi, T. G.O.; 50, 53, 66, 163, 164, 174
Gbadegesin, Olusegun; 97, 98, 102
Geertz, Clifford; 4, 21
Gehman, R.J.; 4, 21, 139, 146
Gennep, Arnold van; 188, 194, 208, 214
George, Akin; 167
Gerima, Haile; 331, 346
Gibson, Reginald; 346
Godianism; 59, 65
Gollmer, Rev. C.A.; 257
Gollwitzer, Helmut; 32
Goshit, Zacharia Damina; 187, 215
Graham, Billy; 74
Grail Message; 59
Gregg, Samuel; 297, 298
Grunbaum, Adolf; 176, 184
Guerrero, Angel; 367, 368, 379, 381, 383

Guthrie, D. S.; 112, 113, 121
Gutiérrez, Gustavo; 341, 346
Haggai, John Edmund; 189, 200, 201, 205, 215
Hallen, Barry; 97, 101, 102
Hallgren, Roland; 121
Harding, Rachel; 332, 337, 346
Haruna; 213, 215
Harvey, Professor Graham; 20
Hastings, Adrian; 161
Healing and health care delivery system in indigenous religions; 112
Healing in Islam; 158
Health, healing and restoring; 111
Henry, Frances; 340, 346
Henry, Sawyer; 133
Herskovits, Melville; 360, 383
Historical strands of religious interaction in Nigeria; 390
Hopkins, Dwight N.; 406
Horton, Robin and Peel, J.D.Y. ; 72, 92
Horton, Robin; 67
Houk, James; 332, 346
Hucks, Tracey; 338, 347
Hucks, Tracy & Stewart, Dianne; 335, 347, 405, 406
Hurston, Zora Neale; 334, 347
Ibigbolade, Simon Aderibigbe; 137
Idowu, Bolaji E.; 4, 11, 19, 23, 25, 36, 65, 98, 112-114, 121, 138, 143, 146, 177, 180, 185, 218, 226
Idris, Mallam Ismaila; 157
Idumwonyi, Mercy; 12, 227
Ifa and the knowledge of human destiny; 99
Ifa as a religion and a source of revelatory knowledge; 95
Ifeka-Moller, C.; 72
Ifemesia, C.C.; 52, 67
Igue Festival among the Benin people; 227
Ihekweazu, E.; 40, 53, 55, 67

Index

Ijo Orile Ede Adulawo Ti Kristi (National Church of Christ); 148
Ika, Etim; 383
Ike, F. & Edozien, N.; 289, 299
Ikenga-Metuh, Emefie; 72, 92, 193, 194, 213, 215
Ikime, Obaro; 52, 67, 269, 276
Imad-ad-Dean Ahmad; 299
Imona, Chief Ekon E.; 364, 377, 384
Indigenous spirituality in the lives and experiences of Christian and Muslim religious founders and leaders; 147
Indigenous spirituality, business ethics and contemporary challenges among the Igbo; 289
Indigenous traditions in motion; 73
Indigenous voices in music performances of contemporary Christian and Muslim Missions; 163
International Congress of Orisa Tradition and Culture; 17, 330, 347
Isichei, Elizabeth; 52, 187, 215
Isiramen, Celestina ; 14, 15, 289, 293, 296, 299
Issues and perspectives on African indigenous religious traditions; 5
Iwara, A.U.; 27, 28, 36
Izalatul-Bid'ah Wa Igamat al' Sunnah; 157
James, William; 133, 135
Jegede, Charles Obafemi; 123
Jehu-Appiah, Jerisdan H.; 148, 161
Jensen, J. S. & Martin, L .H.; 31, 32, 36
Johnson, Elizabeth A.; 309
Johnson, Paul Christopher; 385, 402, 407
Johnson, Rev. James; 55, 237, 238
Johnson, Sylvester O.; 163, 174, 336, 347
Kalu, Ogbu Uke; 6, 39, 40-43, 46, 52, 55, 59, 65, 67, 156, 161, 213, 215, 218, 226
Kamara, Jemadari & Van Der Meer, Tony Menelik; 355, 358
Kamari, Jemadari; 330

Kaplan, Flora E. S.; 15, 16, 236, 243, 311, 312, 322, 325, 326, 328
Kayode, Afolabi; 248, 253
Kegley, Charles K.; 30
Kenny, Joseph; 29
Khariji; 157
Knitter, Paul; 61, 67
Knowledge, power, vitality and representation; 7
Kraemer, H.; 61, 67
Kumuyi, William F.; 149
Kunin; 303
Laduke, Betty; 134
Laguda, Danoye-Oguntola; 138, 143, 145, 146
Language of worship, objects, music and titles in the churches; 155
Larson; 133
Lawal, Babatunde; 249, 253
Lawal, Nike; 120, 121
Lawuyi, Professor Tunde; 20
Leonard, A.; 291, 300
Leonowens, Anna H.; 328
Lere, Pauline Mark; 193, 215
Levy-Bruhl; 24
Lincoln, Bruce; 31, 36
Lindom Thomas; 267, 268
Lindsay, Arturo; 332, 347
Ling, Roth H.; 320, 322, 328
Lisanne Norman; 20
Livingston; 303
Lois, Fuller; 92
Lopes, Nei; 335, 340, 347
Lorentzen, Lois Ann; 406
Lowenthal, David; 253
Lydia's Society; 156
Makinde, M.A.; 96, 102
Maloba, Wunyabari O.; 331, 347
Martinez, Pedro; 368-370, 379, 384
Masuzawa, Tomoko; 134
Matory, Lorand; 330, 347, 381, 384
Mbiti, J.; 4, 21, 25, 218, 226, 228, 243
McCarthy, Brown; 335

McCollough; 133
McCutcheon, Russell T.; 30, 36
Meek, Nigel; 26, 36
Mellor, Stephen P.; 128, 134
Memory, identity and the spiritual experience of an African diaspora community; 385
Mendieta, Eduardo; 406
Métreaux, Alfred; 335, 347
Metuh, Emefie-Ikenga; 4, 21
Mezzana, Daniele; 343, 347
Miller, Ivor L.; 359, 361, 363, 379, 380, 384
Milner Jr., Murray; 135
Missionary activities and African religion; 147
Moghadam, Valentine M.; 302; 309
Mol, Hans; 386, 407
Montagu, Lady Mary Wortley; 311, 328
Morakinyo, Olufemi; 98, 102
Morgenbesier, S. & Walsh, T.; 176, 185
Murphy, Joseph M. & Sanford, Mei-Mei; 135, 246, 253, 334, 344, 347, 407
Murphy, Joseph M.; 334, 347, 403, 407
Nadel, S.F.; 113, 121
NASFAT; 301
Nasseef, Abdulla Omar; 67
National African Religious Congress (NARC); 344
National Agency for Food, Drug Administration and Control (NAFDAC); 297
National Church of Christ in Nigeria; 151, 154
Ndzon Melen Eucharistic Rite; 150
Neiers, Rev. Sister Maria de Paul; 192, 210, 215
Neusner, Jacob; 35
New Pentecostal churches; 149
New Religious Movements (NRMs); 3
Ngum, Fr. P. C. u; 150
Nigerian Baptist Convention; 156

Nigerian indigenous religious traditions (NIRT); 23
Njoku, J.; 296, 300
Nnoli, Okwudiba; 384
Oba, Abdulmumini A.; 135
Obadigie, J.O.; 229, 231, 243
Obafemi Charles Jegede; 8
Obasanjo, Olusegun; 139
Obi, C.A.; 154, 161
Obiandu, M. F.; 226
Oduyoye, M.; 52, 227, 232, 243
Ofo; 45
Ofugha, Omosimuna; 253
Oguejiofor, Obi J.; 286, 287
Ogun Ipole festival; 77
Ogunba, Oyin; 257, 268
Ogunbiyi, Yemi.; 256, 268
Ogundipe-Leslie, 'Molara; 303, 309
Ògúngbilé, Margaret Olusola; 20
Ogunremi, Deji & Adediran, Biodun; 174
Oguntola-Laguda, Danoye; 7, 8, 111, 137
Oha, Obododimma; 14, 277
Ohia, C.P. Chi-na-Eke; 280, 287
Ojo, Matthews A.; 161
Oke, Bishop Wale; 149
Oke, Reverend Adeniran; 148
Okere, T.; 293, 300
Okija Shrine; 293-295,
Okolugbo, E.; 238, 239, 243
Ola, V.U.; 181-185
Olademo, Oyeronke; 15, 301
Olajubu, Oyeronke; 303, 309, 310
Ọlọjọ festival; 72
Olomola, Isola; 92
Olude, Rev. T. Ola; 167
Olumba Olumba Obu; 3
Omabe; 45
Omideyi, Olaolu; 167
Omijeh, M.; 231, 244
Omojola, Bode; 167, 174
One Love Family Movement; 3
Onibere, Oseovo; 13, 14, 269
Onwu, E. N.; 161

Opeloye, M.O.; 165, 174
Opoku, Kofi Asare; 21
Oriere, Ben; 167
Orimolade, Moses; 148
Orisa Sonponna, moral knowledge and responsibility in the age of AIDS and biowarfare; 103
Orisa World Congress; 17
Orisha traditions in the West; 329
Ortiz, Don Fernando; 360, 381, 382, 384
Osborn, T.L.; 74
Oshitelu; 148
Osogbo Heritage Council; 250
Osun and Osogbo, Nigeria; 130
Ọṣun festival; 72
Osun Osogbo Festival, another version; 245
Osun shrine; 132
Osunyemi, Siju; 403, 407
Ottenberg, Simon; 127, 135
Otto, Rudolf; 29
Otu, Vicky; 384
Oviasu, V.O.; 238, 244
Owari festival; 77
Owo; 45
Oyedepo, Bishop; 149
Oyewumi, Oyeronke; 303, 309
Paradigms and conceptual issues in African indigenous religious traditions; 1
Paris, Liana; 161
Parish, Jane; 135
Parrinder, Geoffrey W.; 4, 22-25, 36, 114, 121, 221-223, 226
Peek, Philip M.; 100, 102
Peel, J.D.Y.; 344, 347
Peterson, Kirsten Holst; 72
Philips, Thomas Ekundayo; 167
Physical, spiritual and the formation of shrine; 129
Politics in an African royal harem; 311
Polygamy in religions; 159

Position of women in new Pentecostal churches; 152
Power and secret societies; 137
Power, secret knowledge, and secret societies; 137
Precious Stone Society; 148
Probst, Peter; 12, 13, 245, 253
Puerto Rico; 2
Pye, Michael; 31, 32, 36
Quadiriyya; 157
Quine; 100
Raboteau; 341
Ranger, T.O. and Kimambo, I.N.; 39, 67
Ransome Kuti, Rev. J.J.; 167
Ray, Benjamin C.; 135, 310
Redeemed Christian Church of God; 149
Redfield, Robert; 245, 253
Reis, João José; 337, 342, 347
Religion in traditional structure; 40
Religious specialists and use of indigenous mediums; 150
Rey, Terry; 21
Rey; 406
Rheinstein, M.; 146
Rite of renewal/purification; 155
Rites of passages, defining; 187
Rites, rituals and festivals; 10
Ritzer, George; 29, 37, 304, 310
Robert Arungbaolu Coker; 167
Roman Catholic Church; 154-156, 228, 240
Rotberg & Mazrui; 331
Roth, Guenther & Claus Wittich; 92
Rotimi, Ola; 176, 180-185
Routon, Kenneth; 381, 382, 384
Royal Auxiliary; 156
Rudolph, Kurt; 30, 31, 36
Russell, Bertrand; 138, 146
Rutanga, M.; 347
Sacred/profane dichotomy; 127
Salami, Yunusa; 7, 95, 97, 98, 102
Samartha, S.J.; 61, 67
Sancheze, Ifalola; 161

Sanford, Mei-Mei; 7, 103
Sanneh, Lamin; 48, 67
Sarbah, Mensah; 55
Sat Guru Maharaj Ji Movement; 3
Sawyer, Henry; 133, 135
Schleiermacher, Frederick; 345
Schuler, Monica; 330, 347
Scott, James; 332, 347
Scripture Union (S.U.); 74
Seabrook, William B.; 343, 348
Segun, Mabel; 53
Seideltz, Larry; 133, 135
Settles, Shani; 340, 344, 348
Shaw, T.; 175, 185
Sheffer, Gabriel; 385, 407
Shi'I Islam; 157
Shinner, Larry E.; 135
Shishima, G.S.; 112-114, 121
Shittu, H. & Inuwa, B.; 74, 93
Shorter, Aylward; 150, 162, 296, 300
Shrines and sovereignty in religious life and experience; 123
Simmel, George; 139, 146
Simmons, Donald C.; 384
Slater N.; 317, 328
Slave Trade, Nigerians and Cubans; 459
Smart, Ninian; 5, 22, 32, 388
Smith Abdullahi; 45, 67
Smith, Daniel Jordan; 149
Soyinka, Wole; 10, 182, 185, 267, 268
Sproul, Barbara; 385, 407
Stark, Rodney & Bainbridge, William; 135
Starkey, Peggy; 62, 63, 67
Steven, Stanley; 135
Stevens, Stan; 125
Stewart, Dianne; 16, 17, 348
Stewart; 335, 355
Stride & Ifeka; 164
Suda, Collette; 284, 287
Sudarkasa, Niara; 303, 310
Sufis; 157
Sweet; 330
Taiwo, Olufemi; 96, 101, 102

Tasie, G.O.M.; 52, 67
Taylor, J. V.; 121
Thatcher, P.; 228, 244
Thomas, Tunde; 81, 93
Tijaniyya; 157
Townsend, Henry; 165, 257
Traditional groups; 142
Traditional medicine and other religions; 117
Traditional ruler and indigenous traditions; 70
Trinidad and Tobago; 2
Turaki, Yusuf; 72, 93
Turner, H.W.; 162
Turner, Victor W.; 188, 194, 215
Tylor, E.O. James; 24, 128
Types of secret societies; 140
Ubah, C.N.; 53, 67
Ubesie, Tony; 277, 287, 280, 283, 287
Ugonna, Nnabuenyi; 278, 287
Uka, Kalu; 215
Umejesi, I.; 293, 300
UNESCO; 246, 356
United African Church; 55
Use of water in healing; 151
Uwagboe, O.J.; 238, 239, 244
Uwakwe, Abugu; 135
Uzoma, Rose; 162
Uzukwu; 155
Vaill, Peter B.; 353, 358
Van Binsbergen, Wim; 162
Van Der Meer, Tony Menelik; 17, 349, 388
Van Herik, Judith; 4, 22
Vega, Marta; 338, 339, 348
Verger, Pierre Fatumbi; 109
Vidal, Tunji; 163, 174
Wadud; 304
Wahhabism (Salafism); 157
Wambutda, D. Nimcir; 187, 192, 215
Ward-Price; 326
Warrior; 336
Weber, Max; 138, 146

Index

Weigert; 331
Wenger, Susanne & Chesi, Gert; 135
Wenger, Suzanne; 129, 133, 389
Werbner, Richard; 253
Westerlund, David; 4, 22
Wilmore; 330, 341
Wilson, H. Van Remsselaer; 177, 185
Winners Chapel; 149
Wiredu, Kwasi; 102
Witte, Hans; 254
Wolff, Norma H. & Warren, Michael; 135
Women in Yoruba and Igbo indigenous spirituality; 301
Women Missionary Union; 156
World Council of Churches; 61, 162
Wotogbe-Weneka, Wellington O.; 11, 217
Yoder J. Otis; 74
Yoruba account of predestination; 97
Yoruba conception of fate and the role of *Ifa* divination; 177
Yoruba modern traditional health care delivery system; 118
Yoruba traditional health care delivery methods; 115
Young, Cathy; 26, 37
Young, Karl; 268
Zangbeto cultural festival; 13, 255-268
Zwerling, Philip; 335, 341, 342

Printed in the United States
By Bookmasters